I0446004

PARKLANDS

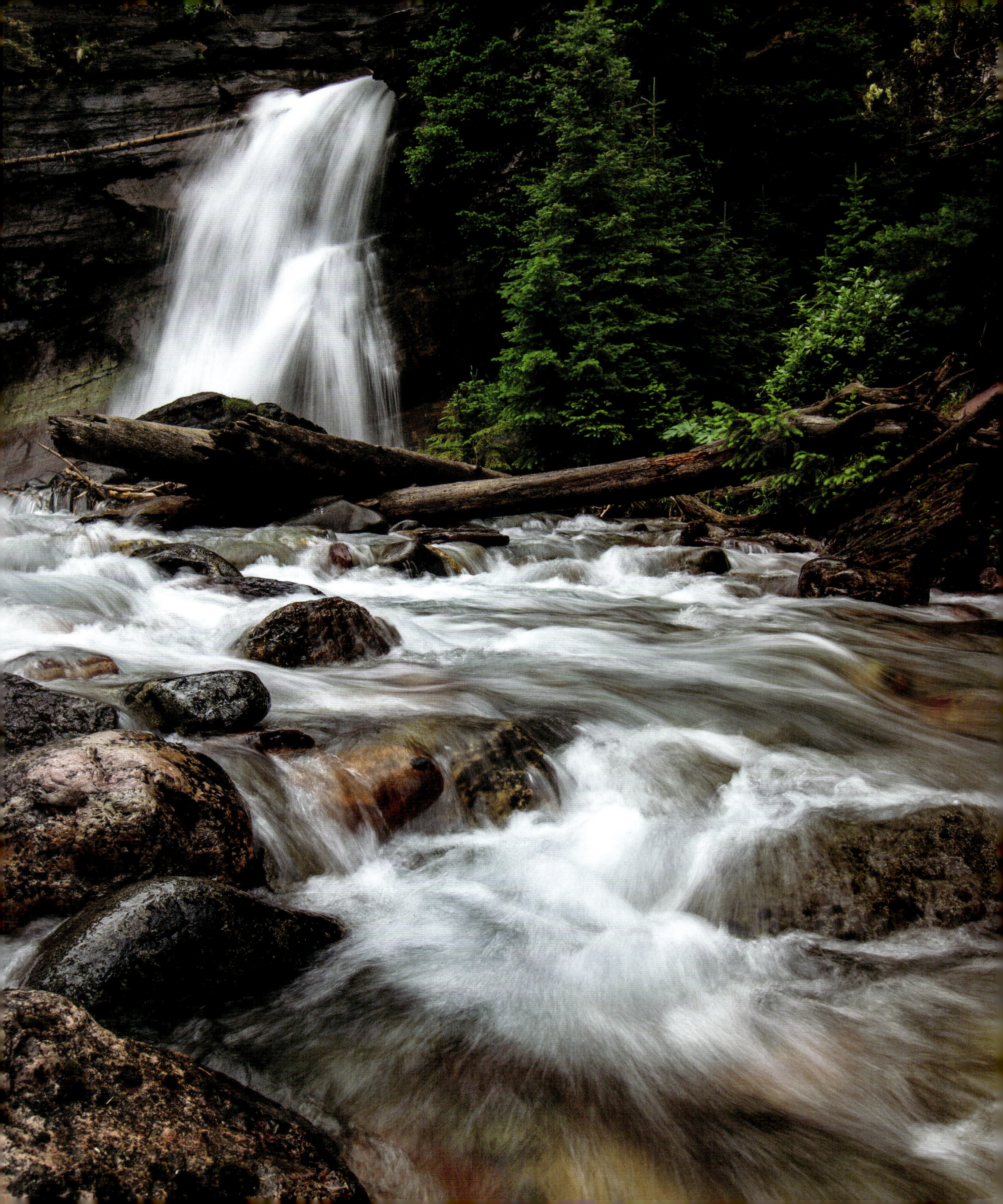

PARK LANDS

America's National Parks and Public Lands

JACOB W. FRANK

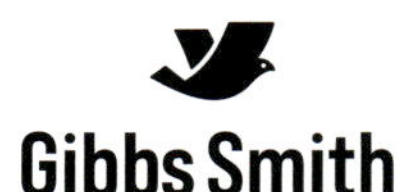

Gibbs Smith

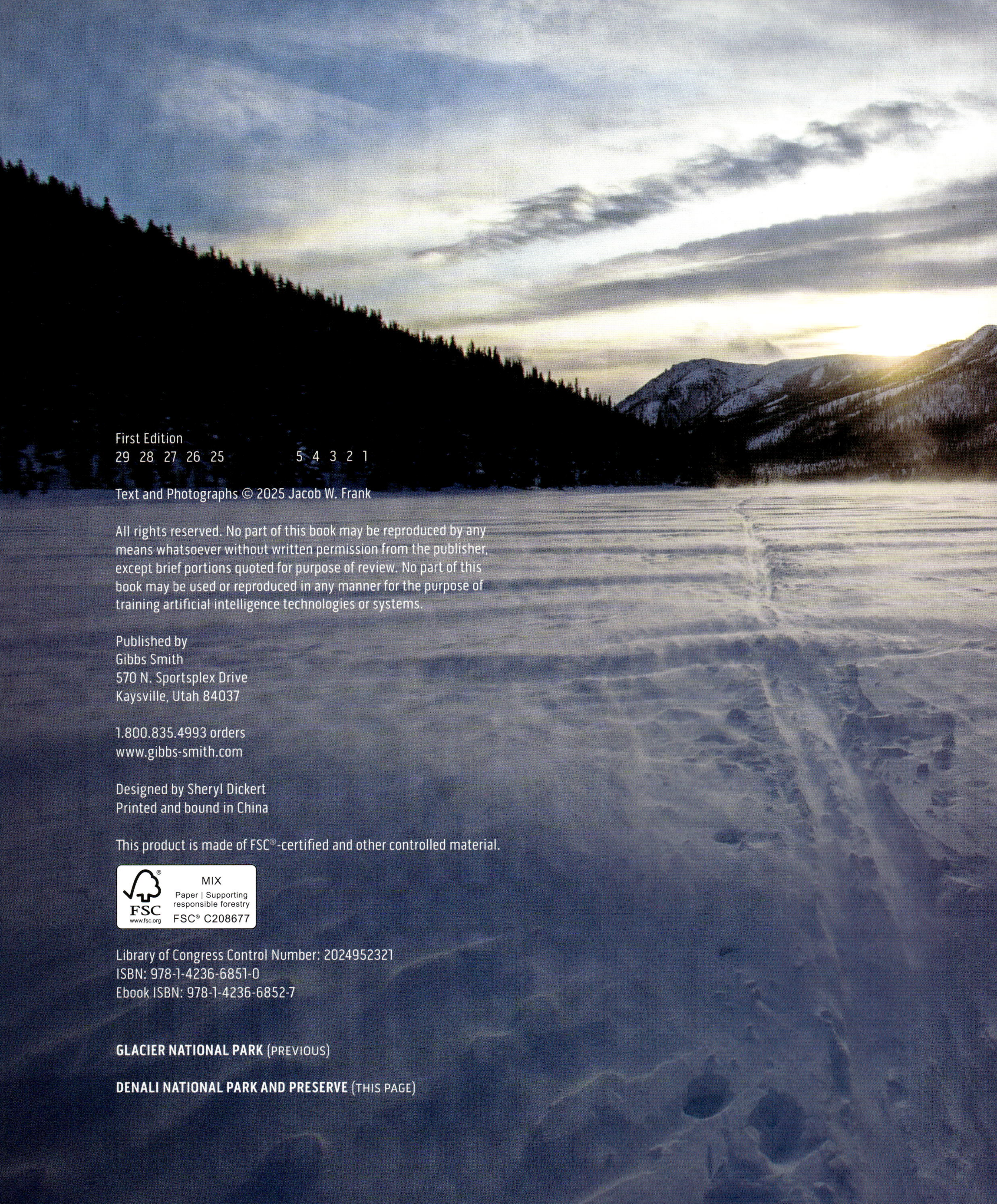

First Edition
29 28 27 26 25 5 4 3 2 1

Published by
Gibbs Smith
570 N. Sportsplex Drive
Kaysville, Utah 84037

1.800.835.4993 orders
www.gibbs-smith.com

Designed by Sheryl Dickert
Printed and bound in China

This product is made of FSC®-certified and other controlled material.

Library of Congress Control Number: 2024952321
ISBN: 978-1-4236-6851-0
Ebook ISBN: 978-1-4236-6852-7

GLACIER NATIONAL PARK (PREVIOUS)

DENALI NATIONAL PARK AND PRESERVE (THIS PAGE)

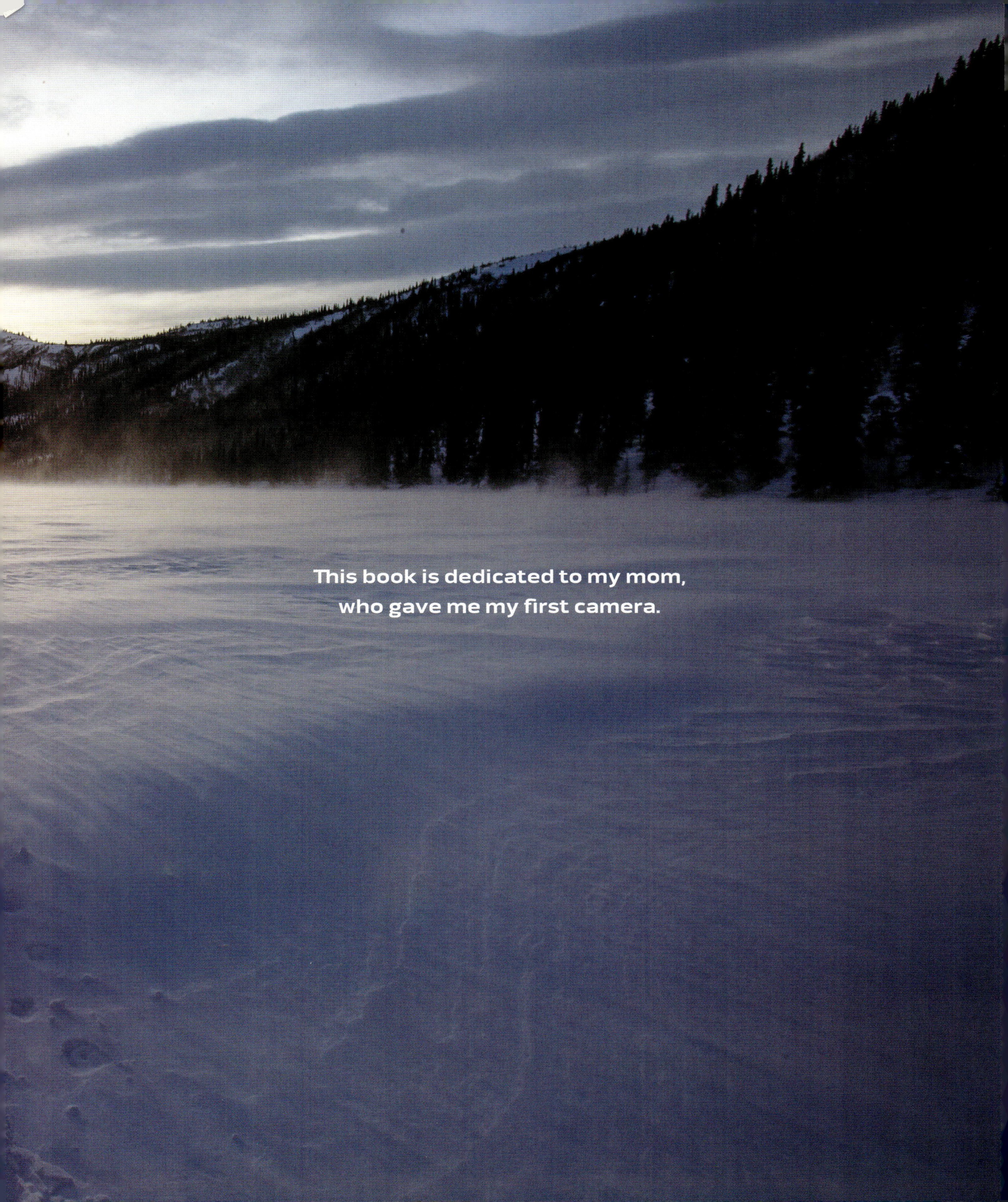

This book is dedicated to my mom,
who gave me my first camera.

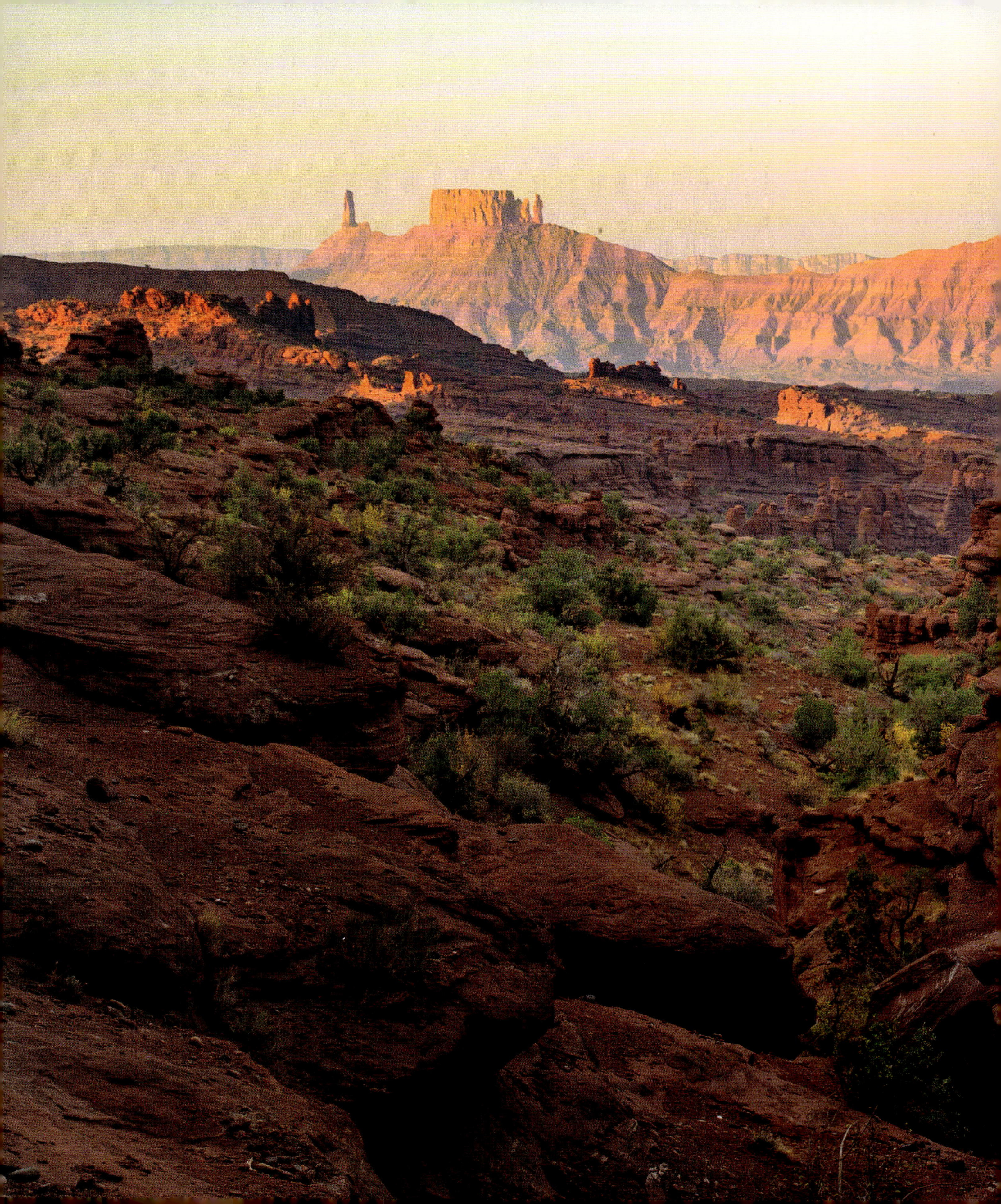

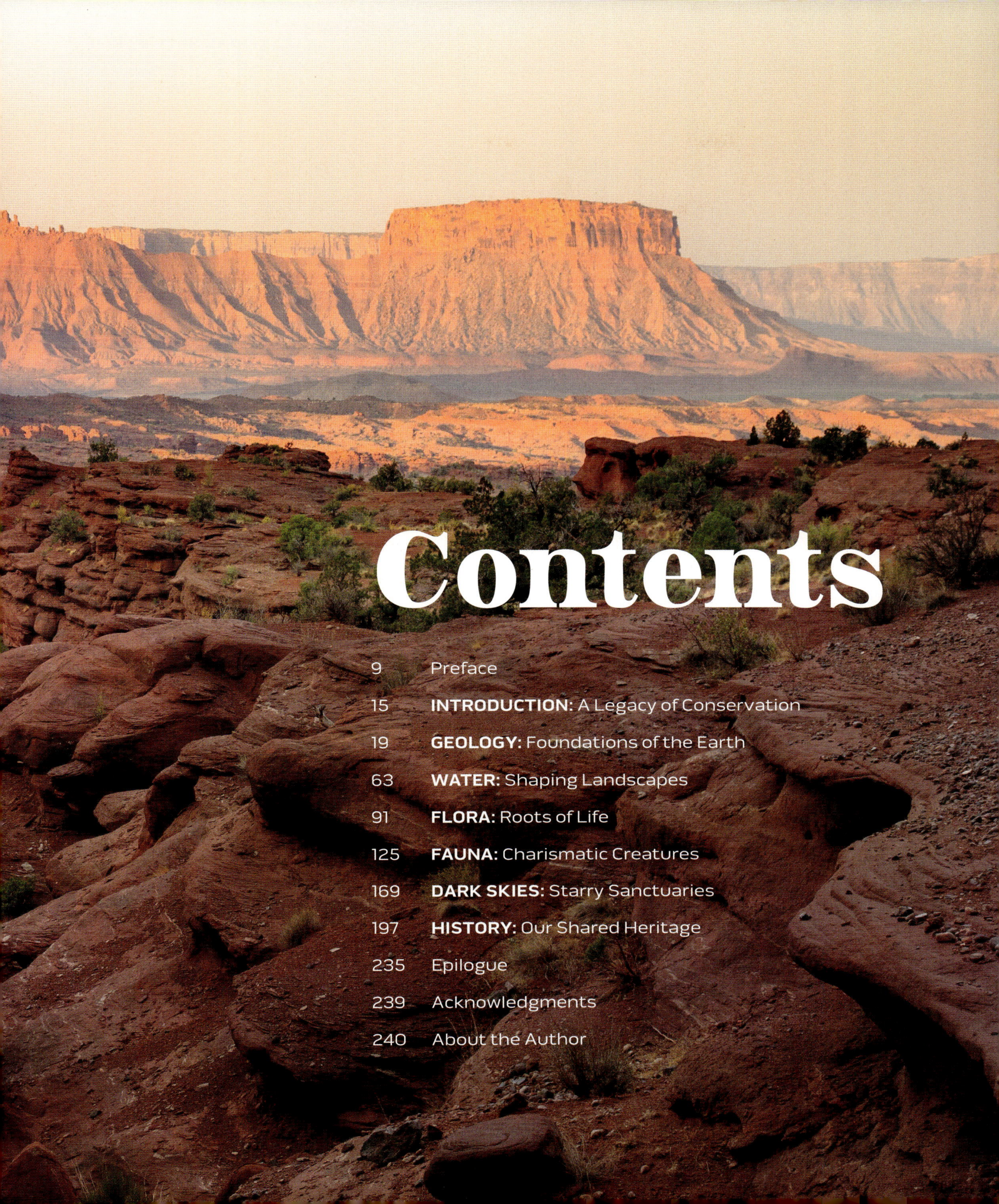

Contents

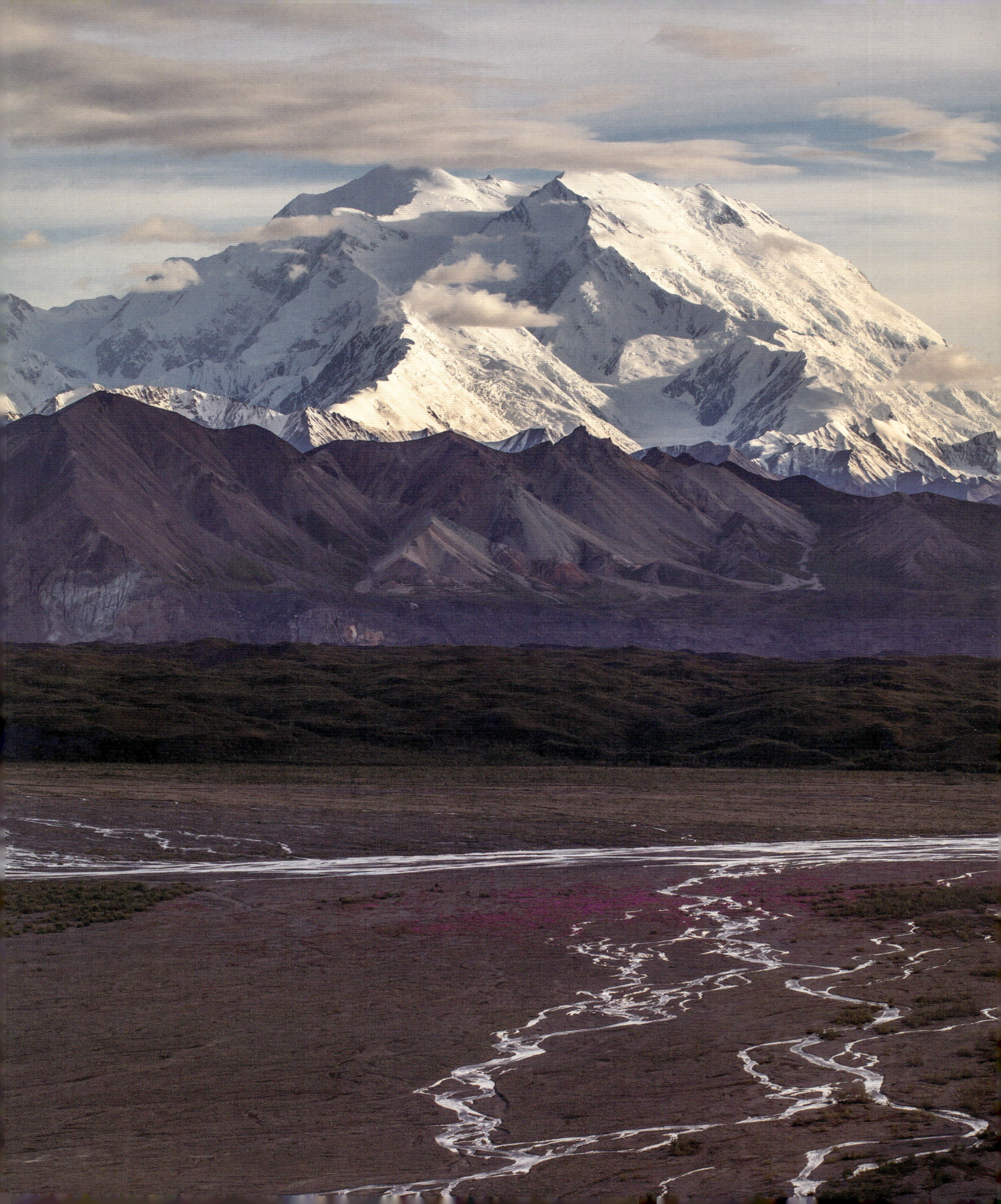

PREFACE

DURING THE MOST NOMADIC SIX YEARS OF MY LIFE, I moved across state lines a total of ten times. Fortunately, before I set off on this path, my mom gave me her old digital camera and urged me to "take pictures" whenever I could. That small piece of advice proved to be some of the most influential I would ever get.

At the outset, my camera was a gateway to the natural world, my trusty companion in exploring and documenting the unknown. Before long, I found myself eager to travel and see new things, so that I could take more photos. The thrill of discovery fueled my desire to explore farther, to wander into new landscapes and capture new experiences. My camera soon evolved into a documentary tool for recording all my adventures. The act of storytelling through photographs became second nature, a language I was learning to speak fluently. To this day, when glancing through my old albums, the sights, sounds, and emotions of each of those moments come flooding back with striking clarity.

The pursuit of capturing these moments became a passion, transcending my camera's original utilitarian purpose. The joy of creating became the ultimate reward, the real driving force behind my desire to capture and craft new stories with my camera.

FISHER TOWERS NATIONAL RECREATION TRAIL (PREVIOUS)

DENALI NATIONAL PARK AND PRESERVE (OPPOSITE) The view from Eielson Visitor Center is breathtaking. One of my favorite times of year is when dwarf fireweed blooms along the Thorofare River bar. This place holds special meaning for me, as it's where my wife, Corrie, and I took our first backpacking trip. The GPS coordinates are even inscribed on our wedding bands.

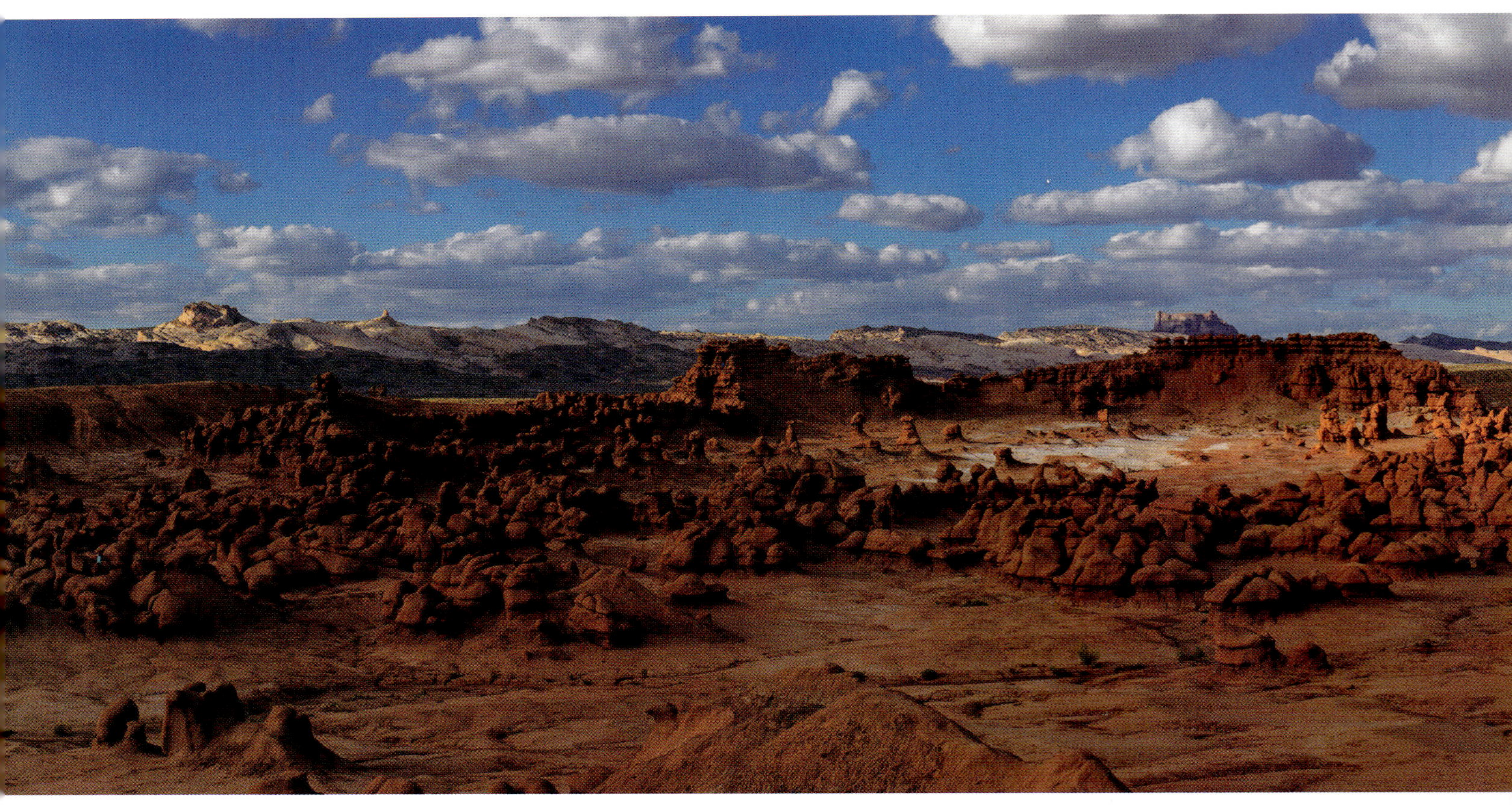

It all started when I was offered a winter internship in Grand Teton National Park. As expected, I was awed by living in the park. Rolling over in bed and seeing the pink alpenglow on the Grand out my bedroom window is something I won't ever forget. Upon completion, I returned to the University of Florida to pursue a master's degree and further specialize in park management and environmental education.

With my freshly minted degrees, I landed a seasonal position at Glacier National Park. That summer proved to be a transformative chapter in my life. It was a season marked by stepping far outside my comfort zone. Surrounded by people who had grown up among the mountains, I was adopted into an outdoor family with a deep wealth of knowledge and enthusiasm. Their eagerness to share their expertise made every day a learning adventure.

Among the many highlights, I hiked 350 miles over three months, immersing myself in the park's breathtaking landscapes. I delved into the world of wildflowers, learning not just their names but their phenology—their life cycles and seasonal rhythms. I chased waterfalls and swam in every backcountry lake I came across.

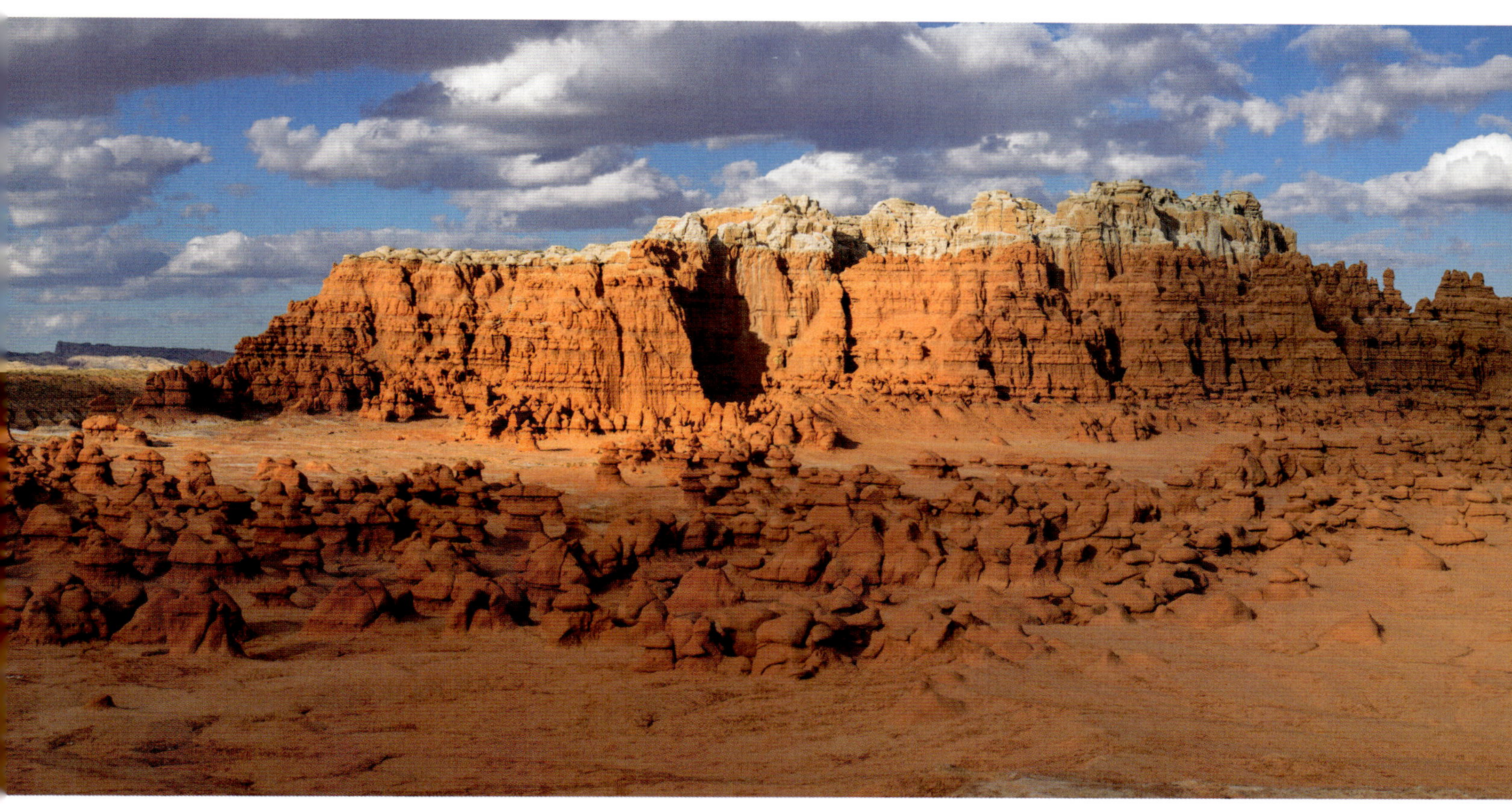

After my unforgettable summer at Glacier, a coworker and I set out on a grand road trip. We navigated our way through fourteen national parks as we drove south from Montana, staying one step ahead of winter. We discovered the awe-inspiring landscapes of the Colorado Plateau for the first time. Canyonlands and Arches National Parks dazzled us with their grandeur, but it was Mesa Verde that left a profound impact. I was moved by what I learned about the Ancestral Puebloans and their rich culture, feeling a mix of surprise and regret for not having learned about them earlier in my life.

GOBLIN VALLEY STATE PARK We had plans to visit Zion National Park for Corrie's birthday to backpack through The Narrows. Unfortunately, that year there was a government shutdown and the park was closed. So, we loaded up our car and decided to check out some state parks near us. Without knowing anything about it before we arrived, we were pleasantly surprised to explore the "goblins" of this beautiful landscape.

In total, our road trip took us through Wyoming, Utah, Colorado, and Nevada, and culminated thirty days later in California, when I was offered a position in Carlsbad Caverns National Park. Living in Carlsbad marked my first experience in a desert environment. With the heat often sweltering, the cool underground caves provided a welcome escape. So, I dove in headfirst, in some cases literally. Exploring caves became a new favorite hobby and I even picked up technical climbing skills for the caves that required ropes and harnesses to explore.

Despite my deep affection for Glacier National Park and my desire to return the following summer, my eyes were set on a new prize. A brief but profound trip to Hyder, Alaska, had left a lasting mark on me. So, when the opportunity arose to live and work in Denali National Park and Preserve, I was overjoyed.

My pilgrimage to the forty-ninth state would begin as far away as possible in the US, starting from Dry Tortugas National Park in Florida. After more than a month and six thousand miles on the road, I arrived in Alaska. That summer in Denali was another turning point in my life, not only because of the stunning landscape I lived in, but also because I met Corrie, who would become my future wife. As a backcountry ranger, she introduced me to hiking and backpacking through trailless wilderness, and together we explored Denali's wonders. While the park is famed for its towering mountain, its diverse flora and fauna are equally captivating. I had thrilling encounters with wildlife, including my first close-up sightings of lynx, wolves, caribou, Dall sheep, and grizzly bears.

With nearly twenty-four hours of daylight, the extended summer days seemed to defy the limits of my endurance. When I made the decision to stay the winter in Alaska, I found that the lack of sunlight can do the opposite. To combat the darkness, Corrie and I escaped to Hawaii for six weeks, where we indulged in backpacking and hiking across Maui, Kauai, and the Big Island.

When we returned to Alaska, the world was beginning to tilt back toward the sun after the winter solstice. With the days gradually lengthening, we spent our afternoons cross-country skiing under the limited sunlight, and at night, I immersed myself in photographing the northern lights. The techniques I had honed while photographing caves proved surprisingly effective for capturing the ethereal beauty of the aurora borealis.

After my second summer in Denali, I discovered AmeriCorps VISTA—a program inspired by the success of the Peace Corps and often referred to as its domestic counterpart. Having enjoyed my time in Utah, I focused my job search there. To my delight, the first opportunity that appeared was working with a nonprofit in Monticello, Utah, at the Four Corners School of Outdoor Education.

Among its many outdoor education programs, its Canyon Country Youth Corps program recruited Navajo youth from the nearby reservation and trained them to perform conservation work on public lands. The role I was applying for involved documenting their efforts—camping in the backcountry with the crews, taking photos and videos, and producing content for their social media platforms. It seemed like a perfect fit for my skills and passions.

That year in Monticello was an adventure of a lifetime. I spent over 120 days camping on public lands, plunging into the diverse beauty of the Colorado Plateau. On our shared days off, Corrie—who was working just down the road at Mesa Verde—and I would embark on car camping excursions to nearby public lands.

During the sweltering summer months, we sought refuge on the San Juan River and in the cool heights of the mountains. It was my first experience with overnight river trips, and the thrill of navigating the rapids became an exhilarating new chapter in my outdoor adventures. I continued to learn about the captivating world of Ancestral Puebloan culture, including their fascination with the celestial world. With the Colorado Plateau renowned for its pristine, dark skies and the absence of northern lights this far south, it felt like a natural progression to channel my passion into photographing the night sky and the Milky Way.

After completing my year in Monticello, Corrie and I learned we would be living together again, this time in Estes Park, Colorado. For Corrie, who grew up in Denver, Rocky Mountain National Park was like her backyard national park. That summer, we immersed ourselves in the alpine splendor. We climbed mountains and toasted with "summit sodas," spent time flat on our stomachs enjoying vibrant alpine wildflowers, and enjoyed the nightly symphony of elk bugling outside our window.

The following winter, we moved to Yellowstone. Shortly after accepting the winter posting, I received an offer for my first permanent position with the National Park Service. In a few months, I would return to Glacier National Park to apply the skills I had honed over the past six years. It felt like a major milestone—proof that all the hard work had finally paid off.

This book chronicles that transformative period in my life. The subsequent chapters detail my creative journey as I evolved as a photographer, adapting my techniques to capture the diverse landscapes and resources I encountered while moving from place to place. During this time, I had few worries and obligations, allowing me to focus primarily on exploring and photographing as much of our country's natural beauty as possible. My goal was to build a portfolio that would enable me to pursue my passion for working with and protecting America's most treasured resources—our public lands.

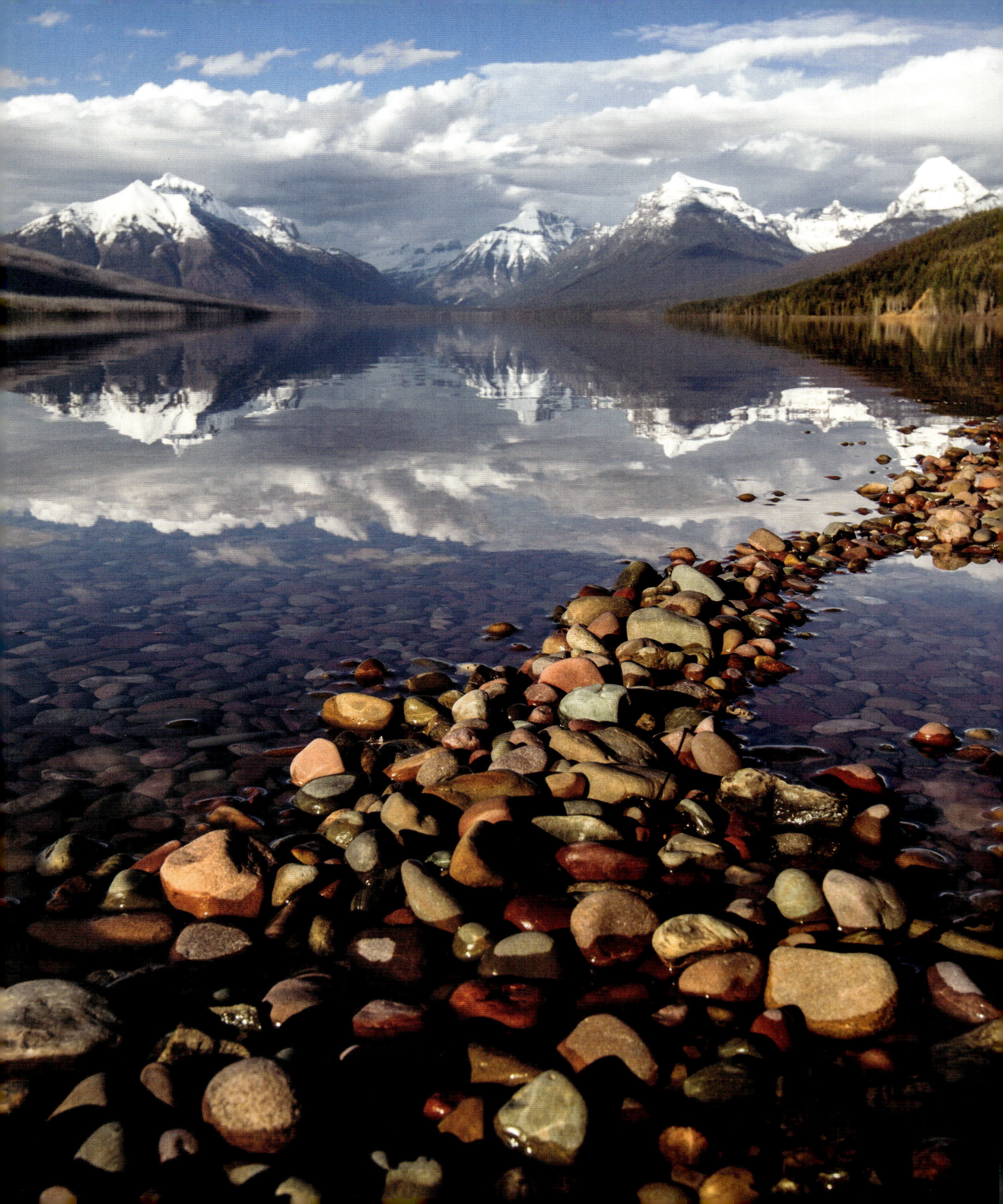

INTRODUCTION
A Legacy of Conservation

THE UNITED STATES SAW THE FORMALIZATION of public lands after the Revolutionary War. As the US expanded westward, the federal government acquired vast tracts of land through treaties, purchases, and conquest and forcible removal of Indigenous peoples. Early on, these lands were seen primarily as economic assets to be sold or given away to encourage settlement and development, such as through the Homestead Act of 1862.

However, by the mid-nineteenth century, thinkers like Henry David Thoreau and conservationists like George Perkins Marsh began advocating for the protection of natural landscapes, arguing that land should be preserved for its aesthetic, spiritual, and ecological values.

In 1864, President Abraham Lincoln signed the Yosemite Valley Grant Act, which granted the Yosemite Valley and the Mariposa Grove to the State of California for preservation and public enjoyment. This was a groundbreaking act because it set a precedent for the concept of protecting natural areas for public use, which would later inspire the creation of the national park system.

In 1872, the creation of Yellowstone National Park is often cited as the birth of the modern public lands movement. It was the first time land was set aside by the US government specifically for preservation and public enjoyment. This idea spread to other parts of the world, inspiring the creation of national parks in countries like Canada, Australia, and New Zealand.

GLACIER NATIONAL PARK Lake McDonald is one of the most photographed lakes in Montana, for obvious reasons. The benefit of living in the area is that I've had the opportunity to enjoy and photograph it in all types of weather and seasons. This afternoon in particular, a small group of us spent the evening along this private beach, skipping stones while we waited for the sun to set. Hard to beat.

Today, nearly 40 percent of the United States is public land, supported by taxpayers and managed by federal, state, or local governments. Of that, roughly 640 million acres of land—about 28 percent of the country—are managed at the federal level by four primary land management agencies.

The Bureau of Land Management (BLM), established in 1946, manages around 247 million acres of public land, primarily in the western states and Alaska. The BLM oversees land for multiple uses, including grazing, mining, recreation, and conservation.

The United States Forest Service (USFS), established in 1906, manages approximately 193 million acres of national forests and grasslands. These lands are used for timber harvesting, recreation, watershed protection, and habitat conservation.

The US Fish and Wildlife Service (USFWS), established in 1940, manages around 89 million acres, primarily through the National Wildlife Refuge System. These lands are set aside for the conservation of wildlife and their habitats.

The National Park Service (NPS), established in 1916, manages about 85 million acres in the form of national parks, monuments, historic sites, and other protected areas. The NPS focuses on preserving natural and cultural resources for public enjoyment and education.

These agencies were created to respond to growing concerns over the misuse and degradation of public lands and resources. Each agency developed a unique mission to address issues such as deforestation, wildlife conservation, public enjoyment of natural spaces, and the sustainable extraction of resources. The overarching goal of these agencies is to balance conservation with resource use, ensuring that public lands remain productive and preserved for future generations.

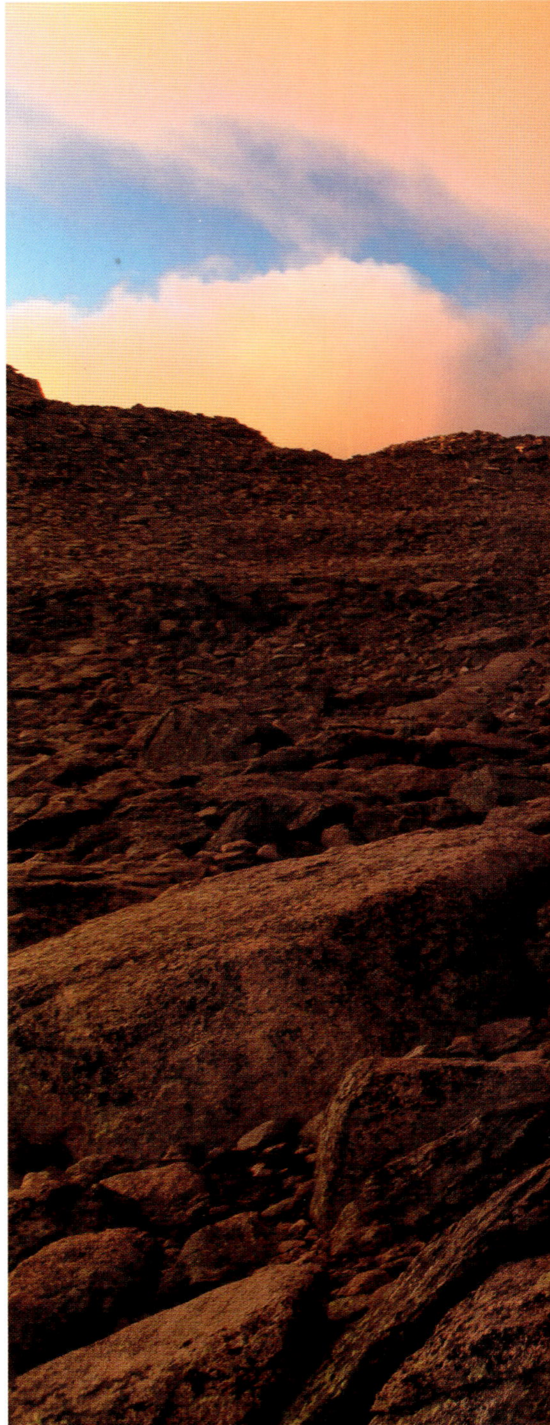

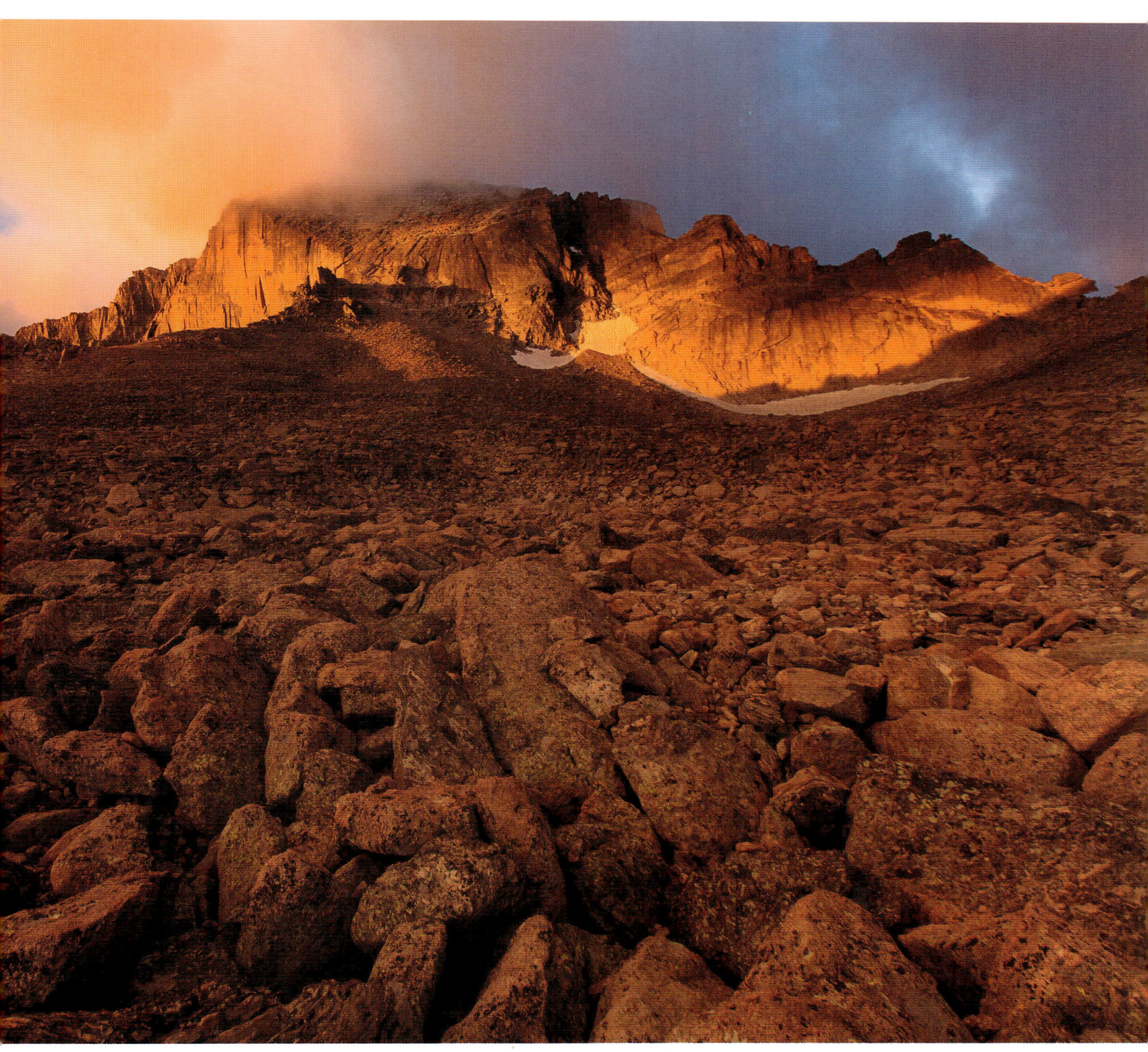

ROCKY MOUNTAIN NATIONAL PARK To celebrate my thirtieth birthday, a group of us backpacked to the Boulderfield at 12,760 feet with some beer and the mission to summit Longs Peak. When we woke up to ice and snow on the route, we decided to bail on the summit attempt. We didn't want to carry the weight back down, so at 6 a.m. we enjoyed the beer along with the sunrise views.

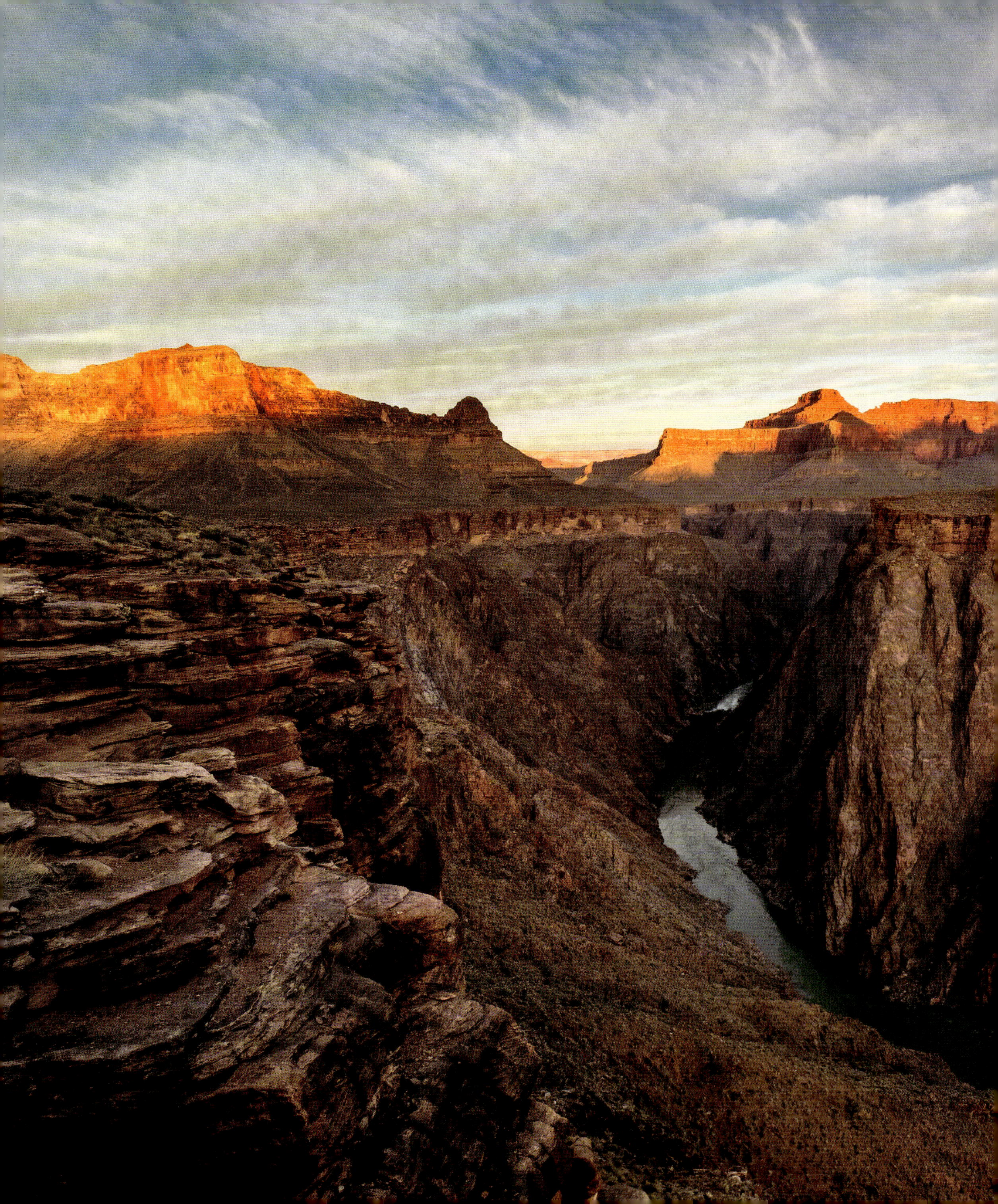

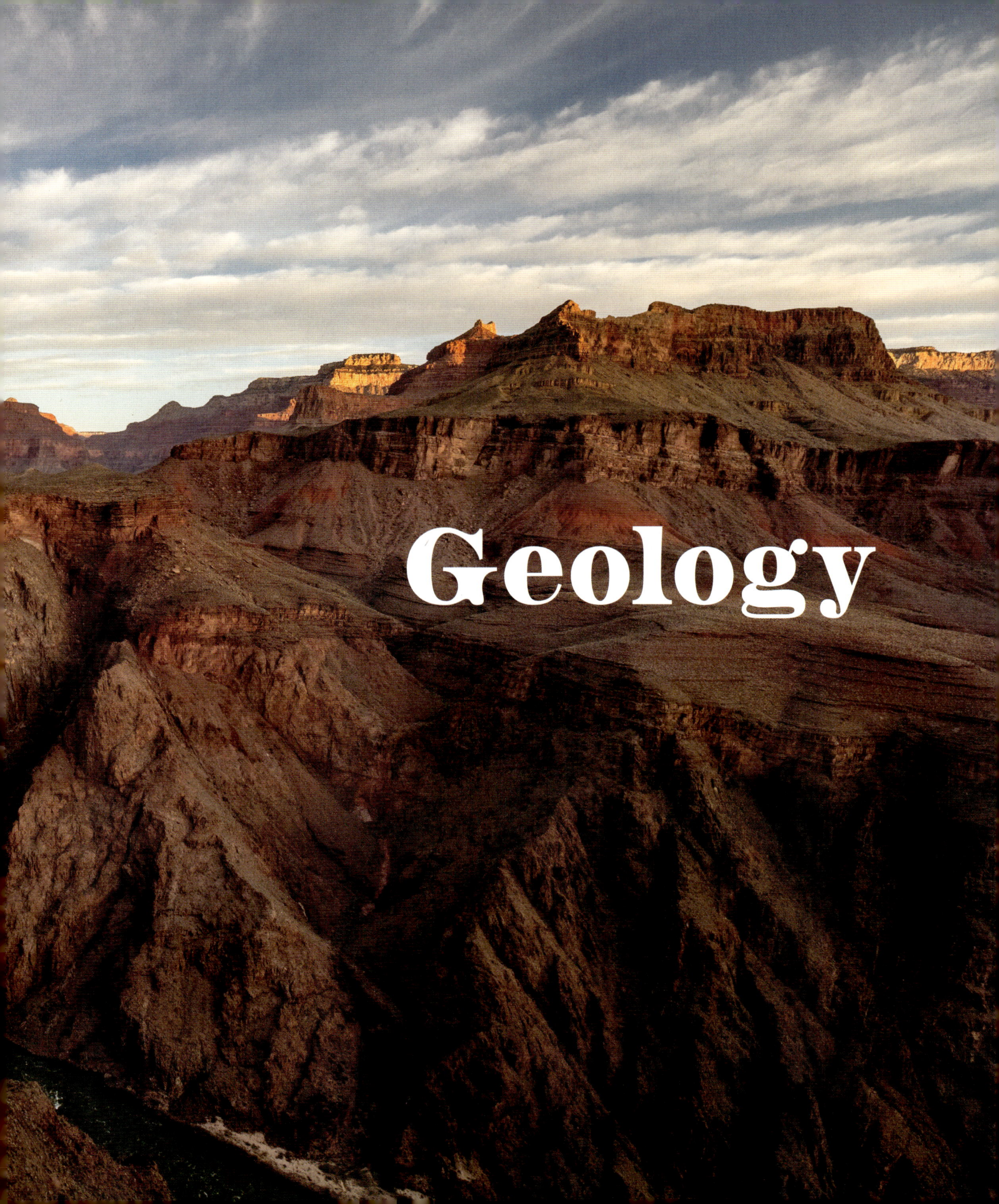

Geology

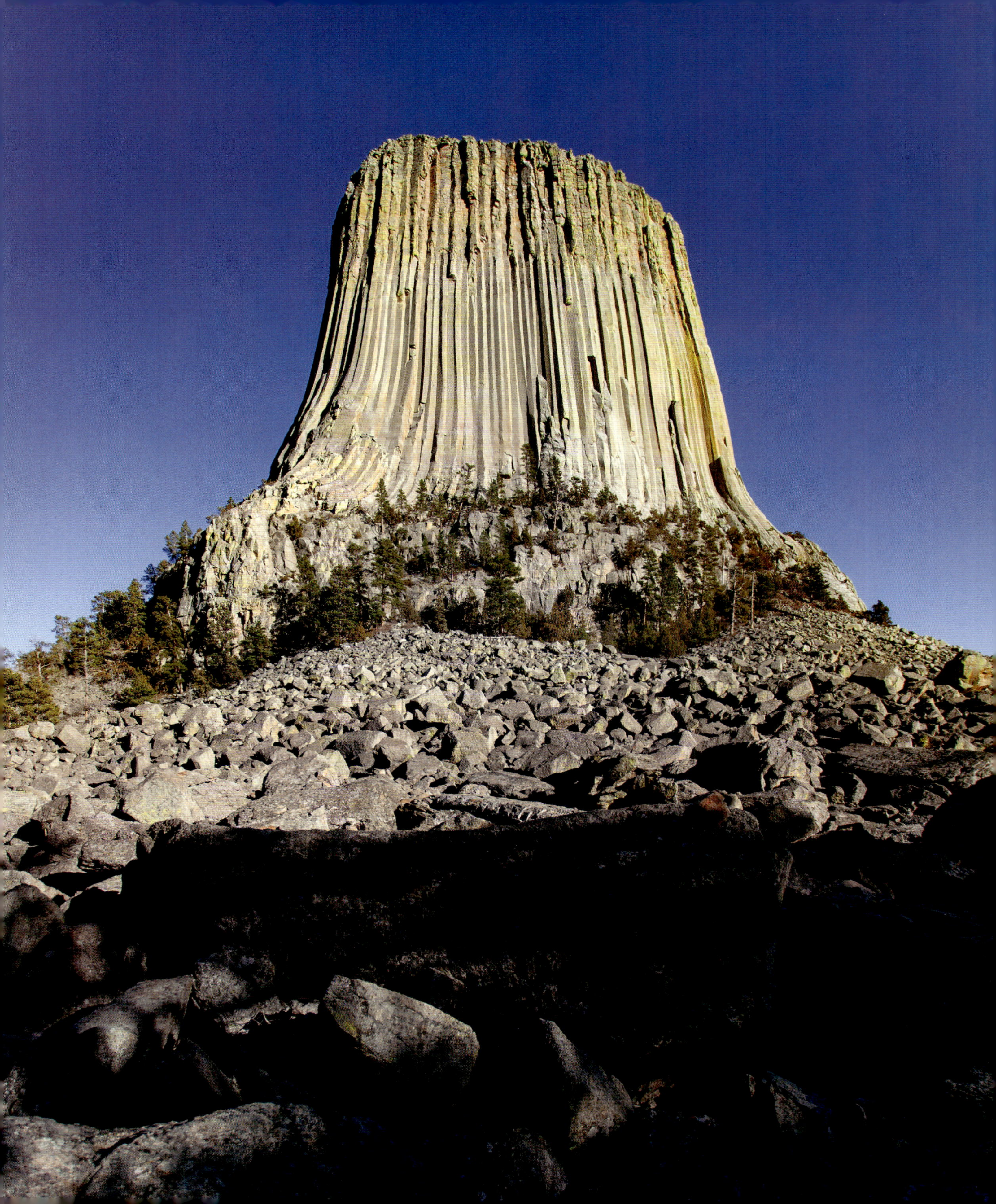

FOUNDATIONS OF THE EARTH

NORTH AMERICA'S GEOLOGY is both diverse and intricate, shaped by a long and dynamic history. This geologic history forms the bedrock of the landscapes on public lands, shaping their unique features and providing a window into the Earth's geological history. From towering mountains to deep canyons, rugged coastlines to expansive deserts, our national parks and public lands showcase a diverse array of geological formations that captivate the imagination and reveal the dynamic forces that have shaped our planet throughout time.

The geologic history of the United States spans billions of years, beginning with the formation of the Earth around 4.6 billion years ago. During this time, the planet was a molten mass, but over millions of years, it cooled, allowing the formation of the first solid crust and oceans.

During the Cambrian Period, around 540 million years ago, the land that would become North America started to take shape. Much of the continent was covered by shallow seas teeming with early marine life. Many marine organisms from that time, such as trilobites, brachiopods, and microorganisms, had shells and skeletons made of calcium carbonate. When these organisms died, their remains settled on the seafloor, gradually accumulating in thick layers. Over time, this sediment turned into solid limestone, preserving fossils of ancient marine life in the rock. Examples of these specimens can be found today throughout the western United States in places like Glacier and Bears Ears, and everywhere in between.

GRAND CANYON NATIONAL PARK (PREVIOUS)

DEVILS TOWER NATIONAL MONUMENT (OPPOSITE) My first visit to "Bear Lodge" was during a cross-country road trip with my family, back when I was too young to fully appreciate what I was seeing. Funny enough, I remember staring at this sacred mountain, feeling a mix of awe and confusion. Since then, I've visited a handful of times, and it still inspires the same feelings.

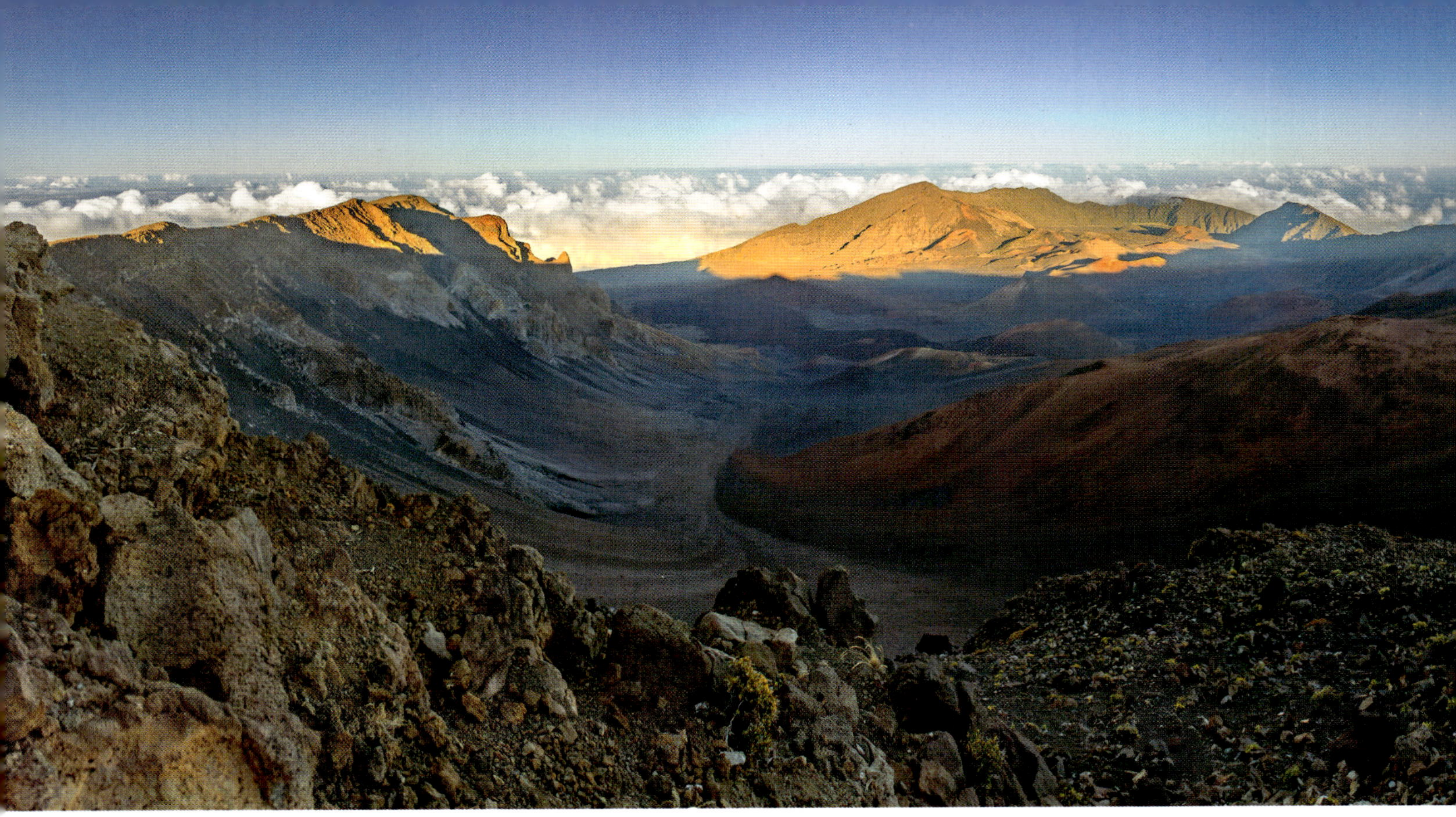

As time progressed, from approximately 480 to 300 million years ago, the Appalachian Mountains were formed. This mountain range emerged from a series of collisions between ancient landmasses, pushing up the Earth's crust and creating some of the oldest mountains in North America, as seen in Great Smoky Mountains and Shenandoah National Parks.

At the beginning of the Cenozoic Era, about 65 million years ago, dramatic changes in the Earth's climate and the landscape started to occur. The most famous event of this time was the mass extinction event that wiped out the dinosaurs, likely due to a combination of volcanic activity and a massive asteroid impact. Following this extinction event, mammals began to dominate. This period also saw the formation of large mountain ranges, like the Rocky Mountains, and continued geological processes that shaped the landscape. These geological wonders can be seen today in Rocky Mountain, Yellowstone, and Glacier National Parks.

The formation of the Grand Canyon started around 5 to 6 million years ago when the Colorado River started to carve through the region's layered sedimentary rocks. The river's powerful flow eroded the rock layers, cutting deeper into the Earth's crust over time. This process was aided by mechanical weathering, such as freeze-thaw cycles, which helped break down and remove rock debris. Chemical weathering–the dissolution of soluble rocks, particularly limestone–also played a role.

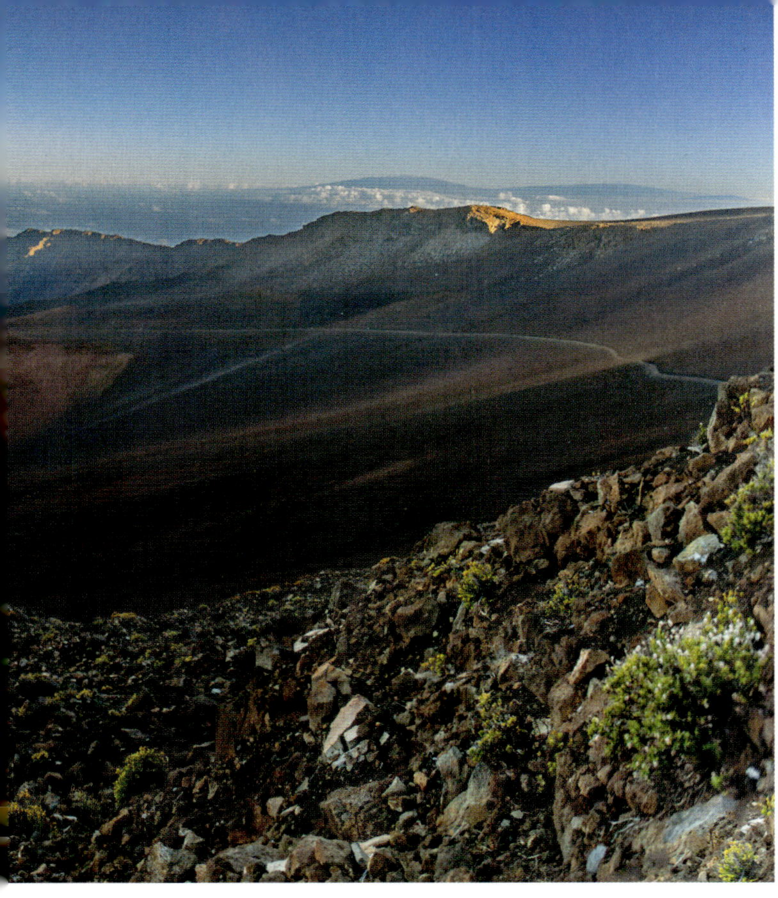

HALEAKALĀ NATIONAL PARK During my only visit to Maui, we planned a backpacking trip to Haleakalā Crater. Before setting out, we watched the sunrise from the summit—a must-do experience. From the rim of the volcano at 10,000 feet, it felt like we were gazing down from heaven—a very windy and chilly heaven.

The Colorado Plateau, where the canyon is located, experienced significant uplift due to tectonic forces, raising the region and allowing the river to cut even deeper. Wind and ice further shaped the canyon's features, and the relentless action of the river, combined with these weathering processes, gradually created the vast, intricate landscape of the Grand Canyon that we see today.

Chemical weathering is also responsible for the formation of many cave systems. The process begins when slightly acidic water, which has absorbed carbon dioxide from the atmosphere or the soil, seeps into the ground through cracks in the Earth's surface. The carbon dioxide reacts with the limestone, dissolving it over time. This chemical reaction creates underground voids and passageways. This primary cave formation is called speleogenesis. Secondary formations—like stalactites and stalagmites—form as water flows through these voids, depositing minerals and creating beautiful and intricate features, called speleothems, which are commonly seen in caves like Carlsbad Caverns.

One of the most significant geological events in recent history was the Ice Ages, which began about 2.5 million years ago and lasted until about 10,000 years ago. During this time, enormous ice sheets covered large portions of North America, including much of Canada and the northern United States. These glaciers were like massive ice blankets that moved slowly across the land, carving out U-shaped valleys, forming new lakes, and shaping the landscape in profound ways. Many of the landscapes protected in places like Yosemite, Glacier, and Grand Teton National Parks were formed by the movement of these glaciers. As the Ice Ages came to an end, the glaciers melted, and the landscape began to recover and change again.

In the past 10,000 years, after the Ice Ages, the landscape of North America continued to evolve. The diverse landscapes we see today, from the deserts of the Southwest to the forests of the Northeast, are the result of ongoing geological processes.

Volcanism has also played a significant role in shaping the North American continent. As the Pacific Plate subducts beneath the North American Plate, it melts, and the resulting magma rises to the surface. This subduction process is responsible for the volcanic activity seen along the Pacific Coast from Oregon to the Aleutian Islands in Alaska and is part of a larger feature known as the Pacific Ring of Fire.

The volcanic activity observed in Yellowstone and Hawai'i Volcanoes National Parks, however, is due to hotspots beneath the North American and Pacific Plates, respectively, rather than subduction, as seen in the Pacific Ring of Fire. Yellowstone sits atop a cooling magma chamber that rises from deep within the Earth's mantle. This hotspot heats the rocks and groundwater, creating the ideal conditions for the highest concentration of geysers in the world.

Similarly, the Hawaiian Islands are formed as the Pacific Plate moves over the Hawaiian Hotspot. Here, magma erupts through the ocean floor, creating volcanic islands. The Big Island of Hawaii is home to some of the world's most active volcanoes, including Kilauea and Mauna Loa, which continue to shape the landscape with their eruptions. These volcanoes produce basaltic lava flows that build up the islands' shield volcanoes, known for their broad, gentle slopes. Over time, volcanic activity has created a diverse landscape of volcanic craters, lava tubes, and rugged terrain. Erosion and weathering further shape the islands, contributing to their varied topography of lush rainforests, rugged cliffs, and coastal plains.

Our national parks and public lands play a crucial role in preserving geologic diversity and promoting scientific research and education. These geological wonders serve as living laboratories for scientists, educators, and visitors alike, offering opportunities to study Earth's processes, uncover ancient fossils, explore the mysteries of geologic time, and admire their beauty.

Public lands face numerous threats to their geological heritage, including resource extraction, climate change, and unsustainable land use practices. By safeguarding the geological treasures found on public lands, we can ensure that future generations have the opportunity to explore, study, and appreciate the rich tapestry of Earth's geological history, fostering a deeper understanding of our planet's past, present, and future.

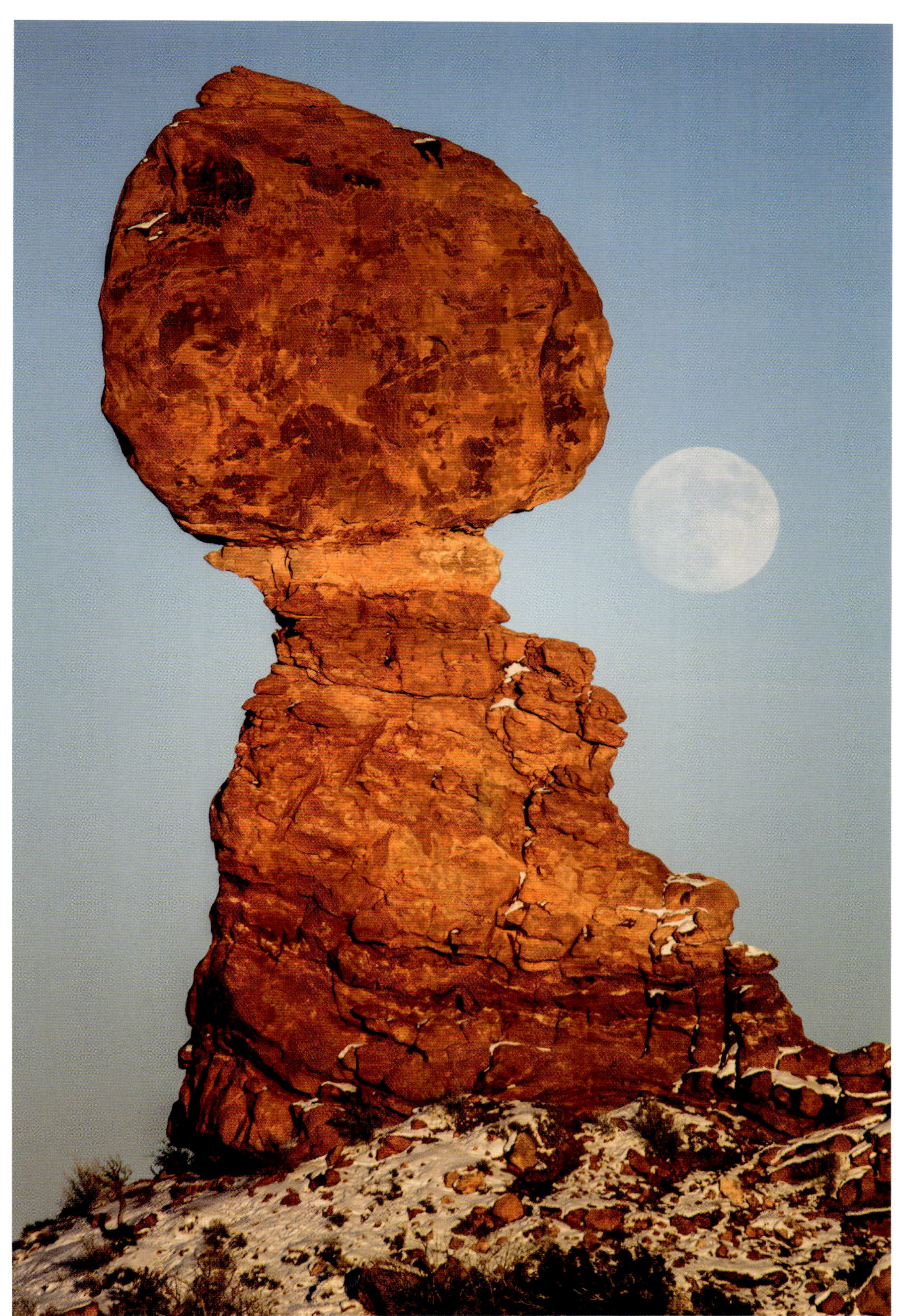

ARCHES NATIONAL PARK

After watching my first supermoon rise in Arches, I made it a habit to catch each full moonrise from a new spot. On this particular winter evening, we had just finished a hike and were on our drive home. As we passed Balanced Rock, I noticed in my rearview mirror that the moon had risen. No planning—just happened to be in the right place at the right time.

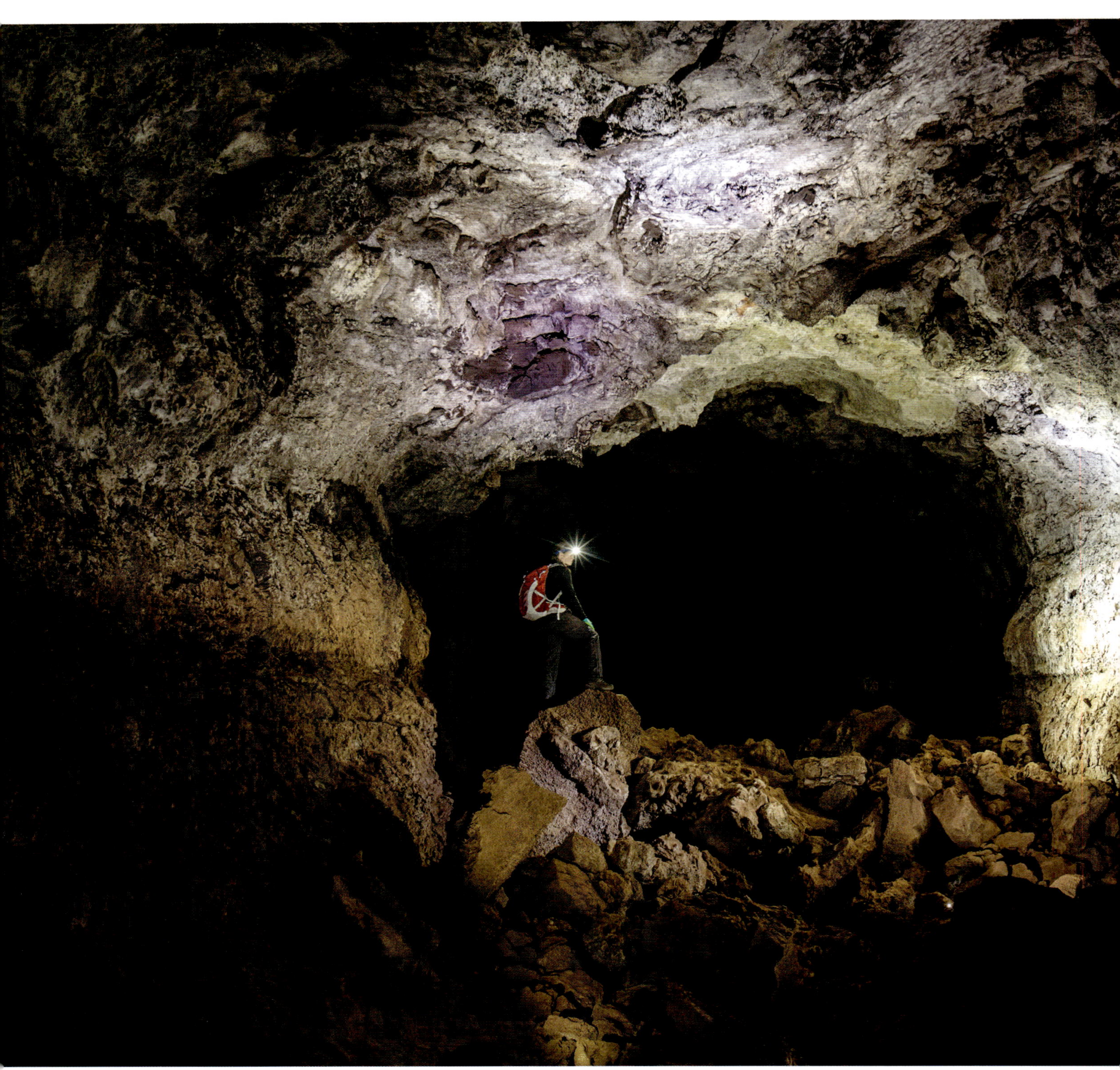

EL MALPAIS NATIONAL MONUMENT

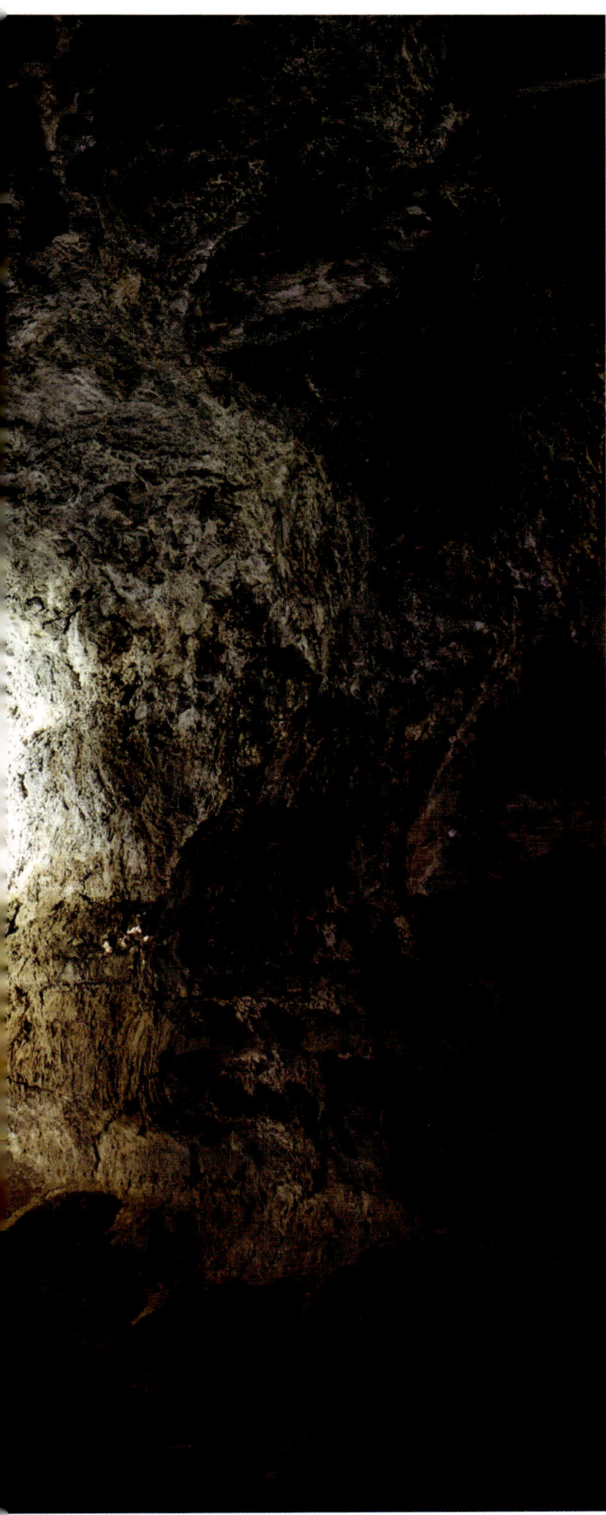

My first off-trail cave trip was on a tour of the Hall of the White Giant in Carlsbad Caverns. Once inside, we immediately started crawling, sliding, twisting, and contorting our way through the cave. The experience was unlike anything I had done before—physically and mentally challenging, like solving a puzzle with your entire body. As we progressed, we reached Matlock's Pinch, the crux of the cave. It's a six-foot-long passage so narrow that you must raise your hands above your head, slide on your stomach, and turn your head sideways to squeeze through.

While I don't consider myself claustrophobic, I had no desire to linger in that tight spot. Eager to get through the pinch quickly, I waited for the person in front of me to give the all-clear before entering. Unfortunately, after I was fully inside the pinch, they called back for me to wait—the person ahead of them was having a panic attack.

At first, I kept my mind occupied with other thoughts. But eventually, anxiety started creeping in. I became acutely aware of how hot and uncomfortable I was. When I tried to shift my body, I couldn't move. I was completely enveloped by rock on all sides. The light from my headlamp reflected off the rock just inches from my face, making the situation worse. Just as panic was about to take over, I managed to bend my elbow enough to switch off my headlamp. In the pitch-black, hyperventilating but unable to take deep breaths due to the tight space, I found myself at a breaking point.

Then, out of nowhere, I had an epiphany: I was crawling through a cave eight hundred feet below the surface of the Earth. "How lucky am I to be doing this?," I thought. My labored breathing eased, and before I knew it, I was laughing uncontrollably. As I lay there, giggling in the dark, the all-clear came again, and I crawled out without issue.

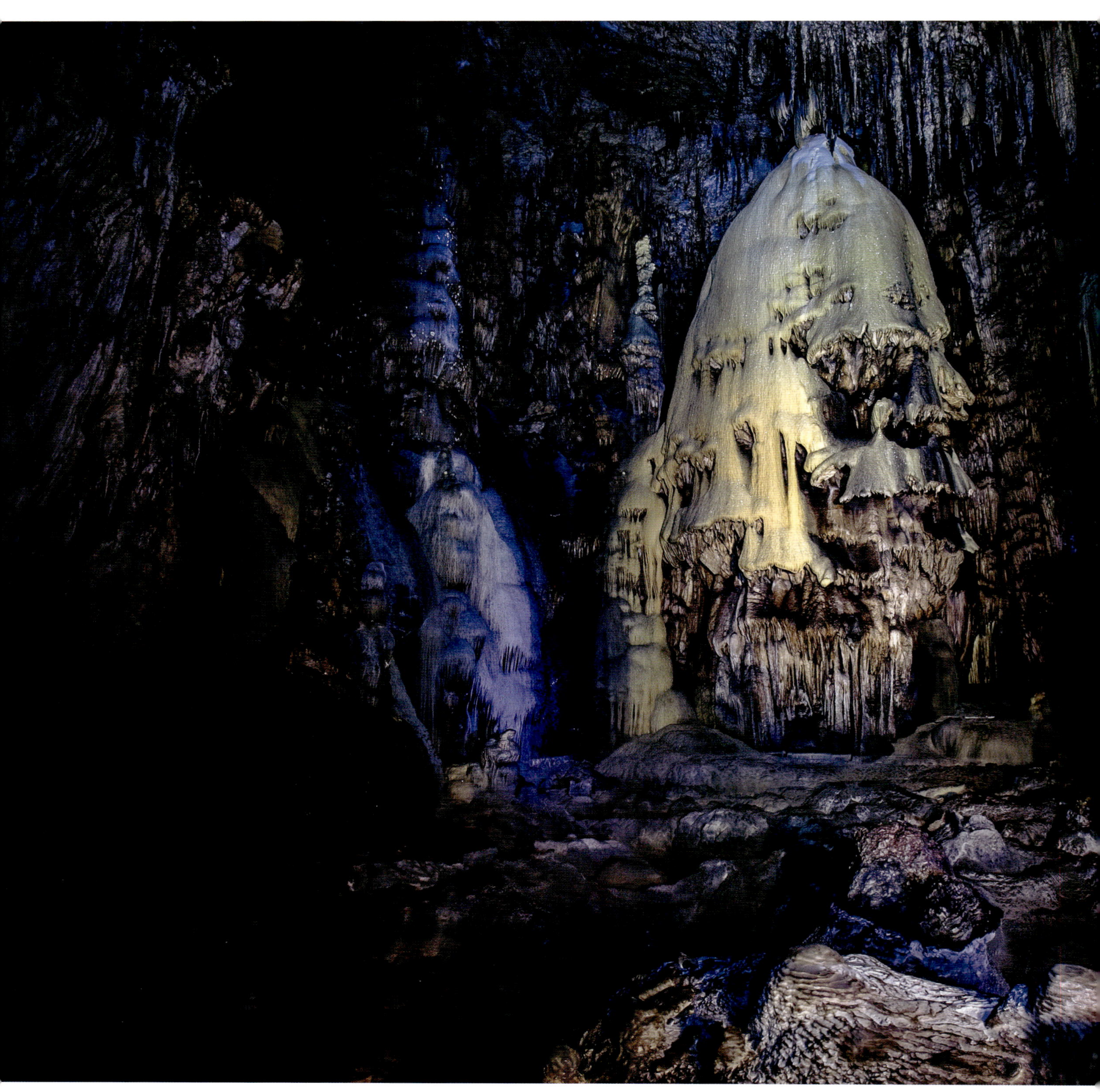

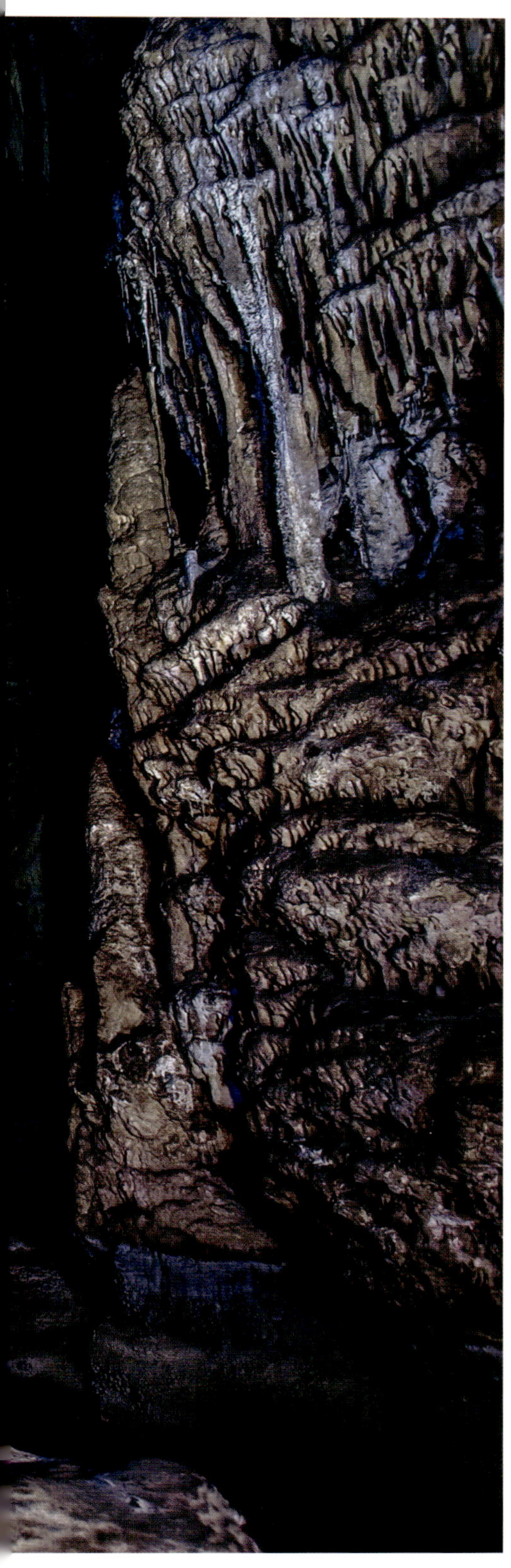

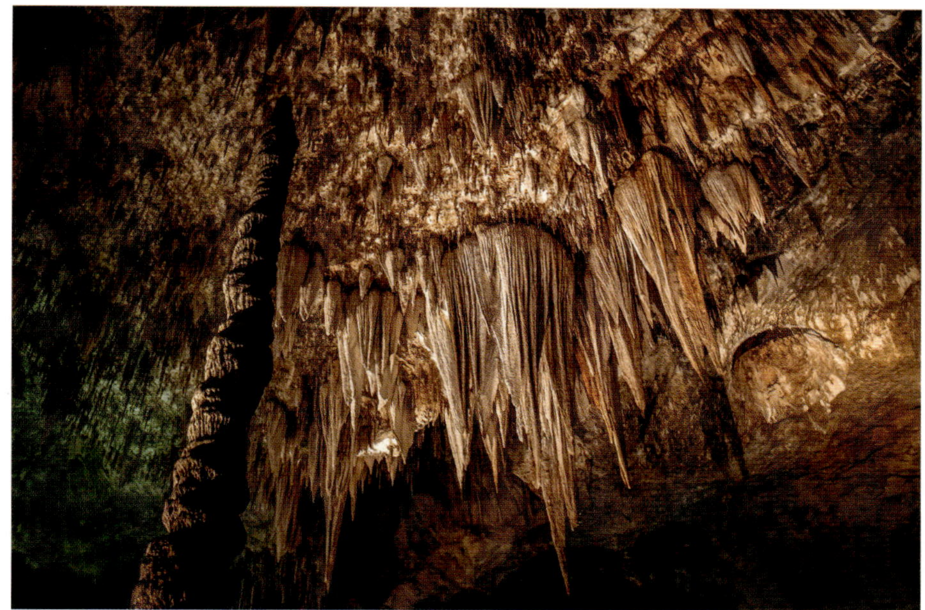

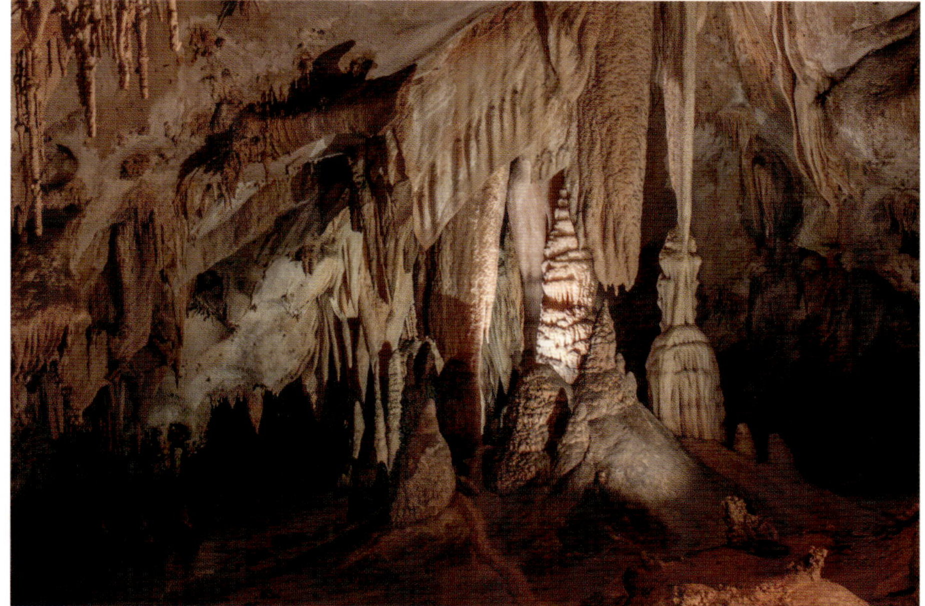

CARLSBAD CAVERNS NATIONAL PARK It wasn't until I lived in, worked at, and explored this park that I truly came to appreciate geology. I had visited other cave systems before, but none as spectacular as this one. The Big Room is more breathtaking than any cathedral I've seen in Europe. One of my favorite shifts was turning on the cave lights, knowing I was the only person there. I'd sit on a small bench, take in the view, and smile, feeling incredibly lucky.

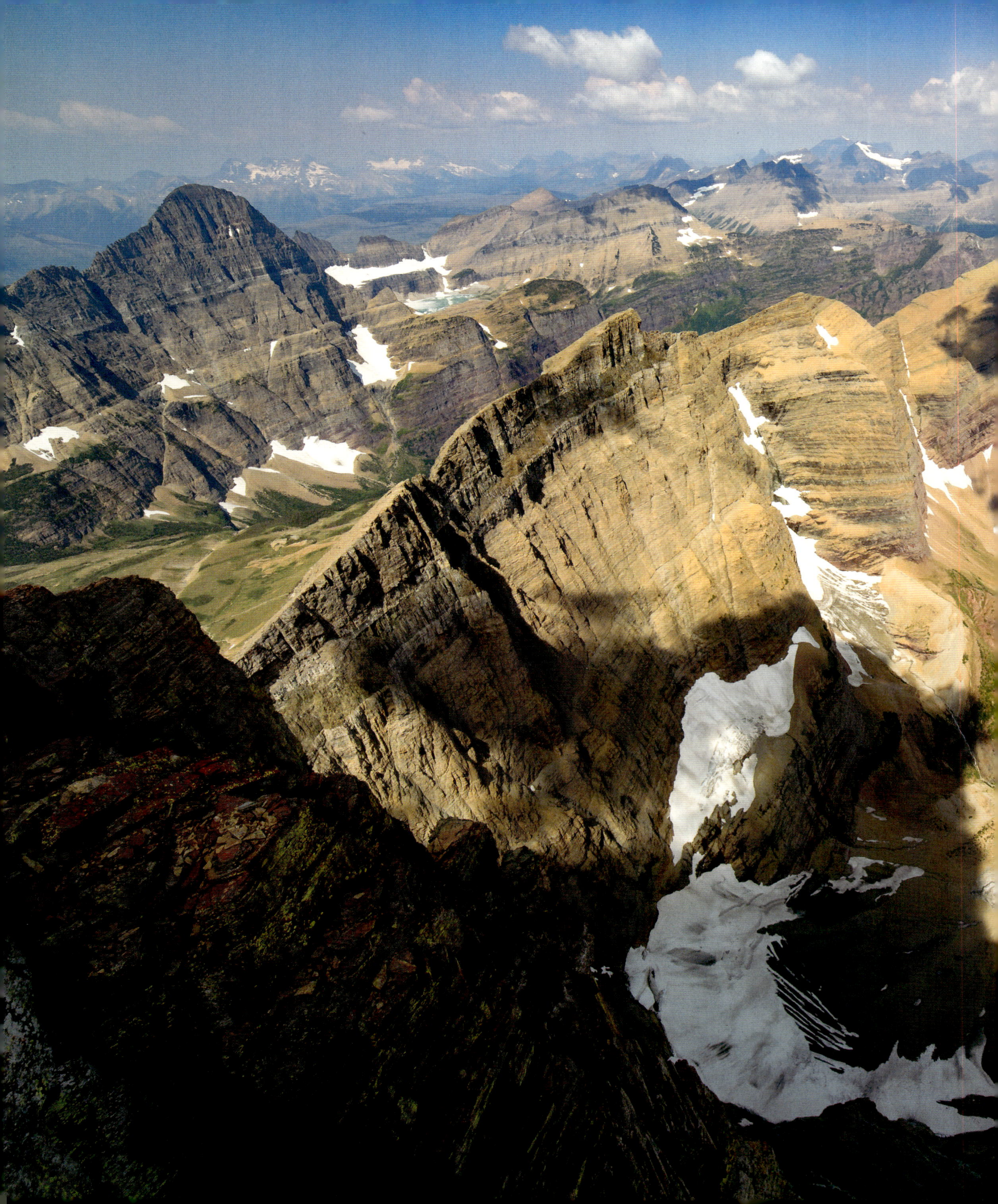

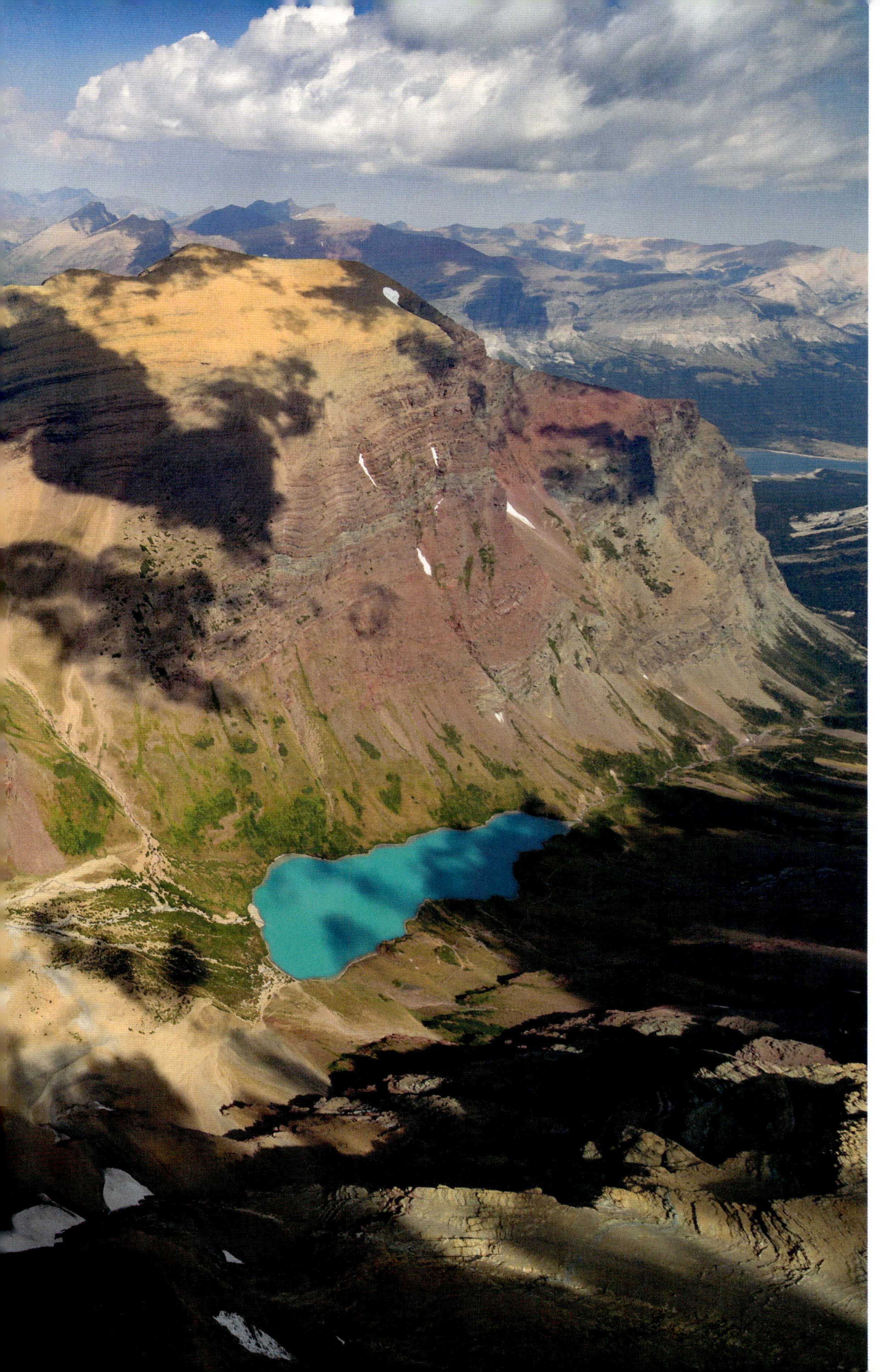

GLACIER NATIONAL PARK
During my first summer in the park, I attempted to climb Mount Siyeh twice but was forced to turn back both times due to extreme wind. Seven years later, on a calm, windless day, I finally reached the summit—just in time to celebrate my birthday. Sitting at the top, I enjoyed a couple of birthday beers while taking in the breathtaking view of Cracker Lake, 4,000 feet below—a perfect reminder that good things come to those who wait.

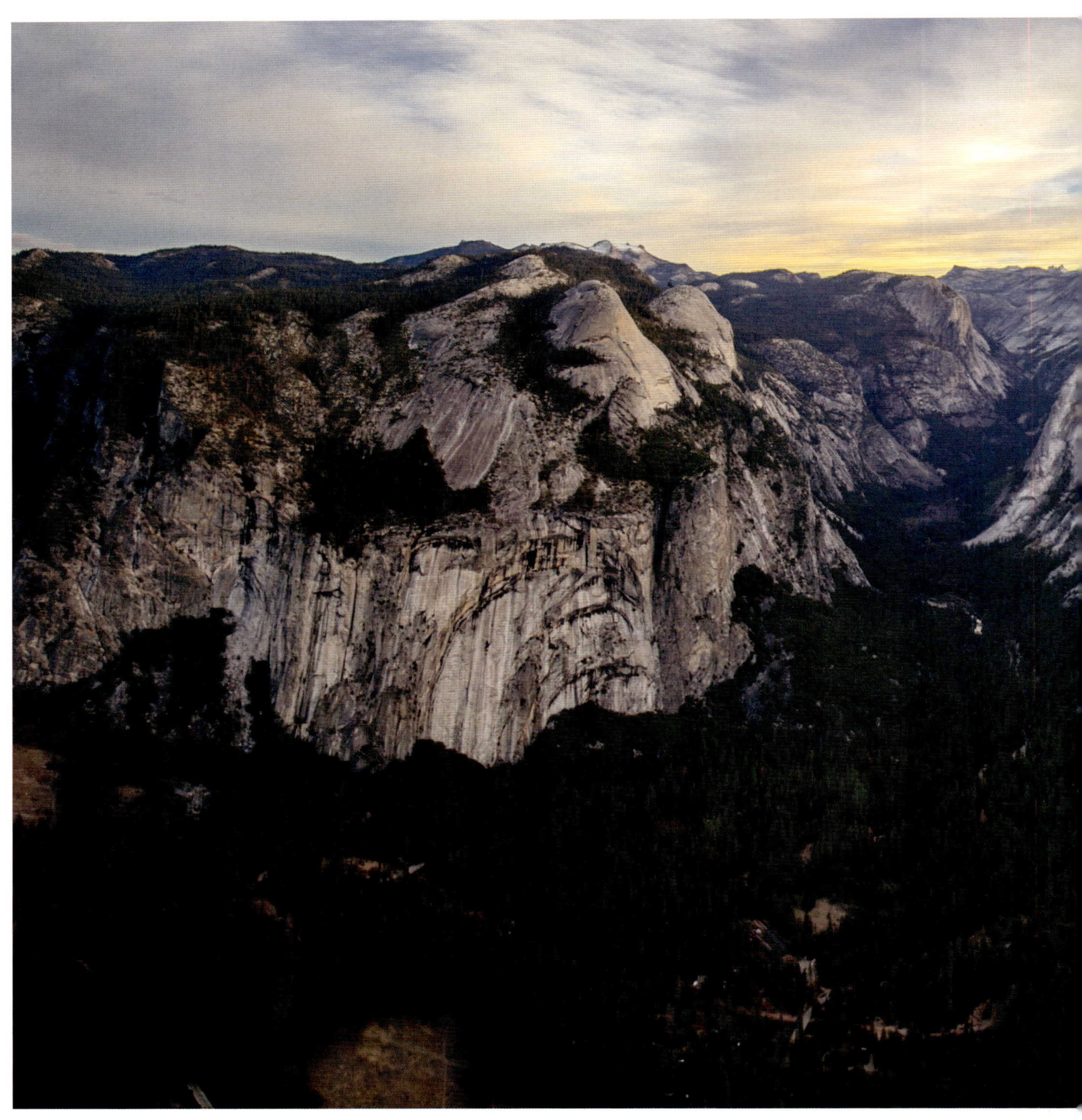

YOSEMITE NATIONAL PARK To celebrate the end of our thirty-day road trip, my friend and I drove to Glacier Point to watch the sunrise. Yosemite was the last of fourteen parks we visited on the trip, and this was the final photo taken before I had to leave for my new job at Carlsbad Caverns. A beautiful way to end a spectacular journey.

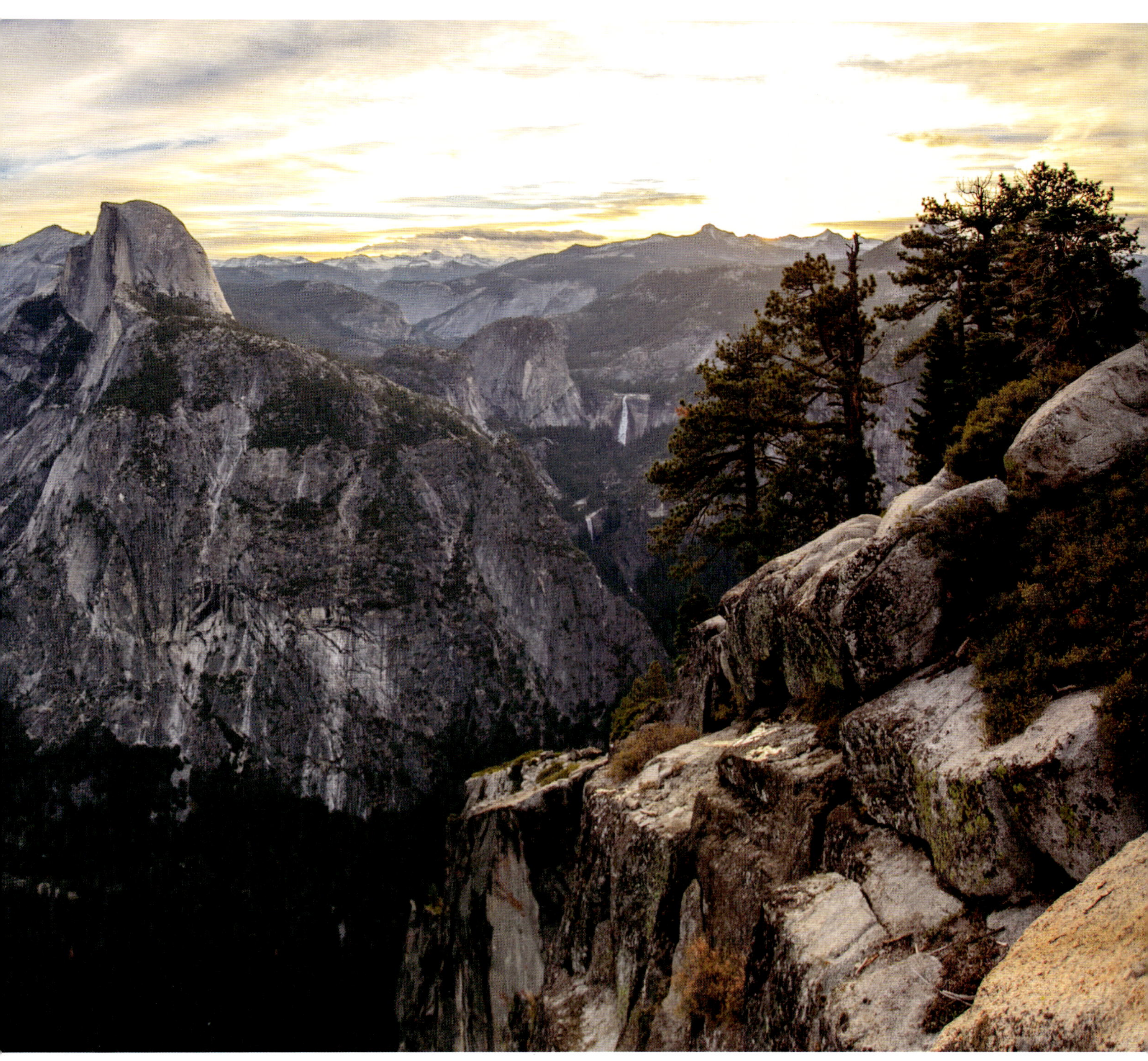

GRAND TETON NATIONAL PARK To celebrate my birthday, I planned a bucket list trip with two friends to summit the Grand Teton. Three weeks before the trip, I had emergency hernia surgery and had to break the news that I couldn't carry more than twenty pounds. Without hesitation, my friends reassured me it didn't matter. So, with seventy-pound packs between them, we set off. High winds and snow nearly forced us to turn back, but on summit day, the weather cleared. We spent the afternoon at the top, soaking in the views and enjoying our hard-earned summit sodas.

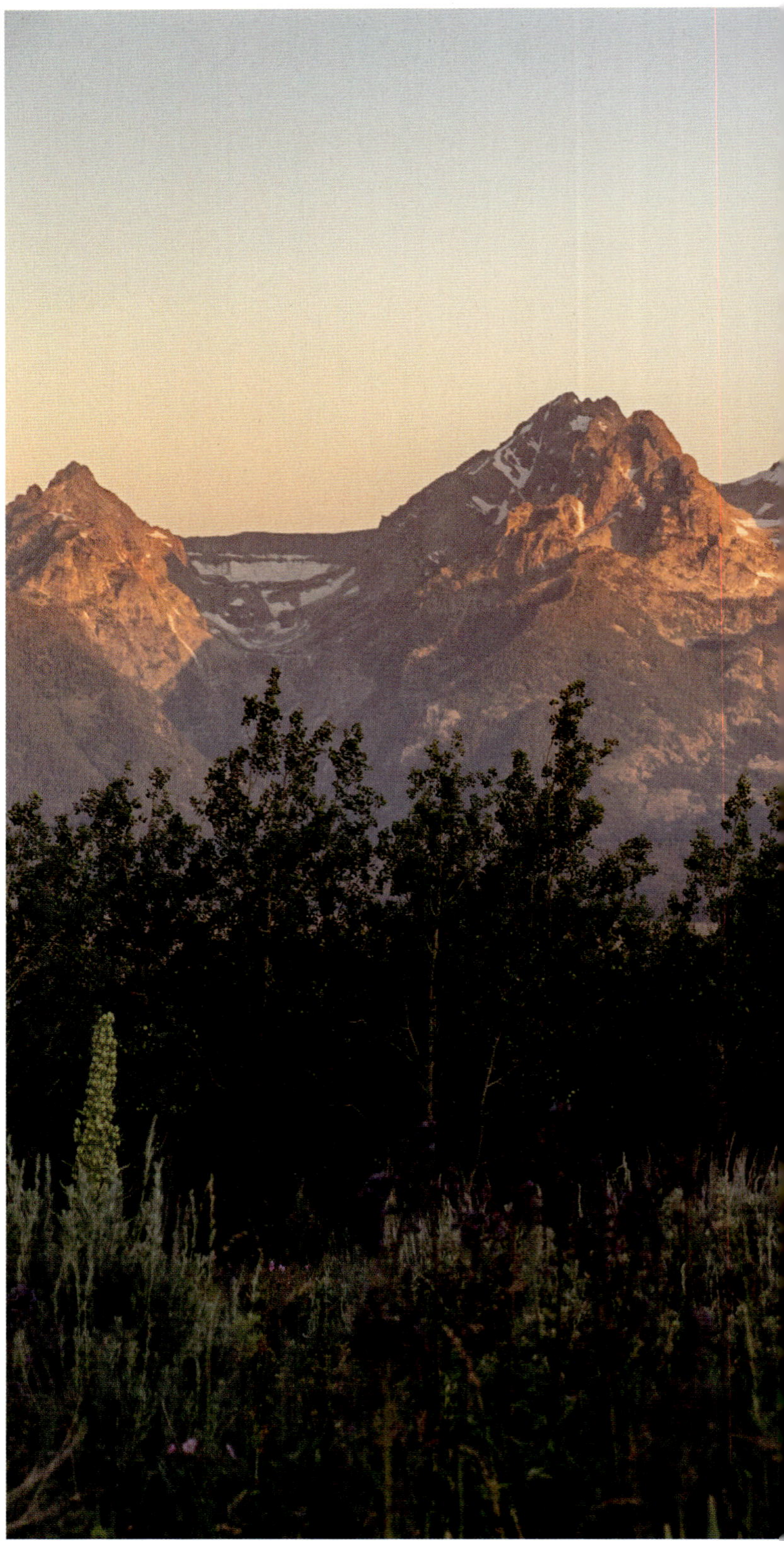

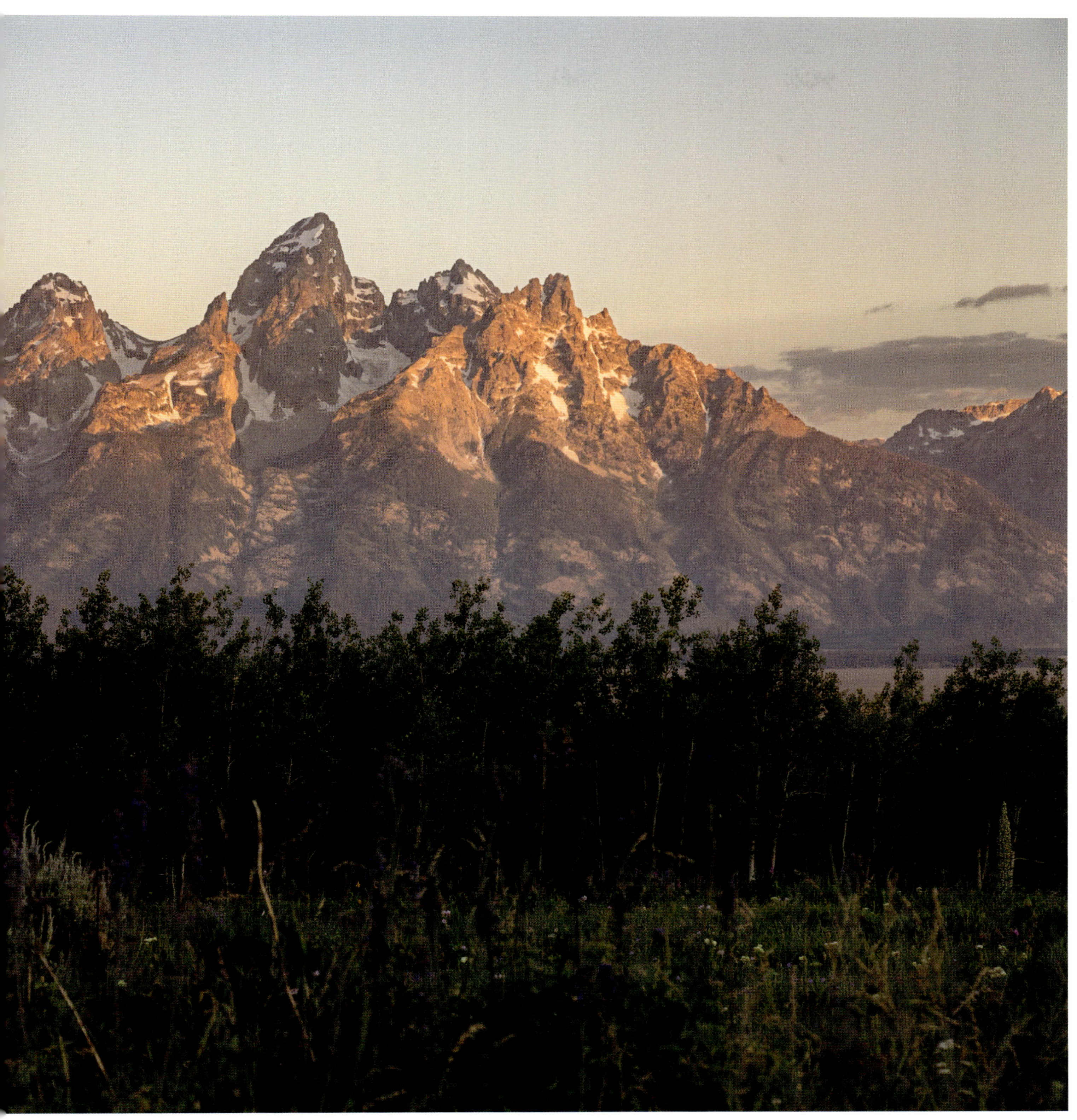

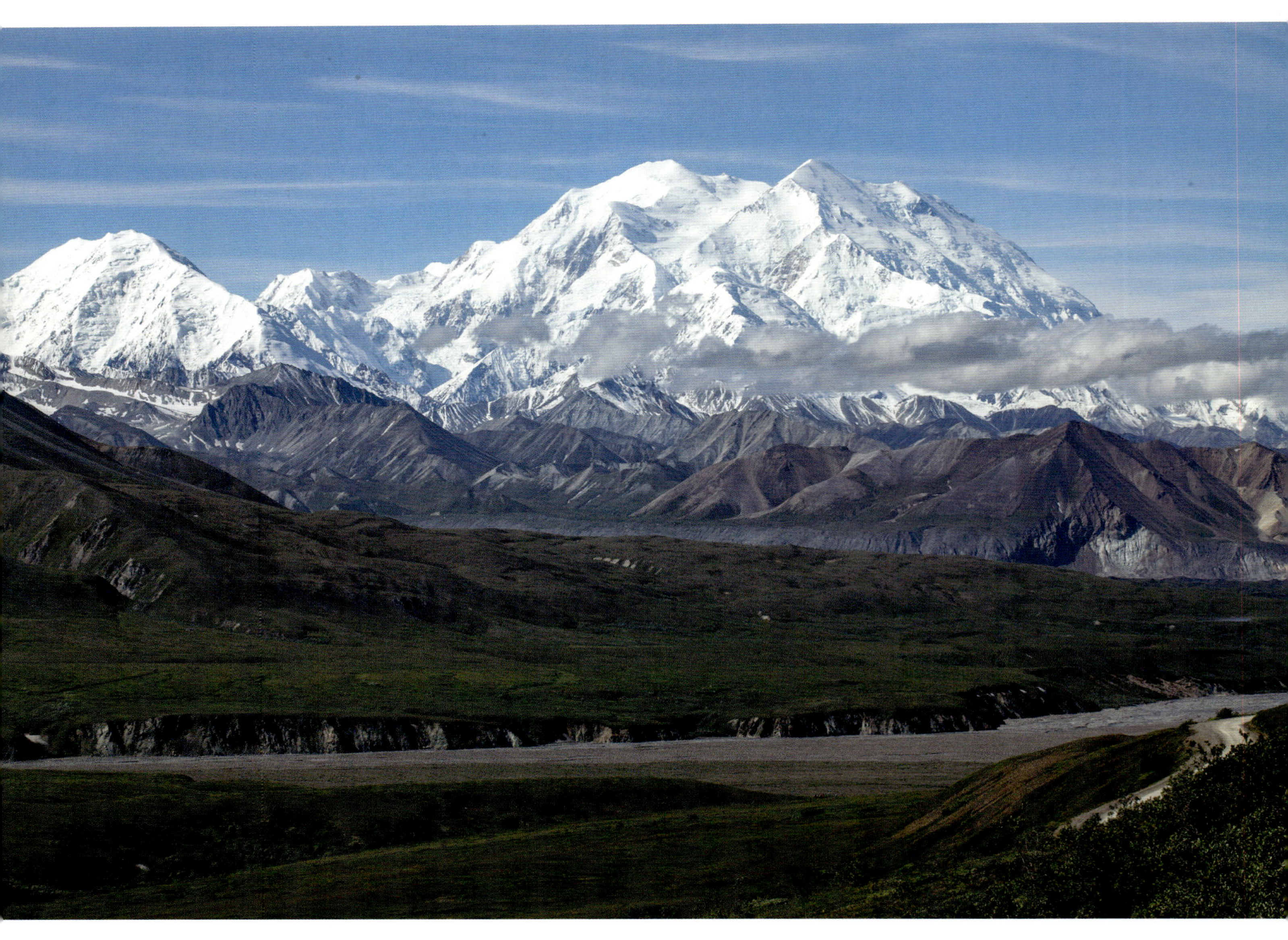

DENALI NATIONAL PARK AND PRESERVE (ABOVE)

DEATH VALLEY NATIONAL PARK (OPPOSITE)

The highest and lowest points in North America, both located in national parks, are separated by 20,592 feet of elevation—20,310 feet above sea level in Denali and 282 below sea level feet in Death Valley.

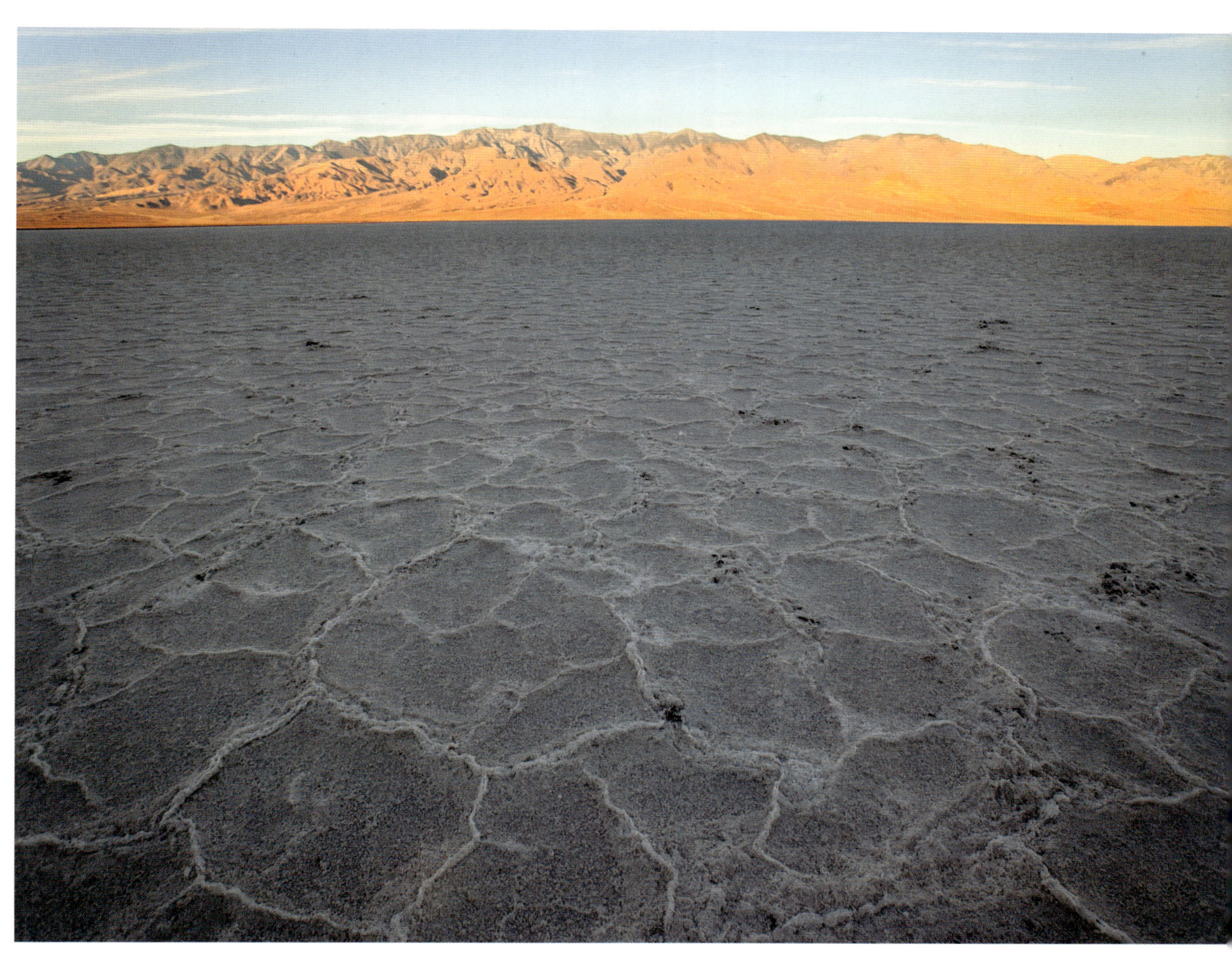

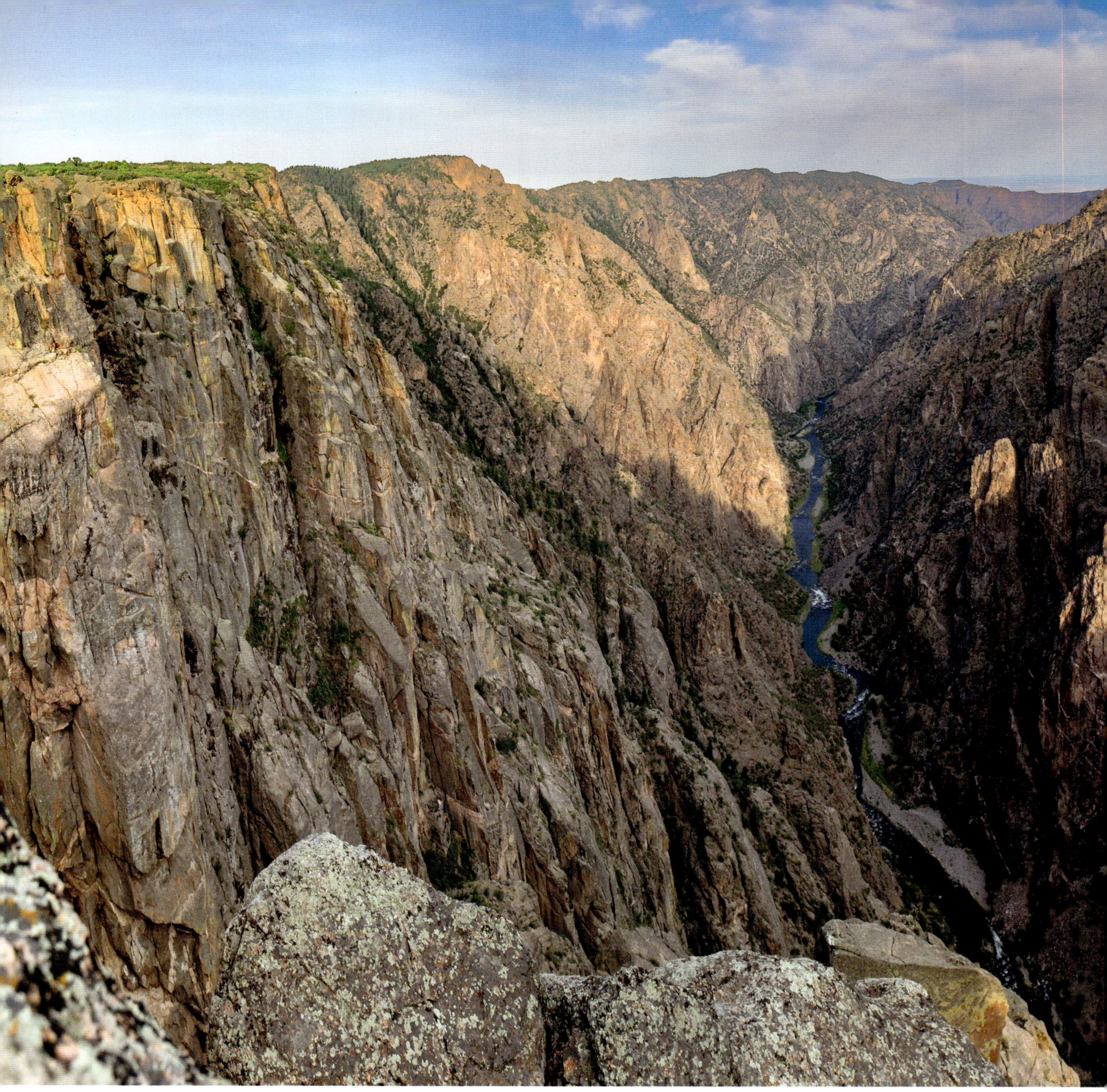

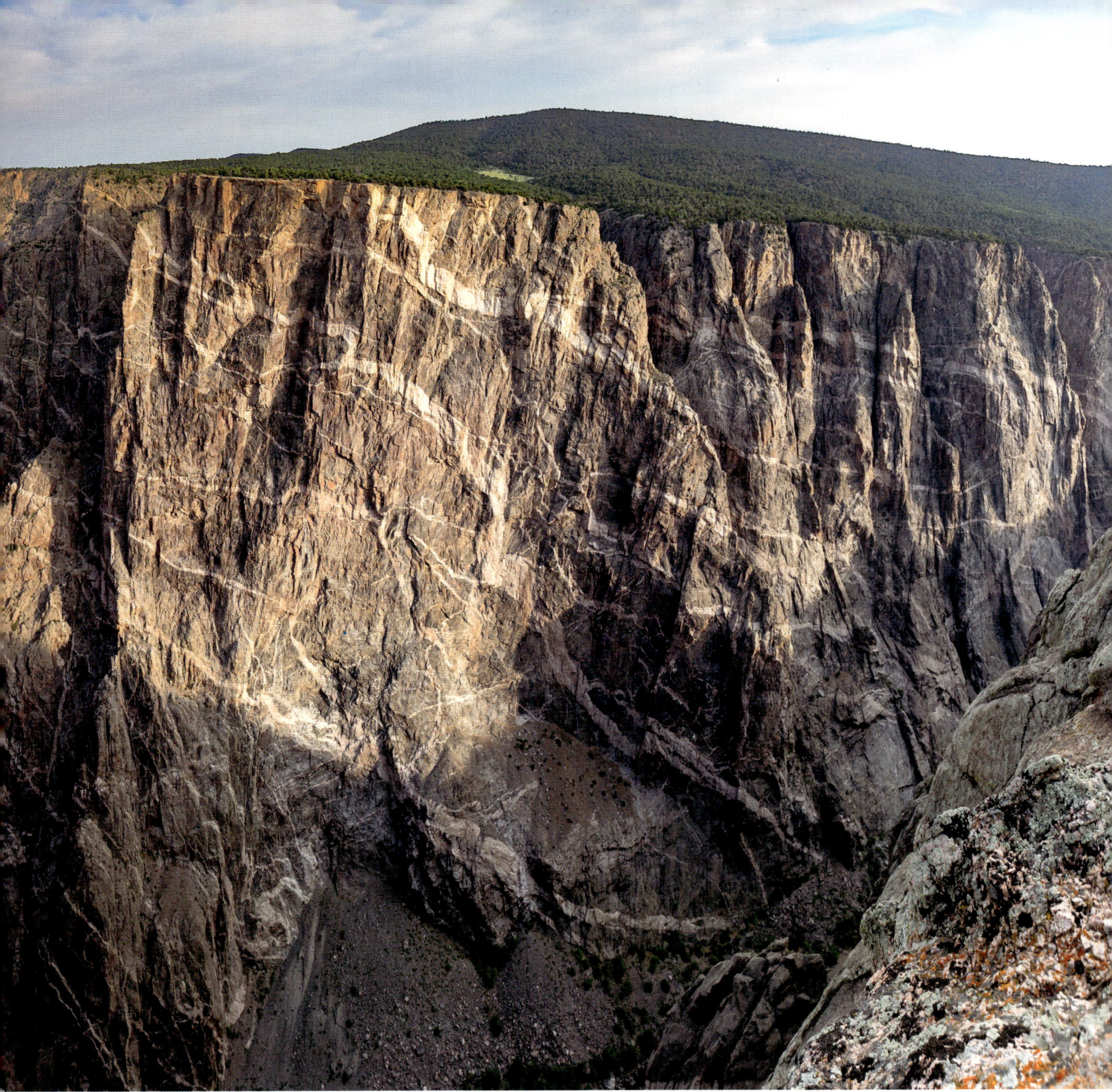

BLACK CANYON OF THE GUNNISON NATIONAL PARK One of the most difficult "hikes" I had ever done at that point in my life was the Gunnison Route down to the river from the South Rim. Dropping over 1,800 feet in just one mile, it felt less like a hike and more like a controlled fall at times. But don't worry—the park installed giant chains to help navigate the steepest, loosest sections on the way up and down.

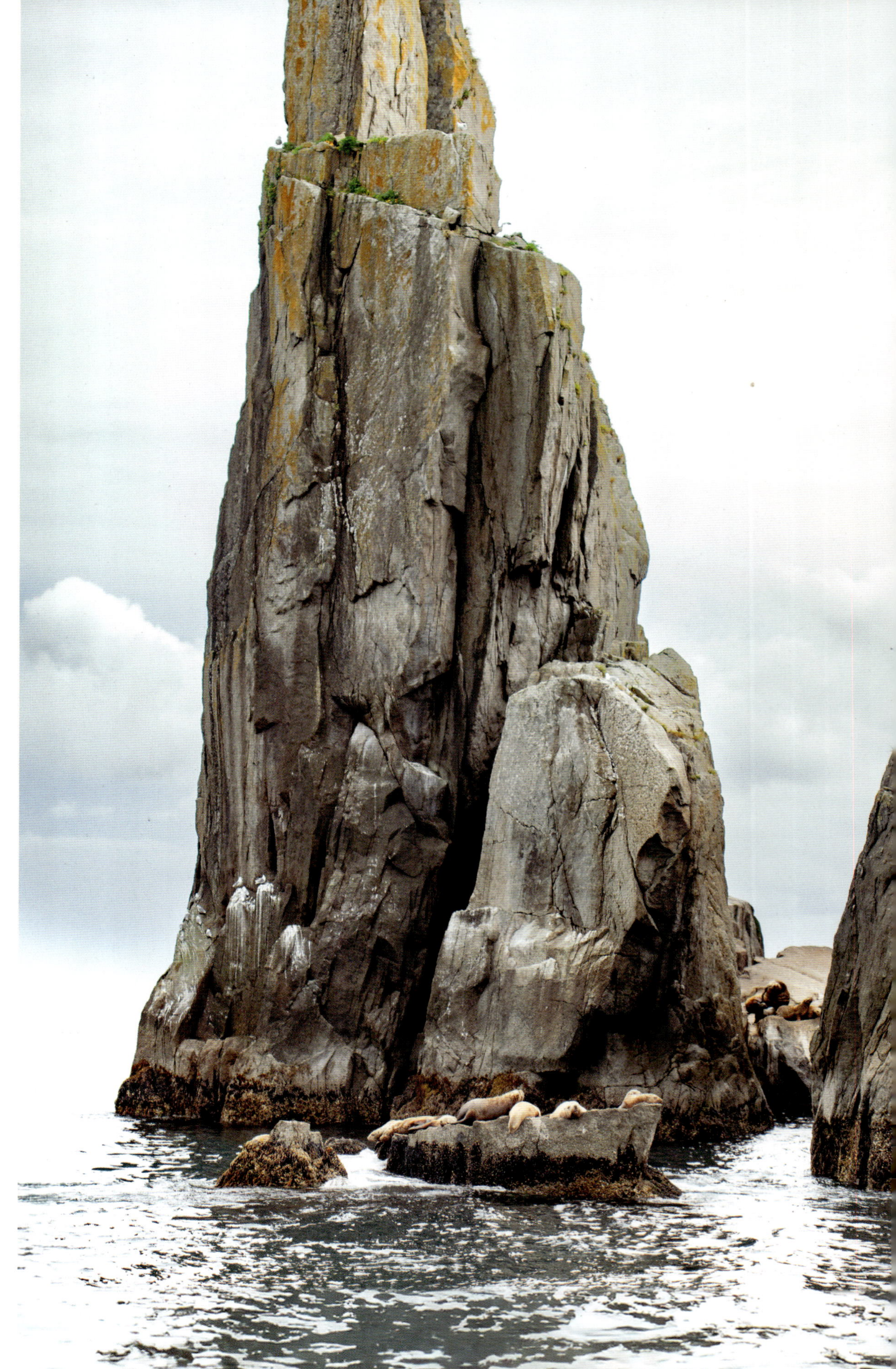

KENAI FJORDS NATIONAL PARK From a distance, these giant pinnacles of granodiorite appeared lifeless. It wasn't until our boat passed by more closely that I saw they were home to thousands of puffins, murres, and auklets. Sea lions were also lounging on the smooth granitic slabs, resting as the waves crashed around them.

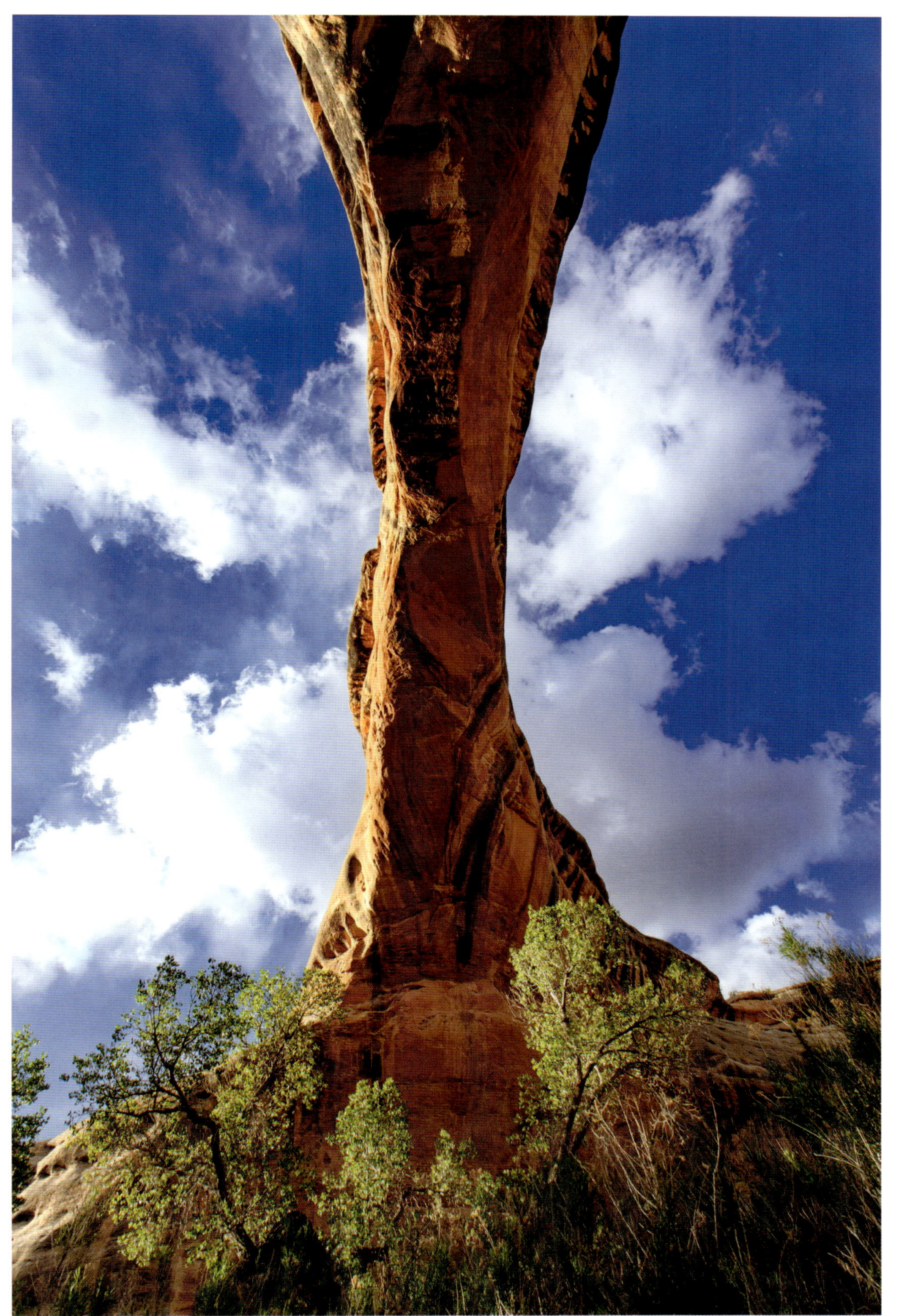

NATURAL BRIDGES NATIONAL MONUMENT
On my first visit to the monument, we took a wrong turn on our planned ten-mile hike and ended up hiking seven miles in the wrong direction. We only realized we had gone the wrong way when we came across backcountry hikers who informed us the fastest way back was to turn around. Those twenty-four miles still hold the record for my longest hike in a day—a record I don't plan on breaking.

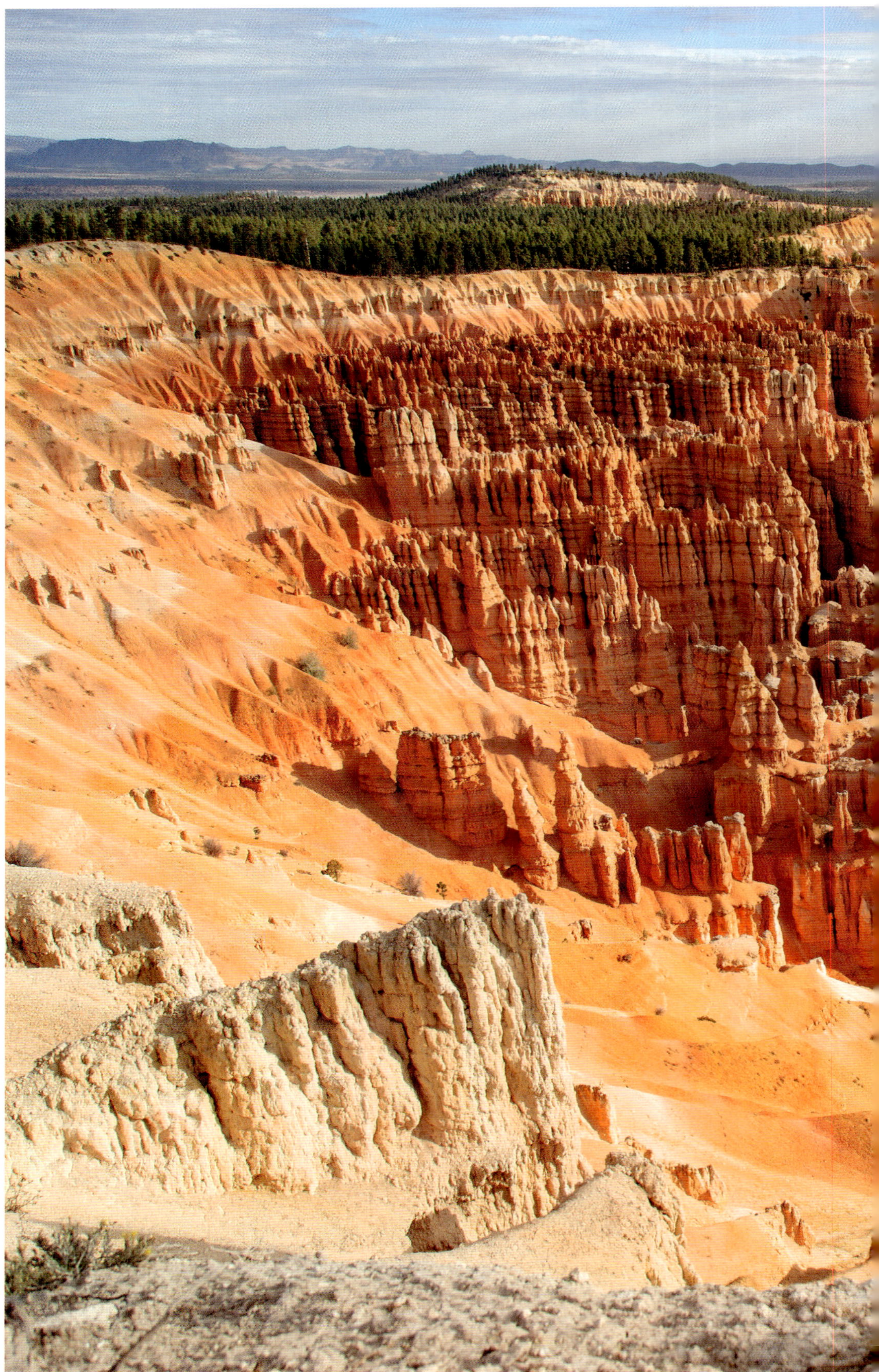

BRYCE CANYON NATIONAL PARK
My first visit to the park was during a large snowstorm and I wasn't able to see much. A few years later I came back with Corrie and we spent a long weekend hiking, birding, and taking in the sweeping vistas of crimson hoodoos and endless horizons.

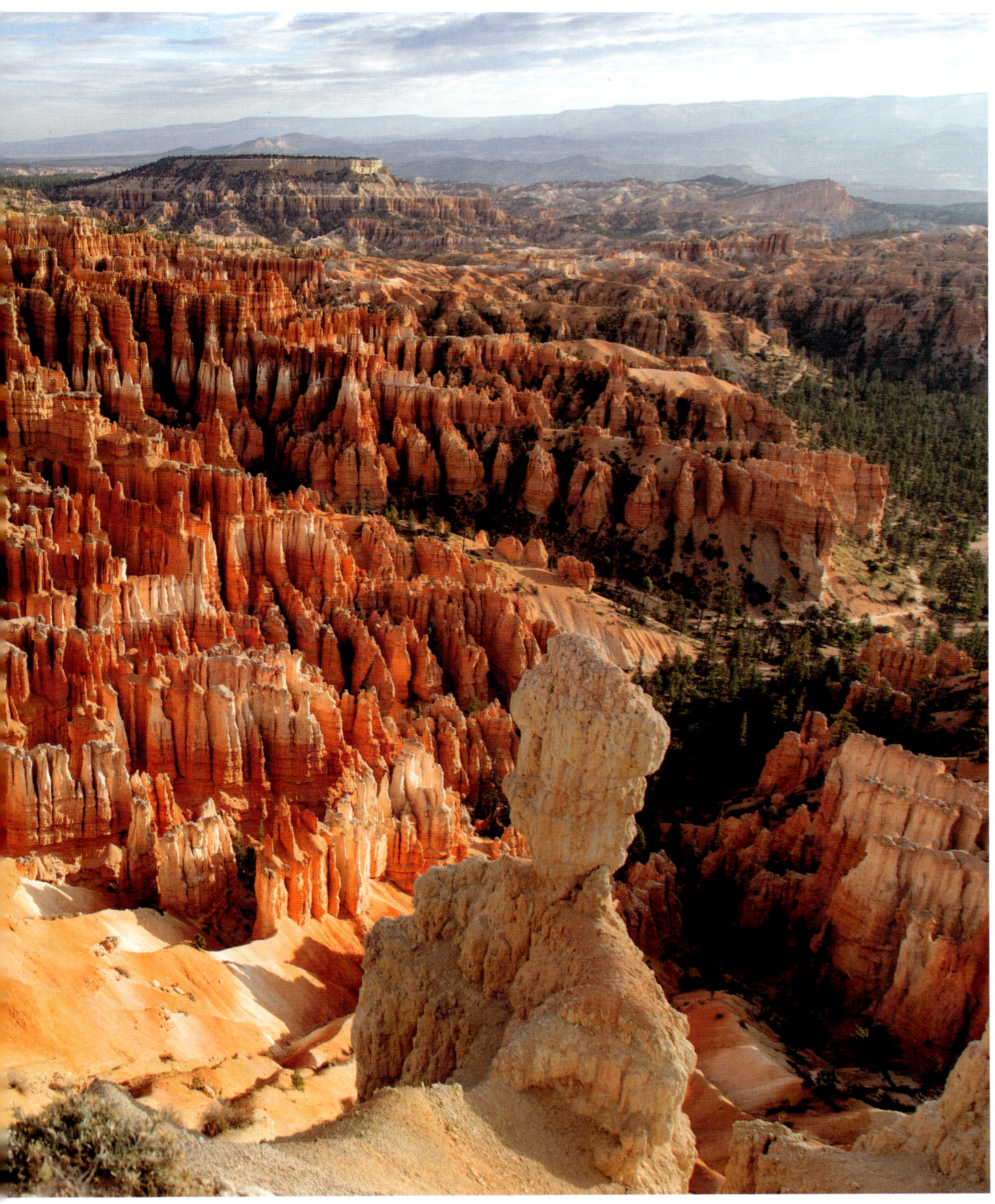

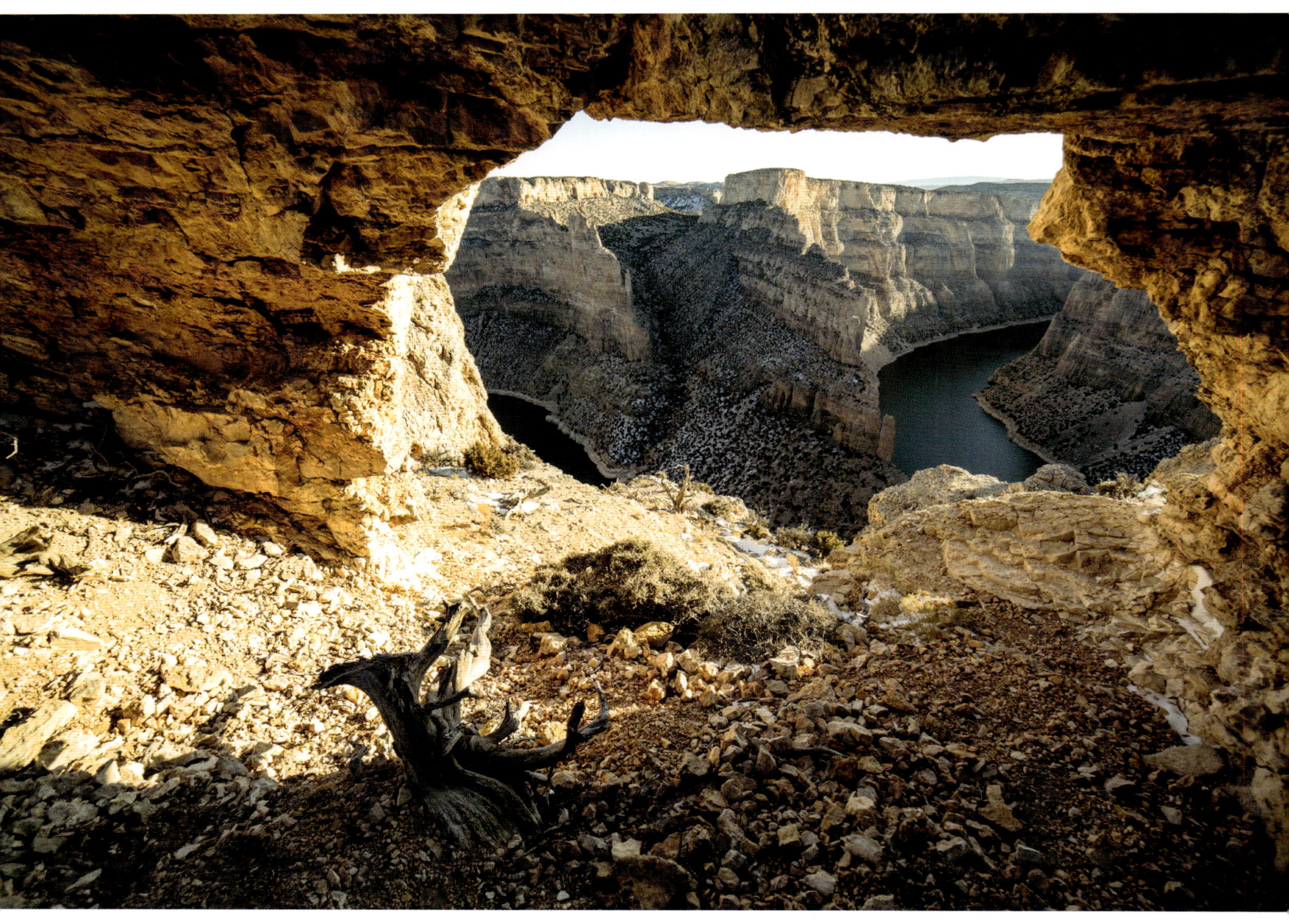

BIGHORN CANYON NATIONAL RECREATION AREA (ABOVE) Growing up, I spent countless days camping and wakeboarding near Yellowtail Dam. It wasn't until twenty years later that I visited to explore the views from the rim. After a cold night of tent camping at -10° F, we were greeted to spectacular sunrise views of the canyon.

GRAND STAIRCASE-ESCALANTE NATIONAL MONUMENT (OPPOSITE) When I lived in Monticello, Utah, I made a to-do list of places I wanted to visit before leaving, and exploring Zebra Canyon was high on that list. Eight years later I finally made it—to celebrate our wedding anniversary. Wading through chilly, chest-deep water while trying to keep my camera dry added to the adventure, but it was well worth the wait!

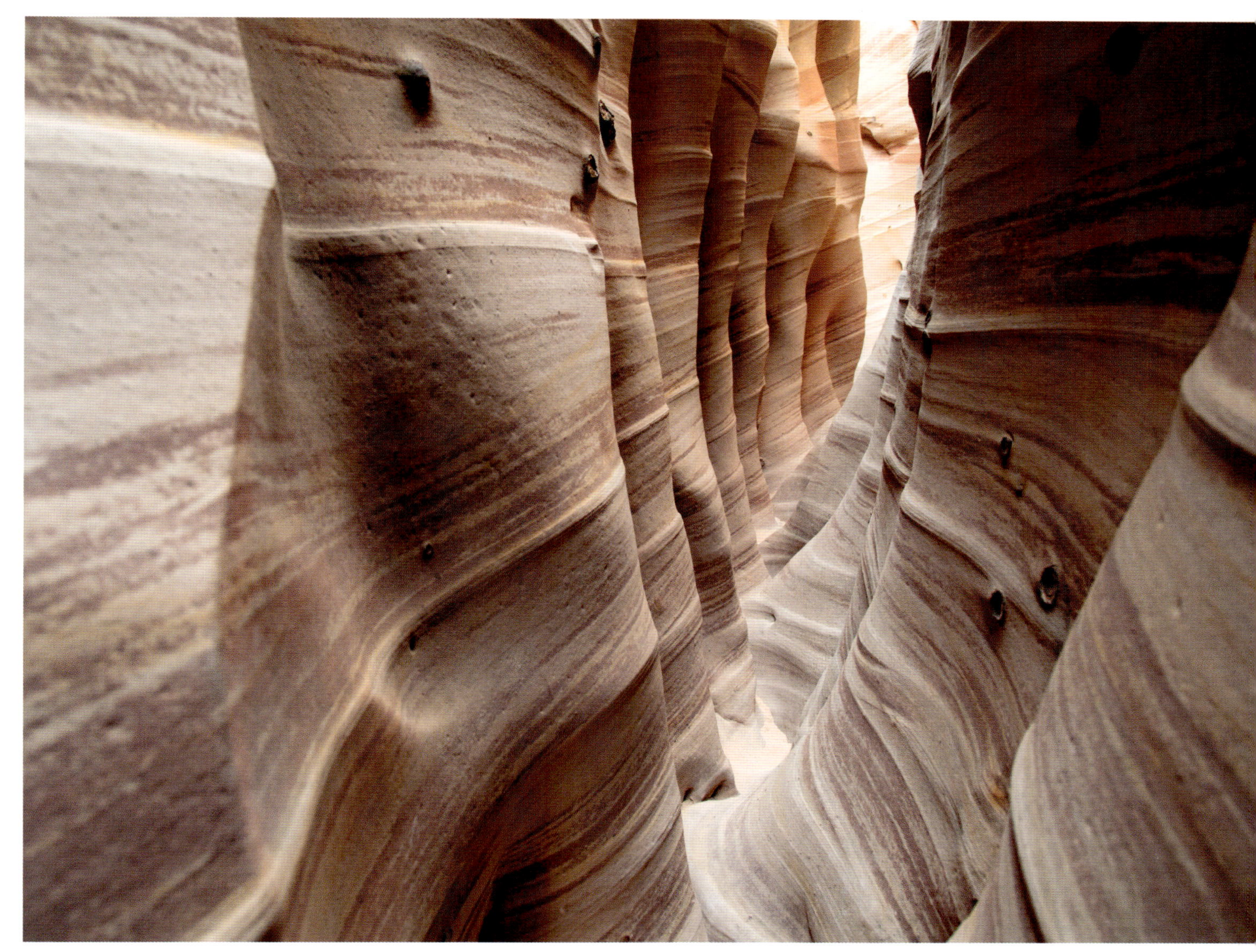

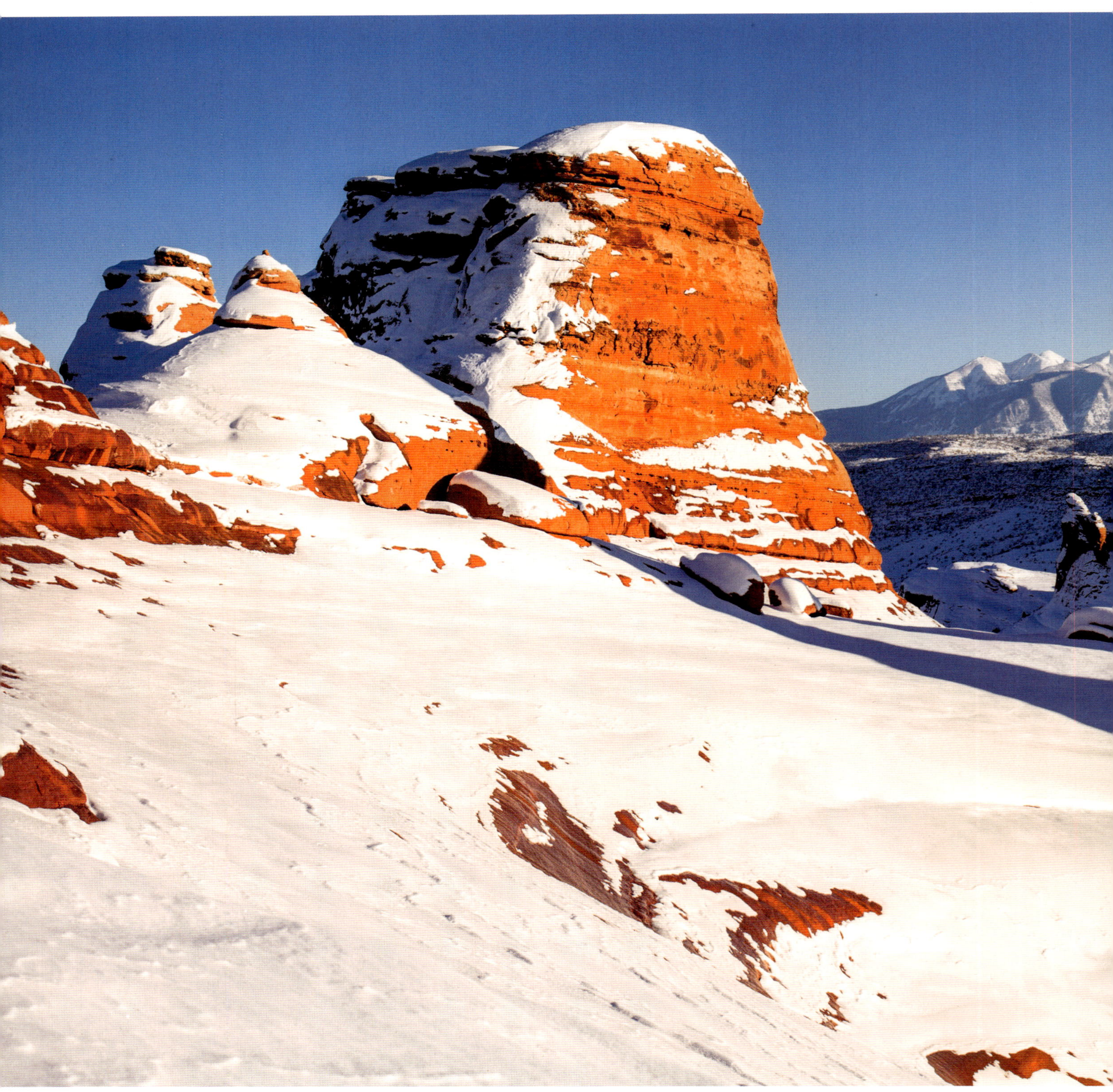

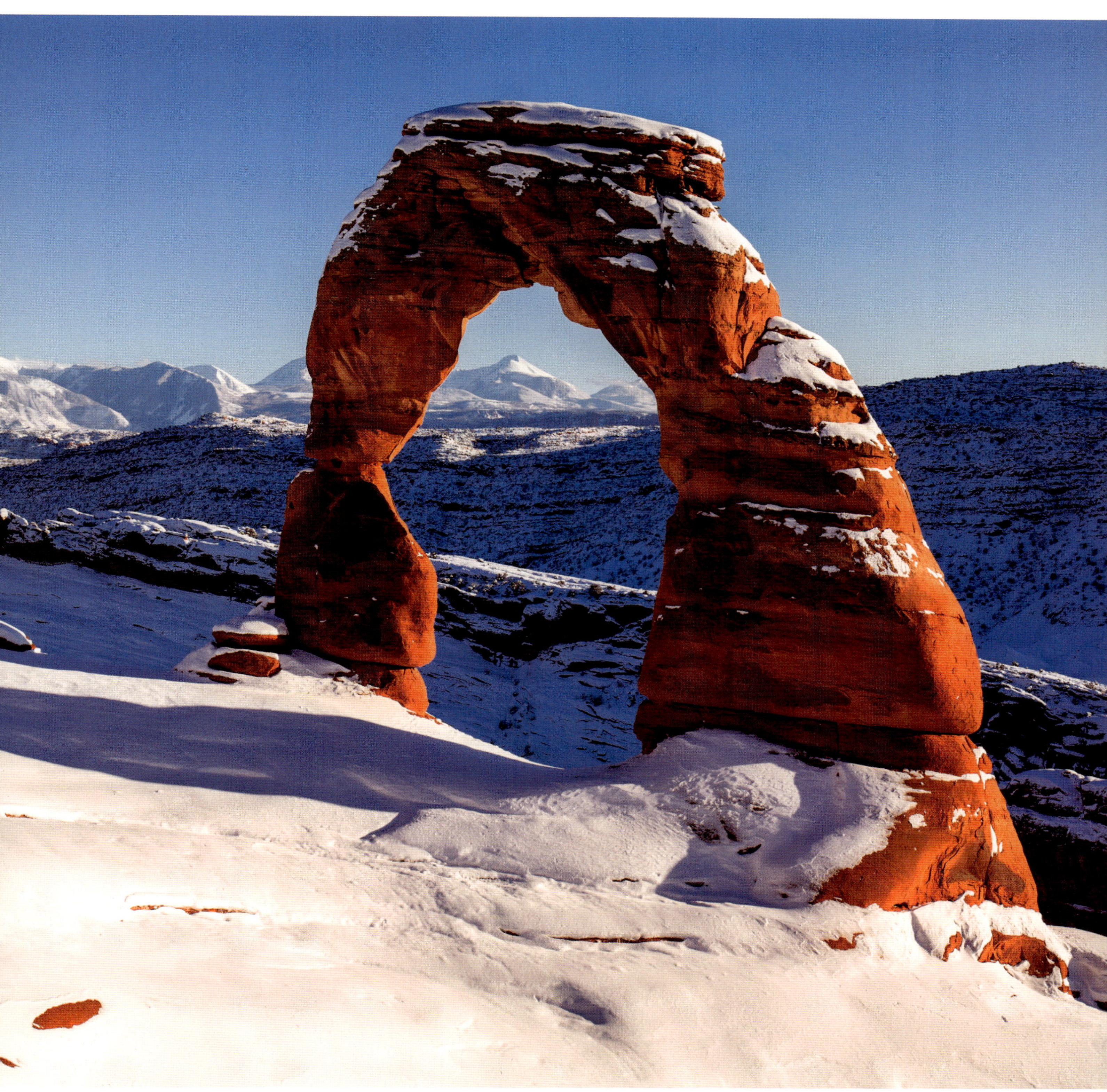

ARCHES NATIONAL PARK My all-time favorite moment in the park was on a hike to Delicate Arch after a big snowstorm. Even though the hike was quite treacherous, seeing the orange landscape with its white blanket made it feel like a brand-new park. The snow also kept most people away, which meant that we were able to enjoy the normally busy destination nearly to ourselves.

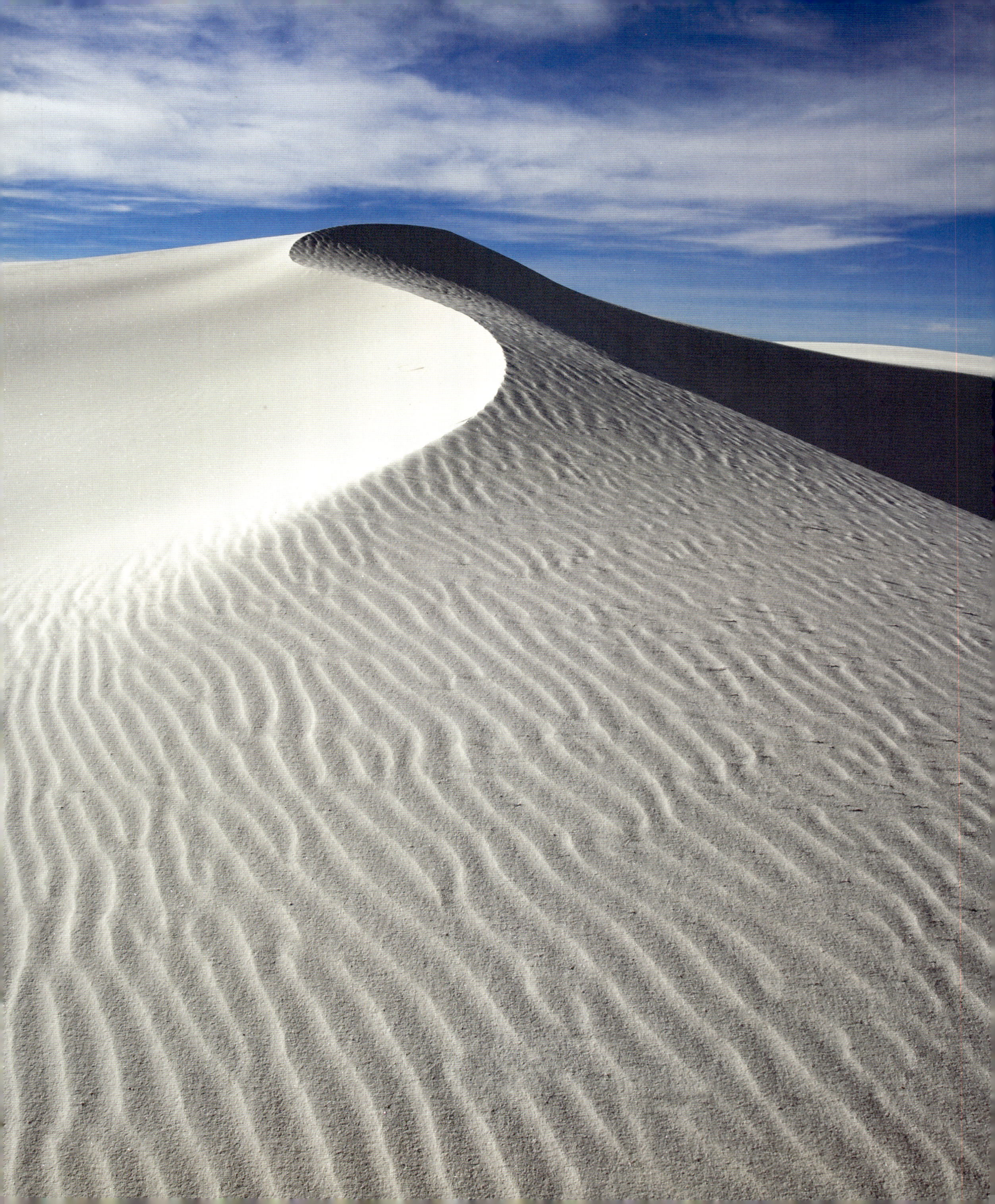

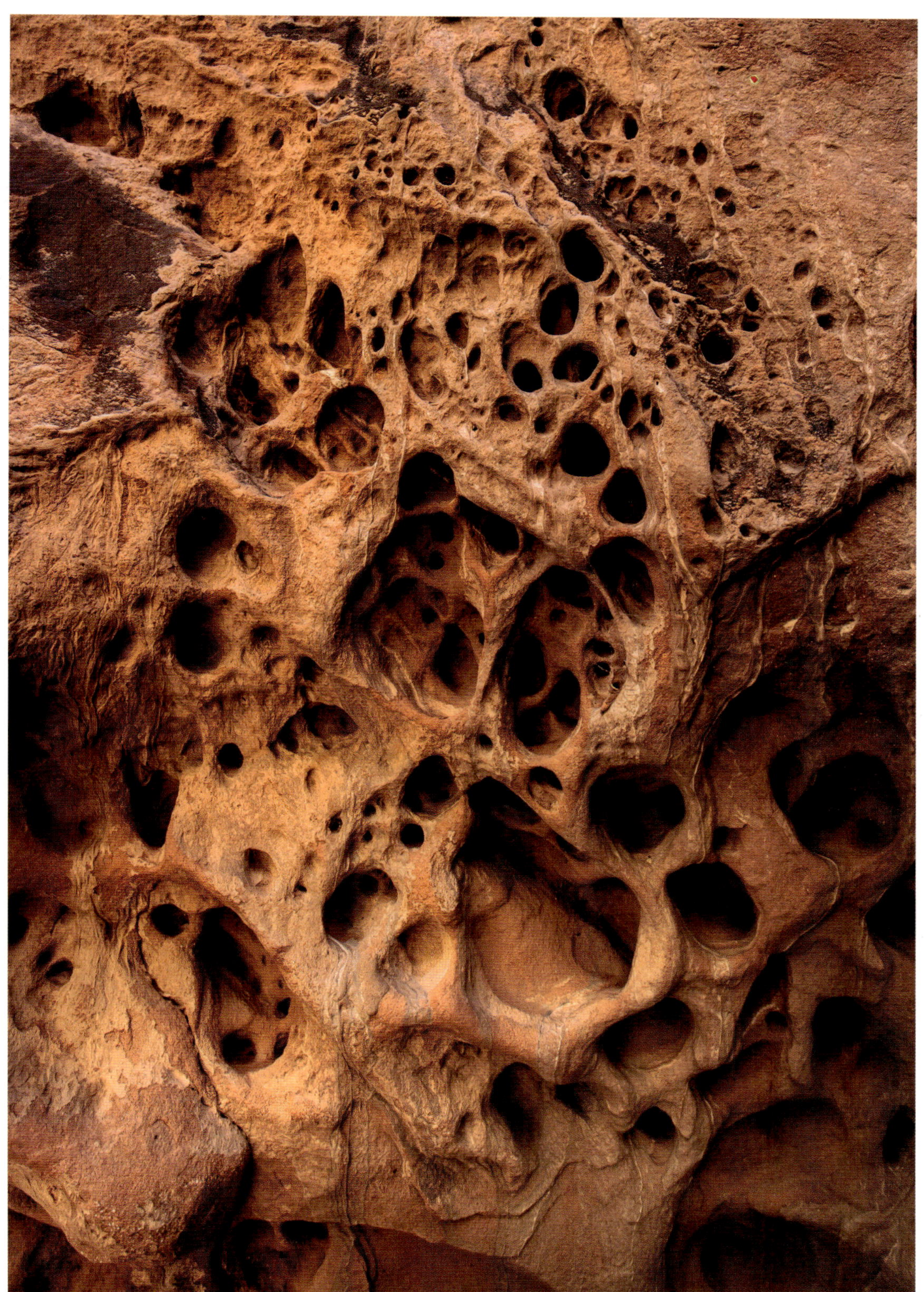

WHITE SANDS NATIONAL PARK (OPPOSITE) While living and working in New Mexico, my roommate and I road-tripped to the park for an overnight backcountry trip in the dunefield. Beyond the day use area, there are endless untouched dunes to explore. To me, the beauty of this park is that the geologic features change rapidly. Depending on the wind and weather, the dunes you see on any visit will never be the same.

ARCHES NATIONAL PARK Even with over 2,000 named arches, there are tons of smaller geologic wonders to discover in the park. Known as honeycomb weathering or "Swiss cheese rock," tafoni are small, rounded, smooth-edged openings in a rock surface, most often found in arid or semi-arid deserts. This feature, found in the Fiery Furnace, is one of my favorite examples.

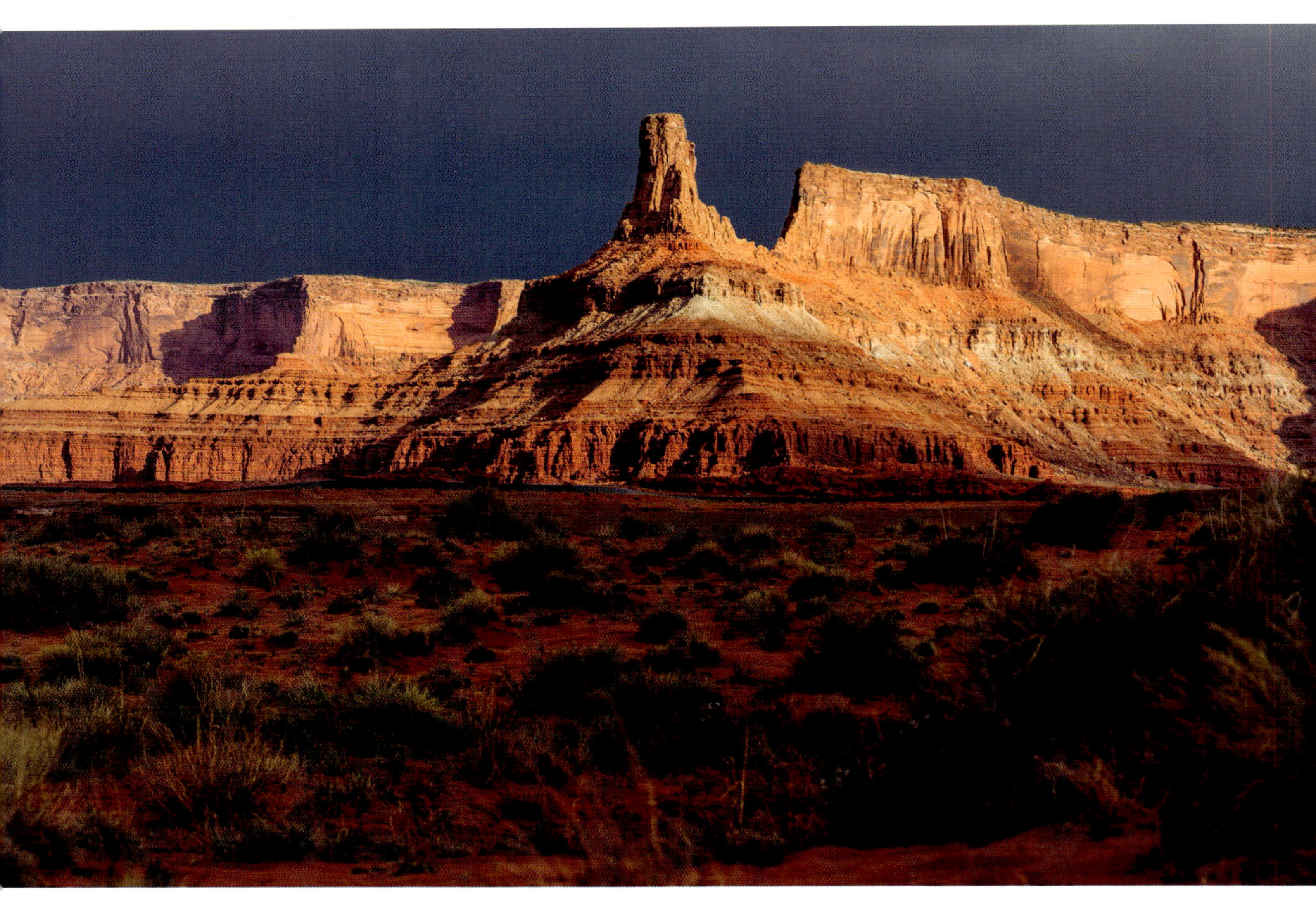

KANE CREEK RECREATION AREA One particular evening we decided to get out of town to do some car camping. After a short drive, we arrived at our roadside campsite. Only after setting up camp did we realize that we had forgotten our stove, but luckily we had some emergency dehydrated meals and a Jetboil. We spent the extra time we saved cooking enjoying the sunset.

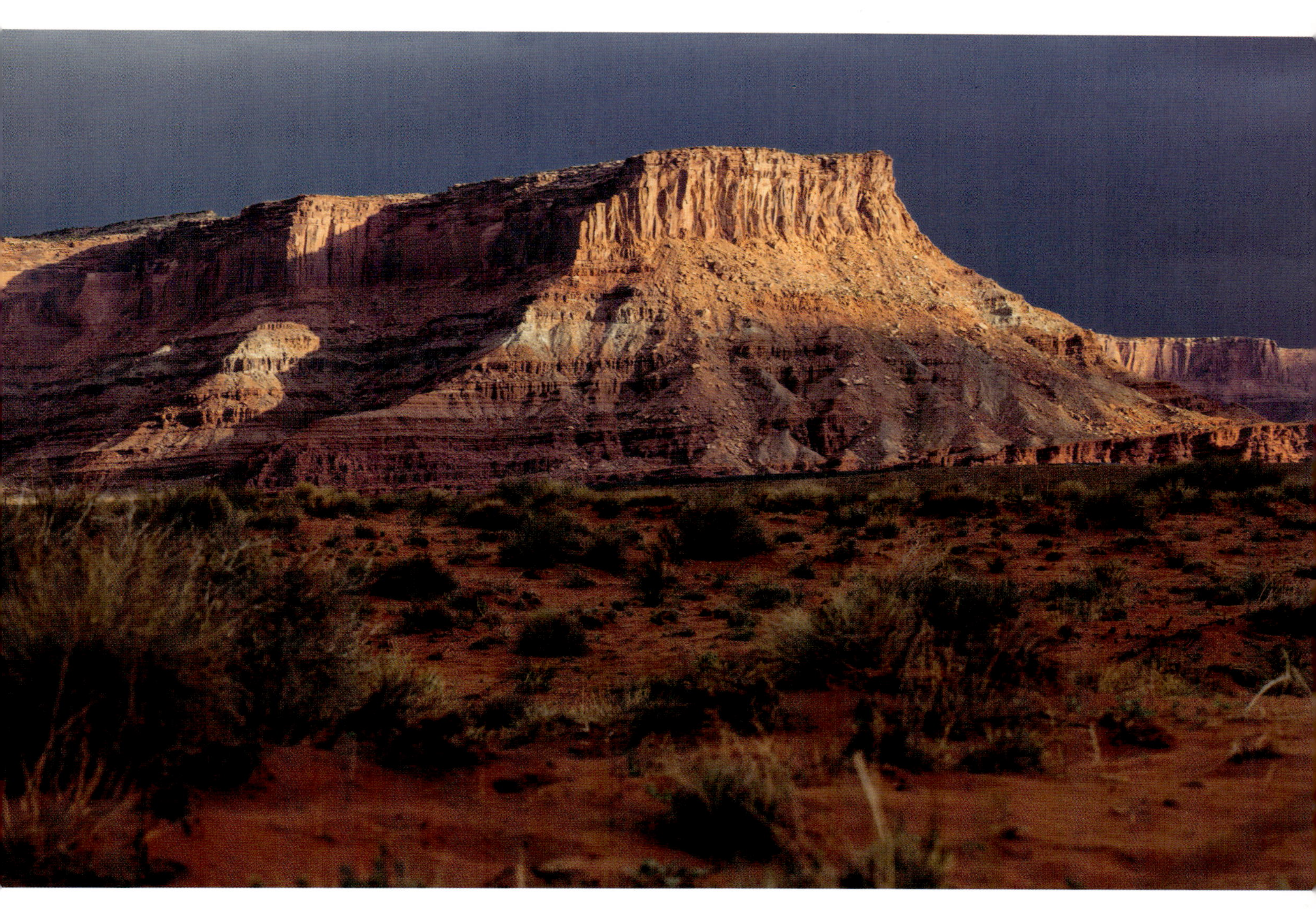

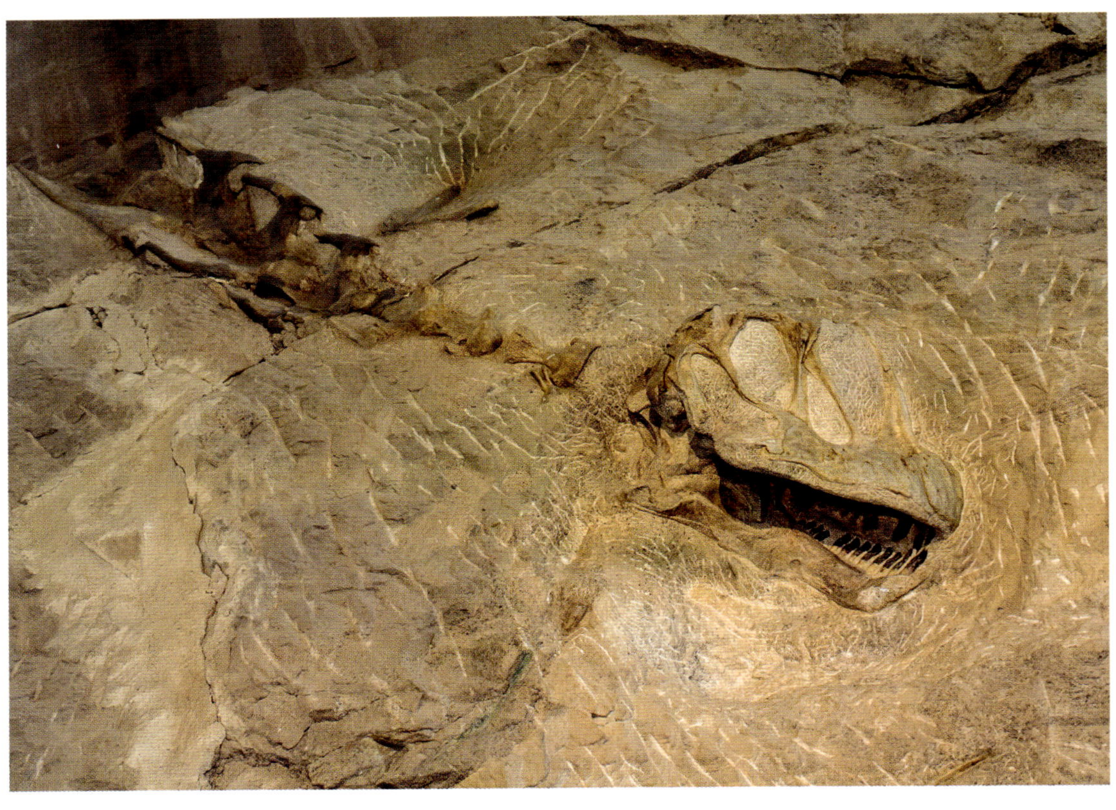

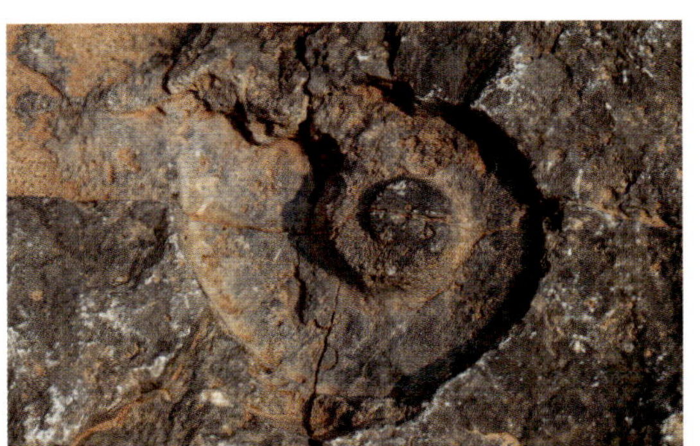

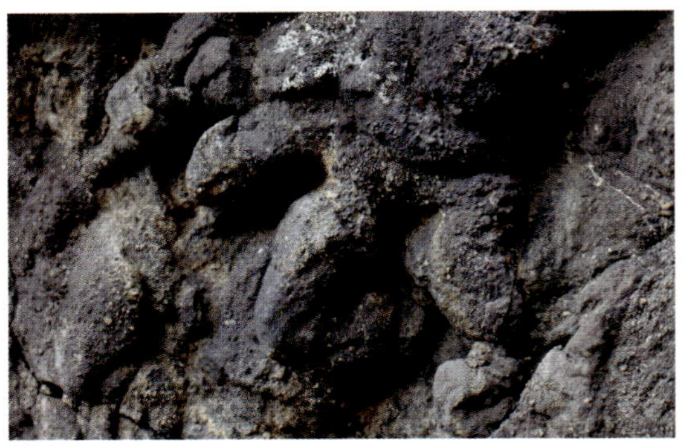

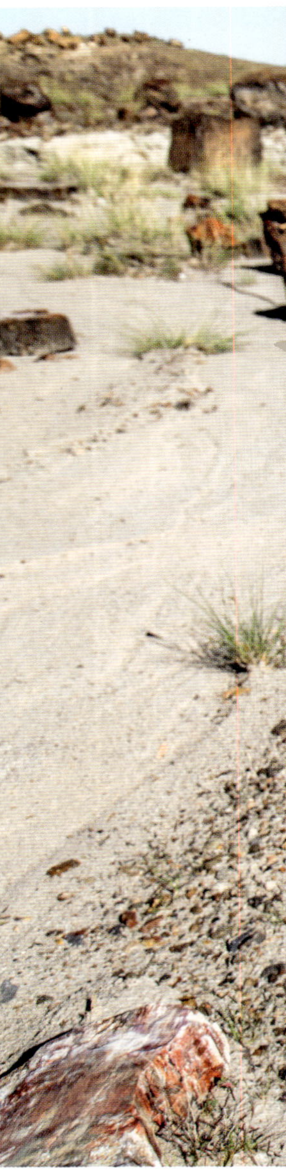

DINOSAUR NATIONAL MONUMENT (TOP) This is my favorite monument. It's hard to believe it doesn't have national park designation. One of the best fossils in the park is the Camarasaurus skull and vertebrae in the Quarry Visitor Center. If you have the opportunity to get on the Green or Yampa Rivers, don't pass it up!

BEARS EARS NATIONAL MONUMENT (BOTTOM LEFT) Along the thirty-five-mile float from Sand Island to Mexican Hat on the San Juan River, one of my favorite things to do is look for marine fossils. Among the many specimens I've found, this nautiloid is one of the best.

DENALI NATIONAL PARK AND PRESERVE (BOTTOM RIGHT) When I first heard that the park had fossilized dinosaur footprints, my curiosity kicked into high gear. Up to that point, I had only seen dinosaur fossils in museums, never in the wild. So, after some planning, we set off into the backcountry with only a rough idea of where to look. It took a bit of wandering, but we finally found this theropod print, perfectly preserved in an overhanging stone.

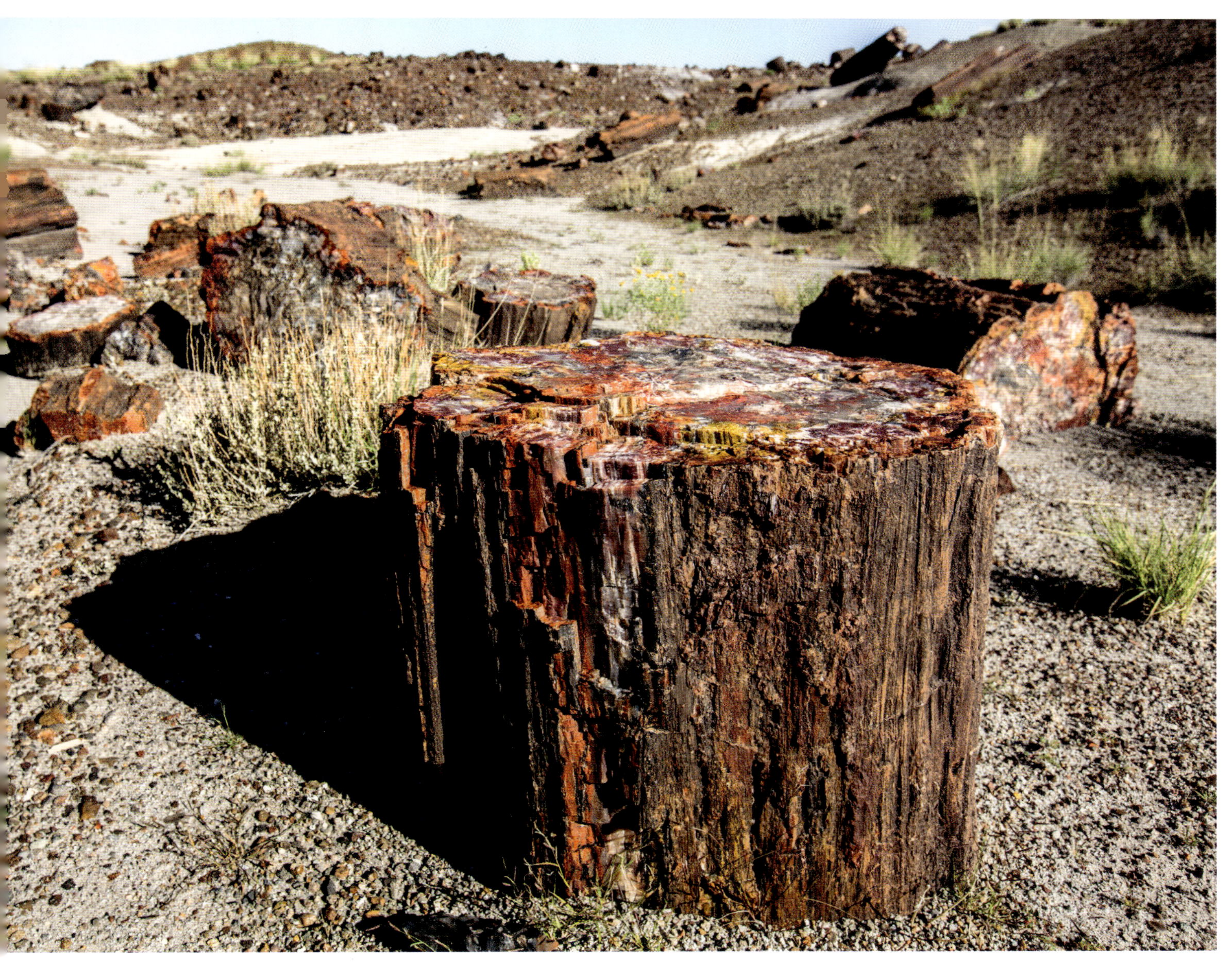

PETRIFIED FOREST NATIONAL PARK I've seen petrified wood in many places, but the specimens in this park are some of the most vibrant I've ever encountered. The various colors reflect trace minerals in the quartz, with iron and manganese contributing significantly to the stunning hues.

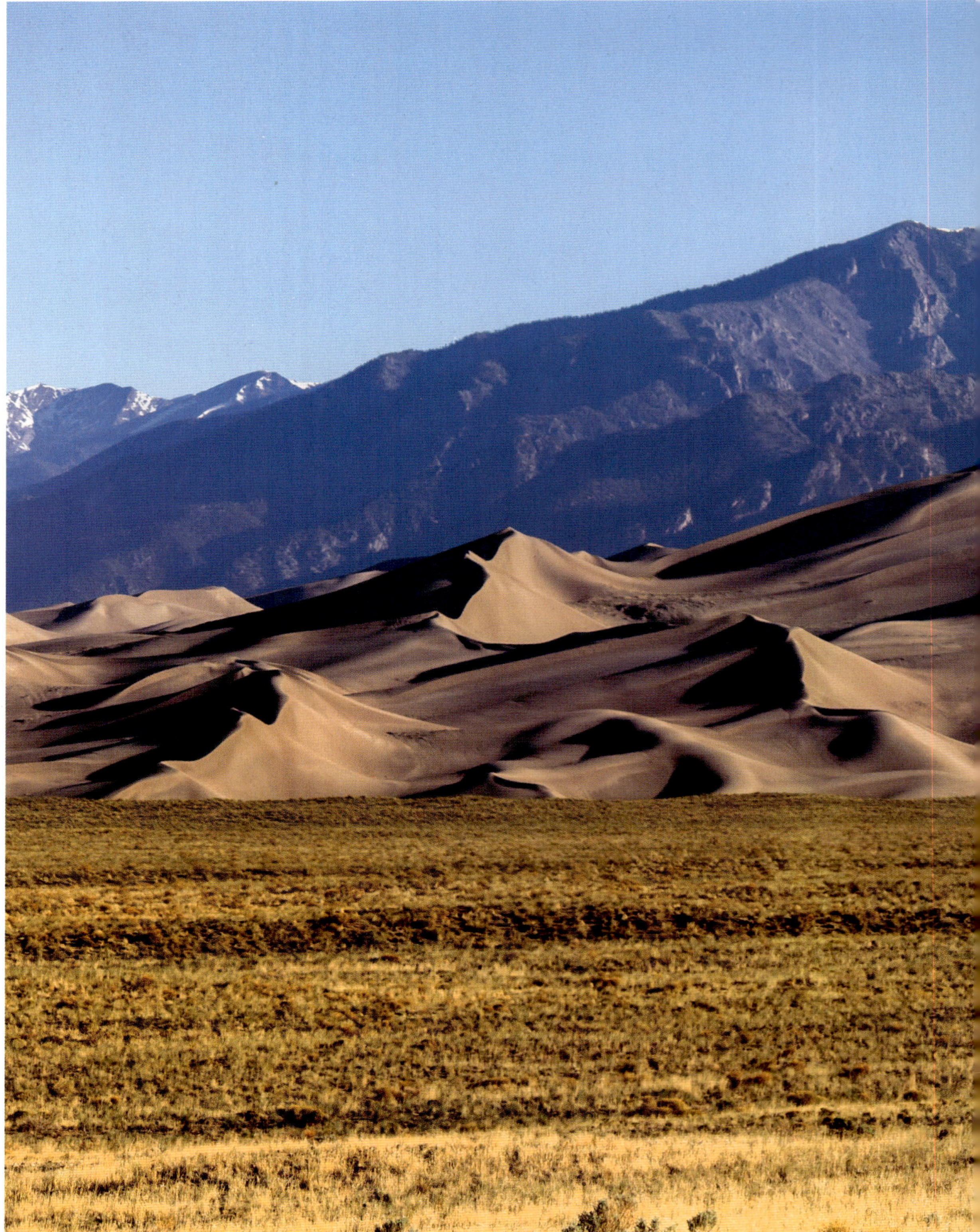

GREAT SAND DUNES NATIONAL PARK AND PRESERVE At the base of the Sangre de Cristo Mountains, 750-foot-tall Star Dune is the tallest in the dunefield. The hike to the top is both fun and challenging—and one that stays with you long after you leave, quite literally. No matter how much I scrubbed, it took a week or two to finally get all the sand off me!

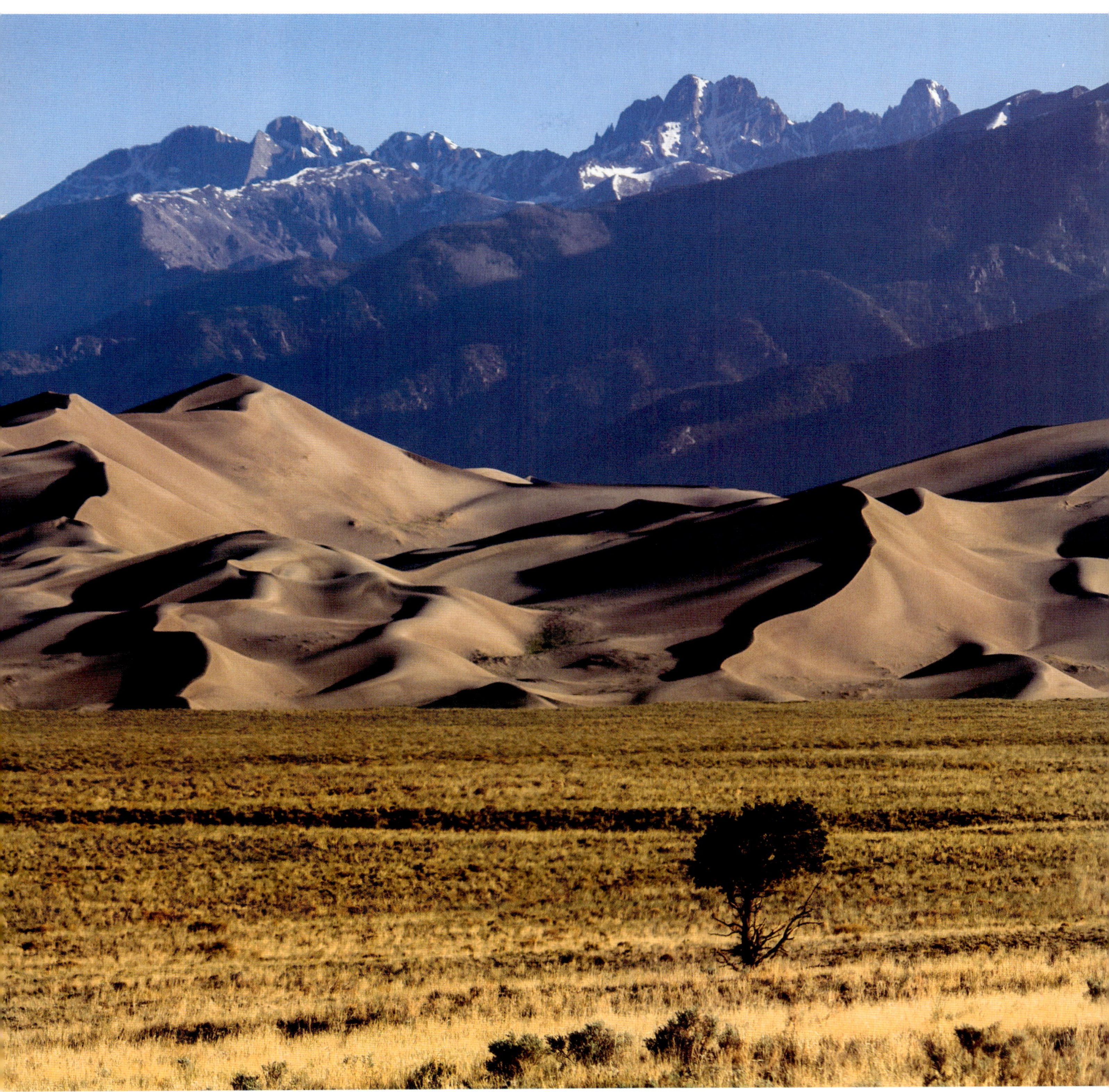

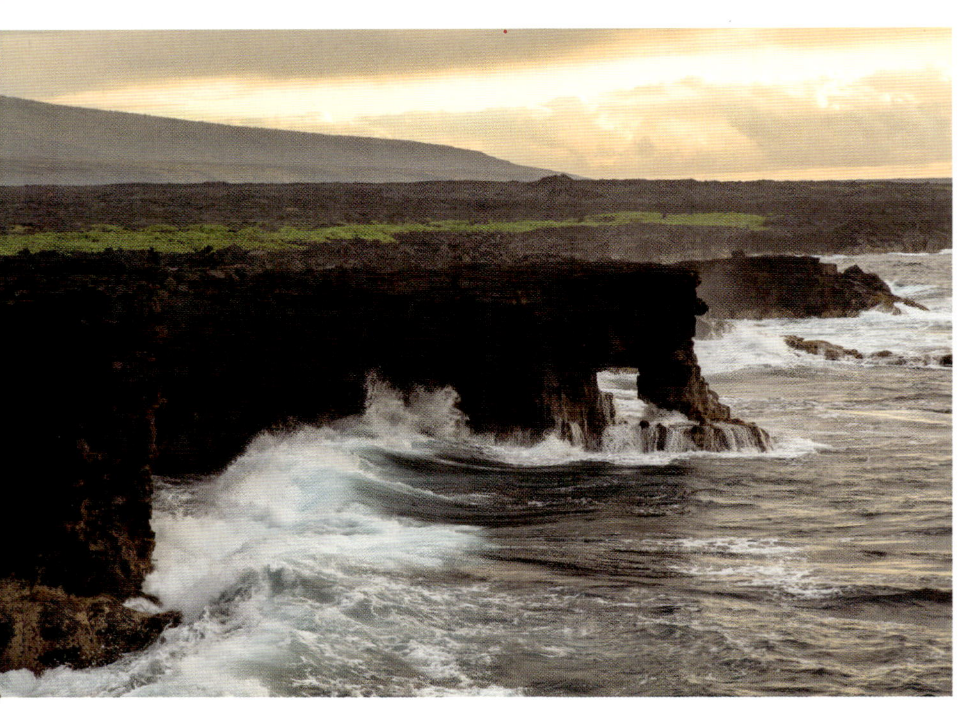

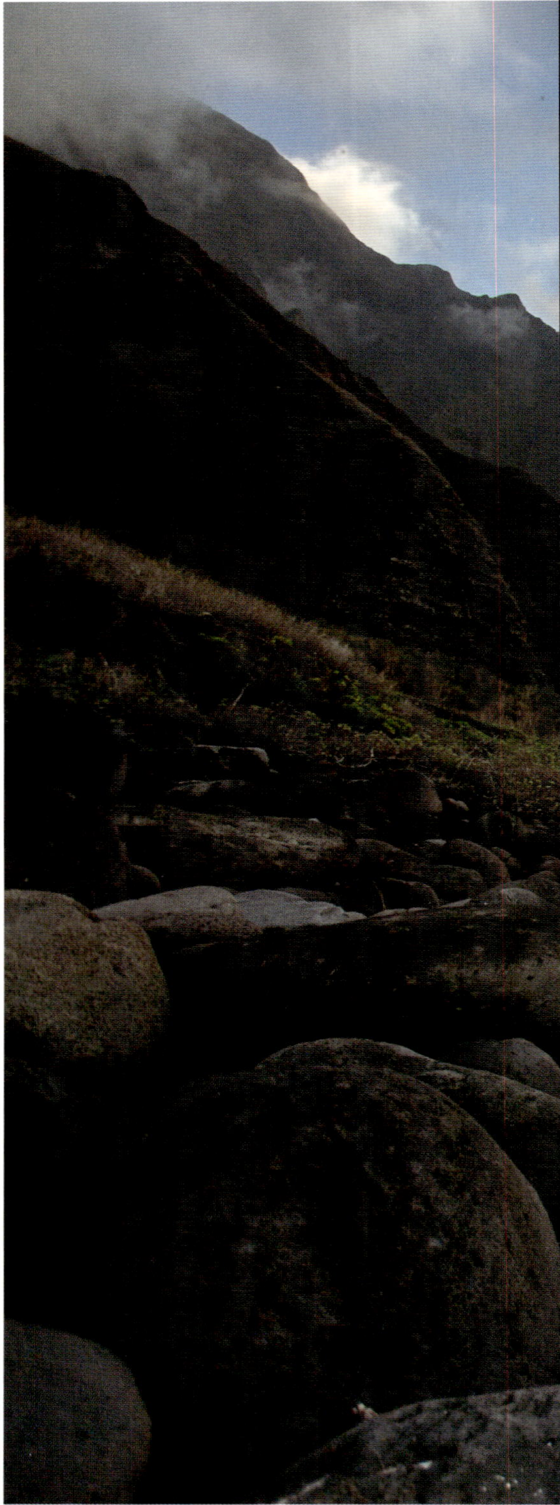

HAWAI'I VOLCANOES NATIONAL PARK (ABOVE) We left our camp at Aupa Point before sunrise to beat the day's heat and were rewarded with the sight of this stunning sea arch just as the sun crested the horizon. The scene was breathtaking—waves crashed powerfully against the cliffs, their energy unmistakable in the golden morning light.

NĀ PALI COAST STATE WILDERNESS PARK (OPPOSITE) Kalalau Beach, the terminus of our twenty-two-mile backcountry trip, is one of the most beautiful campsites I've ever visited. It's a challenging hike, but the views along the trail, including the 1,000-foot Hanakoa Falls, are beautiful. There's a giant cave to explore at the end of the beach and a waterfall where you can take a "refreshing" shower before falling asleep to the sound of crashing waves.

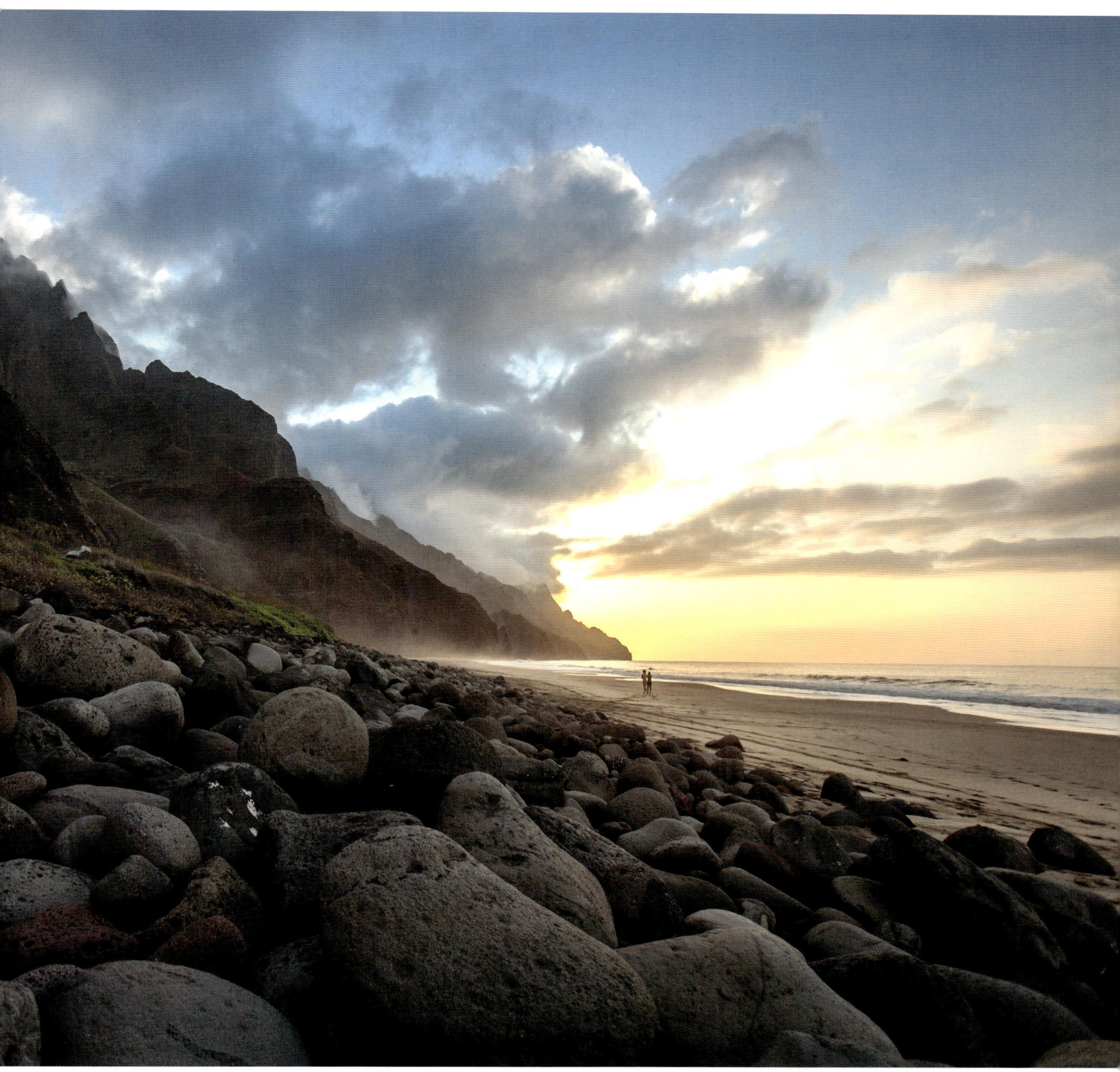

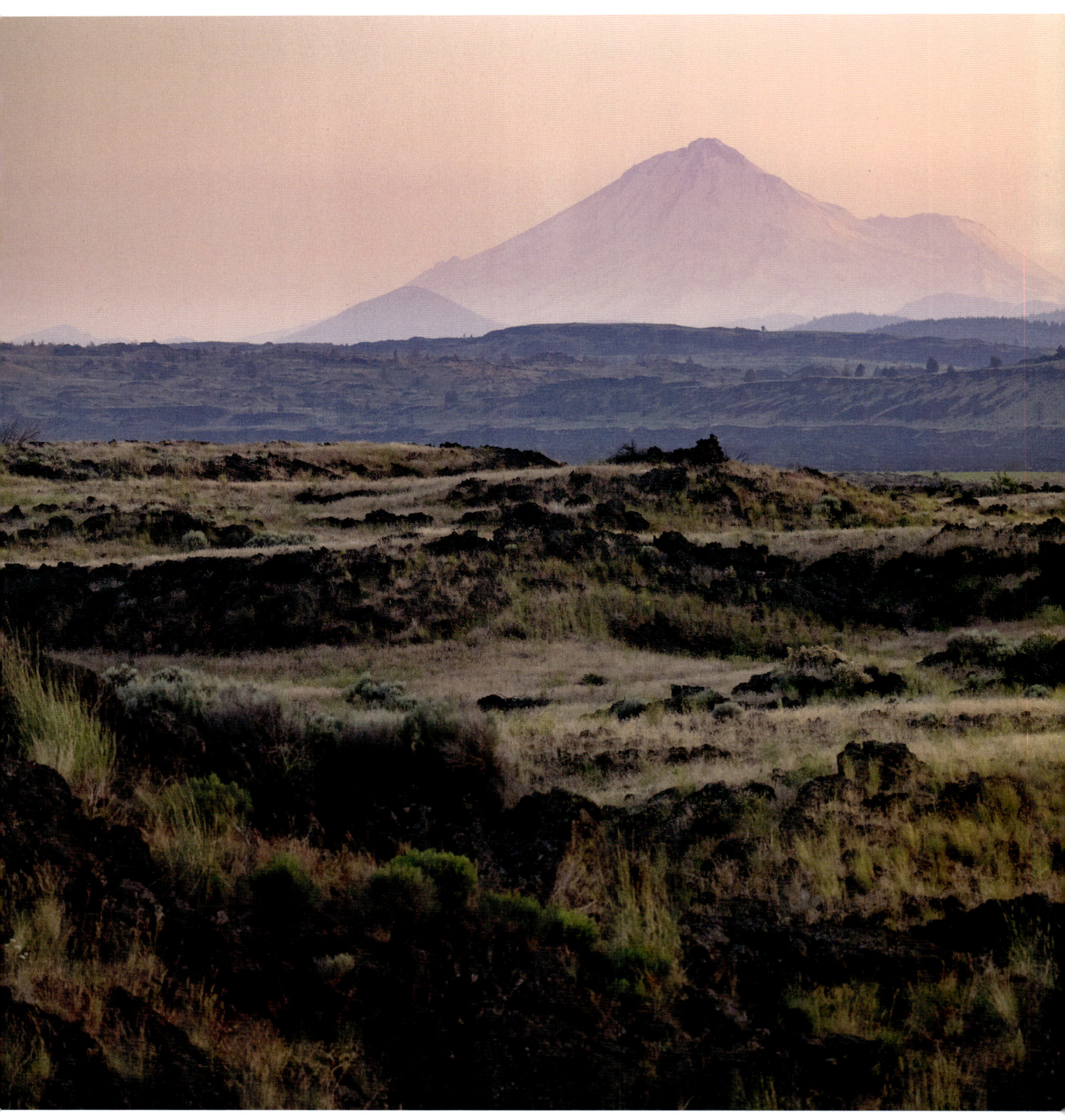

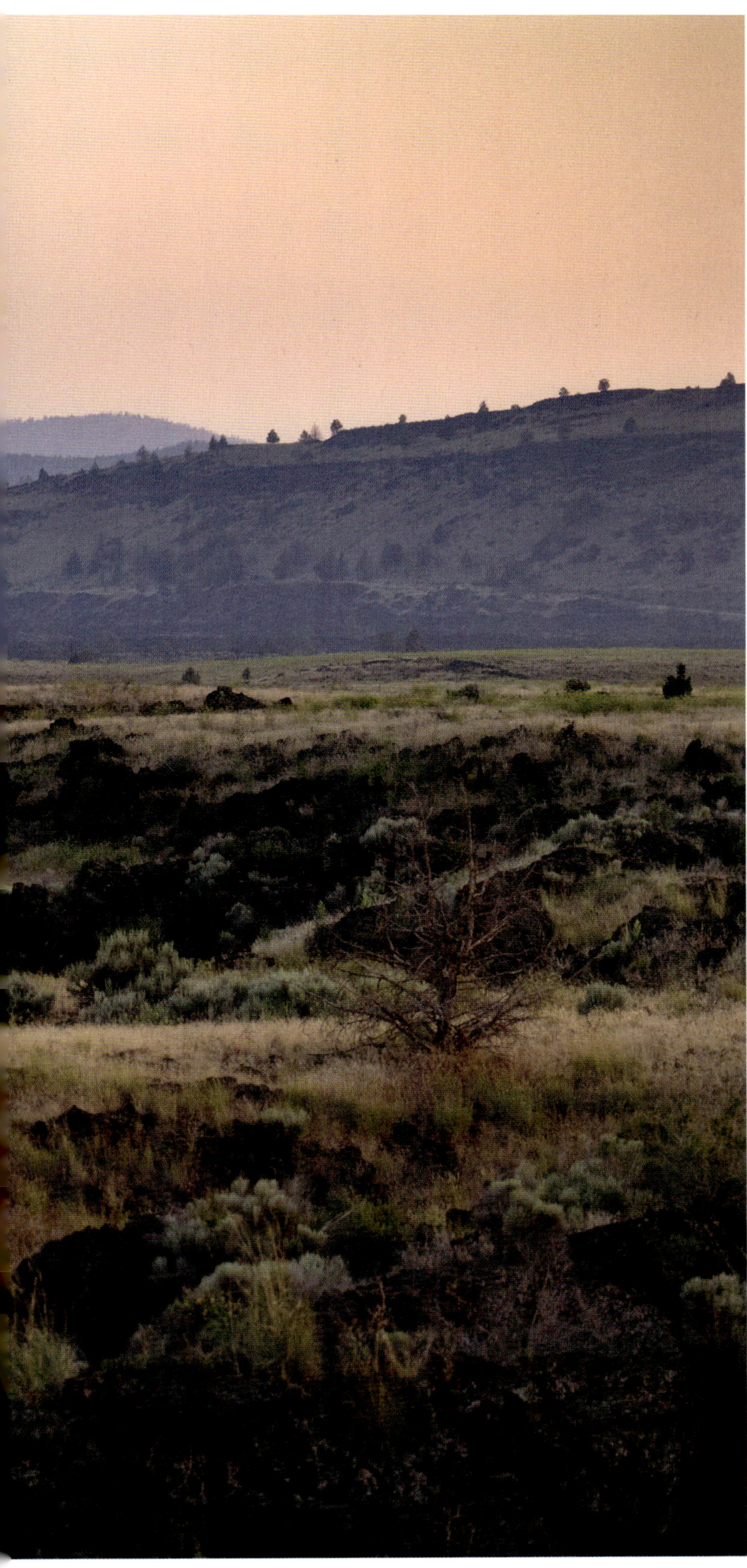

LAVA BEDS NATIONAL MONUMENT Each evening while we were camping at the monument, we set out to find a place to watch the sunset. One of our favorite spots was Captain Jack's Stronghold. Along with its historical and cultural significance to the Modoc people, the compound stratovolcano Mount Shasta towers over the landscape and glows pink in the evening light.

HAWAI'I VOLCANOES NATIONAL PARK During one of our visits to the park, we heard the lava was flowing. Hiking through the lava fields toward the coast, we came across stunning pahoehoe—smooth, billowy formations that looked almost sculpted. We arrived just in time for sunset and sat for a while, watching molten lava spill into the ocean, slowly witnessing the island of Hawaii grow before our eyes.

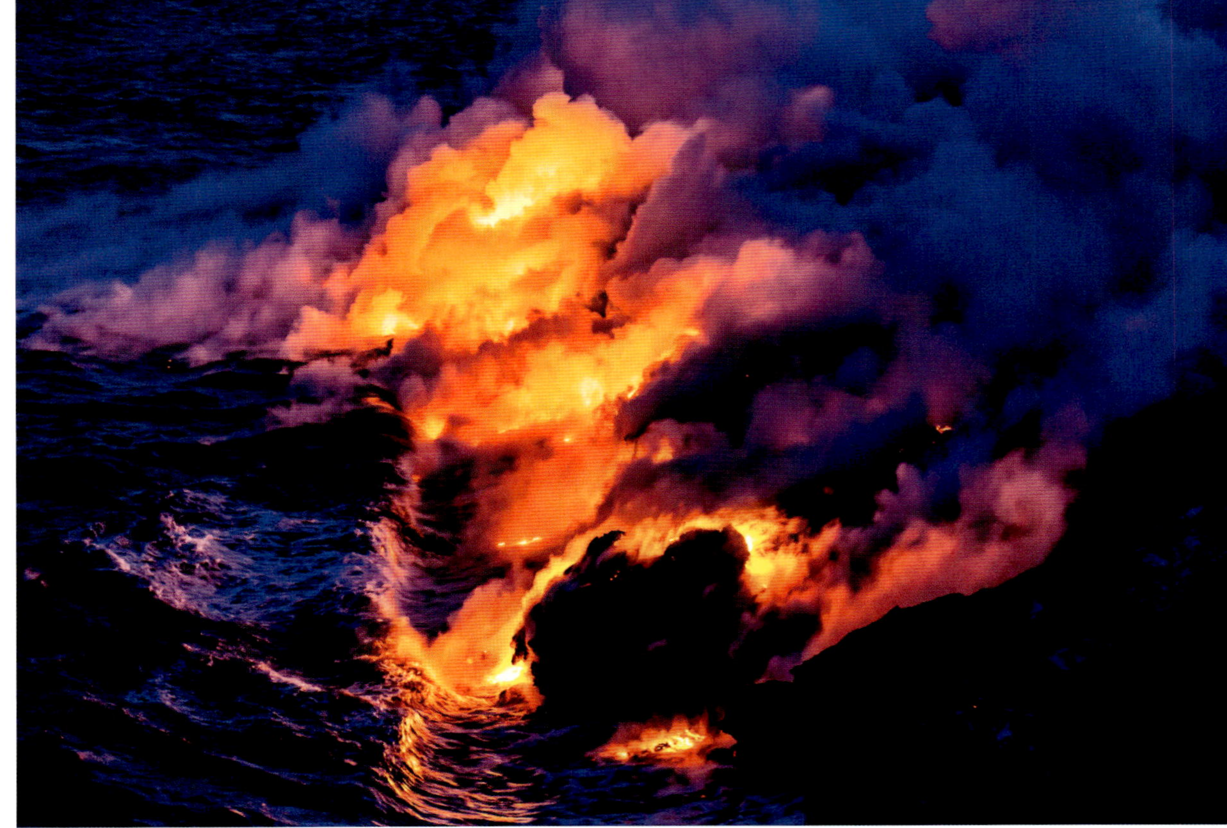

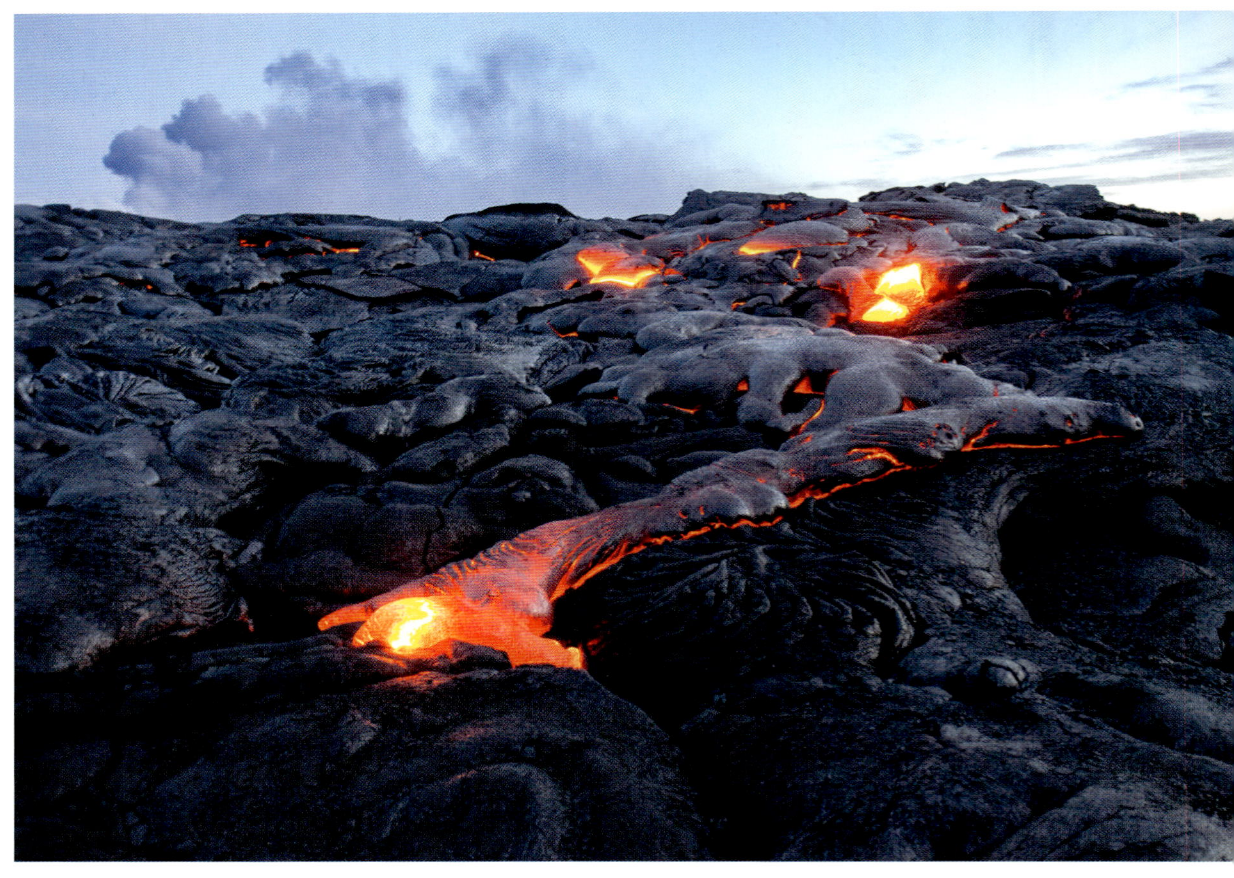

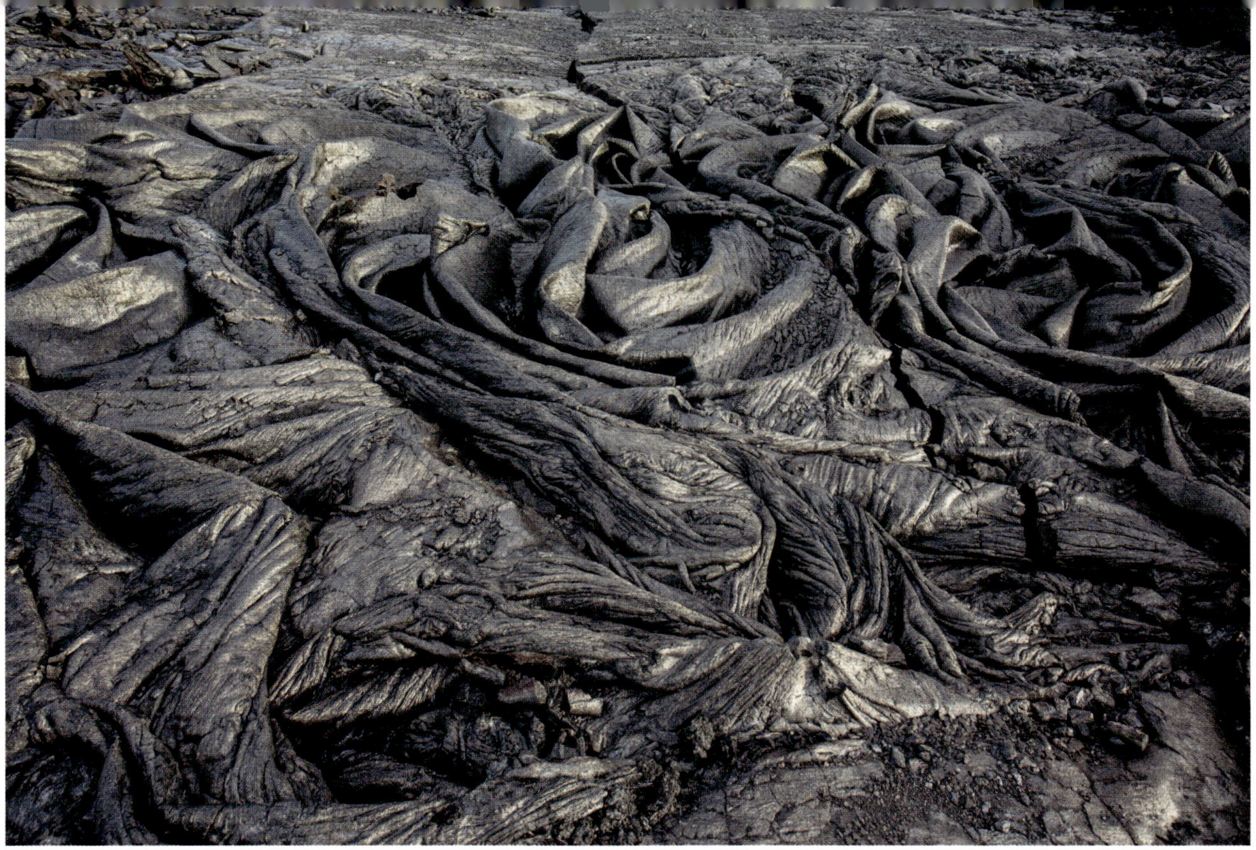

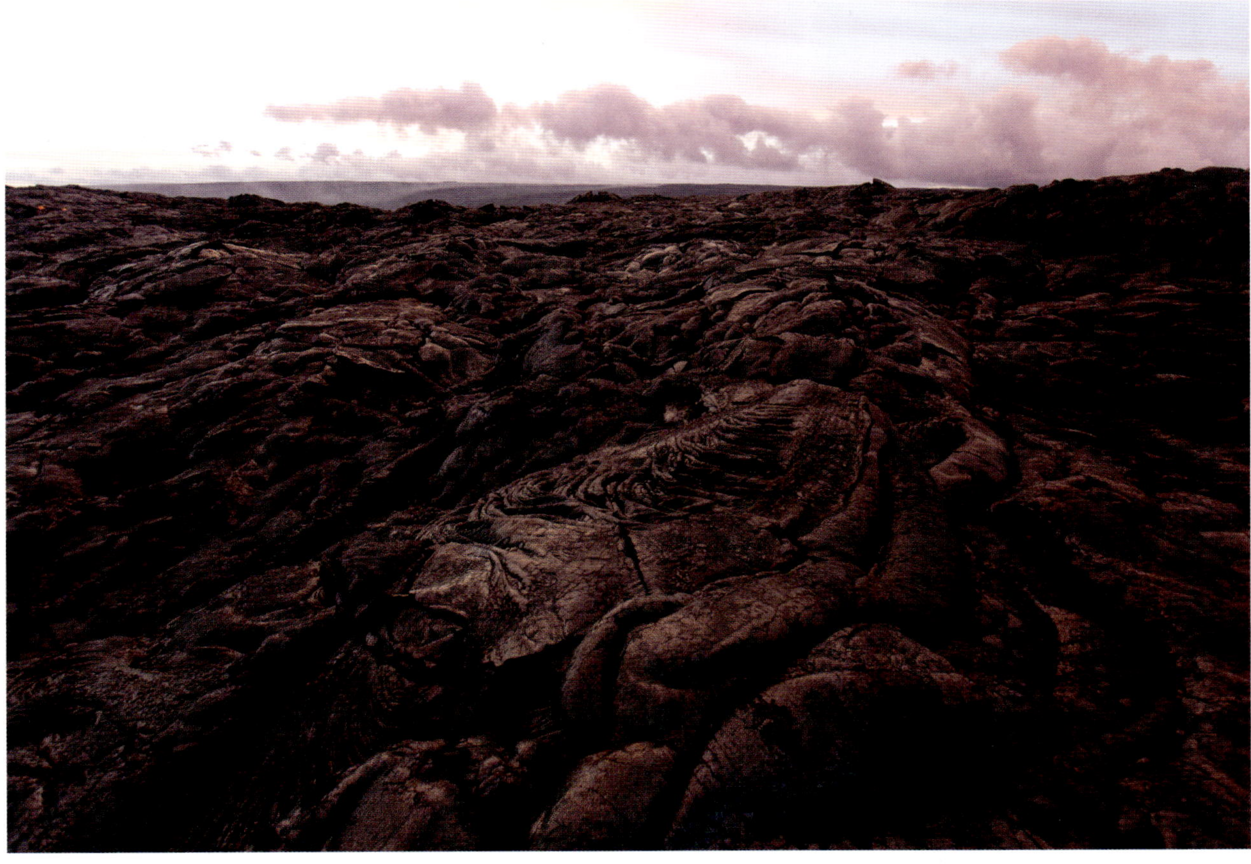

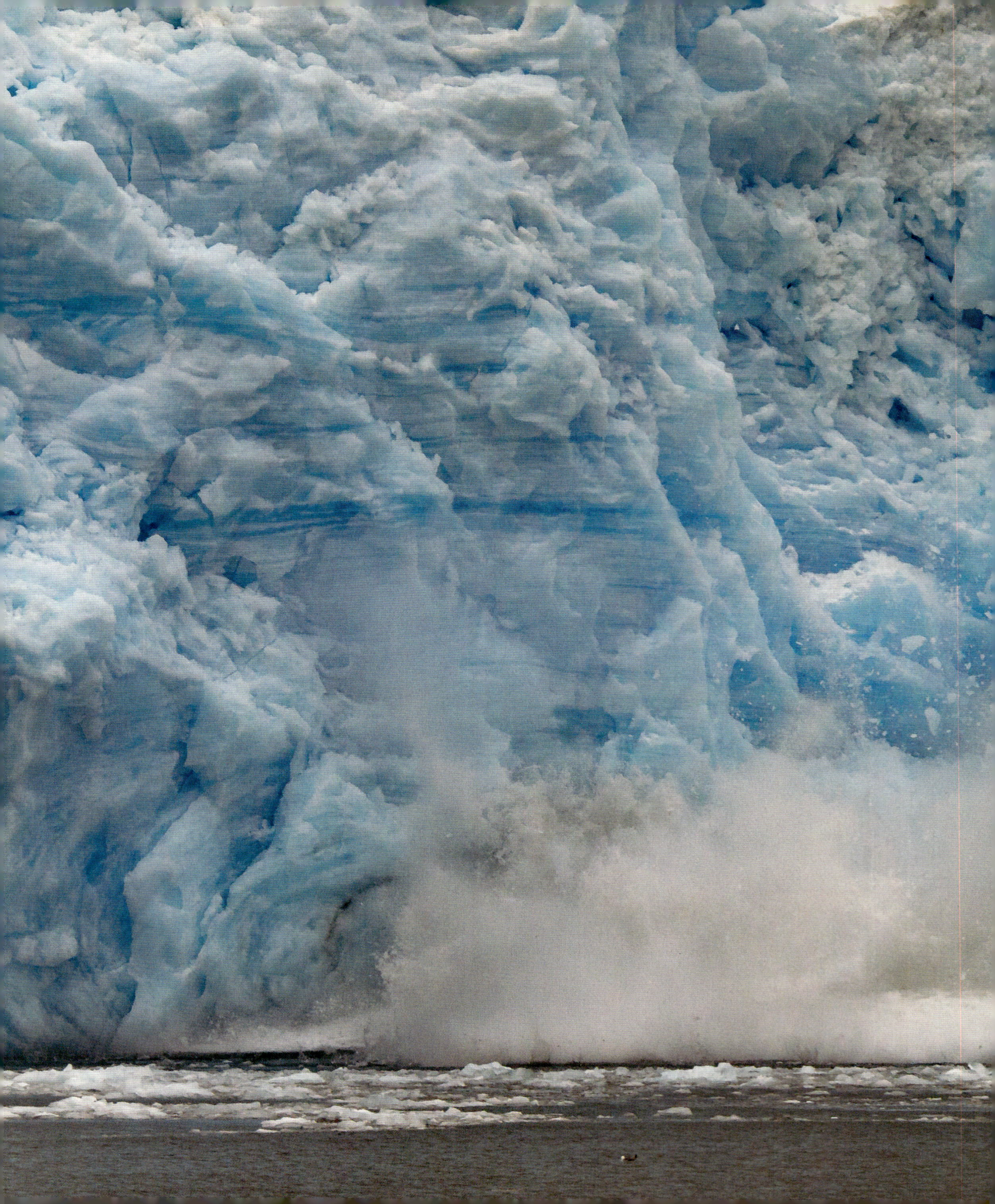

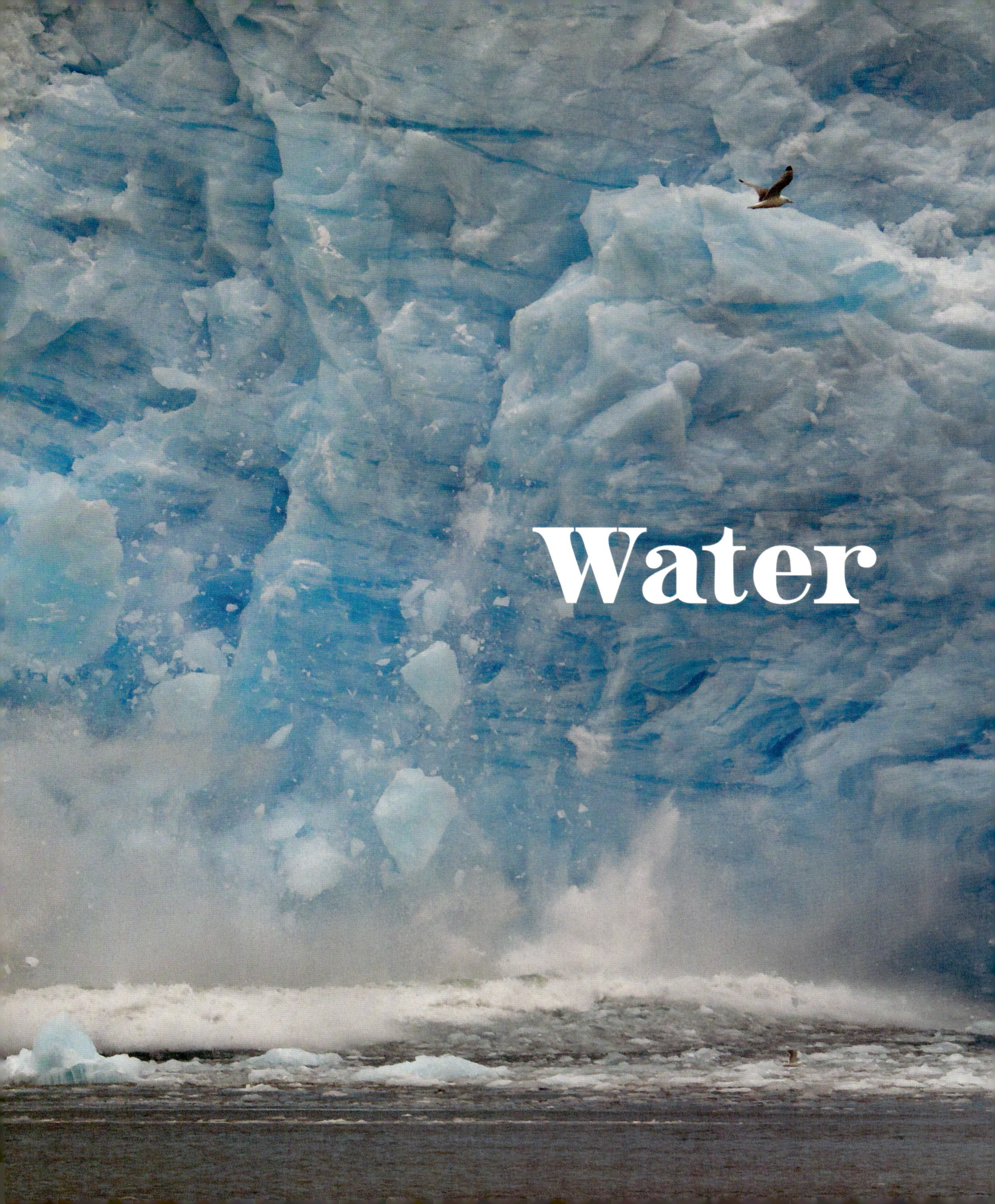

Water

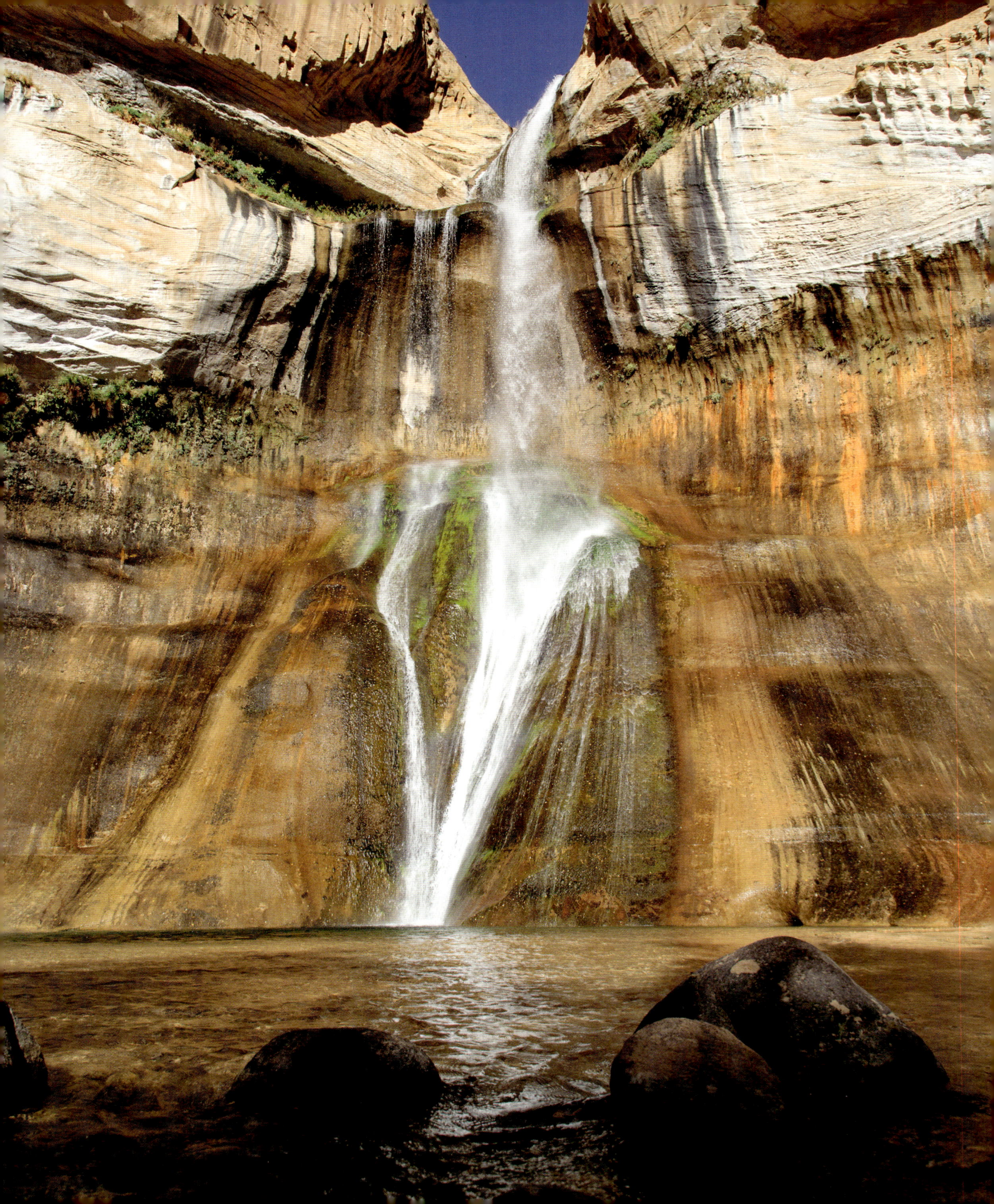

SHAPING LANDSCAPES

WATER IS A FUNDAMENTAL RESOURCE that sustains life, regulates climate, and shapes ecosystems, encompassing a diverse range of forms including oceans, glaciers, and freshwater ecosystems.

Oceans, which cover approximately 70 percent of the Earth's surface, play a critical role in regulating the global climate by acting as massive heat reservoirs. They absorb and redistribute solar energy, which helps to moderate temperatures and influence weather patterns worldwide. Oceans also drive the water cycle through evaporation, contributing to precipitation and the replenishment of freshwater resources. They are home to a staggering diversity of marine life, from microscopic plankton to enormous whales, all of which contribute to ecological balance and support global food chains.

Alternatively, glaciers perform a crucial ecosystem service by acting as essential reservoirs of fresh water and regulating global water supplies. A glacier is a large, slow-moving mass of ice formed from accumulated snow over long periods, typically centuries or millennia. Under the pressure of their own weight, glaciers gradually flow downhill or outward, carving and shaping the terrain as they move. They store about 68 percent of the world's fresh water, releasing it slowly over time through melting, which provides a steady and reliable flow of water to rivers, lakes, and aquifers, particularly during dry periods. This gradual release is vital for maintaining consistent water supplies for agriculture, drinking, and ecosystems, especially in regions dependent on glacier-fed rivers. Additionally, glaciers help regulate regional climates by reflecting solar radiation and influencing atmospheric conditions. As they melt, they contribute to sea level rise, which has significant implications for coastal areas and global climate patterns.

KENAI FJORDS NATIONAL PARK (PREVIOUS)

GRAND STAIRCASE-ESCALANTE NATIONAL MONUMENT (OPPOSITE) Waterfalls in the desert are usually ephemeral, and that's why the year-round flow of Lower Calf Creek Falls is so special. After the short hike through a beautiful canyon, we enjoyed lunch in the shade of the trees and swimming at the base of the falls.

Freshwater ecosystems, including rivers, lakes, wetlands, and streams, are equally important. They support a wide range of biodiversity and provide essential services such as water purification, flood regulation, and groundwater recharge. Rivers and lakes are crucial for drinking water supplies, agriculture, and recreation, serving as lifelines for human and ecological communities alike.

Our public lands play a pivotal role in safeguarding these vital water resources. These lands often encompass key watersheds, wetlands, and riparian zones that are crucial for maintaining water quality and availability. Public lands help regulate water flow, prevent erosion, and filter pollutants before they enter larger water systems. Many national parks such as Glacier, Denali, and Rocky Mountain protect the headwaters of major rivers and lakes. The preservation of these areas ensures that the natural filtration processes necessary for clean water are sustained.

Public lands are also instrumental in addressing the challenges posed by climate change. As global temperatures rise, the impacts on water resources are becoming more pronounced. Changes in precipitation patterns, glacier melt rates, and sea levels can affect water availability and quality. Public lands provide natural buffers against these changes by preserving ecosystems that enhance resilience and adaptability. For example, wetlands like Everglades National Park act as sponges. By providing storage and slowly releasing water, they absorb excess nutrients and sediments from runoff and mitigate the effects of extreme weather events like floods and drought.

Our public lands attract hundreds of millions of visitors each year who seek out water-based outdoor recreational activities. As this number continues to grow, the transportation of aquatic invasive species (AIS) poses a growing threat to freshwater and marine ecosystems by disrupting the natural balance and causing extensive ecological and economic damage. These non-native species—introduced either intentionally or accidentally through human activities—often lack natural predators or competitors in their new environments, allowing them to proliferate rapidly. Their invasion can lead to a range of detrimental effects. For instance, AIS such as zebra mussels can outcompete native species for resources like food and habitat, leading to declines in native biodiversity. They can alter ecosystem functions by changing nutrient cycles, disrupting food webs, and affecting the physical structure of aquatic habitats. AIS may also introduce diseases or parasites that further harm native wildlife.

Our public lands serve as important sites for scientific research and monitoring, which contribute to better understanding and managing of water resources across the country. Research conducted in these areas provides valuable data on water quality, ecosystem health, and the impacts of environmental changes.

Public lands also offer opportunities for education and public engagement, helping to

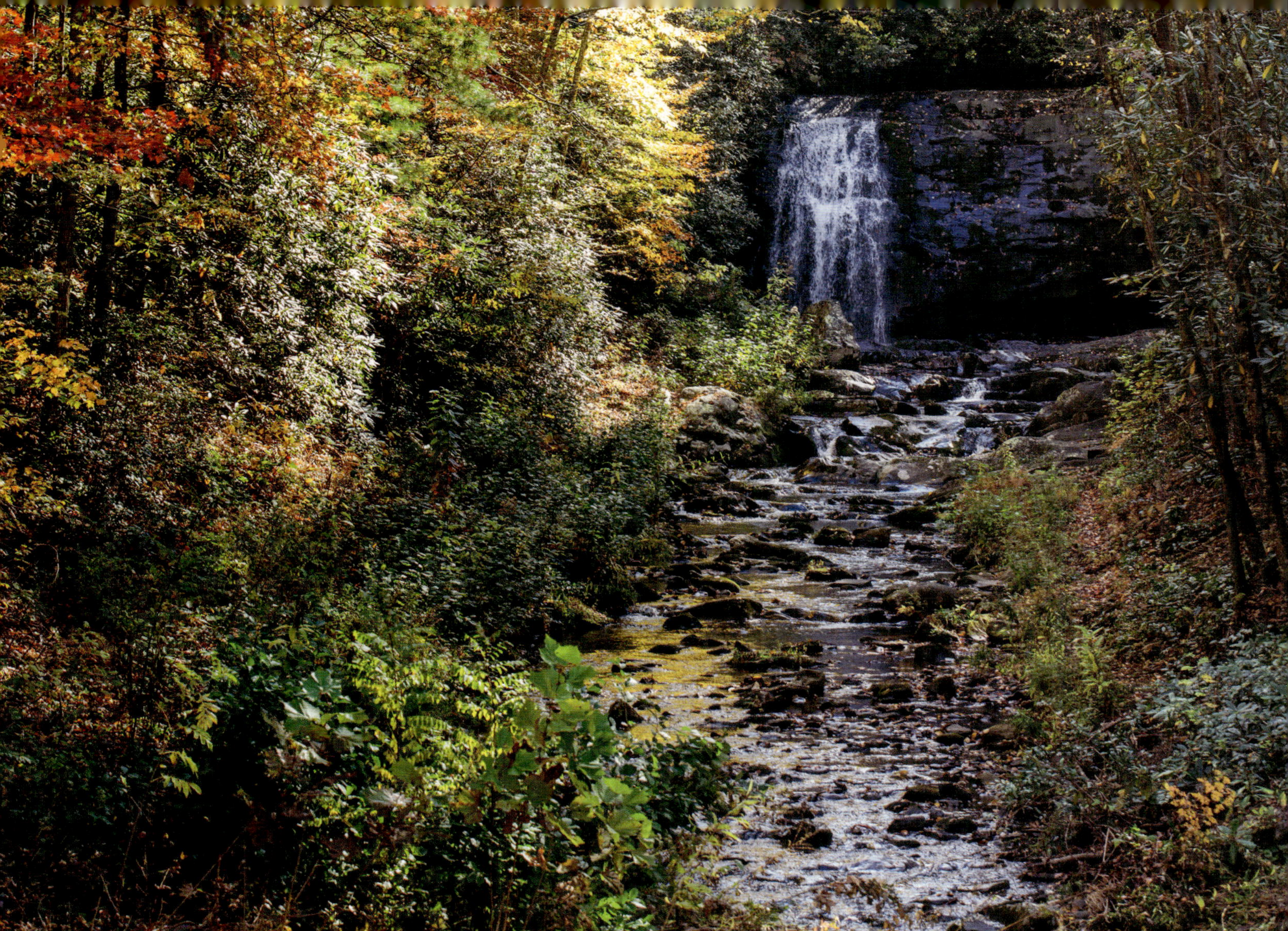

raise awareness about the importance of water and the need for its protection. By fostering a connection between people and nature, public lands encourage stewardship and support for water conservation efforts.

Through effective conservation, management, and public engagement, we can ensure that these natural areas continue to play their critical roles in safeguarding water resources for future generations.

GREAT SMOKY MOUNTAINS NATIONAL PARK On a trip out east we planned to spend a couple days in the park. We didn't have time for long hikes or backpacking trips, so we spent most of our time exploring views near the road. Framed perfectly by the fall foliage, Meigs Falls is tucked away on the far side of Little River and can be easily missed while driving.

We departed from Seward, Alaska, by boat and traveled through Resurrection Bay on our way to Kenai Fjords National Park. The water teemed with wildlife. Along the way, we spotted humpback whales, puffins, sea lions, otters, and orcas, to name a few. As we entered Aialik Bay, I noticed a blue-tinged glacier sandwiched between the low-hanging clouds and ocean far in the distance.

As we got closer, the small blue shape grew larger, revealing more details. What appeared to be tiny hairline cracks from afar were actually enormous crevasses that could easily swallow full-sized vehicles. When we reached our destination, we found ourselves floating among freshly calved icebergs from the mile-wide tidewater glacier in front of us. After a brief talk, the guide said he would remain silent to allow us to absorb the glacier's sights and sounds.

As I watched and photographed, I realized I had no real sense of the glacier's immense scale. Only when birds landed on distant icebergs did I gain any perspective. I had been severely underestimating its size. House-size chunks of ice repeatedly broke off the glacier, crashing and exploding onto a rocky outcrop below. The sound of each impact followed seconds later, echoing throughout the fjord. When ice calved directly into the ocean, massive waves formed, causing the icebergs to bob up and down slowly in the water. It was mesmerizing.

What felt like just a few minutes later, the guide spoke again, saying it was time to return. He asked if the glacier had held our attention the entire time. I found the question odd until I looked at my watch and realized we had been there for over an hour. It felt like we had unknowingly traveled through time.

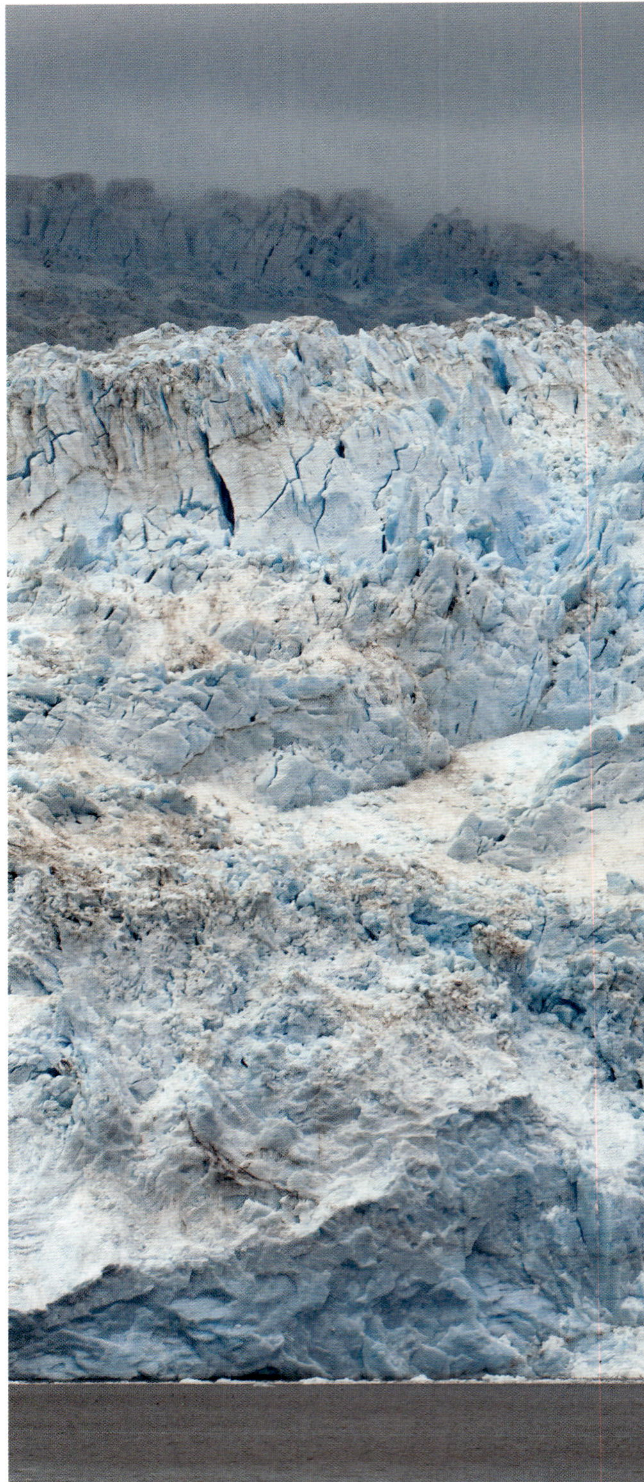

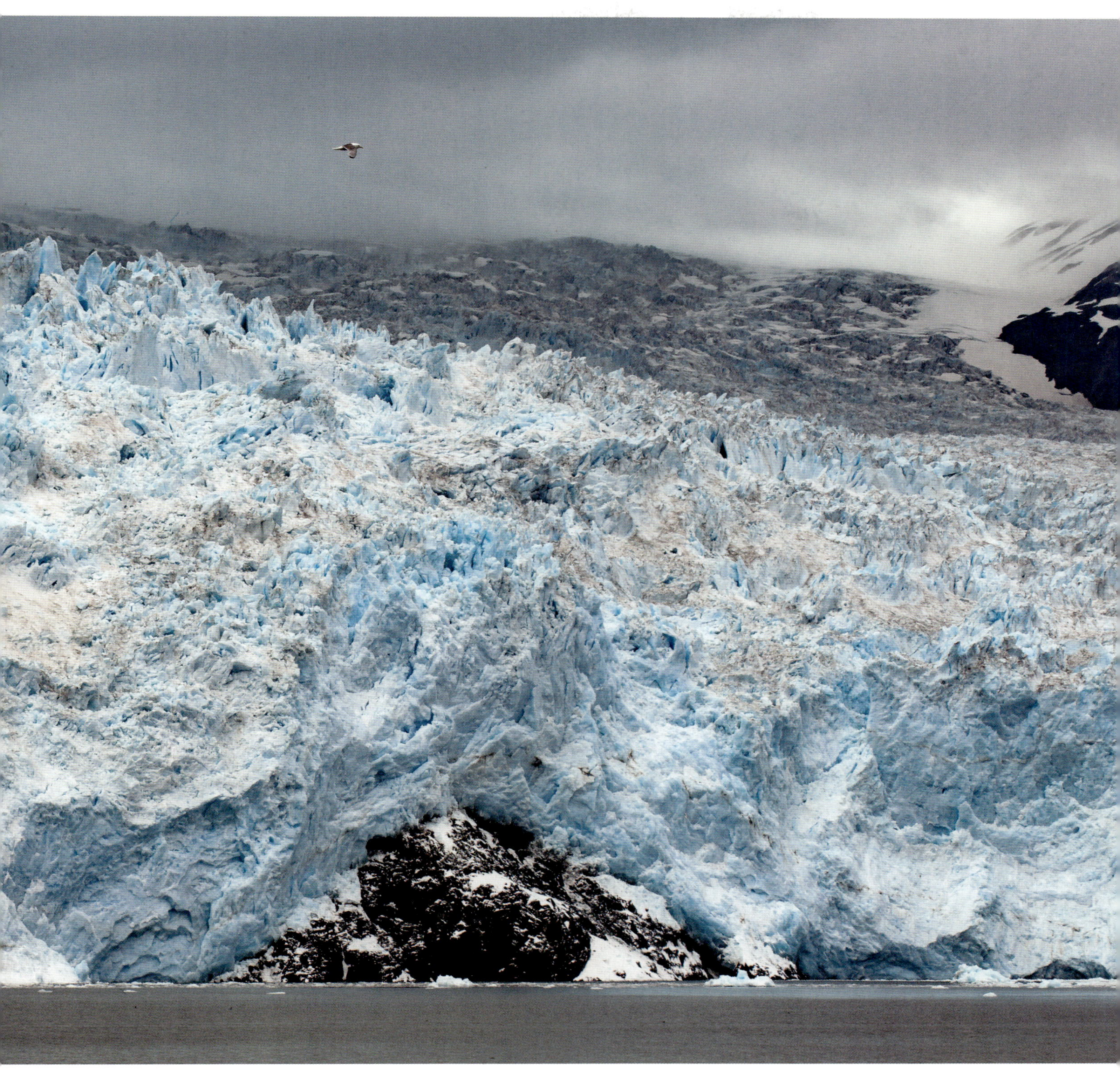

KENAI FJORDS NATIONAL PARK

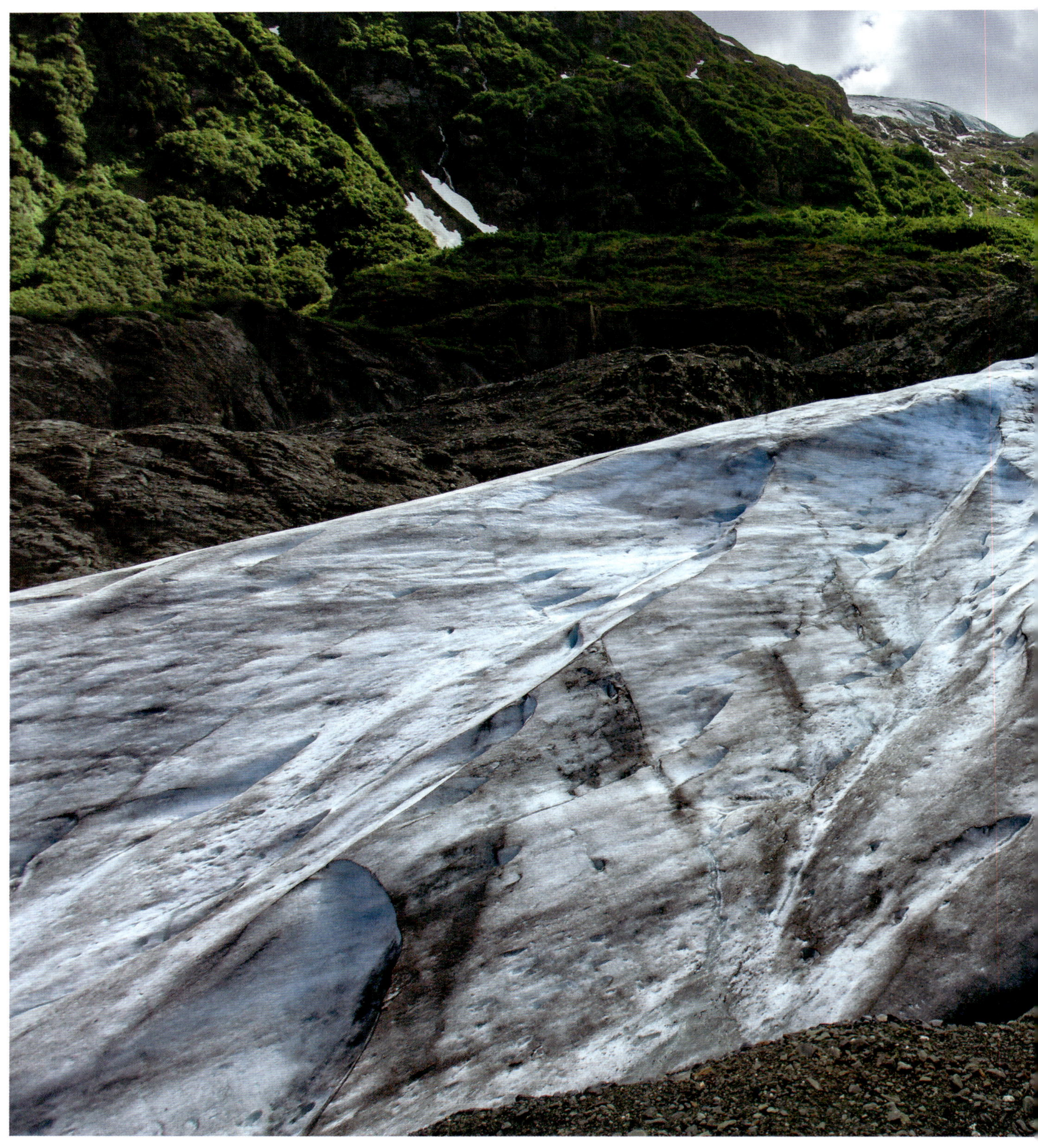

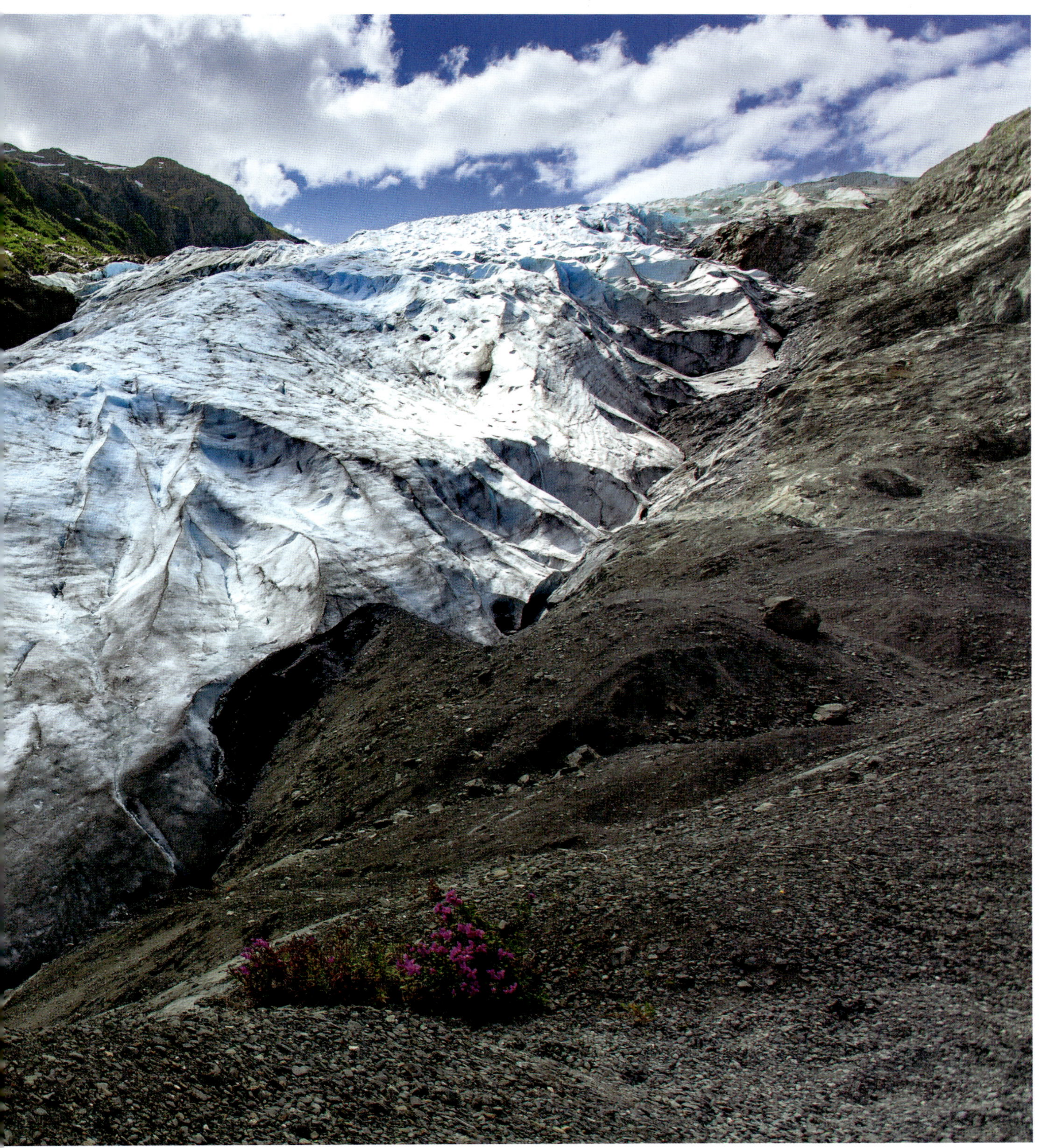

KENAI FJORDS NATIONAL PARK Most the park's glaciers are only accessible by boat, except for Exit Glacier, which flows from the Harding Icefield toward the park's nature center. The hike to the overlook is steep, but the views of the glacier along the trail keep you wanting to see more.

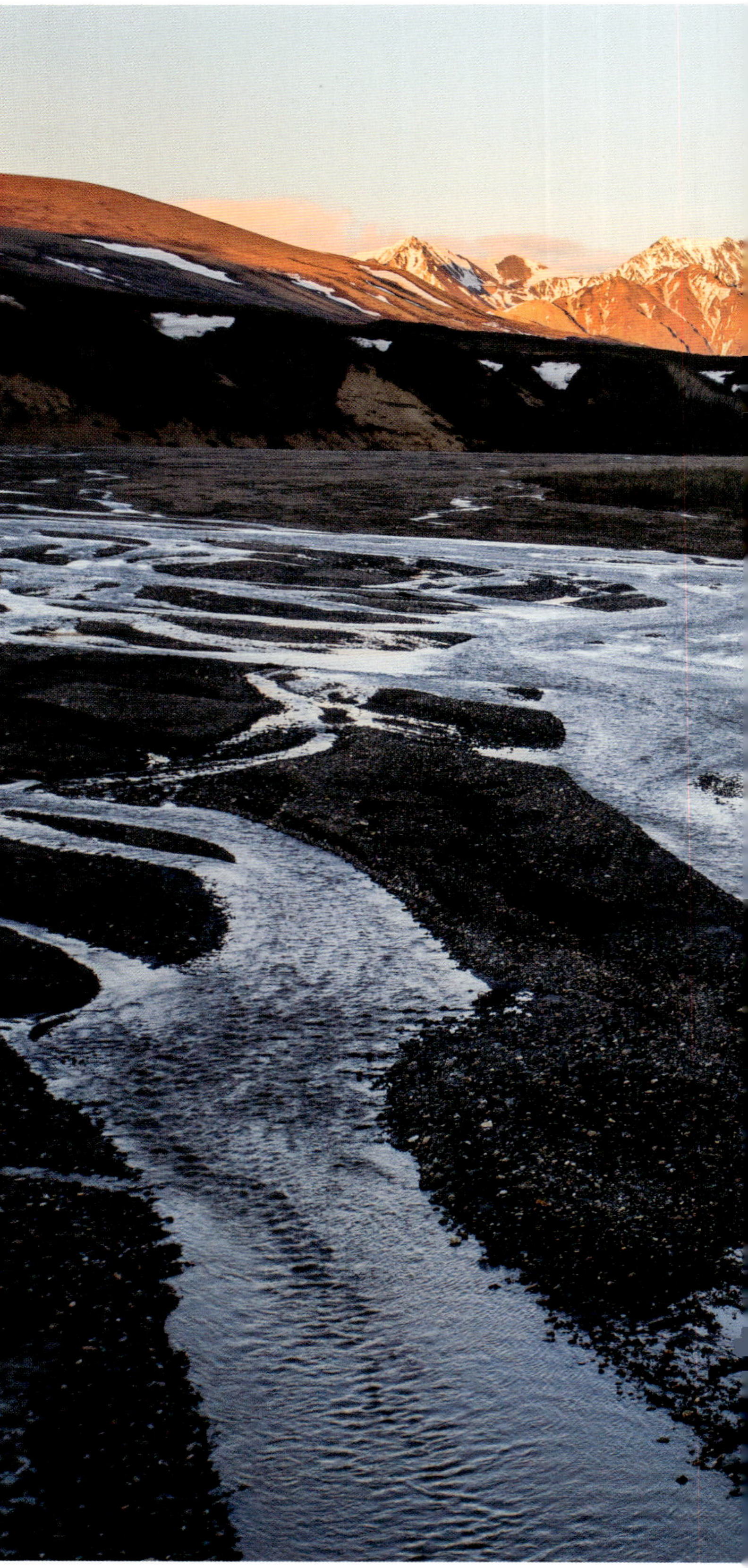

DENALI NATIONAL PARK AND PRESERVE The East Fork of the Toklat River is where Adolph Murie spent his summers studying wildlife, which would influence management policies across the National Park Service. Not too far from here is where I spent two of the best summers of my life. It would also become the namesake for our dog many years later.

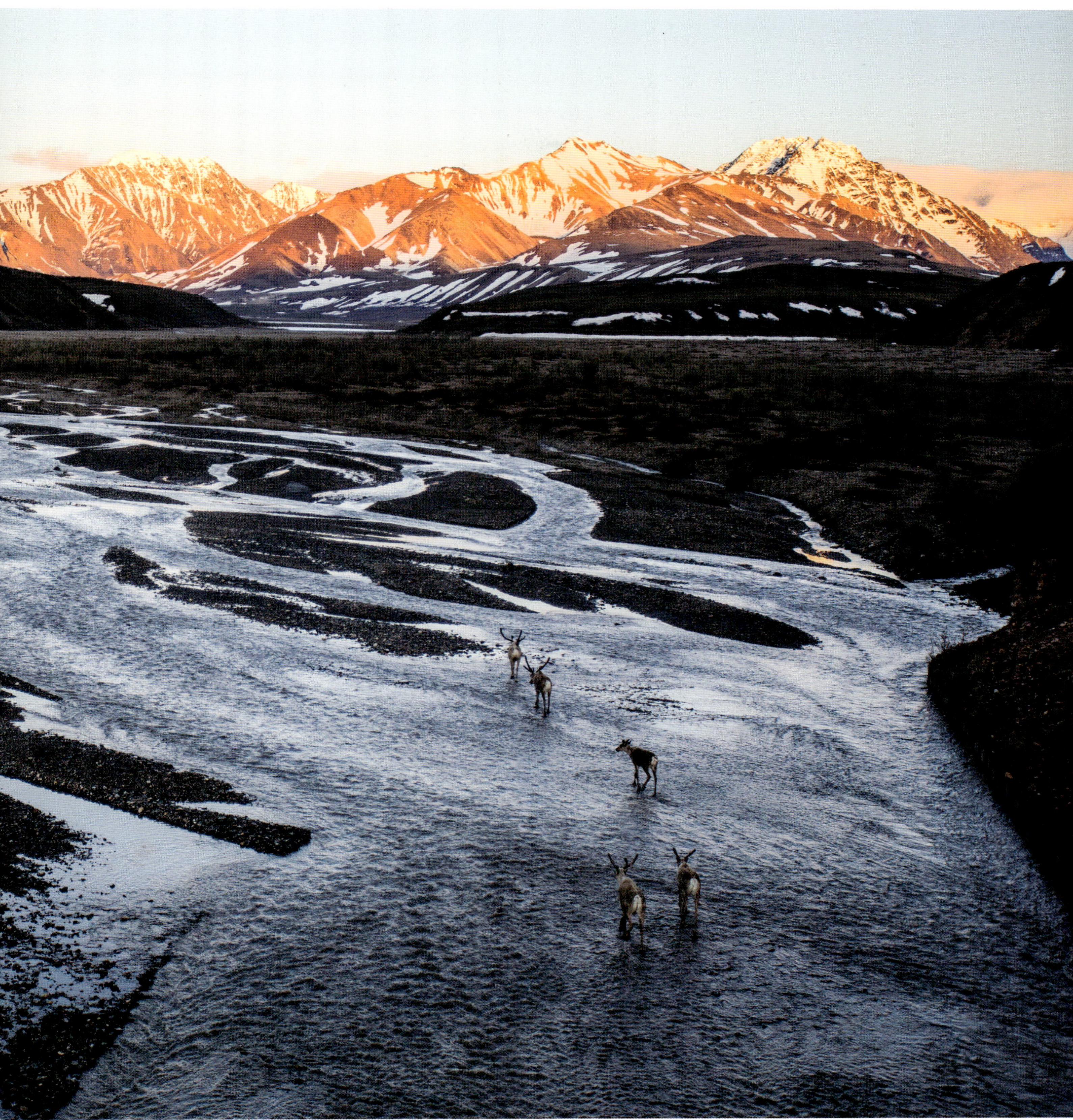

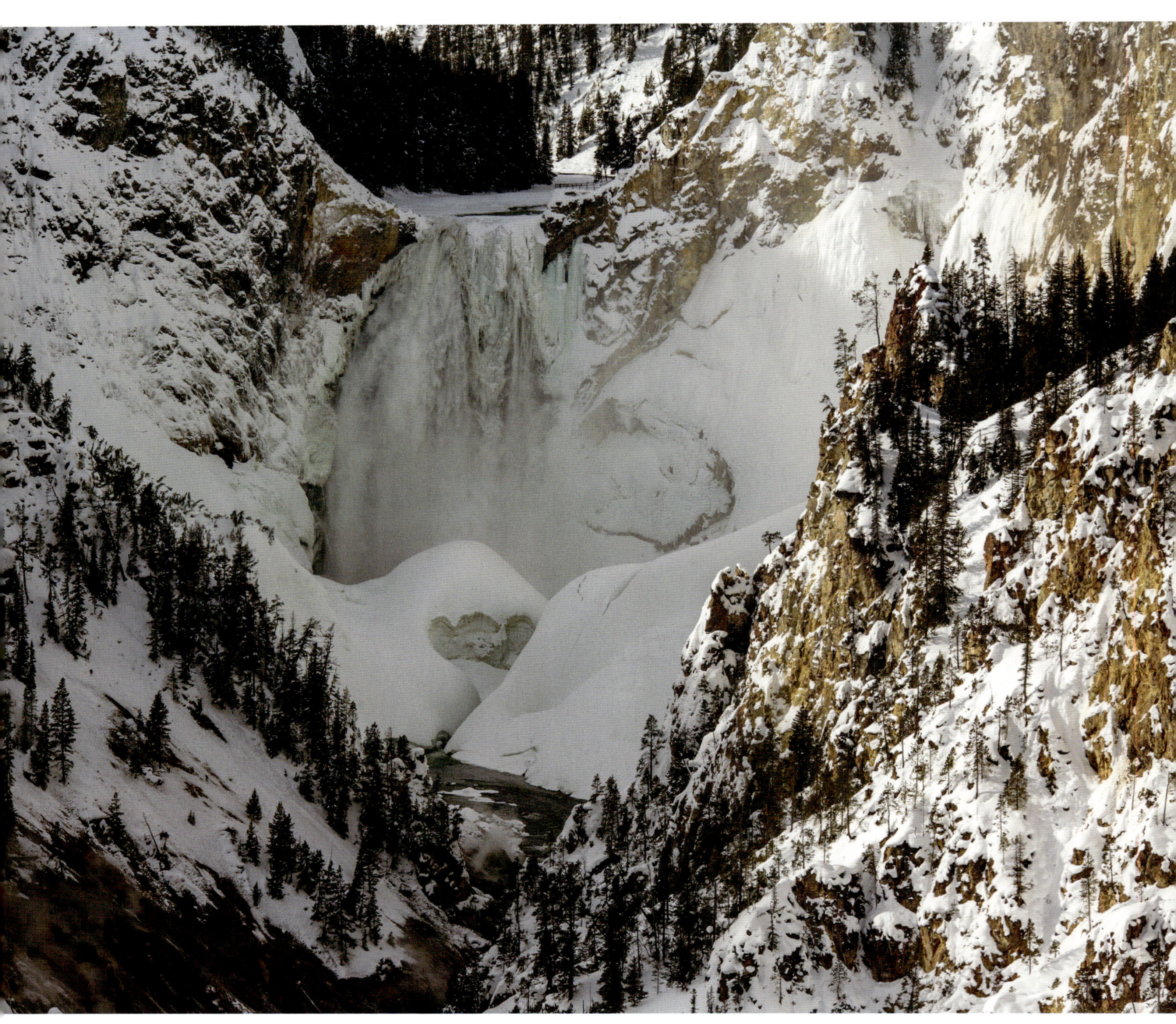

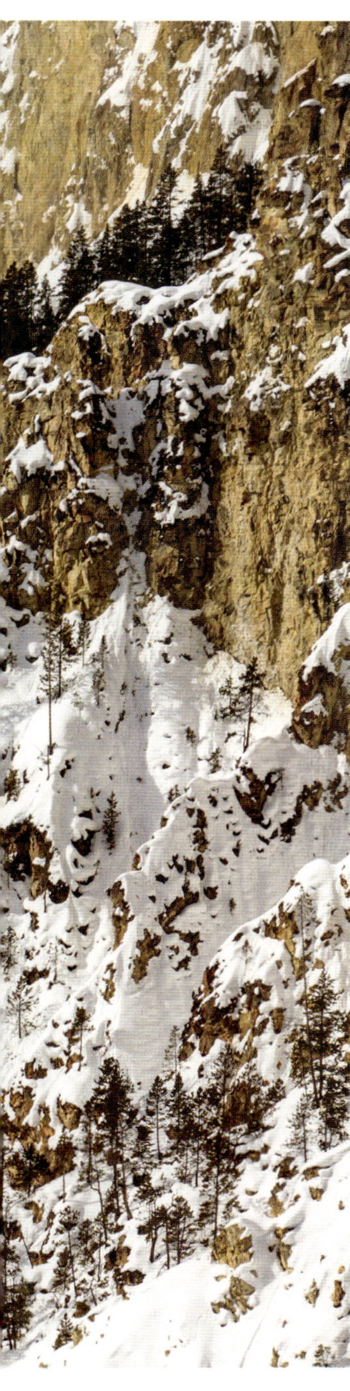

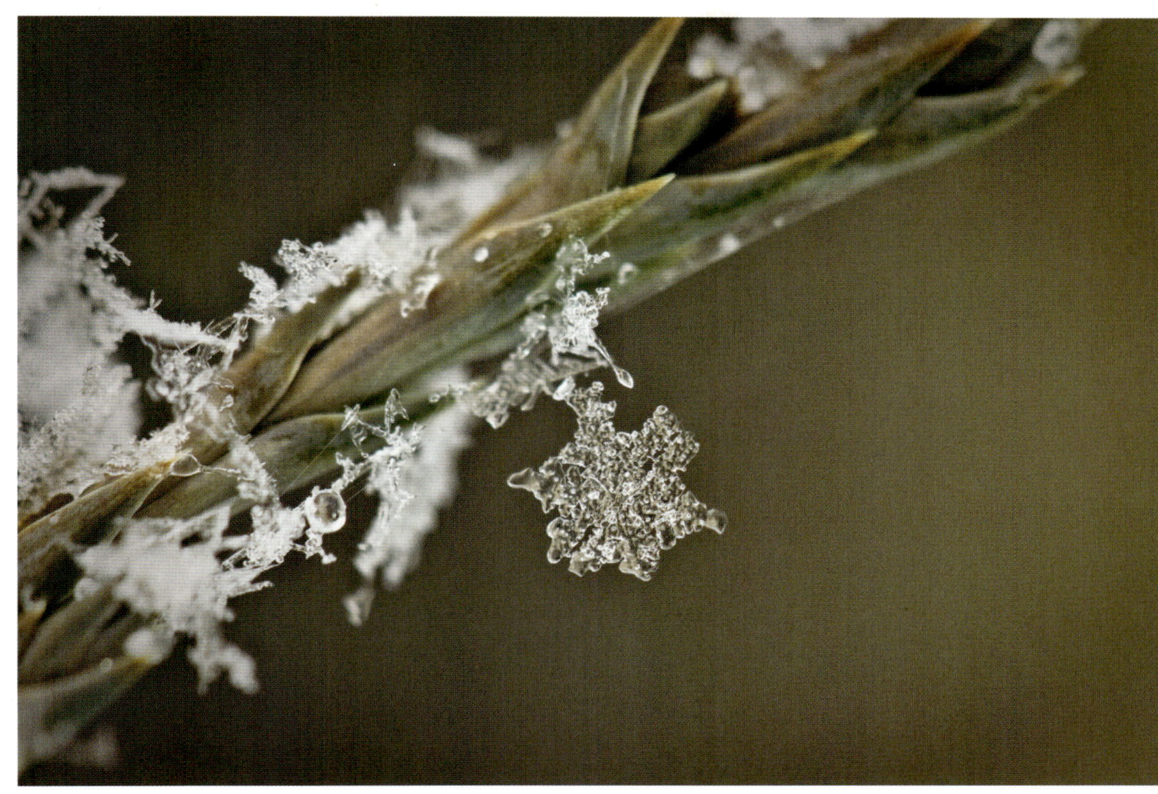

YELLOWSTONE NATIONAL PARK

(OPPOSITE) At 308 feet tall, the Lower Falls flow year-round in the Grand Canyon of the Yellowstone. During the winter, the ephemeral ice dam that forms at the base of the falls can best be seen from Lookout Point on the North Rim. Any time of year in Yellowstone is special, but winter is pure magic.

(ABOVE) In a park with enormous landscapes, snowflakes are a good reminder to not overlook the small stuff.

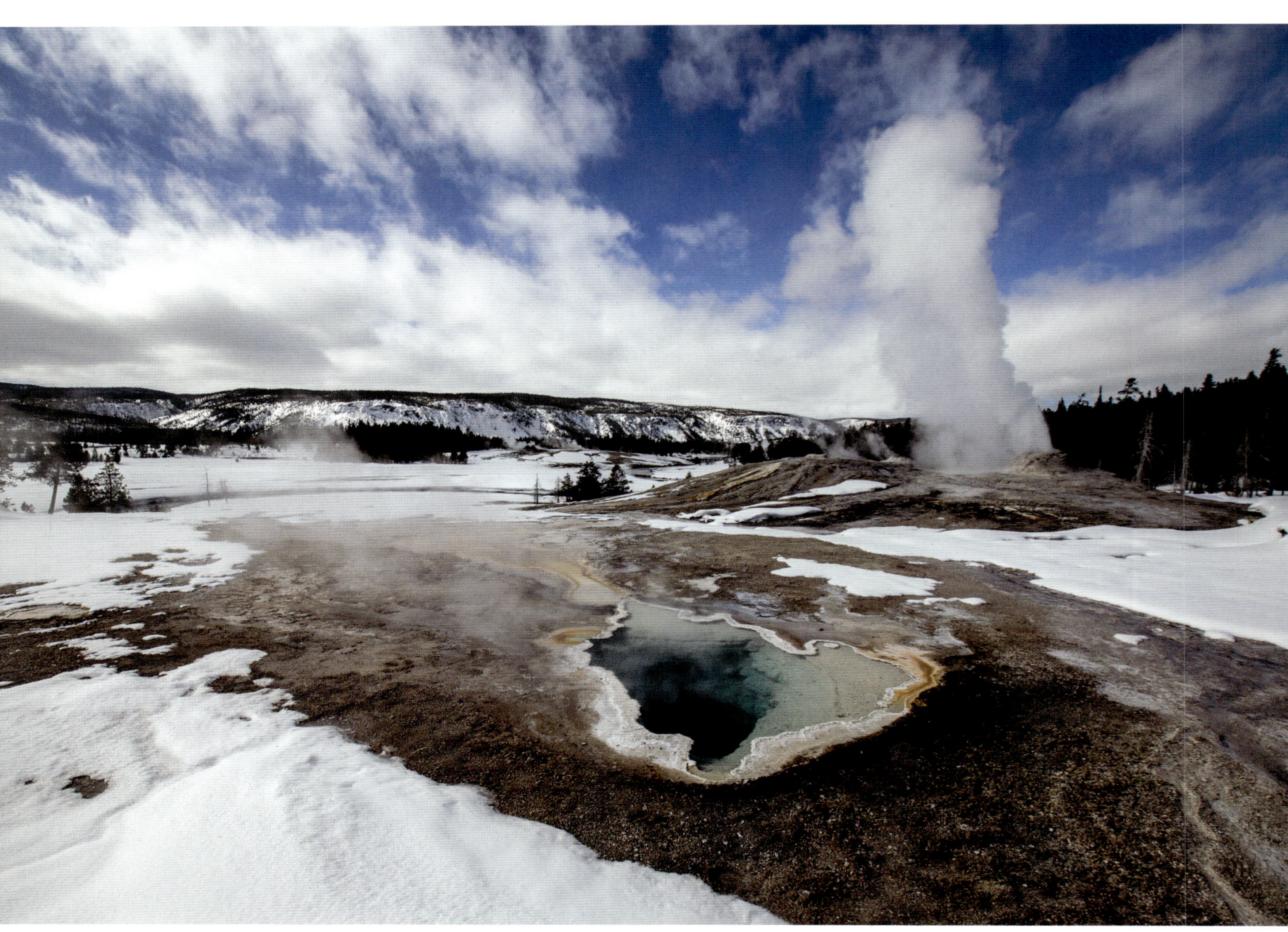

YELLOWSTONE NATIONAL PARK

(ABOVE) A favorite hot spring of mine in any season, Heart Spring provides a beautiful foreground for an eruption of Lion Geyser.

(OPPOSITE) Canary Spring is a must-visit when exploring the Mammoth Hot Springs area. The terraces are constantly changing, due to the deposition of over one ton of travertine each day.

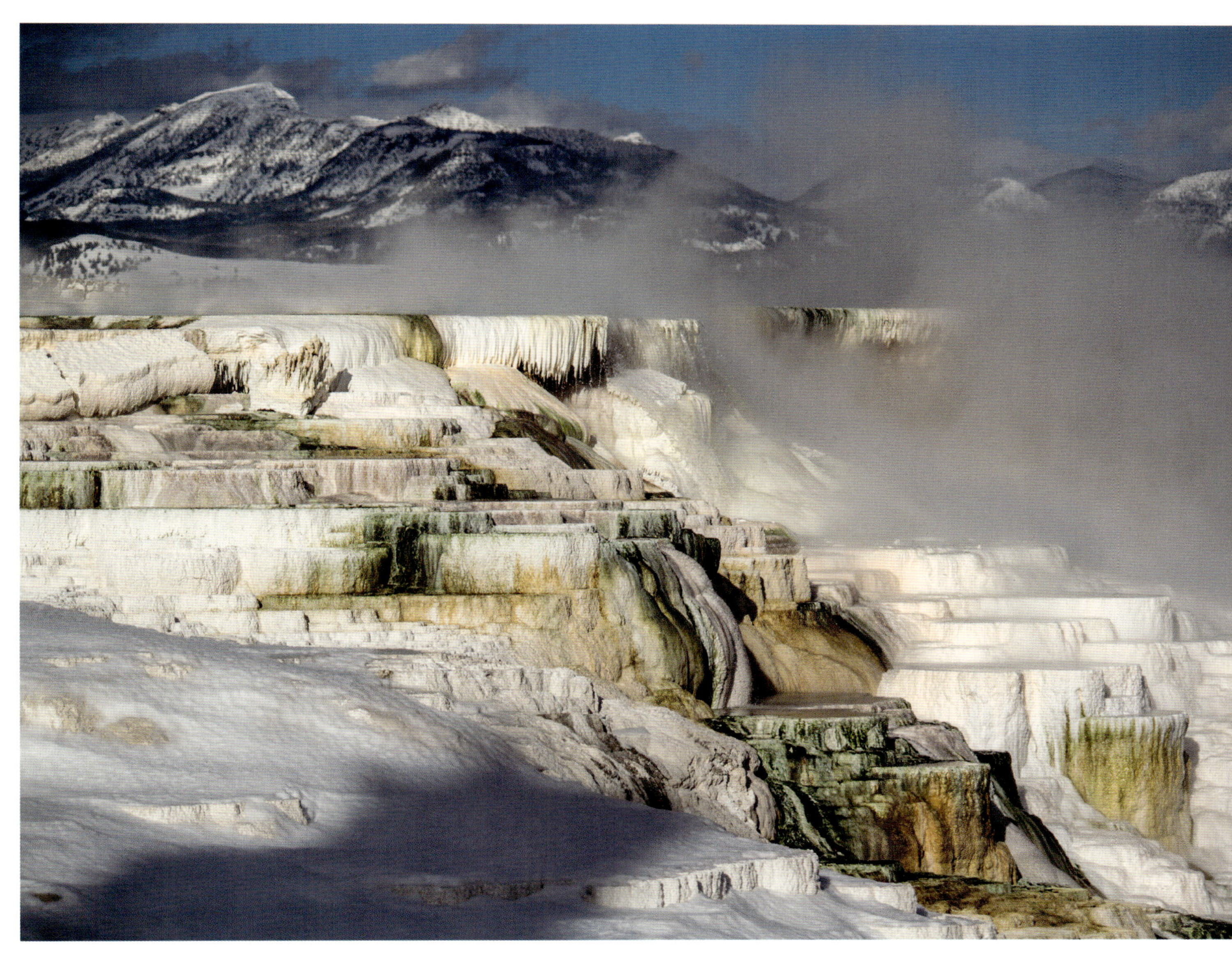

ROCKY MOUNTAIN NATIONAL PARK

There are so many beautiful hikes in this comparatively small park, but Sky Pond stands out as a favorite of mine. It's especially beautiful on a calm day when you get reflections of The Sharkstooth in the water.

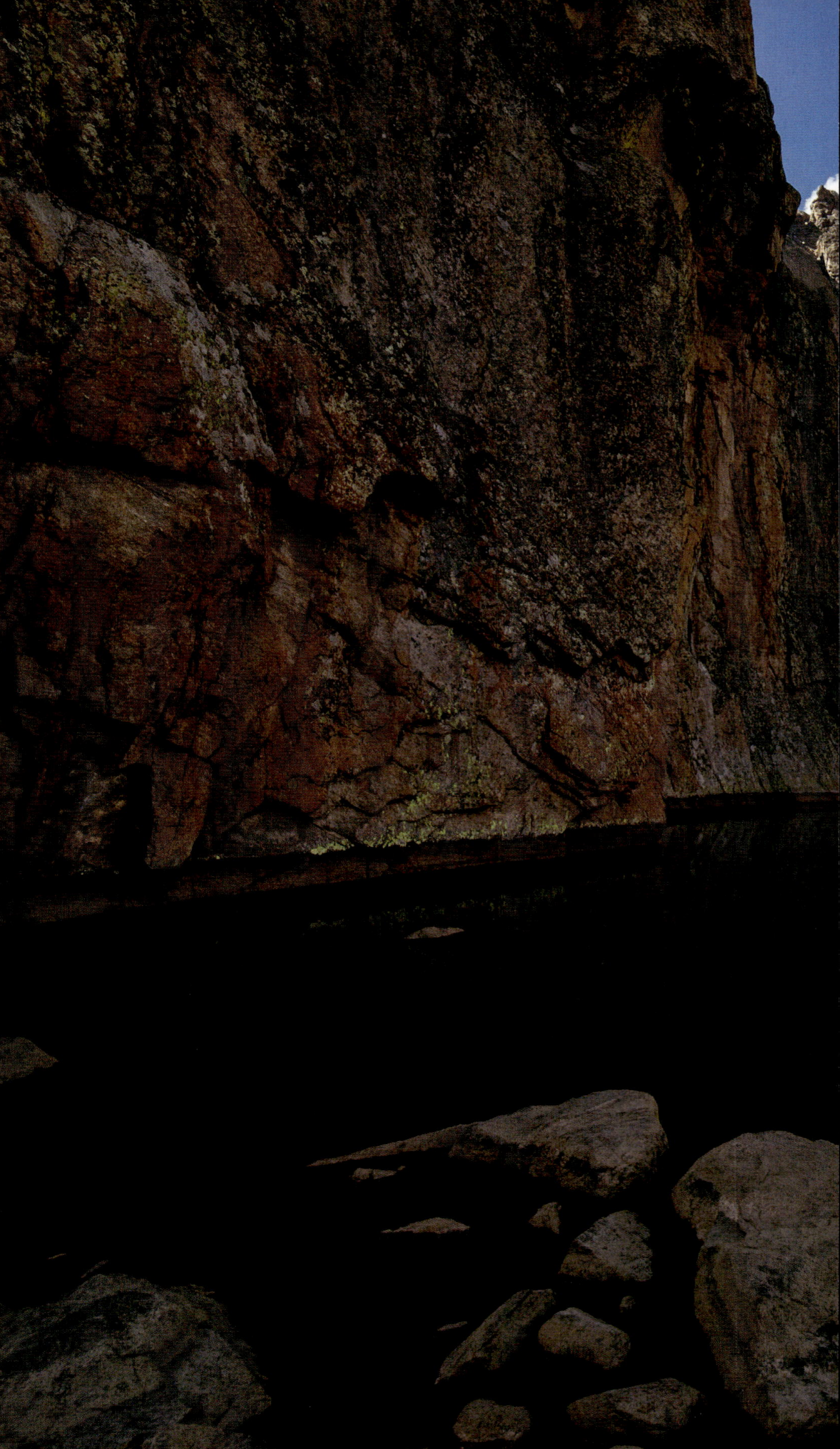

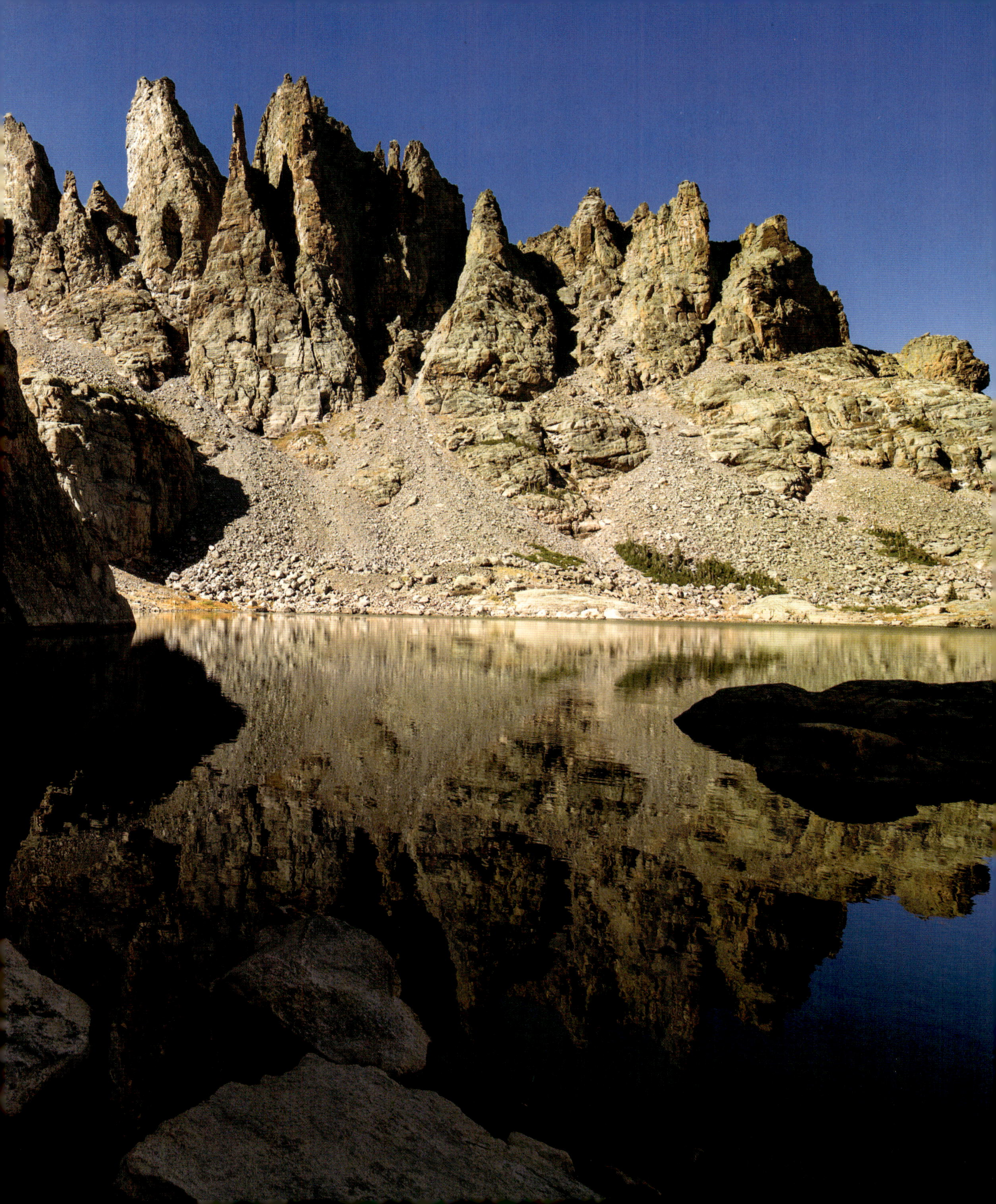

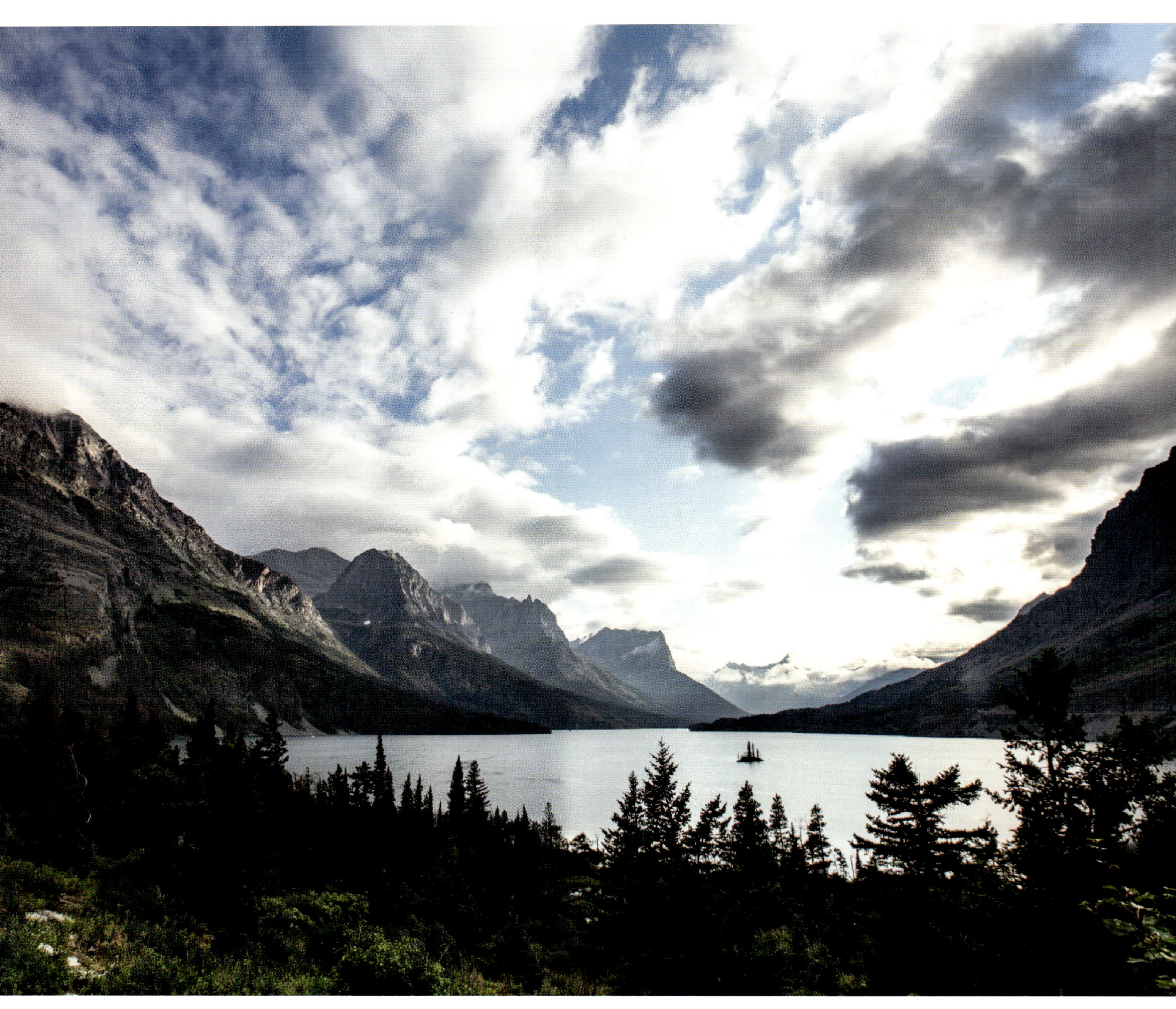

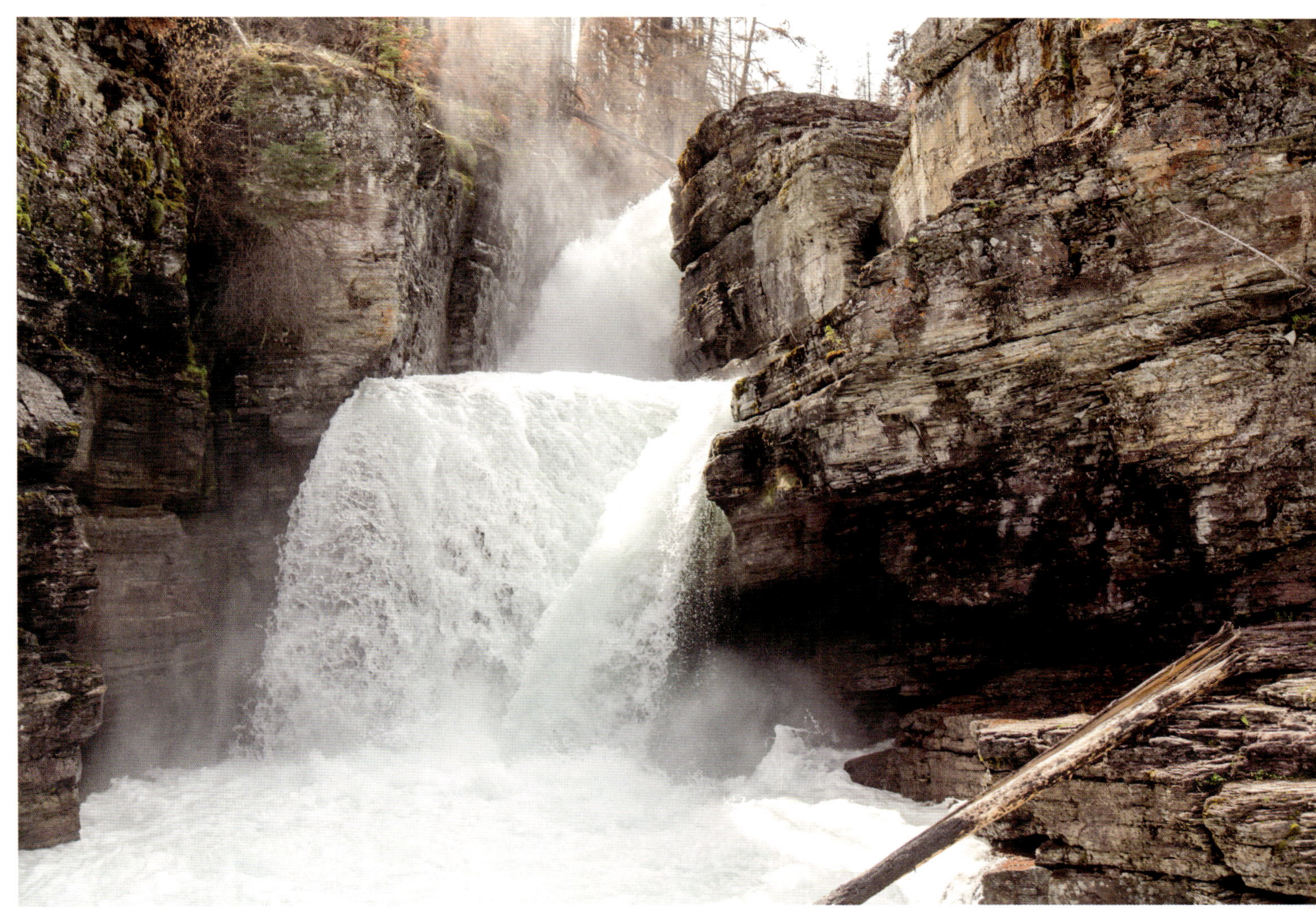

GLACIER NATIONAL PARK

(OPPOSITE) The view of Saint Mary Lake at Wild Goose Island Overlook is perhaps one of the most recognizable scenes in all of Glacier. No matter how many times you drive past, it's always worth a quick stop.

(ABOVE) In my first summer working in Glacier, I led a weekly hike to Saint Mary Falls. Even though I've seen it countless times, it's still a favorite early season destination. Don't forget to hike the extra mile and a half out to Virginia Falls.

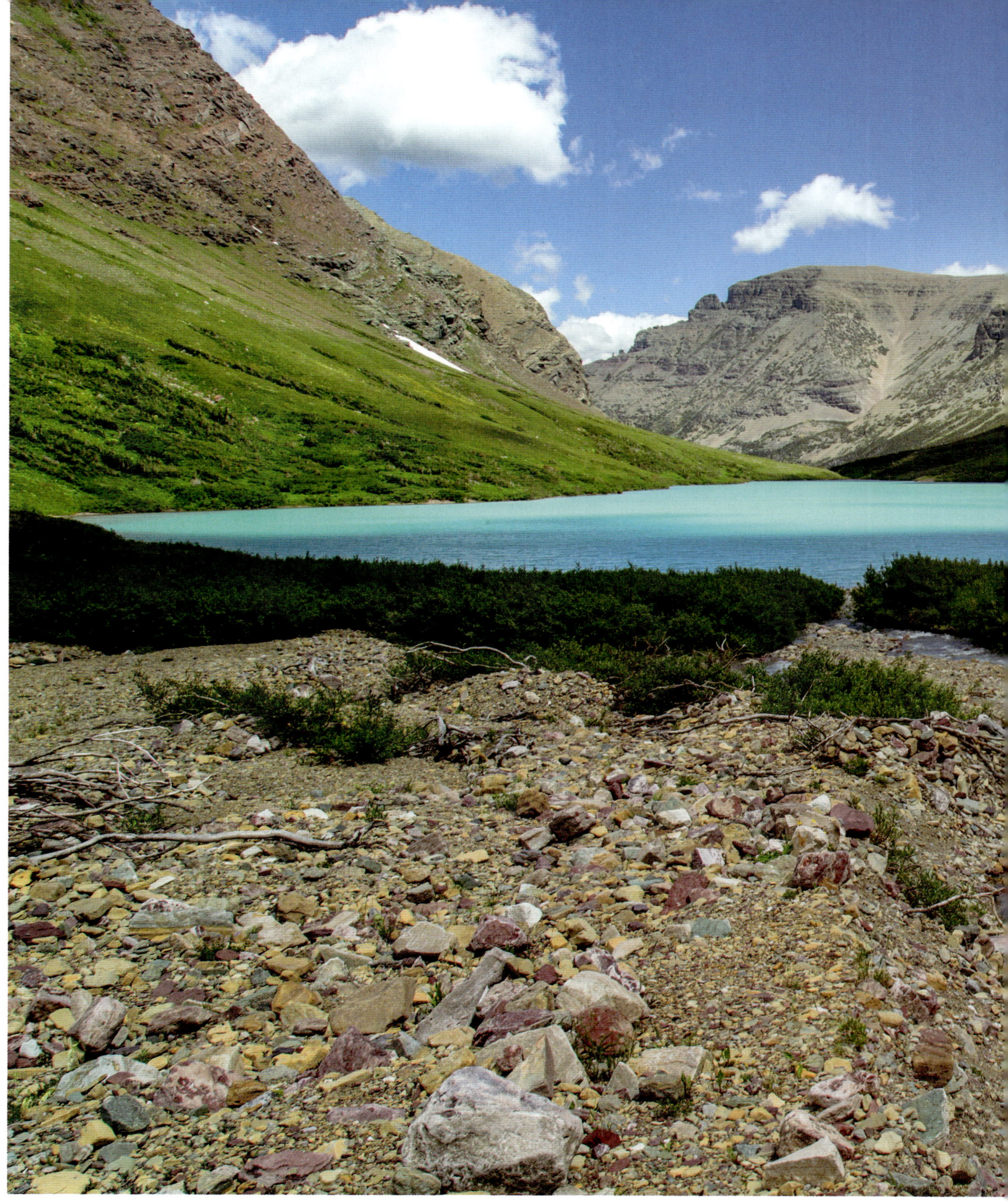

GLACIER NATIONAL PARK Cracker Lake's unmistakable color comes from the "rock flour" carried by meltwater from Siyeh Glacier. The hike to the lake and back can be done in a day, but for those who stay overnight at the backcountry campsite, waking up to a sunrise view of the lake is an experience that's hard to beat.

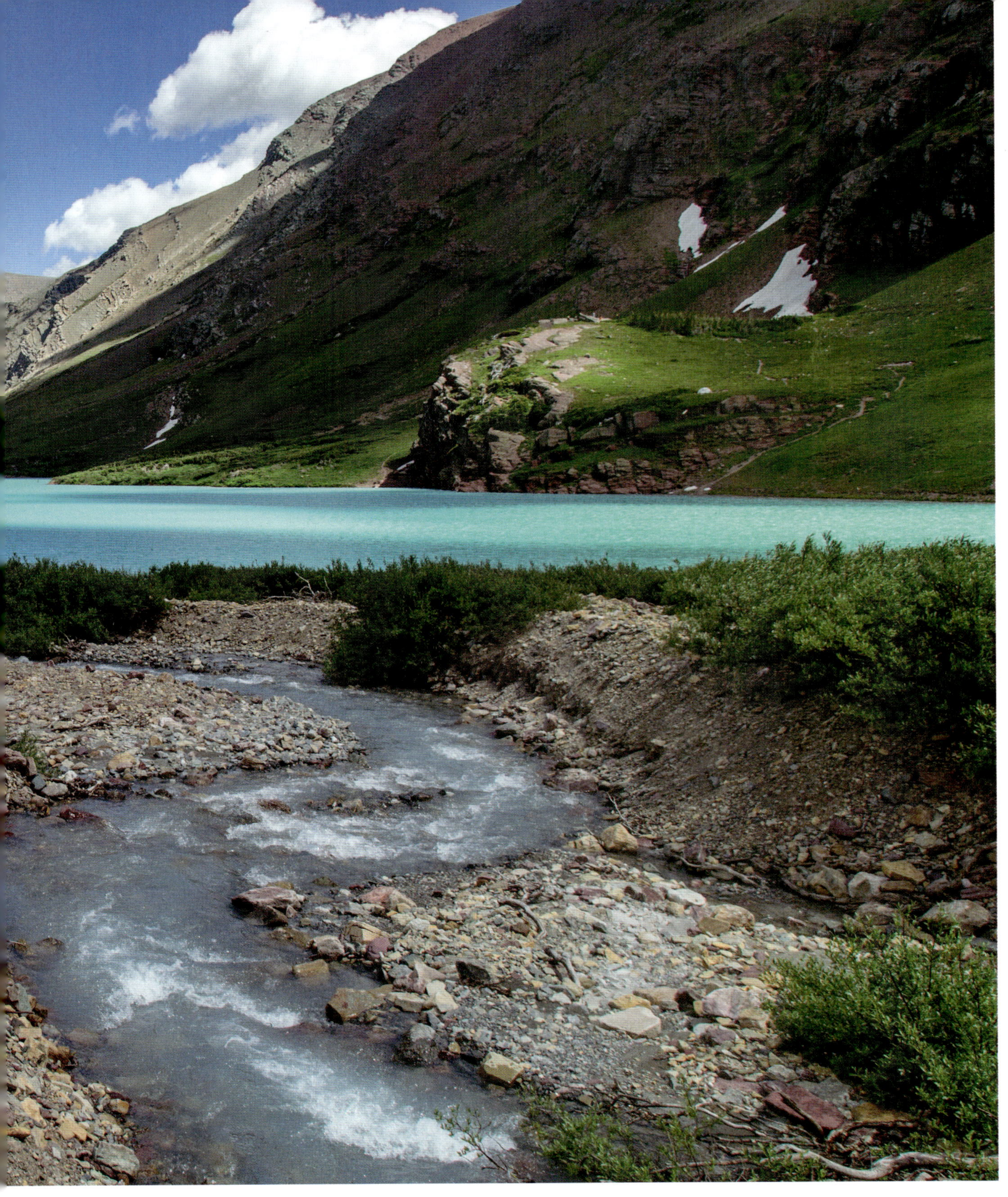

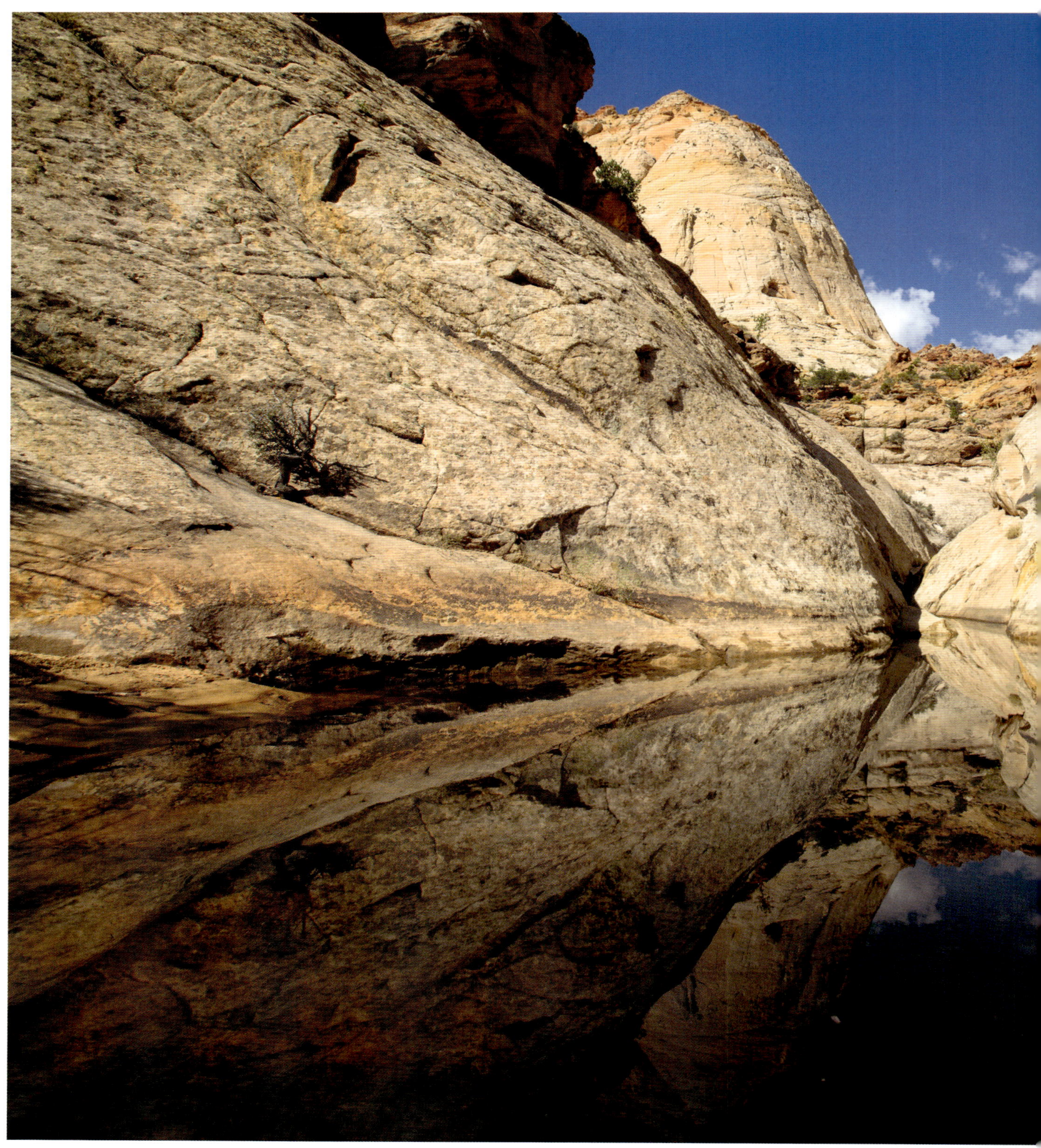

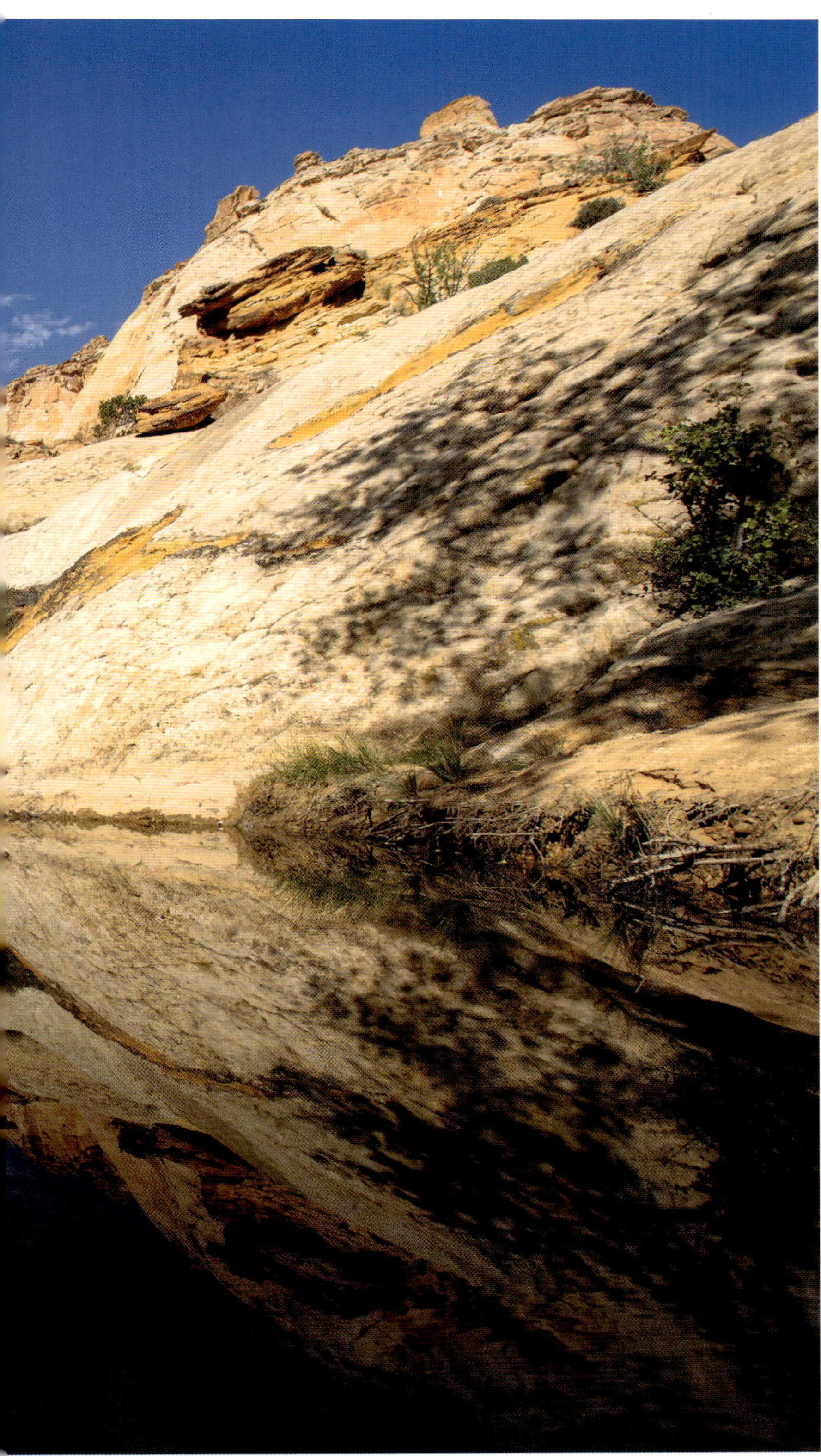

CAPITOL REEF NATIONAL PARK The "Tanks" are natural water pockets carved into the sandstone along the Cassidy Arch Trail. They are replenished after rainstorms and serve as vital reservoirs for the diverse wildlife in this arid desert landscape.

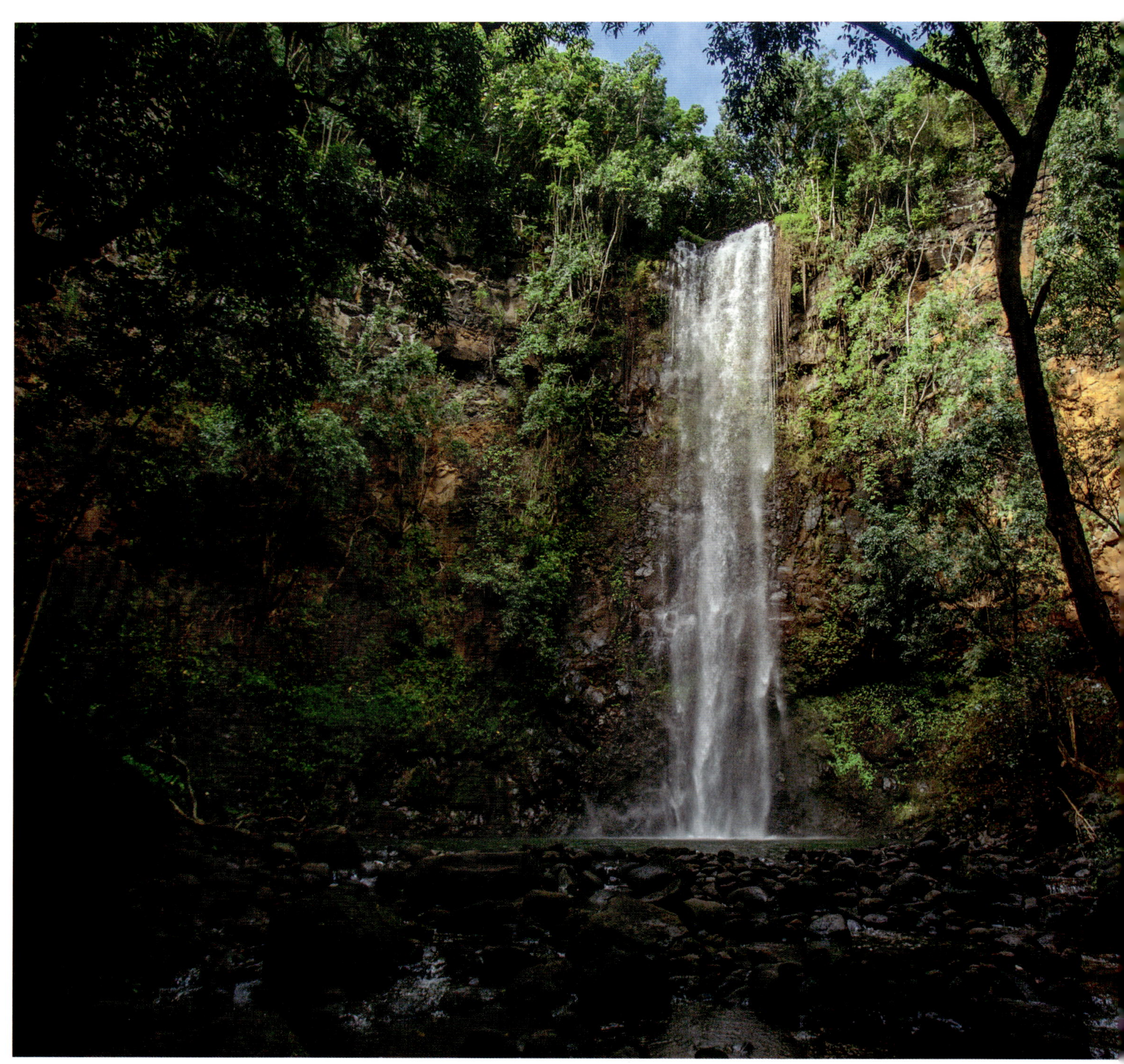

WAILUA RIVER STATE PARK After a few days of long hikes, Corrie and I spent the day kayaking up the Wailua River and capped it off with a short hike to Secret Falls. After lunch, we swam at the base of the falls and took turns on the rope swing back along the river.

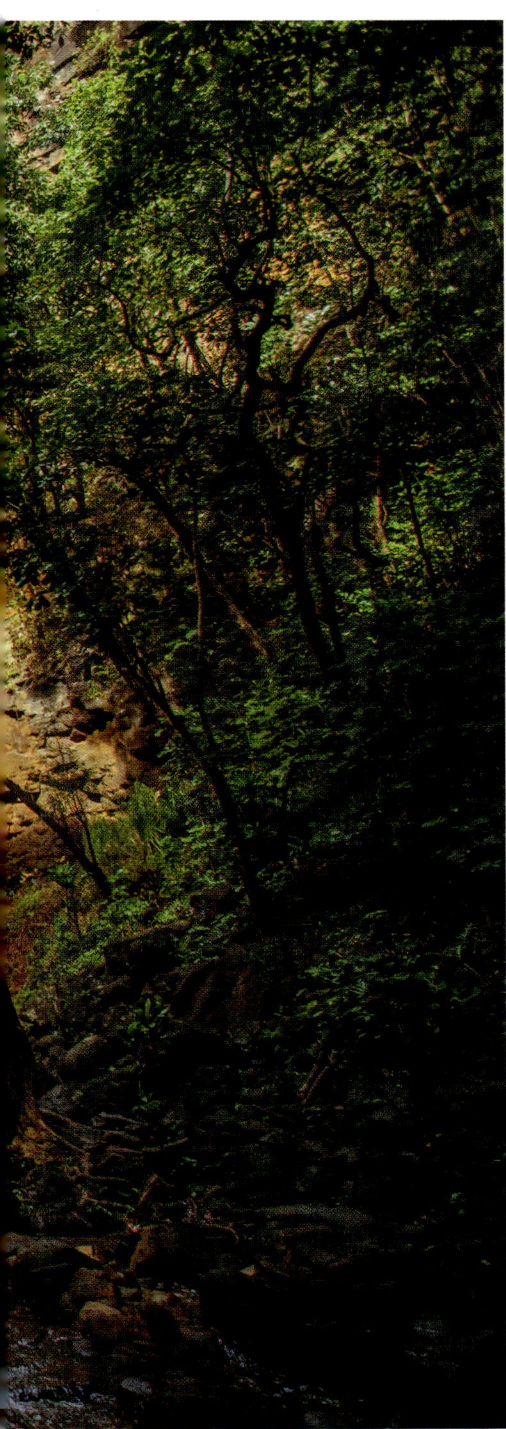

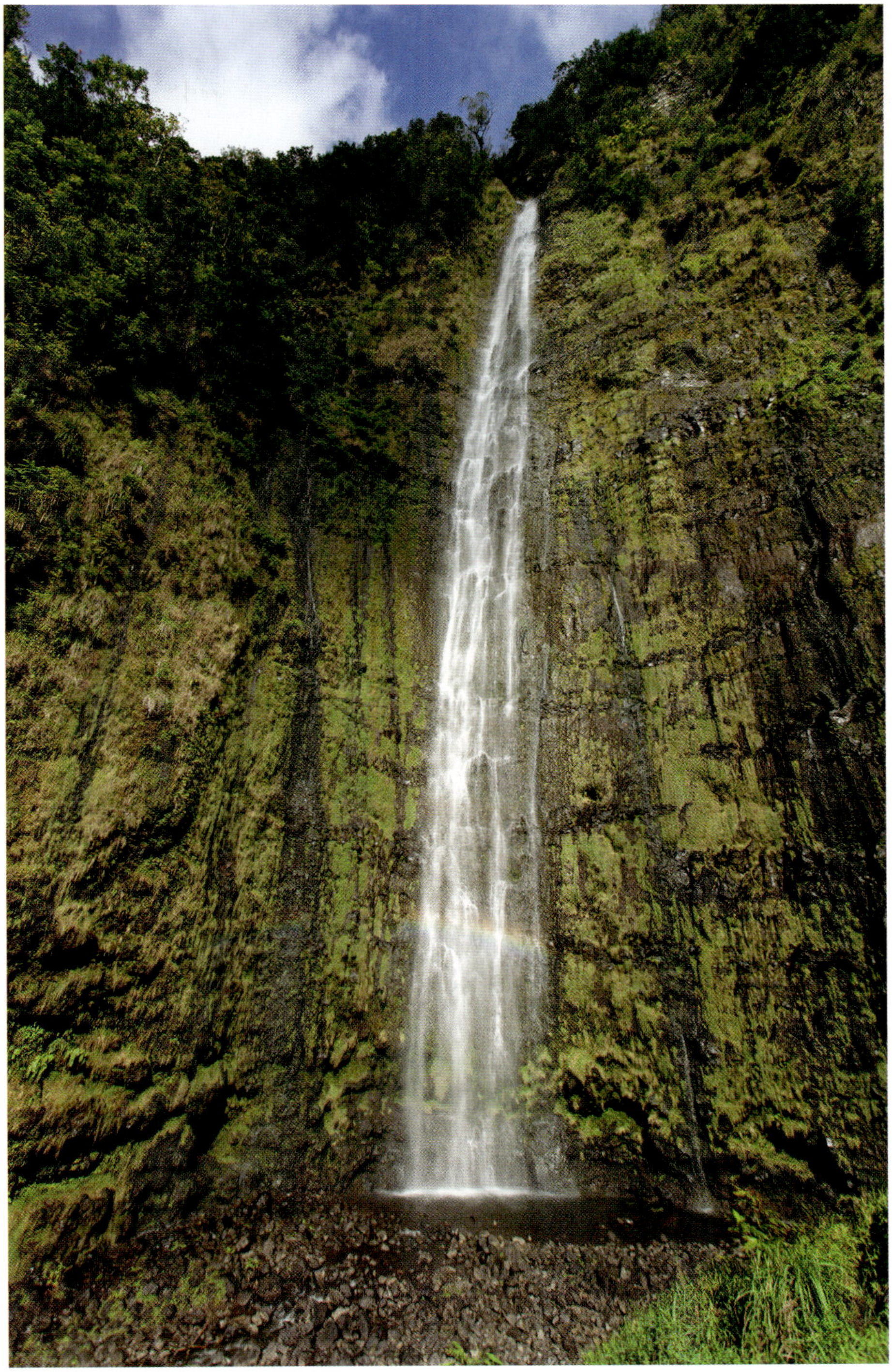

HALEAKALĀ NATIONAL PARK No trip to the Kīpahulu District is complete without a hike through the bamboo forest to the 400-foot Waimoku Falls. On our visit we were also greeted to a partial rainbow at the base of the falls.

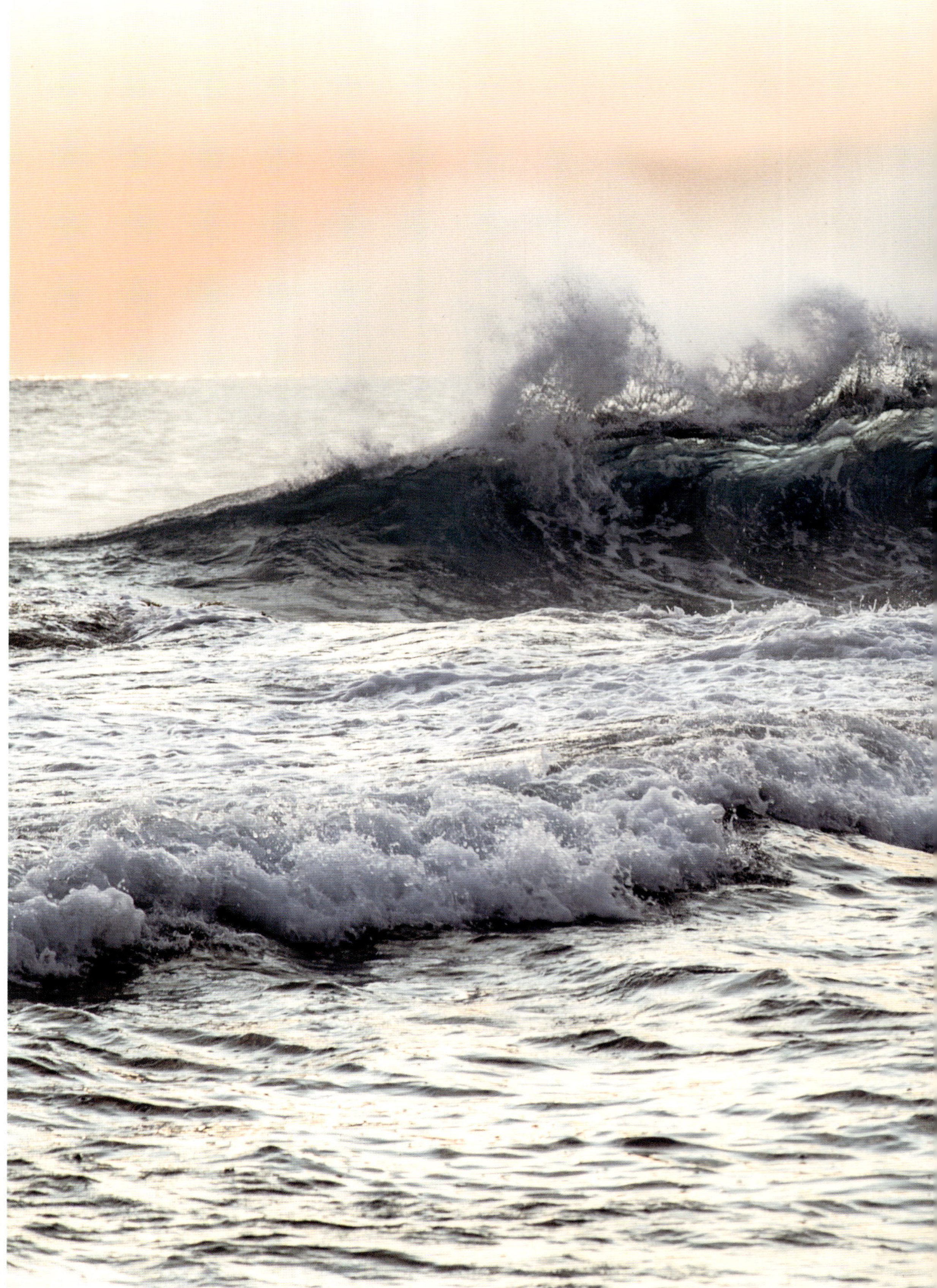

HAWAI'I VOLCANOES NATIONAL PARK On our four-day backpacking trip along the coast, we spent the evenings watching the waves crash along the rocks as we ate dinner. To this day, this trip is the only time I've ever brought a mask and snorkel into the backcountry.

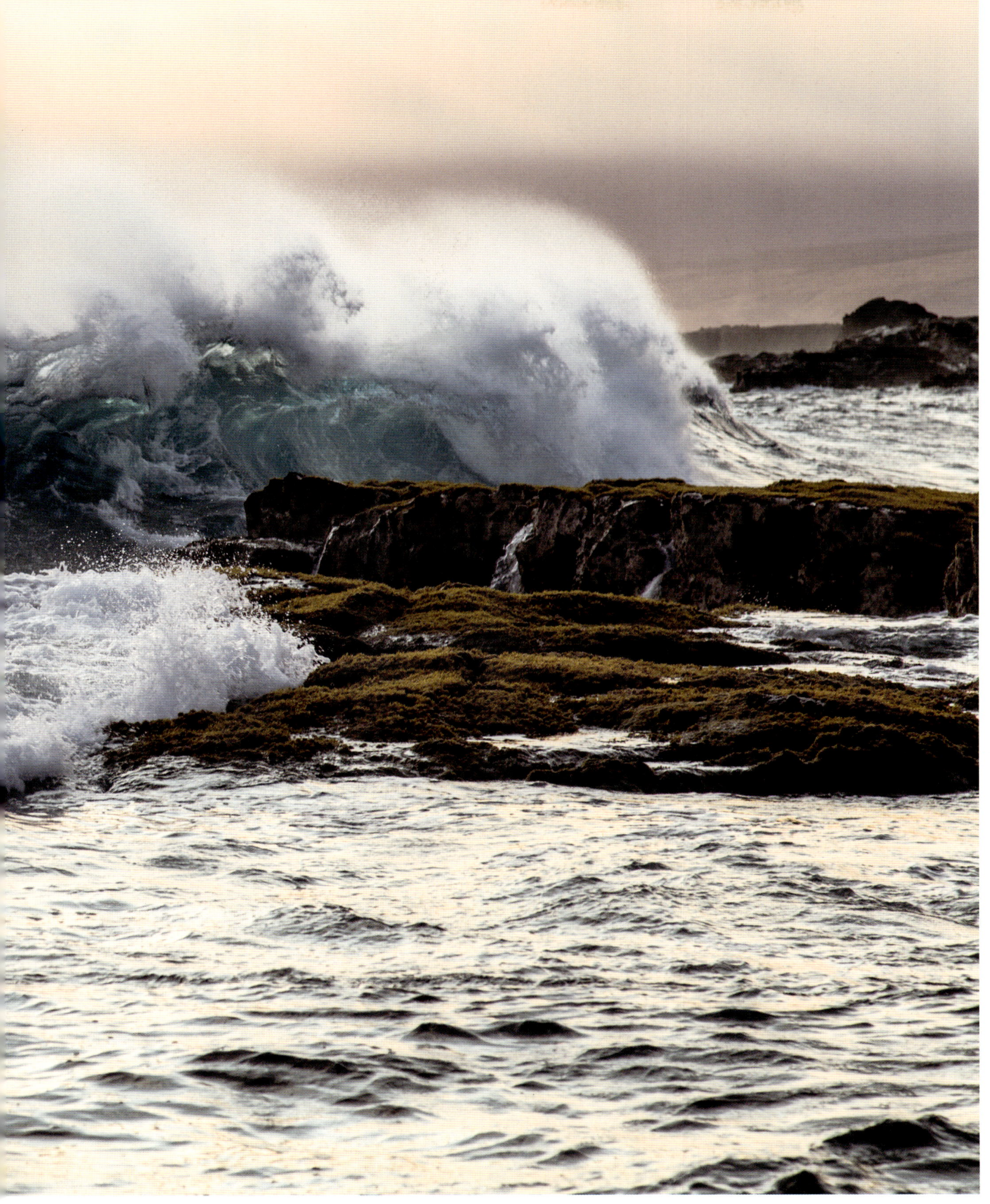

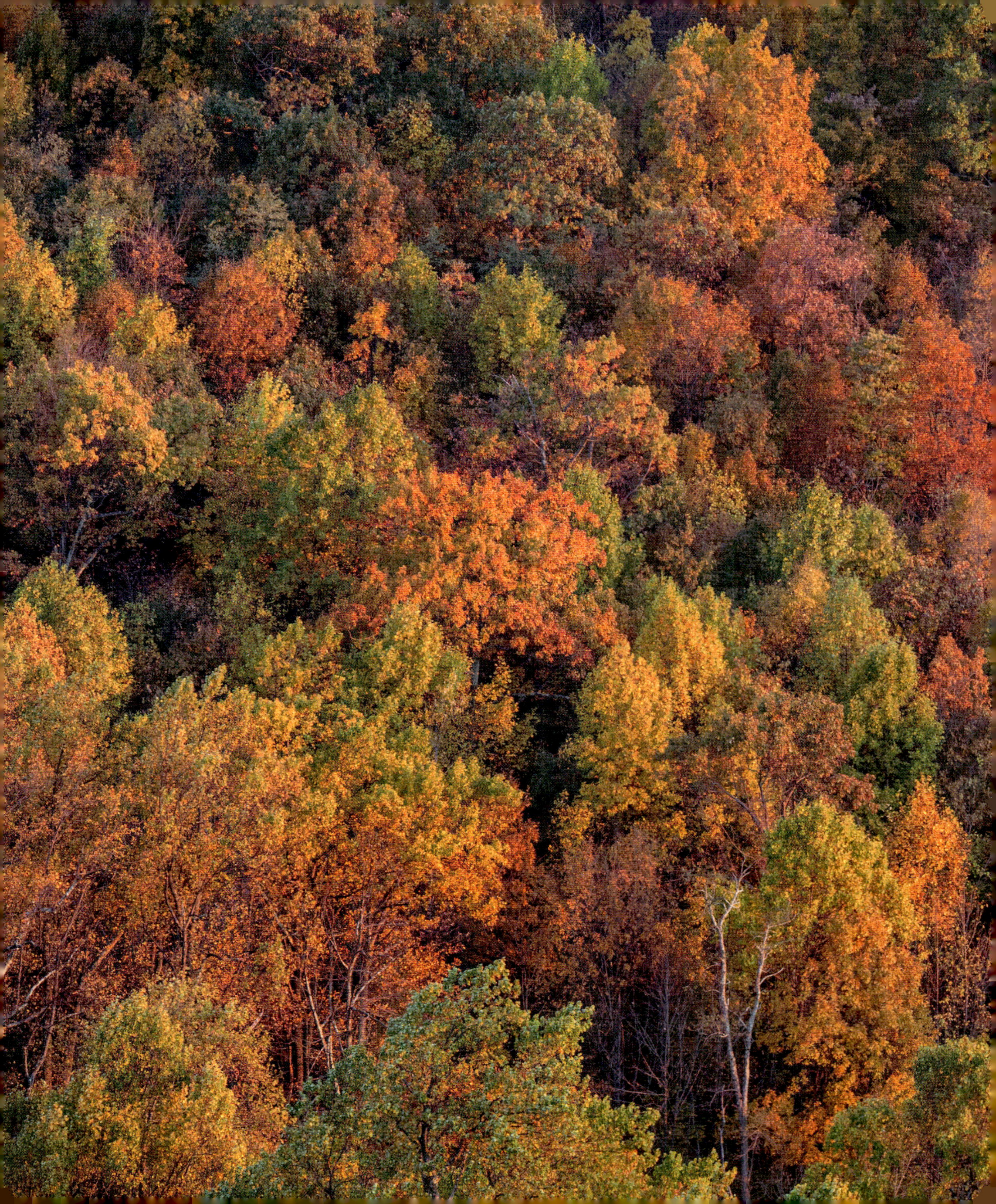

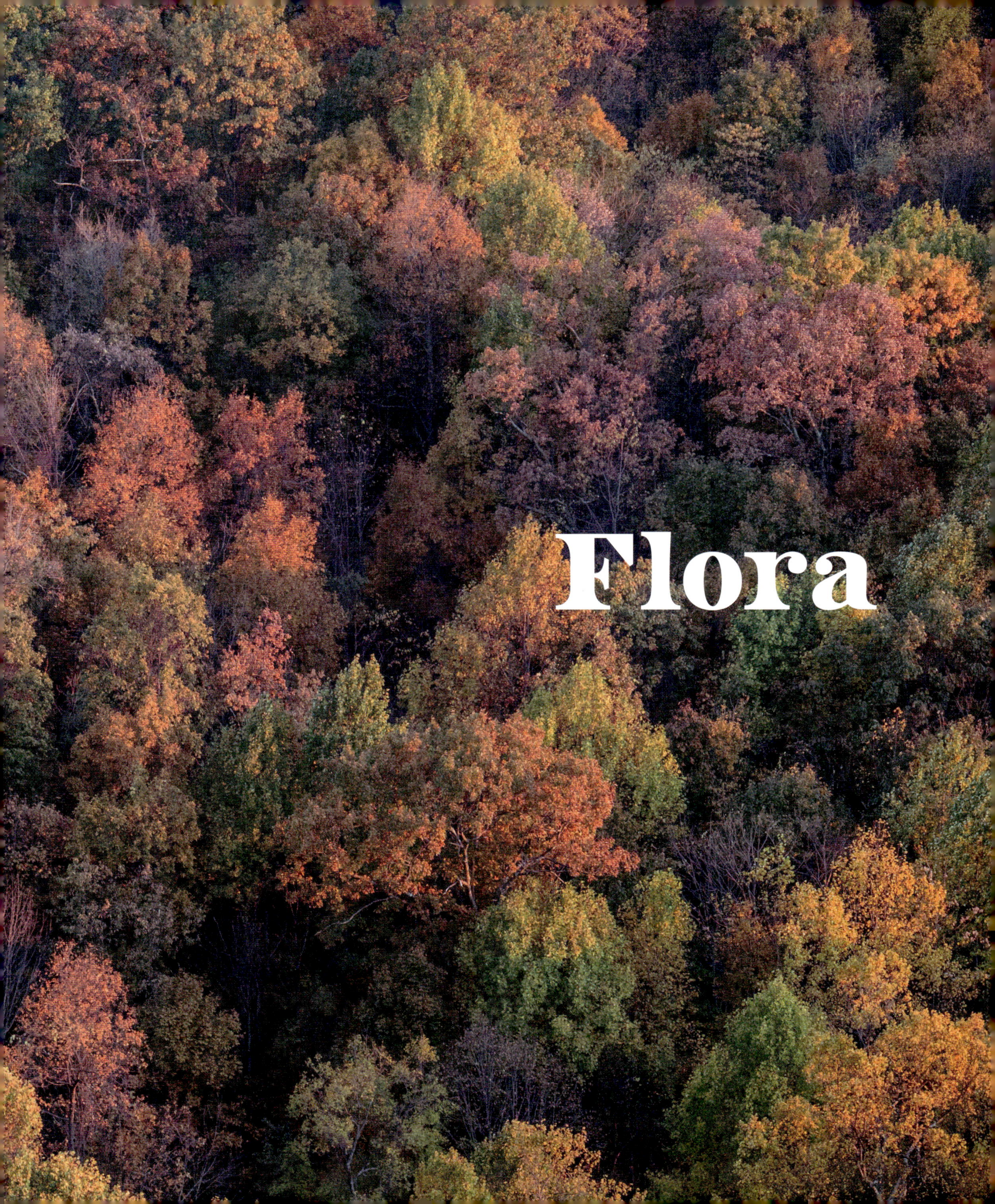

Flora

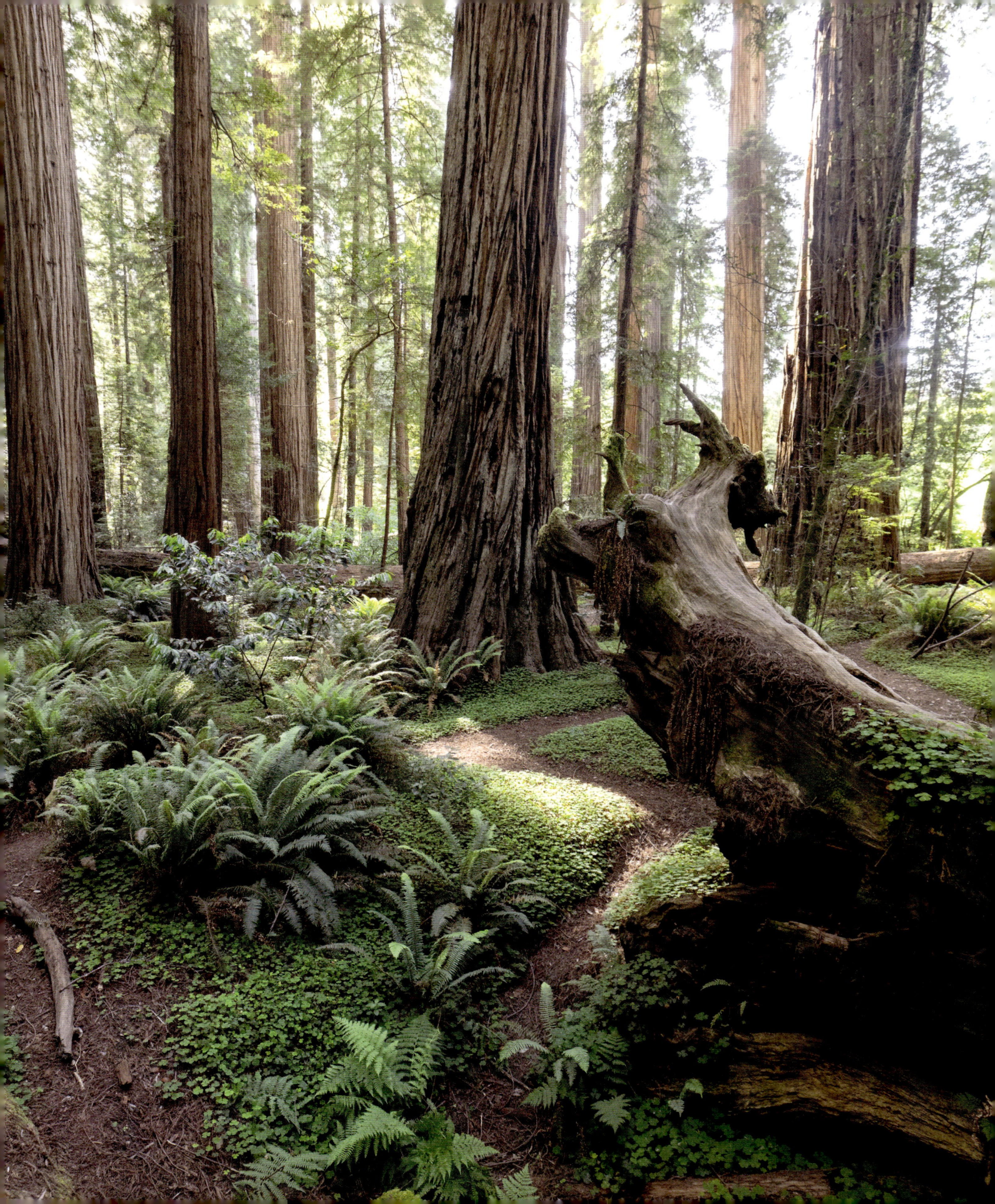

ROOTS OF LIFE

OUR PUBLIC LANDS PROTECT a rich tapestry of plant ecosystems, each uniquely adapted to its environment and contributing to the continent's remarkable biodiversity. These diverse ecosystems range from temperate forests and prairies to arid deserts and tundras, showcasing a wide array of plant life that plays crucial roles in their respective habitats.

Deciduous forests are predominantly found in the eastern United States in parks like Shenandoah and Great Smoky Mountains. This ecosystem is marked by trees that shed their leaves annually. The rich soils of these forests support a diverse understory of shrubs and herbaceous plants, including ferns, wildflowers, and grasses. The changing seasons create a dynamic environment where plants adapt to varying temperatures and light conditions. Deciduous forests are crucial for biodiversity, providing habitat and food for a wide range of wildlife, from insects and birds to mammals.

Also known as boreal forests or taiga, coniferous forests stretch across the northern regions of North America into Alaska. This ecosystem is dominated by coniferous trees such as spruce, fir, and pine, which are adapted to cold climates and poor soils. The dense canopy of coniferous forests offers shelter to many species, including moose, caribou, and various bird species. The forest floor is often covered with mosses and lichens, which thrive in the cooler, shaded environment. These forests play a significant role in carbon storage, helping to regulate global climate.

SHENANDOAH NATIONAL PARK (PREVIOUS)

REDWOODS NATIONAL AND STATE PARKS (OPPOSITE) We spent a few days camping at the Jedediah Smith Campground, exploring all the park had to offer. Wandering among the giant redwood groves is something that doesn't adequately translate to photos. The trees are massively tall, and no matter how hard I tried to photograph them, I found that you really need to see them in person to get a sense of their scale.

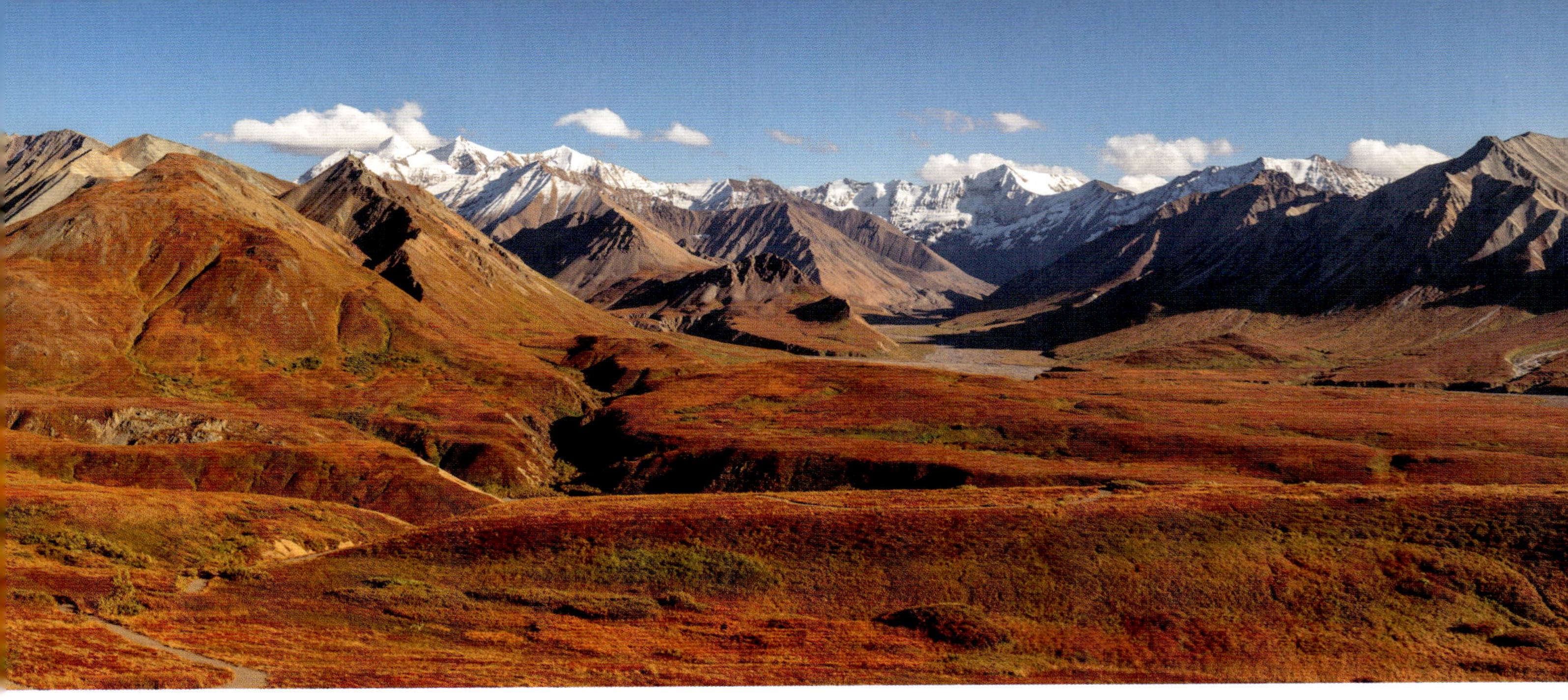

North American deserts, including the Sonoran, Mojave, and Chihuahuan Deserts, are characterized by arid conditions and sparse vegetation. Despite the harsh environment, these deserts host a unique array of plant life adapted to survive with minimal water.

Located in the southwestern United States and northwestern Mexico, the Sonoran Desert is known for its diverse plant life, including the iconic saguaro cactus, as well as ocotillo, creosote bush, and various species of agave and yucca. These plants have developed various adaptations to conserve water, such as waxy coatings, deep root systems, and water-storing tissues. The Sonoran Desert also features seasonal wildflower blooms, which create a dramatic display of color after rare rainfalls.

Extending into the southwestern United States and northern Mexico, the Chihuahuan Desert is known for its diverse array of cacti, yucca, and desert grasses. Plants like the lechuguilla and the ocotillo are well-adapted to the region's varying temperatures and precipitation patterns. The Chihuahuan Desert also experiences seasonal flowering events, with plants blooming in response to summer rains.

The tundra ecosystem is found in the far northern regions of North America, including parts of Alaska. This ecosystem is characterized by its cold temperatures, short growing seasons, and permafrost. The Arctic tundra, as found in Denali National Park and Preserve, is dominated by low-growing plants such as mosses, lichens, and dwarf shrubs. Vegetation is adapted to the cold, nutrient-poor soils and short growing seasons. Plants like Arctic willow and bearberry are common, and many species have developed mechanisms to survive freezing temperatures and strong winds. The tundra provides critical habitat for migratory birds, grizzly bears, and caribou.

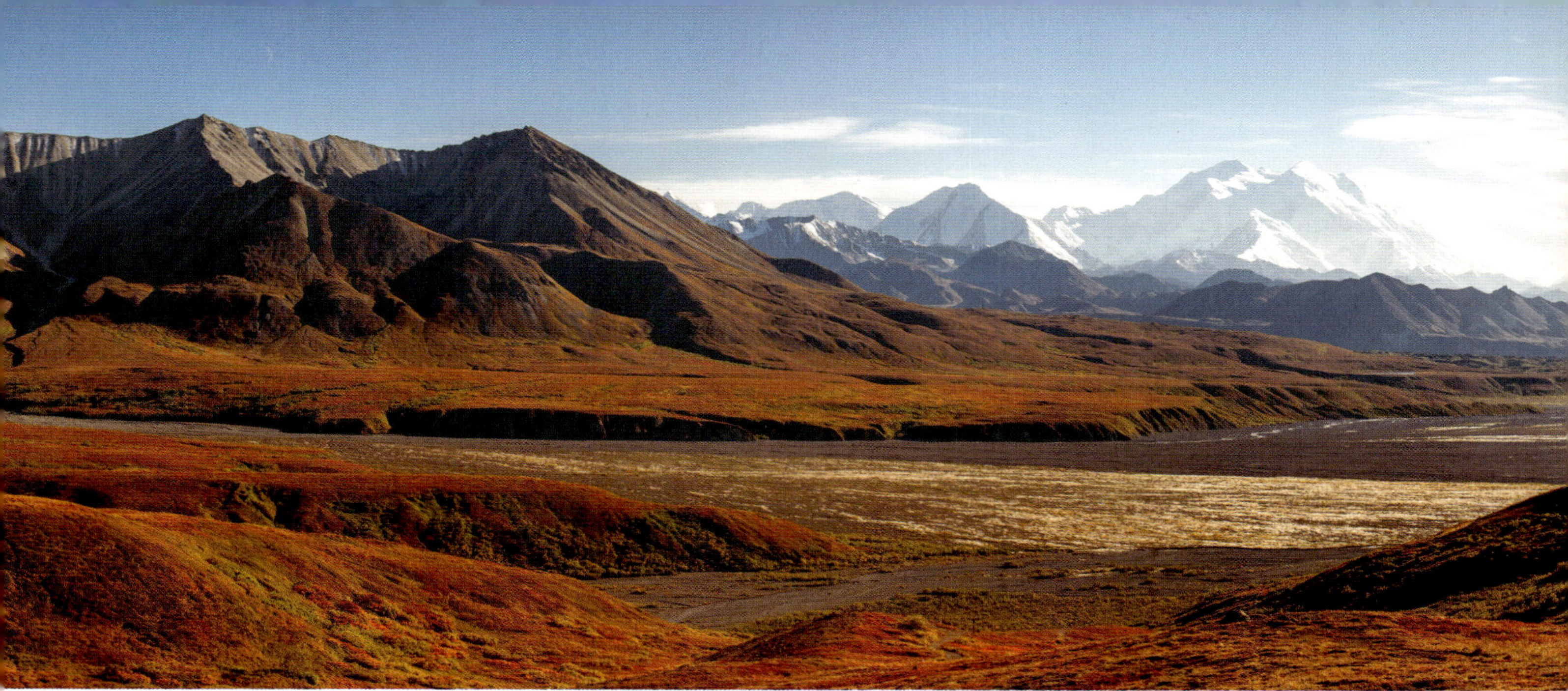

Alpine tundra is found at high elevations in mountainous regions, such as Rocky Mountain and Glacier National Parks. Similar to the arctic tundra, alpine tundra features low-growing vegetation adapted to cold temperatures and high winds. Plants such as alpine grasses, mosses, and dwarf shrubs are common. The alpine tundra supports a variety of specialized wildlife, including pika and ptarmigan.

Wetlands are characterized by their water-saturated soils and diverse plant communities. Swamps, found in areas like Everglades National Park, are dominated by water-tolerant trees such as cypress and mangroves. These wetlands play a crucial role in water filtration, flood control, and providing habitat for a variety of wildlife, including alligators and wading birds.

Hawaii's tropical rainforests are among the most lush and diverse ecosystems on the islands. Found on the windward sides of the islands where high rainfall occurs, these forests are characterized by dense vegetation, high humidity, and rich biodiversity. Native trees like the ʻōhiʻa lehua and Acacia koa are prominent, along with a variety of ferns, orchids, and shrubs.

Our public lands play a vital role in sustaining ecological balance, supporting biodiversity, and providing essential services. Protecting these varied ecosystems ensures the health and resilience of the continent's natural environments and the numerous benefits they provide to both wildlife and human populations.

DENALI NATIONAL PARK AND PRESERVE Fall in Denali is a special time of year. The alpine tundra turns from its various shades of vibrant green to colorful reds, yellows, and oranges. It only lasts a short while, and winter usually isn't too far behind.

During my first summer in Denali, as in every new place I've lived, I set out to photograph and identify as many wildflowers as I could find. I documented a total of 115 species, including one I was unable to identify. When I decided to stay through the winter and return the following year, I set myself a new challenge: to photograph 120 species the next summer. It felt like an achievable goal, given that I could build on my phenologic portfolio from the previous year. I also aimed to solve the mystery of the unidentified species that had stumped both me and the park's botanist.

Using my photos from the previous year as a road map, I returned to specific locations at specific times to re-photograph familiar species. I climbed mountains, trudged through swamps, and hiked in forests, seeking different types of soil, varying elevations, and different sun exposures. As expected, the species from last summer were all there. Additionally, I researched new species to understand when and where I might find them.

Later that summer, I reached out to the park's botanist to share details about my mystery species. A week later, I received an email confirming its identification as Dane's Dwarf Gentian (*Gentianella tenella*). Interestingly, the location where I found it was outside its known flowering range, making it new to that area of the park.

By the end of the season, after the late bloomers had finished, I tallied my total and had far surpassed my goal, identifying 185 species. To top it all off, the regional Alaska botanist heard about my project and offered to collaborate on an idea I had for a wildflower poster. After some back-and-forth, I designed and produced the "Wildflowers of Denali" poster. A framed copy still hangs on my office wall, a reminder of that summer and of the beauty in all things, both big and small.

DENALI NATIONAL PARK AND PRESERVE

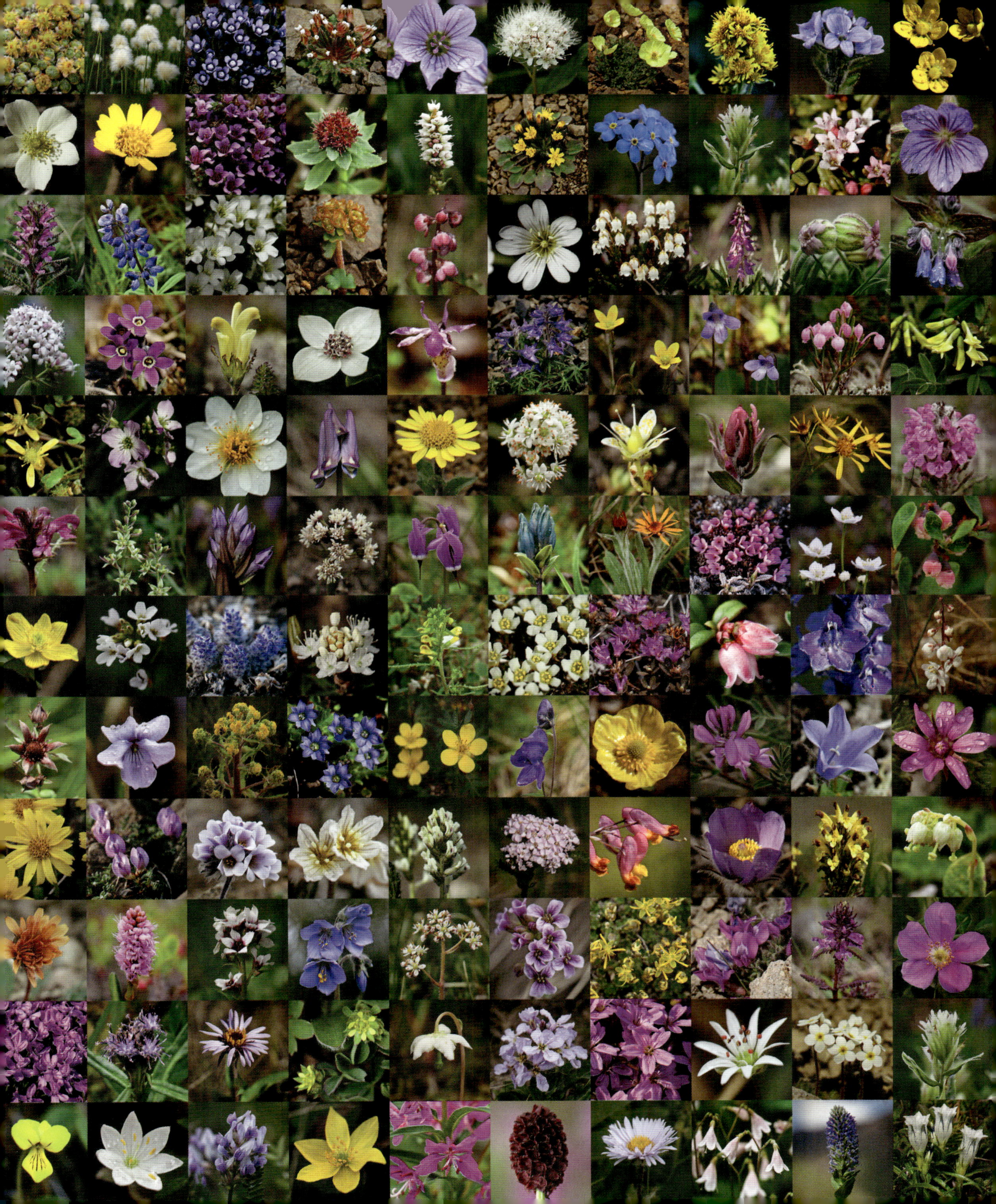

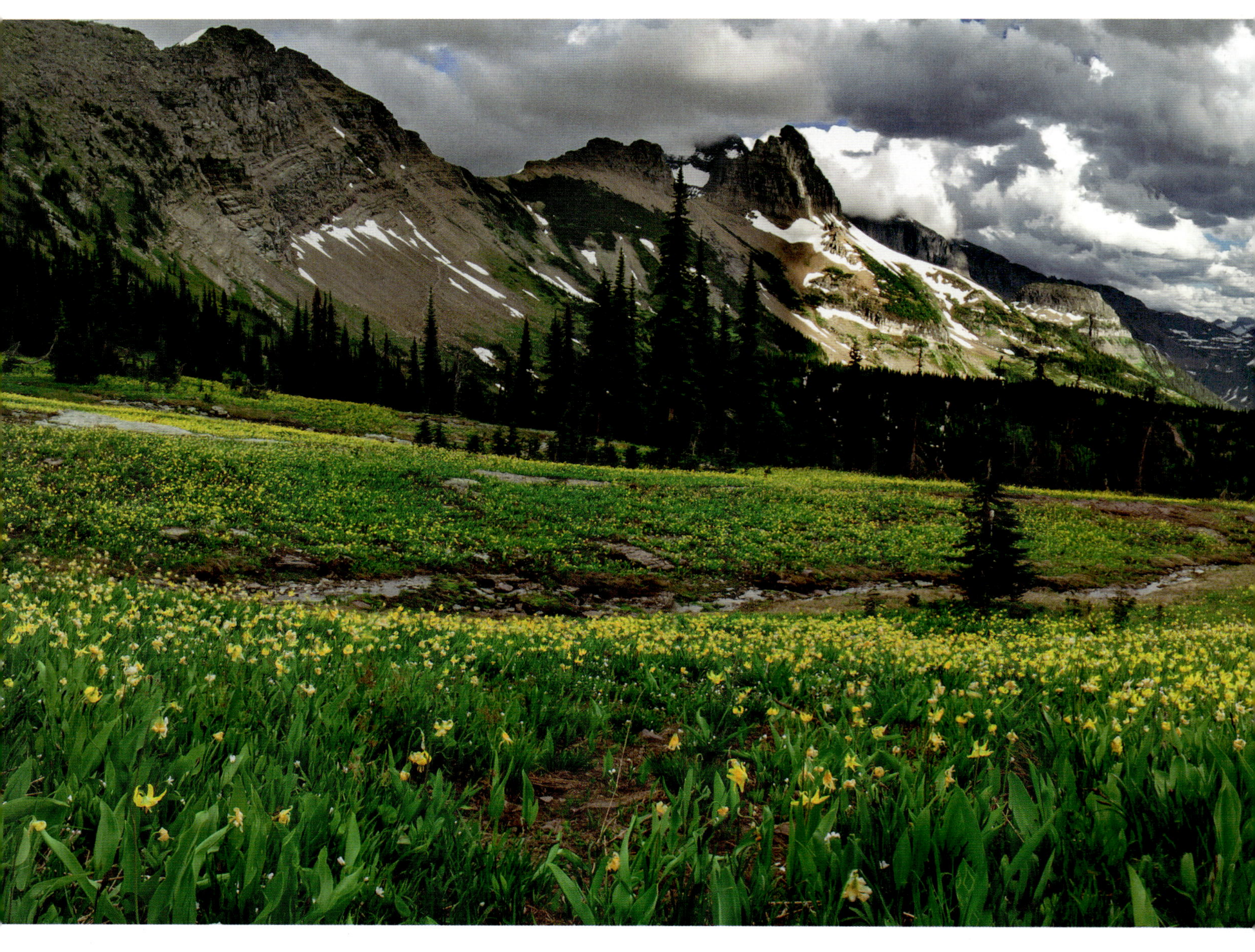

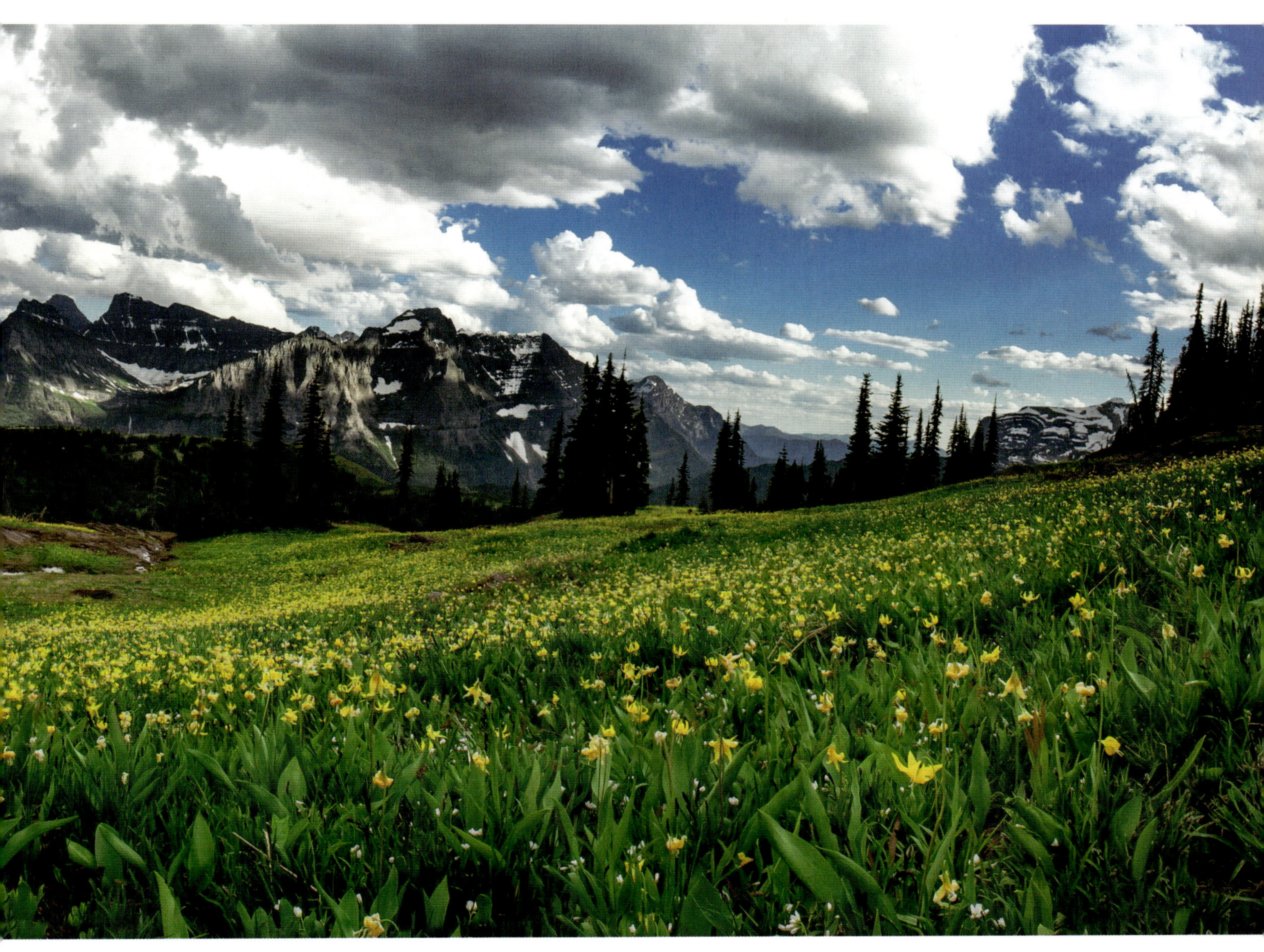

GLACIER NATIONAL PARK It was on my first hike along the Highline Trail that I fell in love with wildflowers. I had never seen an entire field of them before, and this meadow—bursting with vibrant glacier lilies—was absolutely mesmerizing.

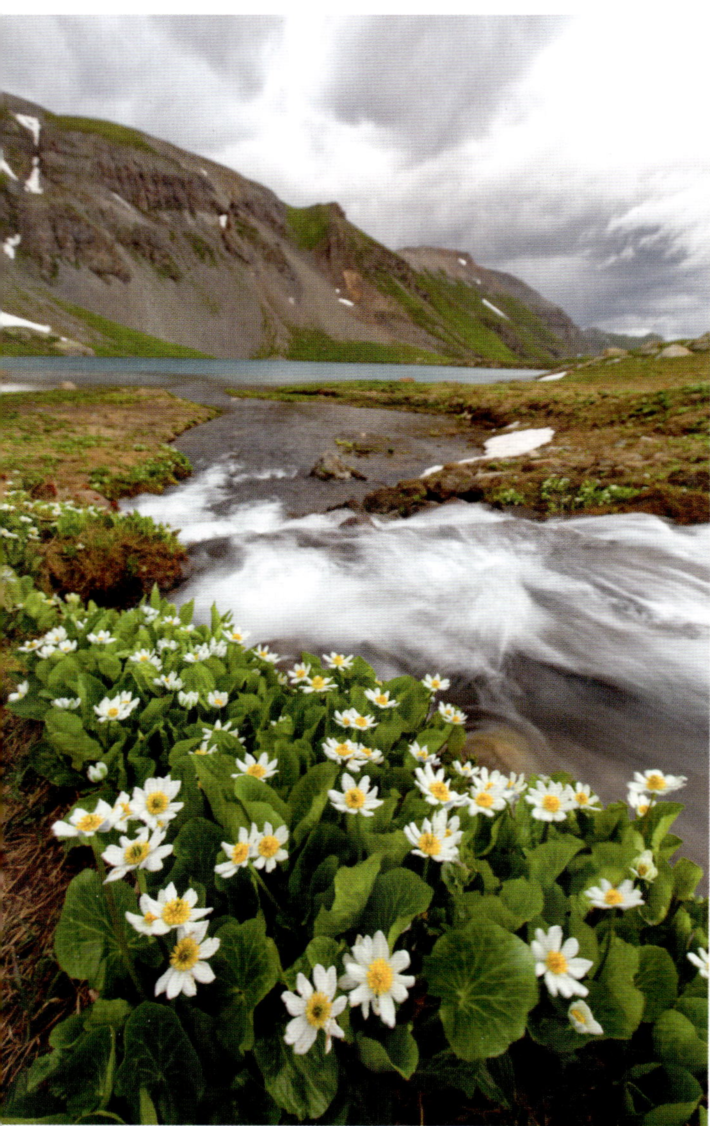

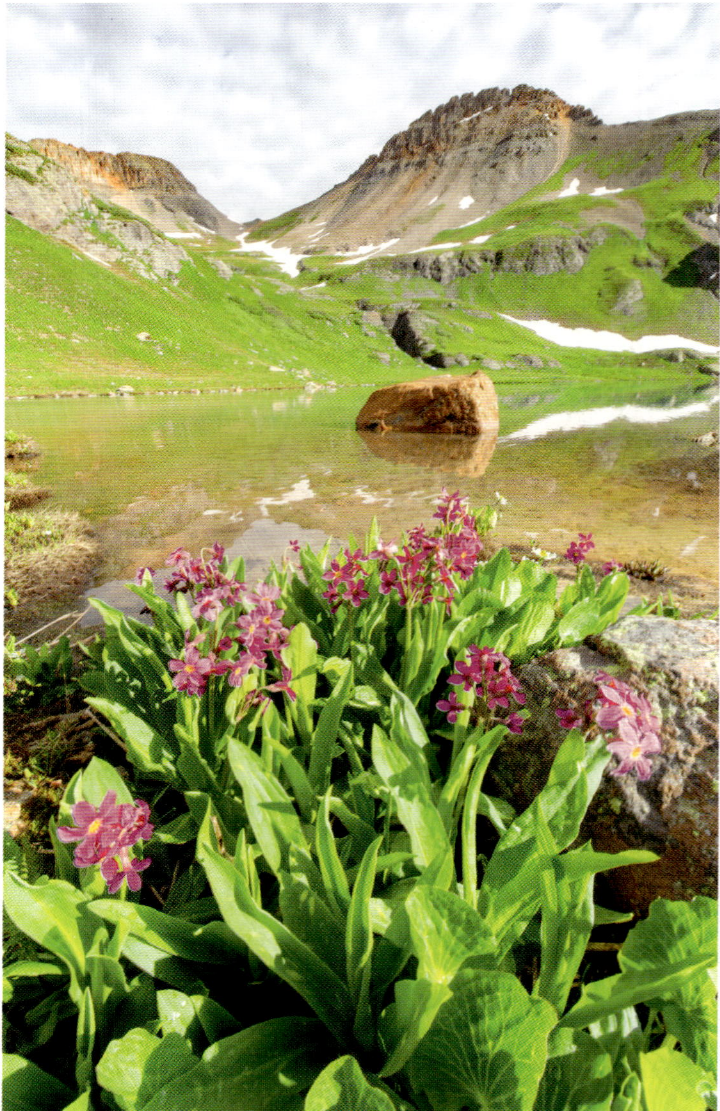

SAN JUAN NATIONAL FOREST While in Durango, Colorado, for our friends' wedding, we planned a backcountry trip to nearby Ice and Island Lakes. Despite it being August, the high elevation meant the wildflowers were just beginning to bloom. As a surprise, two other friends day-hiked in—each carrying a backpack full of beer. We spent the afternoon swimming and unwinding by the lake until an afternoon thunderstorm rolled in, sending us into our tents, where we listened to the thunder crash and echo through the mountains.

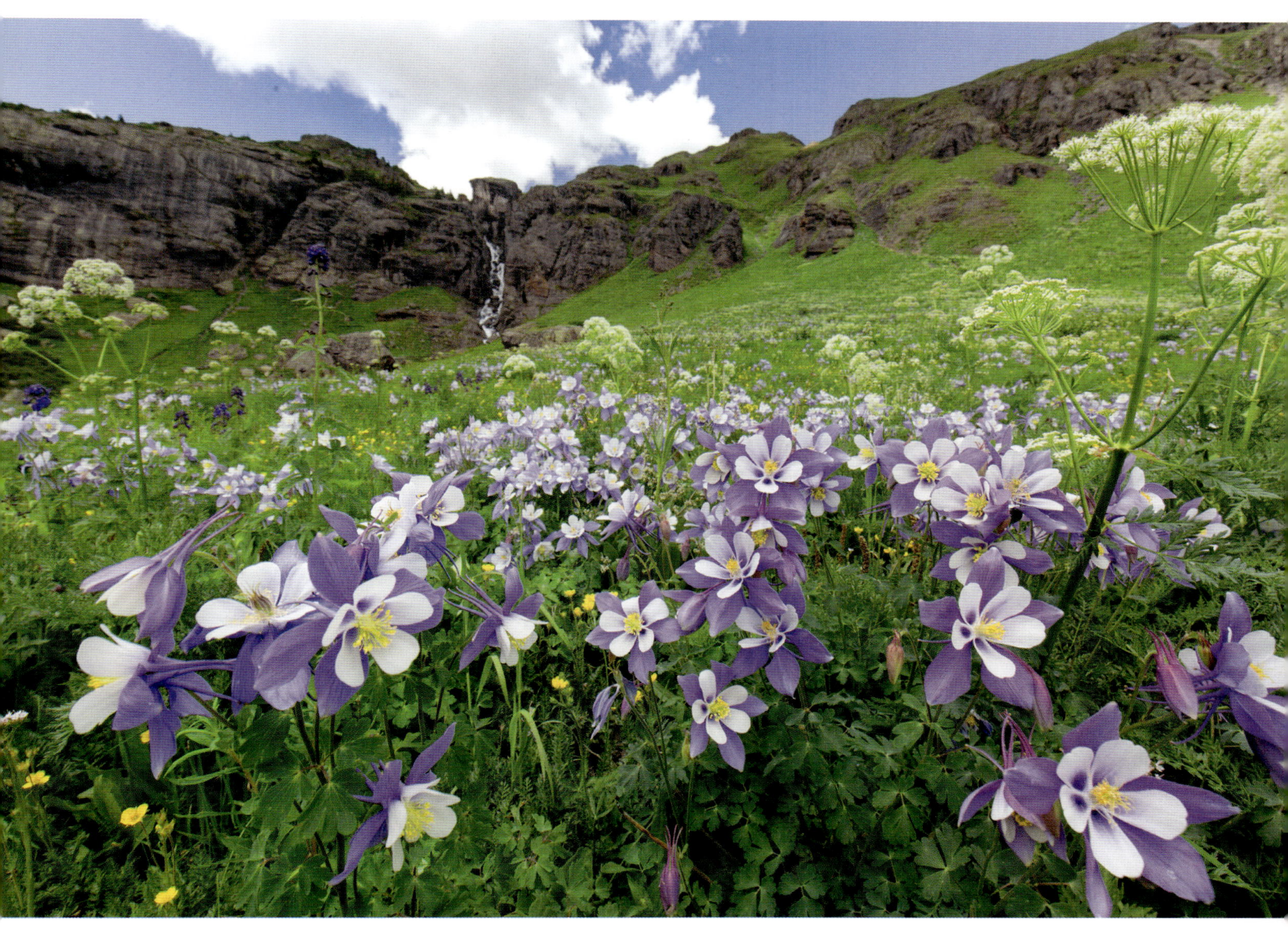

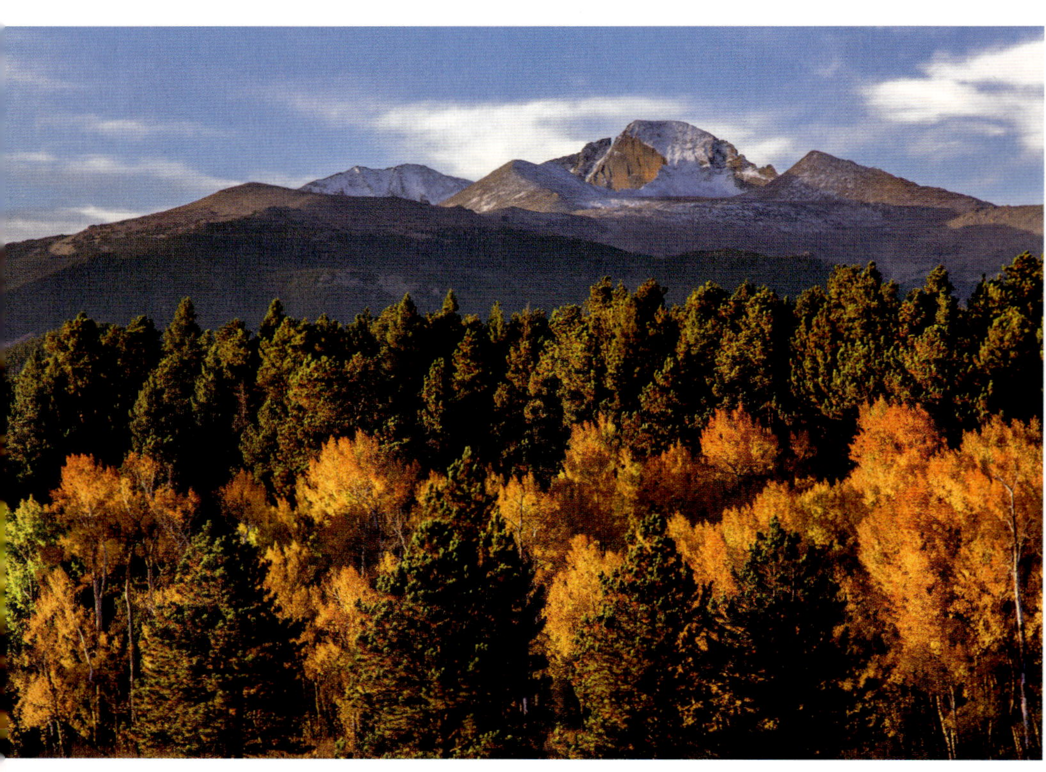

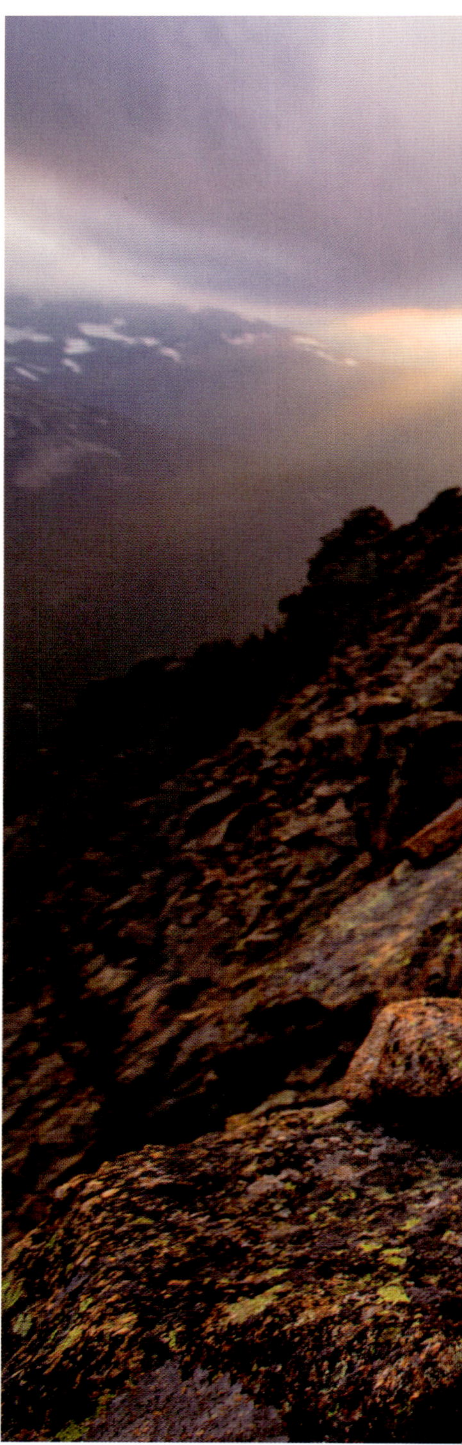

ROCKY MOUNTAIN NATIONAL PARK Whether you're wandering through vibrant alpine meadows in the summer or watching golden aspens set the landscape ablaze in the fall, this park showcases an incredible display of biodiversity.

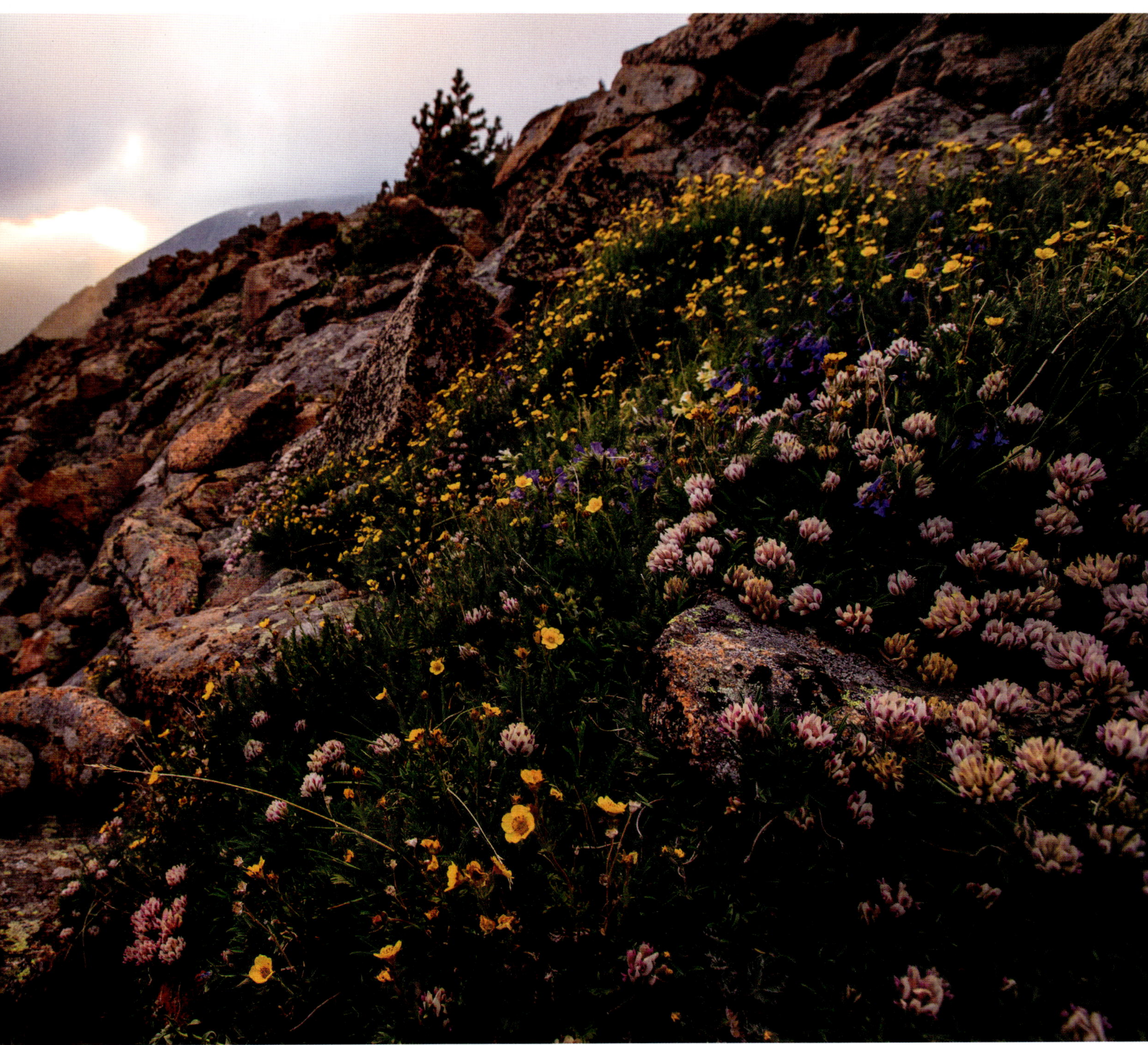

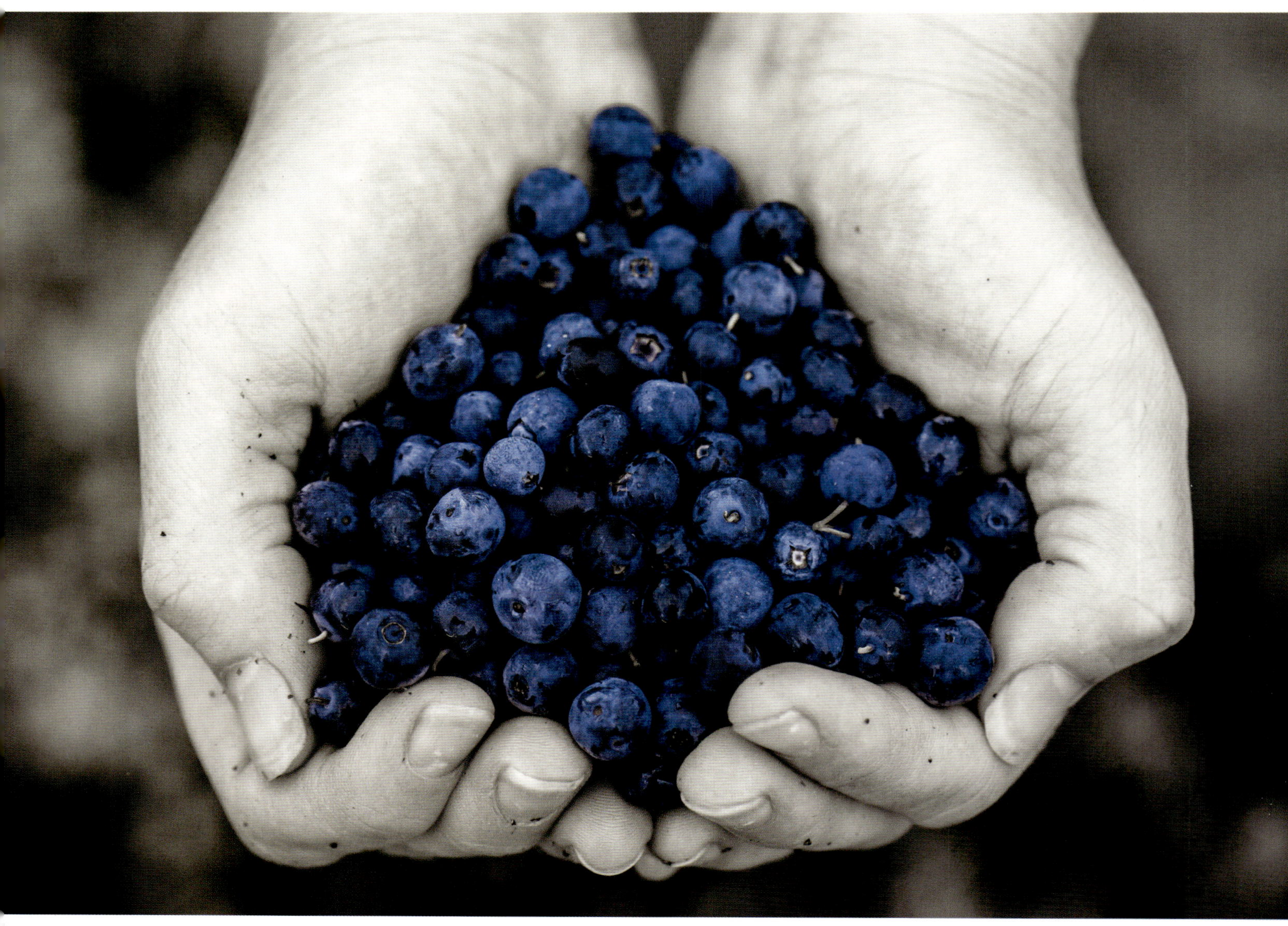

DENALI NATIONAL PARK AND PRESERVE

(ABOVE) Once wildflower season fades, berry season takes over. While many berries in the park are edible, none compare to the sweet, juicy blueberries. With daylight lingering late into the evening, there's plenty of time to gather a few pints after work—just enough to make your weekend waffles even better.

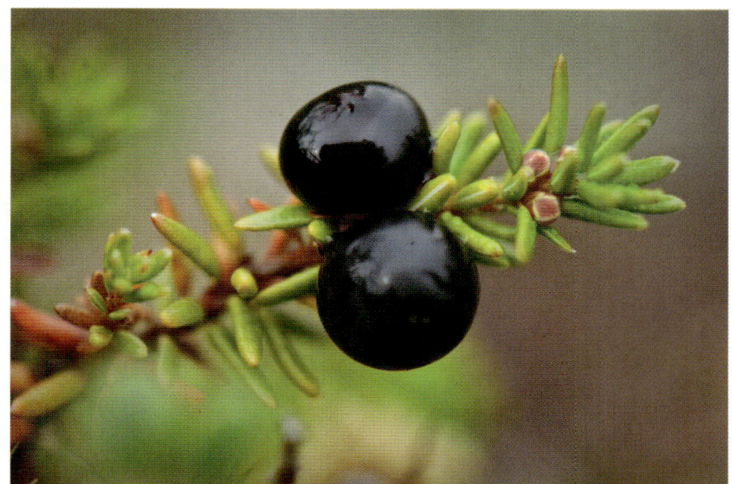

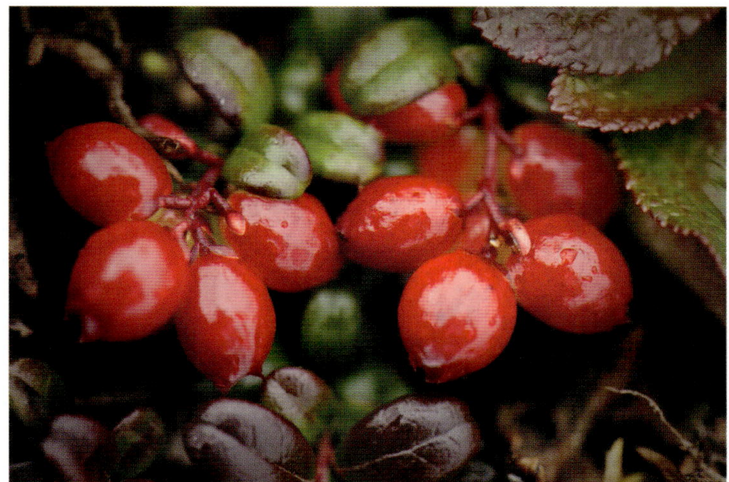

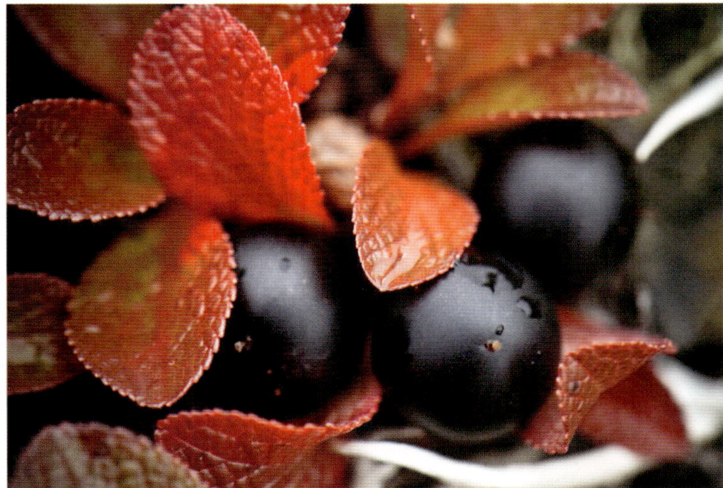

(TOP) Crowberries; (CENTER) Cranberries; (BOTTOM) Bearberries.

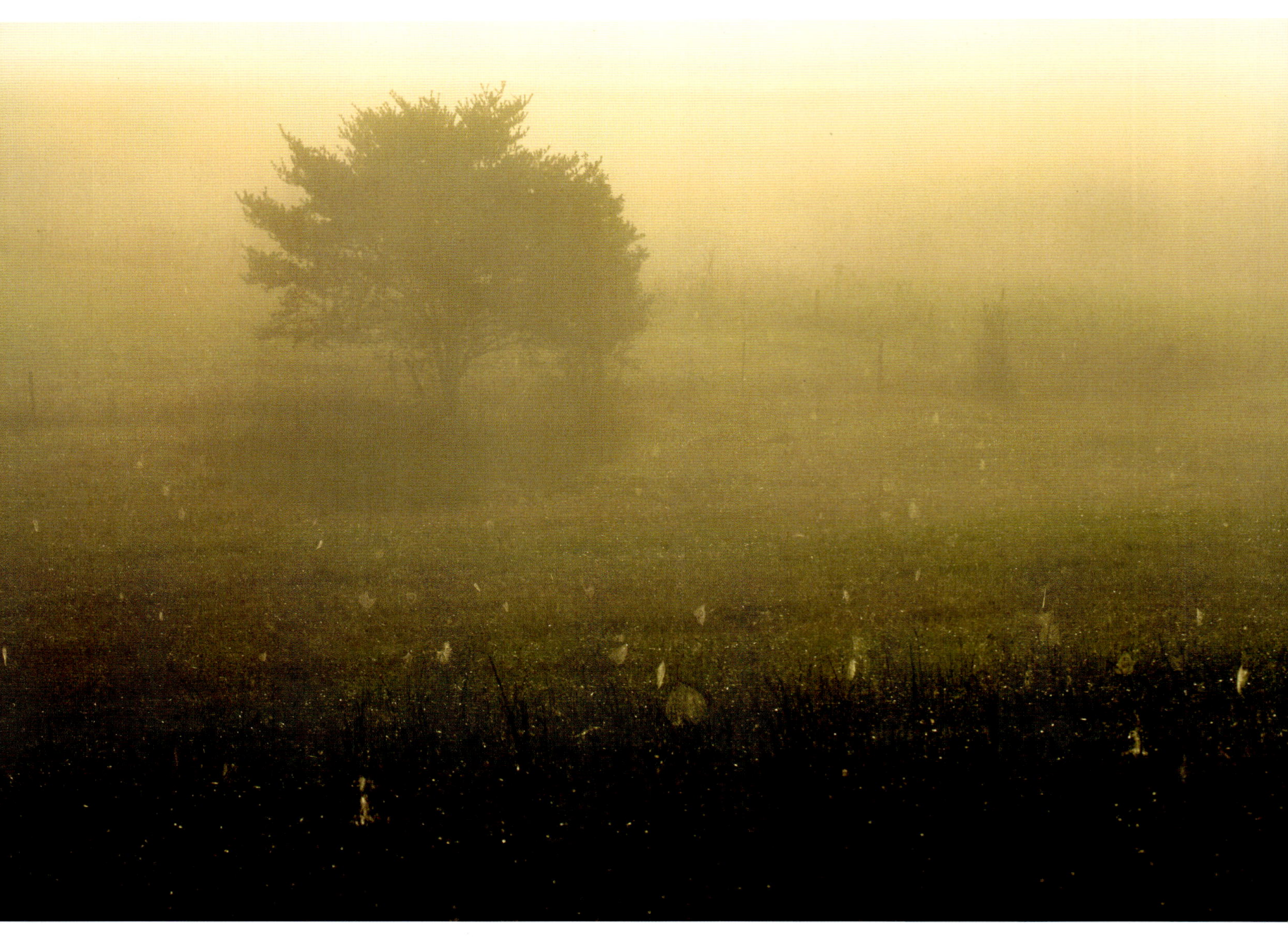

GREAT SMOKY MOUNTAINS NATIONAL PARK

(ABOVE) We woke up early to catch the sunrise in Cades Cove. As the morning fog slowly burned off, we could see the dewy spider webs glistening in the meadow surrounding a lone tree.

(OPPOSITE) Later that same morning we explored the historic Cable Mill and the fall color. Before we left for the day we watched a living history presentation at the blacksmith's, where I learned to make nails.

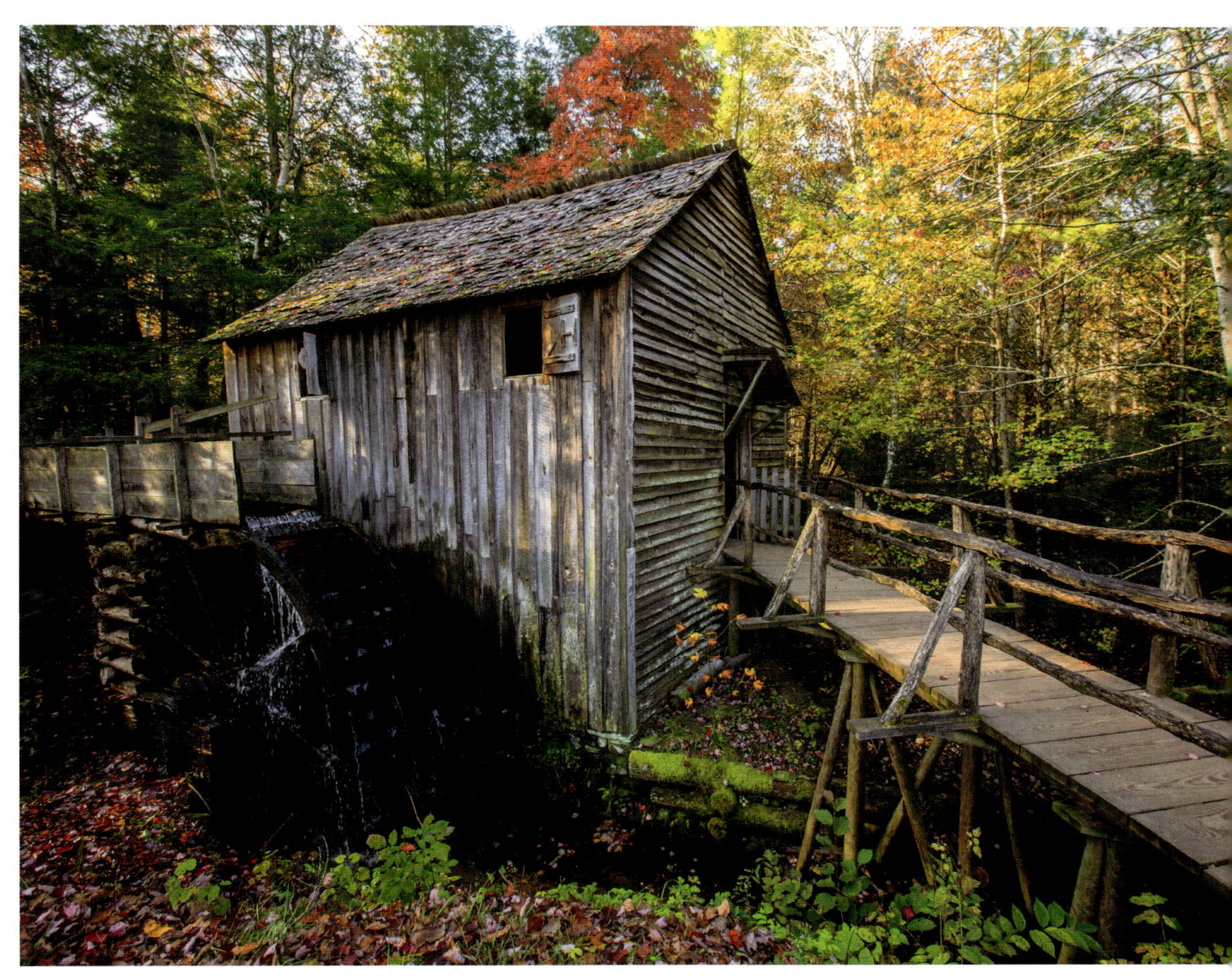

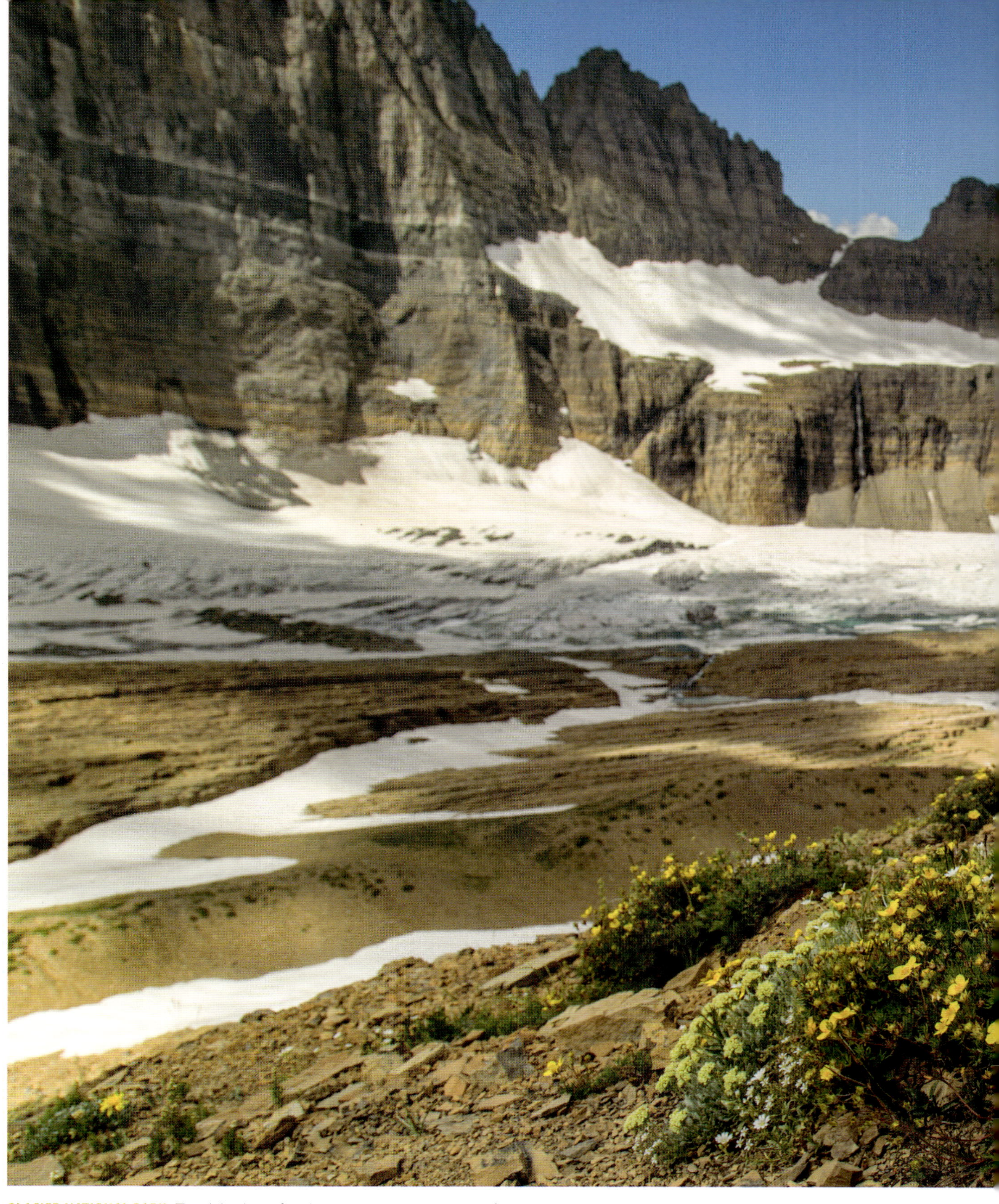

GLACIER NATIONAL PARK The alpine is my favorite ecosystem, a place where life thrives against all odds. I'm always amazed by the resilience of nature—how plants manage to take root in the most unexpected places, even on exposed, windswept mountainsides.

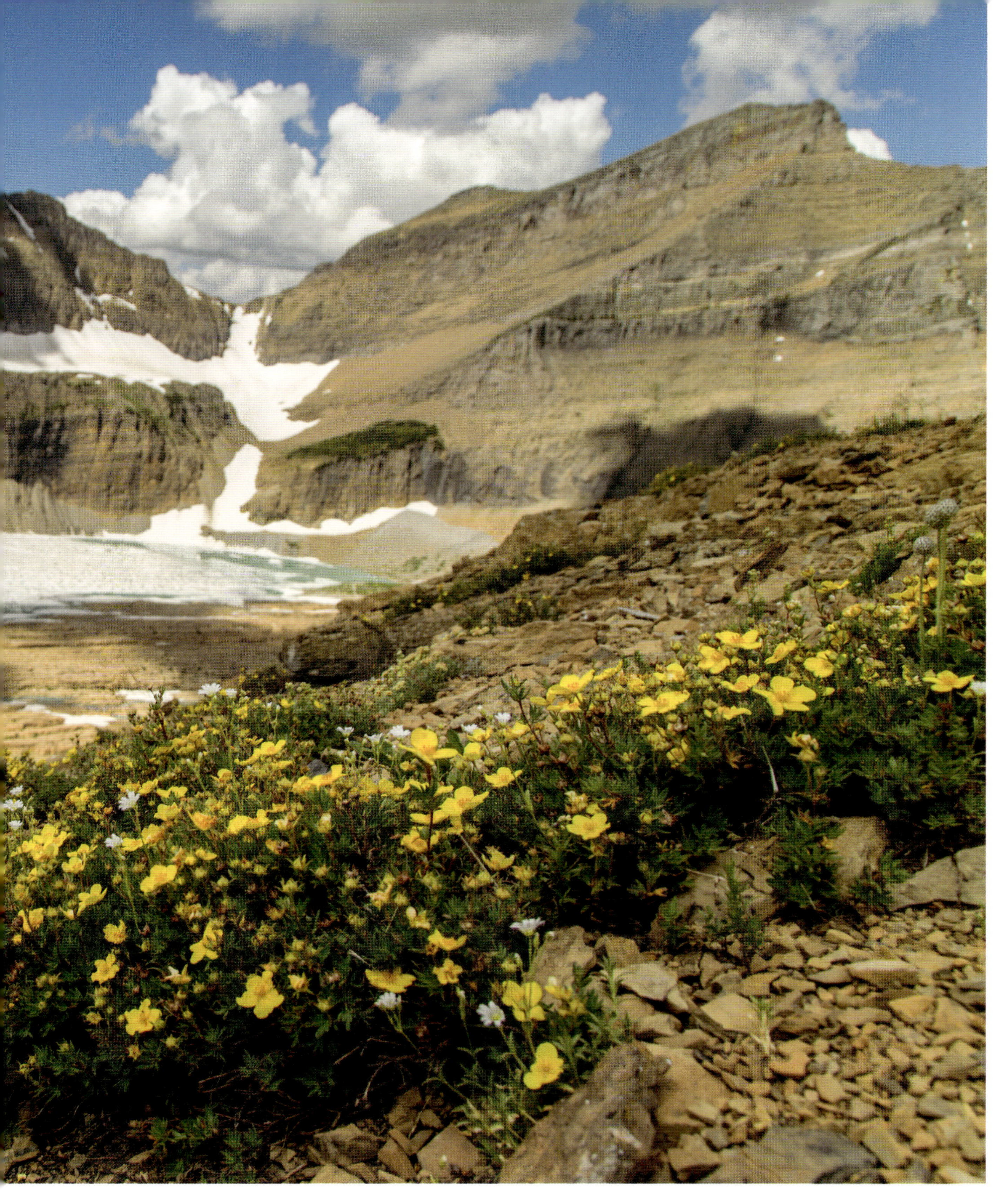

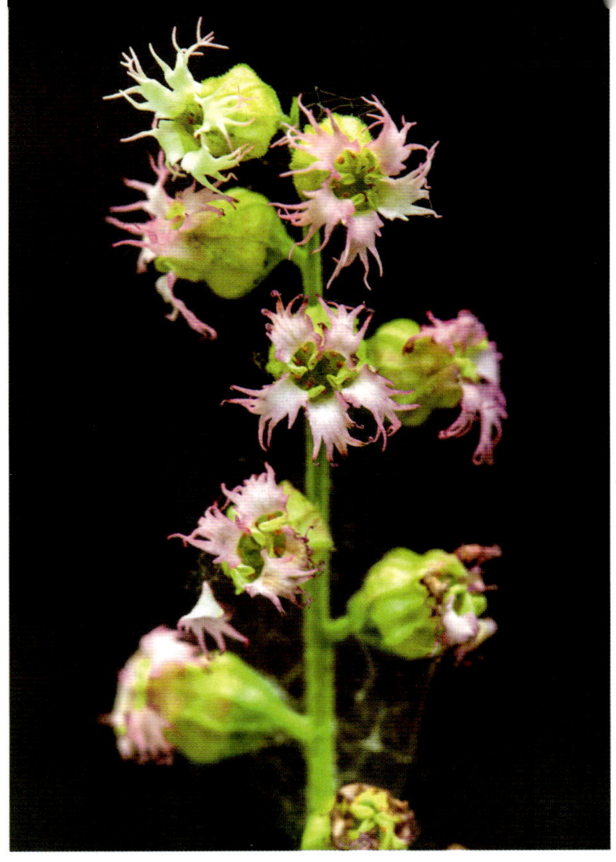

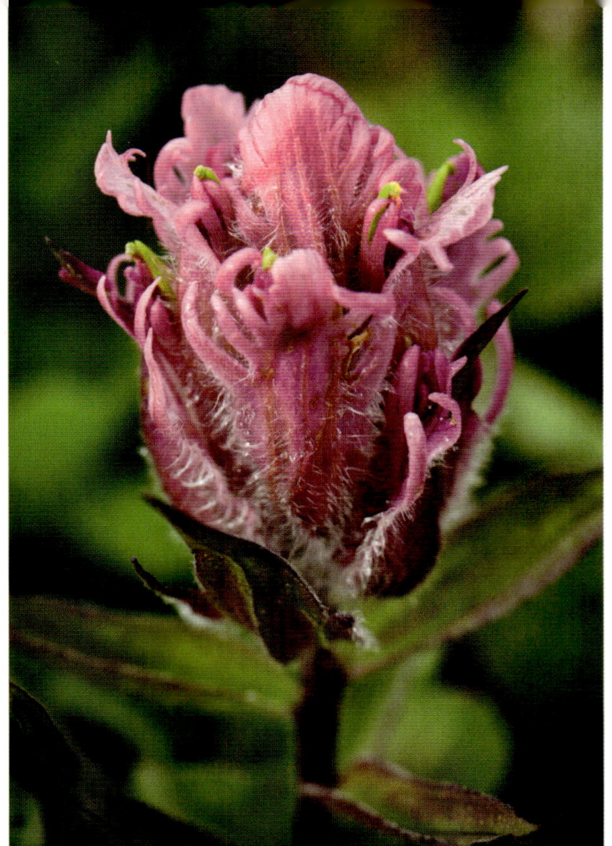

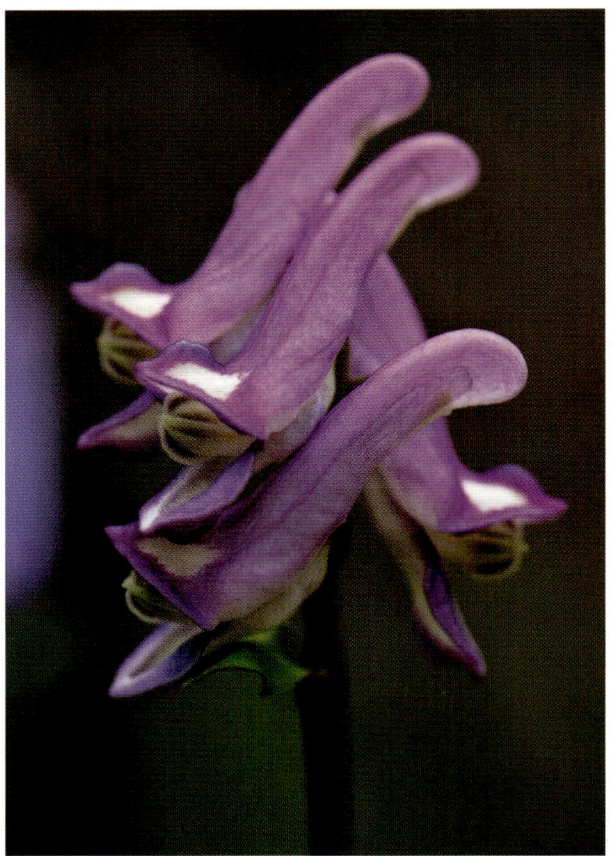

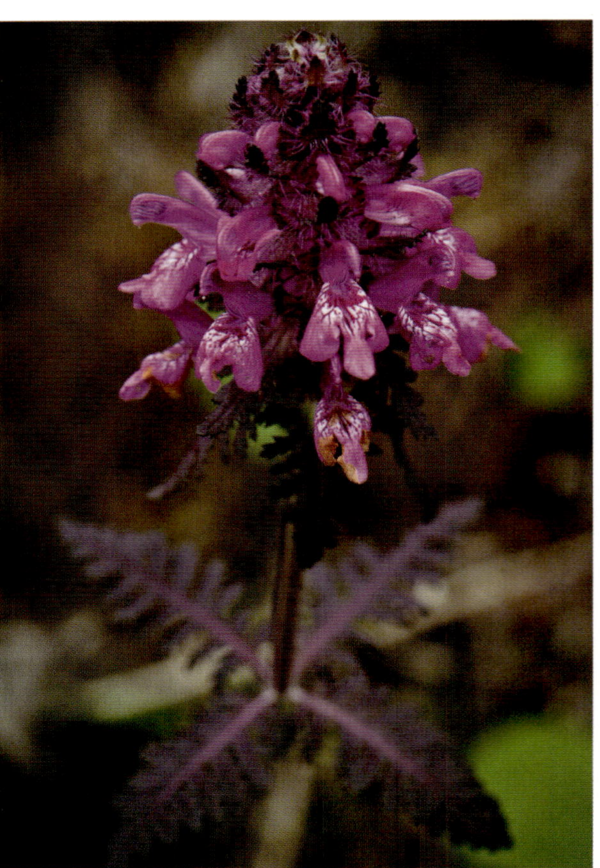

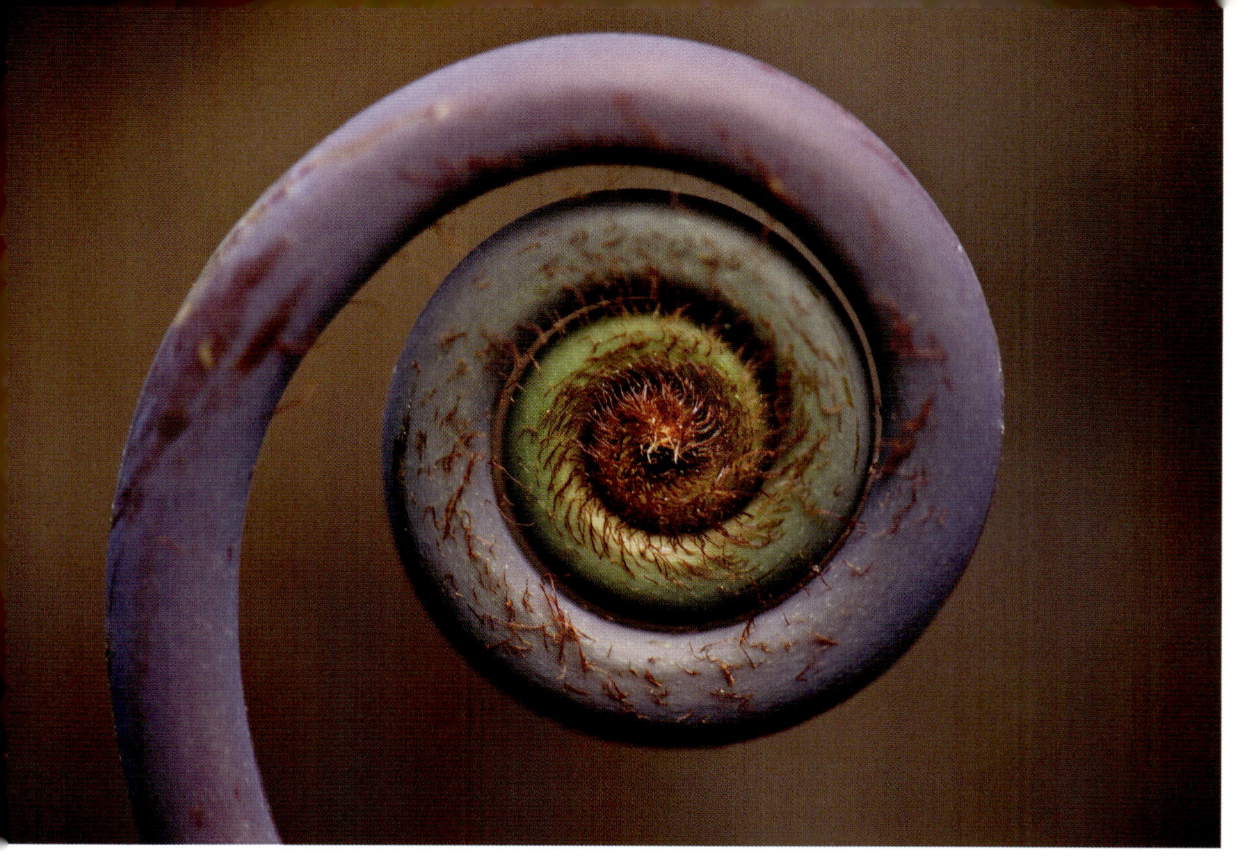

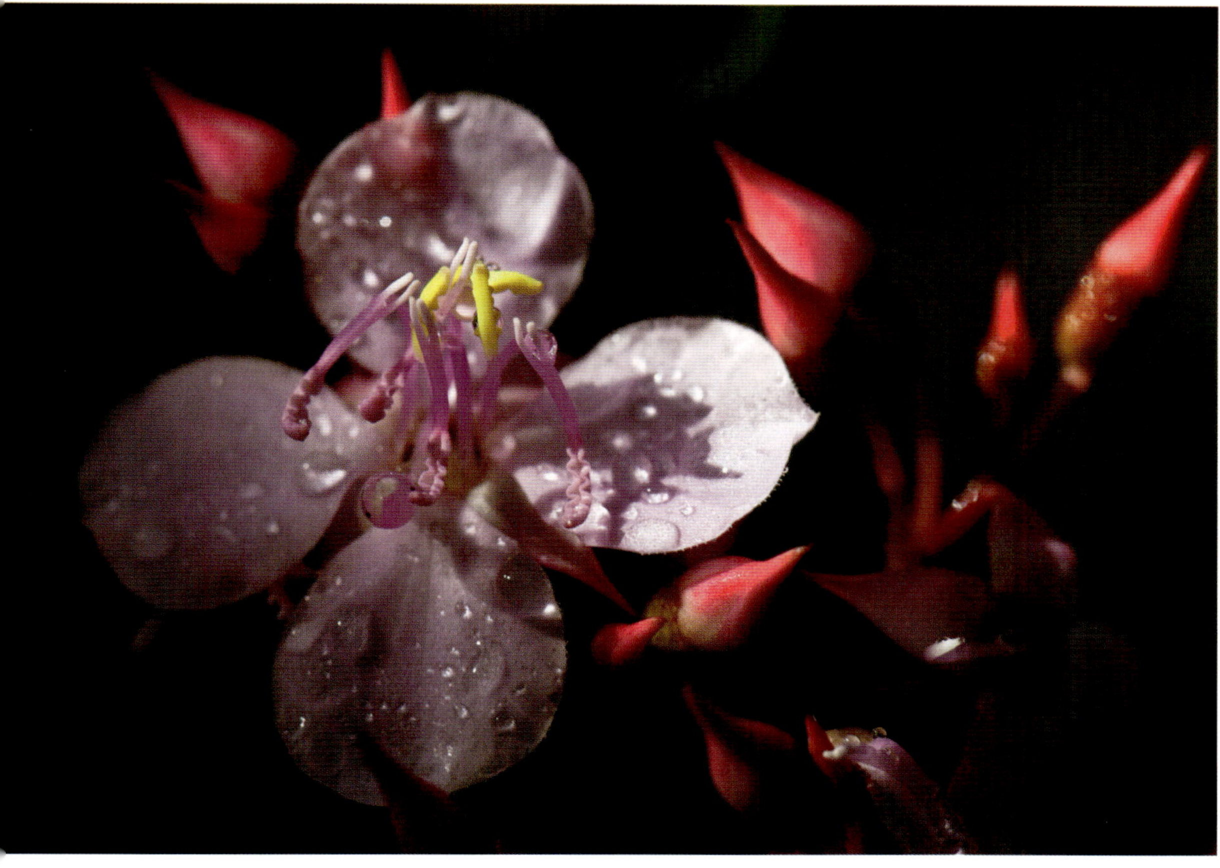

These are a few of my favorites from Alaska and Hawai'i.

DENALI NATIONAL PARK AND PRESERVE

(OPPOSITE, TOP LEFT)
Fringe cups

(OPPOSITE, TOP RIGHT)
Elegant paintbrush

(OPPOSITE, BOTTOM LEFT)
Few-flowered corydalis

(OPPOSITE, BOTTOM RIGHT)
Whorled-leaf lousewort

KOKE'E STATE PARK

(TOP)
Fern fiddlehead

(BOTTOM)
Native begonia

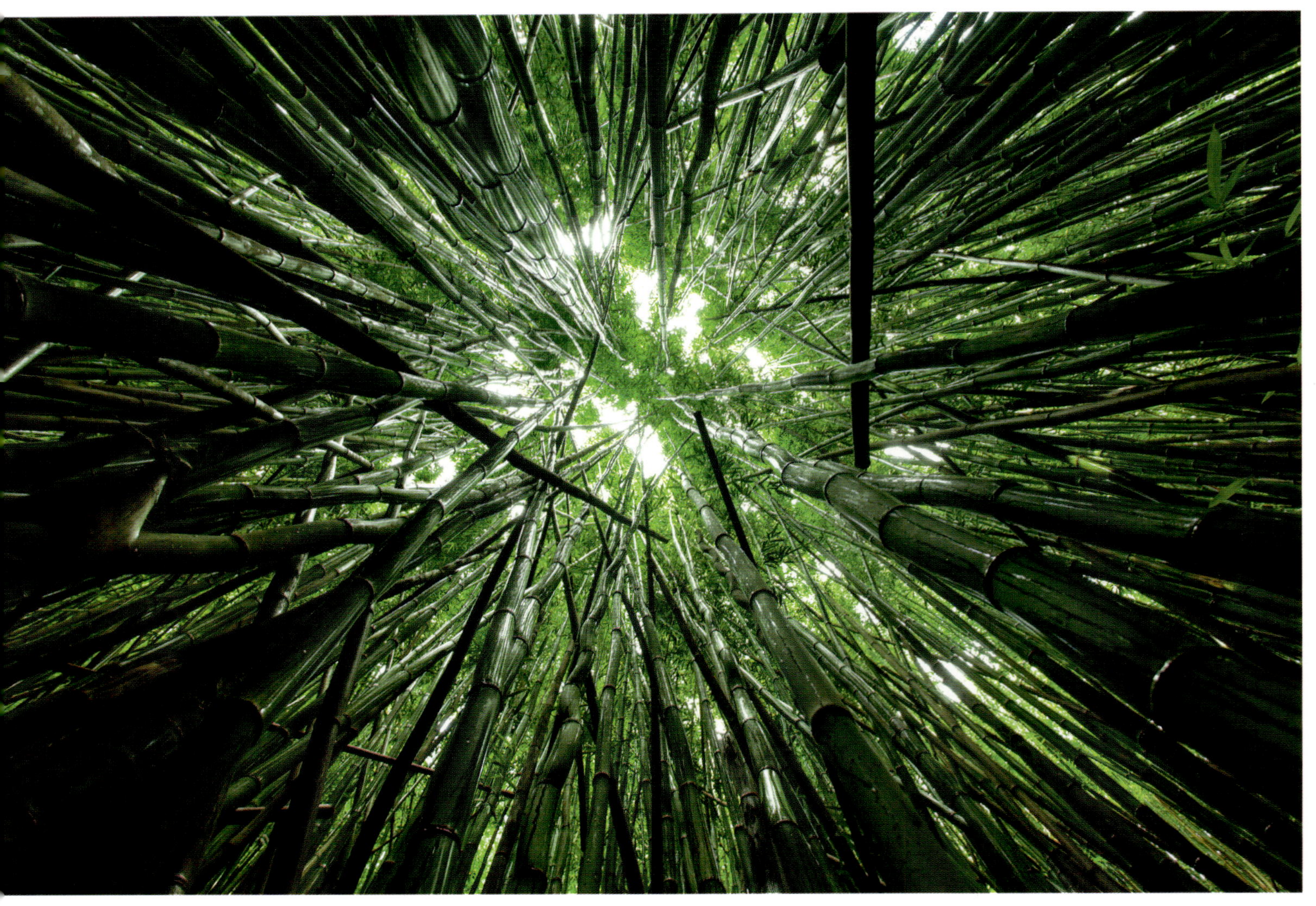

HALEAKALĀ NATIONAL PARK

One of the fun things about photographing forests, whether bamboo or aspen, is that they challenge you to look at things from a different perspective.

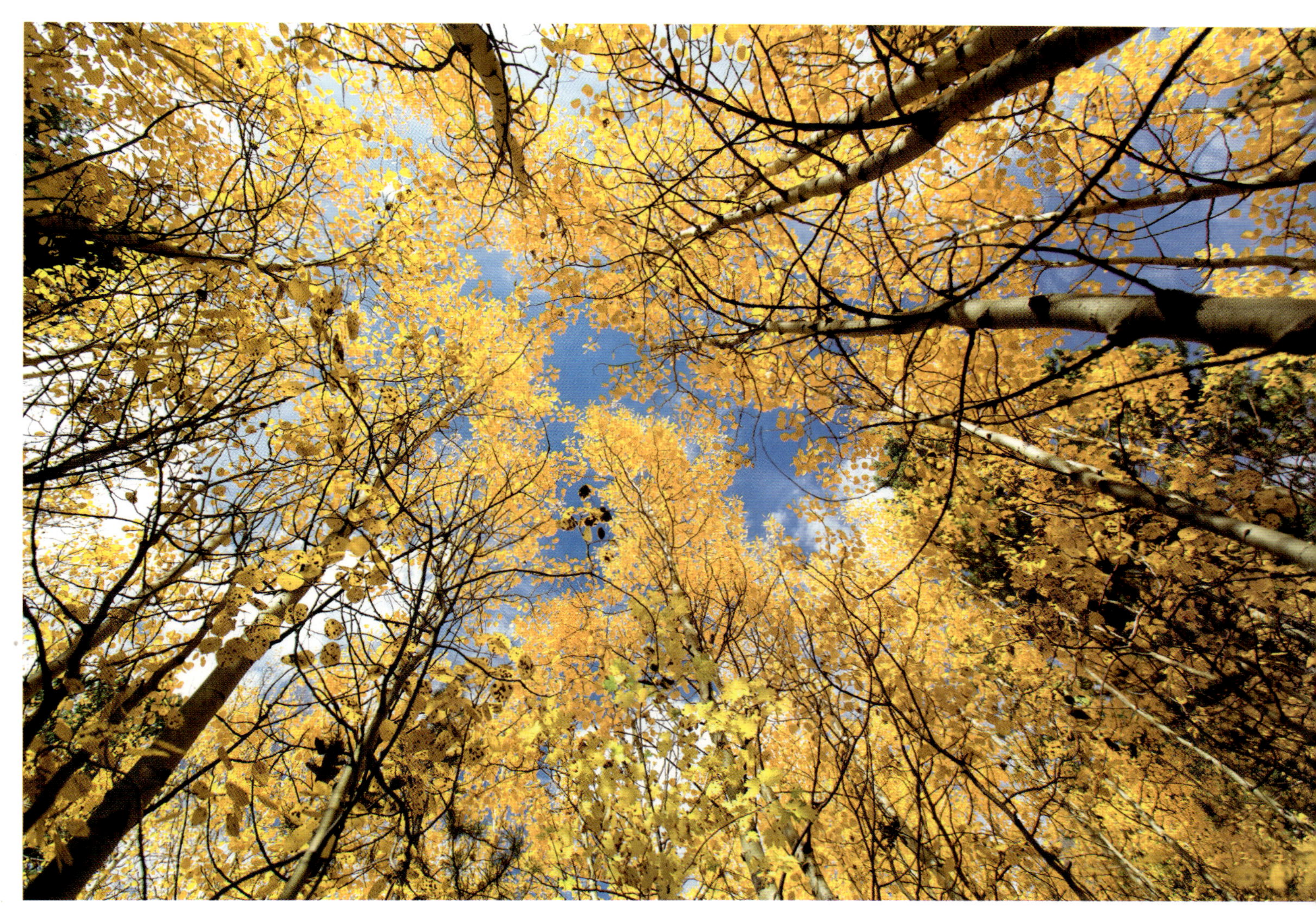

ROCKY MOUNTAIN NATIONAL PARK

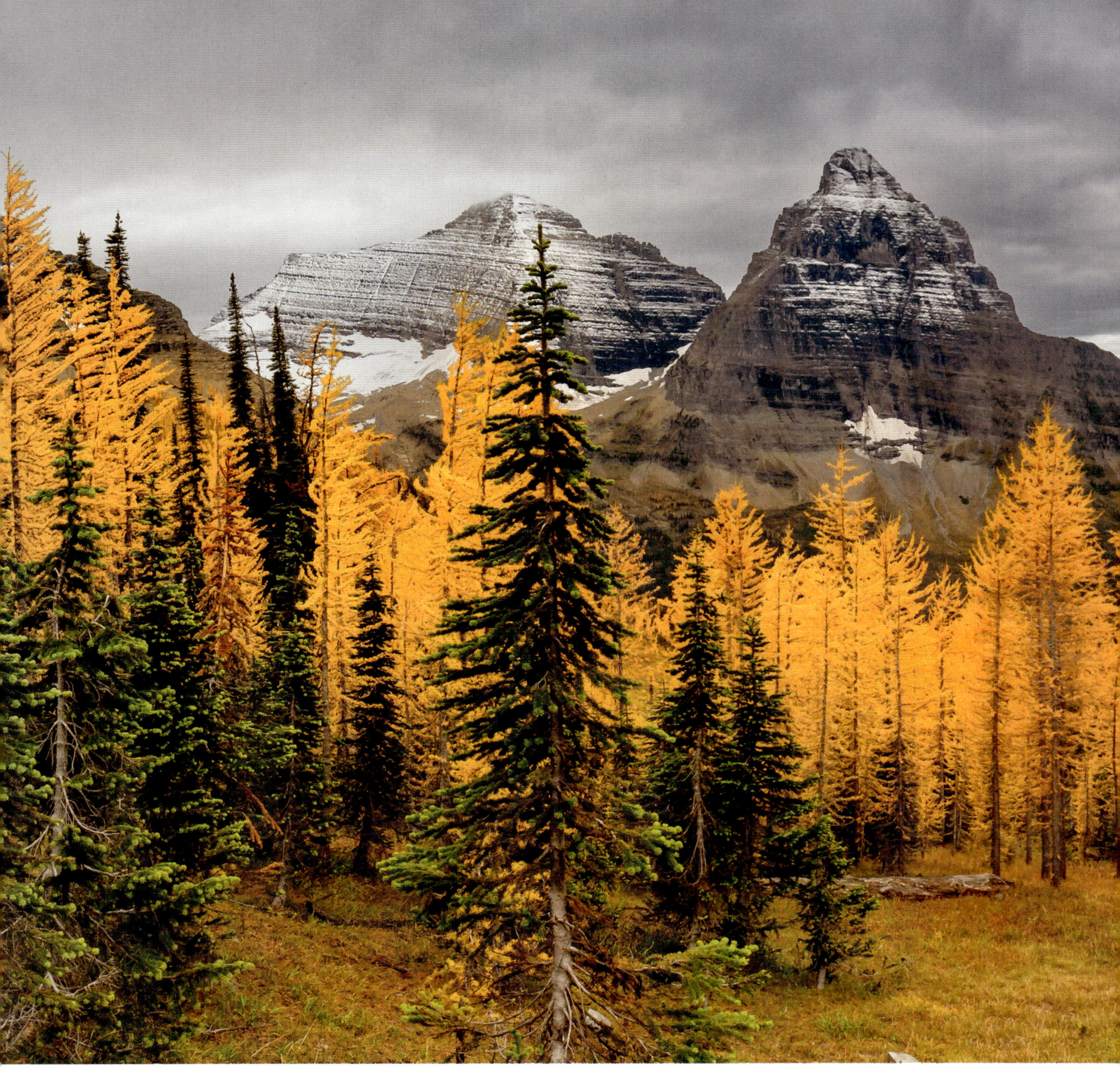

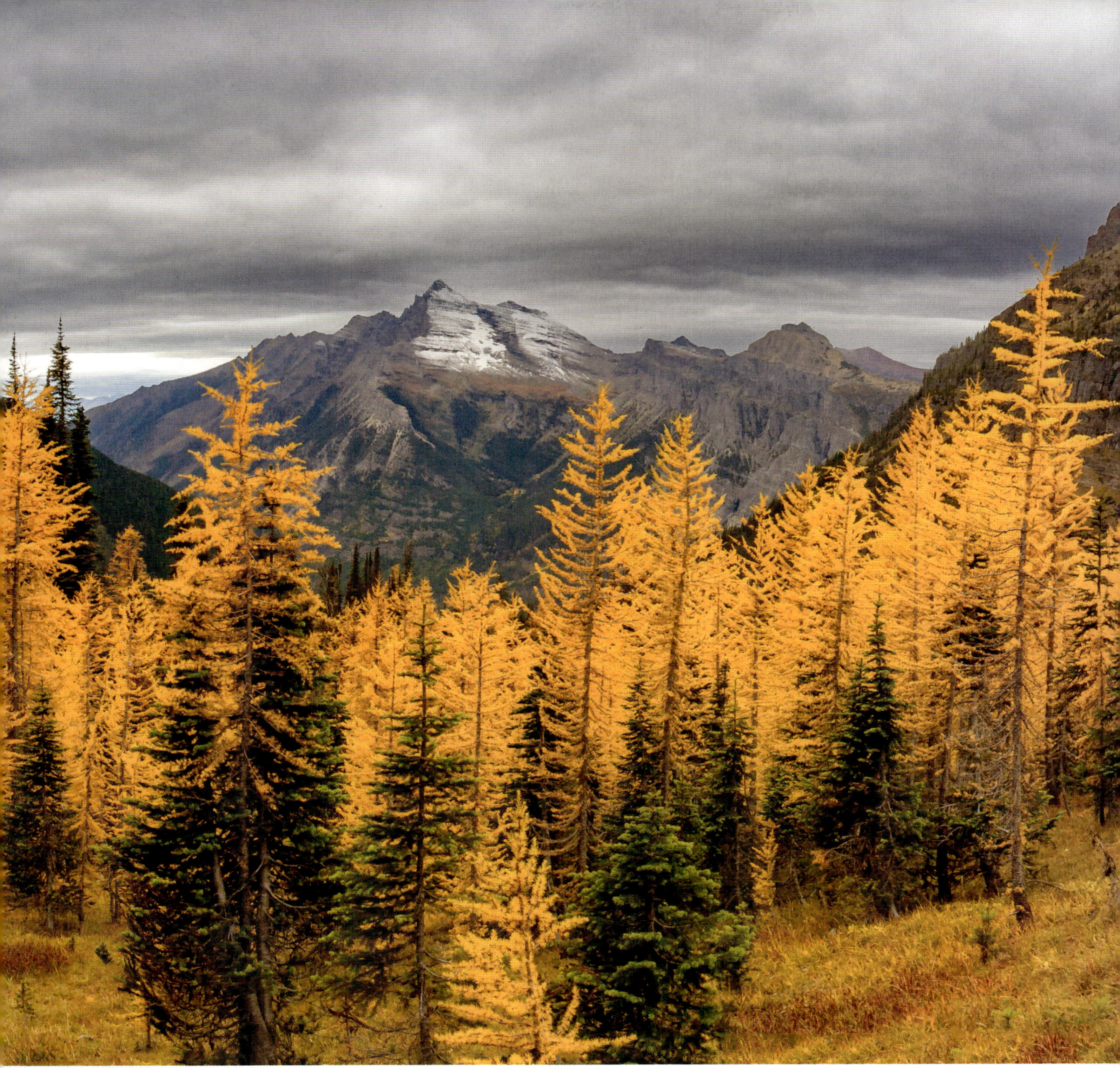

GLACIER NATIONAL PARK After my first season in Glacier, I planned a backcountry trip into the North Fork area of the park. The highlight of the trip was the fall color of the larches. Unlike other conifers, these deciduous trees lose their needles each year.

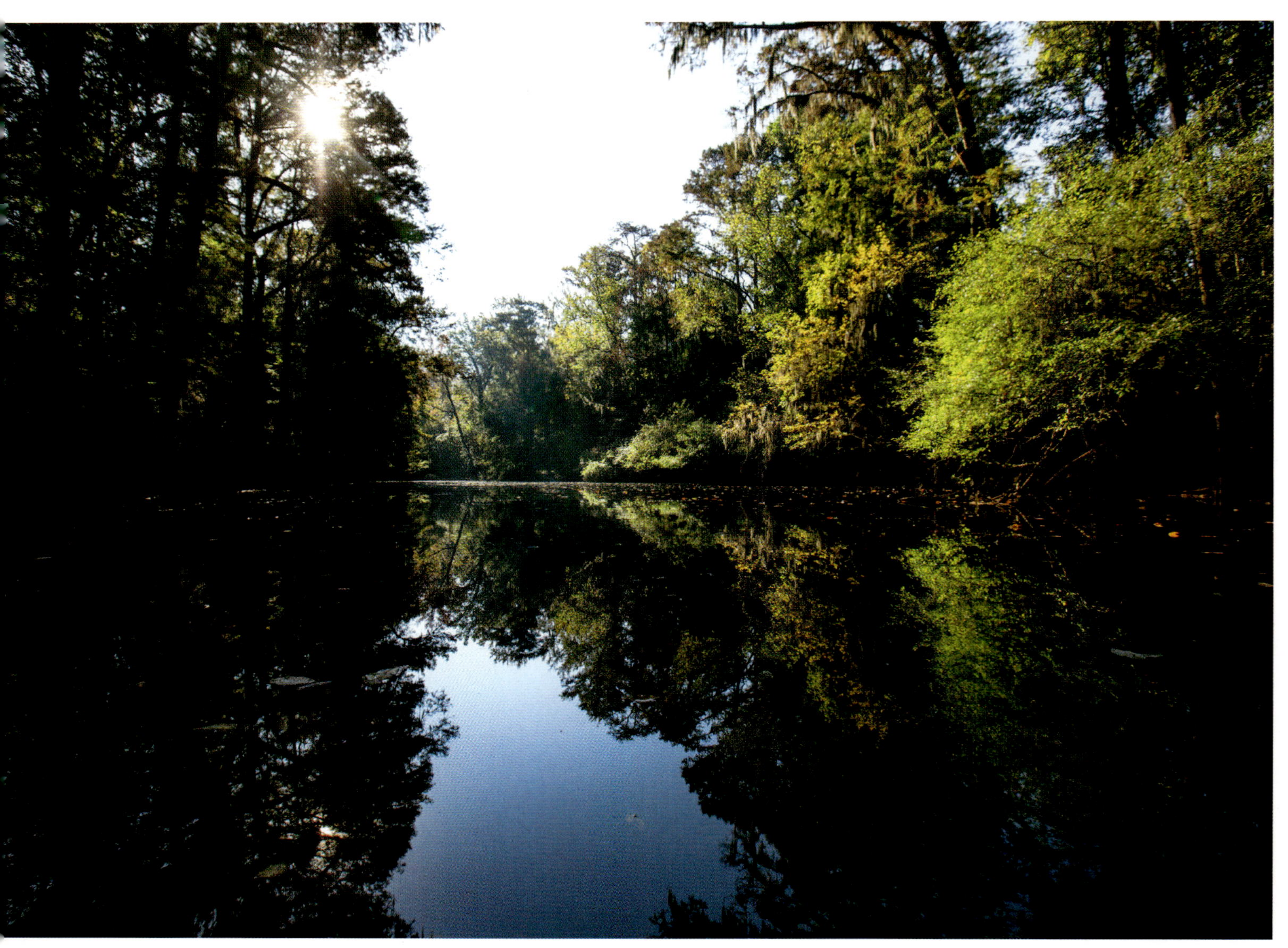

CONGAREE NATIONAL PARK This park is home to the largest intact expanse of old growth bottomland hardwood forest remaining in the southeastern United States. Our favorite part of this trip was exploring Cedar Creek with our kayaks where we were greeted by a family of river otters.

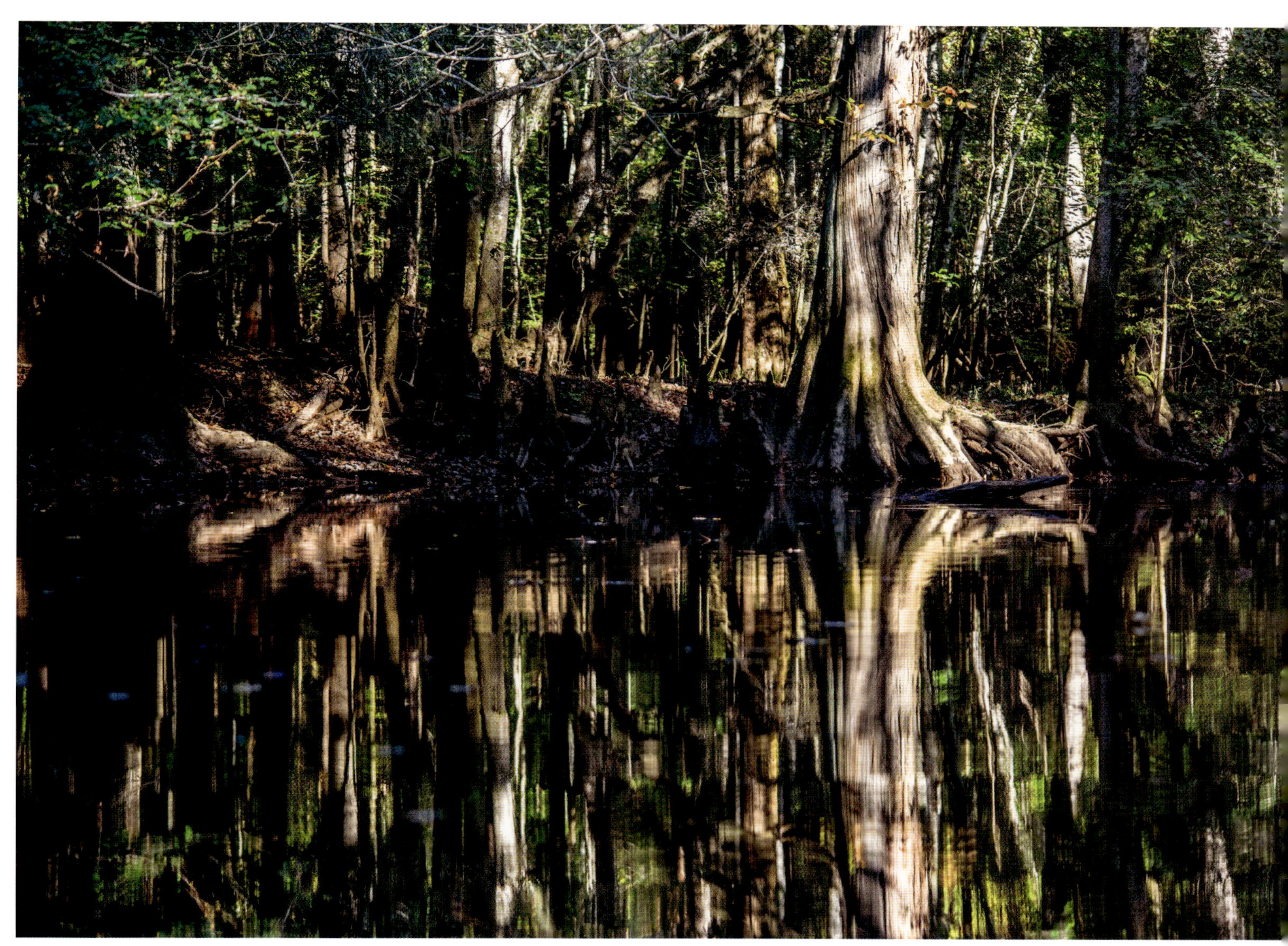

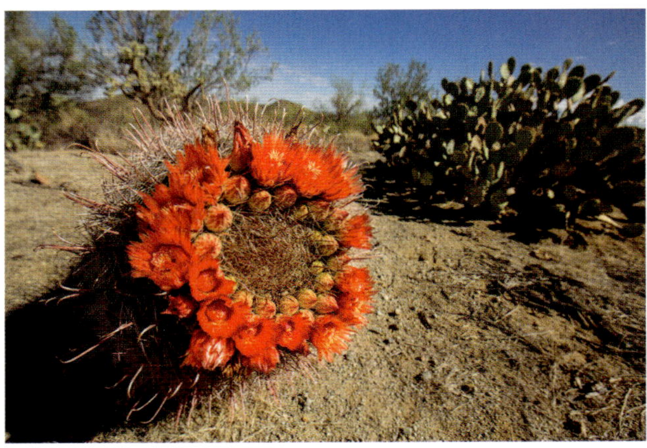

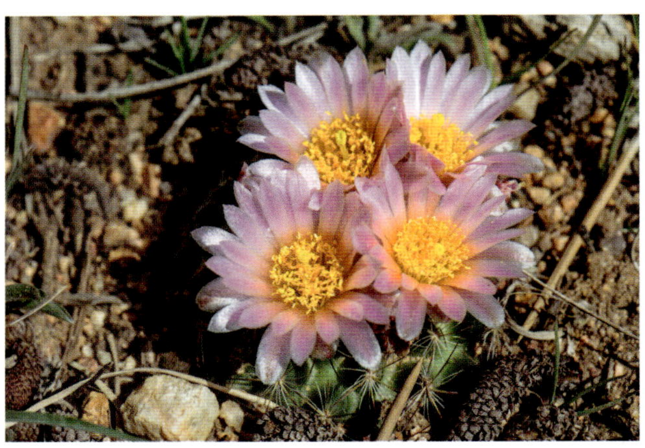

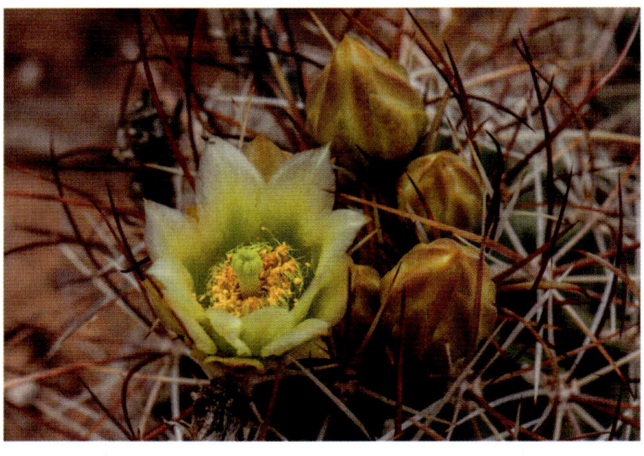

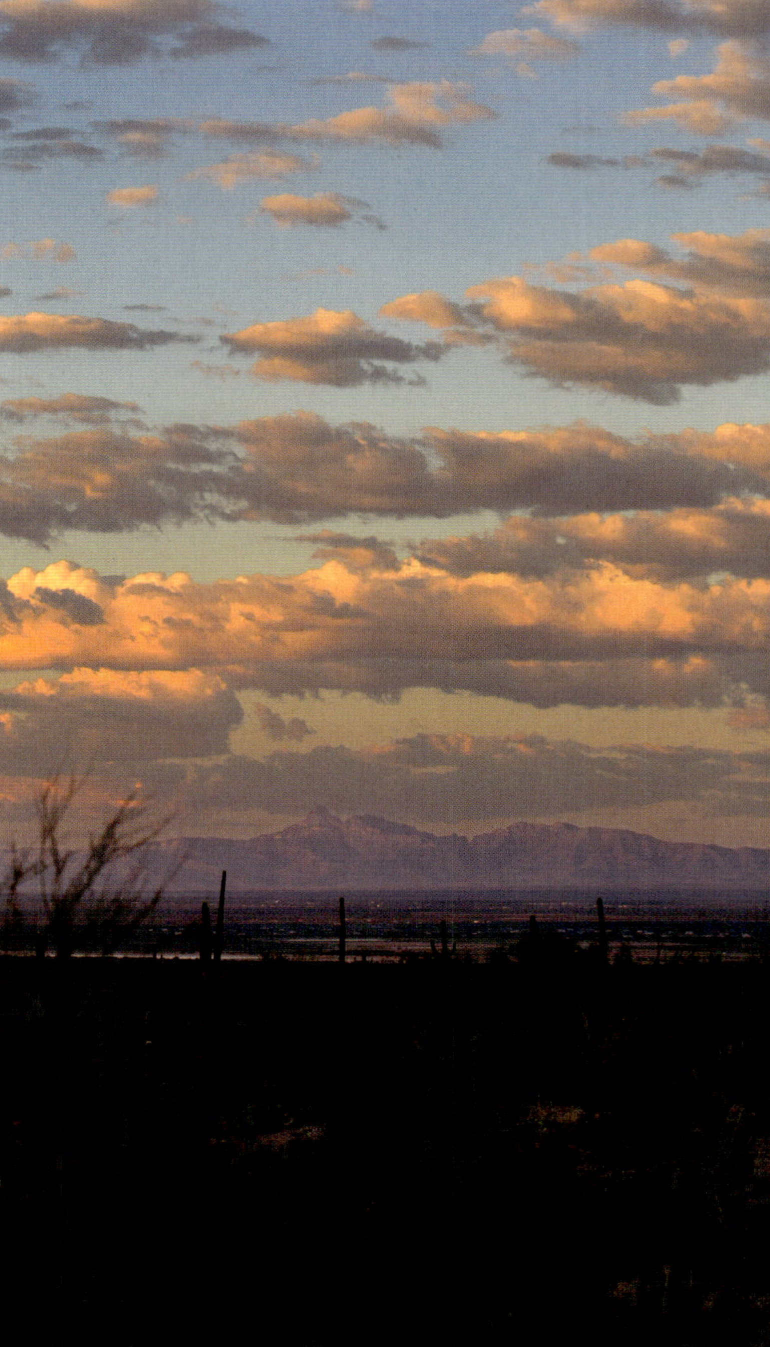

SAGUARO NATIONAL PARK (TOP AND OPPOSITE)

NATURAL BRIDGES NATIONAL MONUMENT (CENTER AND BOTTOM)

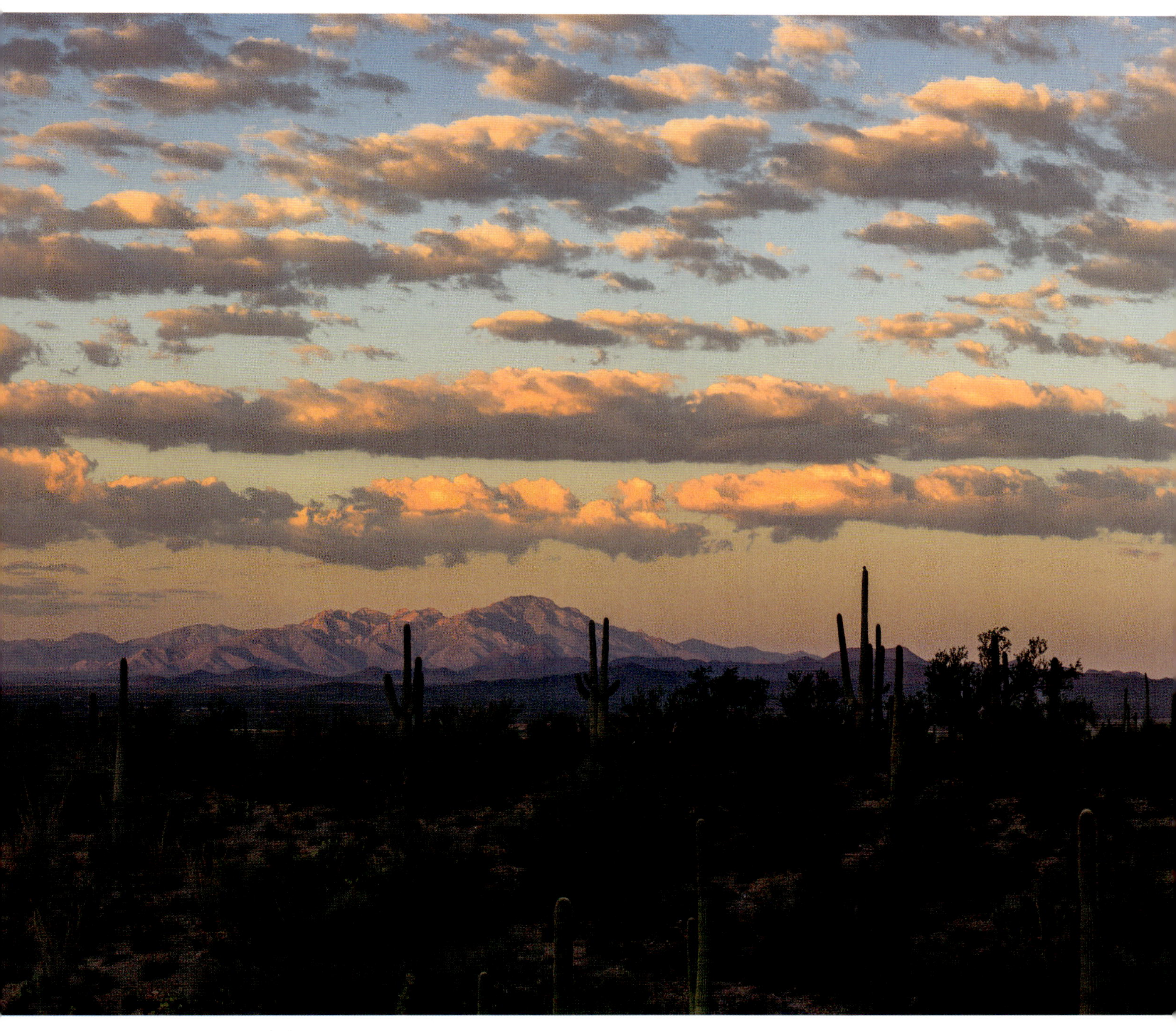

Cacti come in all shapes and sizes. When hiking, its usually best to avoid these spiny species, but they too have some beautiful blooms.

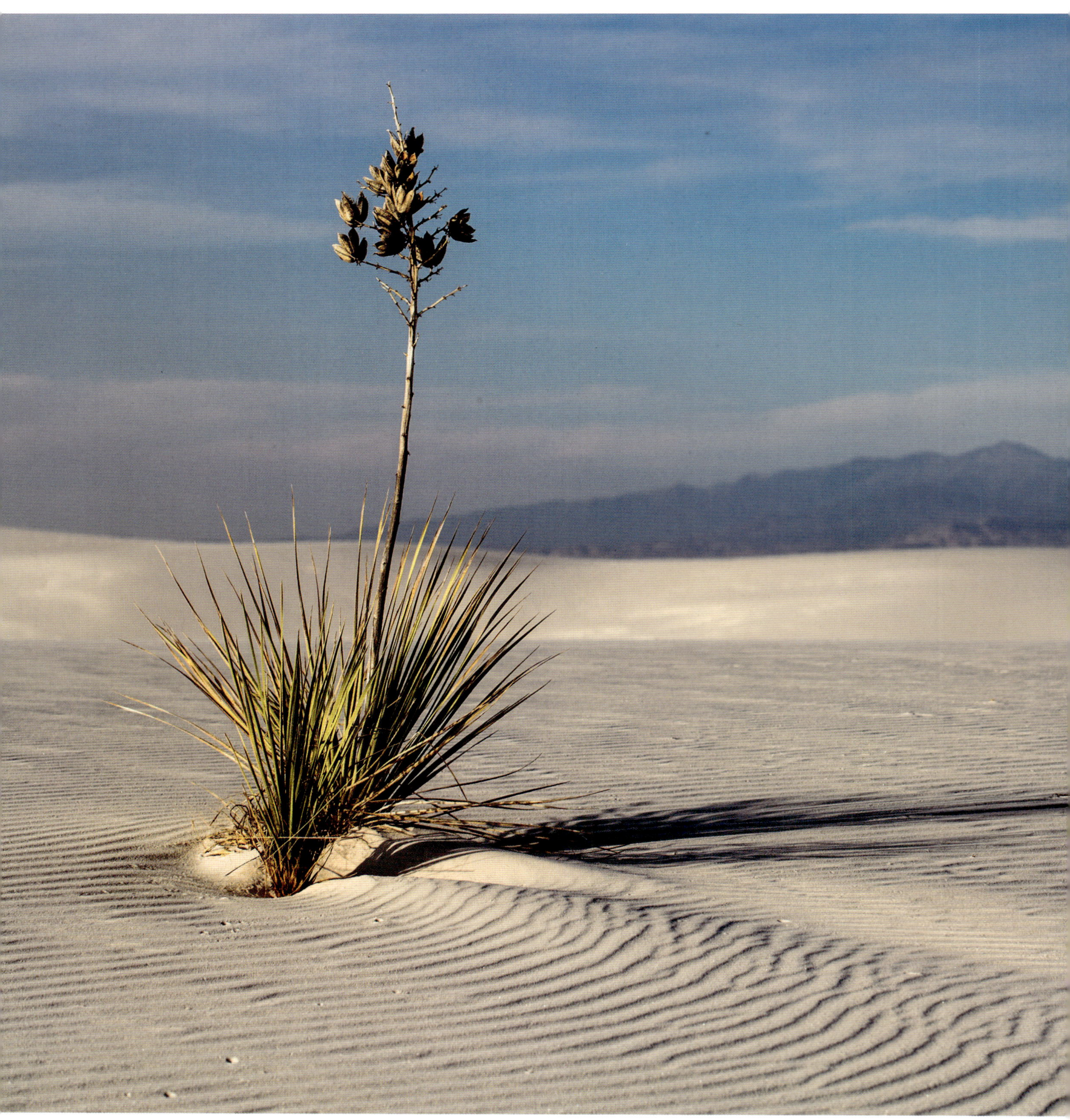

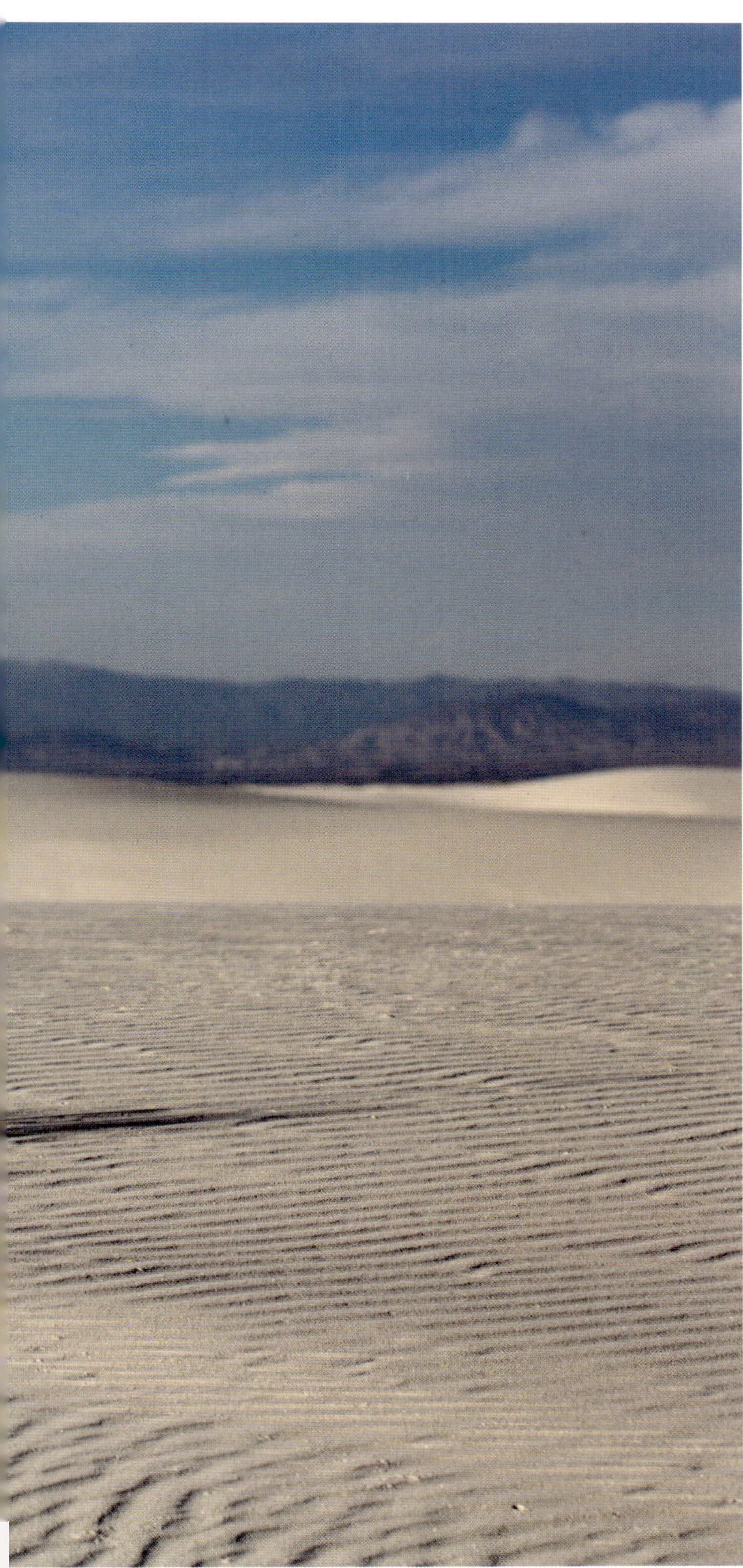

WHITE SANDS NATIONAL PARK A lone banana yucca holds strong as the sea of gypsum sand shifts around it.

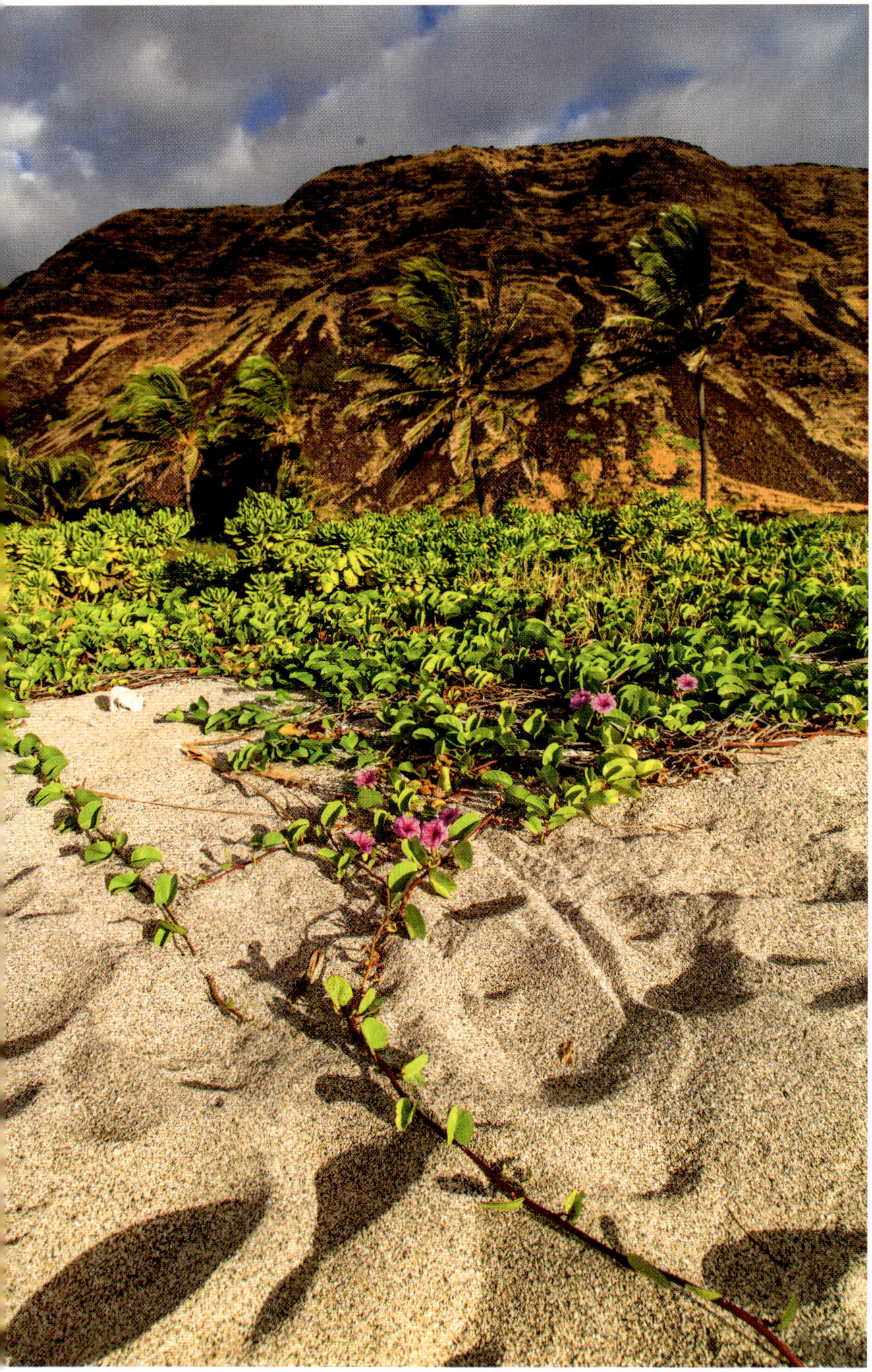

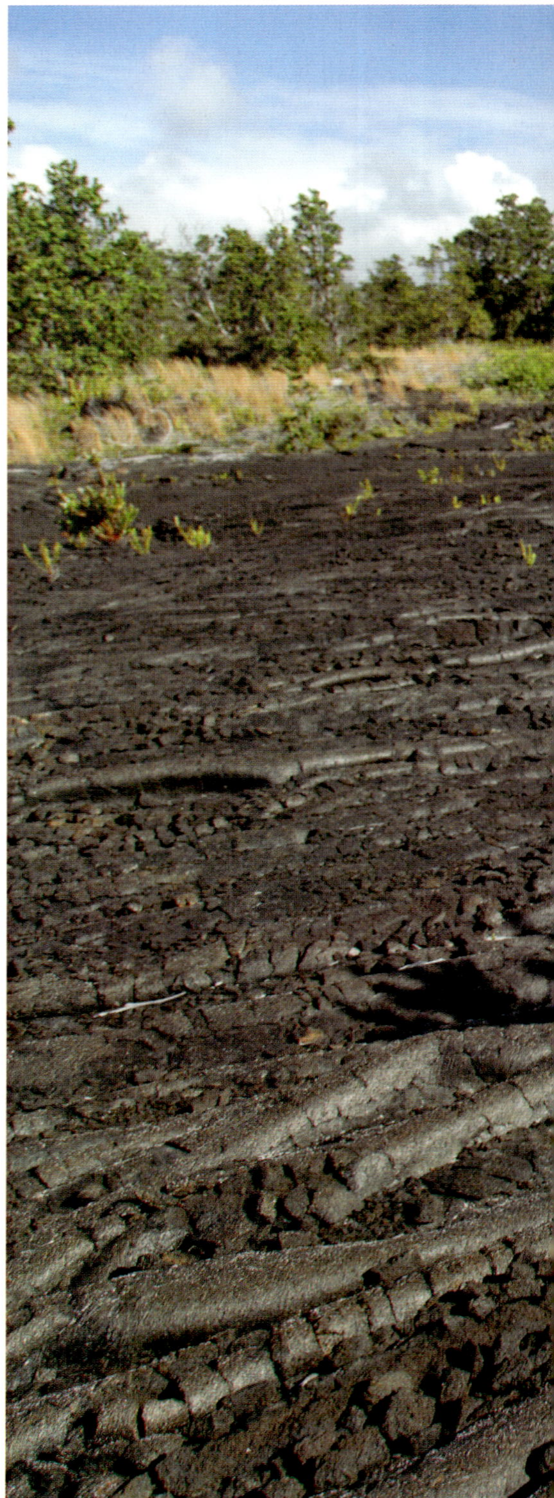

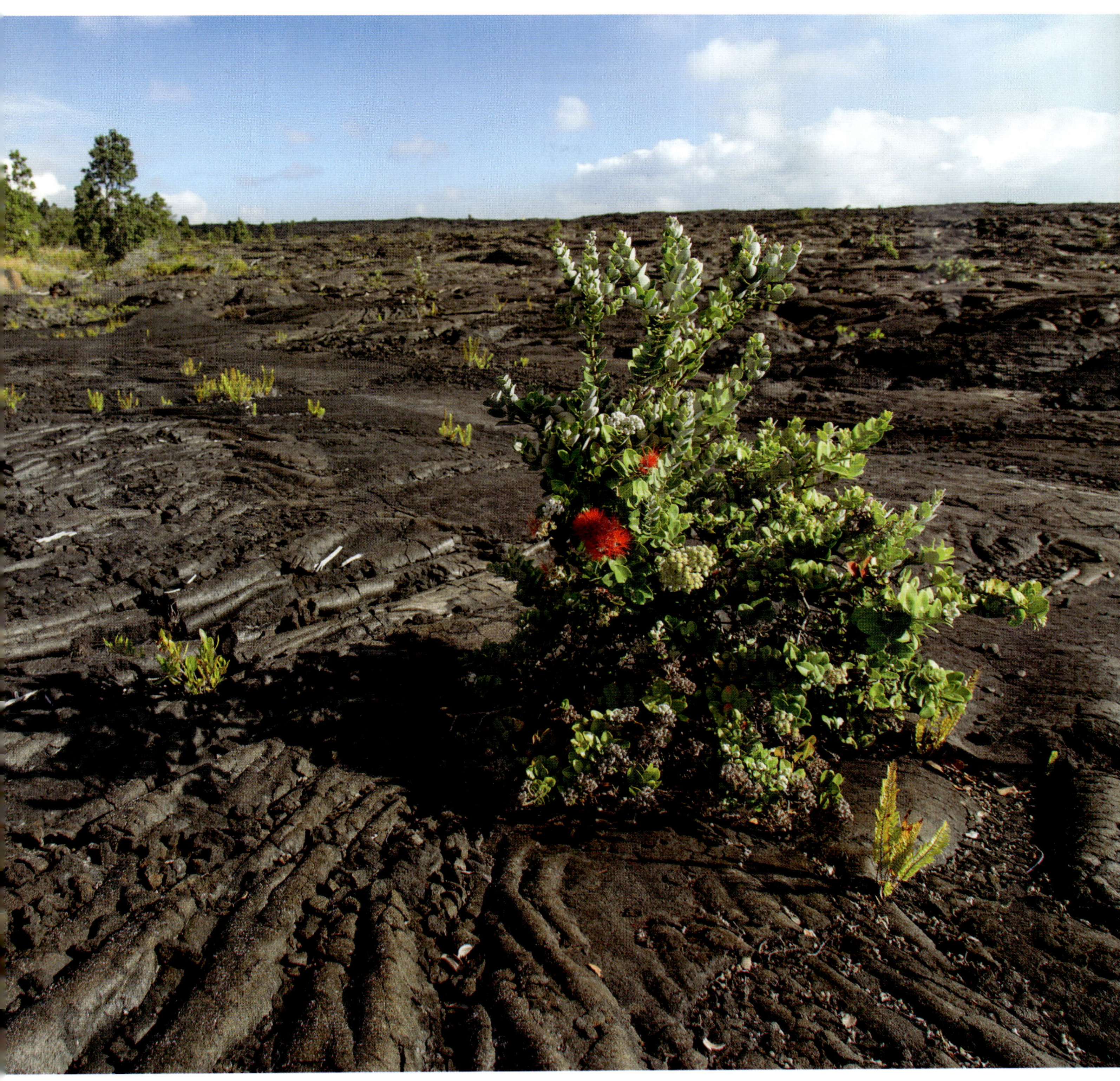

HAWAI'I VOLCANOES NATIONAL PARK On our backcountry trip to the coast, we came across two species thriving in some unlikely places—beach morning glory at Halepē and 'ōhi'a lehua, growing from a lava field.

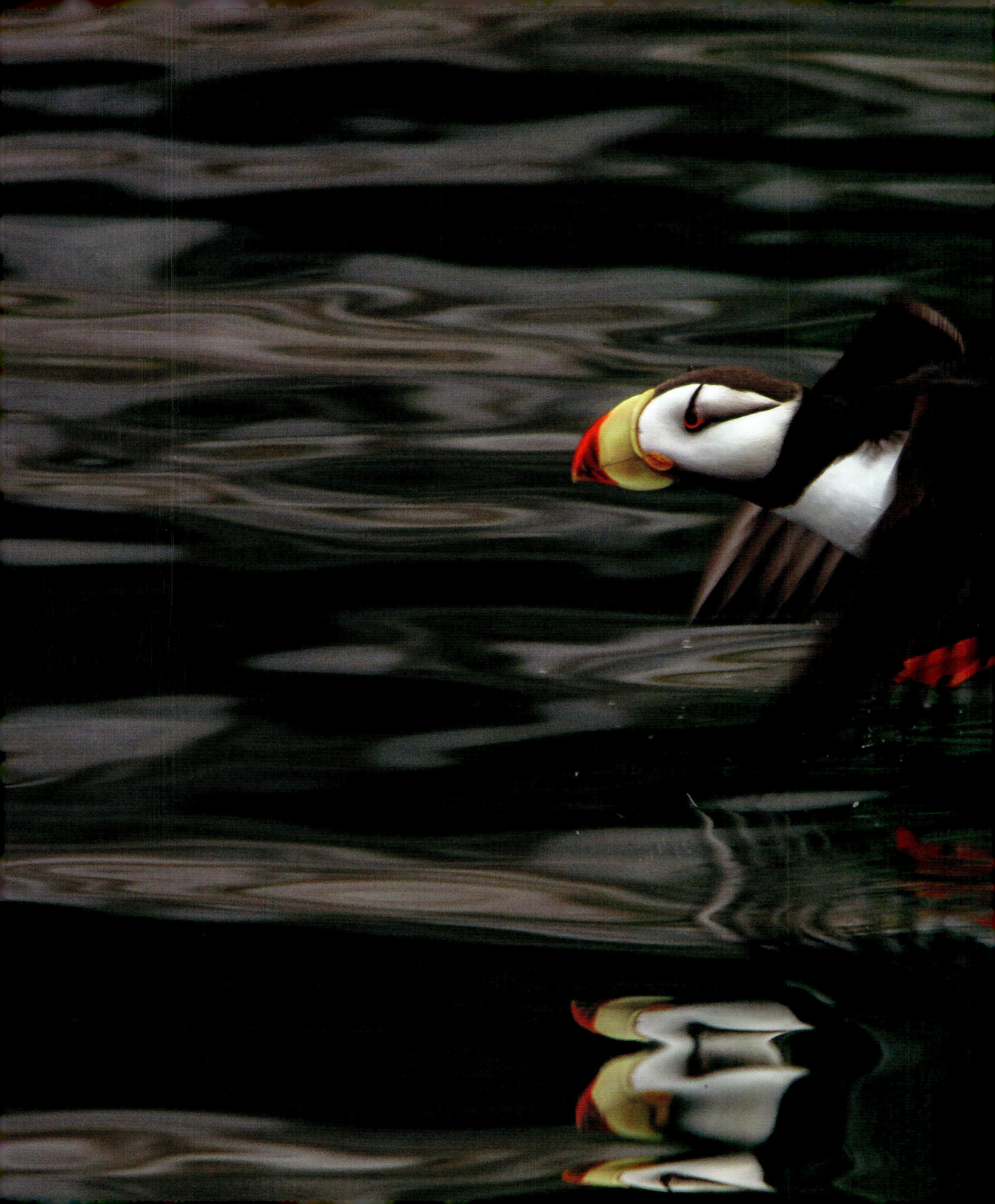

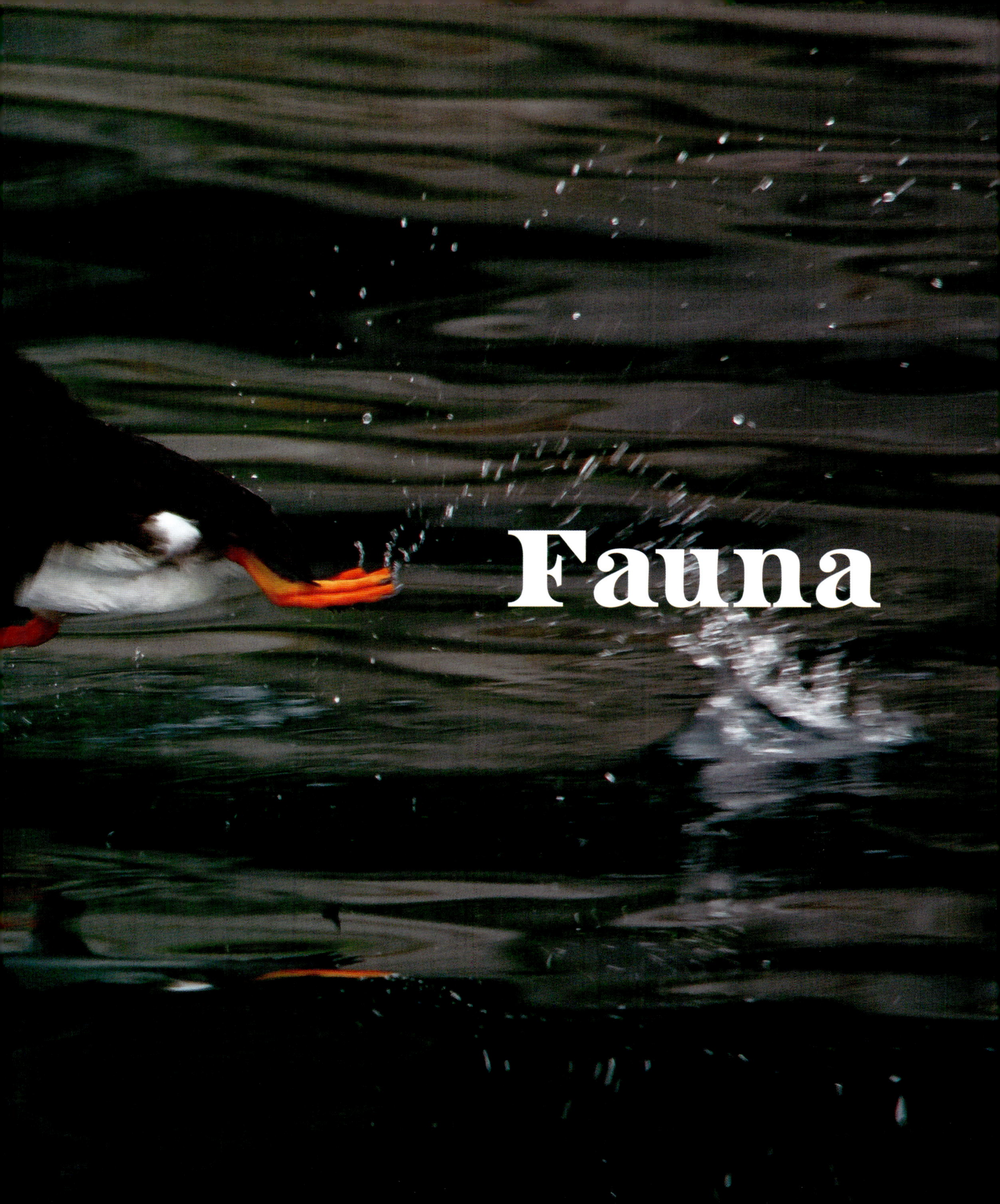

Fauna

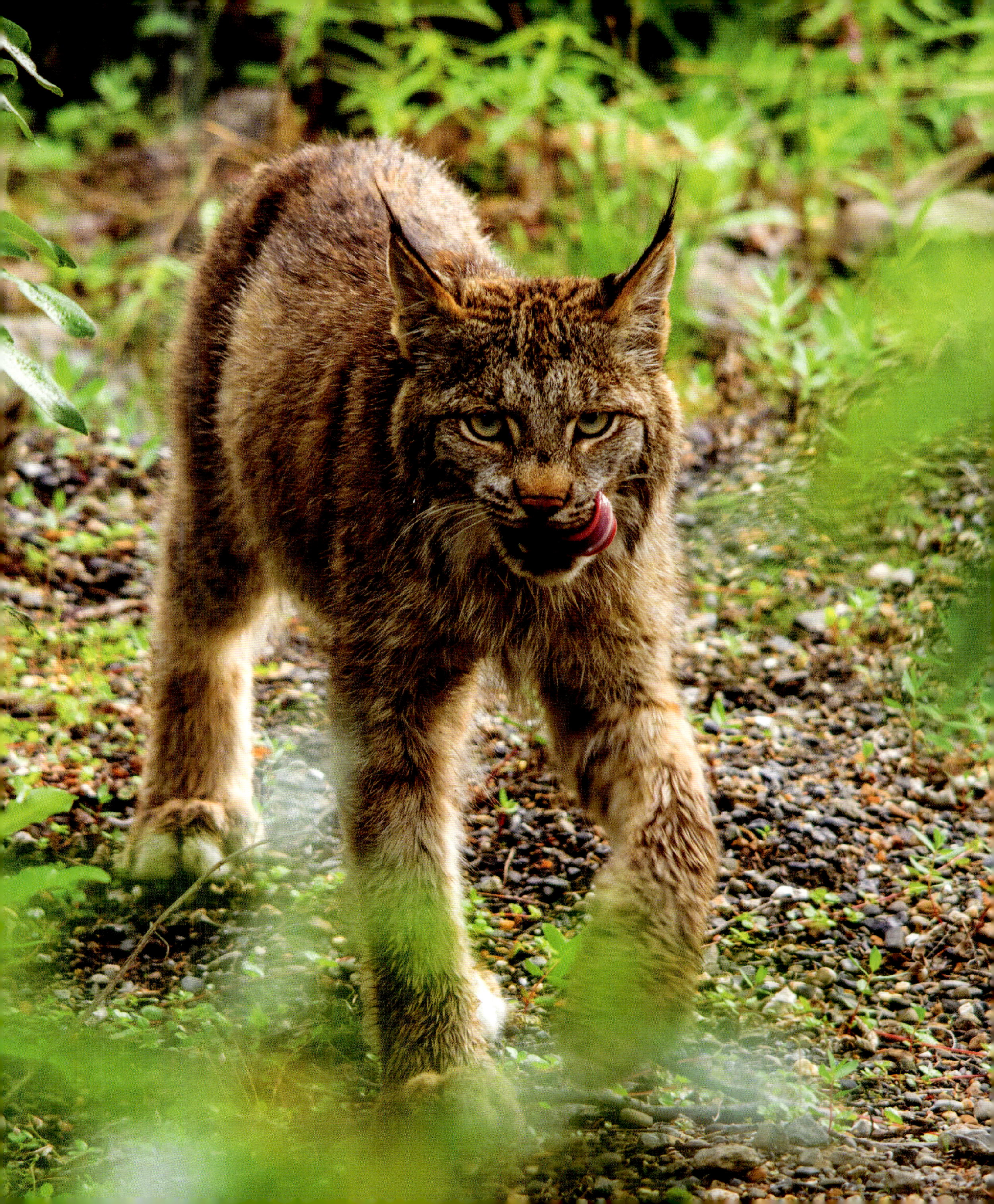

CHARISMATIC CREATURES

OUR PUBLIC LANDS ARE ESSENTIAL for protecting ecosystems and implementing conservation measures that benefit numerous species, including mammals, birds, reptiles, amphibians, insects, fish, and marine life. By safeguarding these critical habitats and applying effective management strategies, public lands play a vital role in preserving biodiversity, supporting healthy ecosystems, and maintaining ecological balance.

For megafauna, public lands are vital to their long-term survival. Large animals such as bison, elk, bears, mountain lions, and wolves require vast, undisturbed territories to roam, hunt, and reproduce. Public lands protect these species from habitat loss and fragmentation caused by urbanization, agriculture, and infrastructure development.

Public lands also serve as critical migration corridors, enabling species to move between different habitats in search of food, mates, and suitable environmental conditions. These corridors are vital for maintaining genetic diversity and ensuring the long-term survival of wildlife populations. By preserving these routes and minimizing barriers such as roads and development, public lands support the health and resilience of wildlife populations across the country.

KENAI FJORDS NATIONAL PARK (PREVIOUS)

DENALI NATIONAL PARK AND PRESERVE (OPPOSITE) From my porch, I watched as a lynx skillfully hunted and devoured two ground squirrels. After its meal, it retreated into the bushes, pausing to groom itself with quiet confidence. Just before disappearing into the forest, it glanced in my direction—a fleeting but unforgettable moment. This was one of my all-time favorite wildlife sightings.

Migratory birds rely heavily on public lands, which offer crucial stopover habitats where they can rest, feed, and breed during their long migrations, often spanning thousands of miles. Without these protected areas, migratory birds would face severe challenges from habitat loss, human disturbances, and environmental degradation. Public lands also safeguard key breeding and wintering grounds, which are vital for the reproductive success and health of bird populations. Conservation efforts on these lands, including habitat restoration and invasive species control, help ensure the ecological conditions that migratory birds need to survive and flourish, even as they face growing environmental pressures.

Marine and aquatic wildlife also heavily depend on public lands, particularly in areas where freshwater systems and coastal environments are safeguarded. These protected areas help maintain water quality and preserve breeding and spawning grounds critical for the survival of fish, amphibians, and marine species. Coastal public lands play a significant role in protecting vital marine ecosystems like coral reefs, seagrass beds, and mangroves, which serve as nurseries and feeding grounds for countless marine organisms, including fish, sea turtles, and marine mammals. By shielding these aquatic habitats from pollution, overfishing, and habitat destruction, public lands contribute to the long-term health of marine and freshwater ecosystems, ensuring that aquatic wildlife continues to thrive.

Insects, though often overlooked, benefit significantly from the protection offered by public lands. These areas provide diverse and undisturbed habitats that are essential for the survival of many insect species, including critical pollinators like bees and butterflies. Insects play key roles in pollination, nutrient cycling, and serving as food for other wildlife. Public lands, which are largely free from harmful pesticide use, urban sprawl, and agricultural practices, help ensure the survival of both common and endangered insect species. By preserving these habitats, wildlands contribute to the stability and resilience of insect populations, which are crucial for maintaining broader ecosystem health and the stability of food webs.

Wildlife in the United States faces a variety of significant threats, including habitat loss, climate change, pollution, and human-wildlife conflict. Habitat loss—driven by urban development, agriculture, and deforestation—fragments ecosystems and reduces available space for wildlife. Climate change exacerbates these problems by altering habitats, shifting migration routes, and threatening species unable to adapt quickly enough. Pollution, especially from pesticides and industrial waste, degrades ecosystems and harms wildlife. Additionally, human-wildlife conflict, through overhunting, poaching, and vehicle collisions, places further stress on species. These threats are interconnected and compounded by invasive species and disease, underscoring the importance of conservation efforts on public lands to mitigate these risks.

Maintaining biodiversity on public lands is essential for the health and stability of ecosystems. Biodiversity ensures that ecosystems function effectively, with different species performing essential roles such as pollination, seed dispersal, and population regulation. A rich variety of fauna supports natural processes like nutrient cycling, soil health, and water filtration, which benefits other wildlife within these ecosystems and the human communities that rely on them. A diverse array of species also enhances ecosystem resilience, allowing habitats to adapt to changes such as climate shifts or disease outbreaks. By supporting a wide range of species, public lands contribute to genetic diversity, which is crucial for the long-term survival of wildlife populations. In preserving biodiversity, public lands safeguard the continued functioning of natural systems and the many services they provide to both nature and society.

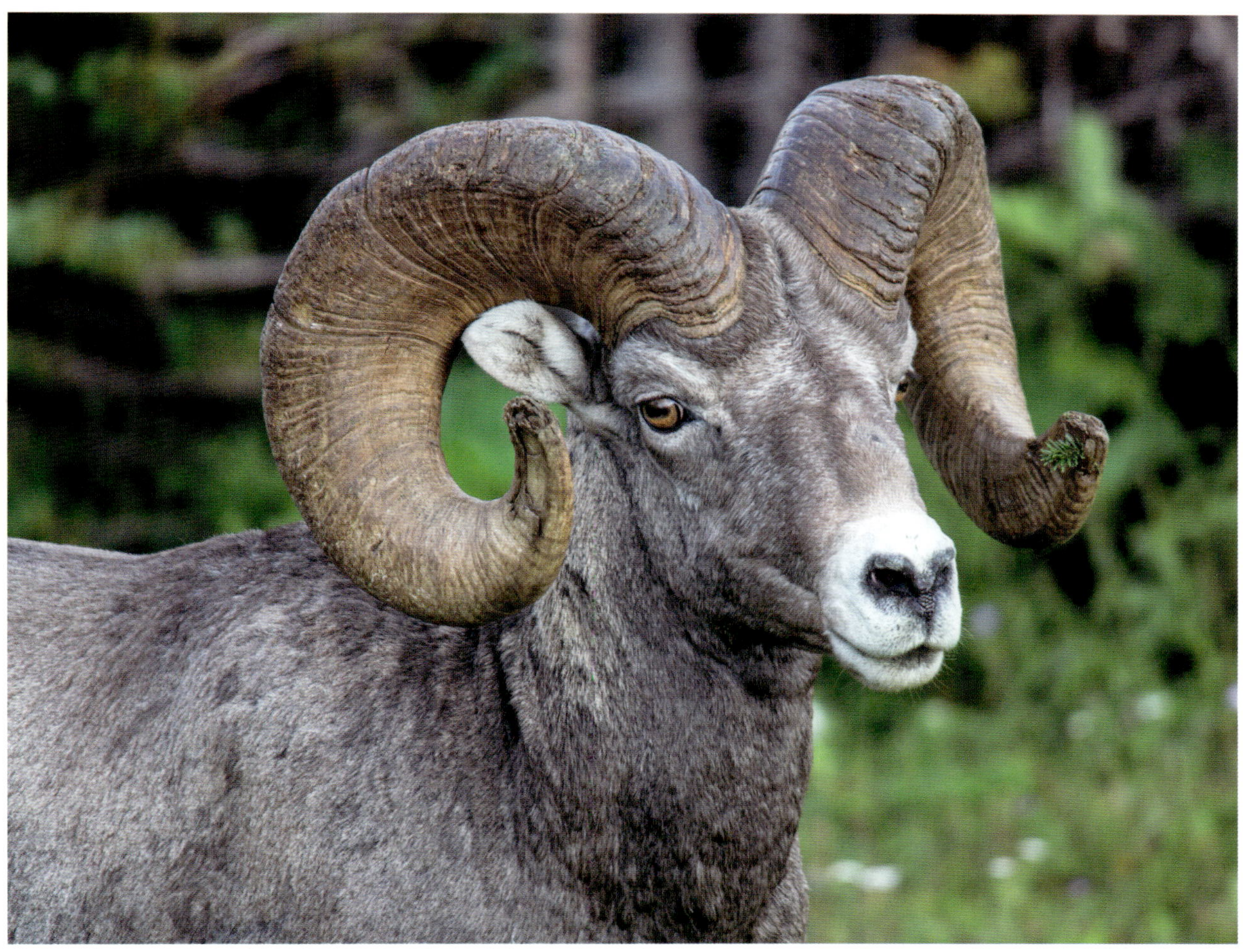

GLACIER NATIONAL PARK The largest of the many bighorn rams that live near the Logan Pass Visitor Center.

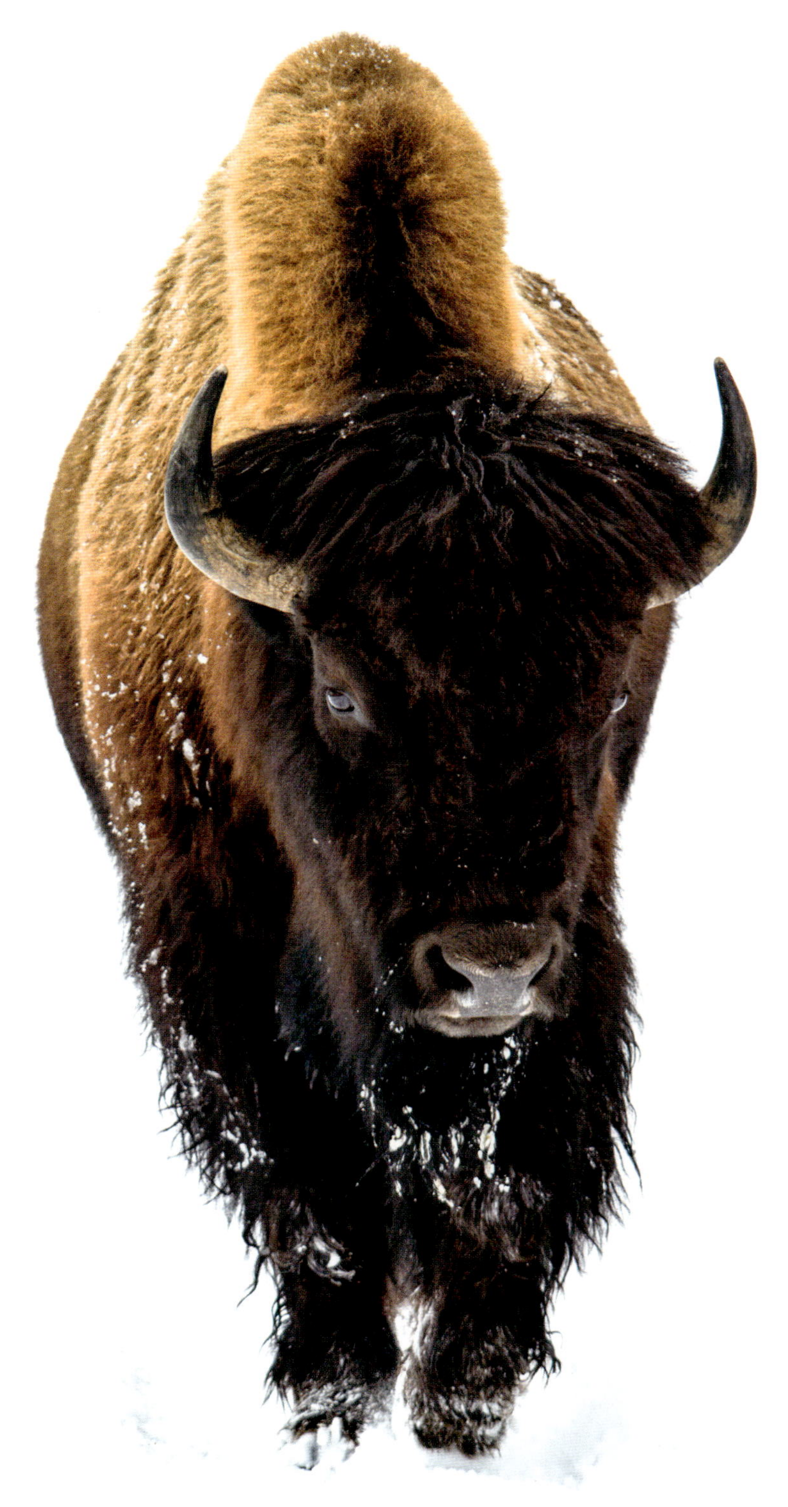

Each winter in Yellowstone, thousands of bison migrate from their summer range in Lamar Valley to the park's North Entrance in Gardinier, Montana, passing through Mammoth Hot Springs on the way. During this time, it's fairly common to see bison grazing or resting in people's yards, sometimes making it difficult to get in or out of your house. Of all the places I've lived and all the wildlife encounters I've had, Yellowstone remains the only place where you can use the excuse, "Sorry I was late; there was a bison blocking my front door," and people will understand.

On one particular night, I was abruptly woken from a deep sleep—I felt the house shaking. Initially, I thought it was an earthquake. Yellowstone sits atop a giant cooling magma chamber known as the Yellowstone Caldera. This active geological feature is responsible for the park's geysers, hot springs, and thousands of small earthquakes each year, most of which go unnoticed. After I came to my senses, I realized the shaking movement was erratic, starting and stopping at uneven intervals, not like the other times I had felt an earthquake. Then I heard a familiar sound—a low-pitched grunt coming from outside our bedroom window. I grabbed a light and shined it through the window to find a huge bull bison scratching itself against the side of our house. Full-grown bulls can weigh as much as two thousand pounds–large enough to shake a house, apparently. It didn't seem like he was going to stop anytime soon, so I opened the window and told him to leave us alone, which he did.

The following morning, we woke up, made coffee, and relaxed on the couch while waiting for the heater to warm the house. After about fifteen minutes, I realized that the heat was blowing cold air. Despite a basic inspection of the thermostat and checking our propane tank level, I couldn't figure out the issue. After a phone call and a short time later, a repairman came to inspect the system and informed us that our seismic gas shutoff valve just needed resetting. Putting two and two together, we determined that the bison shook the house enough to trigger the valve, cutting off the gas flow to our home, as it was designed to do during an earthquake.

YELLOWSTONE NATIONAL PARK

YELLOWSTONE NATIONAL PARK A lone bull elk stands proudly before Yellowstone's Antler Peak. It never ceases to amaze me that these animals can regrow such massive antlers—up to twenty pounds—in just a few months.

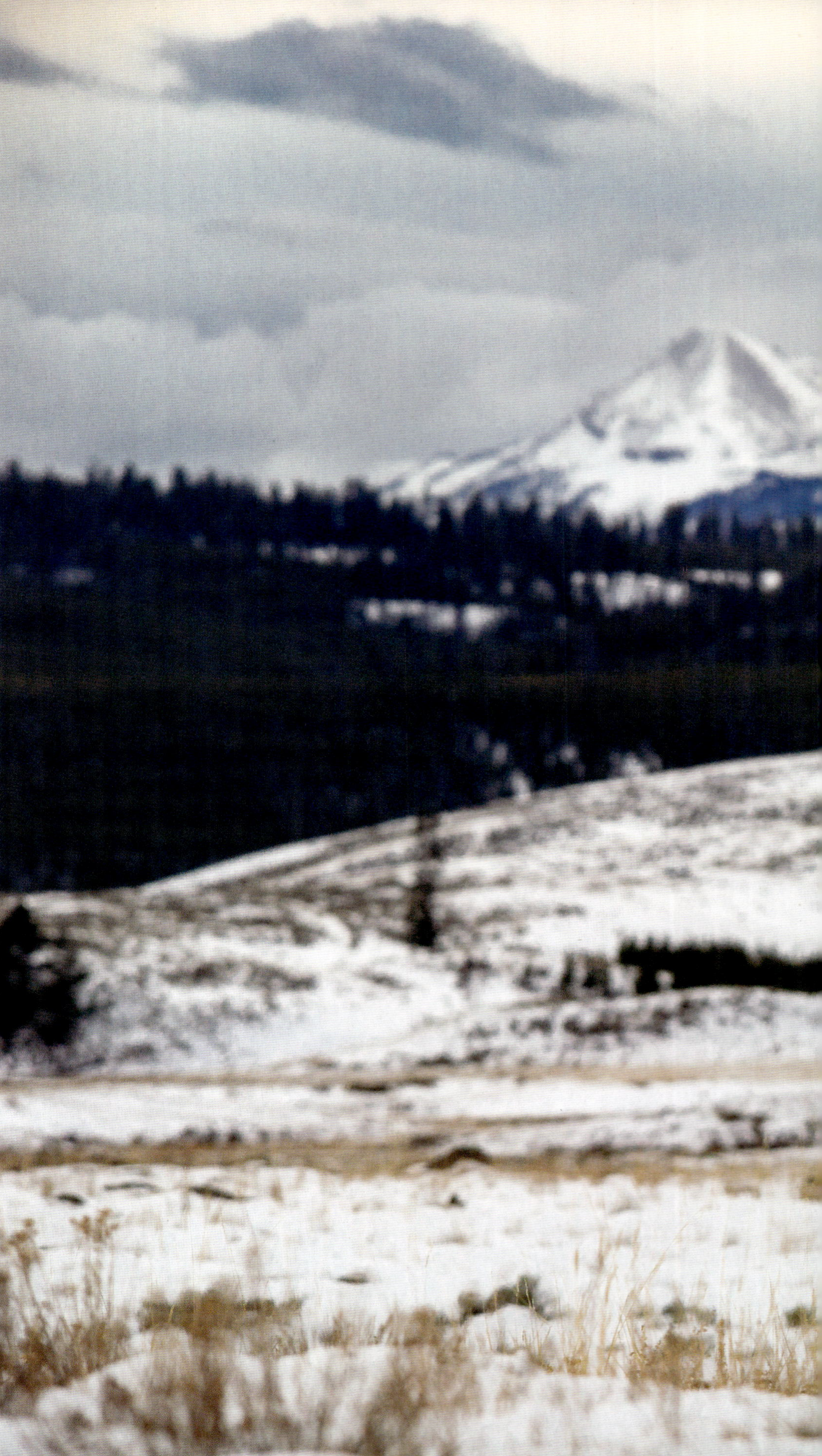

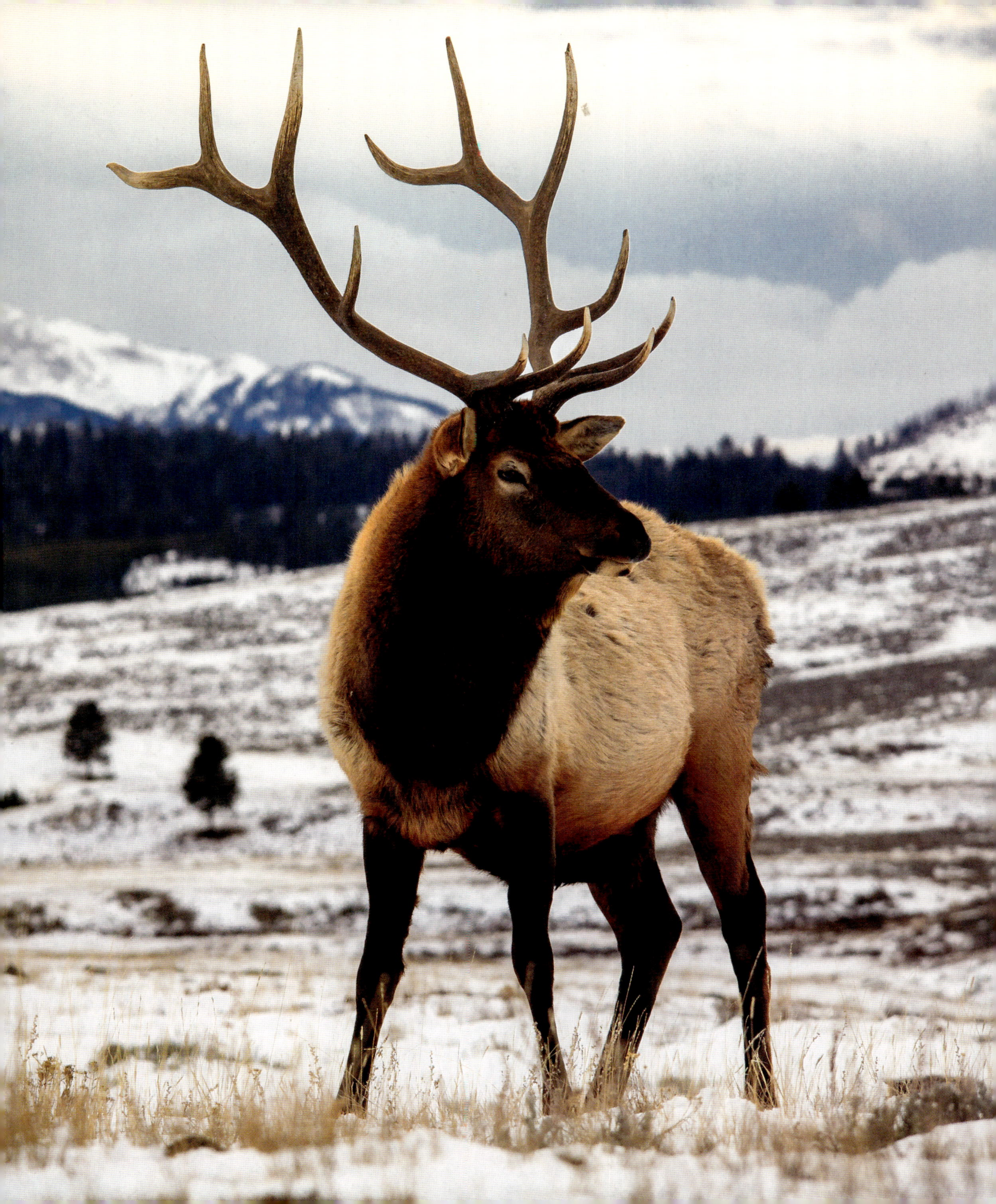

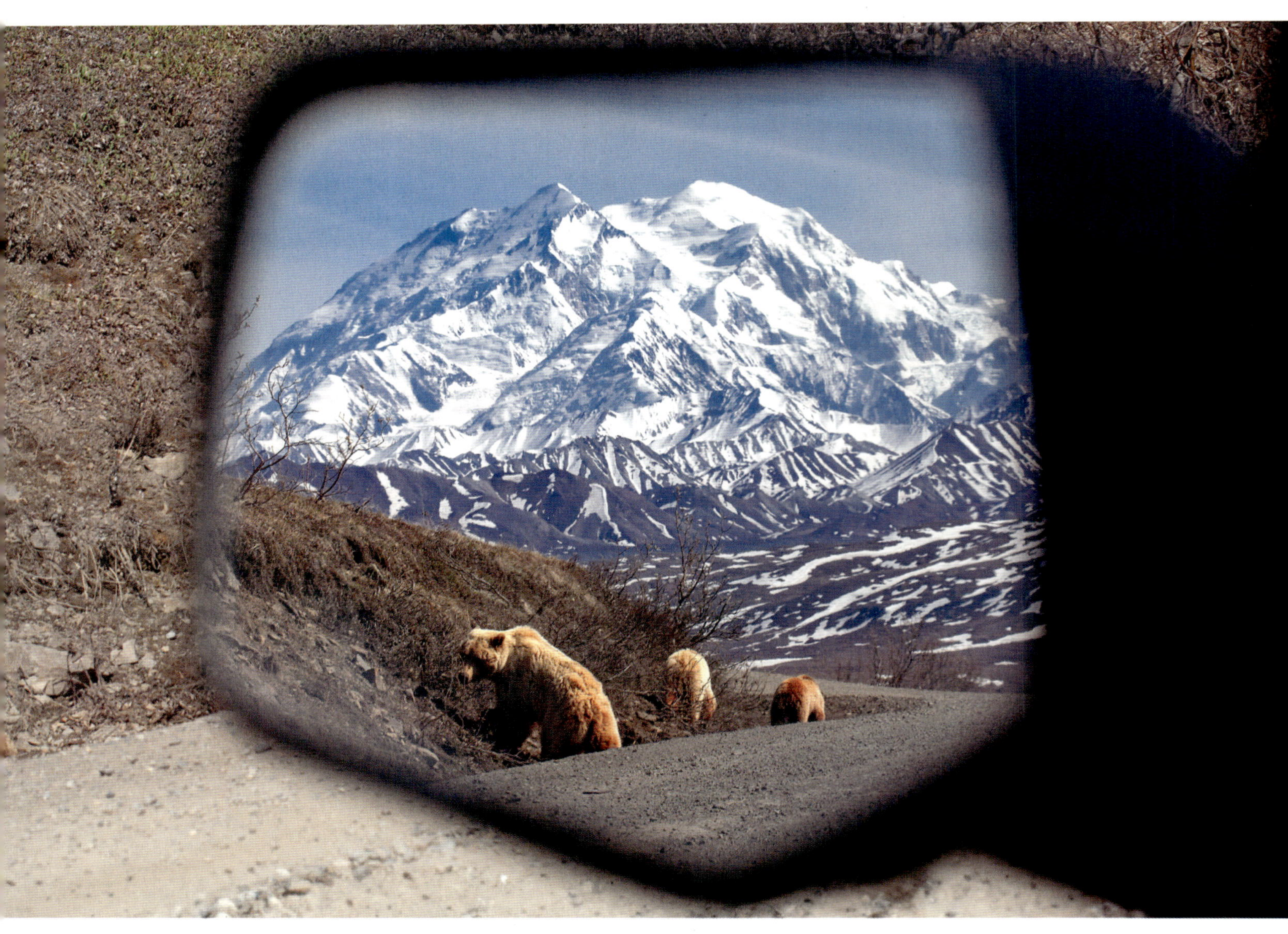

Two of my favorite grizzly sightings stand out vividly in my memory.

DENALI NATIONAL PARK AND PRESERVE The first happened when I pulled over to let a sow and her cubs pass. As they walked by, I happened to glance in my side-view mirror and realized The Mountain was perfectly framed behind them. I waited, hoping for the perfect shot, and just before they disappeared from view, the sow paused, turned, and gave me just enough time to capture the moment.

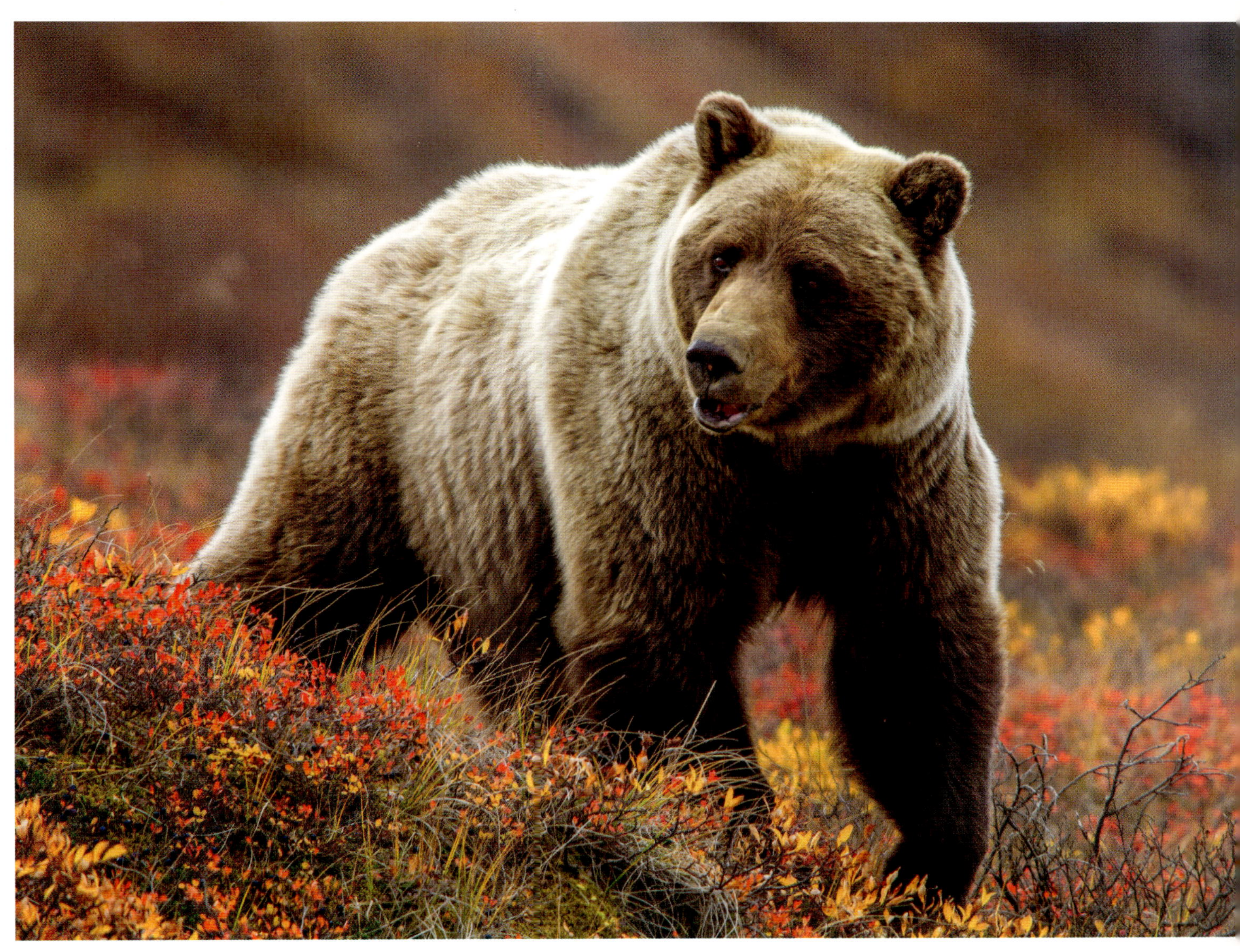

(ABOVE) The second sighting took place in the same area but with a different bear family. A mother and her older cubs were grazing on blueberries, completely unfazed by our presence. Our entire bus sat in hushed awe for nearly twenty minutes, so silent that we could hear the soft sound of their lips plucking berries from the bushes.

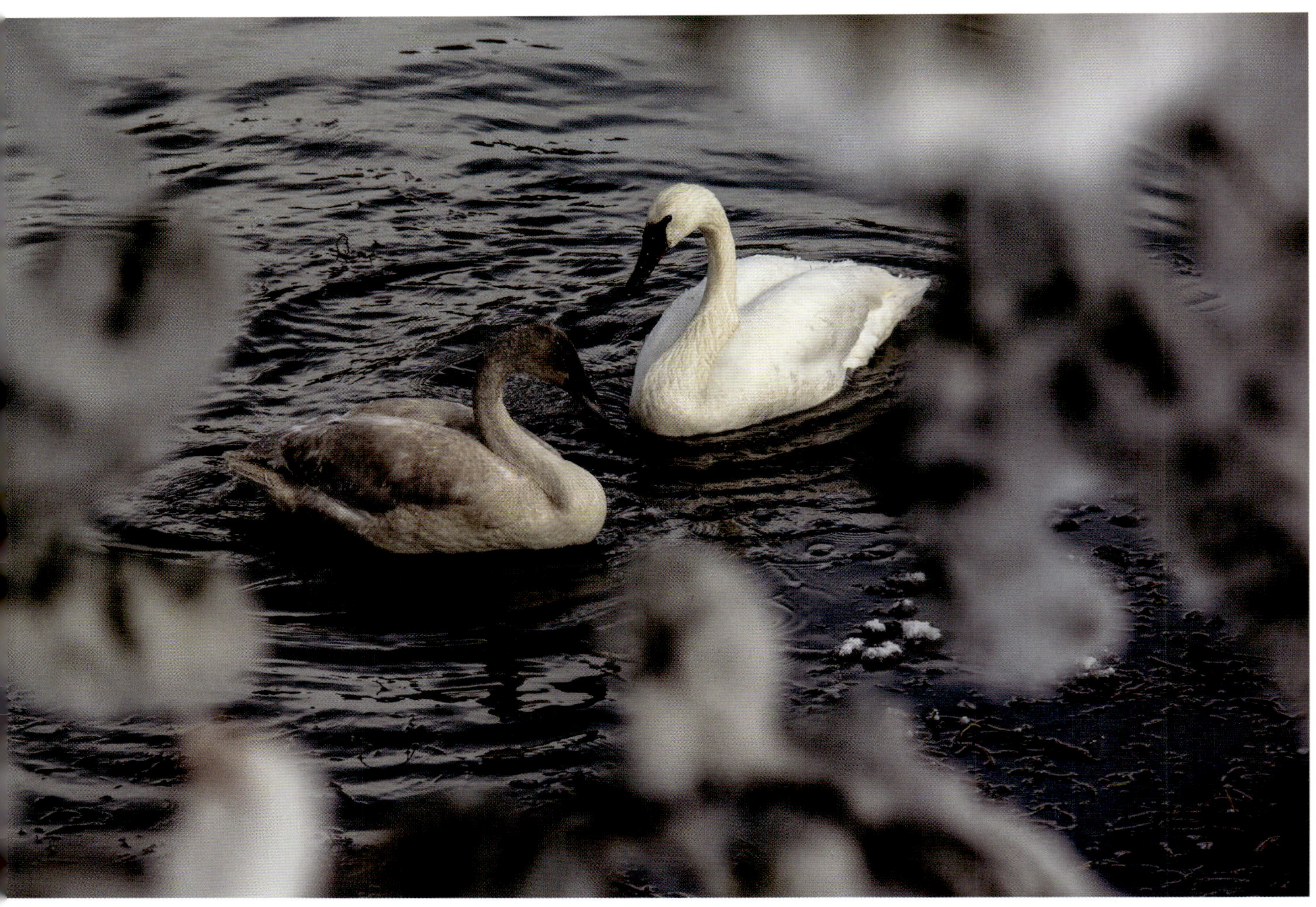

YELLOWSTONE NATIONAL PARK

(ABOVE) Trumpeter swans are slowly making a comeback in the park after nearing extirpation. Thanks to thermally influenced waters that remain ice-free year-round, some swans never leave, spending their entire lives there. Seeing one up close for the first time is striking—not just because of their elegance, but because of their sheer size. They're massive!

(OPPOSITE) My first close wolf encounter in the park happened in winter, and I almost missed it. The wolf was lying down, blending into the landscape, and there was no one else around. I pulled over and climbed into the passenger seat for a better angle. After a while, it slowly stood, stretched in a deep "downward dog," then silently slipped out of sight. This was a quiet, powerful moment I'll never forget.

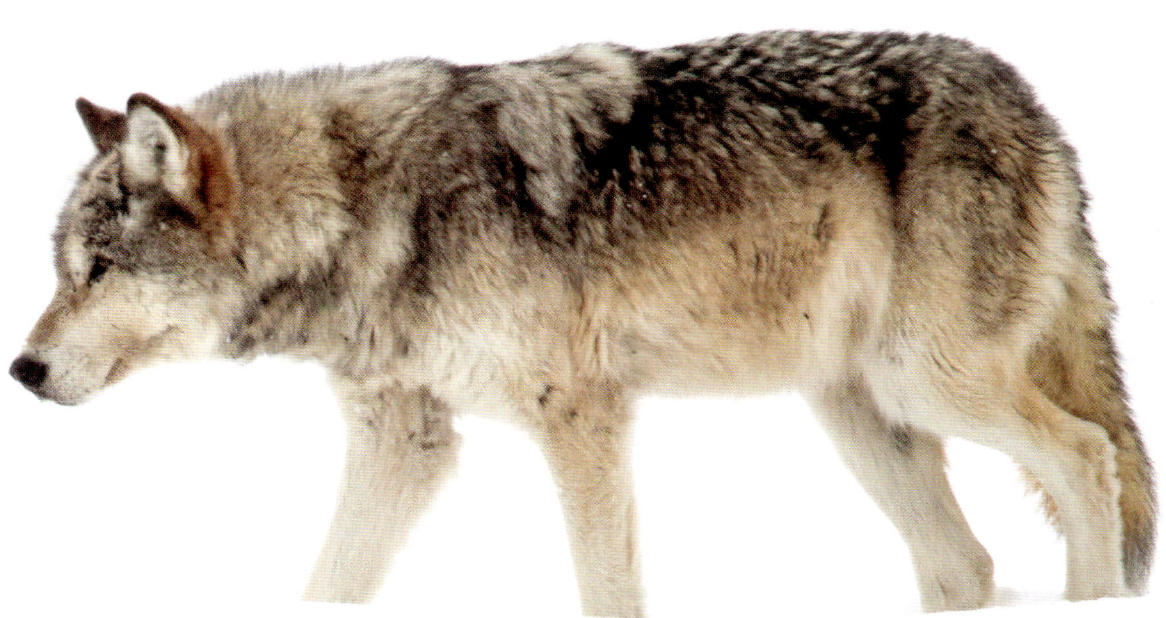

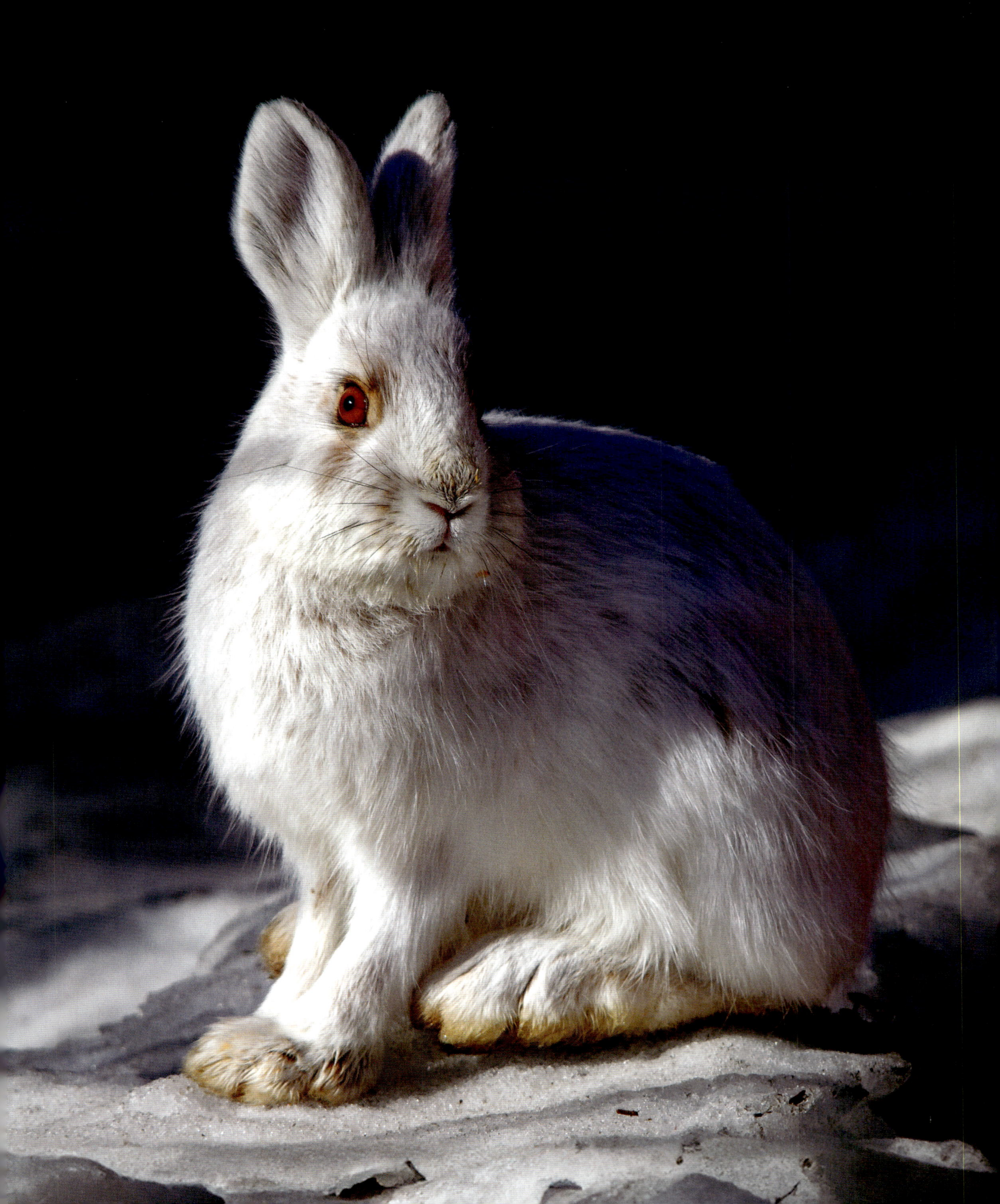

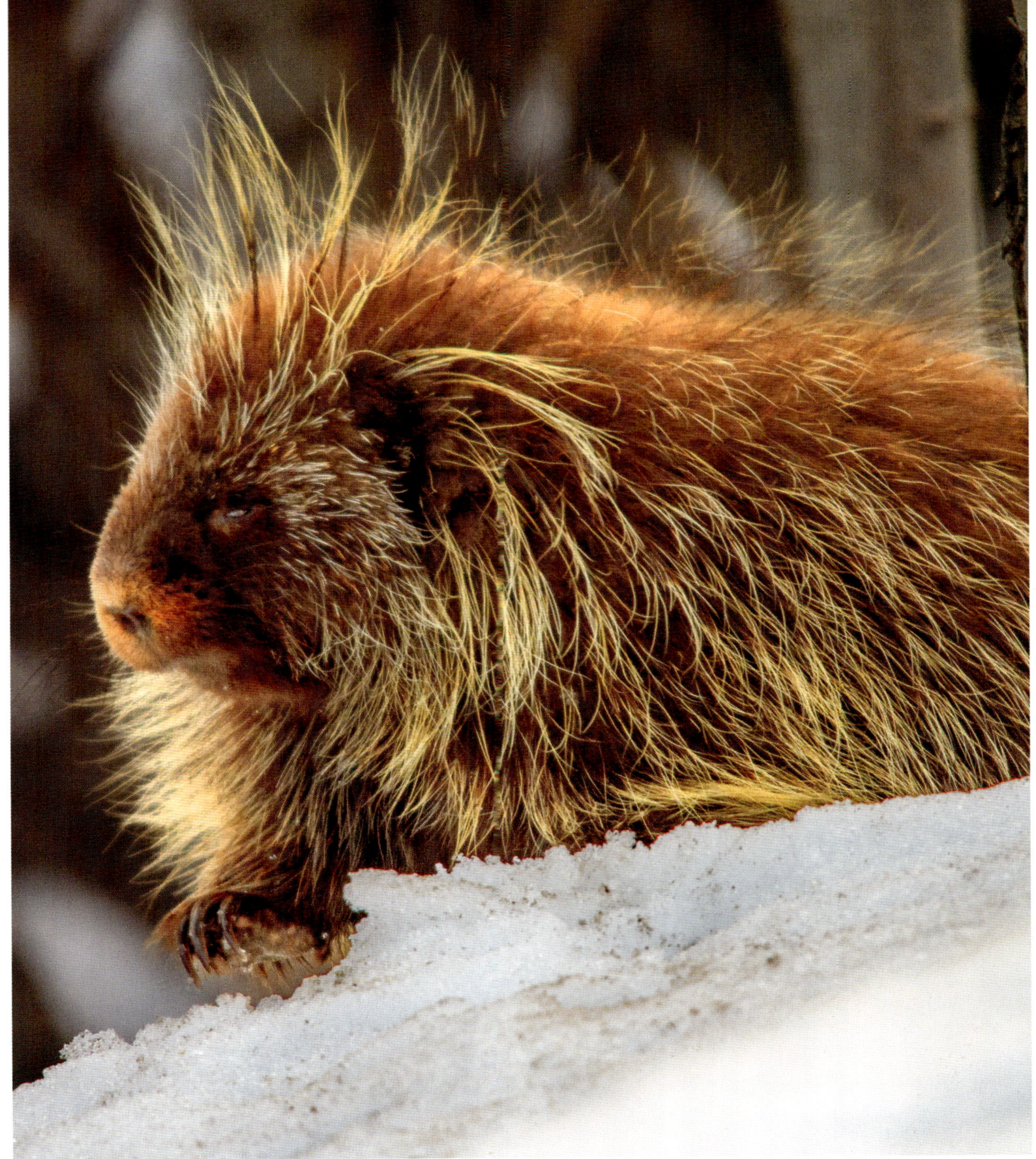

DENALI NATIONAL PARK AND PRESERVE

(OPPOSITE) On my first morning in the park, I spotted a snowshoe hare sunning itself just behind my cabin—my first-ever sighting of one.

(ABOVE) Later that week, during an evening drive, we saw a porcupine crawling over a snowbank—another first for me.

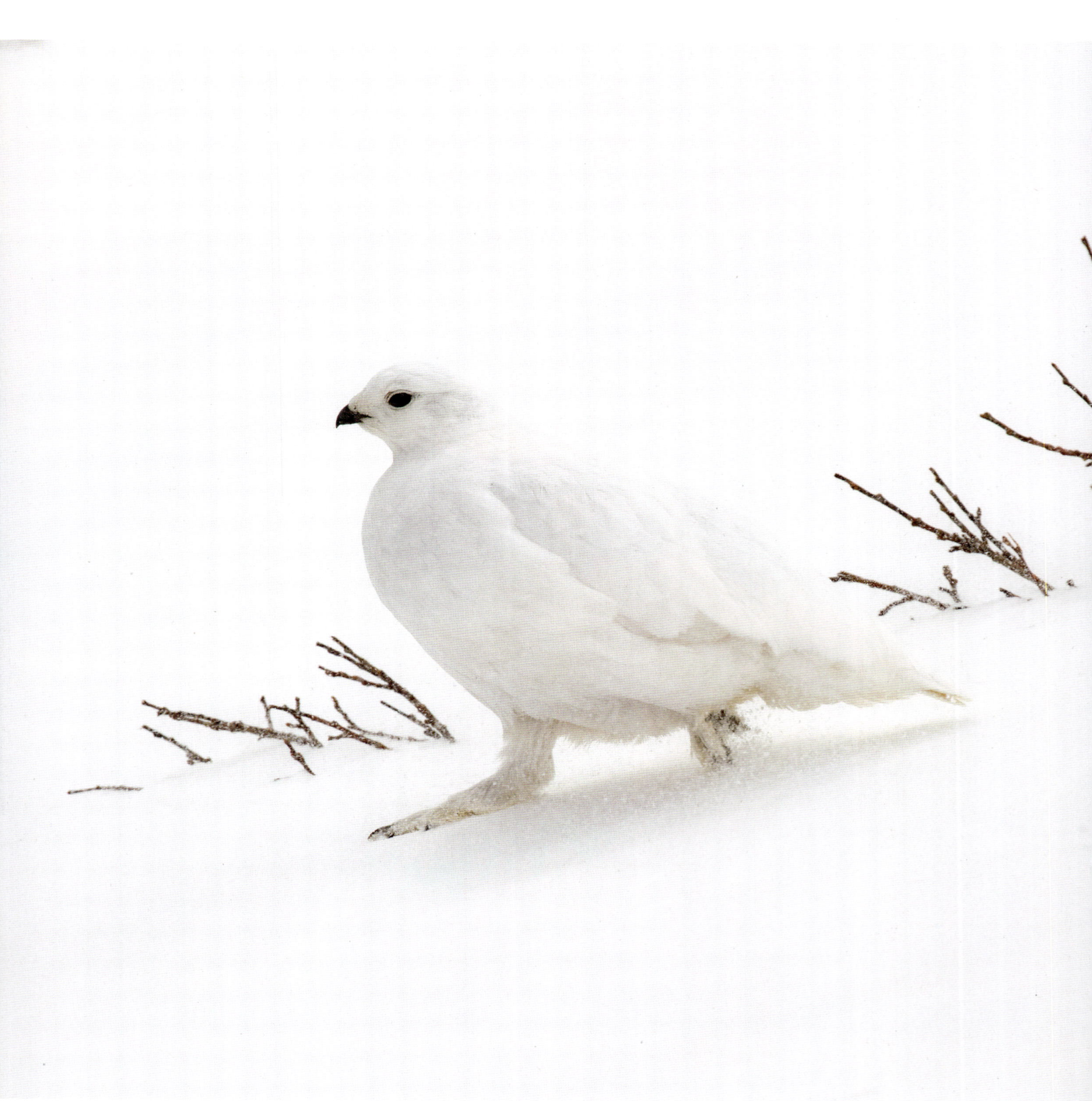

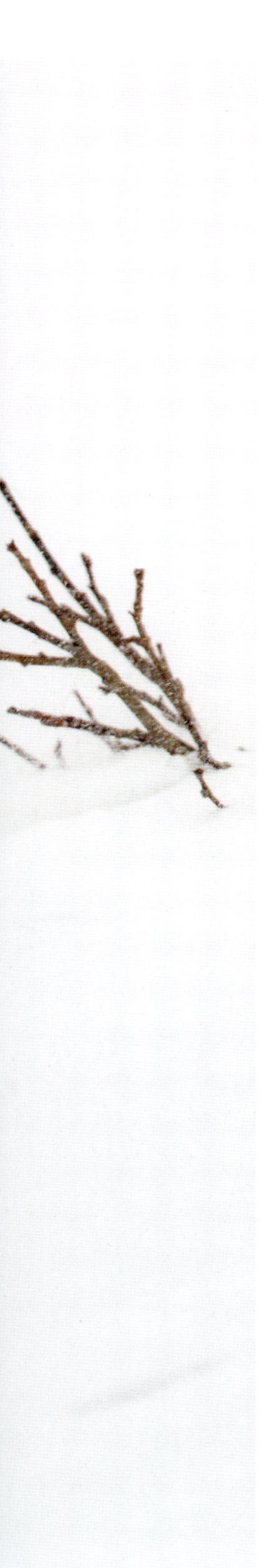

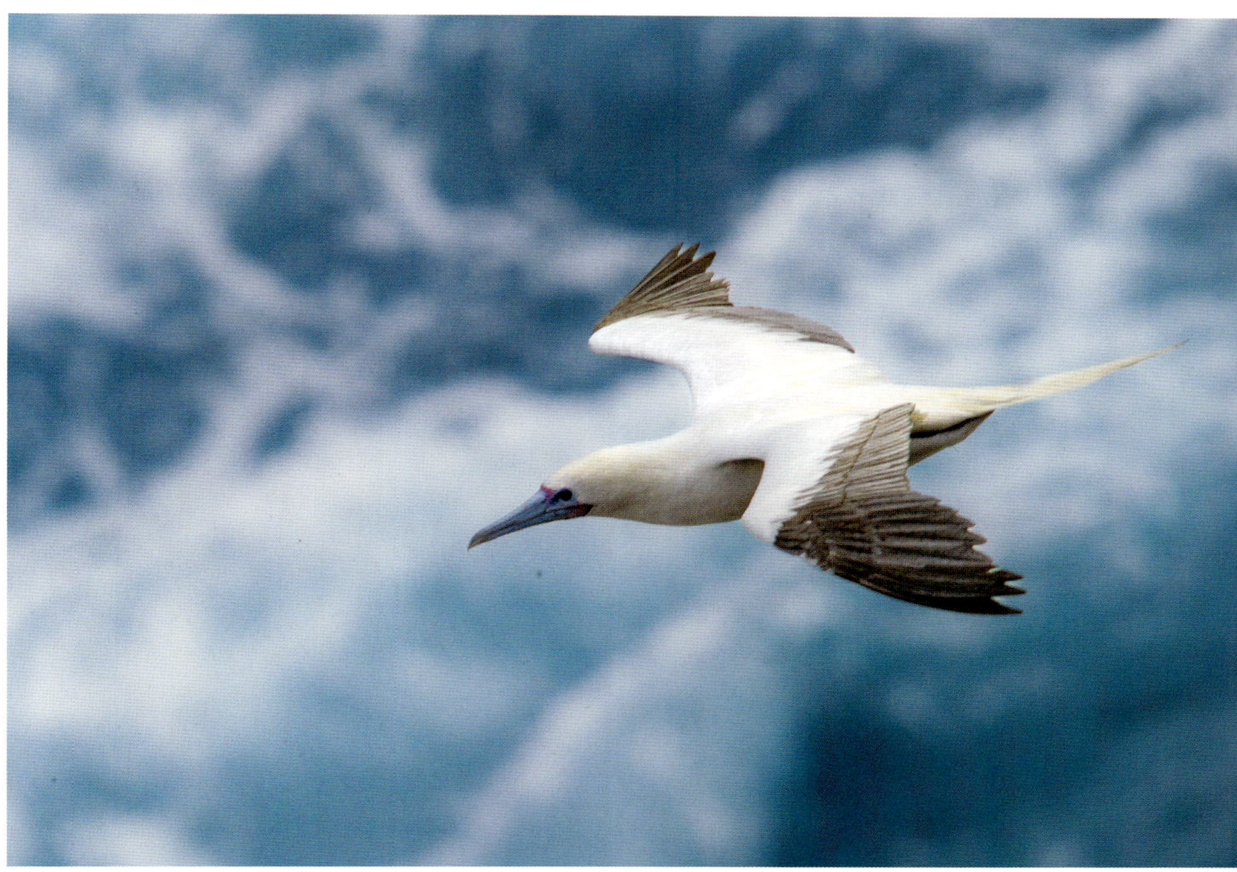

KĪLAUEA POINT NATIONAL WILDLIFE REFUGE (ABOVE) We spotted this red-footed booby off the coast of Kauai while exploring the refuge. I especially love when I get the chance to photograph a bird from an elevated position.

ROCKY MOUNTAIN NATIONAL PARK (OPPOSITE) To celebrate my friend's birthday, we headed up to the park for a weekend of snowshoeing in the mountains. On our way down from Flattop Mountain, we stumbled upon a group of white-tailed ptarmigan. It was my first time seeing them in their winter plumage—a perfect surprise to cap off the adventure.

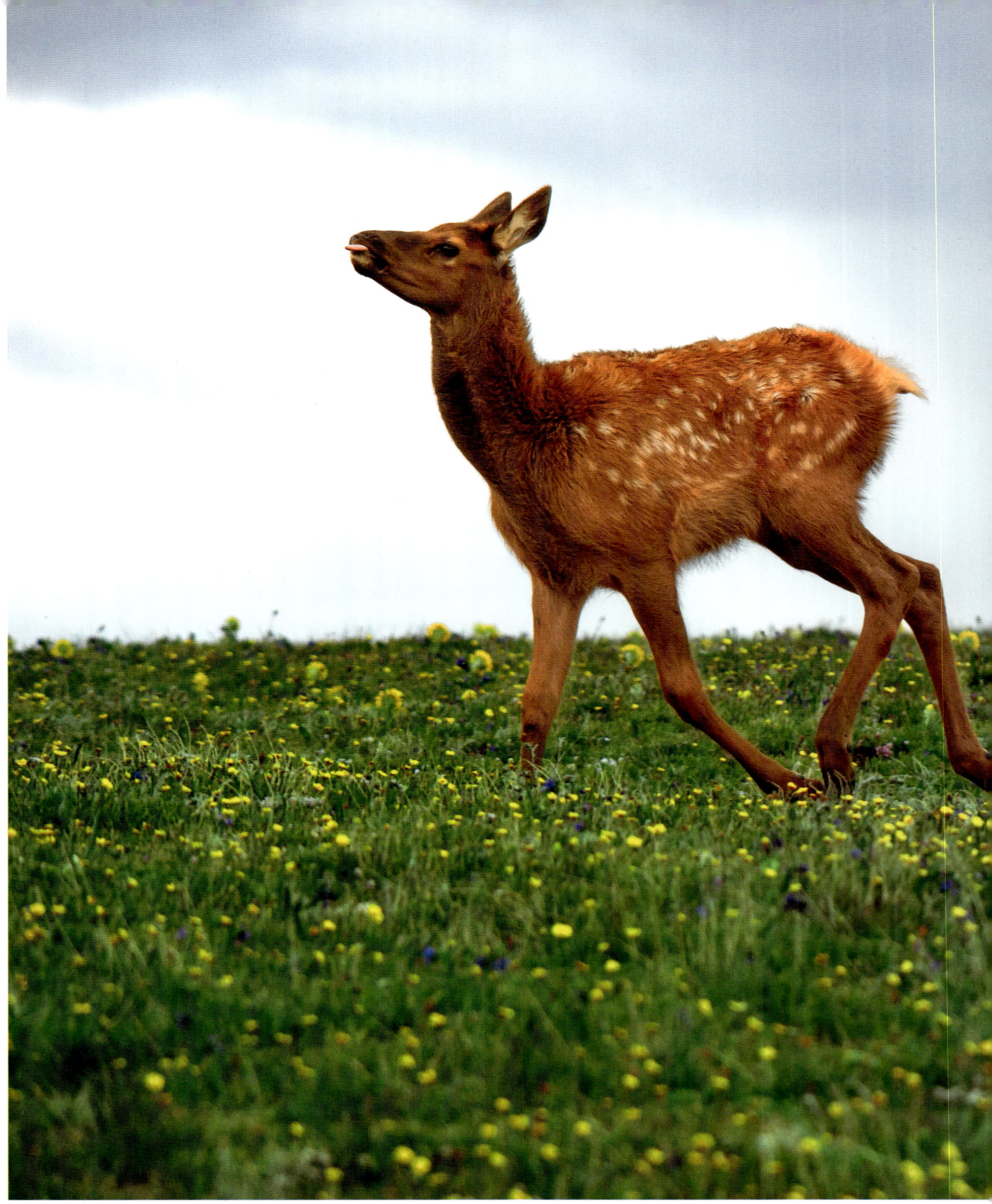

ROCKY MOUNTAIN NATIONAL PARK On a sunny afternoon at 12,000 feet along Trail Ridge Road, two elk calves bounded through the tundra, kicking up tufts of summer grass as they raced across the open expanse.

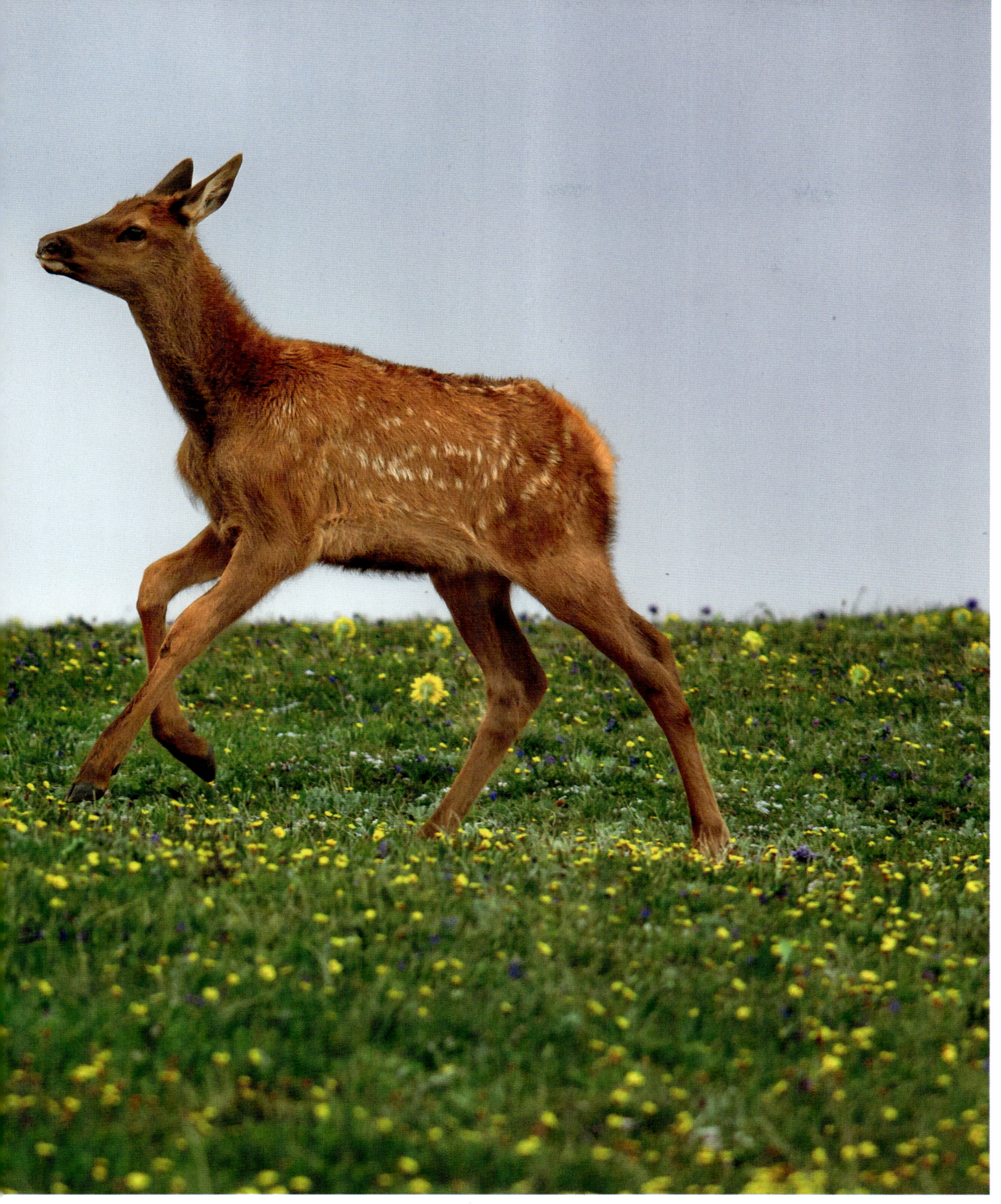

DENALI NATIONAL PARK AND PRESERVE On a trip to Alaska for our friends' wedding, we planned a visit to Wonder Lake to reconnect with our old stomping grounds. While hiking along the shoreline, we stumbled upon one of the largest caribou I've ever seen, grazing peacefully by the water's edge.

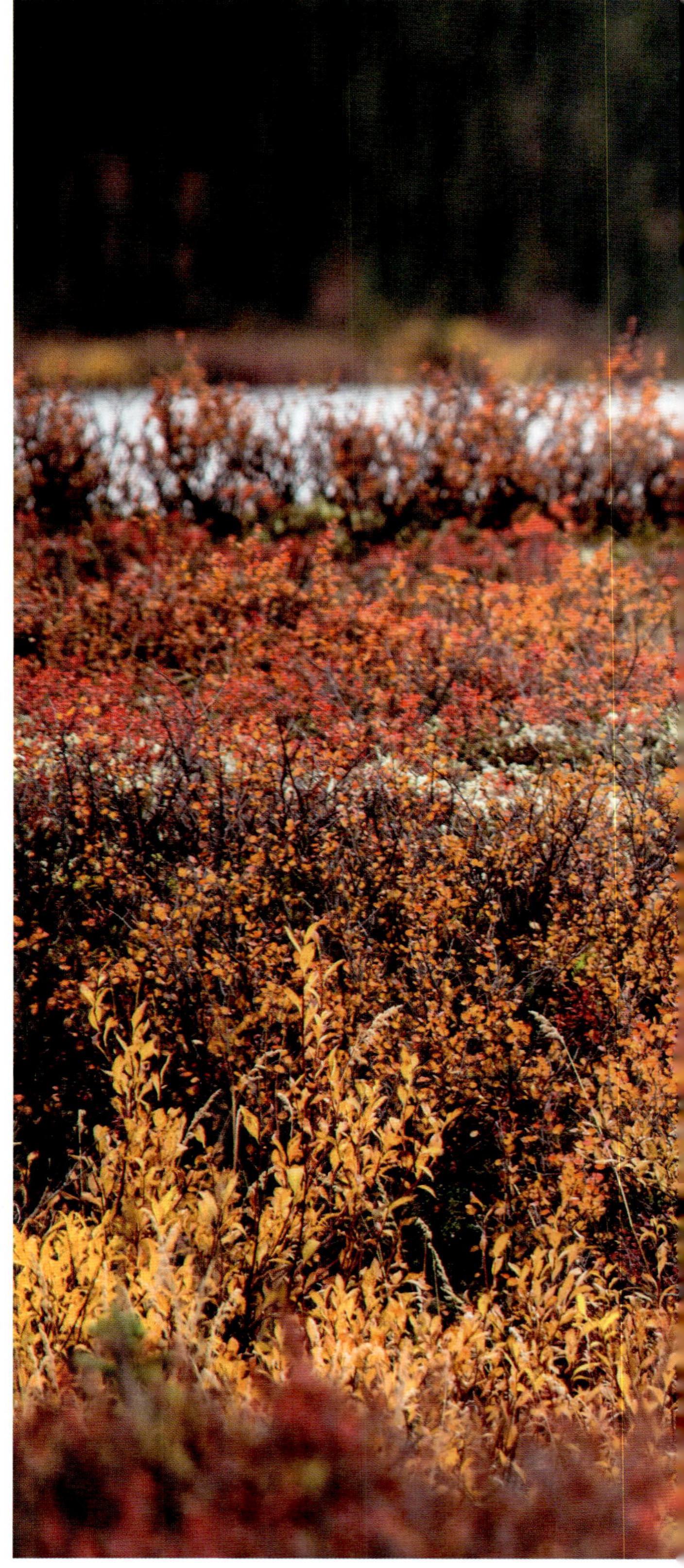

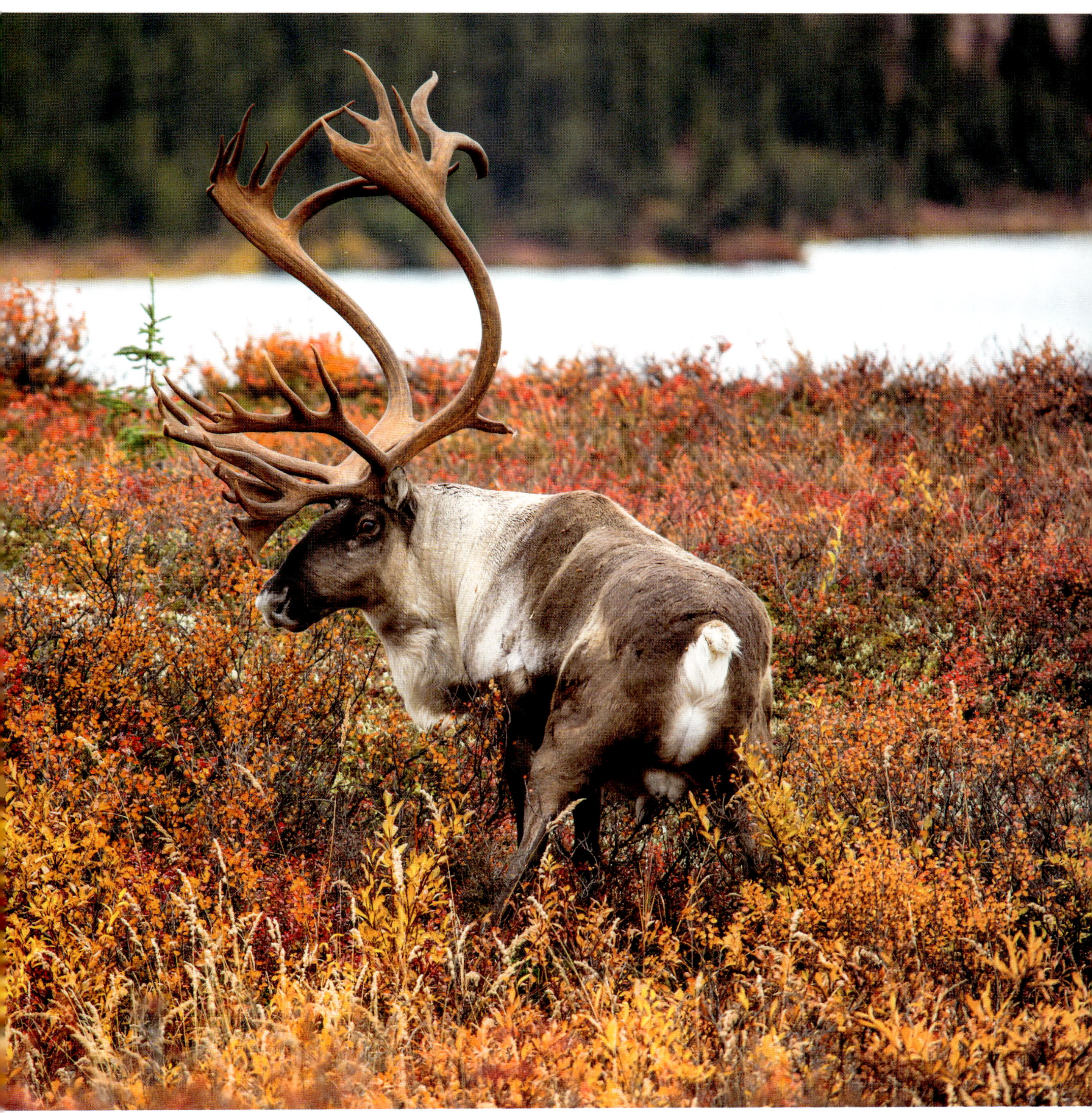

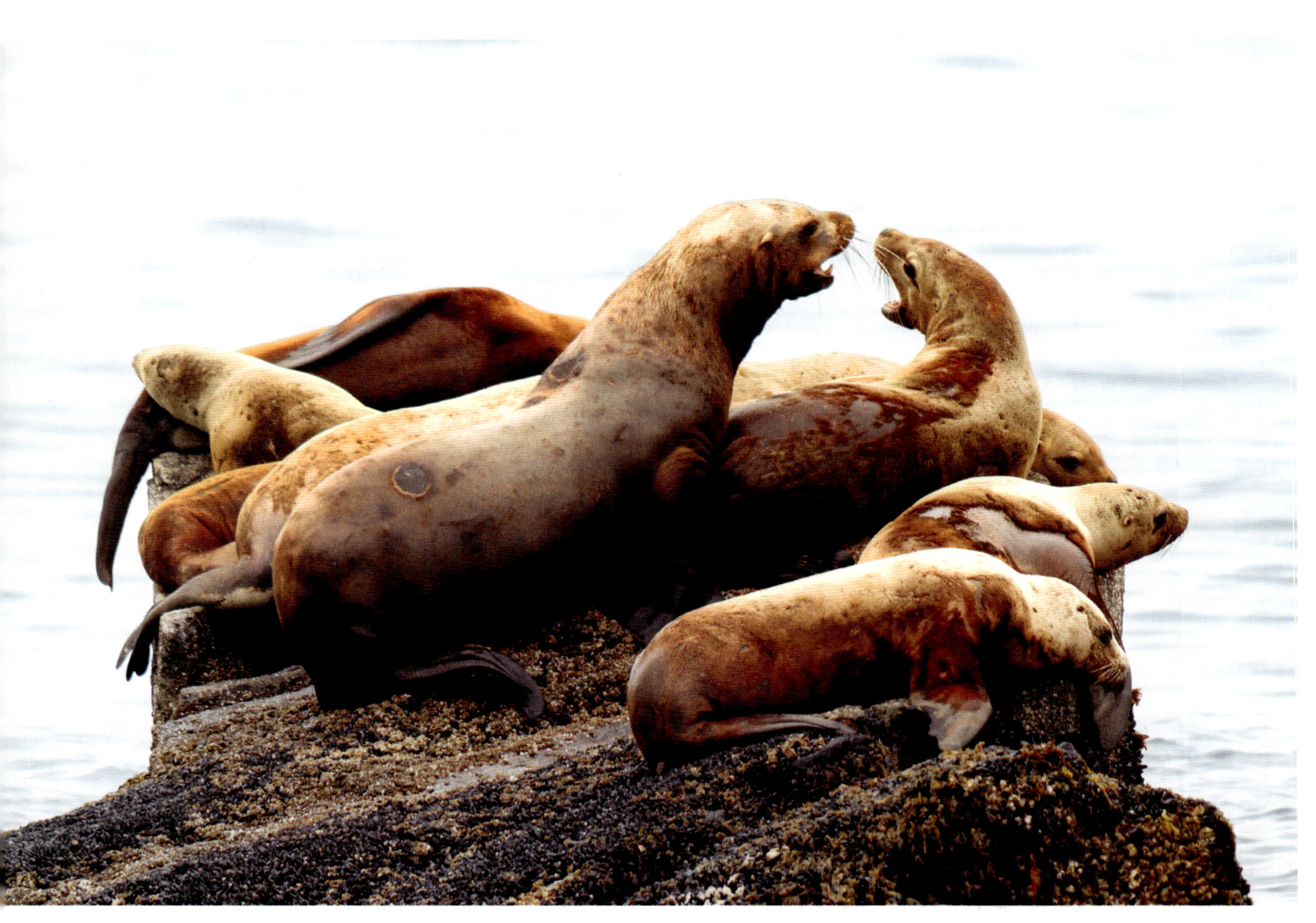

KENAI FJORDS NATIONAL PARK (ABOVE) Steller sea lions jostling for the best napping spot in Resurrection Bay.

REDWOODS NATIONAL AND STATE PARKS (OPPOSITE) While kayaking on the Smith River, we noticed some movement along the shore. As we paddled closer, we found this river otter eating a lamprey. We could hear the sound of the otter crunching through the bones as it feasted.

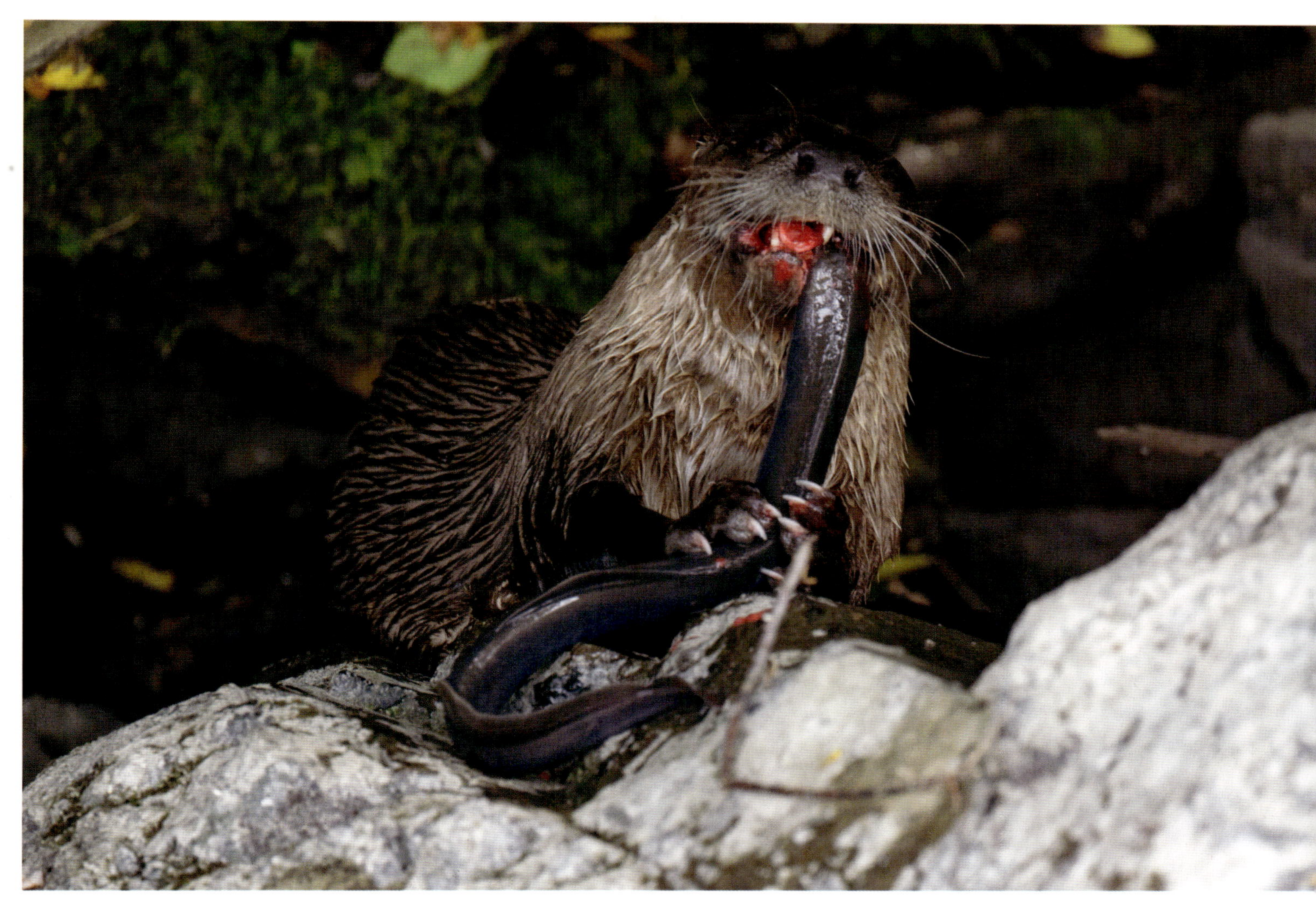

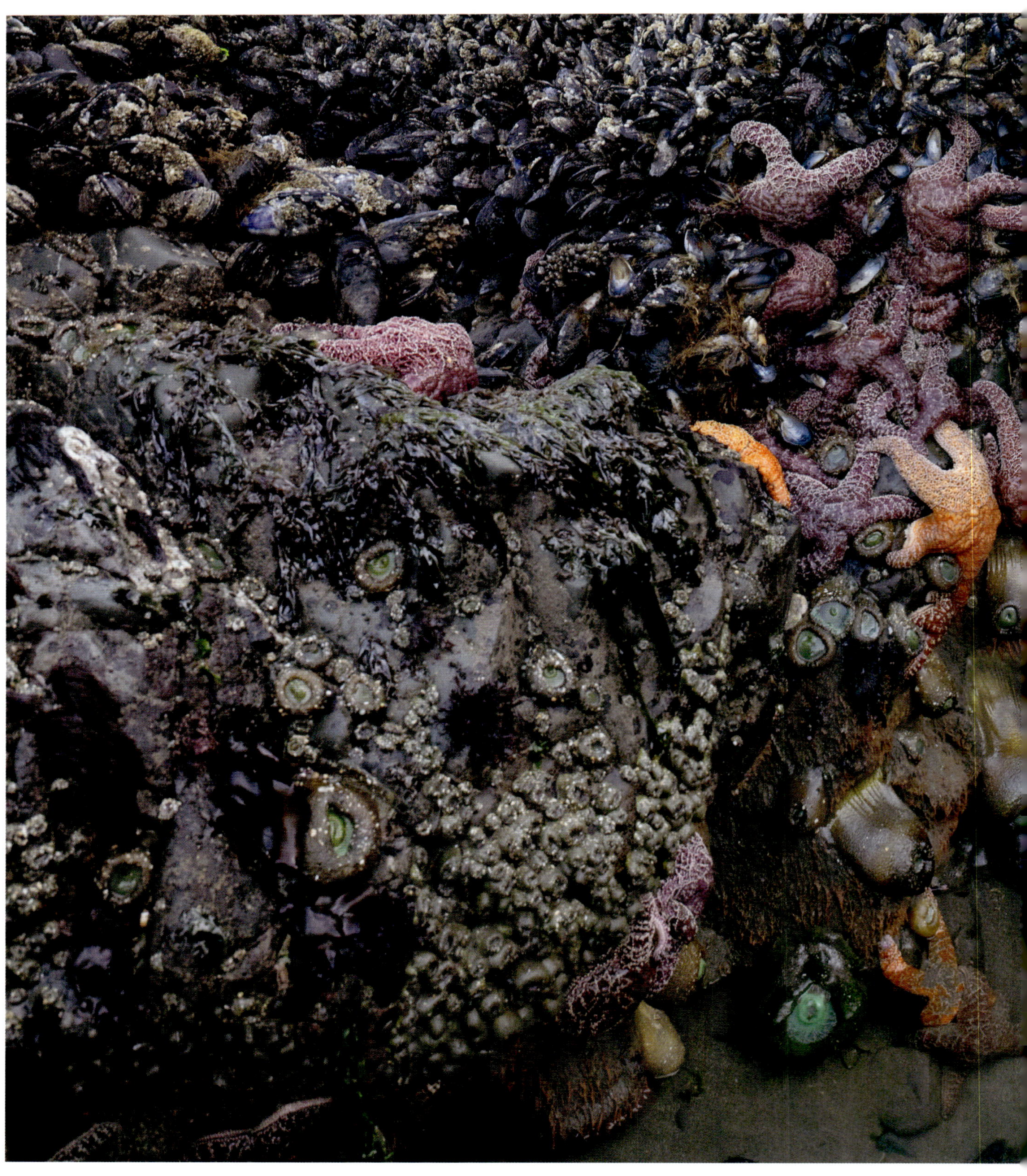

REDWOODS NATIONAL AND STATE PARKS On our last day, conditions were ideal for us to explore the tide pools during sunrise at Enderts Beach.

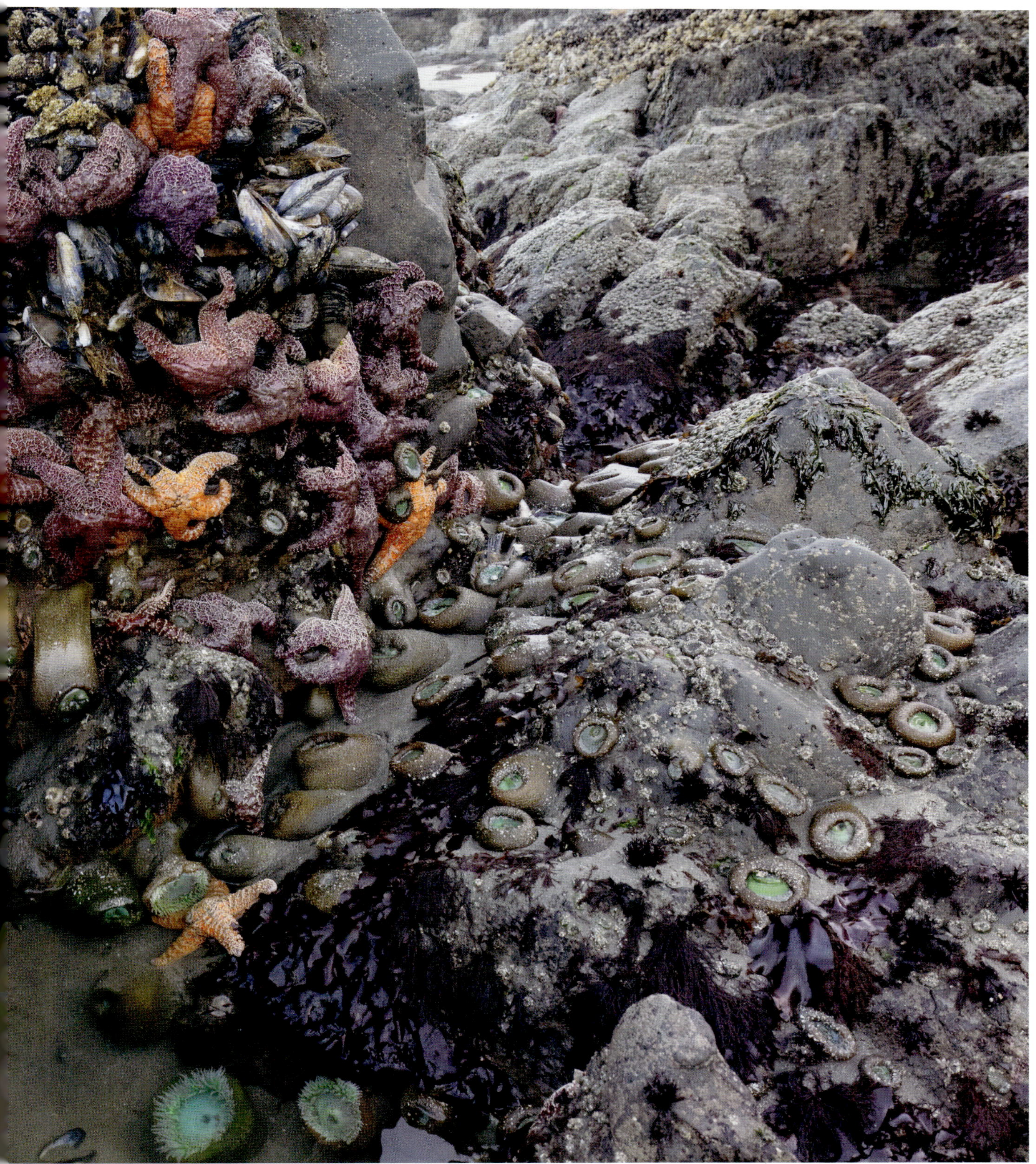

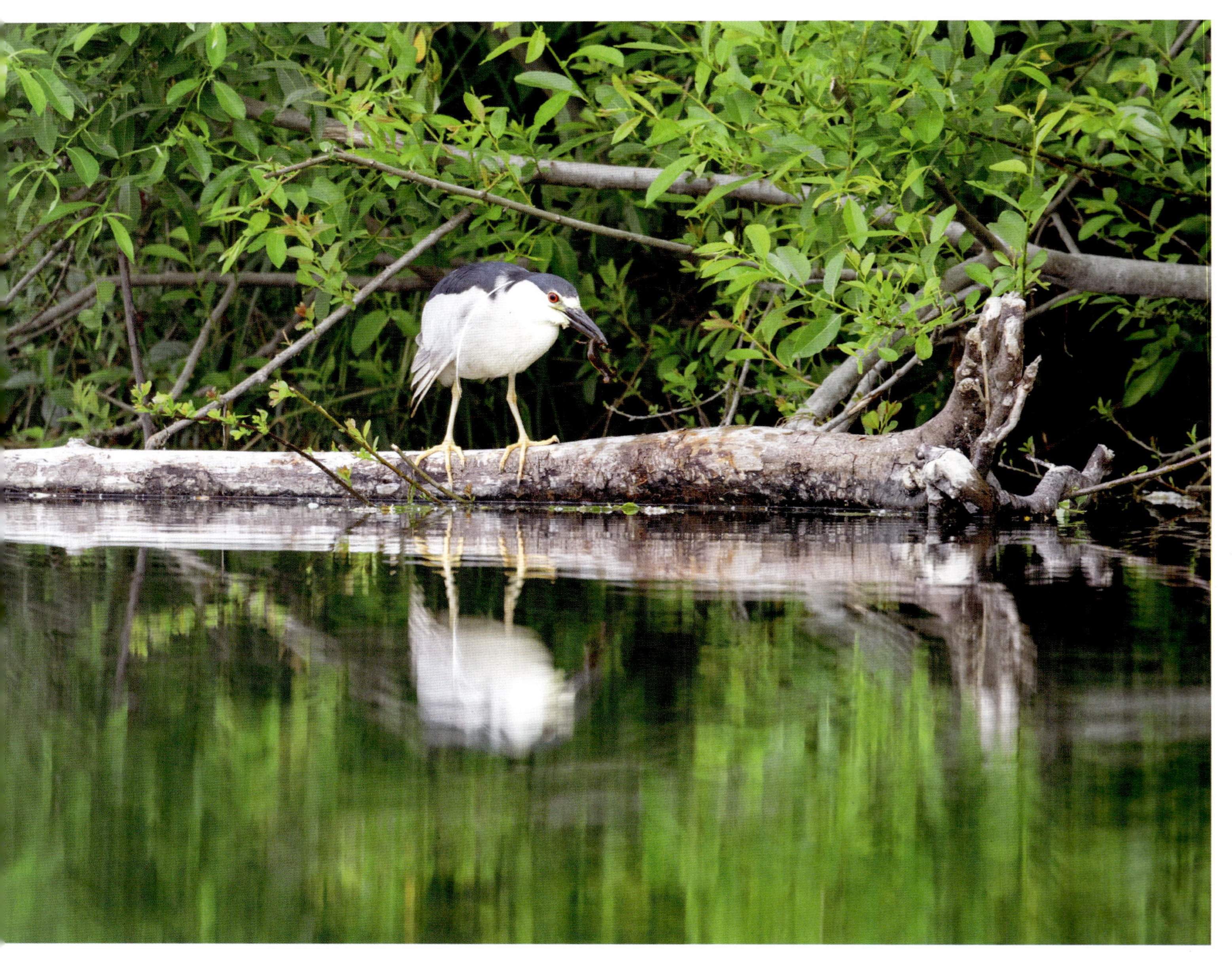

REDWOODS NATIONAL AND STATE PARKS (ABOVE) A black-crowned night heron catches a salamander while perched on a log along the Smith River.

CONGAREE NATIONAL PARK (OPPOSITE) A river cooter suns itself on a log along Cedar Creek.

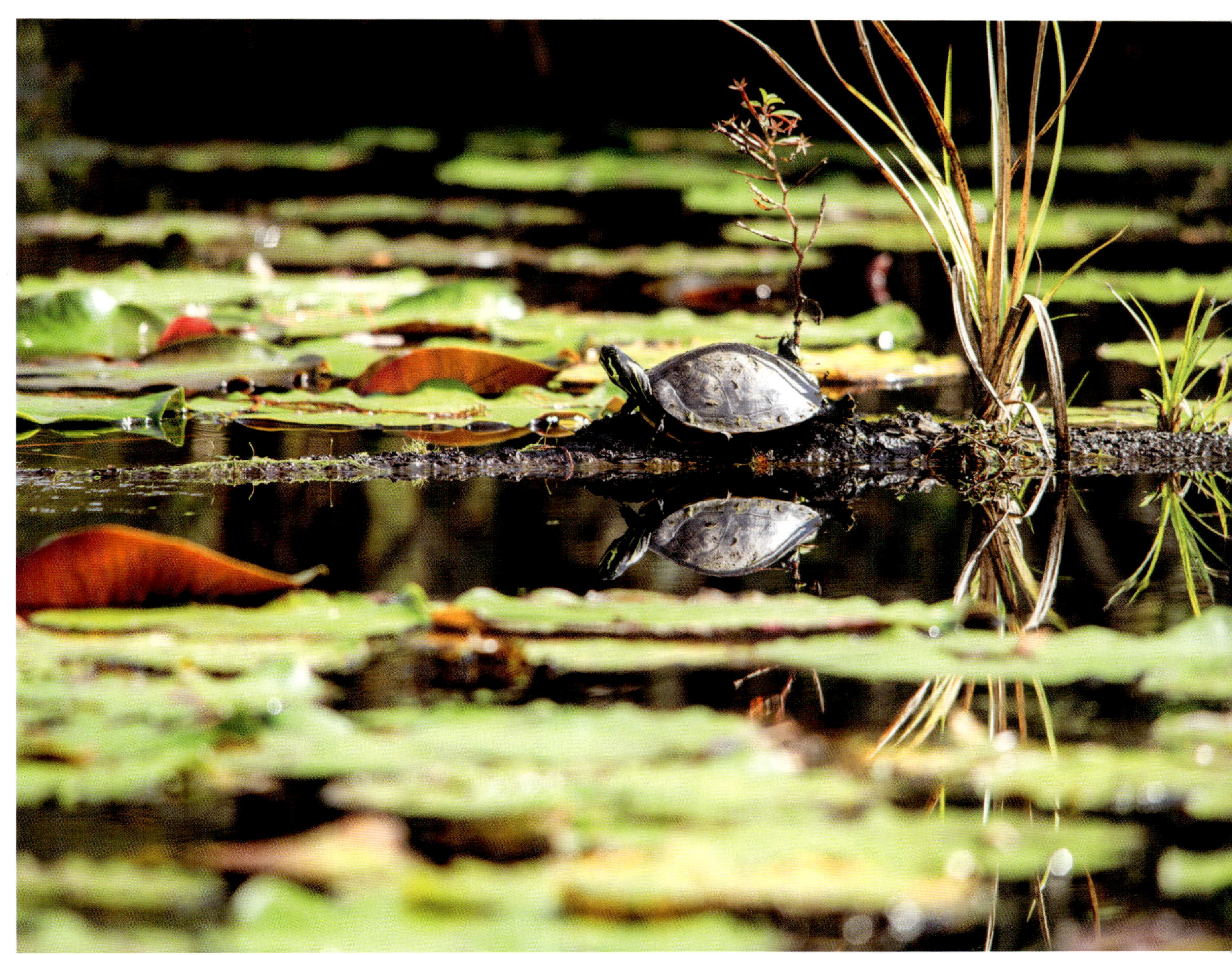

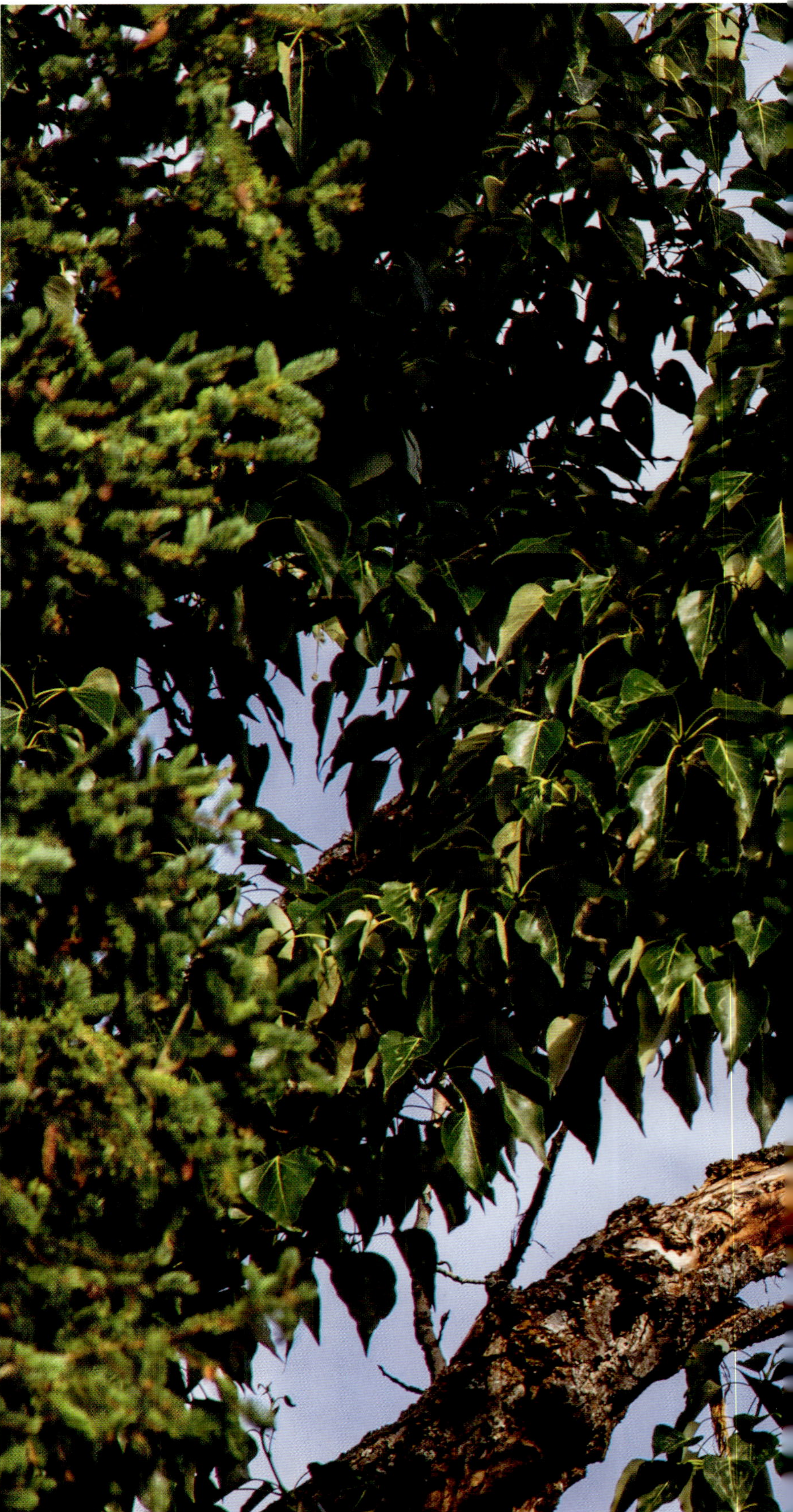

GLACIER NATIONAL PARK Shortly after it delivered a fish to its chick, this adult bald eagle perched on a nearby branch, watching its young enjoy their meal.

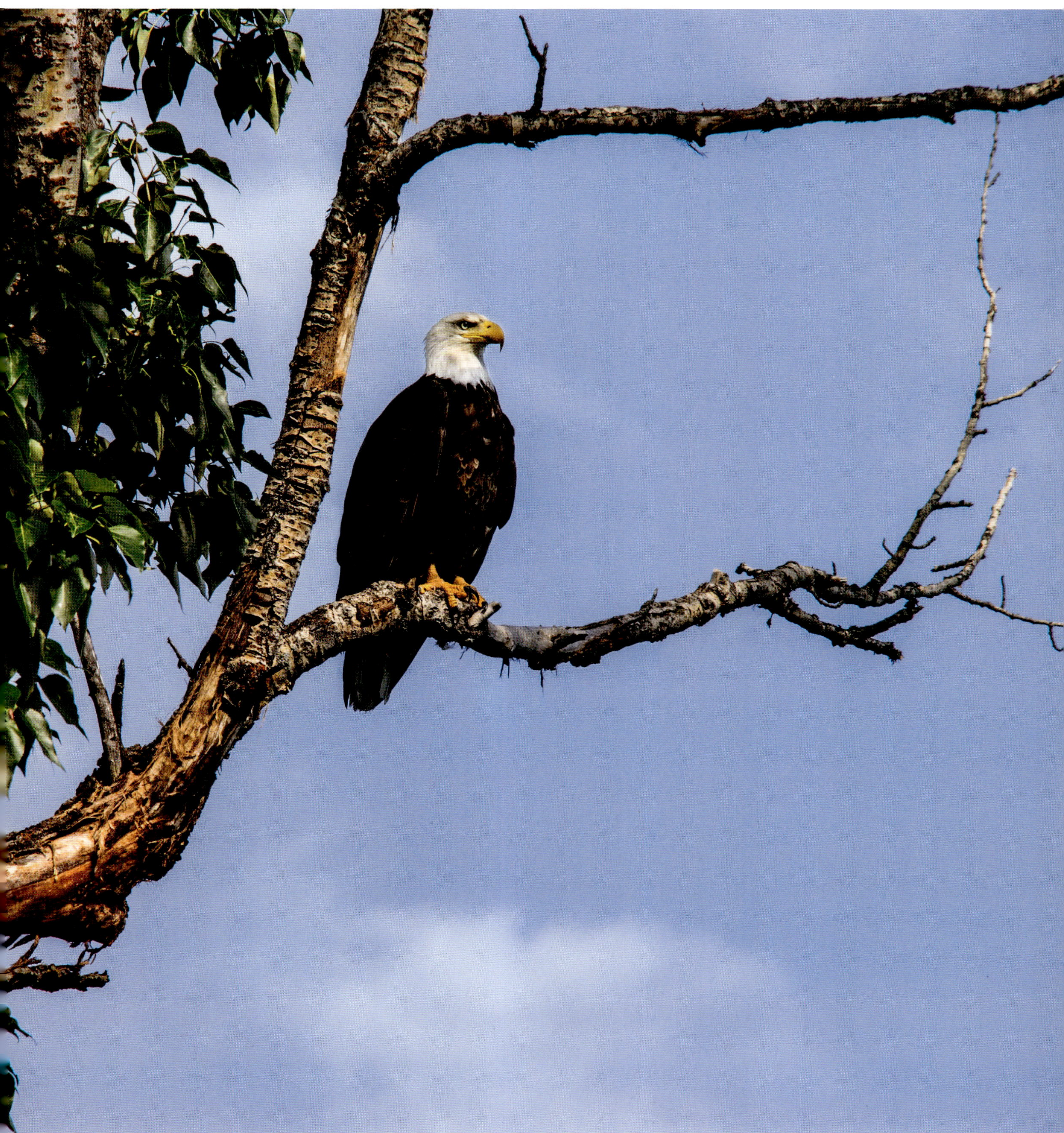

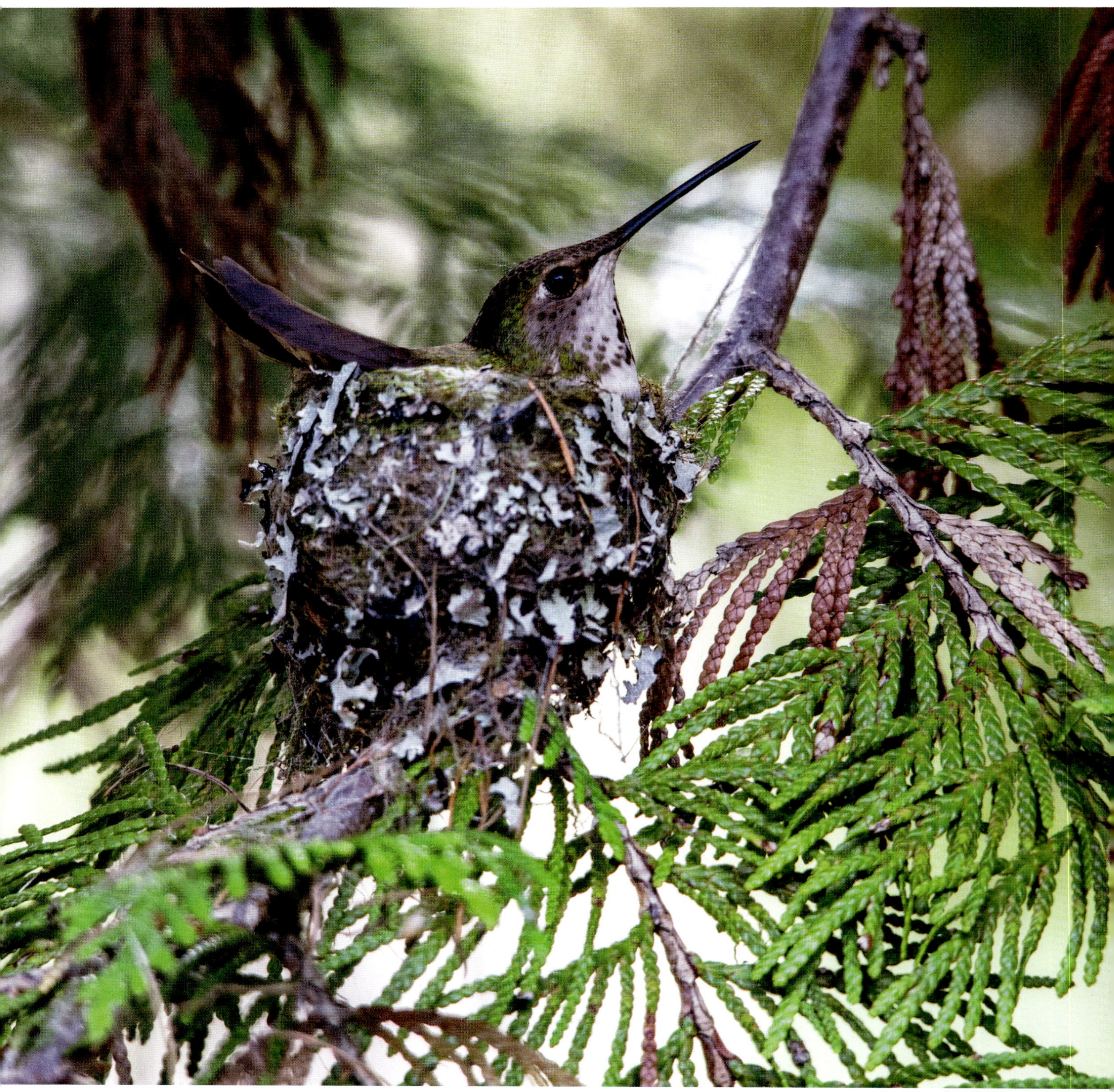

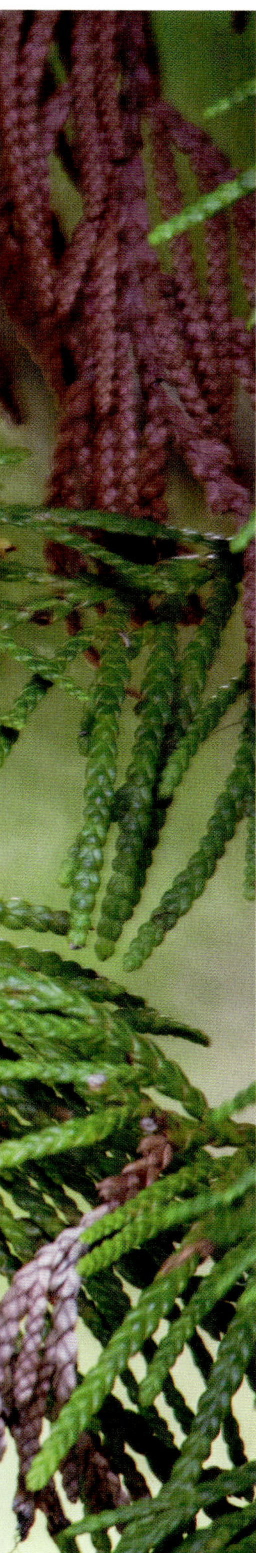

HULLS GULCH RESERVE (BELOW) On a spring road trip to Boise, Idaho, we took our dog, Toklat, for a hike through a local nature reserve. Along the way, we spotted a handful of birds, including a vibrant yellow warbler and a striking lazuli bunting—small but dazzling highlights of the day.

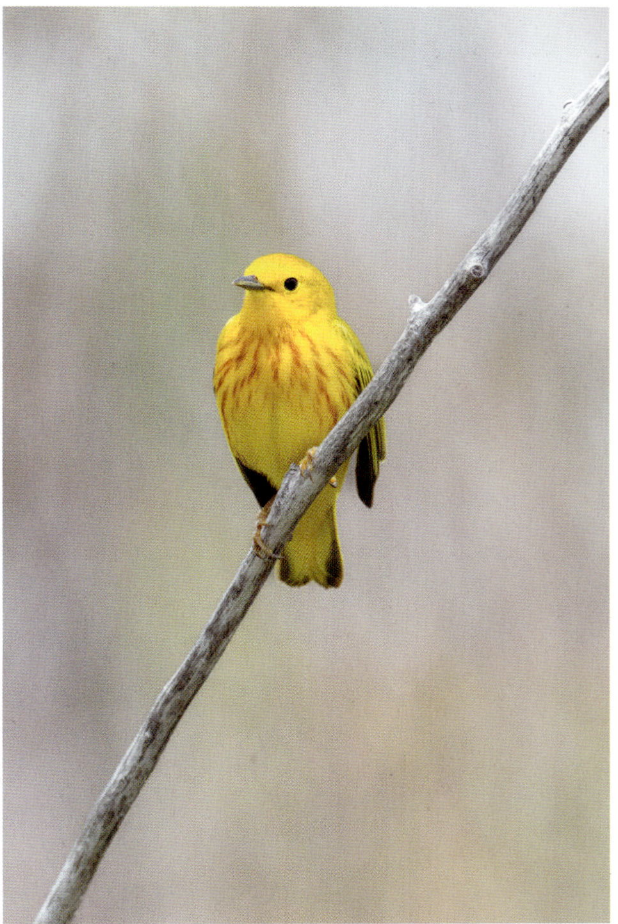

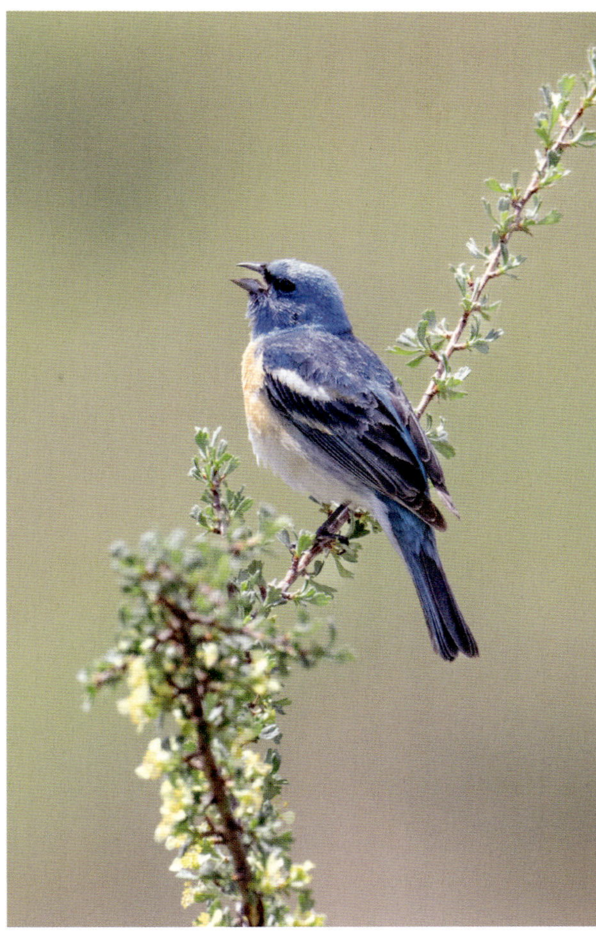

GLACIER NATIONAL PARK (OPPOSITE) I've seen plenty of bird nests over the years, but this rufous hummingbird nest—no bigger than a golf ball—stands out as my all-time favorite.

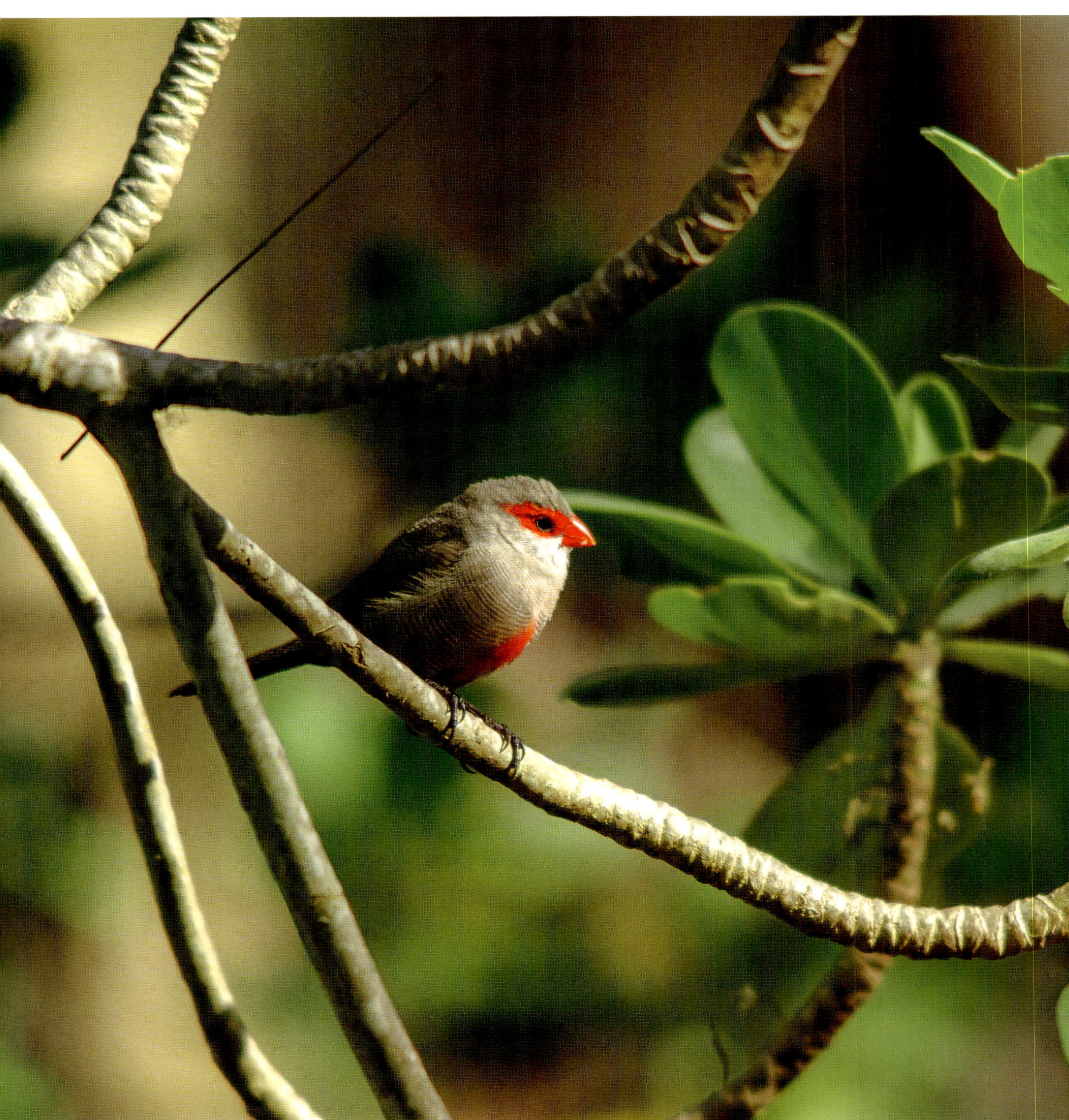

HAWAI'I VOLCANOES NATIONAL PARK A common waxbill perched in the afternoon sunlight.

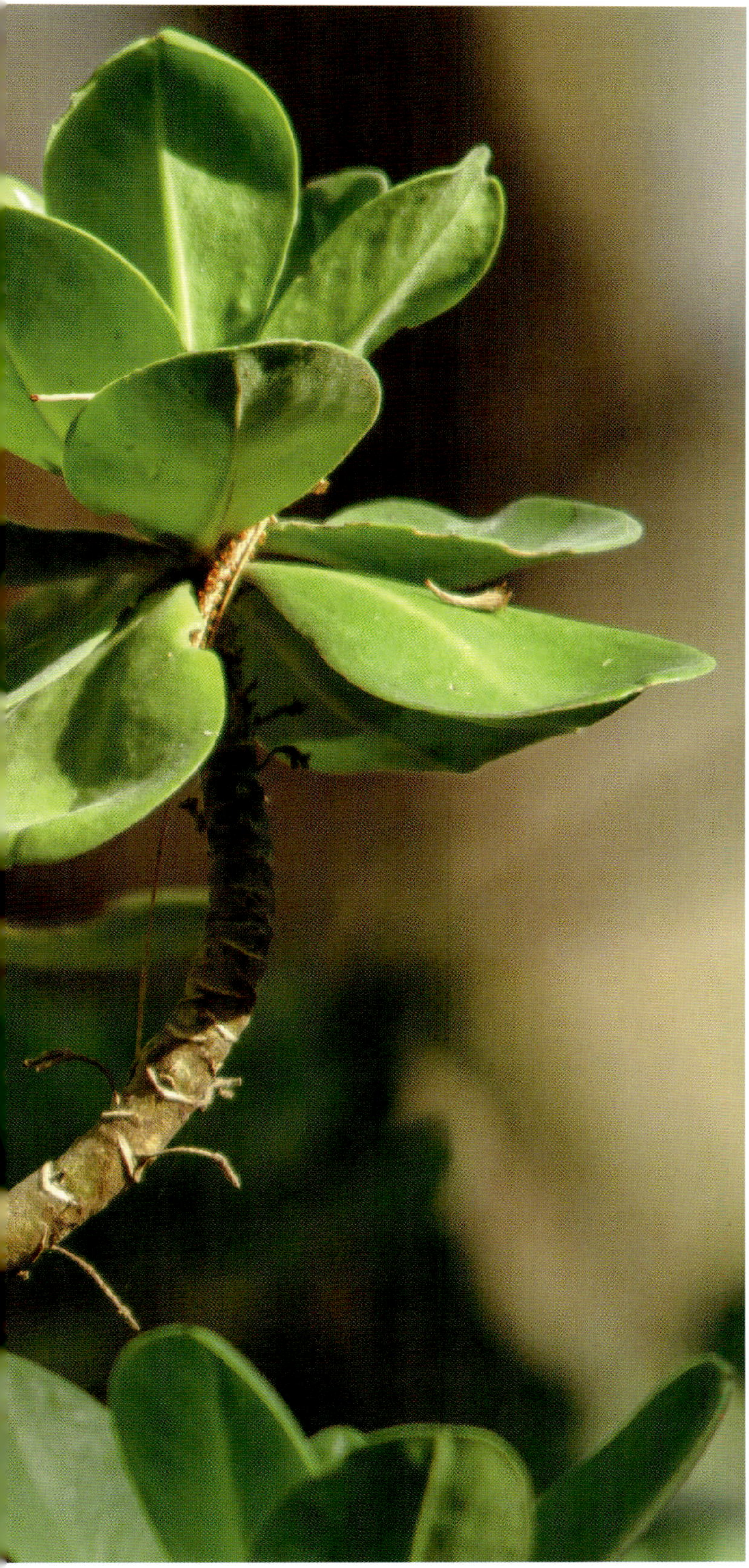

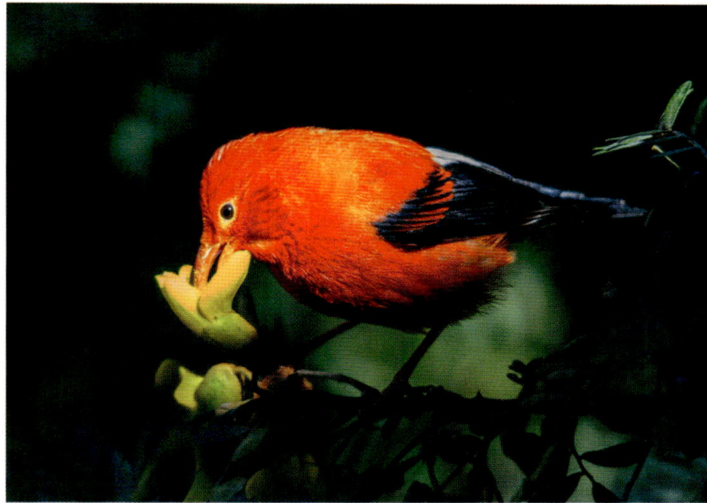

HALEAKALĀ NATIONAL PARK (ABOVE) We spent hours birding, searching specifically for the endemic ʻiʻiwi. But, of course, it wasn't until we returned to camp to make breakfast that one landed right next to us—proving once again that nature has its own timing.

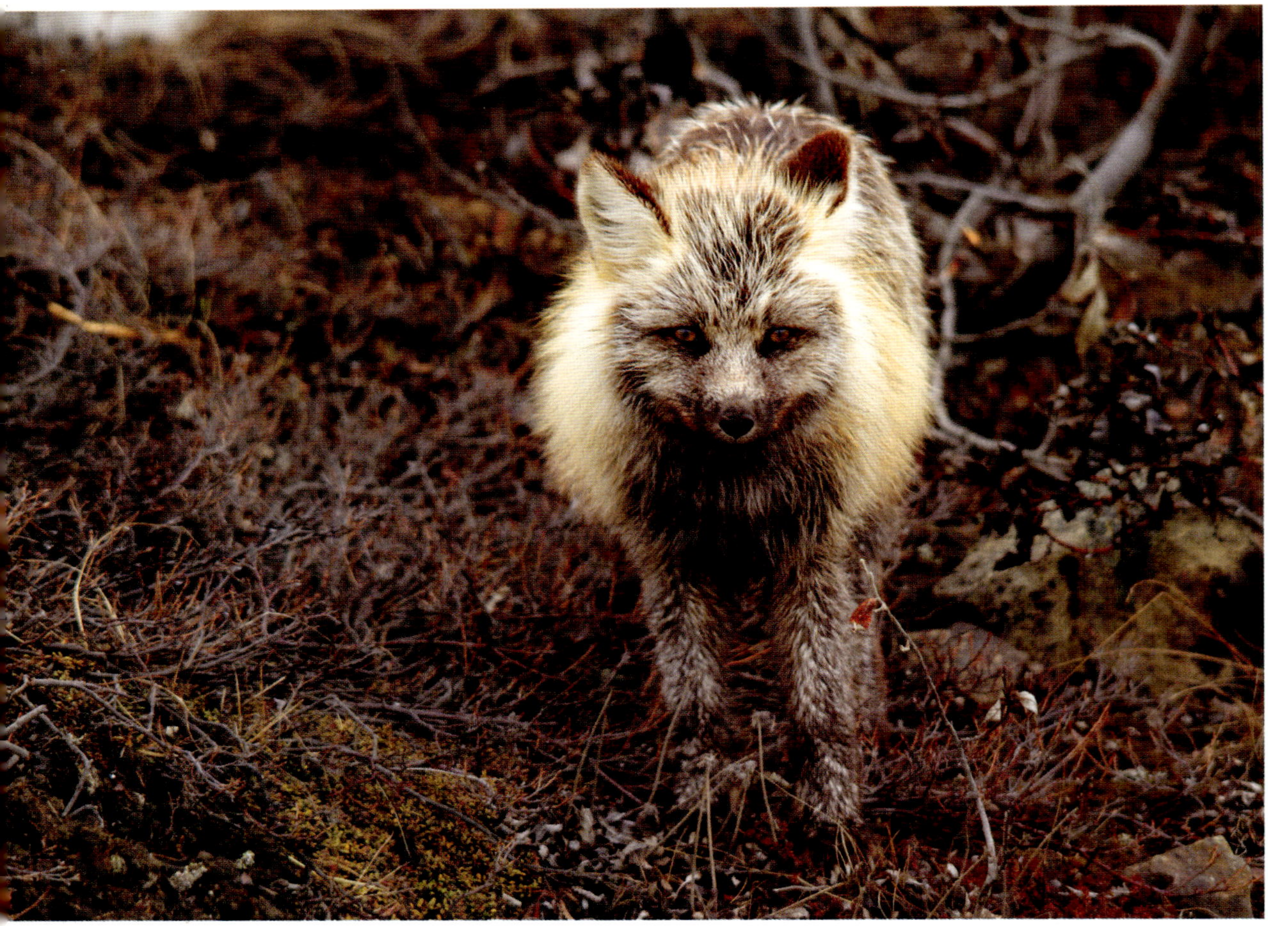

DENALI NATIONAL PARK AND PRESERVE (ABOVE) This uniquely colored red fox spent its time hunting near my house in the park. After a few weeks of seeing it, I was finally able to grab a photo.

BLACK CANYON OF THE GUNNISON NATIONAL PARK (OPPOSITE) While on a morning birding hike on the North Rim, we were briefly visited by this curious coyote.

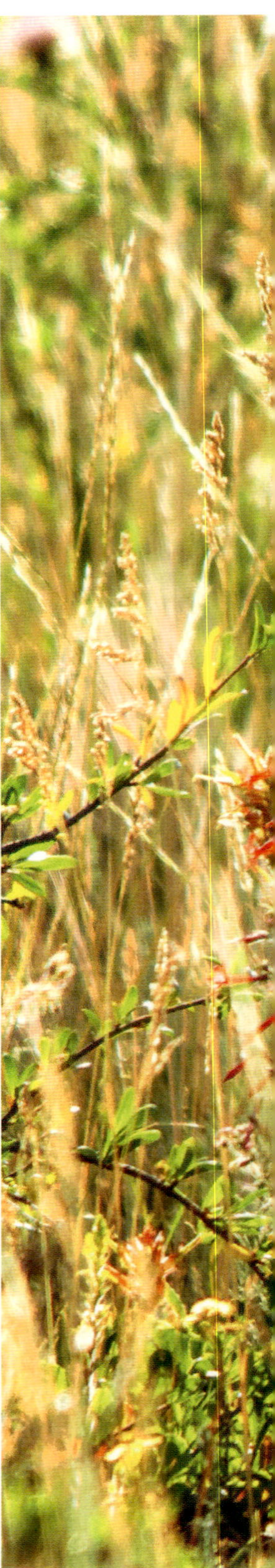

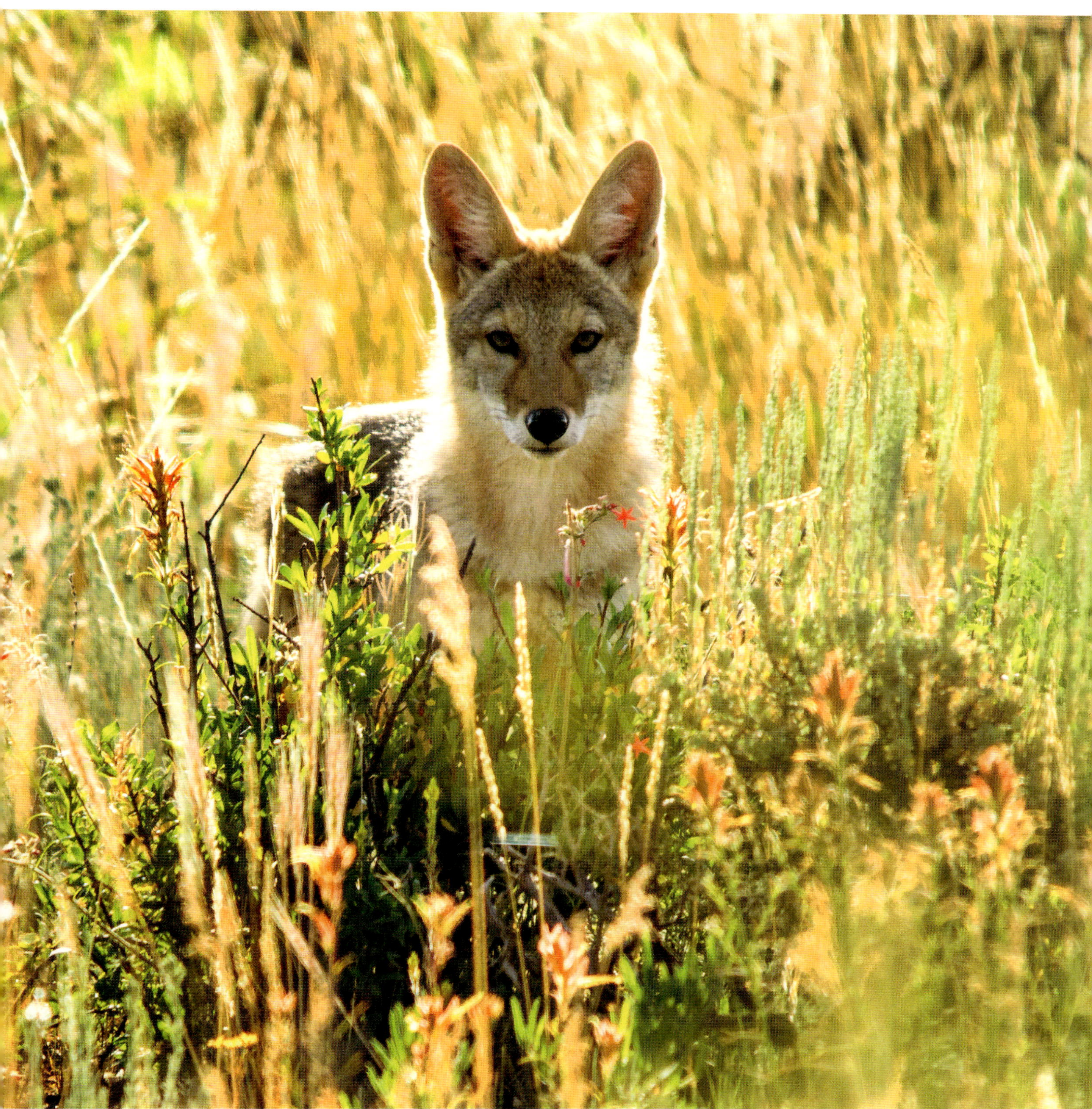

LAVA BEDS NATIONAL MONUMENT
From a distance, we couldn't tell what kind of bird it was. As we got closer, we were surprised to find a chipmunk, precariously perched on the end of a branch, swaying with the wind.

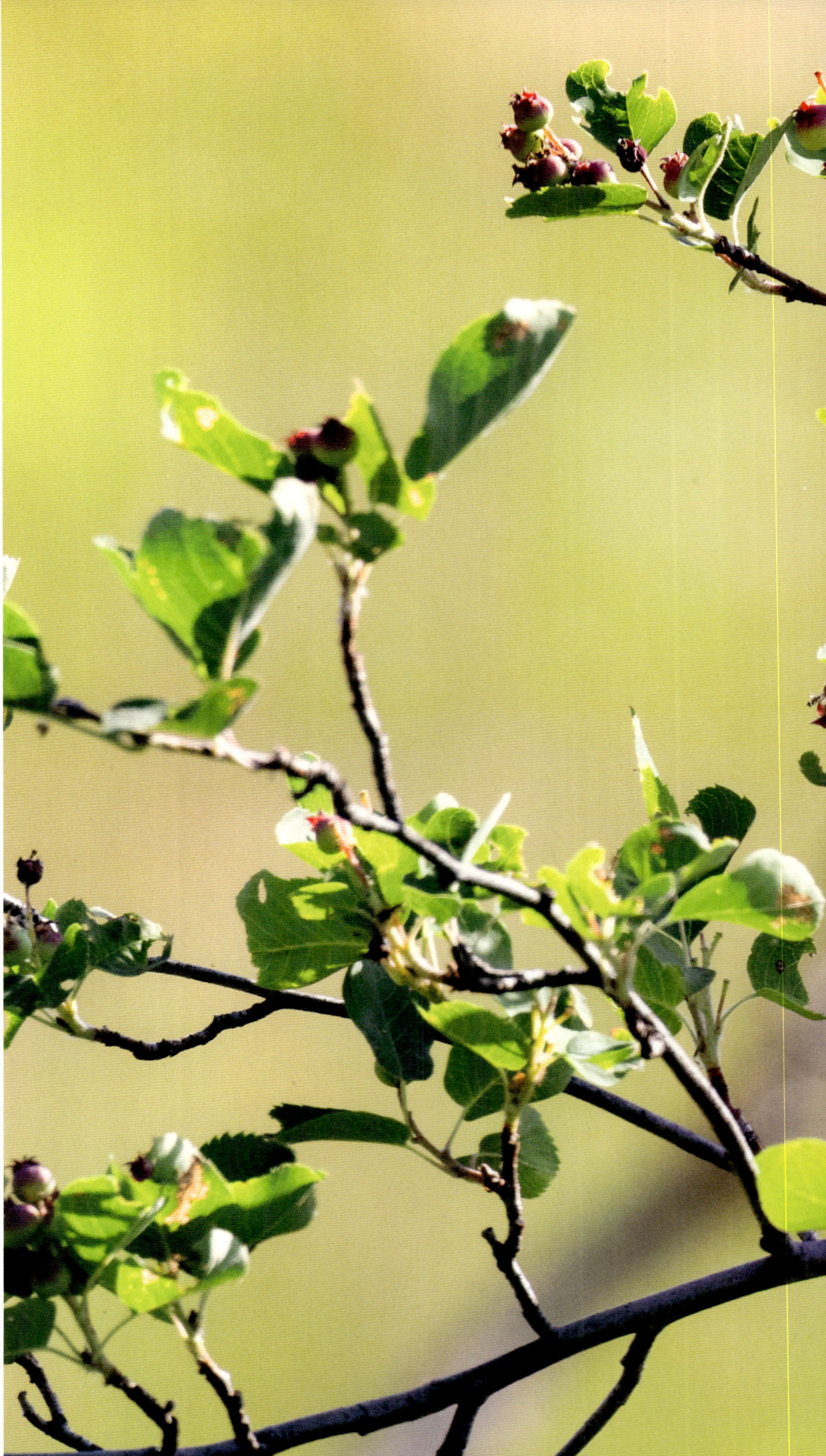

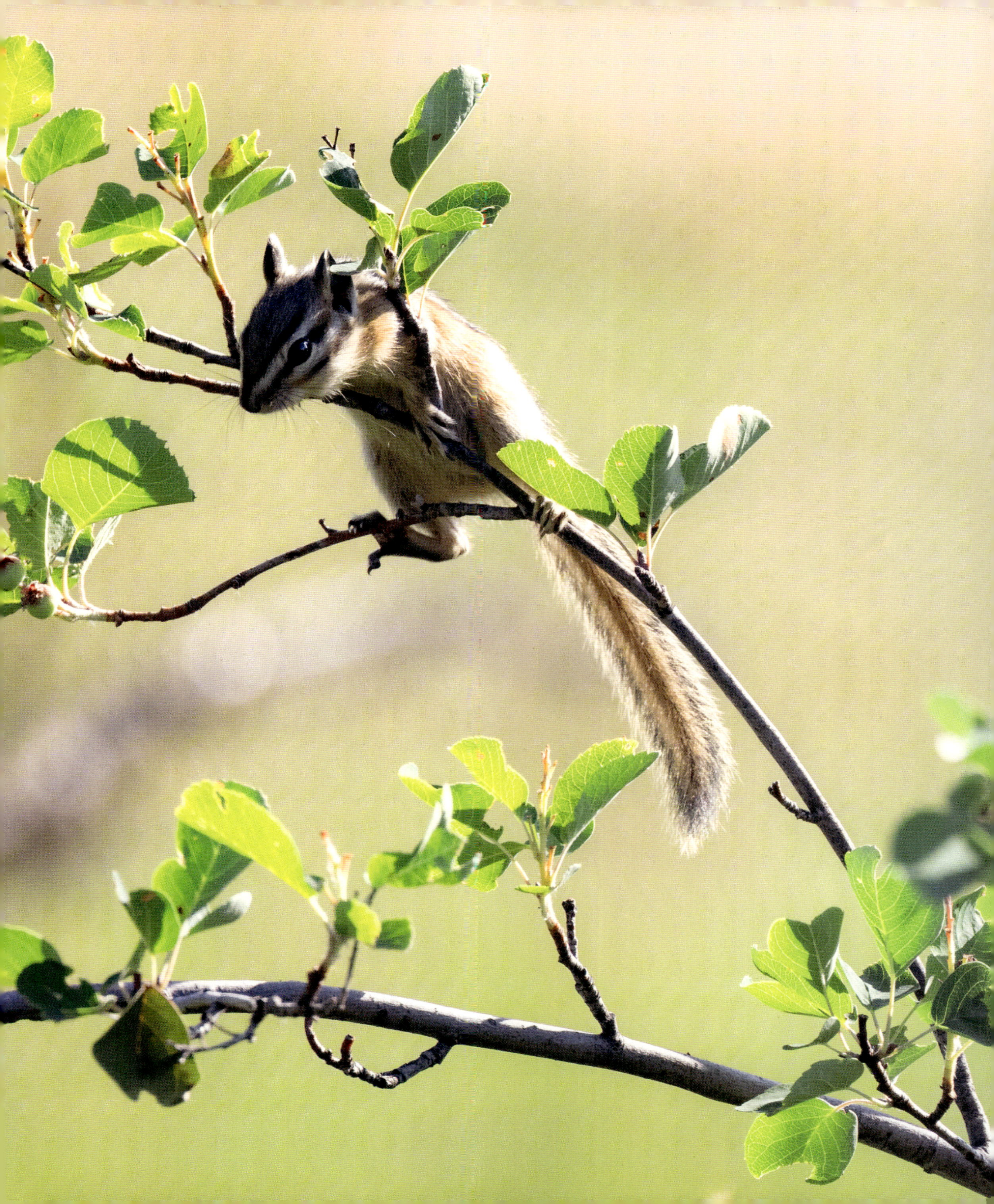

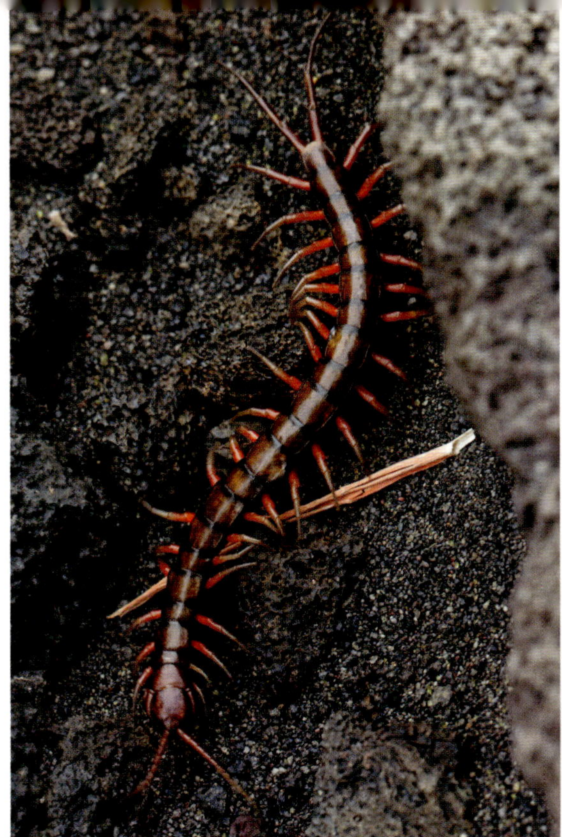

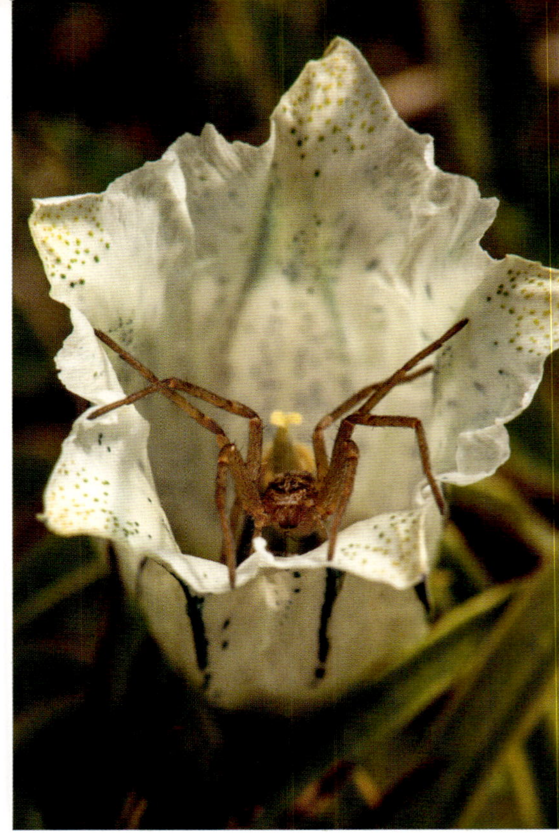

HAWAI'I VOLCANOES NATIONAL PARK (TOP LEFT) We spotted this centipede while backpacking along the coast.

DENALI NATIONAL PARK AND PRESERVE (TOP RIGHT) A wolf spider sought shelter from the wind inside a glaucous gentian.

ROCKY MOUNTAIN NATIONAL PARK A ladybug perched delicately on the petal of a wood lily.

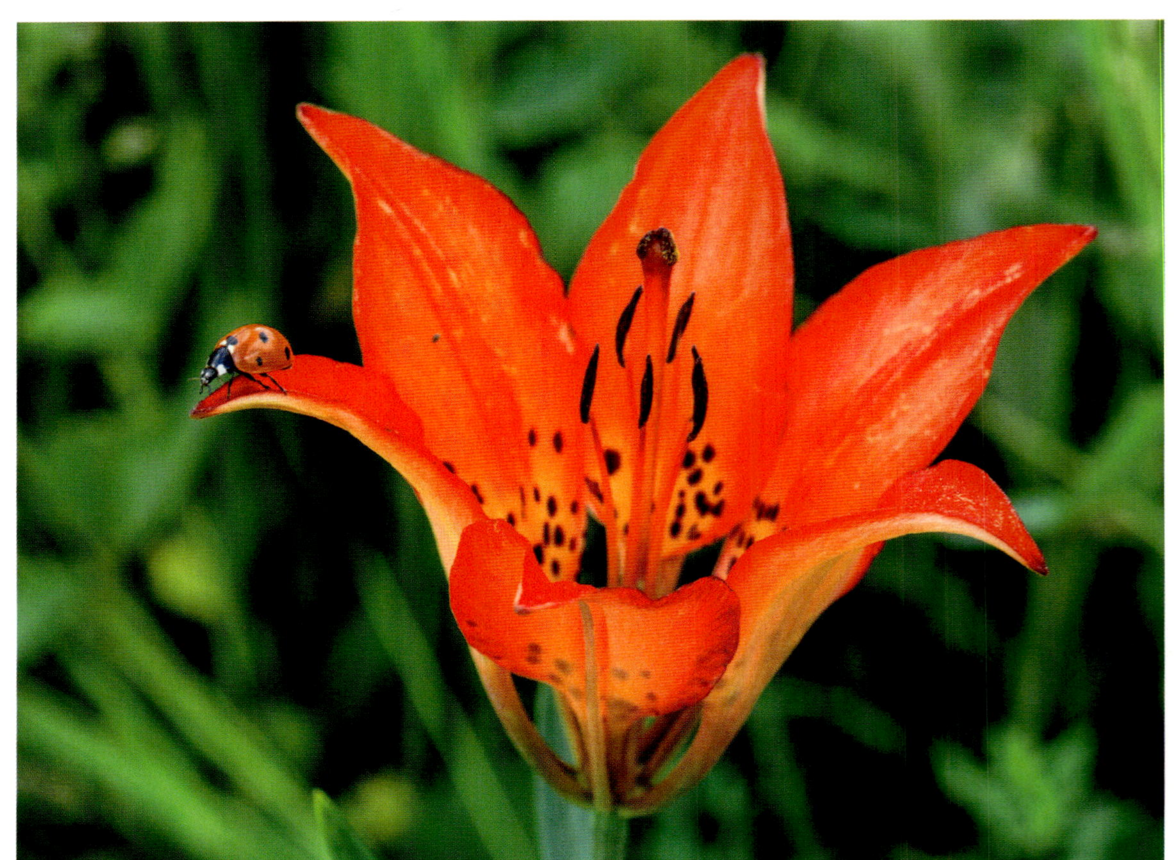

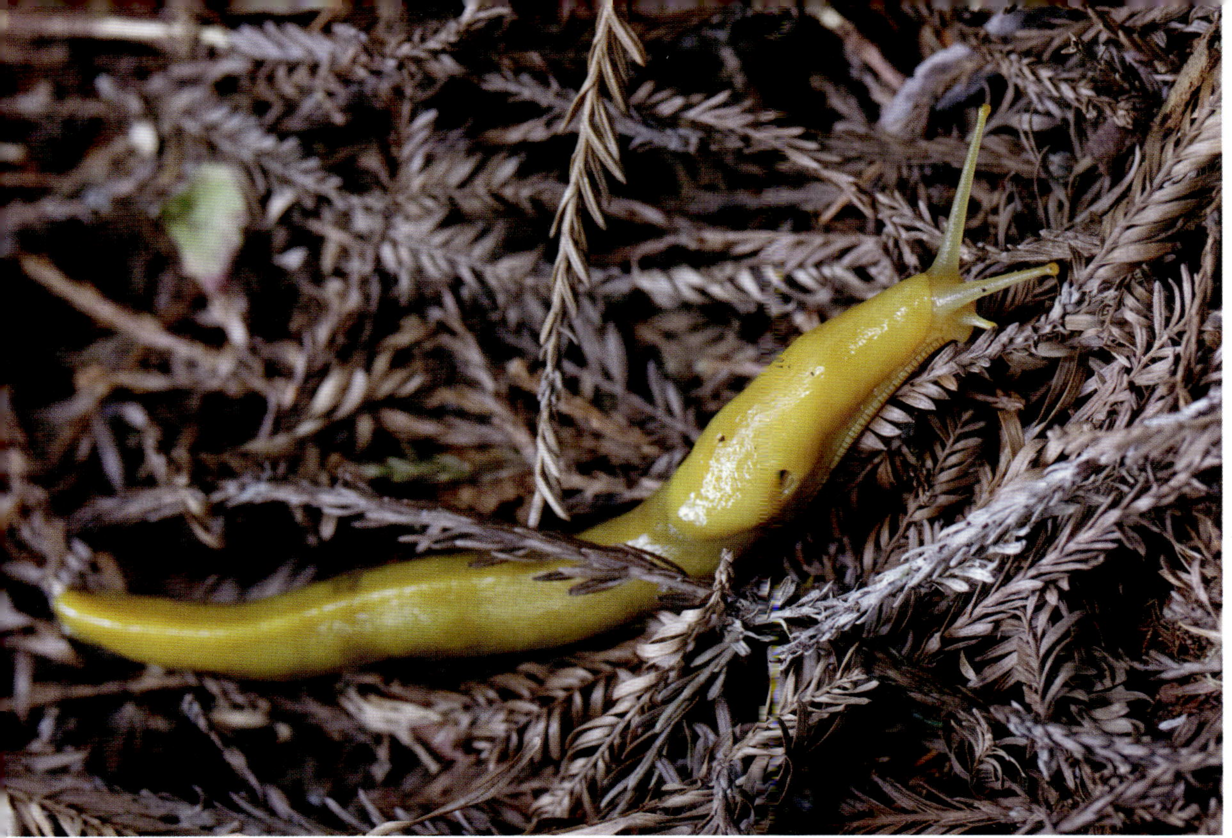

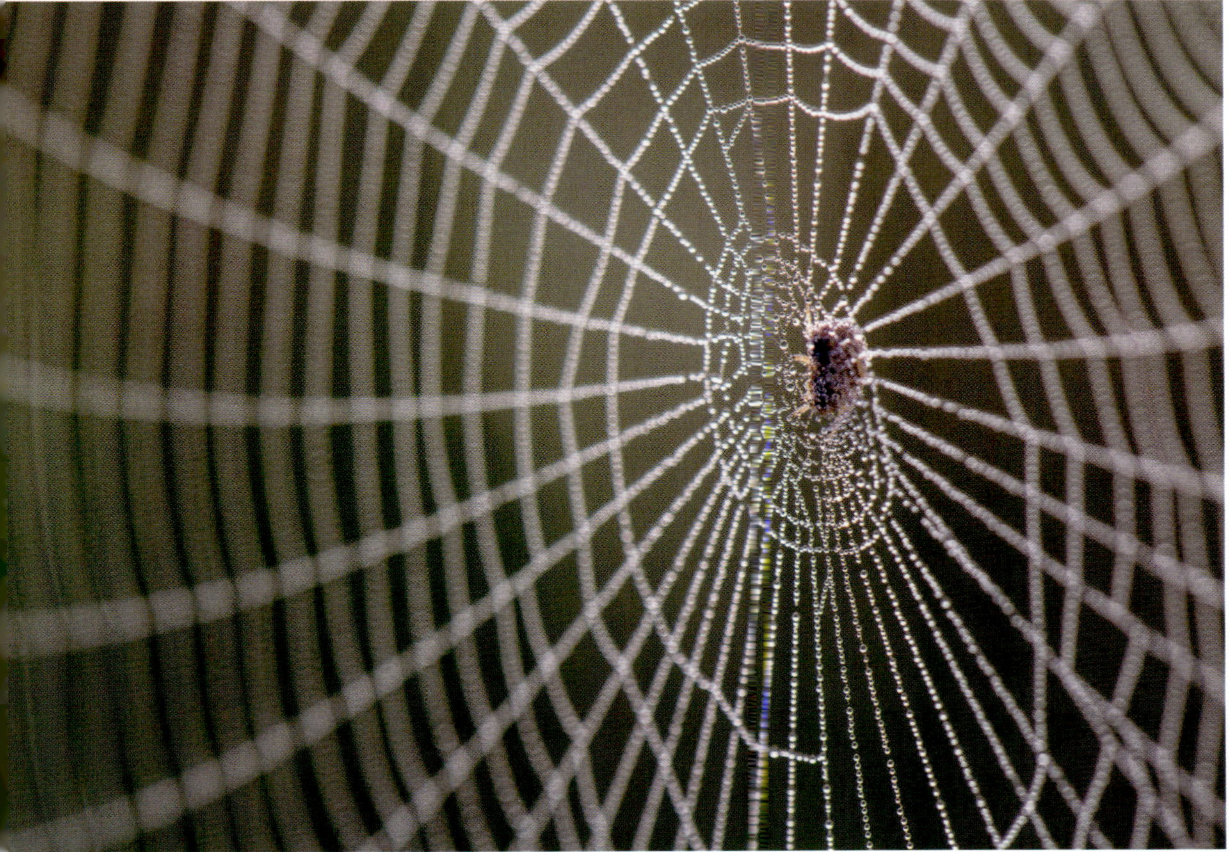

REDWOODS NATIONAL AND STATE PARKS (TOP)
A banana slug glided through the lush understory of a redwood grove.

GREAT SMOKY MOUNTAINS NATIONAL PARK (BOTTOM)
Morning dew collected on a spider and web at Cades Cove.

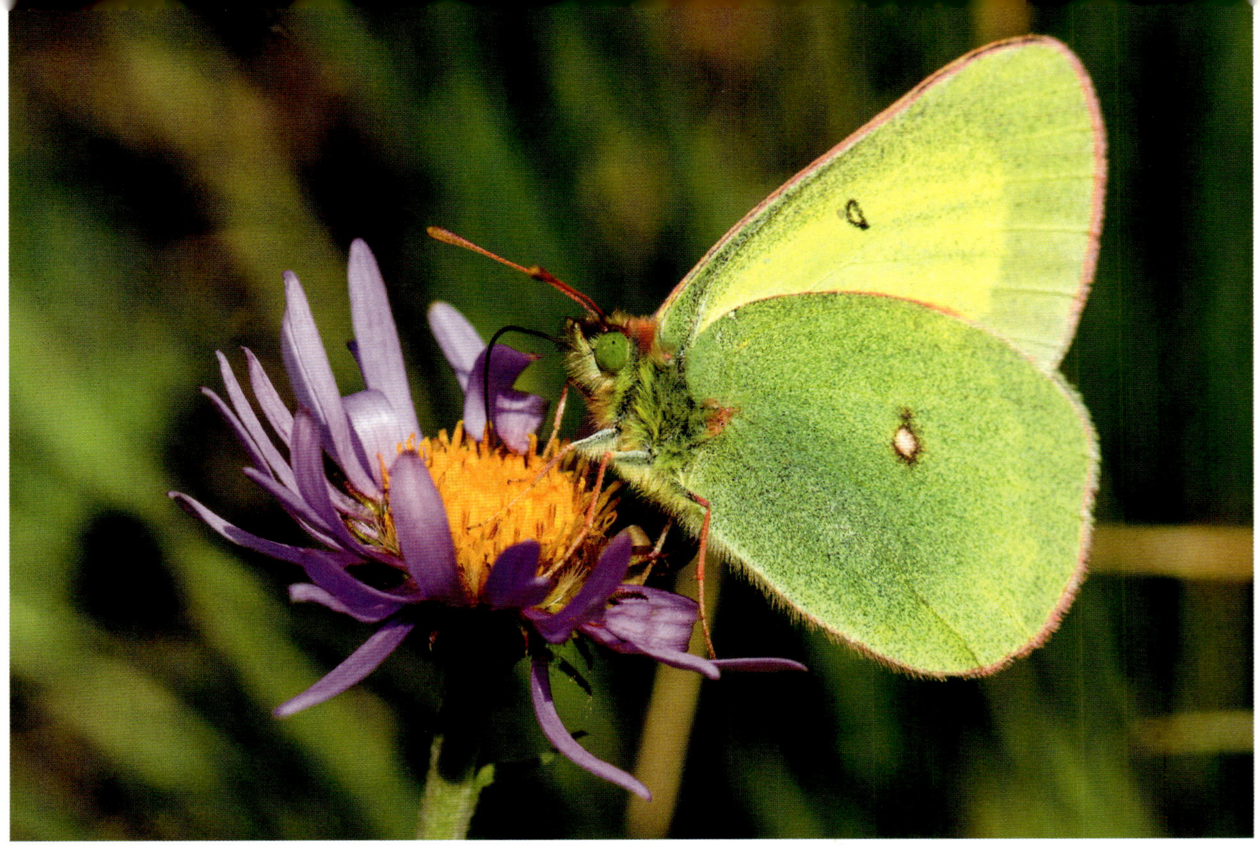

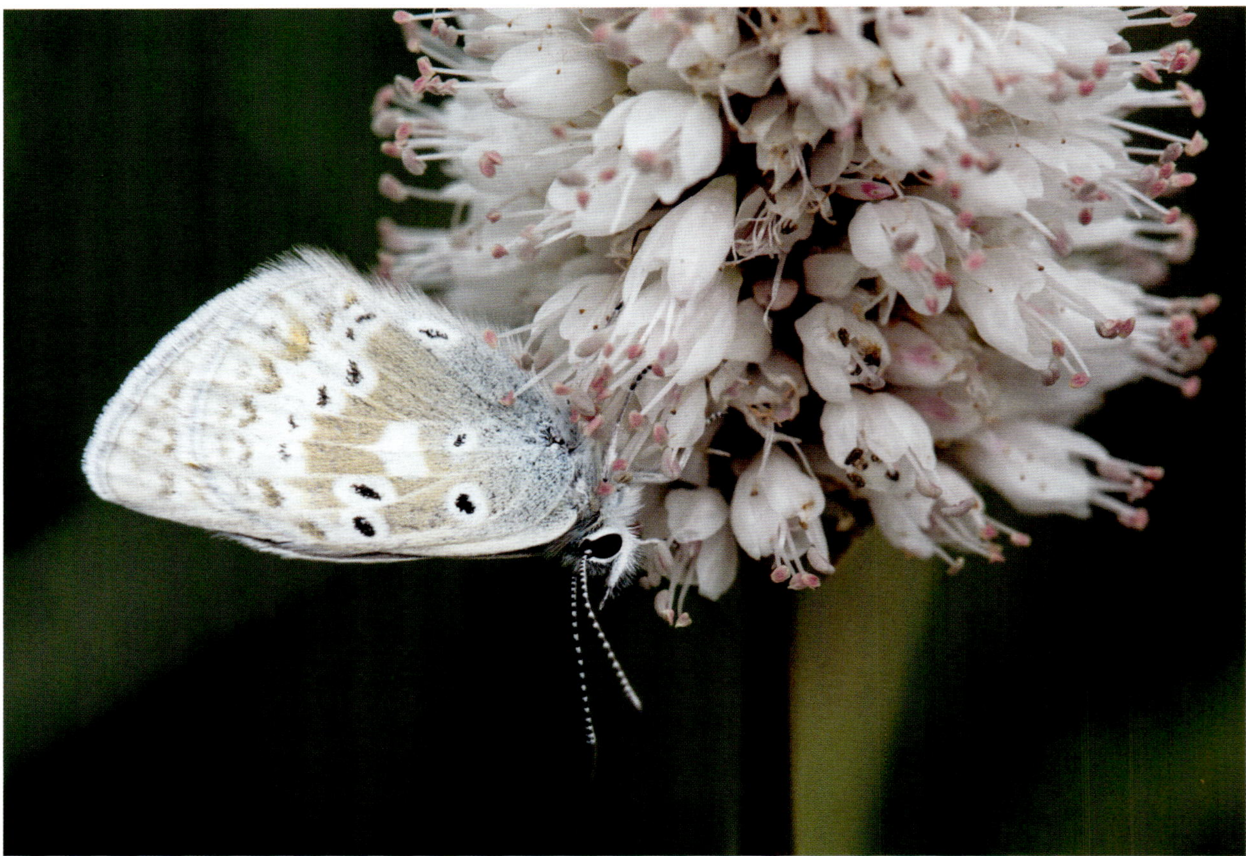

MESA VERDE NATIONAL PARK (TOP); **DENALI NATIONAL PARK AND PRESERVE** (BOTTOM).

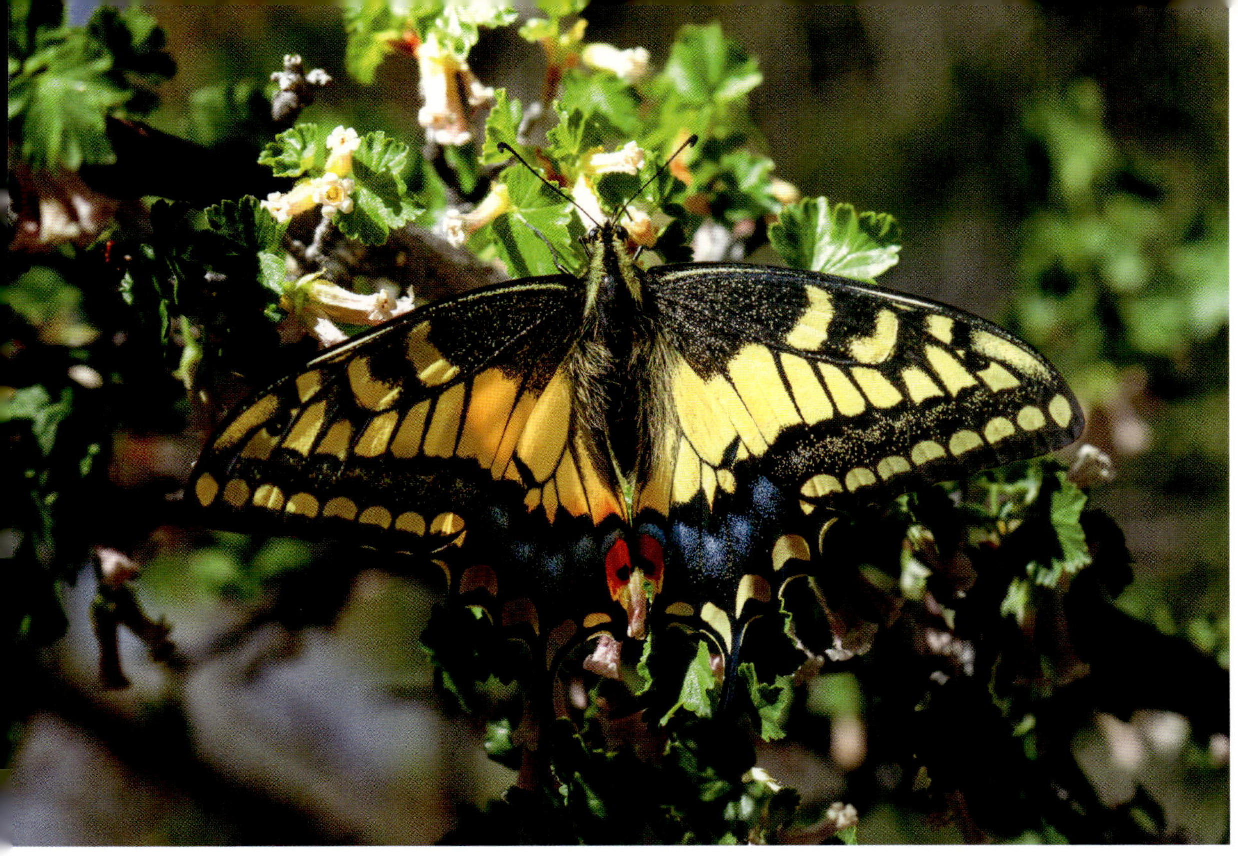

Pollinators play a vital role in maintaining healthy ecosystems. They help fertilize plants, enabling the production of fruits, seeds, and the next generation of vegetation that sustains wildlife and people alike.

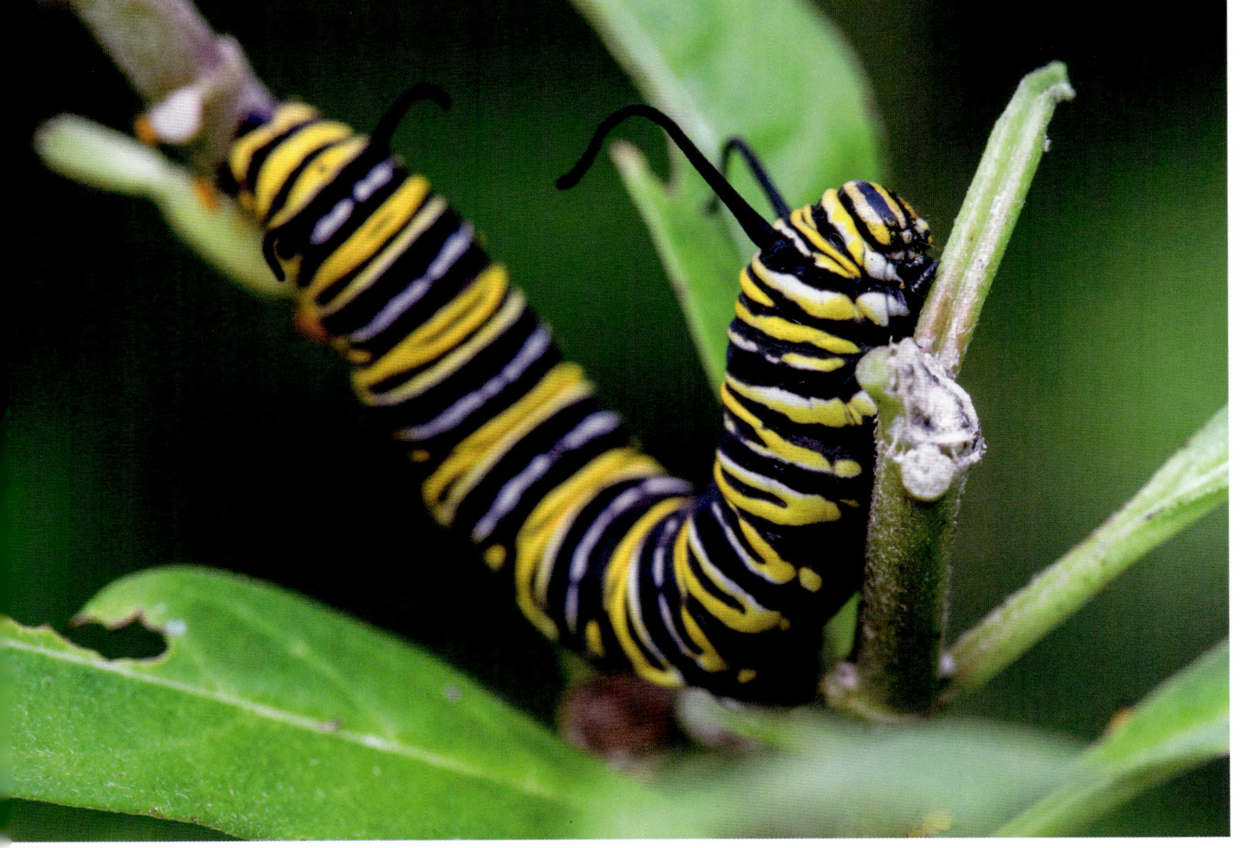

GREAT SAND DUNES NATIONAL PARK AND PRESERVE (TOP); **GRAND CANYON NATIONAL PARK** (BOTTOM).

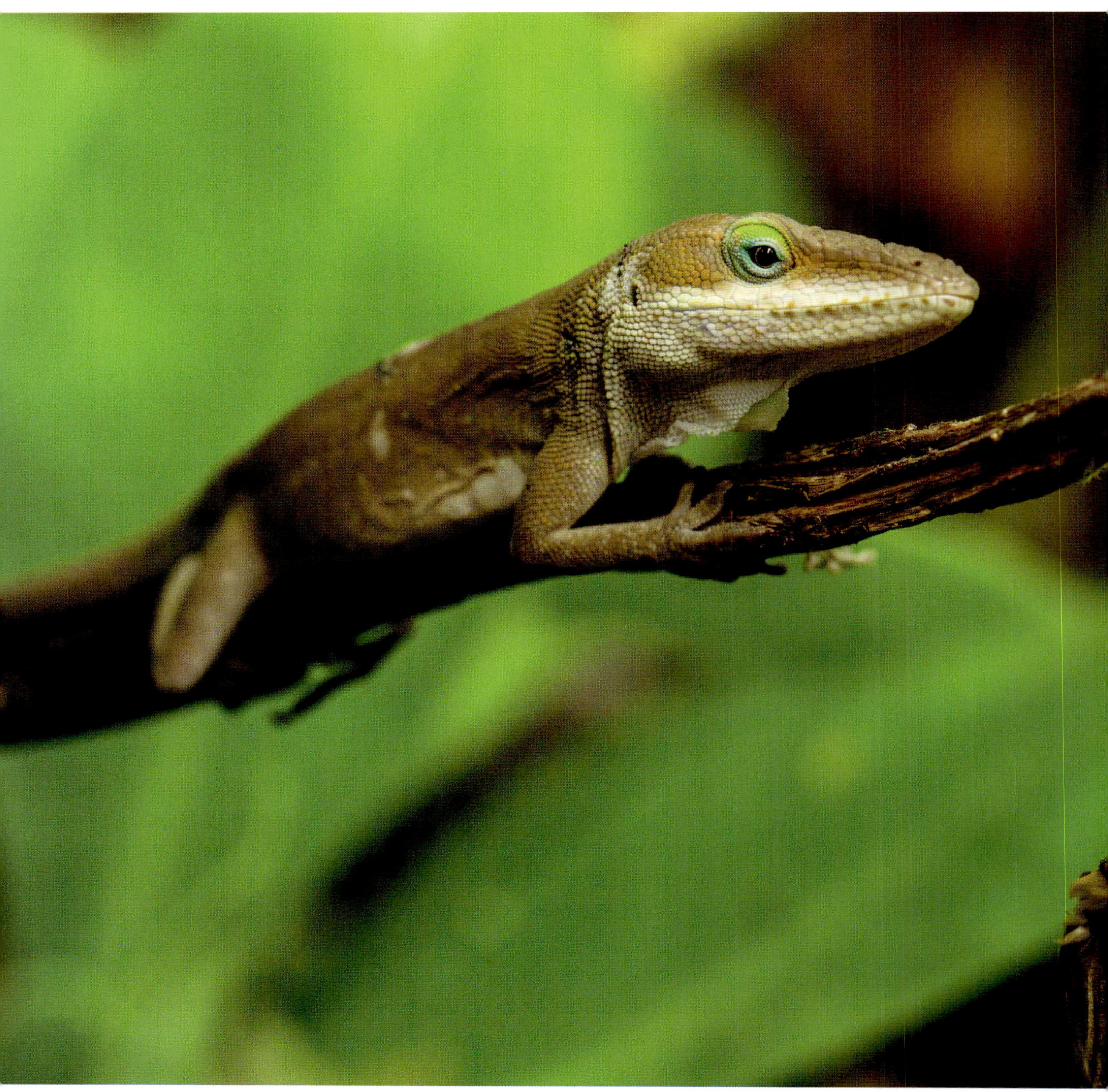

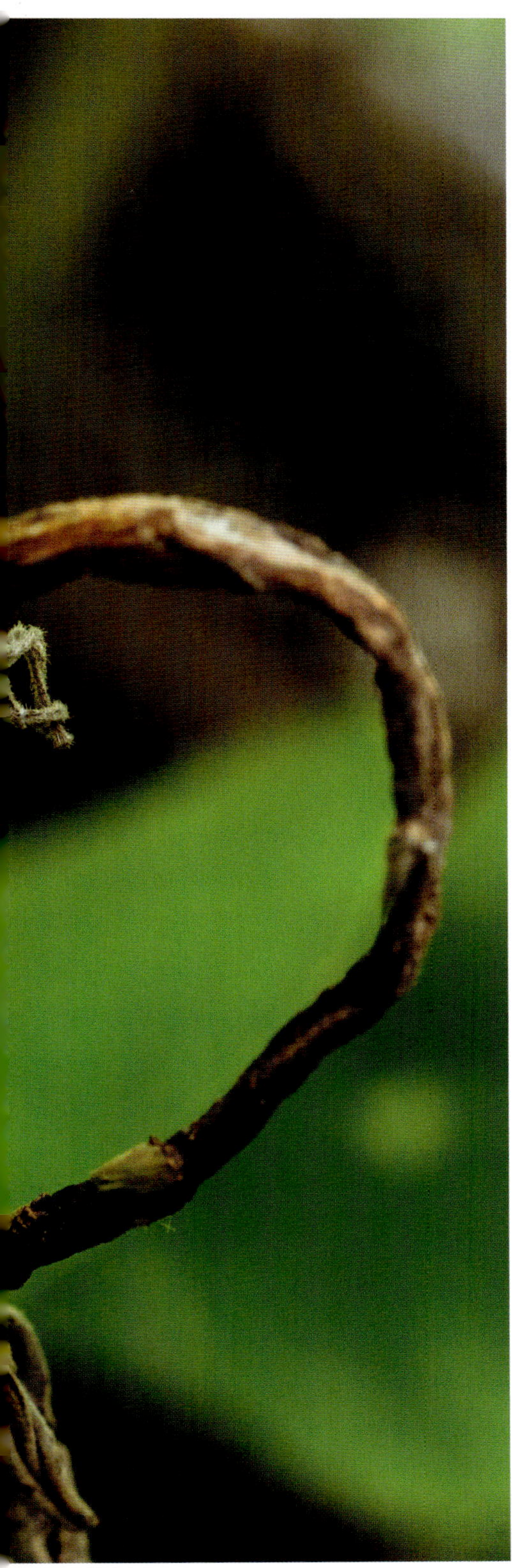

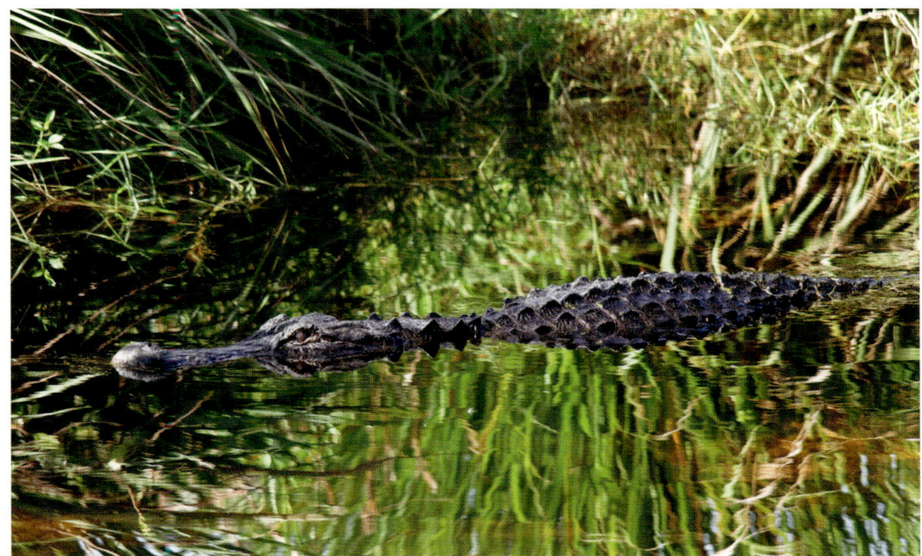

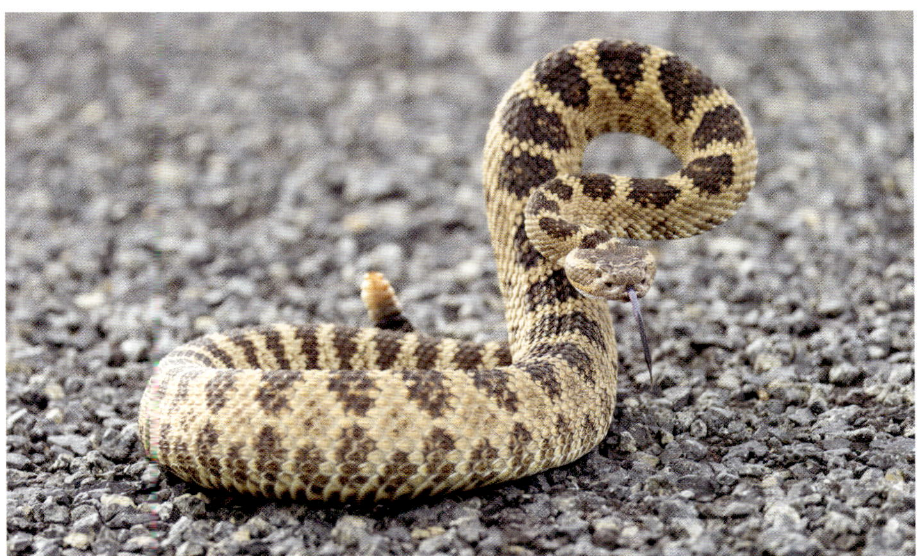

Reptiles are fascinating creatures that play key roles in ecosystems as both predators and prey.

'ANINI BEACH PARK (OPPOSITE) Green anole perched on stem.

EVERGLADES NATIONAL PARK (TOP) Alligator reflecting in the water.

LAVA BEDS NATIONAL MONUMENT (BOTTOM) Western rattlesnake ready to strike.

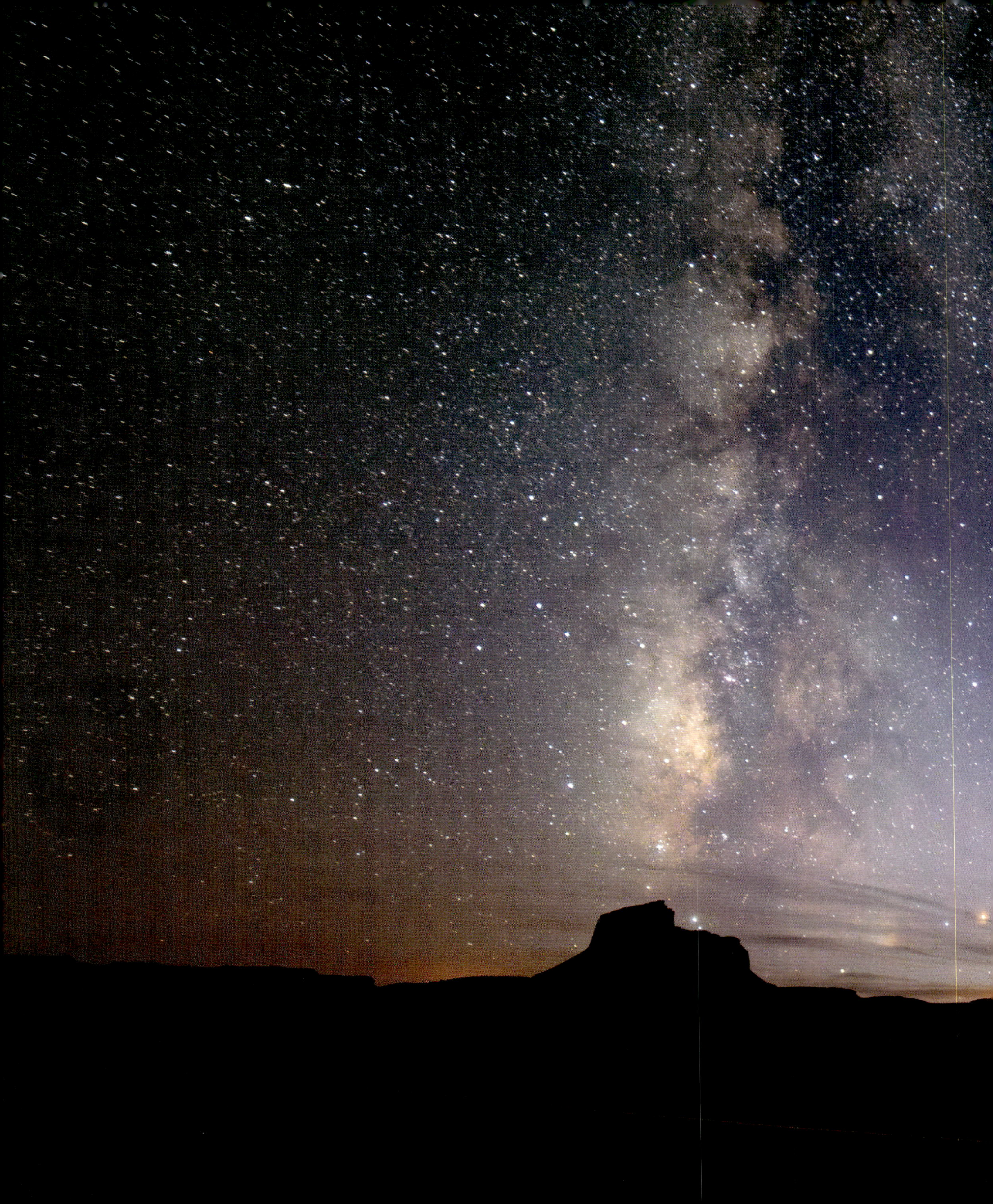

Dark Skies

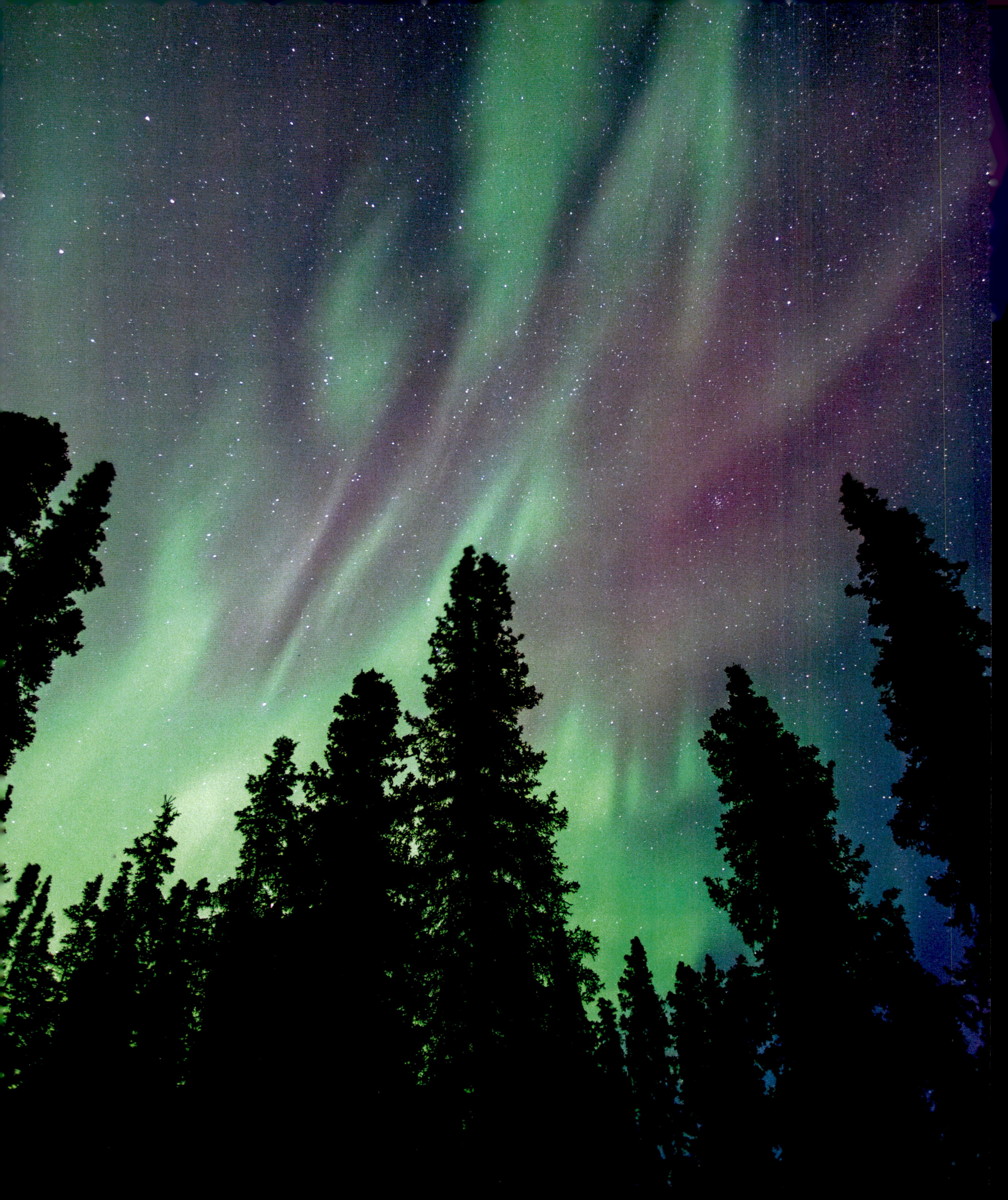

STARRY SANCTUARIES

THE IMPORTANCE OF DARK NIGHT SKIES extends far beyond their aesthetic beauty, profoundly affecting plants, animals, and humans in myriad ways. For countless species, the darkness of night is not merely the absence of daylight but a critical component of their ecological and physiological processes. For plants, the night sky plays a key role in regulating various aspects of their growth and development. Many plants, particularly those adapted to temperate climates, rely on the diurnal cycle of light and darkness to time critical biological events. The length of the night can influence flowering times, seed germination, and photosynthesis. Plants that bloom at night often rely on nocturnal pollinators such as moths, which are attracted to their nighttime fragrance and visual cues. The absence of artificial light allows these plants to maintain their natural rhythms and synchronize their life cycles with the appropriate pollinators, ensuring successful reproduction and survival. Without the natural night cycle, these processes can become disrupted, leading to reduced plant diversity and ecological imbalance.

CANYONLANDS NATIONAL PARK (PREVIOUS)

DENALI NATIONAL PARK AND PRESERVE (OPPOSITE) Faint aurora dances above the trees on a fall night.

For animals, the night sky is equally indispensable, as many species have evolved to utilize darkness as part of their survival strategies. Nocturnal animals, such as owls, bats, and insects, have adapted to the night environment to avoid predators, find food, and reproduce. Bats use echolocation to navigate and hunt for insects in the dark, while owls rely on their acute hearing and night vision to hunt small mammals. Additionally, many species of insects, like fireflies, use bioluminescence as a method of communication and mating during the night. The clarity of the night sky, free from the interference of light pollution, is crucial for these animals to carry out their nighttime activities effectively. Artificial lighting can disrupt their natural behaviors, leading to disorientation, decreased reproductive success, and even population declines. Therefore, preserving the natural darkness of the night sky is essential for maintaining the health and balance of nocturnal ecosystems.

For humans, the night sky has historically been a source of wonder and inspiration, playing a significant role in cultural, scientific, and practical aspects of life. Stargazing has been a fundamental part of human culture, inspiring myths, navigation systems, and scientific inquiry throughout history. The visibility of celestial objects like stars, planets, and the Milky Way provides a connection to the broader universe, fostering a sense of wonder and curiosity. Moreover, astronomical observations have been crucial for understanding the cosmos, advancing scientific knowledge, and guiding exploration. The study of celestial bodies has led to significant discoveries about the nature of the universe and our place within it.

In addition to viewing the Milky Way, the viewing of the aurora borealis (northern lights) has profoundly impacted human cultures, scientific understanding, and even societal behaviors. Throughout history, this mesmerizing natural light display has been a source of wonder, inspiration, and sometimes even fear. Today, auroras continue to captivate both scientists and the general public. They have become a symbol of natural beauty and a subject of widespread interest in popular culture and tourism. The impact of the aurora on human history is a testament to its profound beauty and its ability to inspire both wonder and scientific curiosity.

The encroachment of light pollution poses a serious threat to the night sky and its associated benefits. Artificial lighting from urban areas, roads, and other sources can obscure the visibility of stars and other celestial phenomena, diminishing the experience of stargazing and affecting astronomical research. Light pollution not only interferes with the ability to observe the night sky but also disrupts the natural behaviors of both animals and plants. For humans, overexposure to artificial light at night can lead to health issues, including disrupted sleep patterns, increased stress, and a range of sleep disorders. Studies have shown that

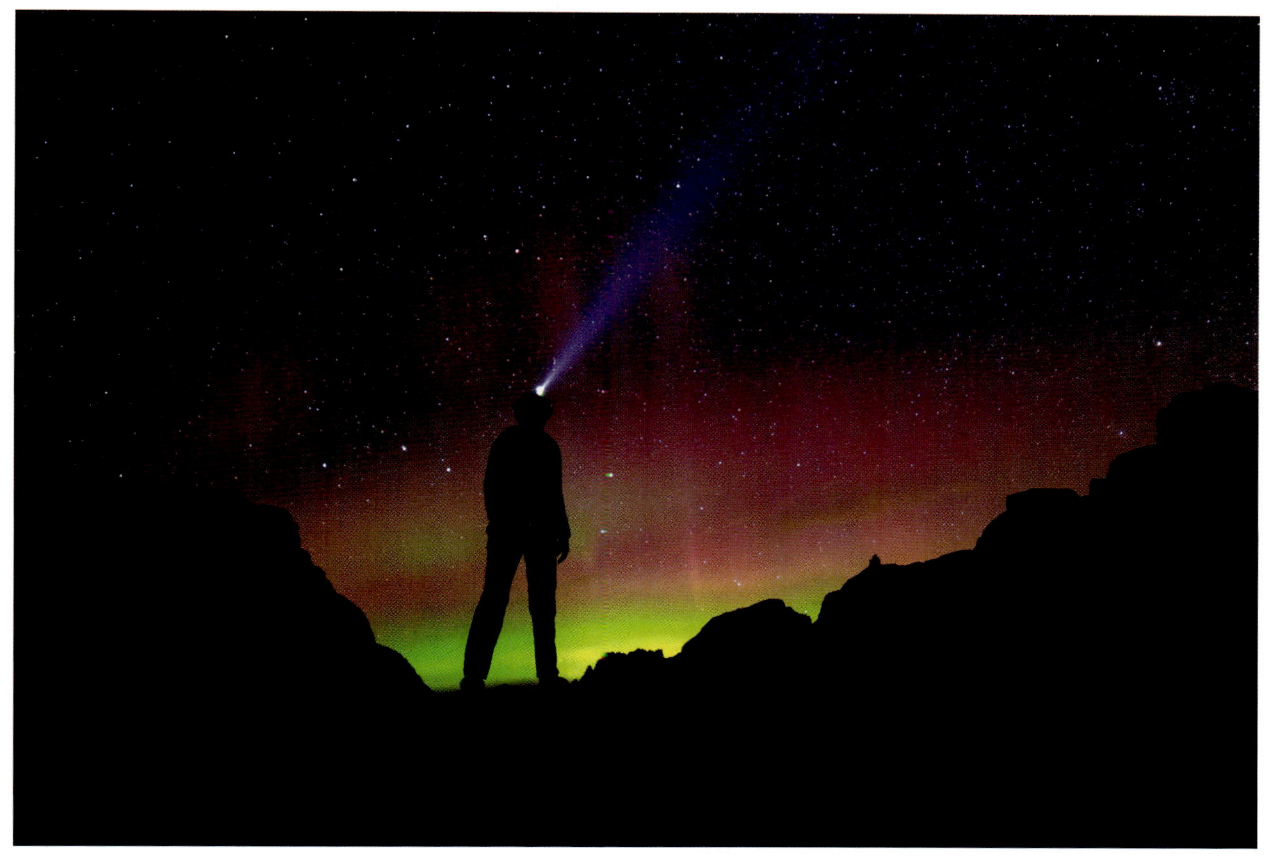

GLACIER NATIONAL PARK Hearing that a solar storm was expected, we drove up to Logan Pass to watch the aurora dance above the Garden Wall.

exposure to artificial light can interfere with circadian rhythms, which regulate various physiological processes and affect overall well-being.

Preserving the natural night sky is therefore critical for maintaining the health of ecosystems and the quality of human life. Efforts to reduce light pollution, such as implementing more efficient outdoor lighting and designing lighting fixtures that minimize skyglow, can help mitigate the negative impacts on wildlife and human health. Additionally, creating dark sky preserves and reserves on our public lands can provide protected areas where the night sky remains free from artificial interference, allowing both people and wildlife to experience and benefit from the natural darkness. By fostering a greater appreciation for the night sky and recognizing its importance, we can work toward preserving this vital aspect of our natural environment and ensuring that future generations can continue to enjoy its beauty and benefits.

The first time I set out to photograph the night sky, I didn't realize how little I understood about it. Without any knowledge of astronomy, it was difficult to capture the images I had envisioned. After a little research and a lot of trial and error, I learned that you can plan your night sky shots well in advance. The only unpredictable factor is whether or not the clouds will cooperate.

When I was invited to my cousin's wedding on Oahu the following summer, I started planning a shot. I had visited Hawai'i Volcanoes National Park the previous winter and witnessed the glowing Kīlauea Caldera at night. While I took some photos, the orientation of the Milky Way in winter didn't allow for the shot I was hoping for. After checking the moon phases for the summer, I decided to visit the Big Island a week before the wedding to try and make the picture in my mind a reality.

On the first night in the park, the weather was clear—time to see if all my planning would pay off. I walked to the back side of the Jaggar Museum and was greeted by a scene I'll never forget: the open Earth, the Kīlauea Caldera, glowing up into the sky, and the core of the Milky Way arching perfectly overhead, just as I had imagined. Despite the wind, cool temperatures, and my lack of proper clothing, I couldn't bring myself to leave. I stayed until my fingers were unable to operate my camera, and then I stayed a little longer, ignoring my camera and just taking it all in.

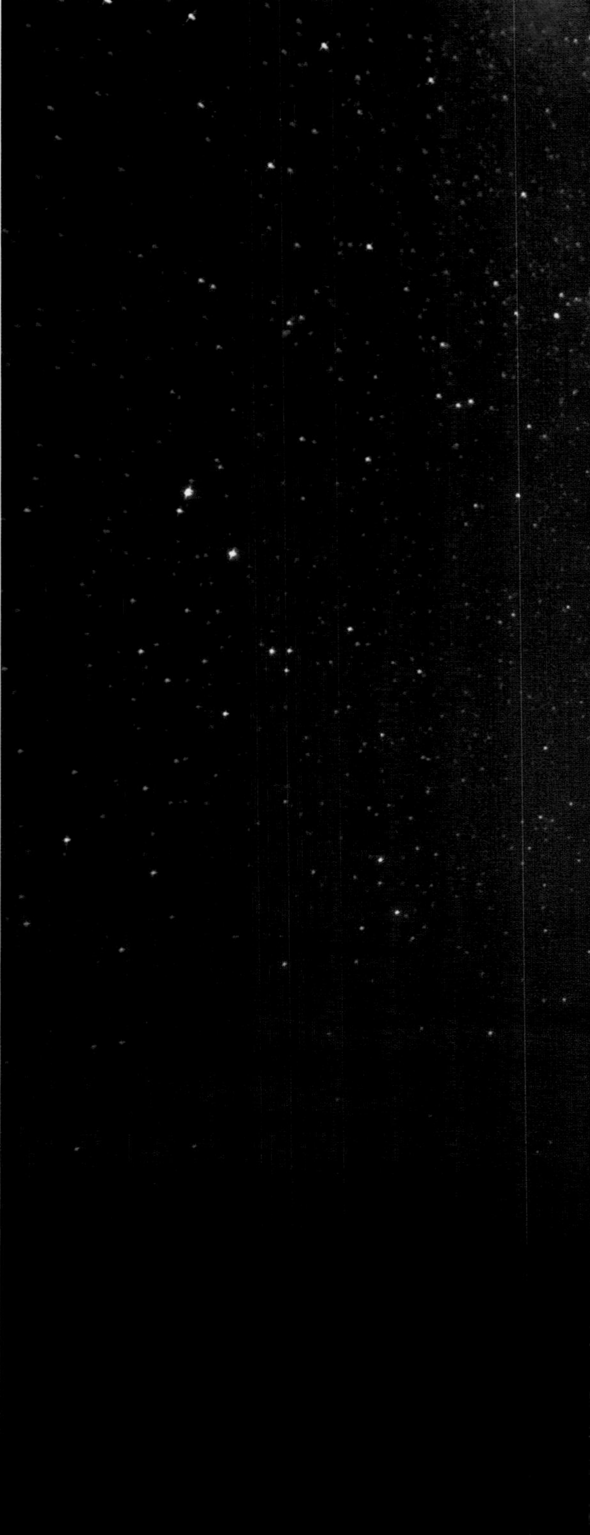

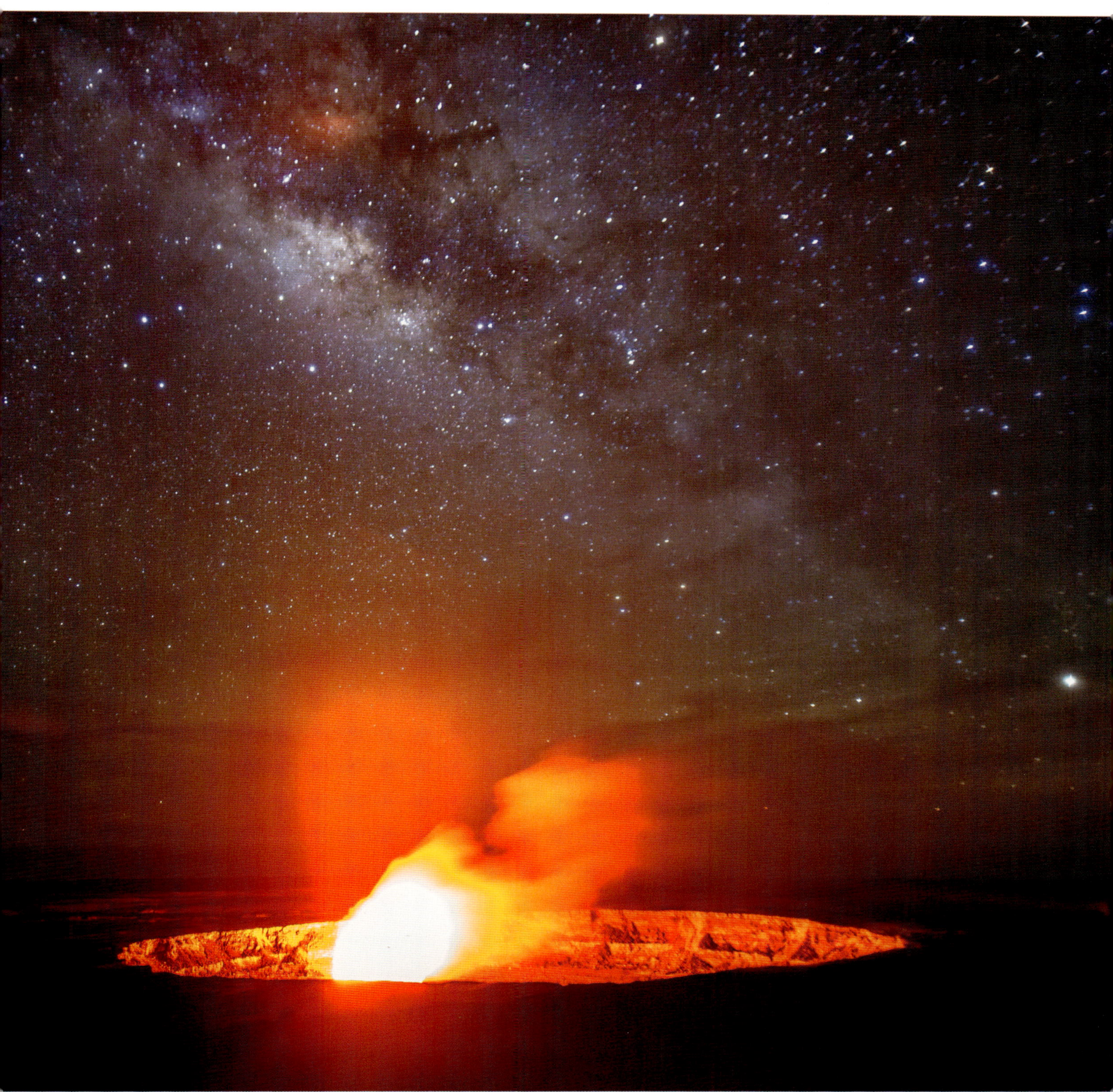

HAWAI'I VOLCANOES NATIONAL PARK

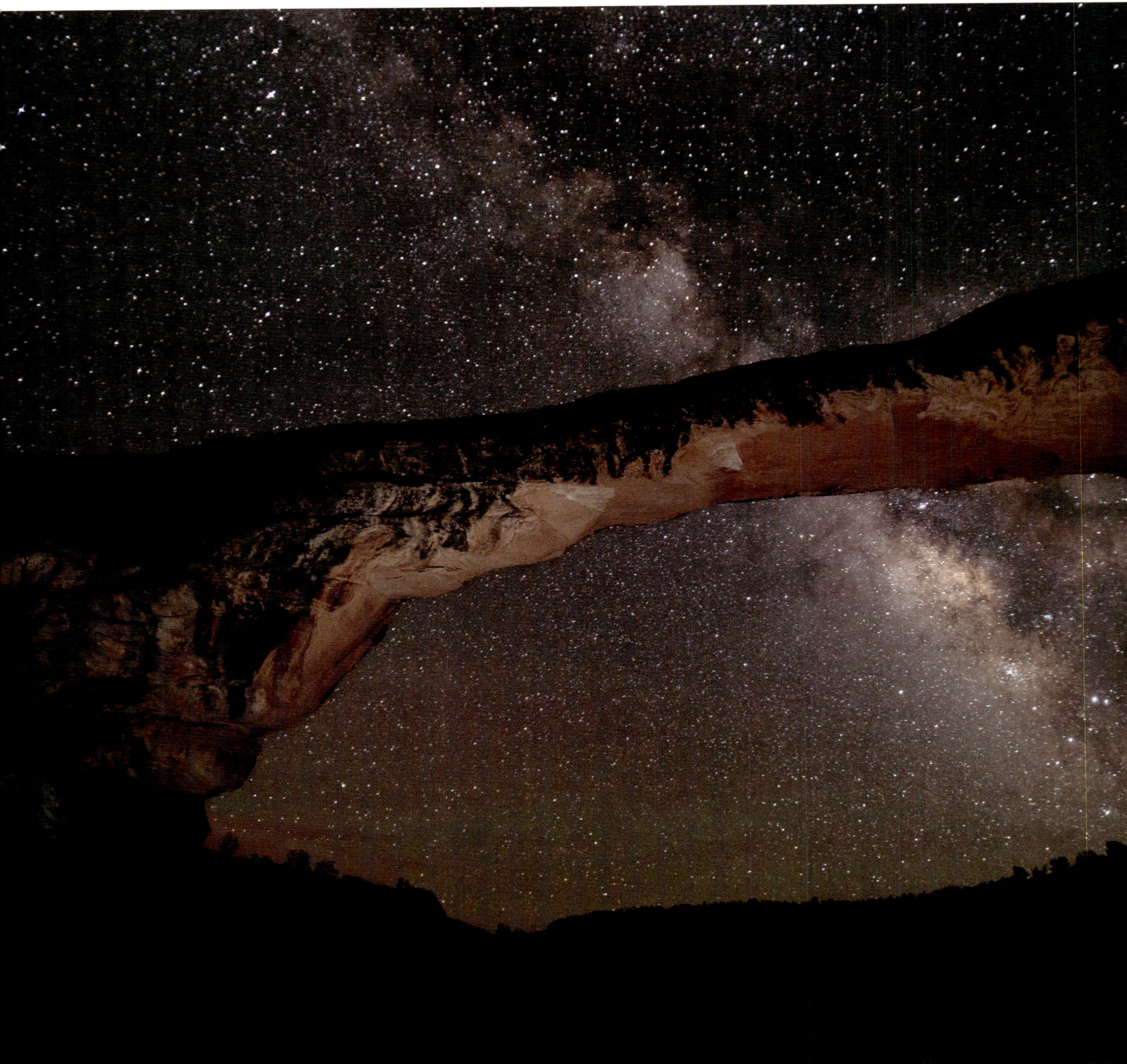

NATURAL BRIDGES NATIONAL MONUMENT It was one of the darkest skies I've ever witnessed—clear and untouched after a recent rainstorm on a new moon night. Once our eyes adjusted, the starlight was so intense that you could see your own shadow cast across the landscape.

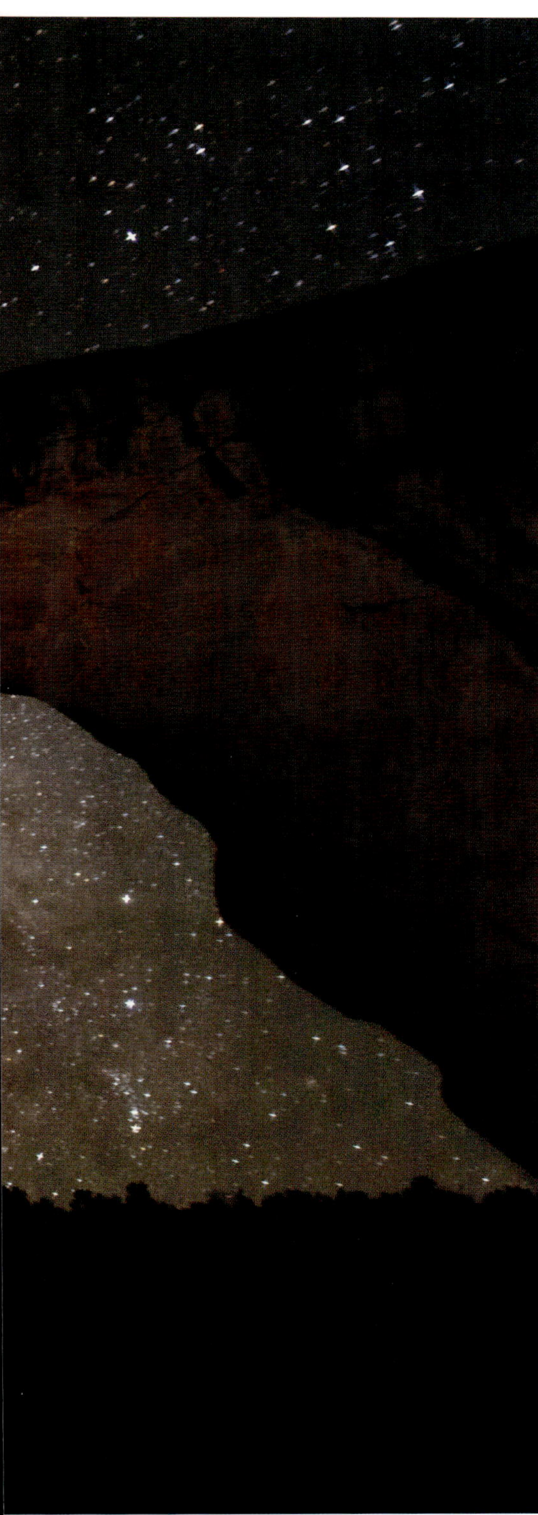

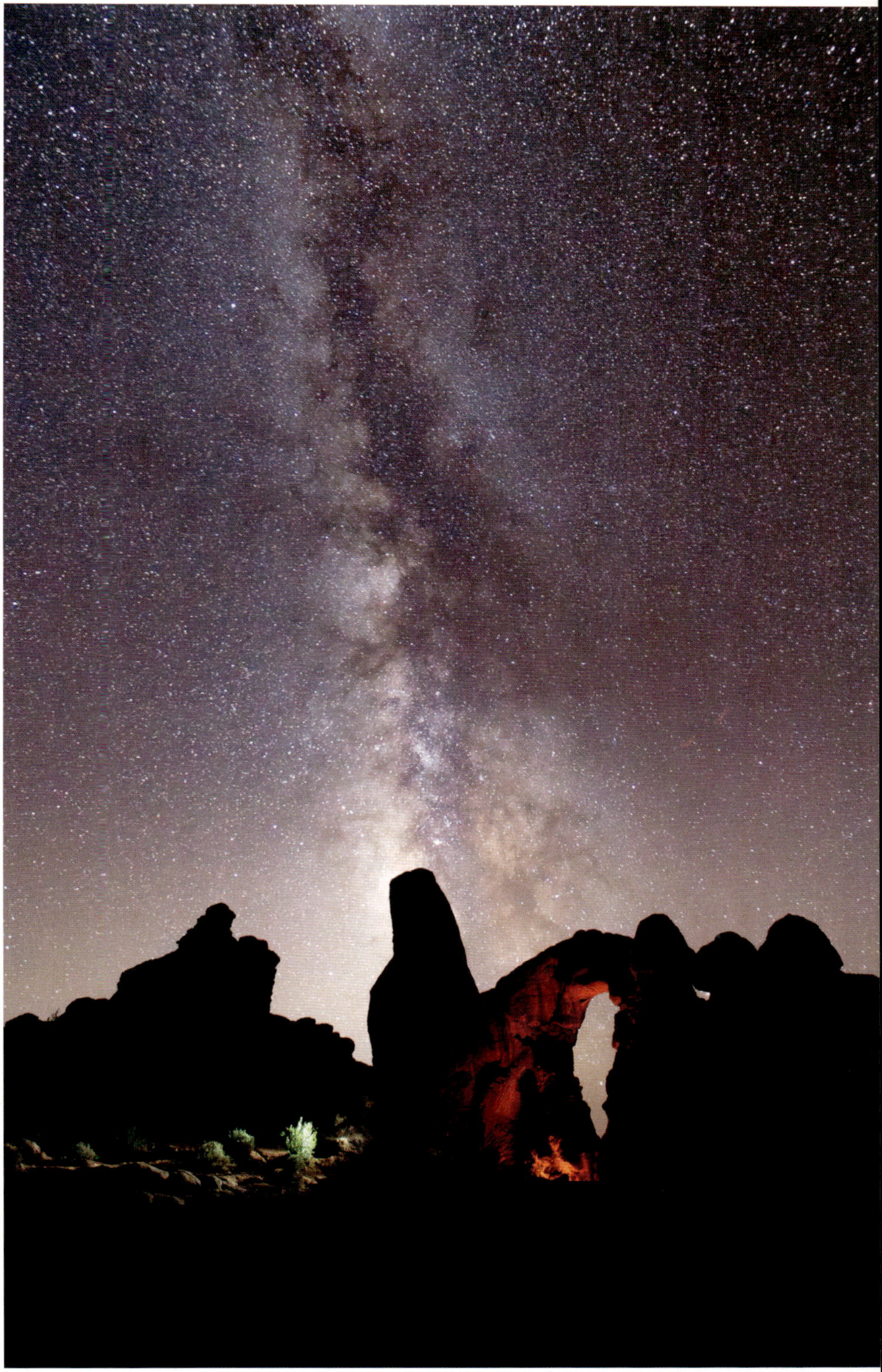

ARCHES NATIONAL PARK My friend was in town visiting and wanted to learn night photography, so we spent the night exploring the Windows and capturing the stars as they slowly moved across the sky.

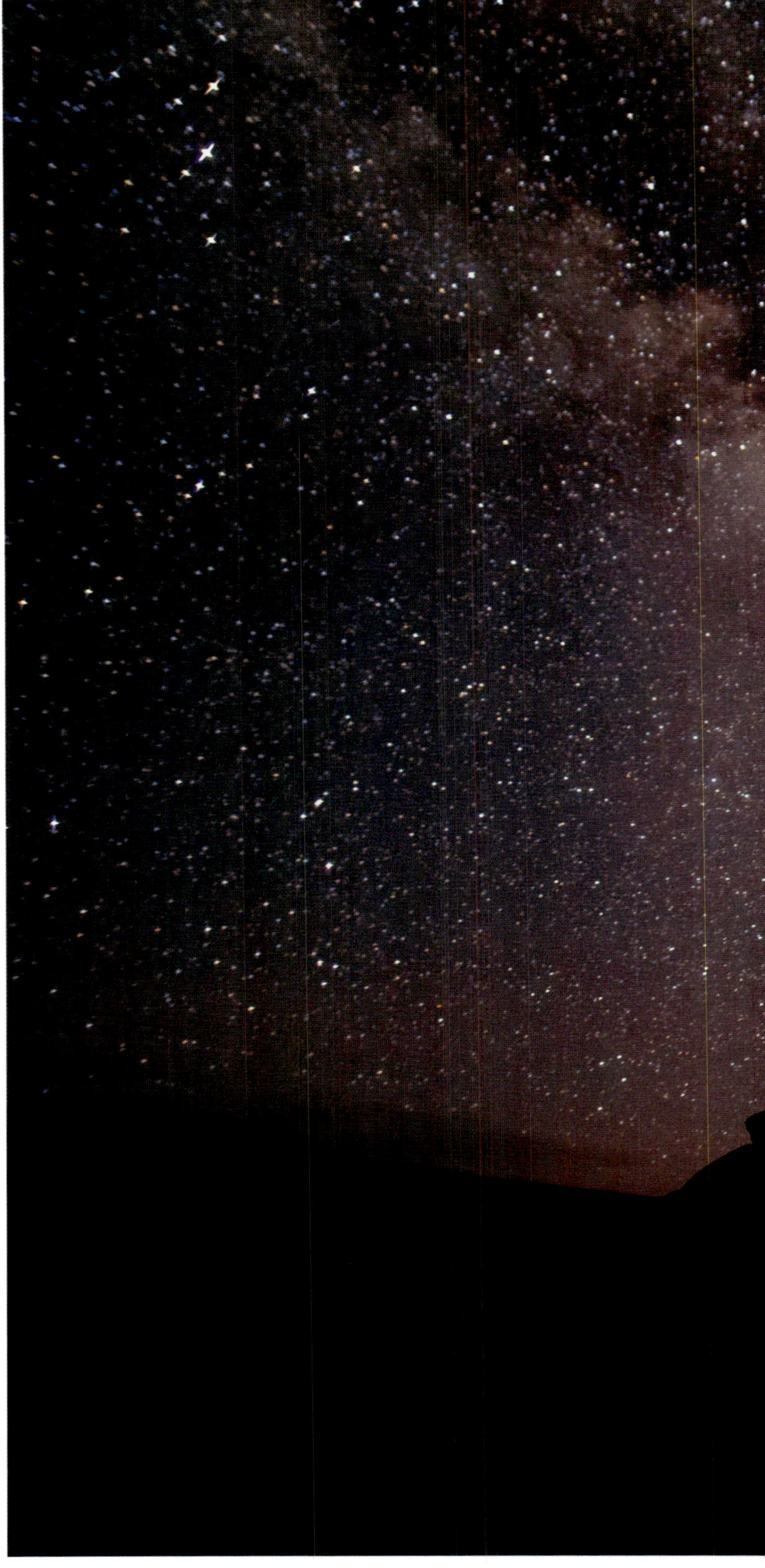

ARCHES NATIONAL PARK My friend and I hiked up to Delicate Arch in the quiet desert night. Even though this is one of the first night photos I've captured, it remains a favorite.

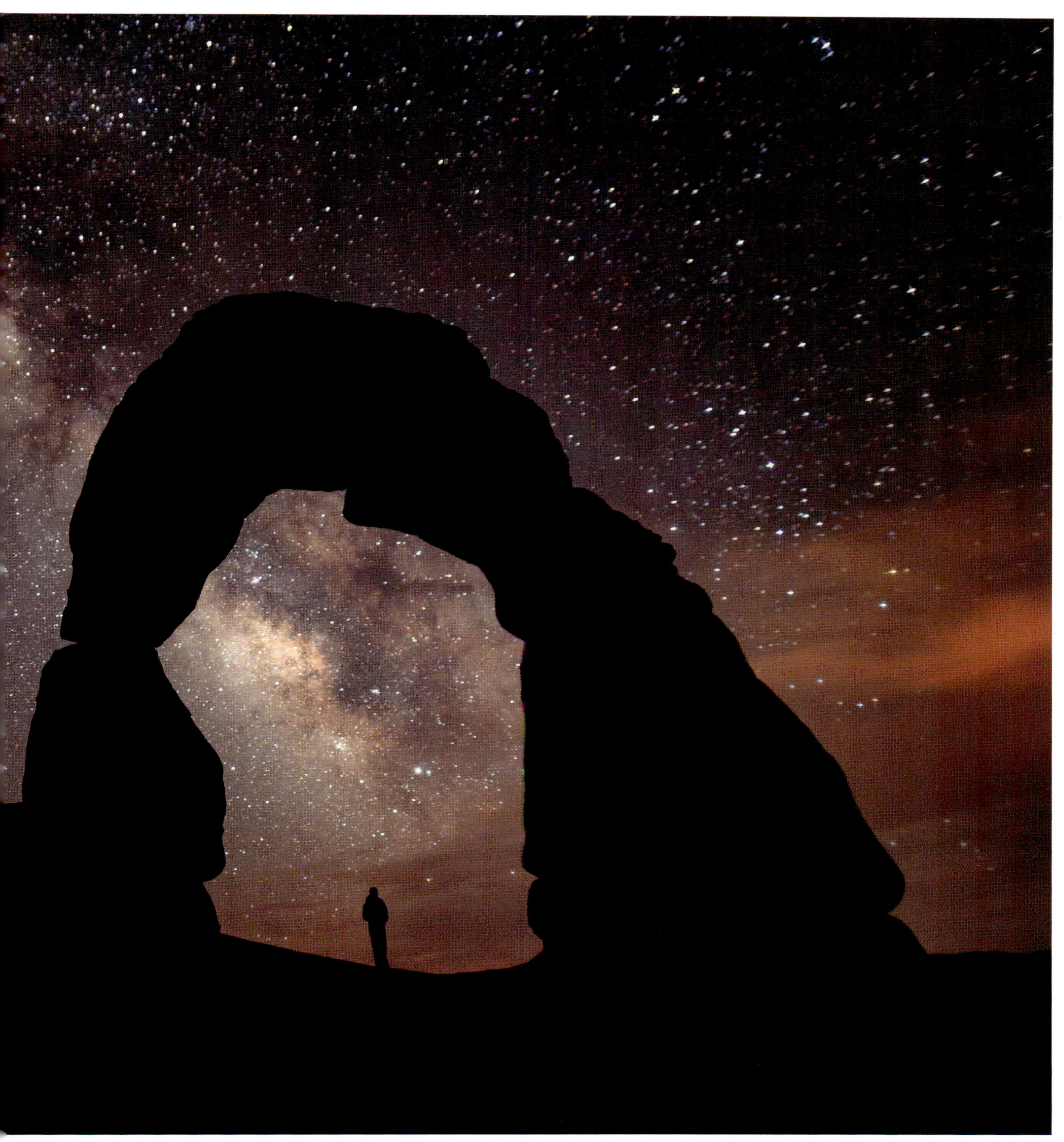

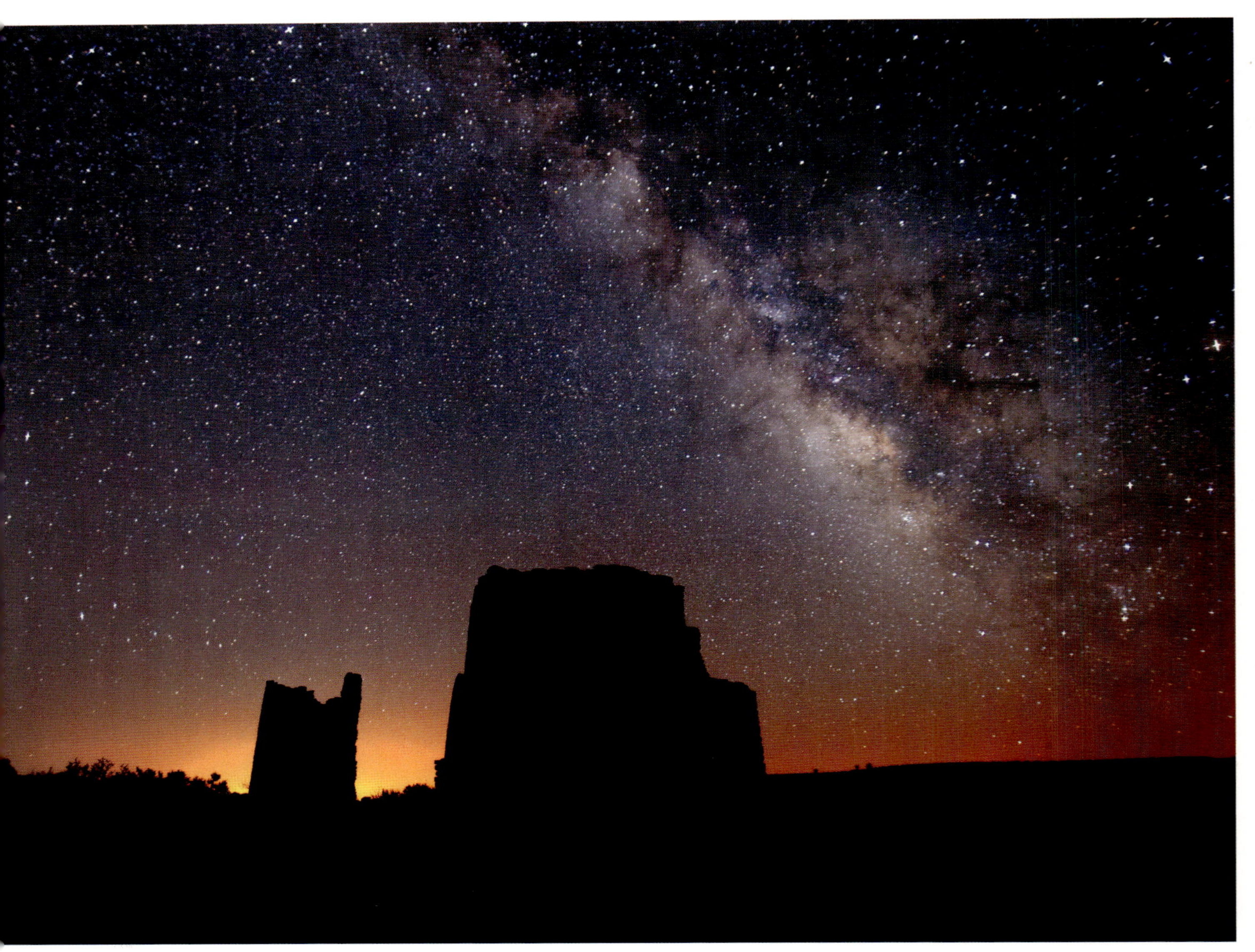

HOVENWEEP NATIONAL MONUMENT

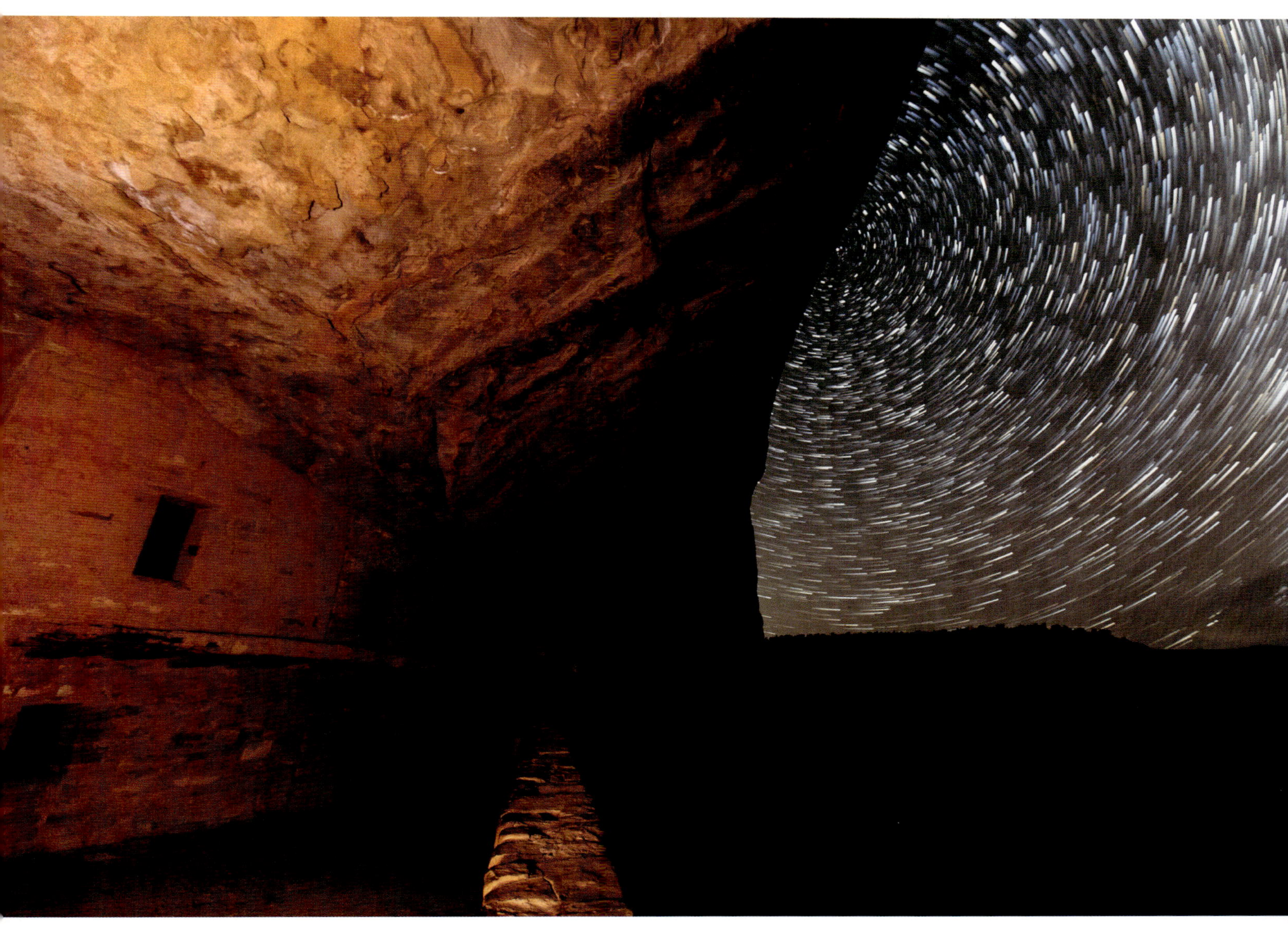

MESA VERDE NATIONAL PARK

The Ancestral Puebloans looked to the night sky as a vital guide, using the stars, moon, and planets to track time, mark seasons, and align their structures with celestial events. Their deep understanding of the cosmos shaped their cultural practices and connected them to the rhythms of the natural world.

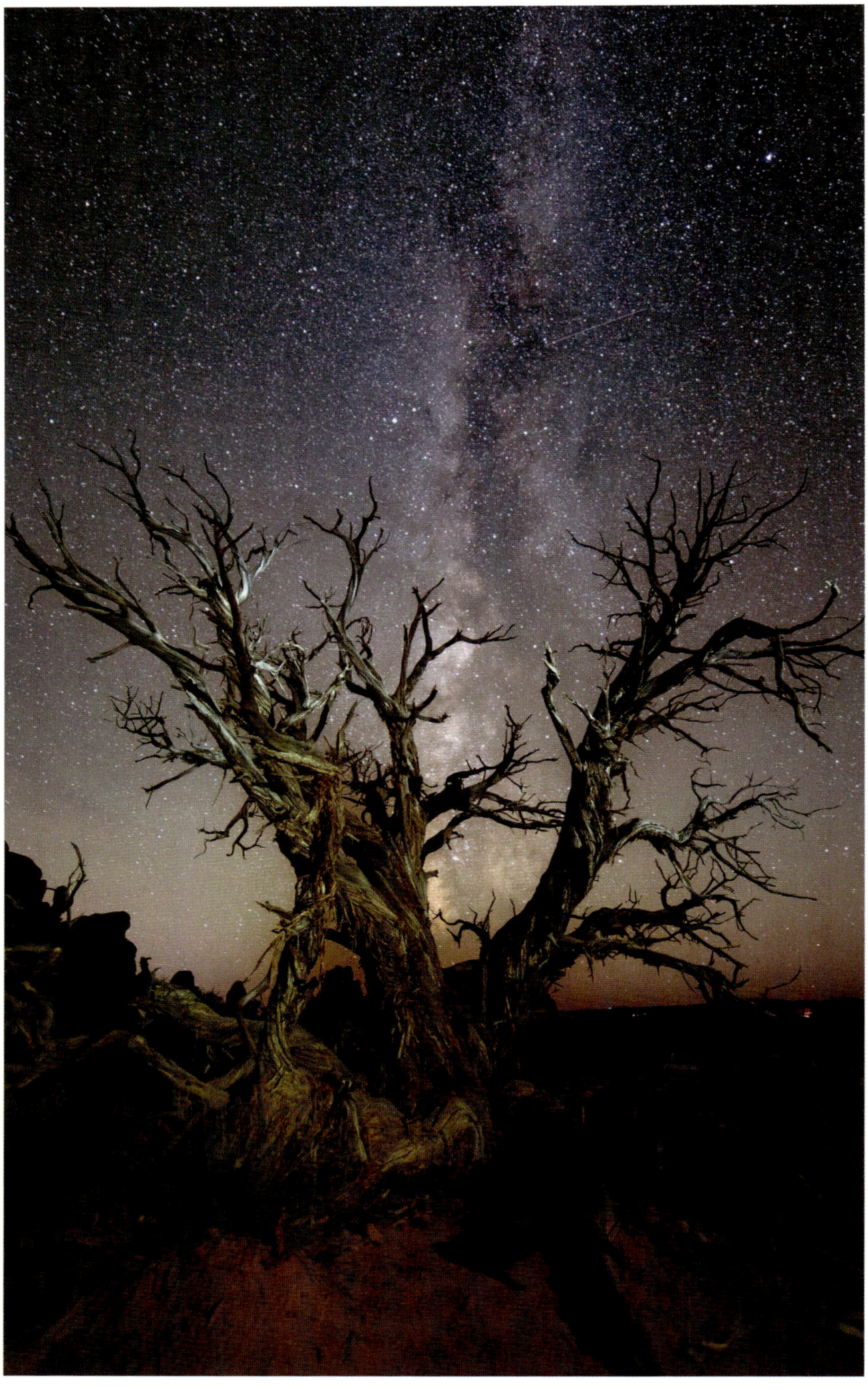

ARCHES NATIONAL PARK I'd noticed this pinyon tree during a past visit to the Windows, and thought it might make a fun foreground.

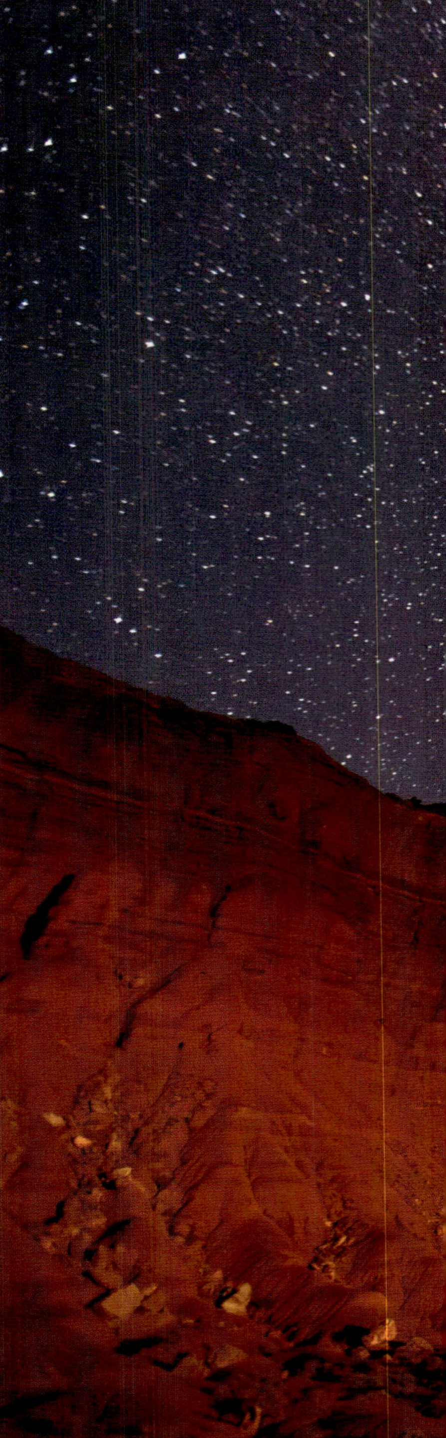

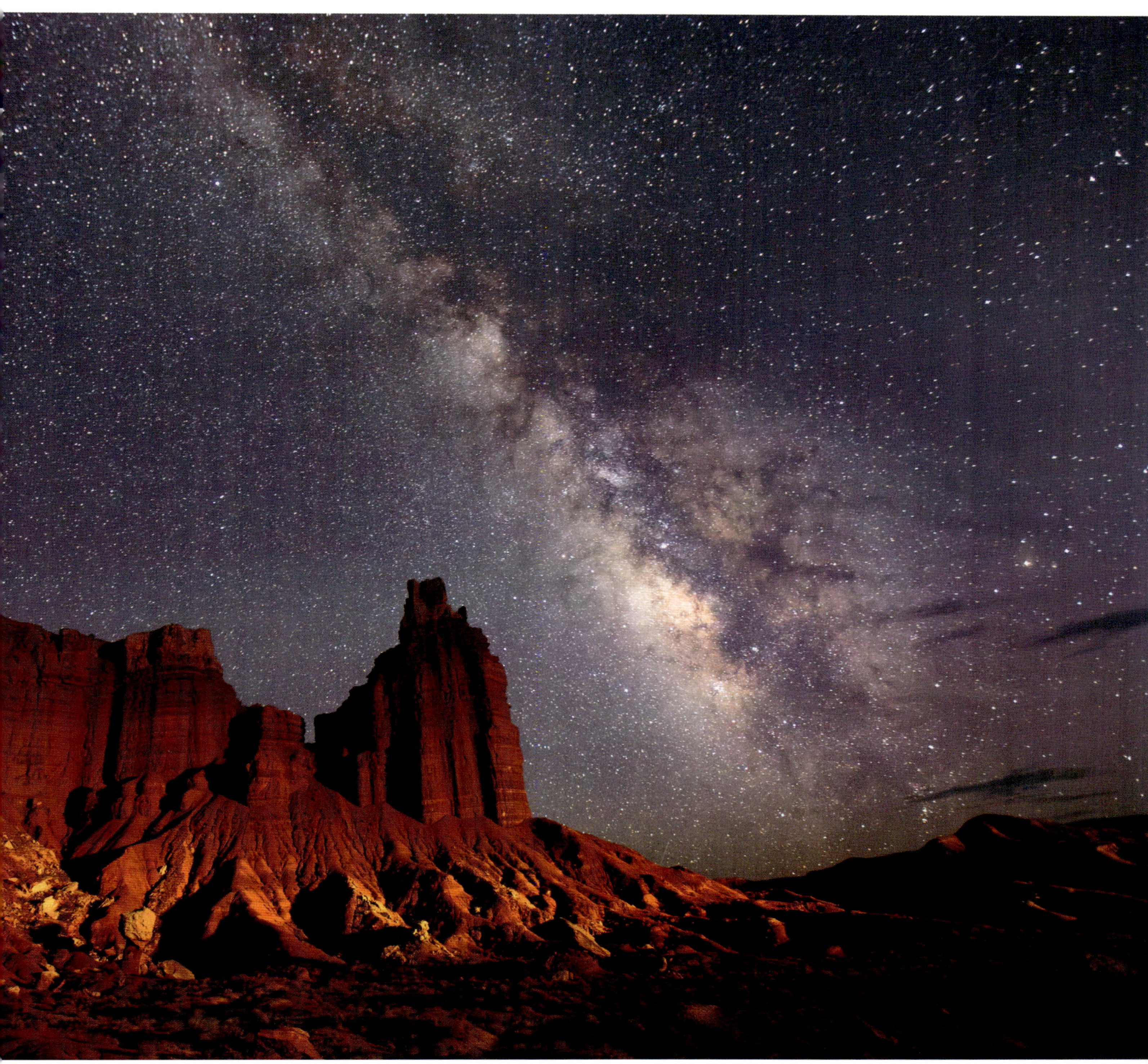

CAPITOL REEF NATIONAL PARK While photographing Chimney Rock, a car driving along the highway illuminated the cliffs. At first, I thought it had ruined my shot, but when I reviewed the photo, I was pleasantly surprised by how it turned out. A happy little accident!

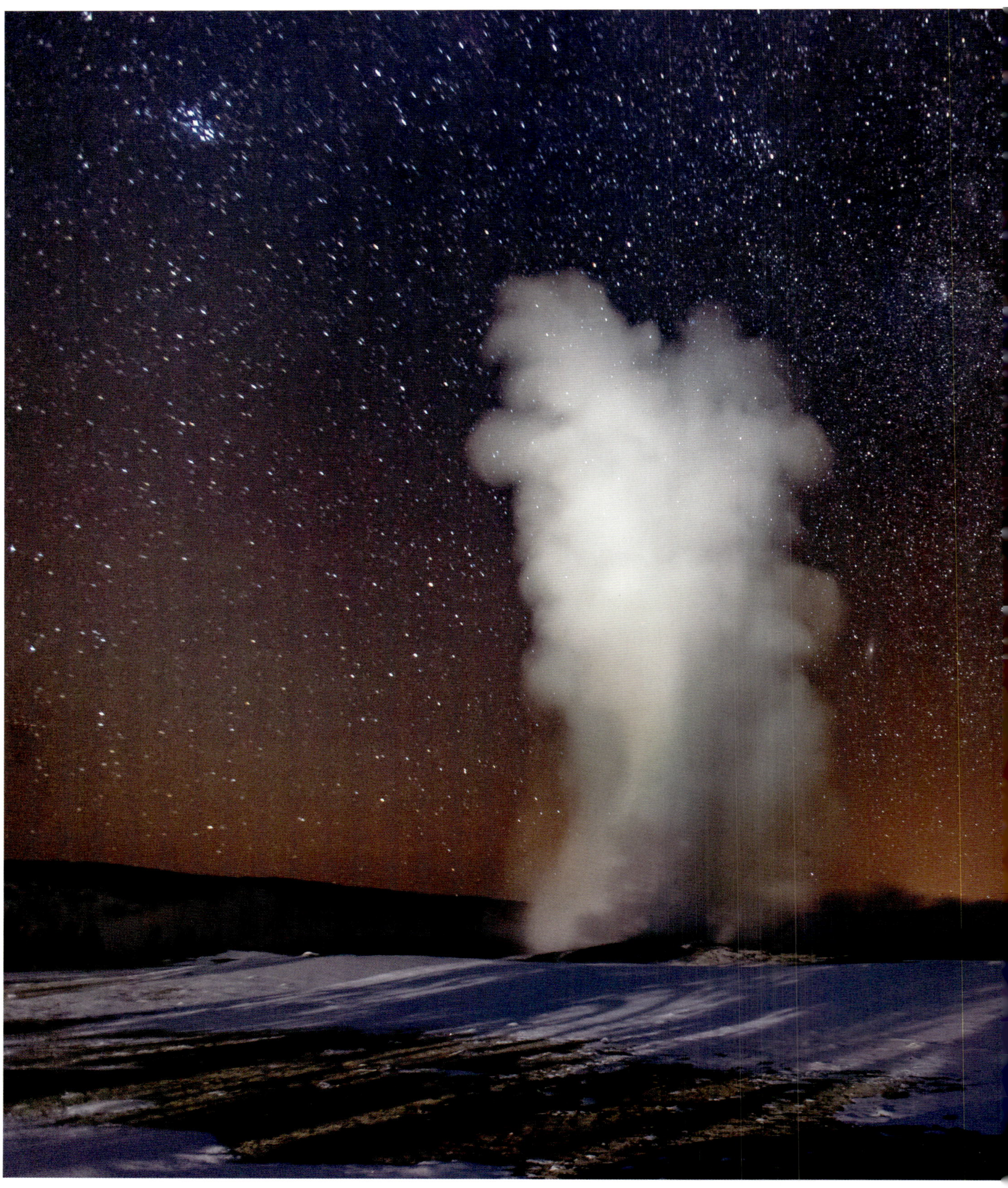

YELLOWSTONE NATIONAL PARK On a winter visit to Old Faithful, I ventured out to photograph the night eruption. I'm fairly certain I was the only one there for that eruption, braving the -20°F temperature. The stillness of the park, combined with the steam rising in the still air, made for an unforgettable and solitary experience.

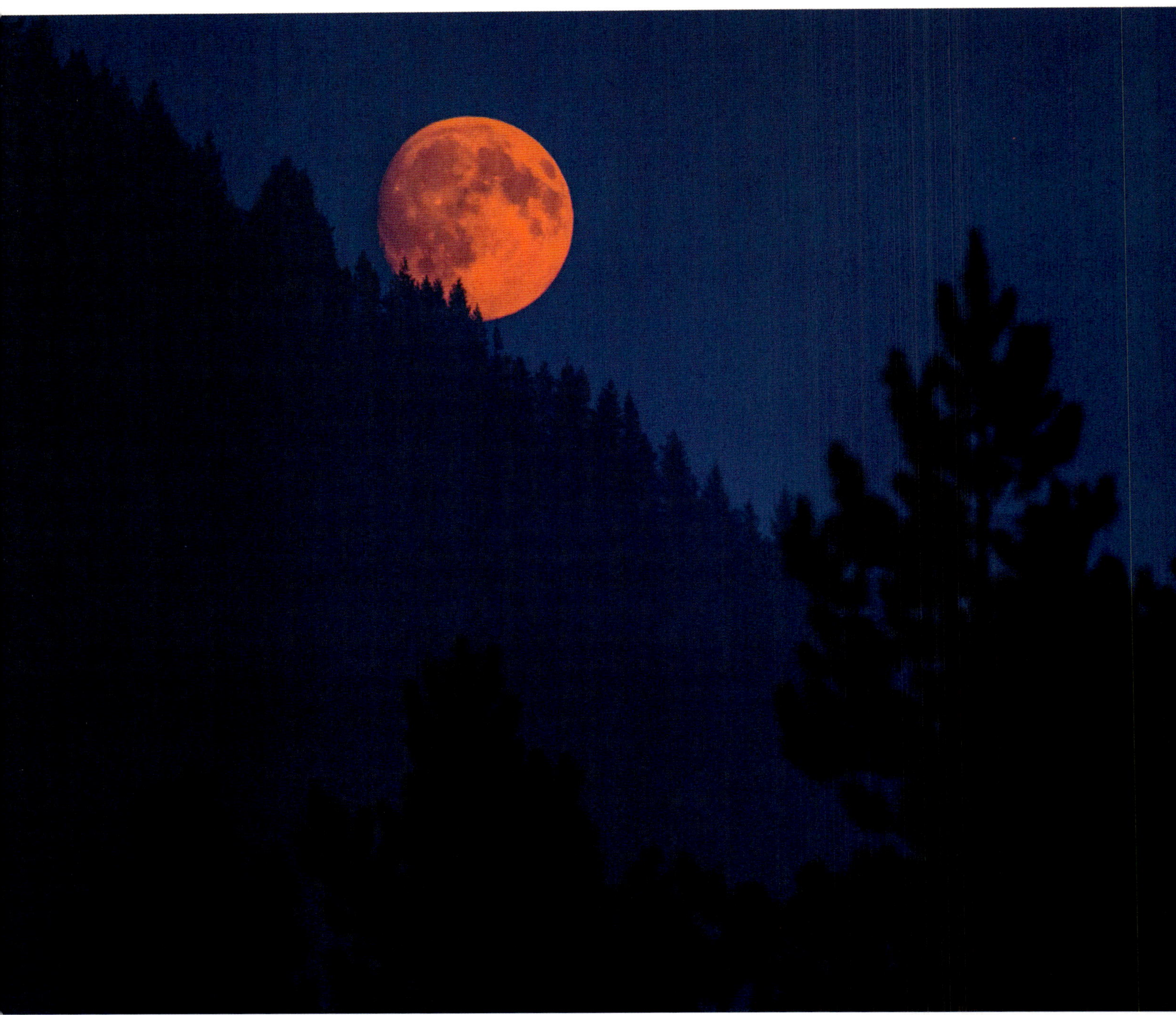

GLACIER NATIONAL PARK (ABOVE) A nearby wildfire created the perfect conditions for a true "blood moon" moonrise one summer evening.

HAWAI'I VOLCANOES NATIONAL PARK (OPPOSITE) The glow of Halema'uma'u illuminated the night sky while we camped at Kulanaokuaiki Campground.

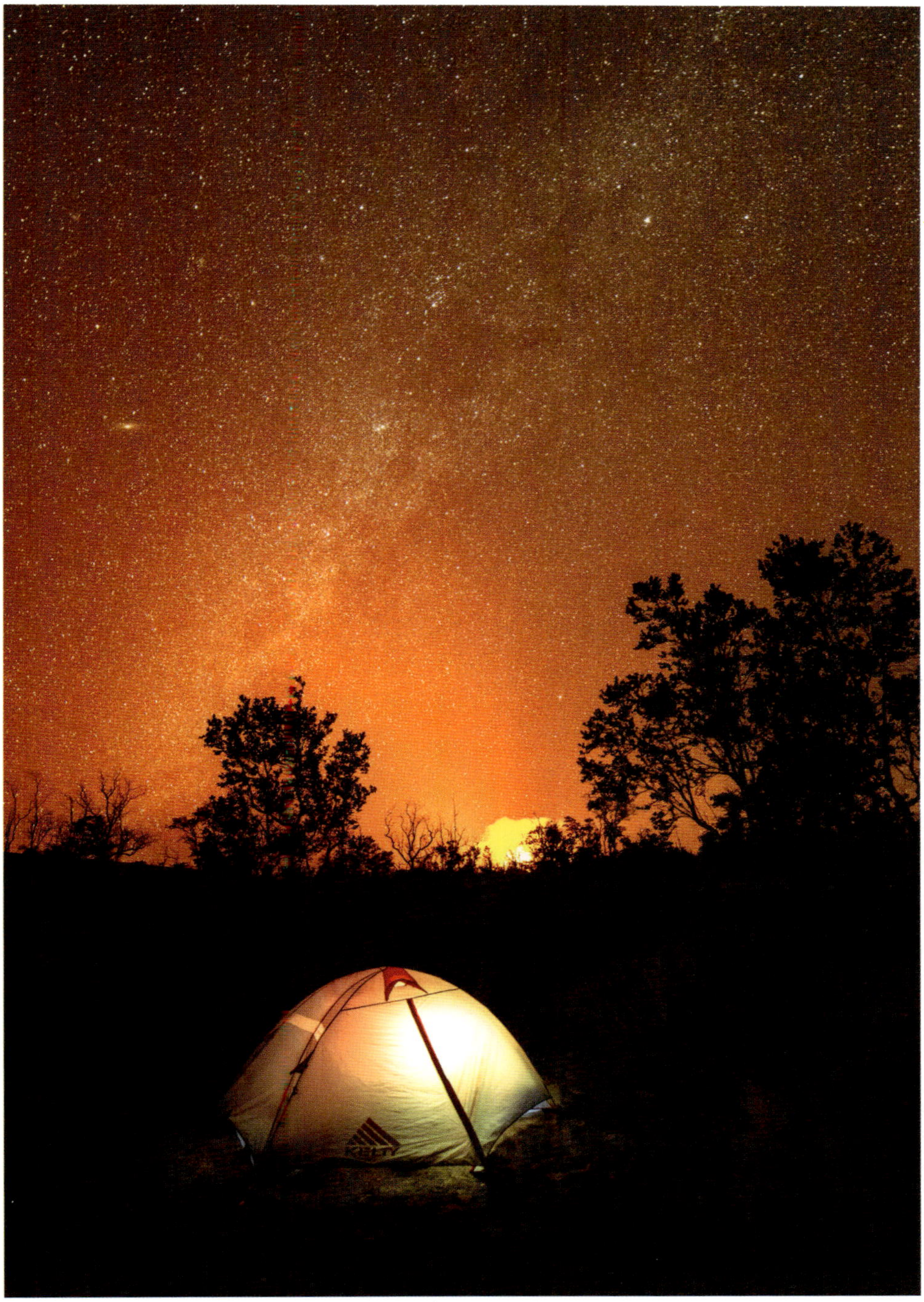

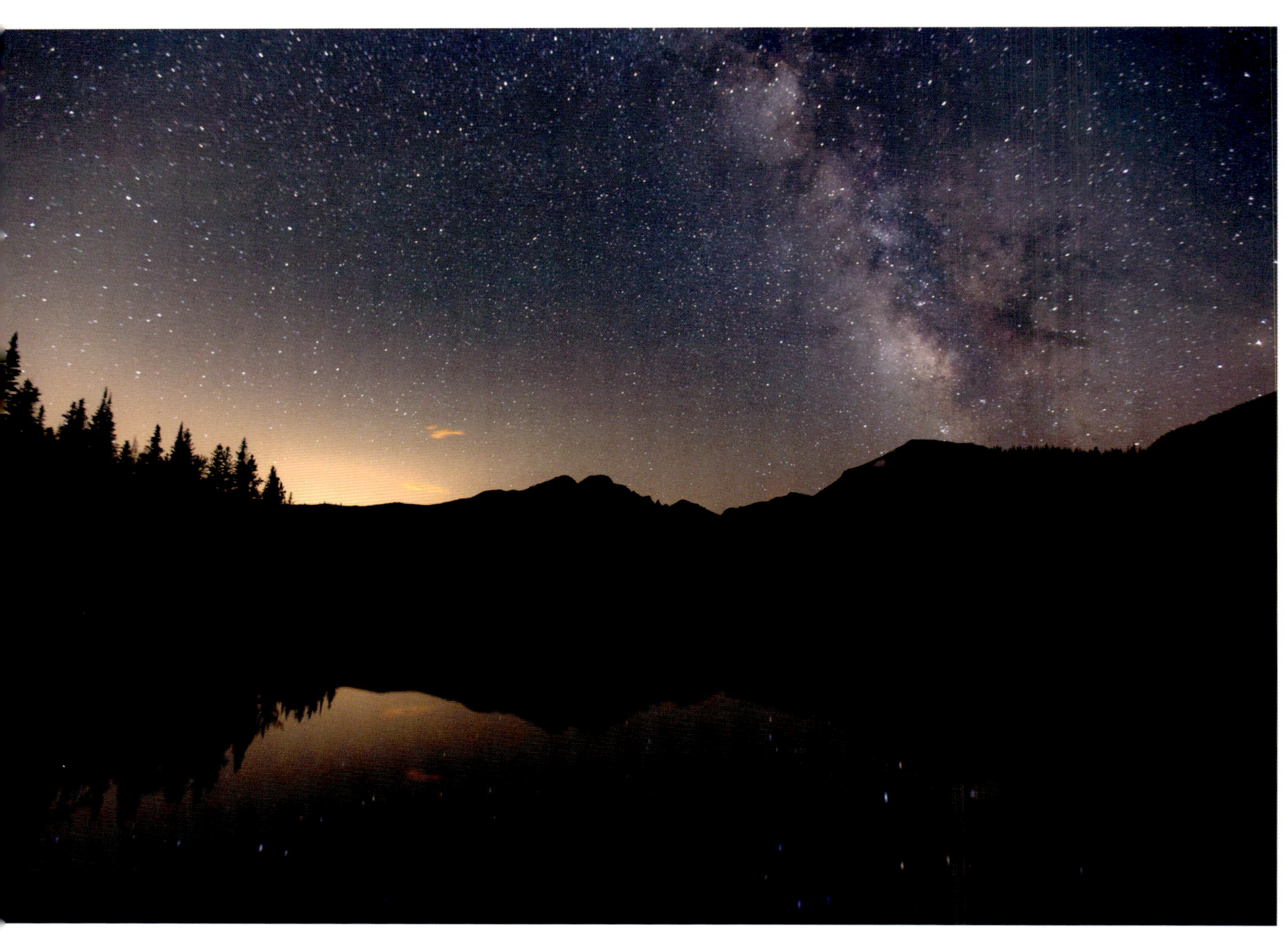

ROCKY MOUNTAIN NATIONAL PARK (ABOVE) My friend and I went on a night hike around Bear Lake so he could see the Milky Way. The skyglow from Denver can be seen over the Longs Peak silhouette.

GLACIER NATIONAL PARK (OPPOSITE) The Milky Way and aurora are usually in opposite parts of the sky. That's why I was so excited when I had the opportunity to fit them both in a single frame while watching this solar storm at Logan Pass. It wasn't until I got home that I noticed that I had also captured a meteor!

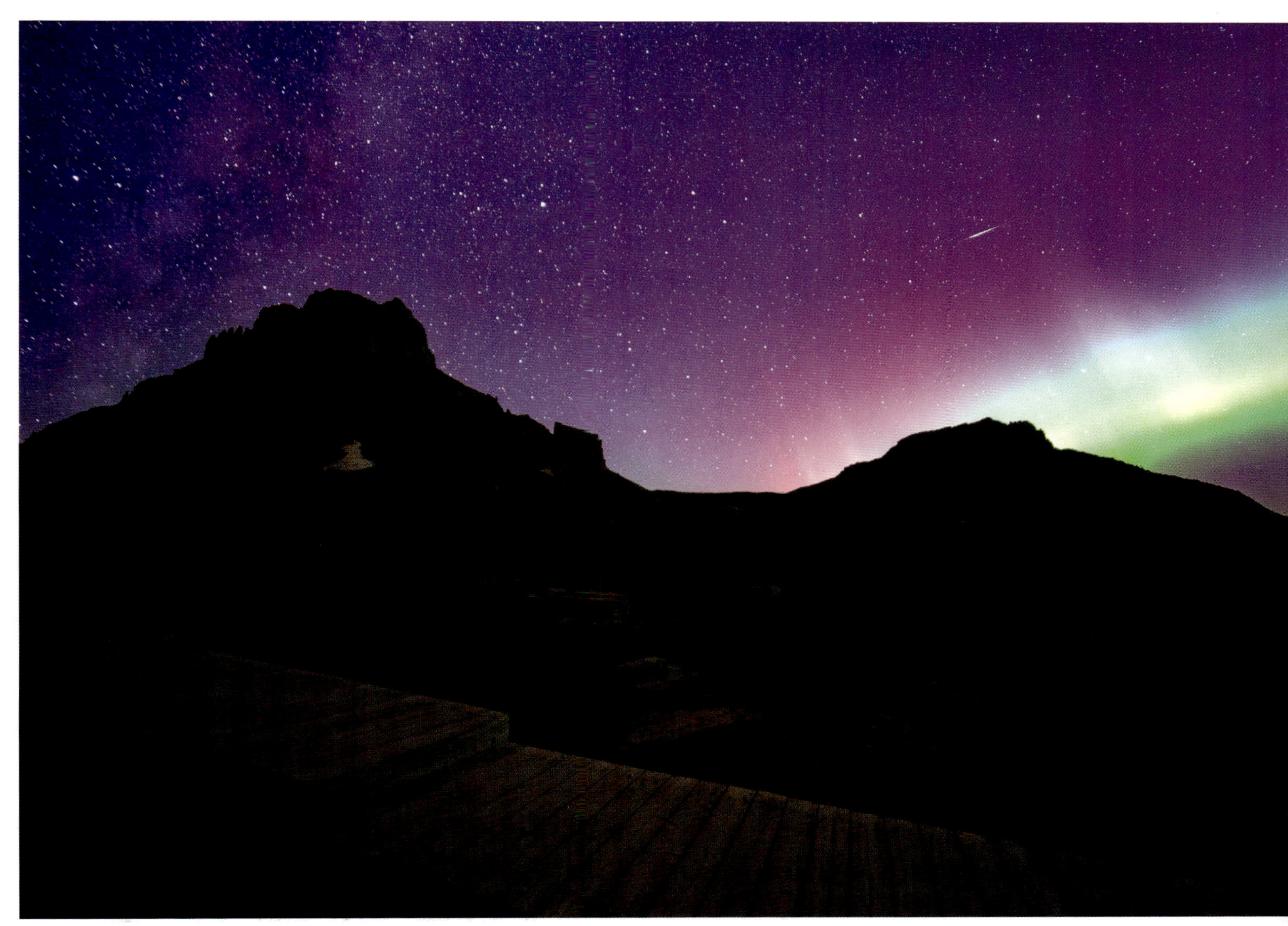

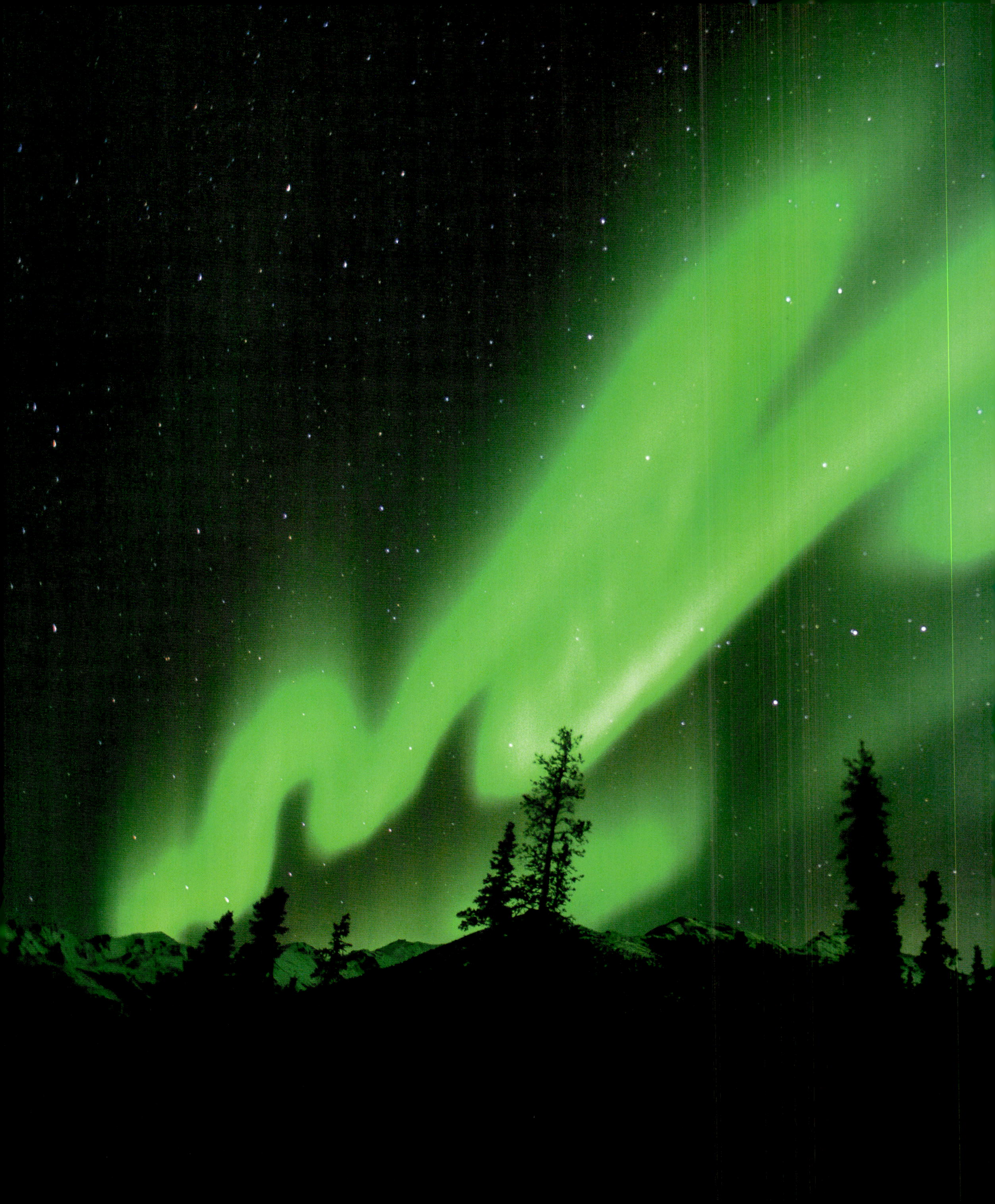

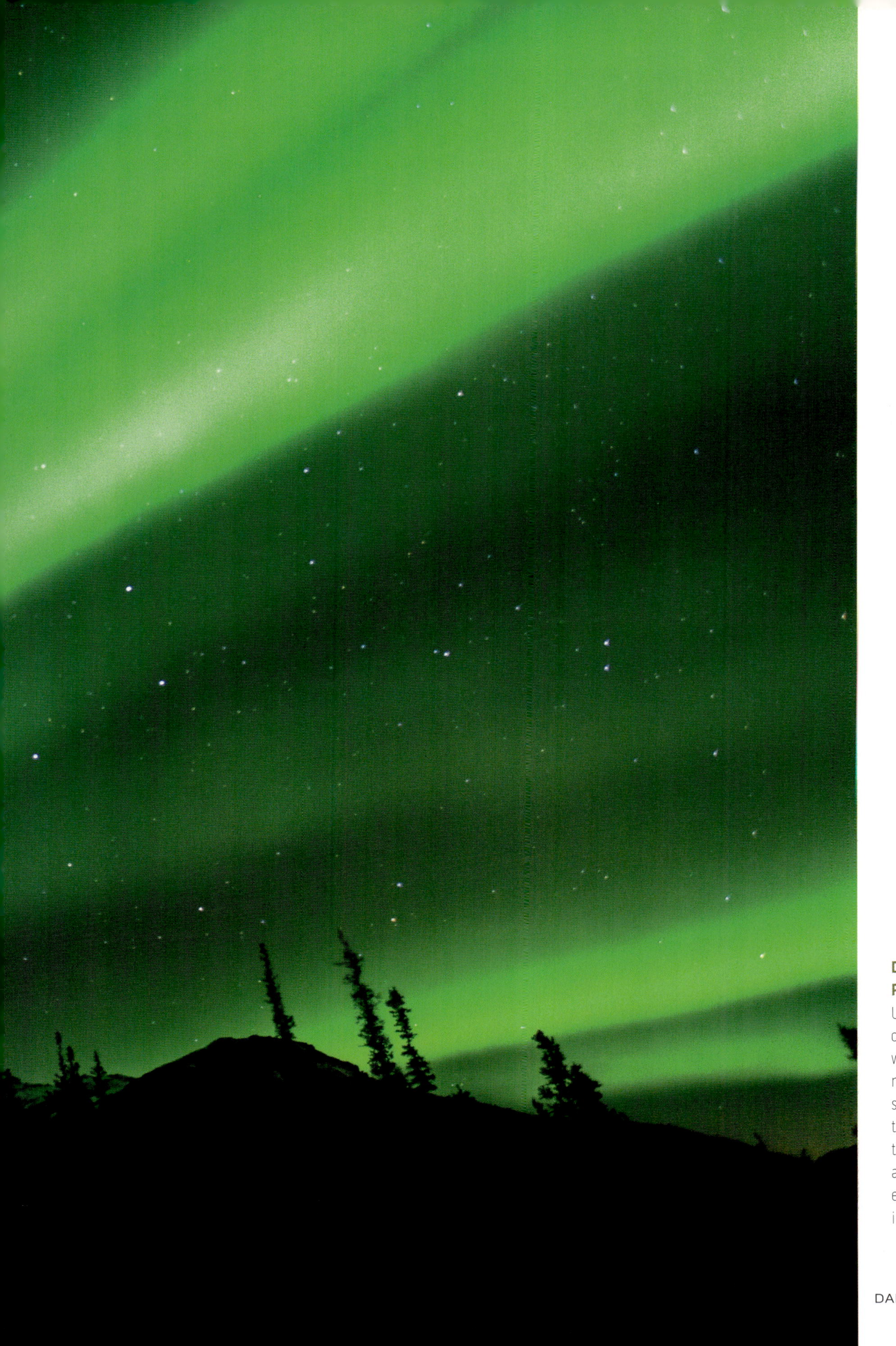

DENALI NATIONAL PARK AND PRESERVE
Up until this photo, most of the auroras I had seen were just a faint glow on the northern horizon. But this storm was different—it was the first time I could see the aurora curtains dance across the sky with my naked eye. This is the night I fell in love with the aurora.

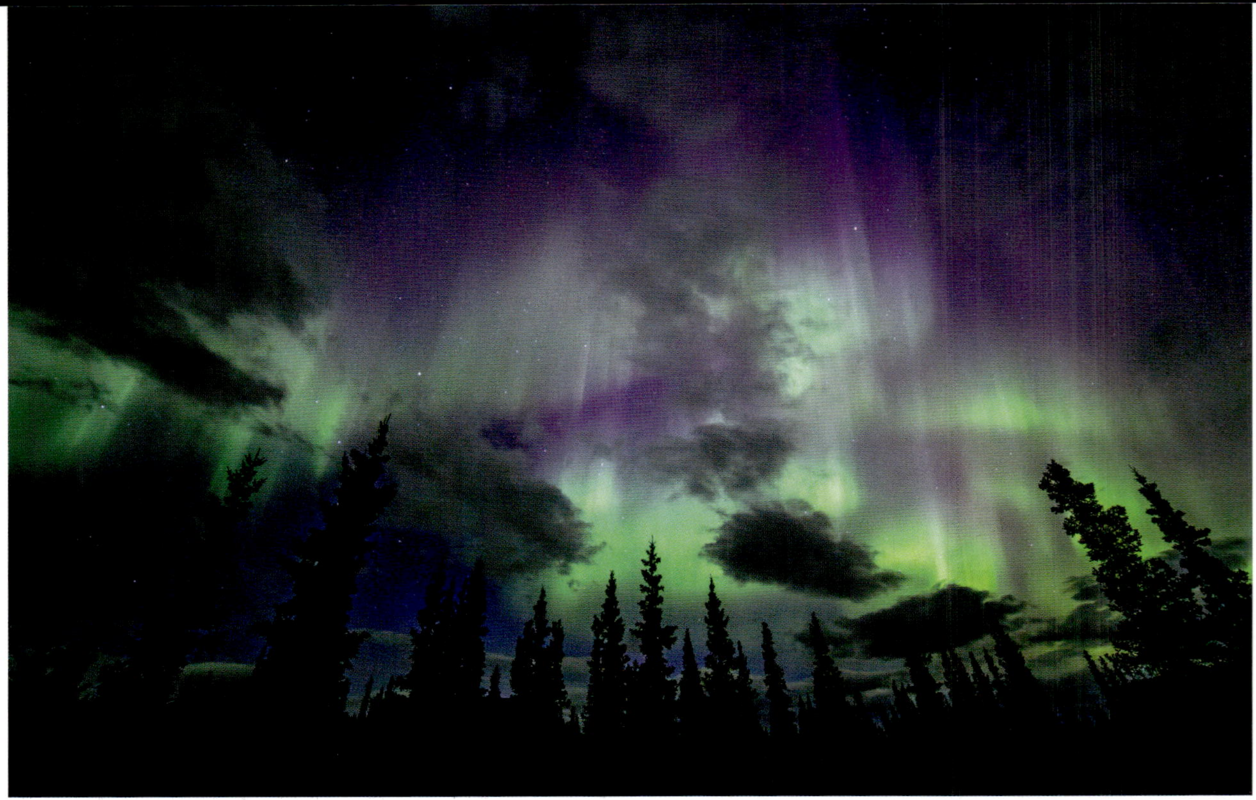

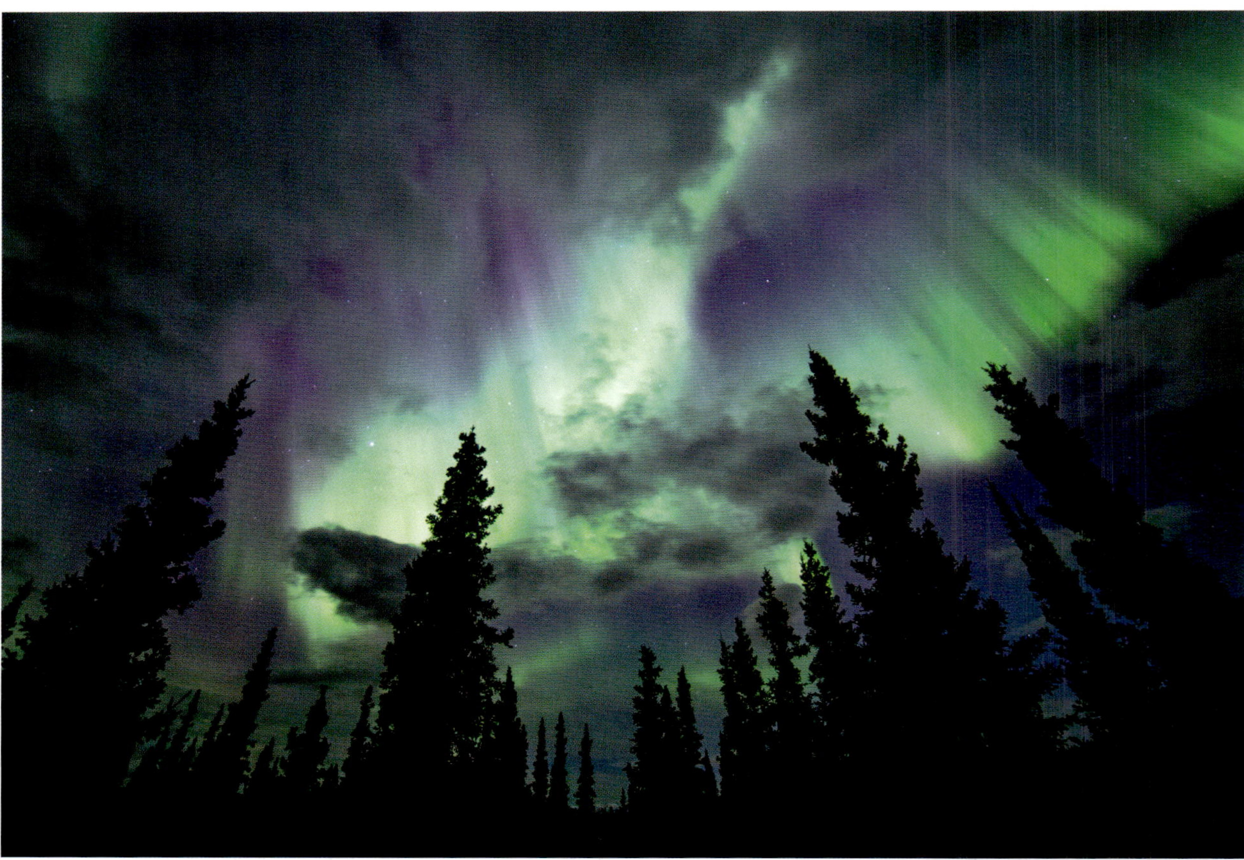

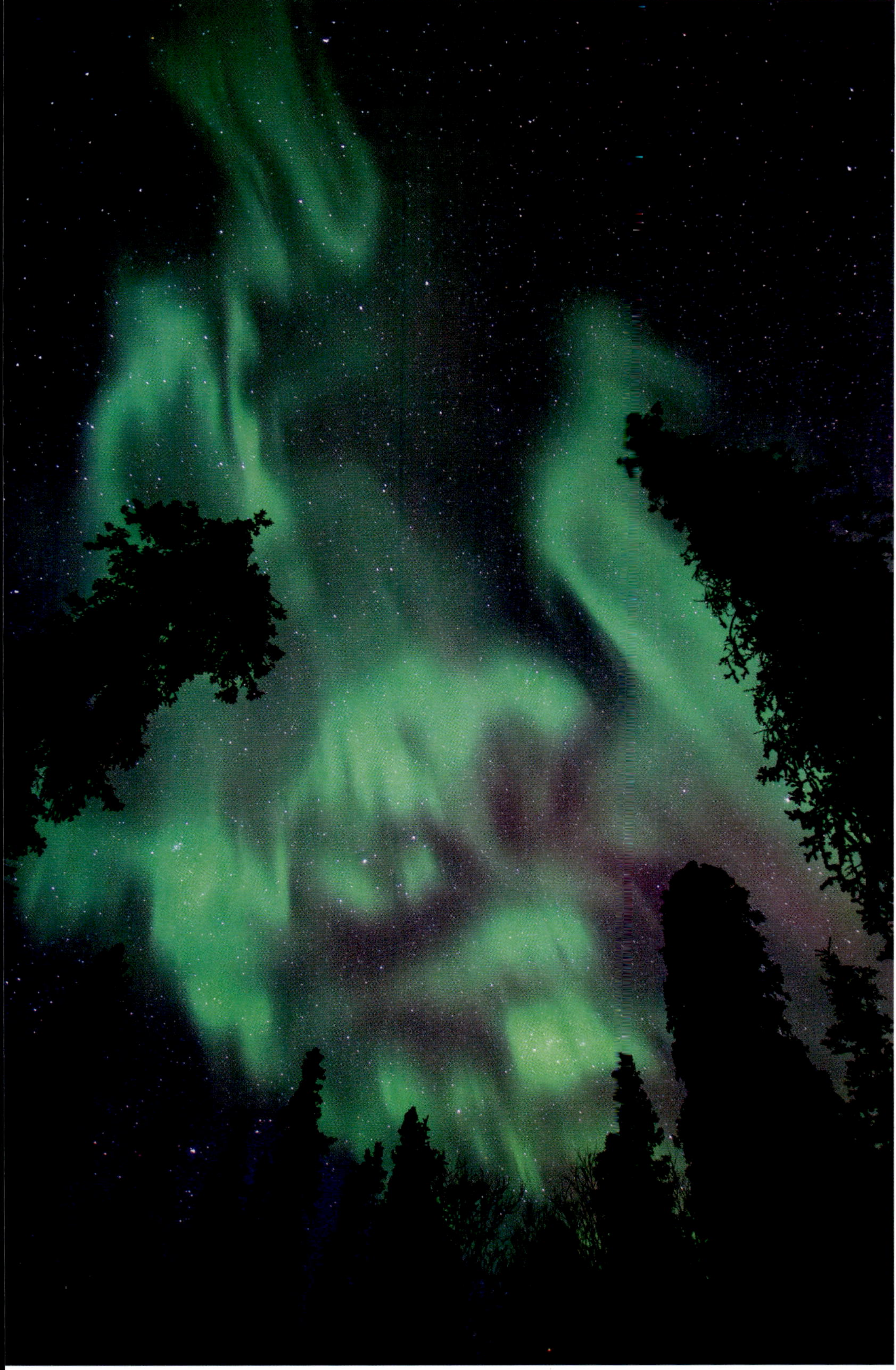

One thing I usually do when the northern lights are forecasted is chug water before bed. That night, when I woke up to use the outhouse, the aurora was just starting. By the time I grabbed my camera, it flared up, casting green flames above the trees. The sky came alive in a way I'll never forget—one of my favorite memories in the park.

DENALI NATIONAL PARK AND PRESERVE
Captures from one of the strongest solar storms I've ever witnessed. At times, the entire sky was so bright that I turned off my headlamp, no longer needing it to navigate.

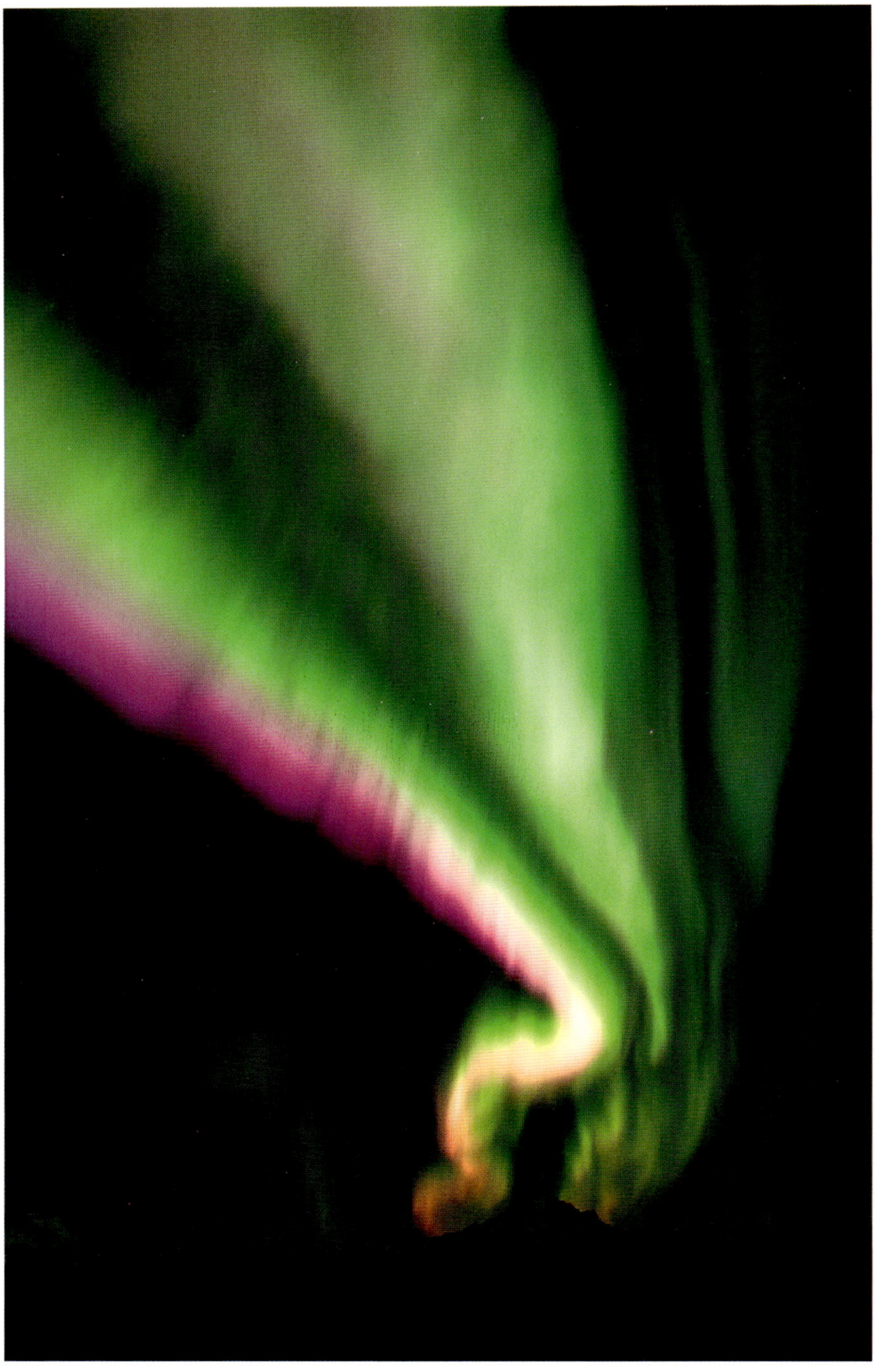

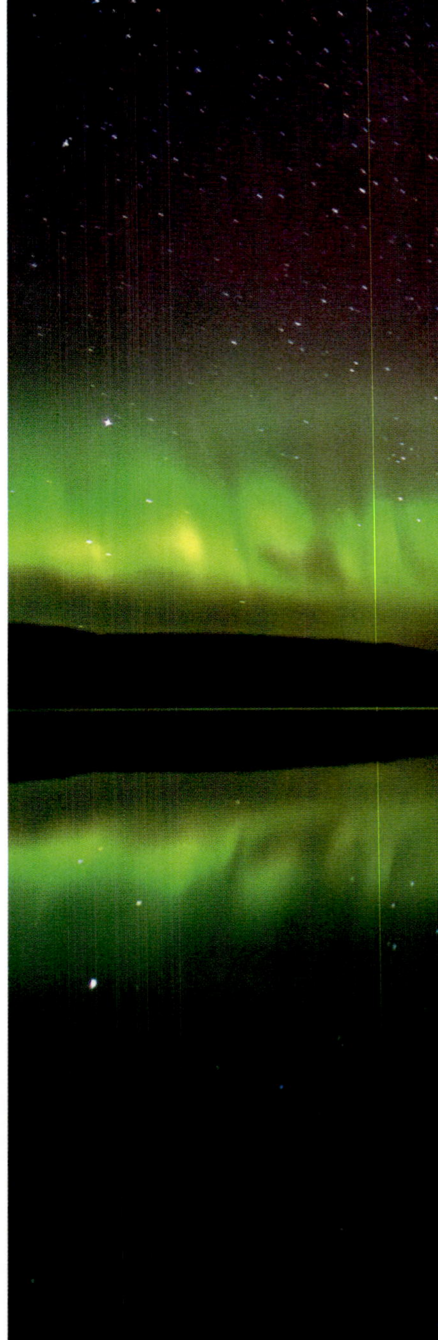

DENALI NATIONAL PARK AND PRESERVE This storm was the first time I had seen colors other than green. It remains the fastest-moving aurora I have ever seen. The curtains streaked completely across the sky from east to west. Pure magic.

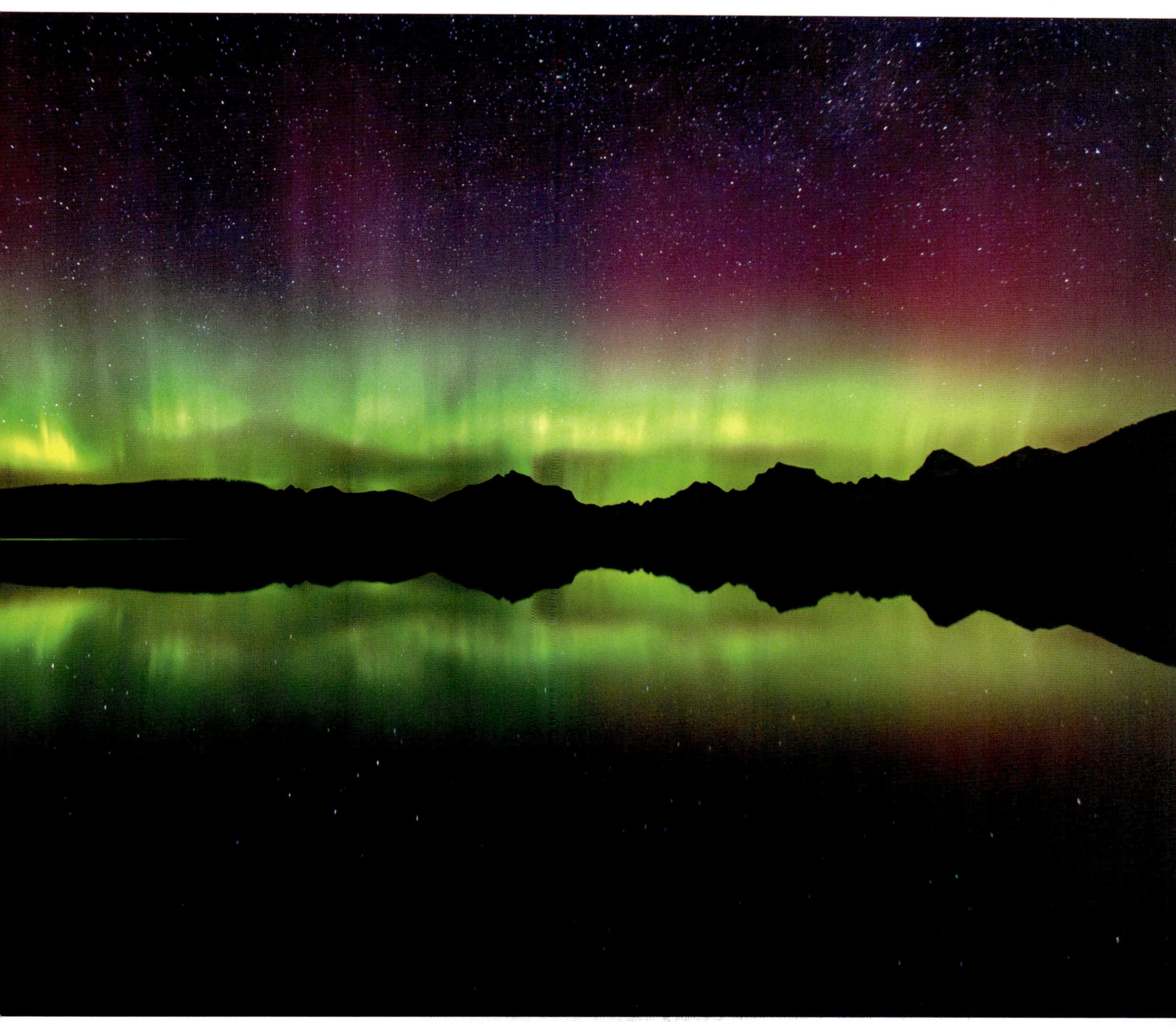

GLACIER NATIONAL PARK Up to this point, I had never seen the aurora over water. It was by pure chance that I was able to watch this solar storm all night reflecting in Lake McDonald.

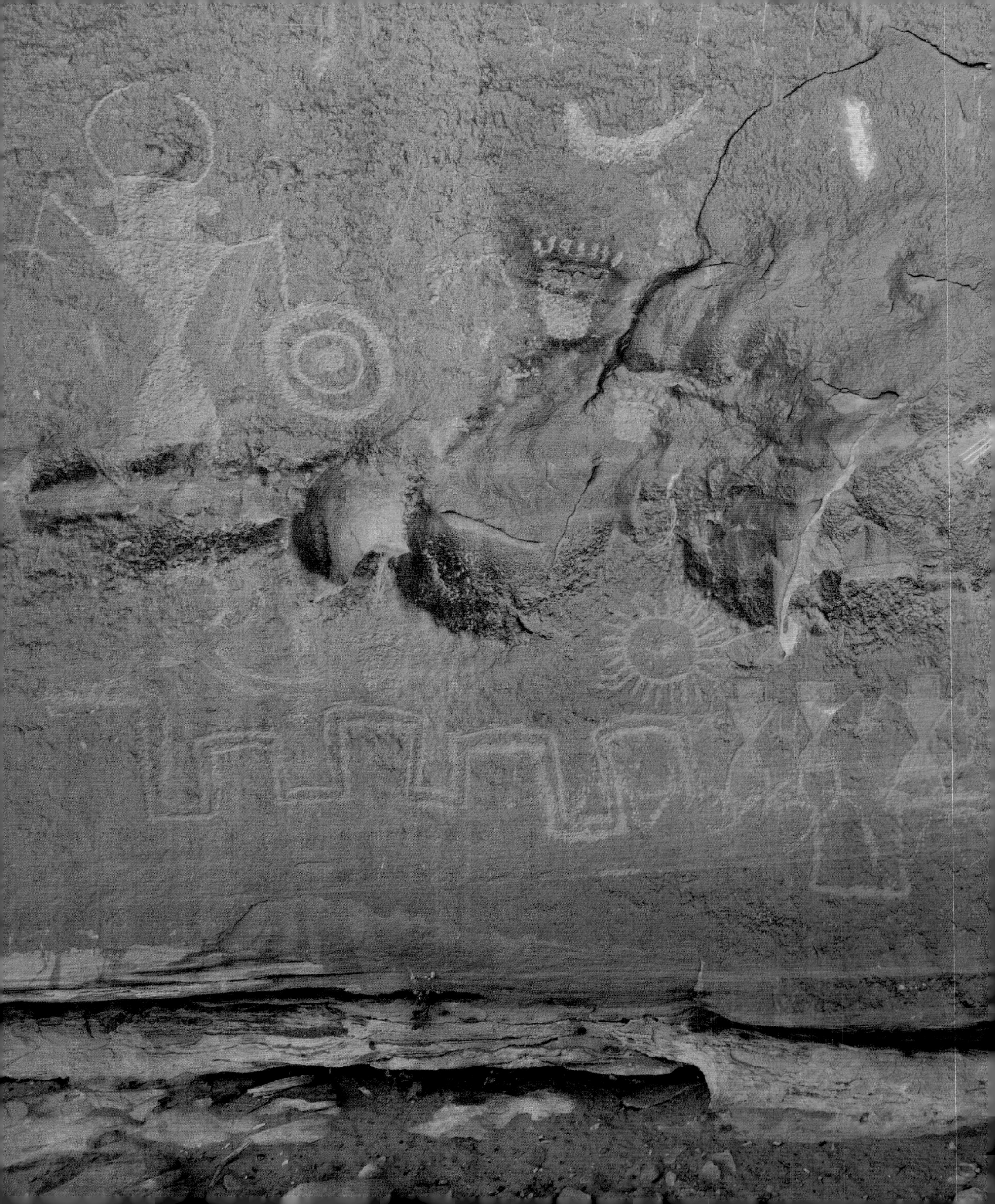

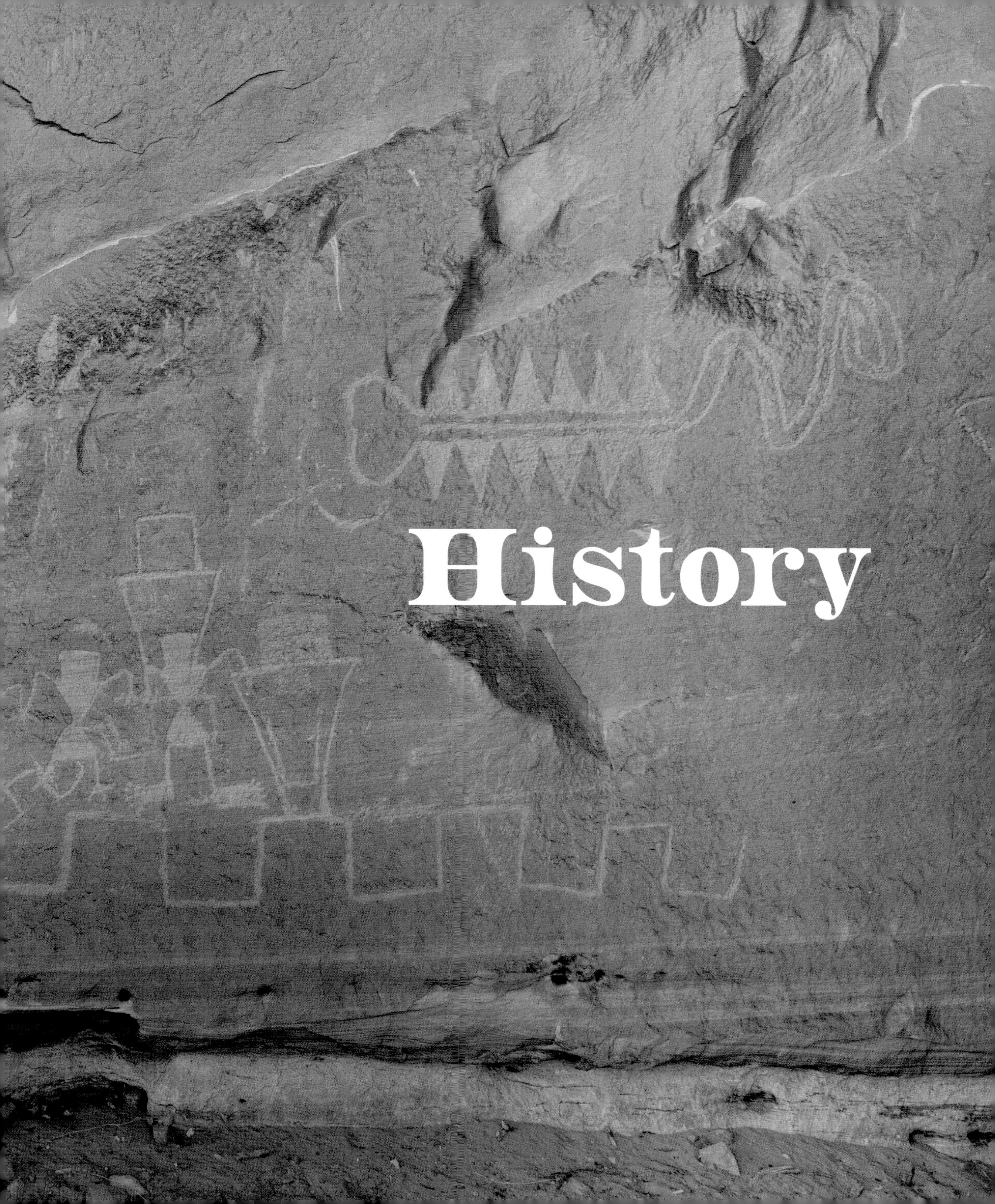

History

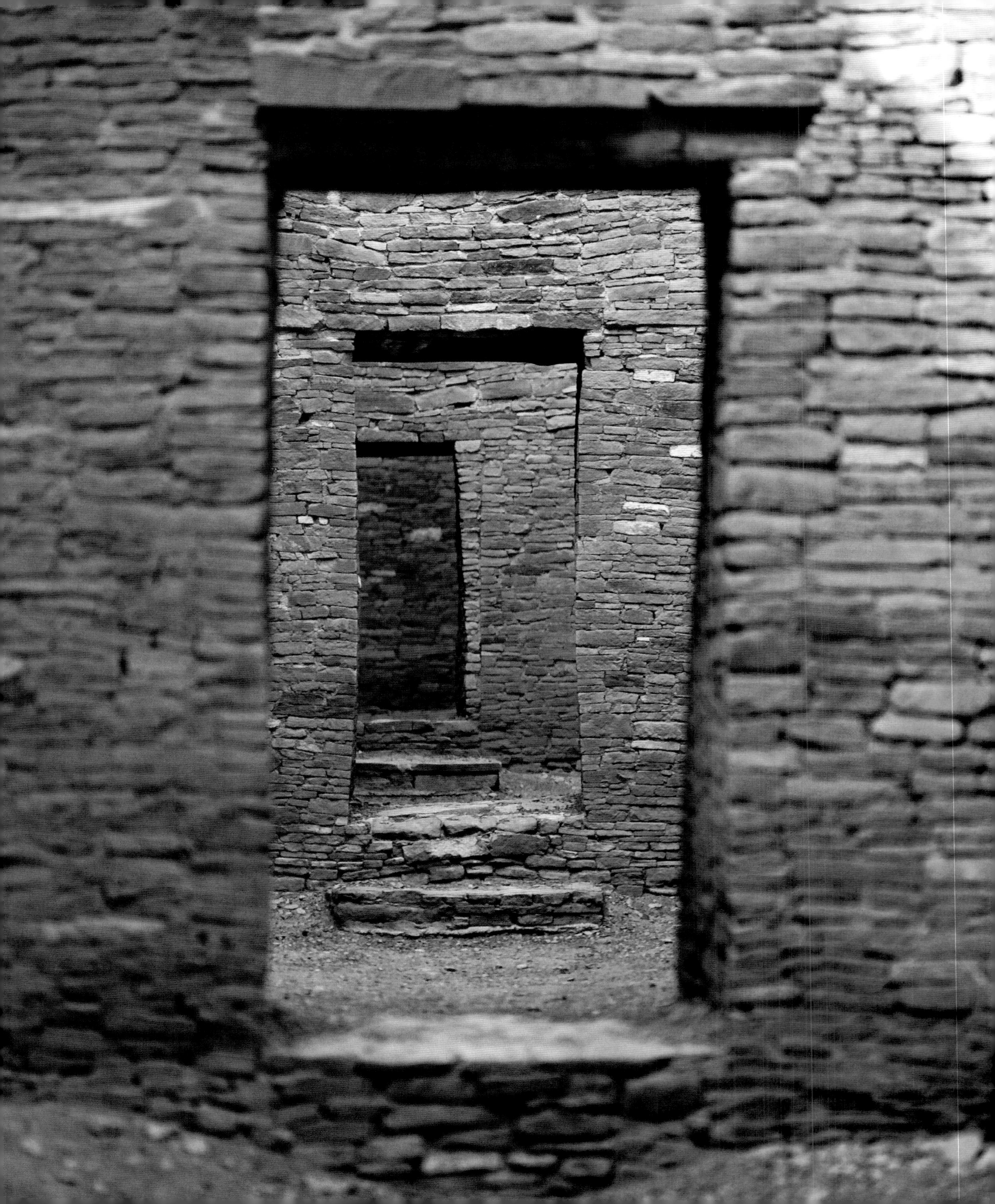

OUR SHARED HERITAGE

OUR NATIONAL PARKS not only protect stunning landscapes and natural resources but also serve as living museums that safeguard America's history, culture, and identity. These public lands offer a window into the nation's diverse past, preserving important sites and telling the stories of the people, events, and movements that have shaped—and continue to shape—our country.

National parks preserve iconic places from the birth of the United States, such as Independence Hall, where the Declaration of Independence and US Constitution were signed. These sites tell the story of America's fight for independence and the creation of its democratic ideals. They also commemorate key Civil War battlefields, memorializing the soldiers who fought and helping us understand the deep divisions that led to the conflict, its costs, and its lasting impact on American society.

Parks highlight the Industrial Revolution, telling the stories of textile mills and factory workers who were central to the country's rapid industrialization. They explore the labor struggles and social changes of the time, as well as the experiences of the millions of immigrants who arrived in search of a new life.

The fight for racial equality is preserved at sites key to the Civil Rights Movement, which tell the story of the struggle for justice for Black Americans. National parks also reflect the complex history of westward expansion, exploring its impact on American Indian Tribes, who often paid a great cost as the US expanded its territory. Finally, parks honor the heritage of Indigenous peoples, the original caretakers of these lands, whose cultures thrived long before European settlement.

GRAND STAIRCASE-ESCALANTE NATIONAL MONUMENT (PREVIOUS)

CHACO CULTURE NATIONAL HISTORICAL PARK (OPPOSITE) Exploring the passageways of Pueblo Bonito was the first time I had the chance to walk among such a massive structure. I was able to move through the walls, feeling the history around me in a way that felt intimate and awe-inspiring.

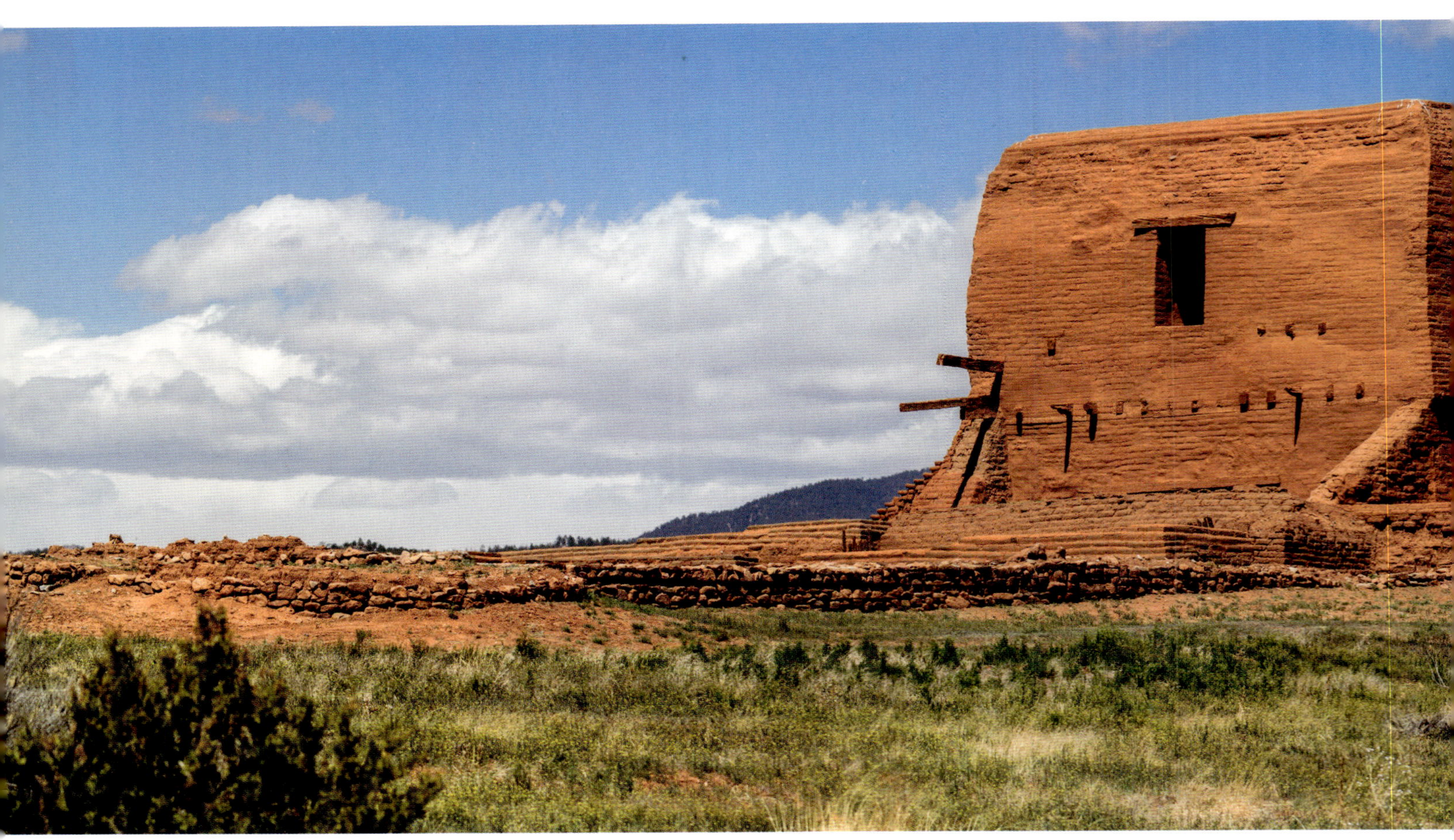

The latest research shows that humans have been living in North America and Tularosa Basin, the area which now encompasses White Sands National Park, for at least 23,000 years. These areas often hold profound cultural, spiritual, and historical significance for the Tribes and communities who have a deep-rooted connection to them. The traditions, stories, and historical practices of these Indigenous groups are intimately tied to the landscapes within these parks. Recognizing this, many national parks work to honor and integrate the Indigenous histories and cultural narratives associated with their lands into their interpretive programs and visitor experiences.

Land acknowledgment is a traditional custom that dates back centuries in many Native nations and communities. Today, land acknowledgments are used to recognize Indigenous peoples who are the original stewards of the lands on which we now live and recreate. A growing number of land management agencies engage in co-management agreements with Indigenous Tribes, allowing these communities to play an active role in site administration and decision-making. Such partnerships not only enhance the effectiveness of conservation strategies but also provide a platform for Indigenous voices and perspectives in the stewardship of these public lands.

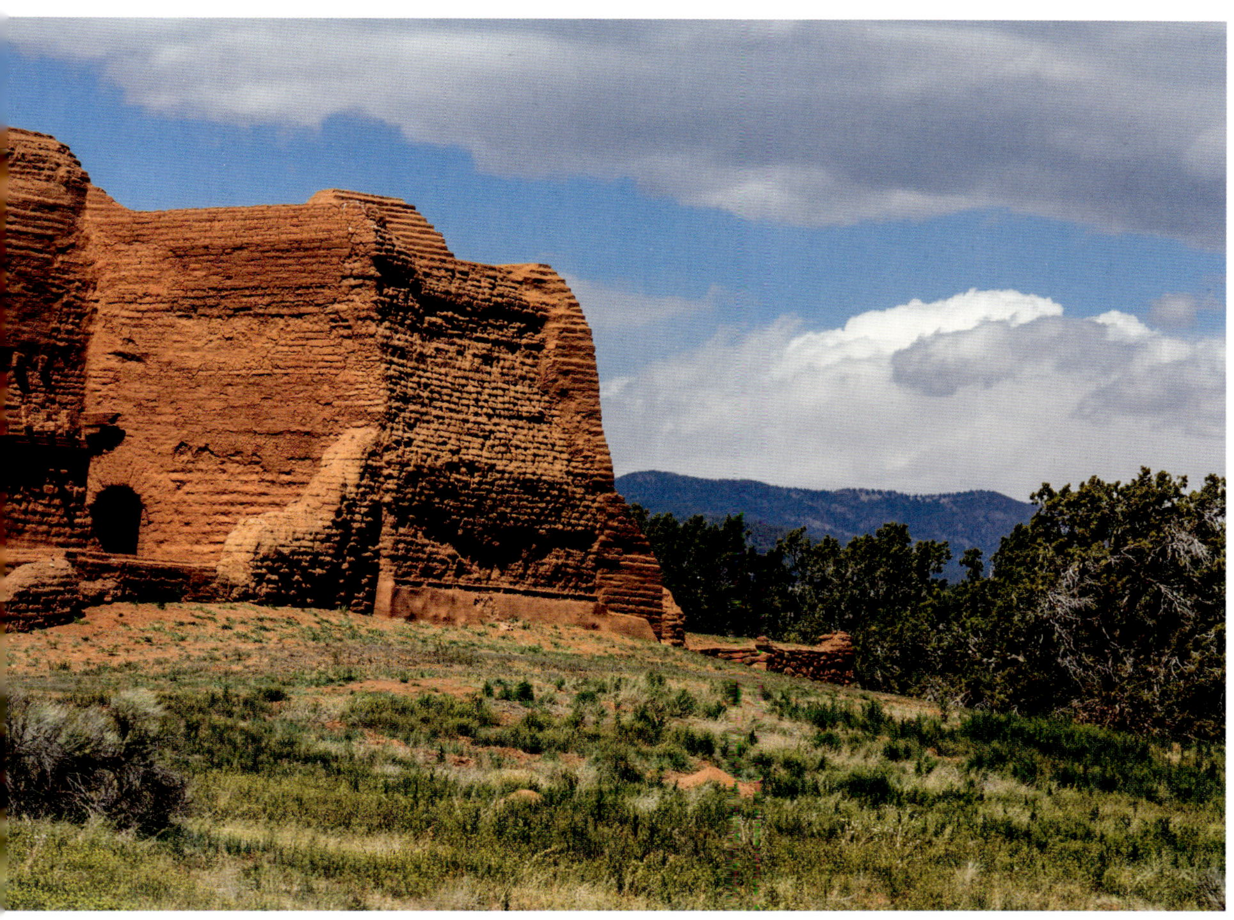

PECOS NATIONAL HISTORICAL PARK
On a road trip out west, we happened upon this park by accident. While visiting, we learned that it was home to Spanish missionaries, Ancestral Puebloans, the Santa Fe Trail, and the westernmost Civil War battle.

Many Indigenous communities continue to hold ceremonies and practice traditions that are linked to the ancient sites, and their ongoing connection to these places is an important aspect of preserving their cultural identity. Collaboration with these Tribes helps to ensure that their perspectives and needs are respected, and that traditional practices can continue in harmony with conservation efforts.

National parks in Hawaii serve as vibrant settings for modern Hawaiian cultural events, seamlessly blending the natural beauty of these landscapes with the rich traditions and practices of Native Hawaiian culture. These parks, which include notable locations such as Pu'uhonua O Hōnaunau National Historical Park, offer unique opportunities for cultural expression and preservation, reflecting the deep connection between the land and the people.

While it's possible to find evidence of Indigenous cultures across the country, the Colorado Plateau, particularly the Four Corners Region (Arizona, New Mexico, Utah, and Colorado), holds an abundance of Indigenous artifacts, especially those of the Ancestral Puebloans, due to environmental and cultural factors. The region's arid climate has preserved materials like wood, textiles, and adobe structures that would typically decay in more humid

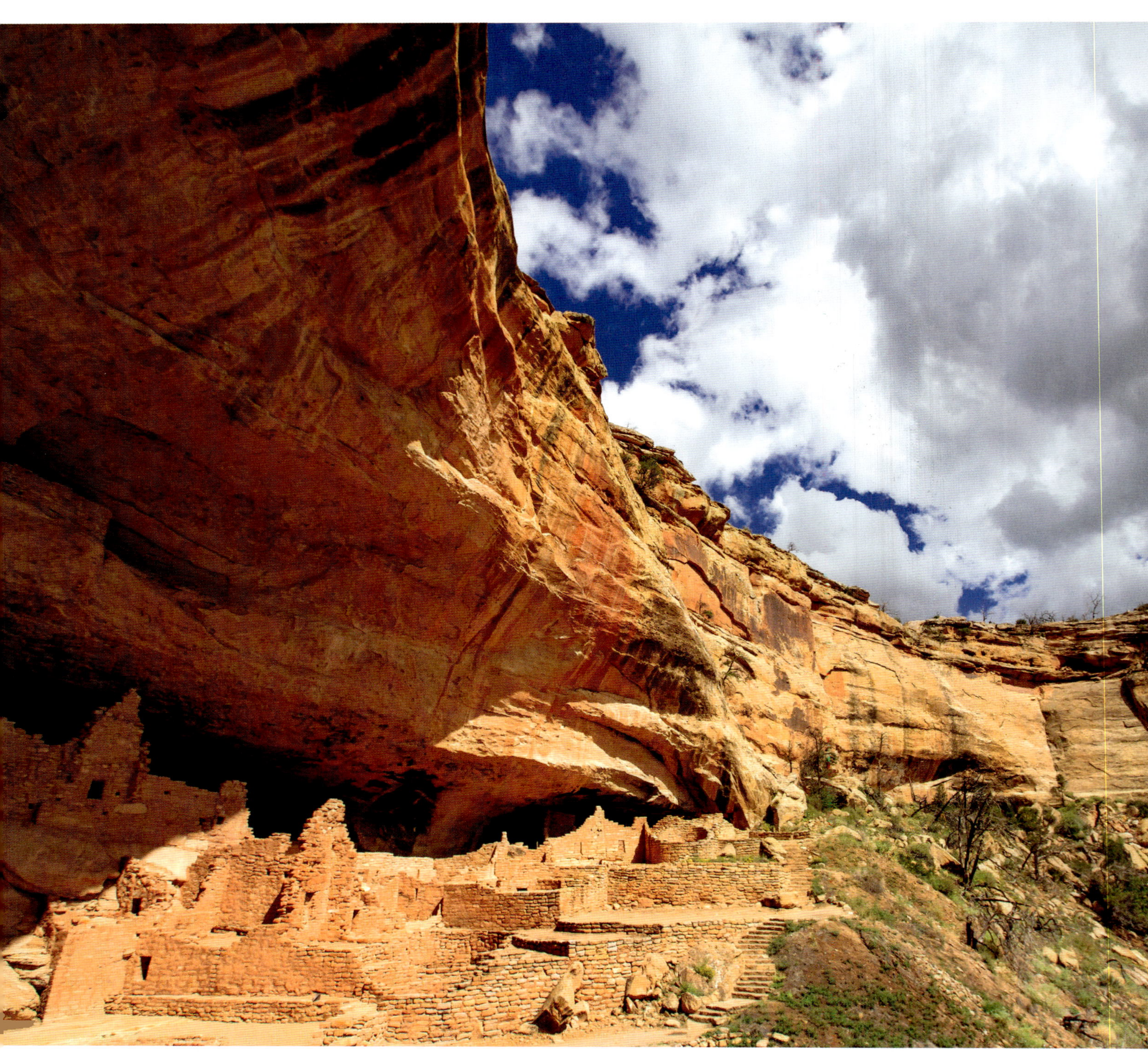

MESA VERDE NATIONAL PARK Long House, the second-largest cliff dwelling in the park, rests beneath a towering alcove. We had the entire site to ourselves for over an hour, climbing ladders and exploring its fascinating features.

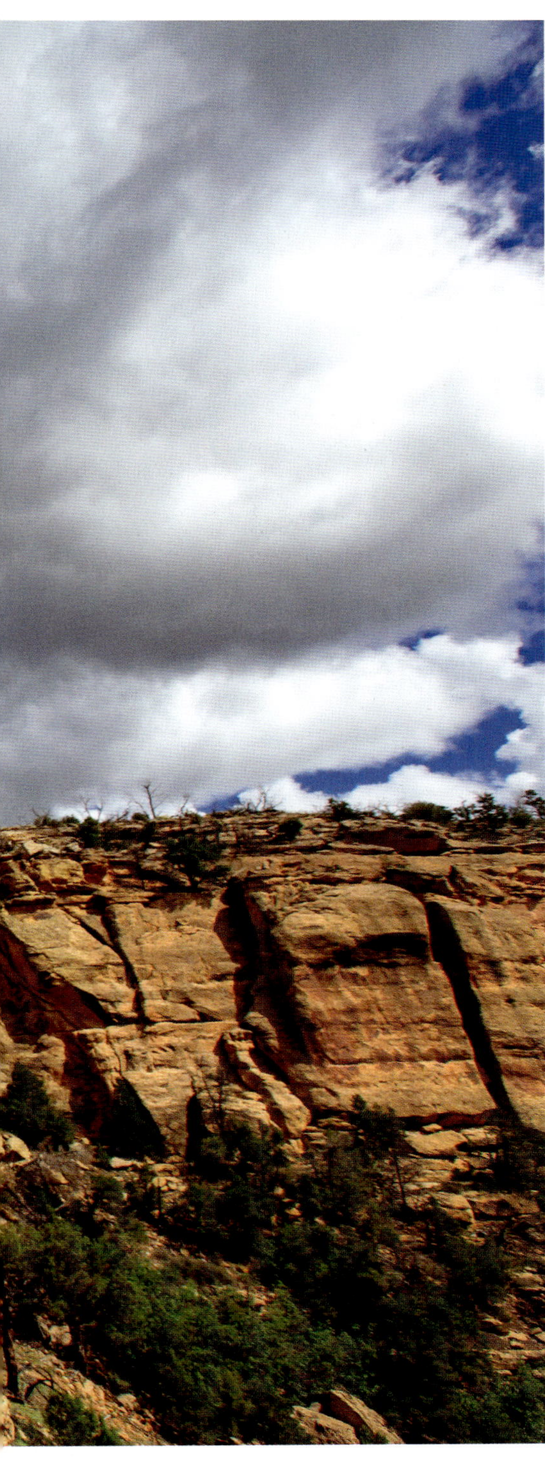

areas. The durable cliff dwellings and pueblos of the Ancestral Puebloans have survived for centuries, offering a rich record of their civilization.

Unlike more nomadic Indigenous cultures in other parts of the United States, the Ancestral Puebloans were settled, creating permanent structures and leaving behind a substantial material legacy. Many artifacts are found in sheltered locations, such as caves and cliff alcoves, which further protected them from the elements. The region's geology and low vegetation also make it easier for archaeologists to conduct surveys and excavations, leading to more discoveries.

Public lands, like Mesa Verde National Park and Chaco Culture National Historical Park, play a vital role in protecting these cultural resources. The impressive dwellings, ceremonial sites, and agricultural fields of the Ancestral Puebloans provide valuable insights into their way of life, and public lands ensure these sites are preserved from development and vandalism. These places also remain spiritually significant to the Hopi, Zuni, and Pueblo peoples, the descendants of the Ancestral Puebloans.

However, modern threats such as climate change and increased tourism pose challenges to the preservation of these ancient sites. Public land agencies actively monitor and mitigate these risks through conservation efforts, ensuring that these cultural treasures are preserved for future generations. By protecting both physical sites and intangible cultural heritage, public lands honor the legacy of Indigenous cultures and strengthen our connection to these ancient civilizations. Indigenous peoples continue to play a key role in the stewardship of these lands, fostering partnerships that uphold conservation and cultural preservation for the future.

With two months between jobs at Carlsbad Caverns and Denali, I seized the opportunity to visit my cousin, who was stationed in Albuquerque, New Mexico. Equipped with my newly acquired camping gear, we searched for a place to hike and camp for a long weekend. After some looking, I discovered that Chaco Culture National Historical Park wasn't too far away.

It took about an hour to reach the park entrance after we turned onto the sixteen-mile washboard dirt road. Securing a campsite was easy since the campground was empty. Over the next few days, we hiked and drove to as many sites as possible. While each site was memorable, one experience stood out.

As we hiked the Pueblo Alto loop trail, we gazed down at Pueblo Bonito, the park's largest and most famous great house. This massive structure covers over three acres and once stood five stories tall in some sections, with around 650 rooms. While soaking in the views, I noticed some "rocks" in the dirt that seemed out of place. Upon closer inspection, I realized they were actually pottery sherds.

Up until then, the only artifacts I had ever seen were behind glass in museum exhibits at Mesa Verde. Finding a significant pottery sherd like this in the wild—and being able to hold it—was an entirely new experience. Initially, I focused on the details of the paint. But when I flipped it over, something even more amazing caught my eye—a single fingerprint, preserved in the hardened clay. Judging by its size, I guessed it was a thumbprint. I placed my thumb over the print and felt the ancient ridges against my own, as if shaking hands with someone from nine hundred years ago. After some time, I carefully returned it to the ground, hoping that someone else might discover it one day and have a similar experience as me.

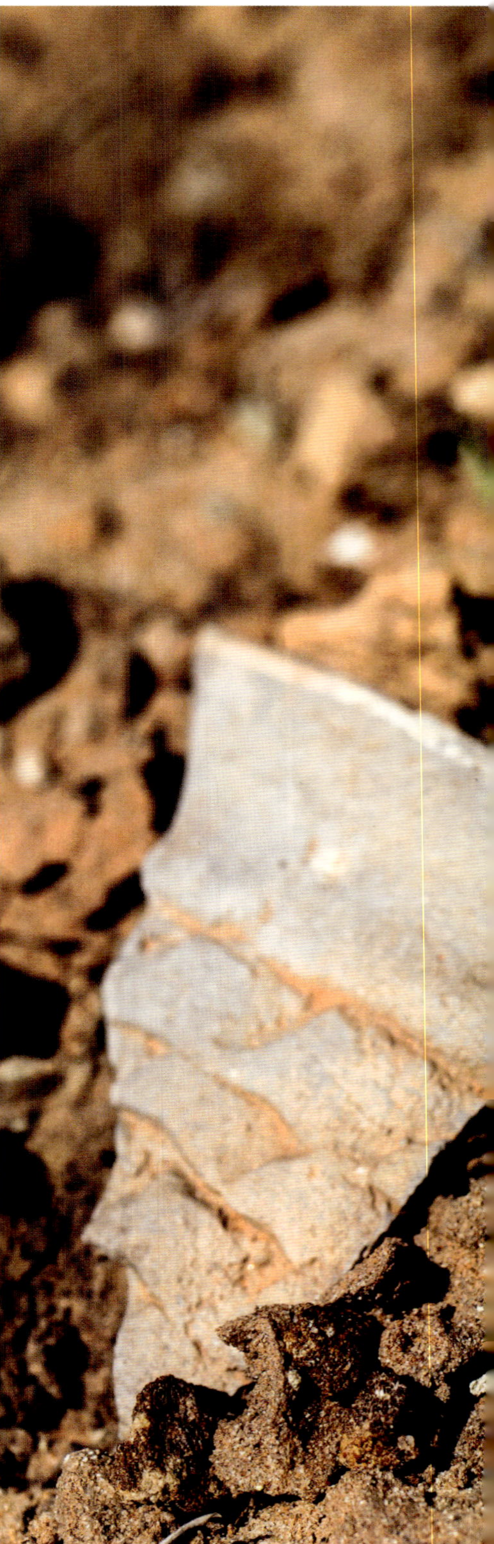

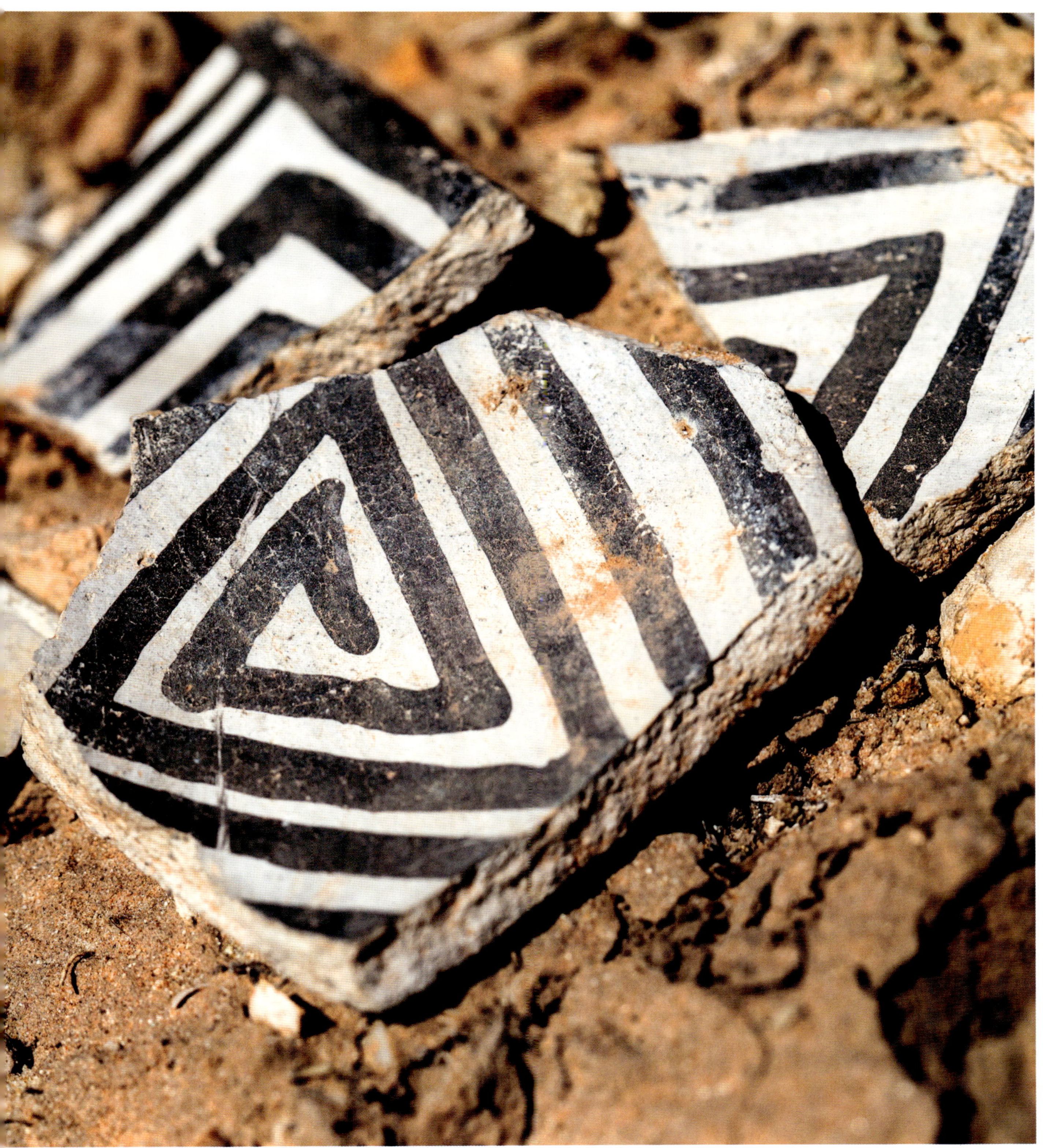

CHACO CULTURE NATIONAL HISTORICAL PARK

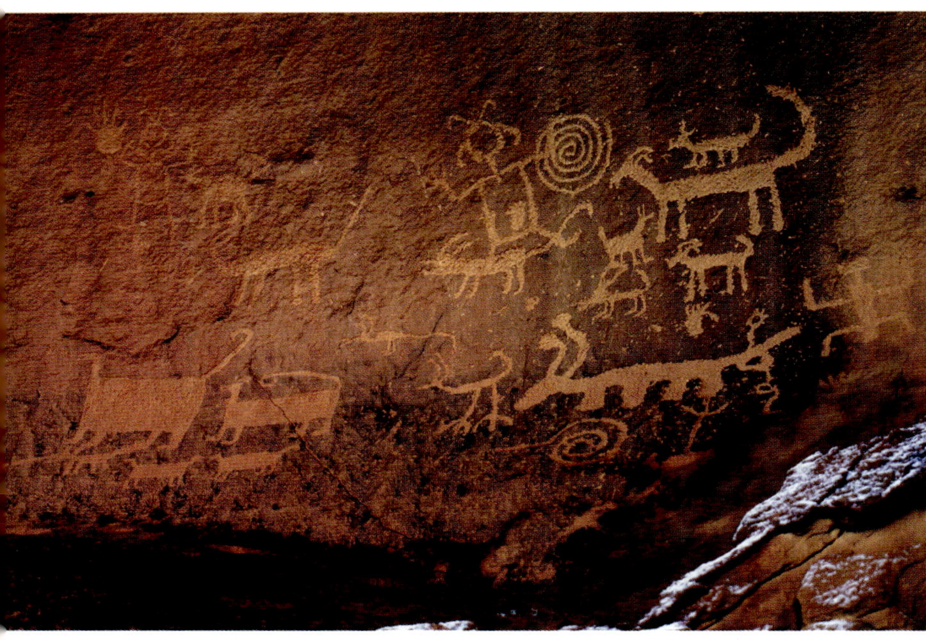

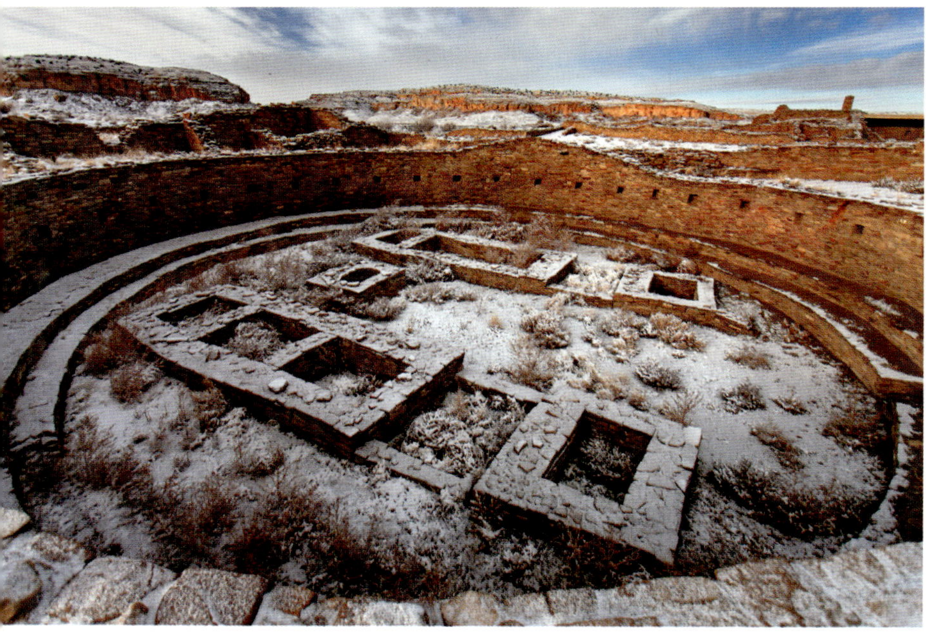

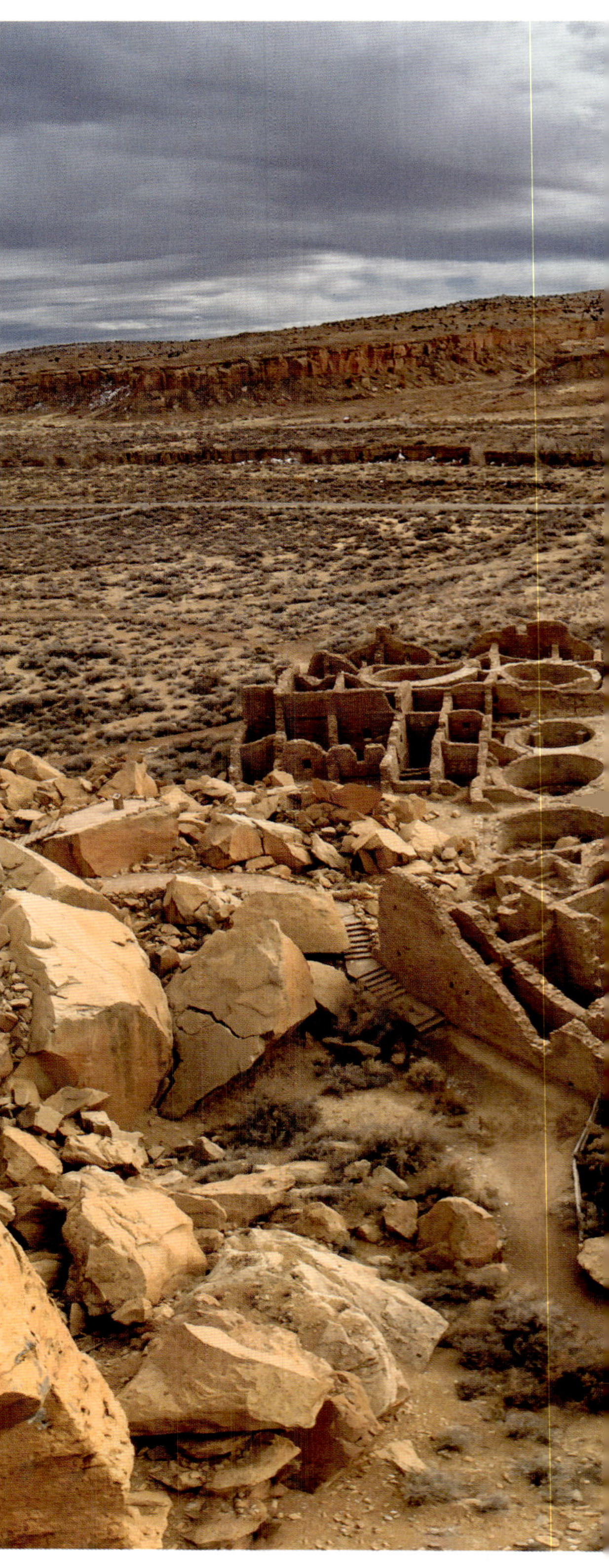

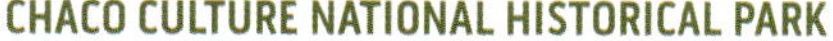

CHACO CULTURE NATIONAL HISTORICAL PARK

(TOP) Una Vida petroglyph panel.

(BOTTOM) Pueblo Bonito kiva with a fresh dusting of snow.

(OPPOSITE) View of Pueblo Bonito from the Pueblo Alto loop trail.

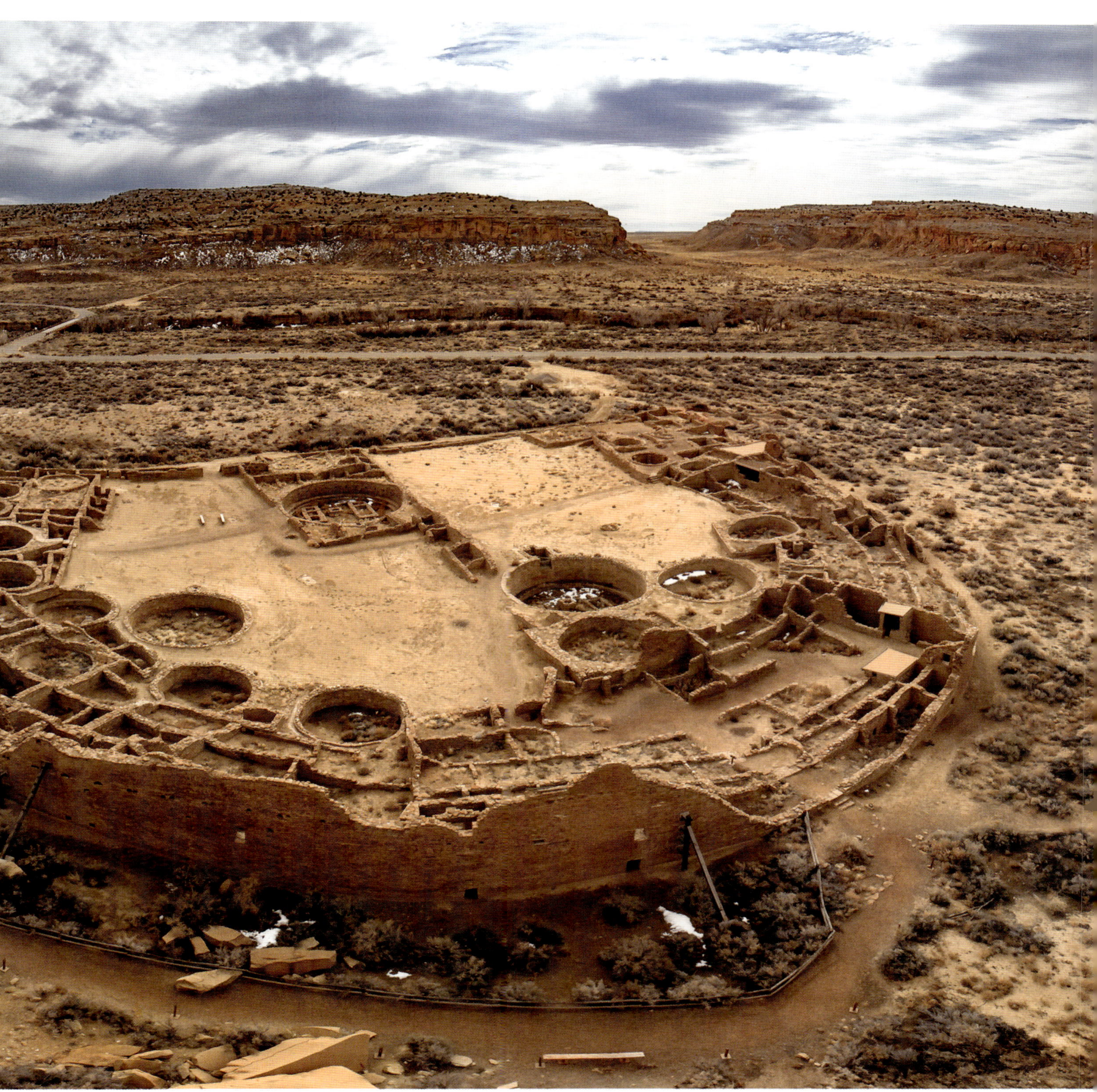

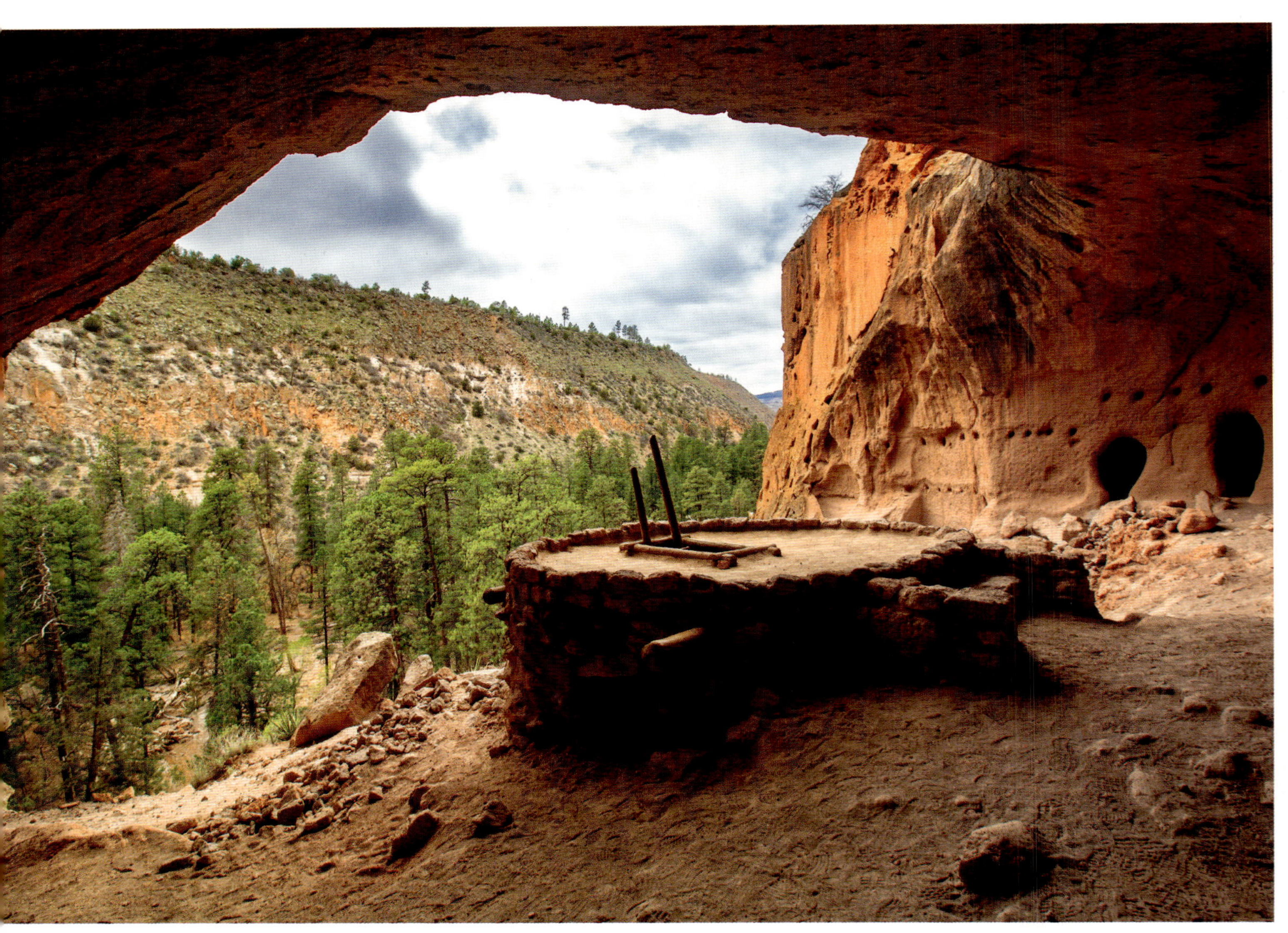

BANDELIER NATIONAL MONUMENT (ABOVE) My favorite hike within the monument was the trail to Alcove House. At the end of the short trail you must climb 140 feet up using stone stairs and a series of four wooden ladders.

(OPPOSITE) What makes the monument stand out to me is the type of dwellings compared to other parks. Ancestral Puebloans carved "cavates" in the soft volcanic tuft, revealing the resourcefulness and artistry of the people who once lived in Frijoles Canyon.

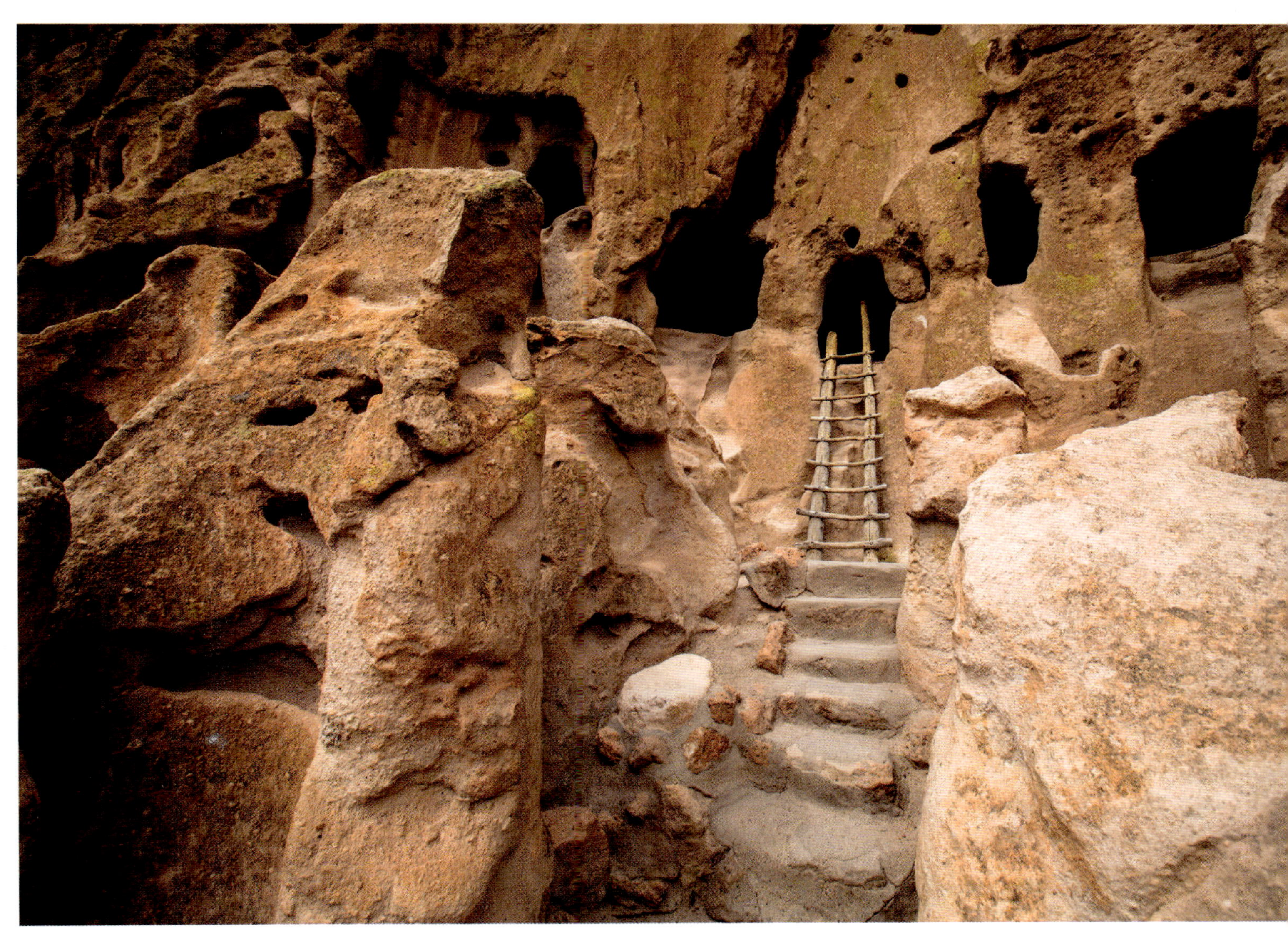

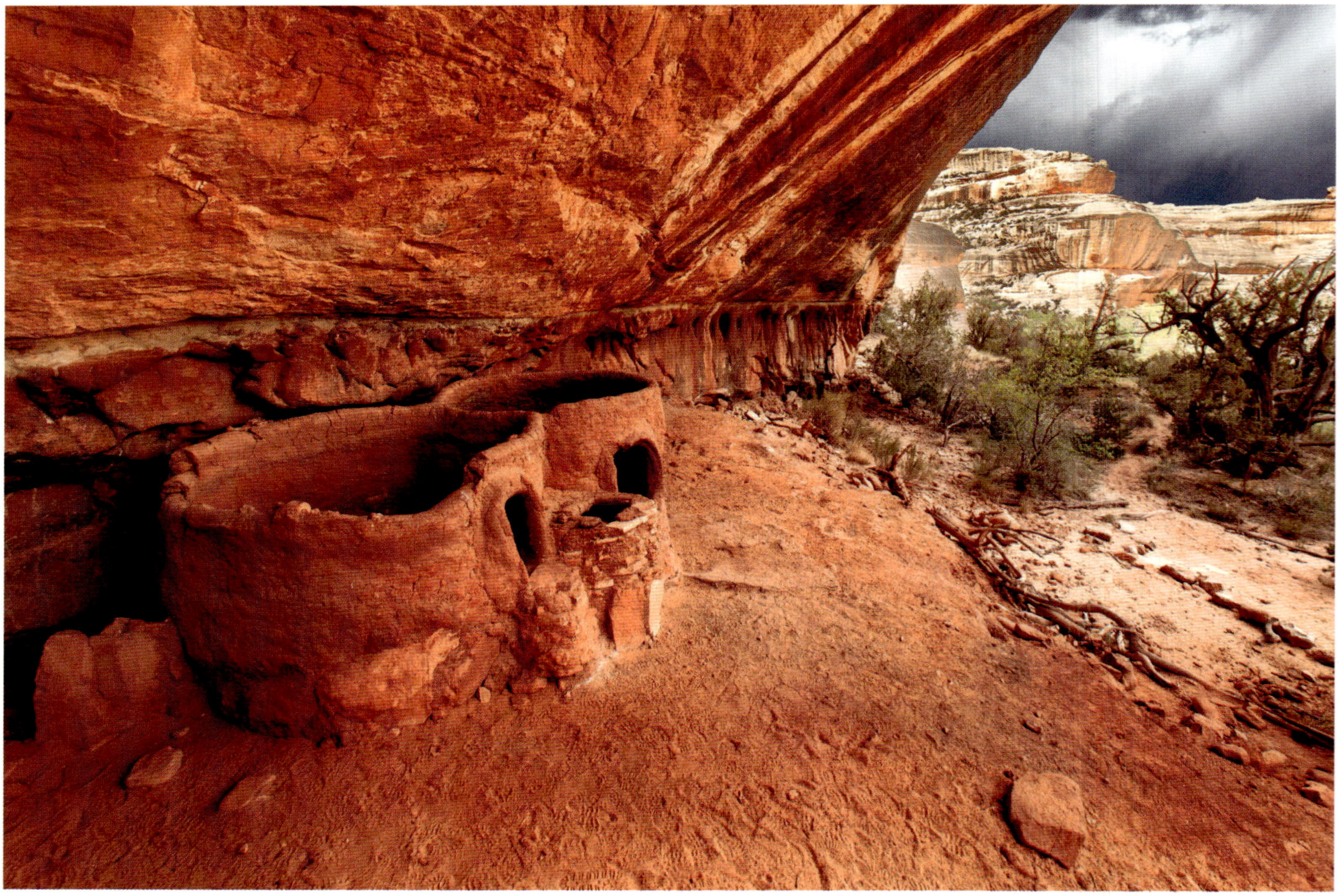

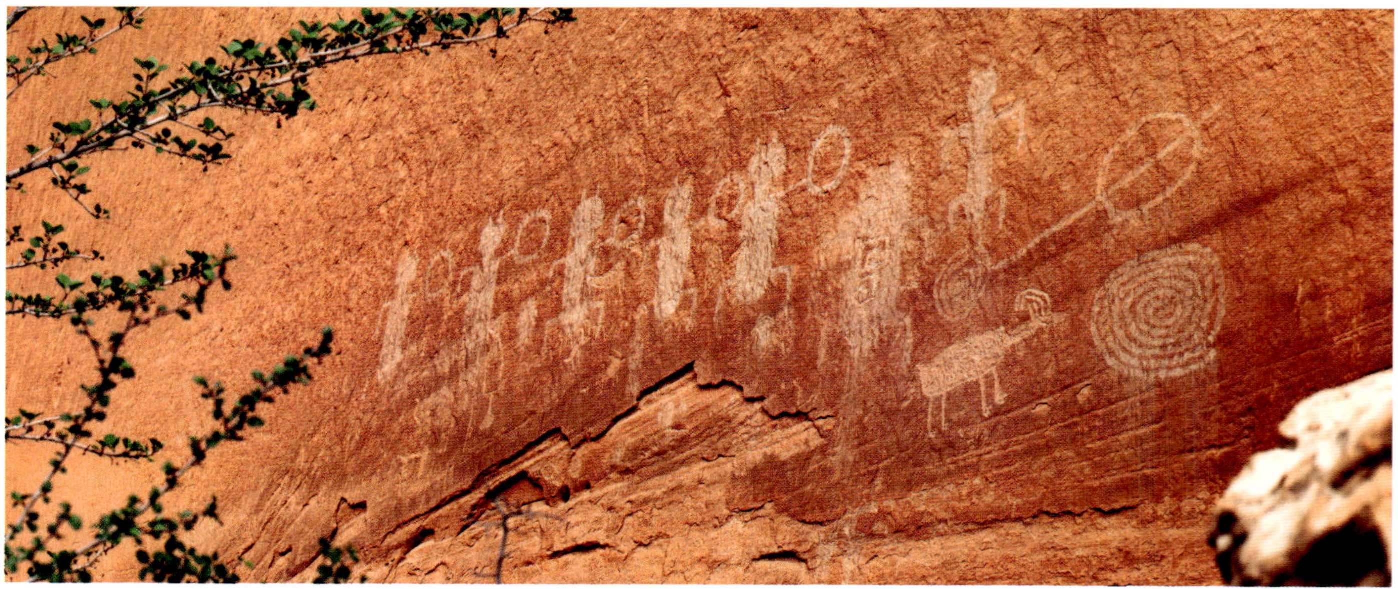

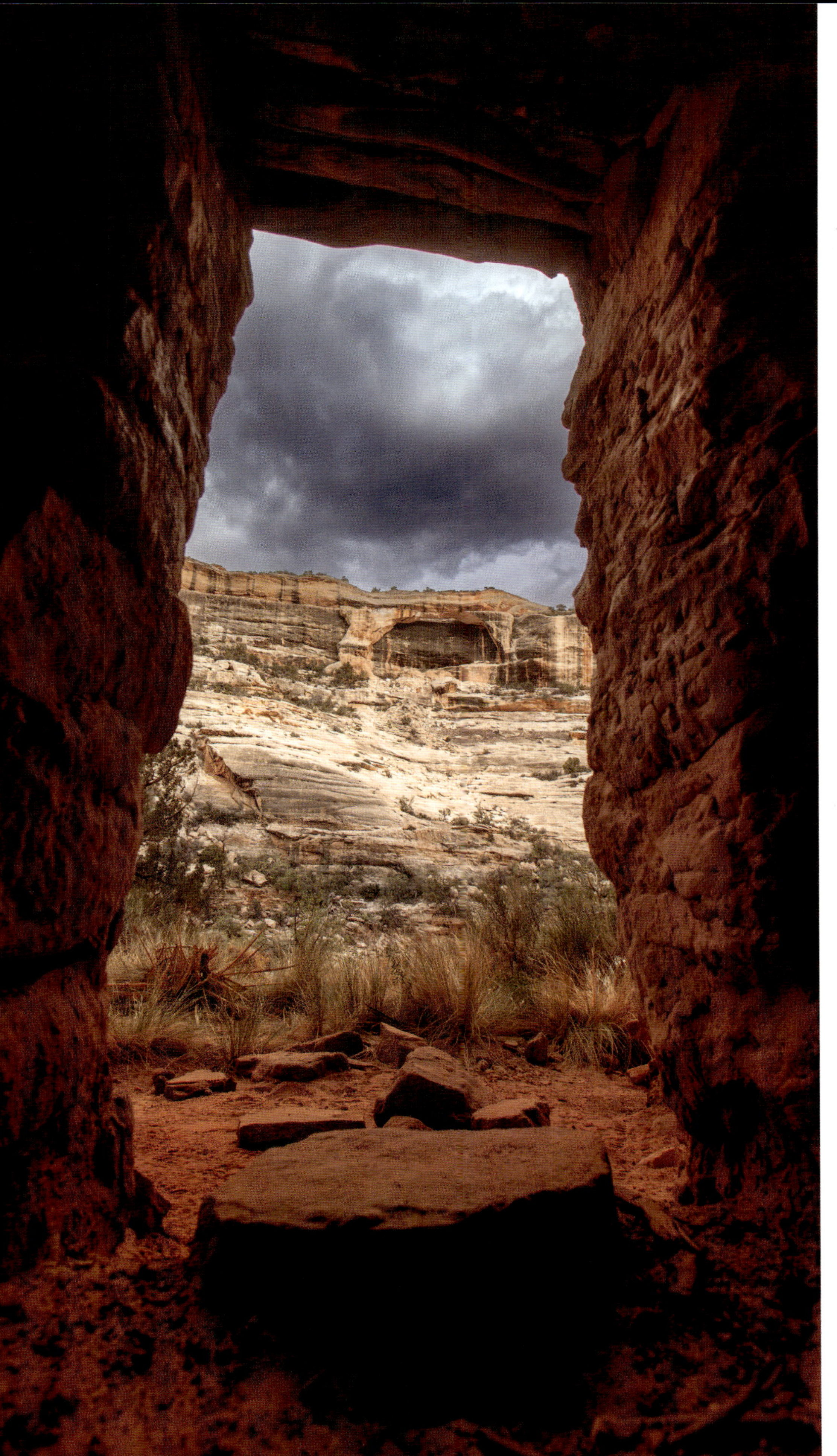

NATURAL BRIDGES NATIONAL MONUMENT

In addition to the three natural bridges for which the monument was established, there are numerous Ancestral Puebloan sites including structures and rock art panels. The most popular site, Horse Collar Ruin, can also be viewed from near the road along the canyon rim.

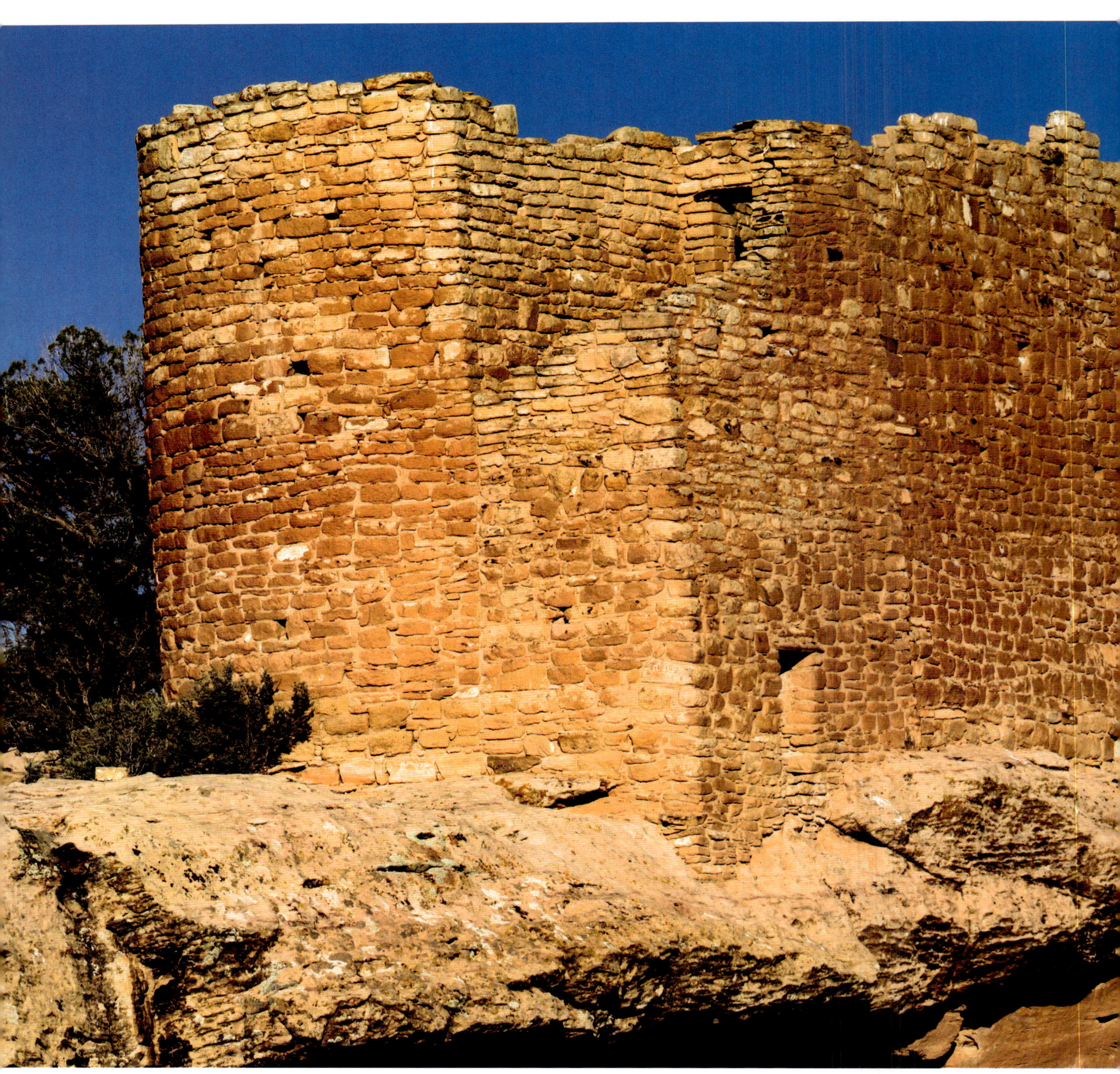

HOVENWEEP NATIONAL MONUMENT The moon rises between the two towers of Hovenweep Castle during a late afternoon hike on my first visit to the monument.

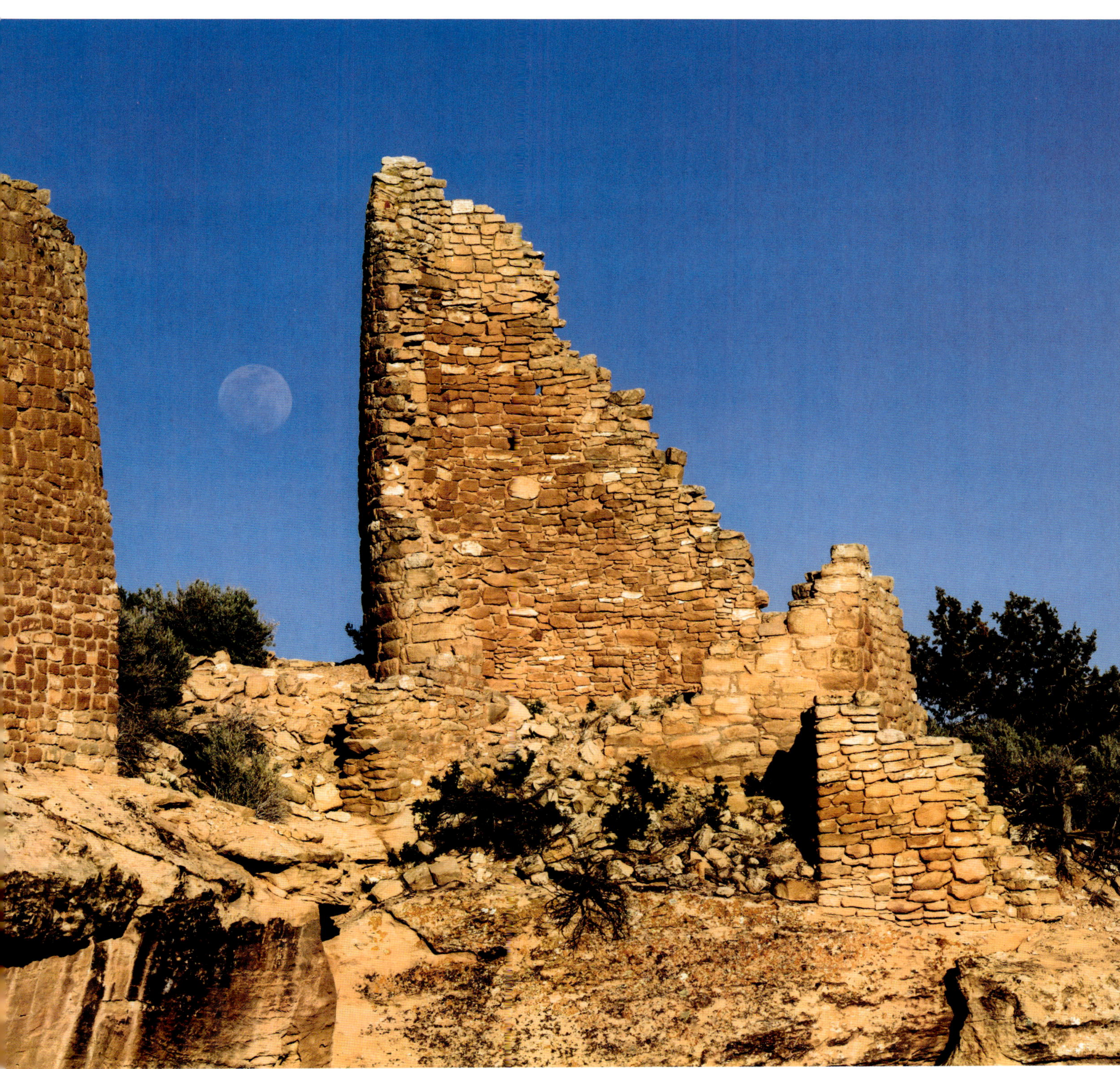

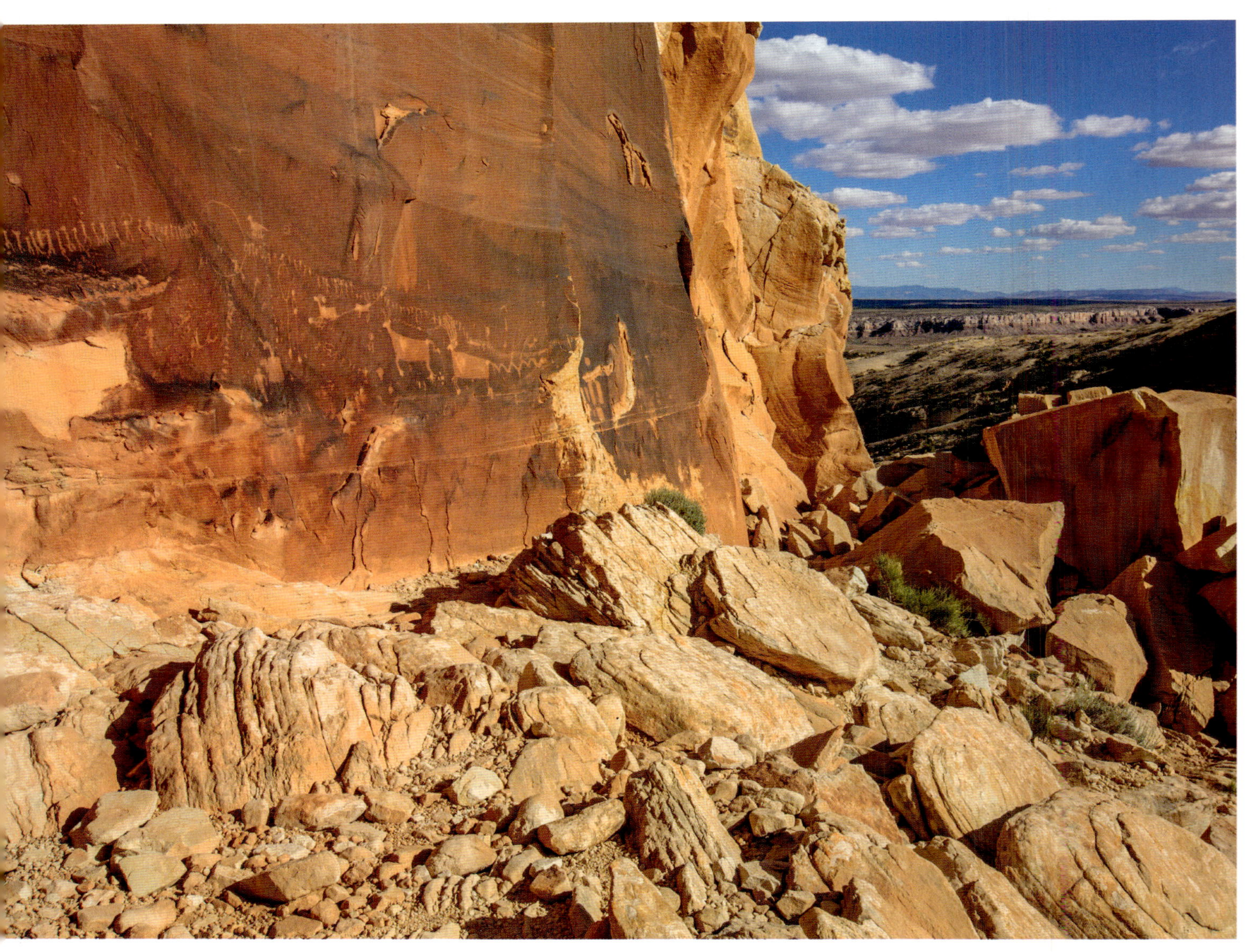

BEARS EARS NATIONAL MONUMENT Two of the most popularized features of the monument, Procession Panel (ABOVE) and House on Fire (OPPOSITE) both live up to their expectations.

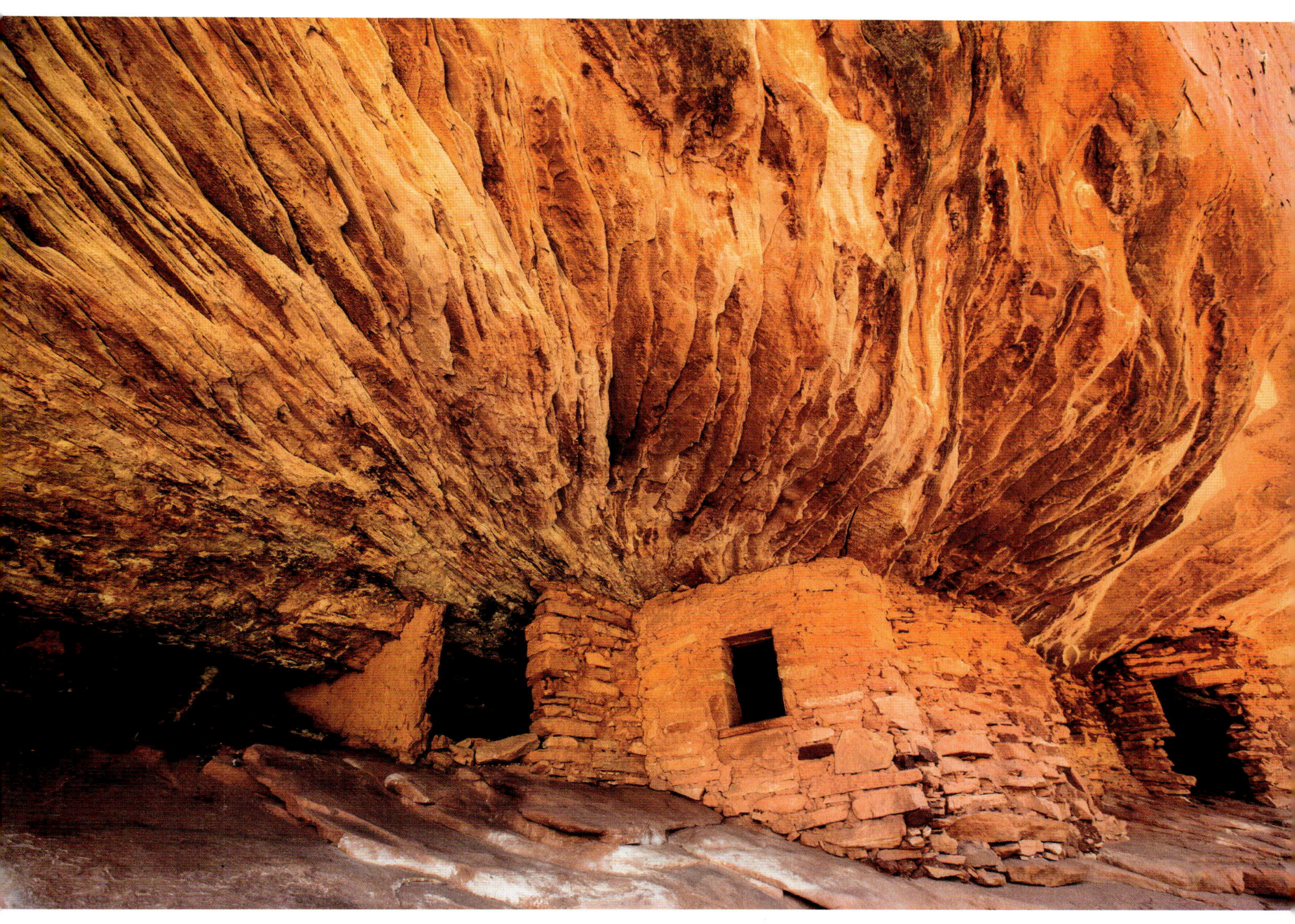

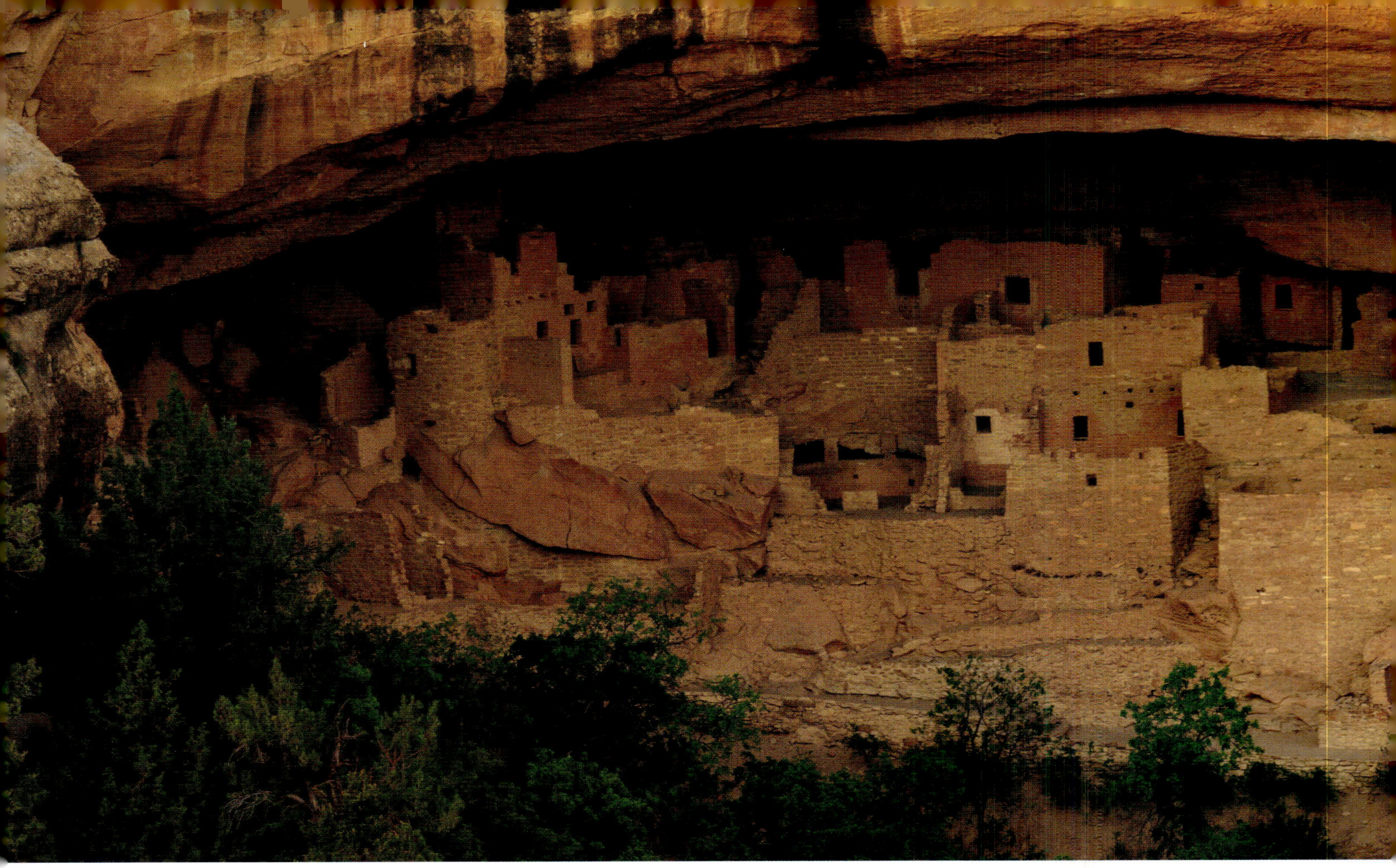

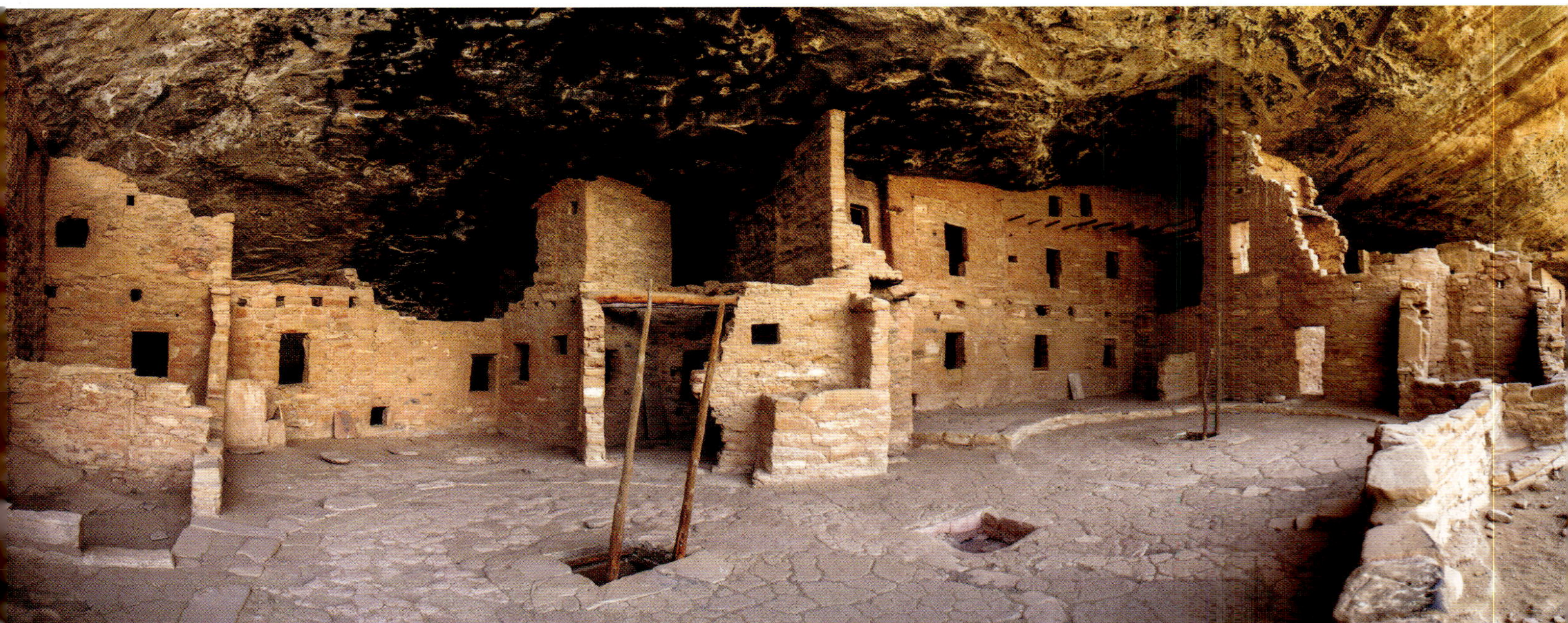

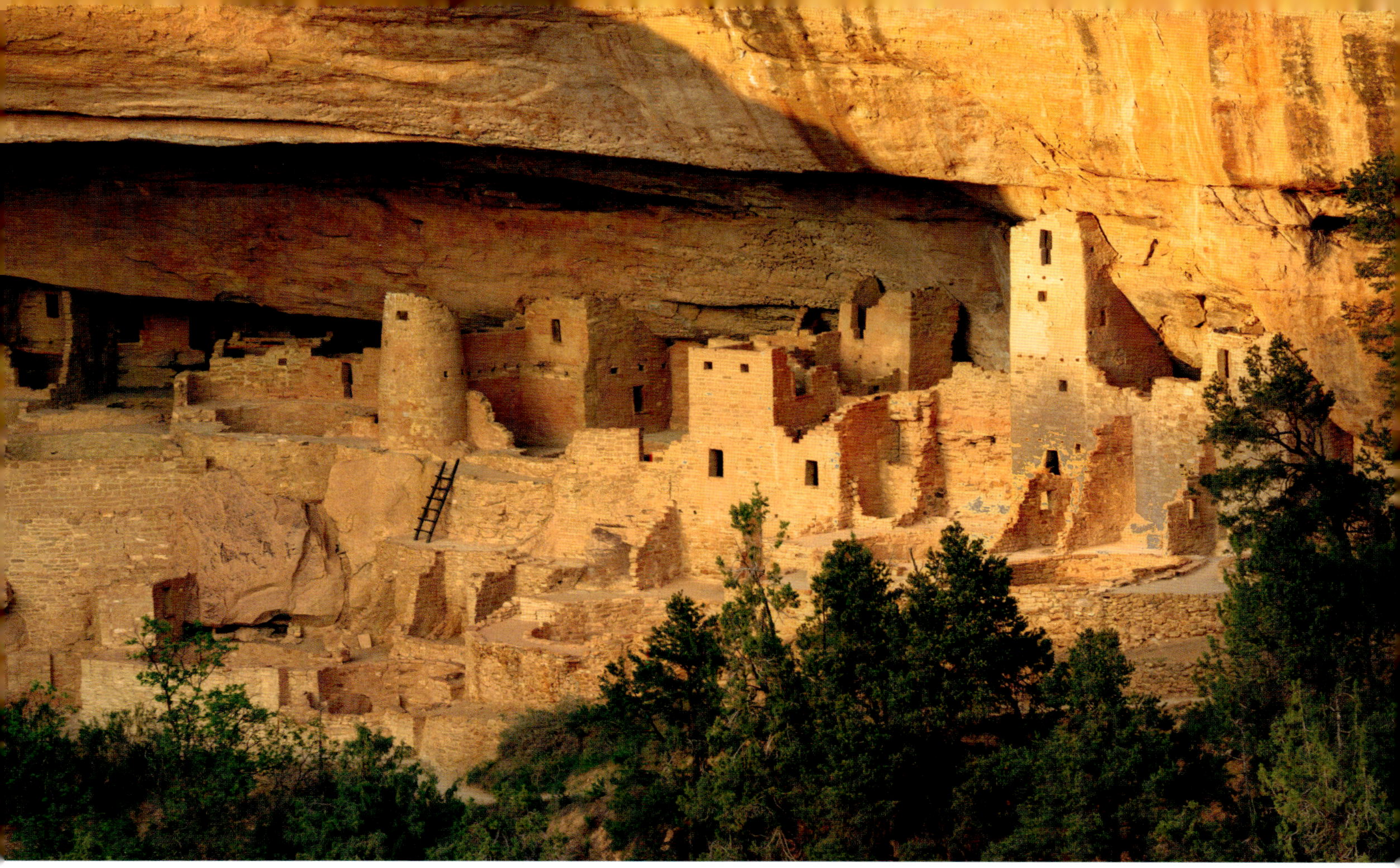

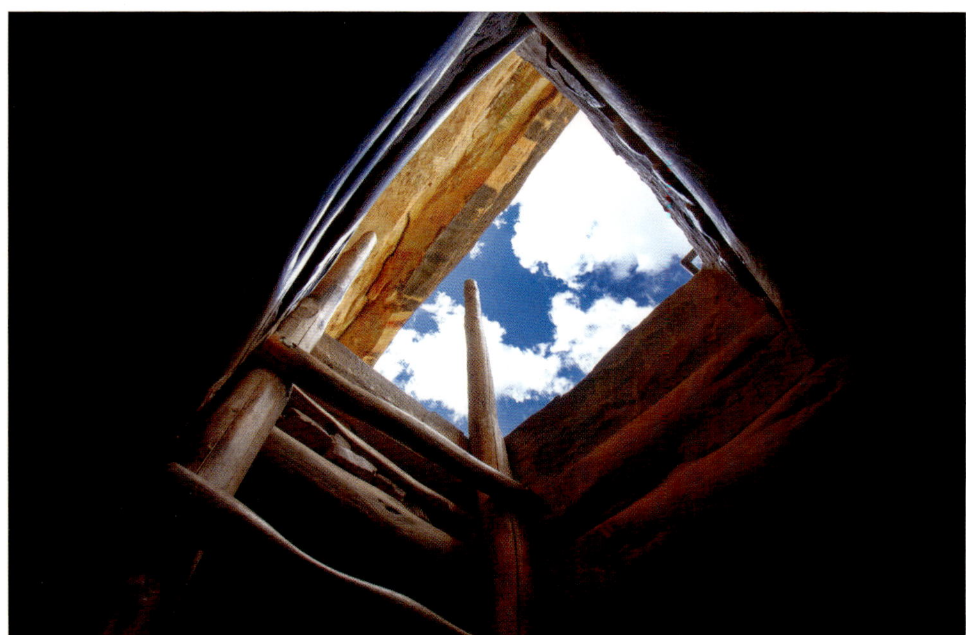

MESA VERDE NATIONAL MONUMENT

(TOP) Watching the afternoon light on Cliff Palace is my first memory of visiting the park. From the overlook, it appears like a diorama, but once you walk among the dwellings, you get a sense of the size and scale of the site.

(BOTTOM AND OPPOSITE) A smaller but equally interesting dwelling is Spruce Tree House. In this site, you can climb down into the restored kivas, which are the ceremonial structures, symbolic of the Sipapu, a sacred opening through which Pueblo peoples believe their ancestors emerged into the present world.

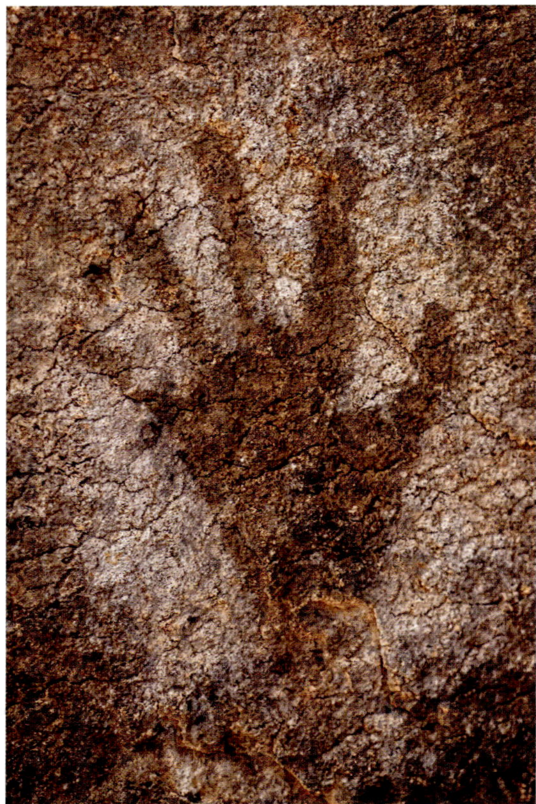

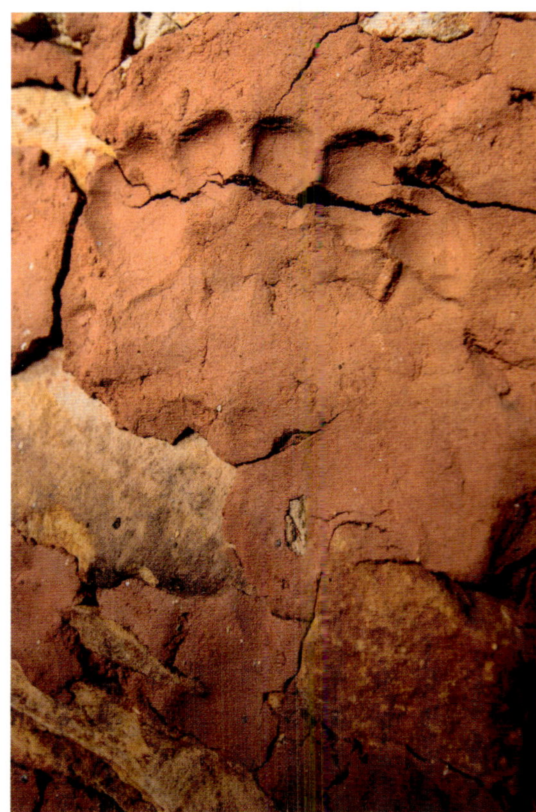

HOVENWEEP NATIONAL MONUMENT (TOP LEFT)

BEARS EARS NATIONAL MONUMENT (TOP RIGHT) My favorite evidence of humans I've come across is this footprint preserved in clay mortar.

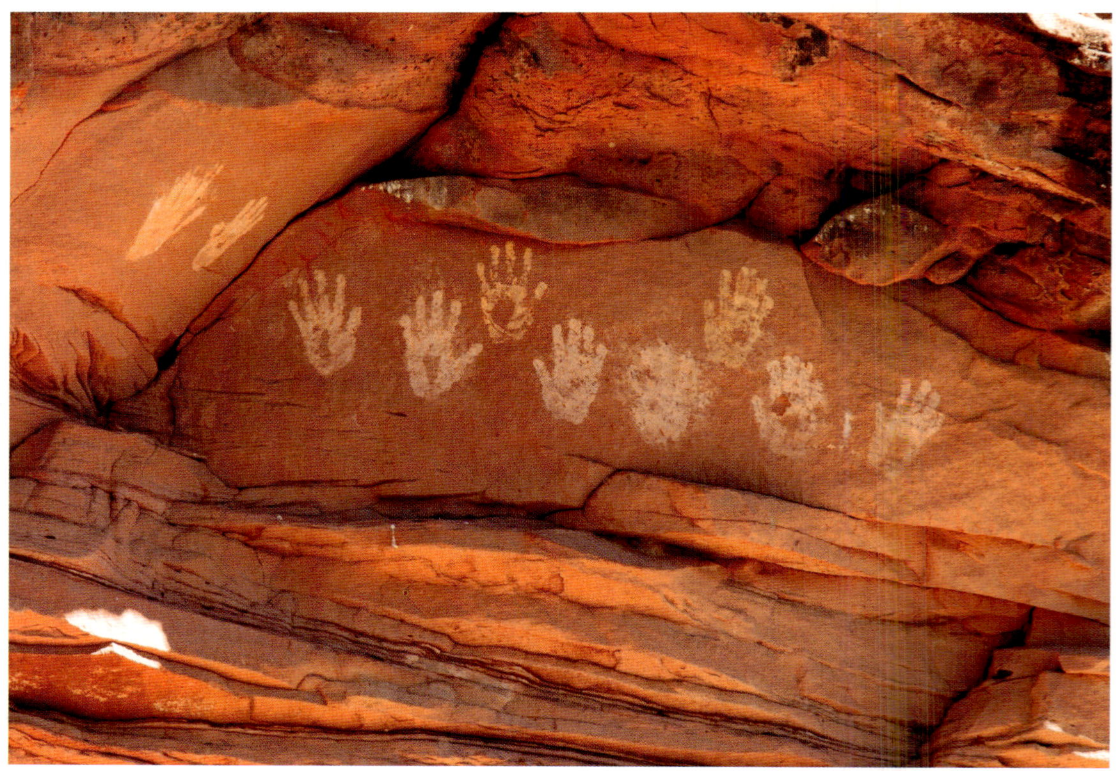

BEARS EARS NATIONAL MONUMENT (BOTTOM)

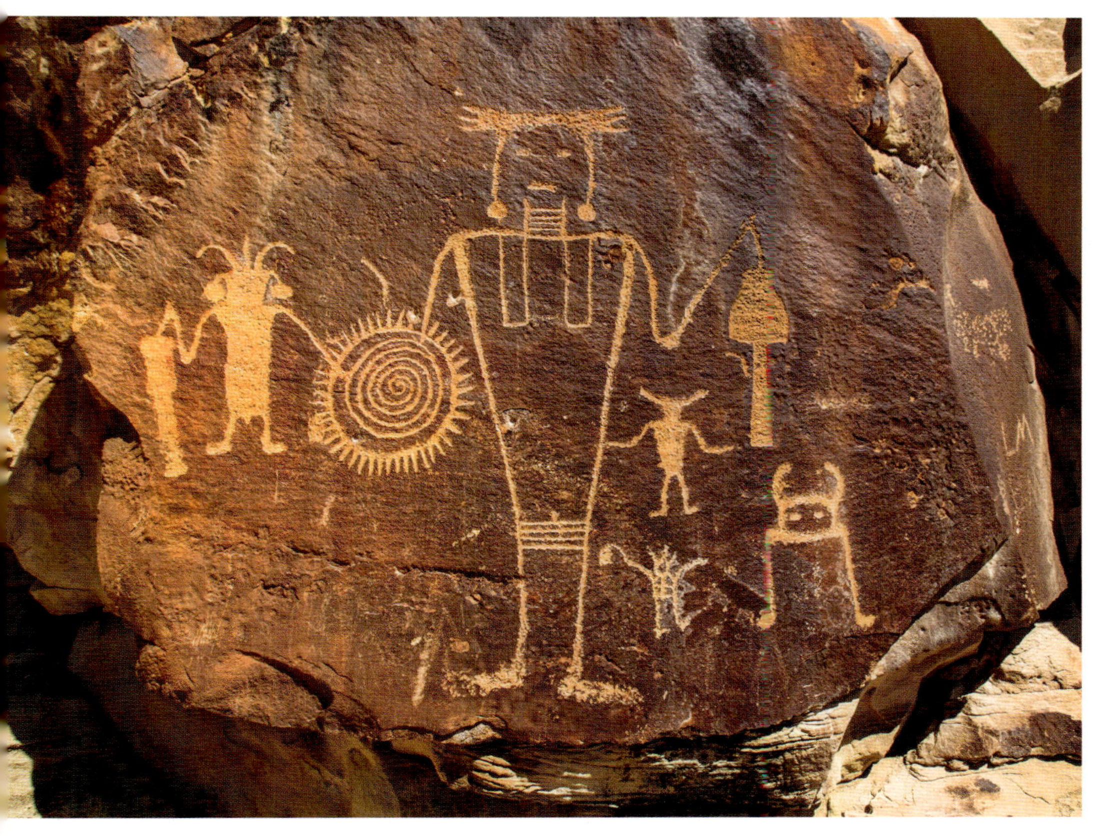

Rock art is broadly grouped into two categories: pictographs and petroglyphs. Pictographs are painted onto a rock surface using natural pigments like charcoal, ochre, or plant dyes. Petroglyphs are images or symbols carved, pecked, or chiseled into the surface of a rock.

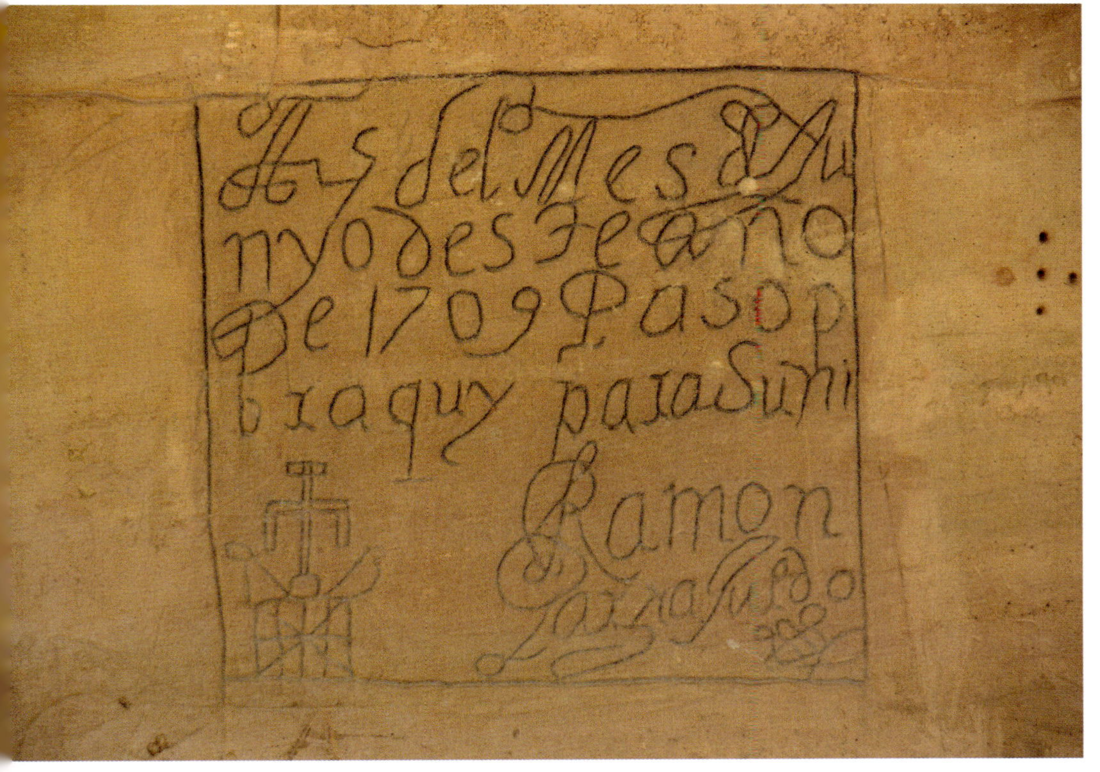

DINOSAUR NATIONAL MONUMENT (TOP)

EL MORRO NATIONAL MONUMENT (BOTTOM)

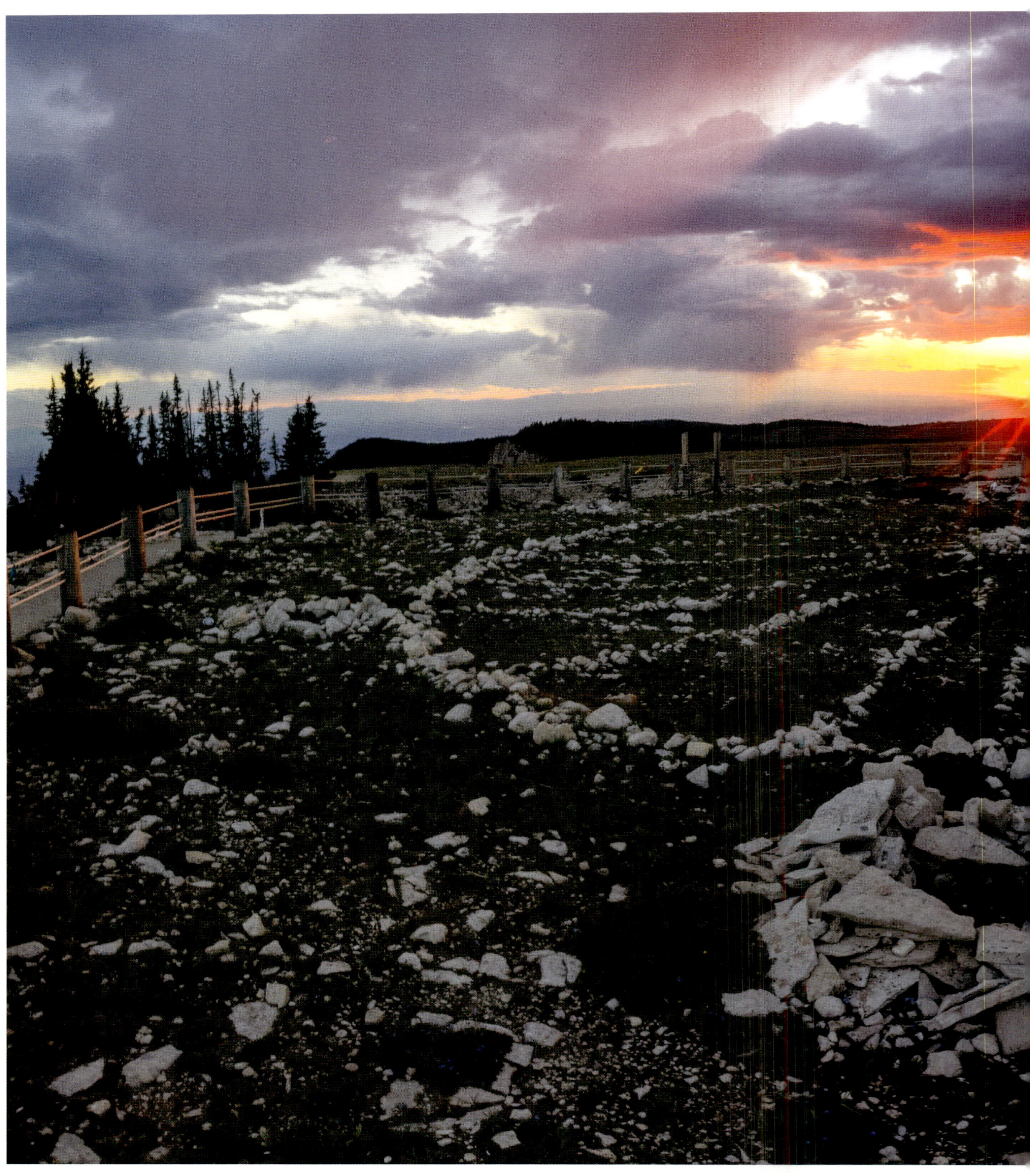

BIGHORN NATIONAL FOREST At nearly 10,000 feet, the Medicine Wheel is a sacred site to many American Indian Tribes, past and present. While camping on the forest, we hiked up to the wheel to take in a sunset by ourselves.

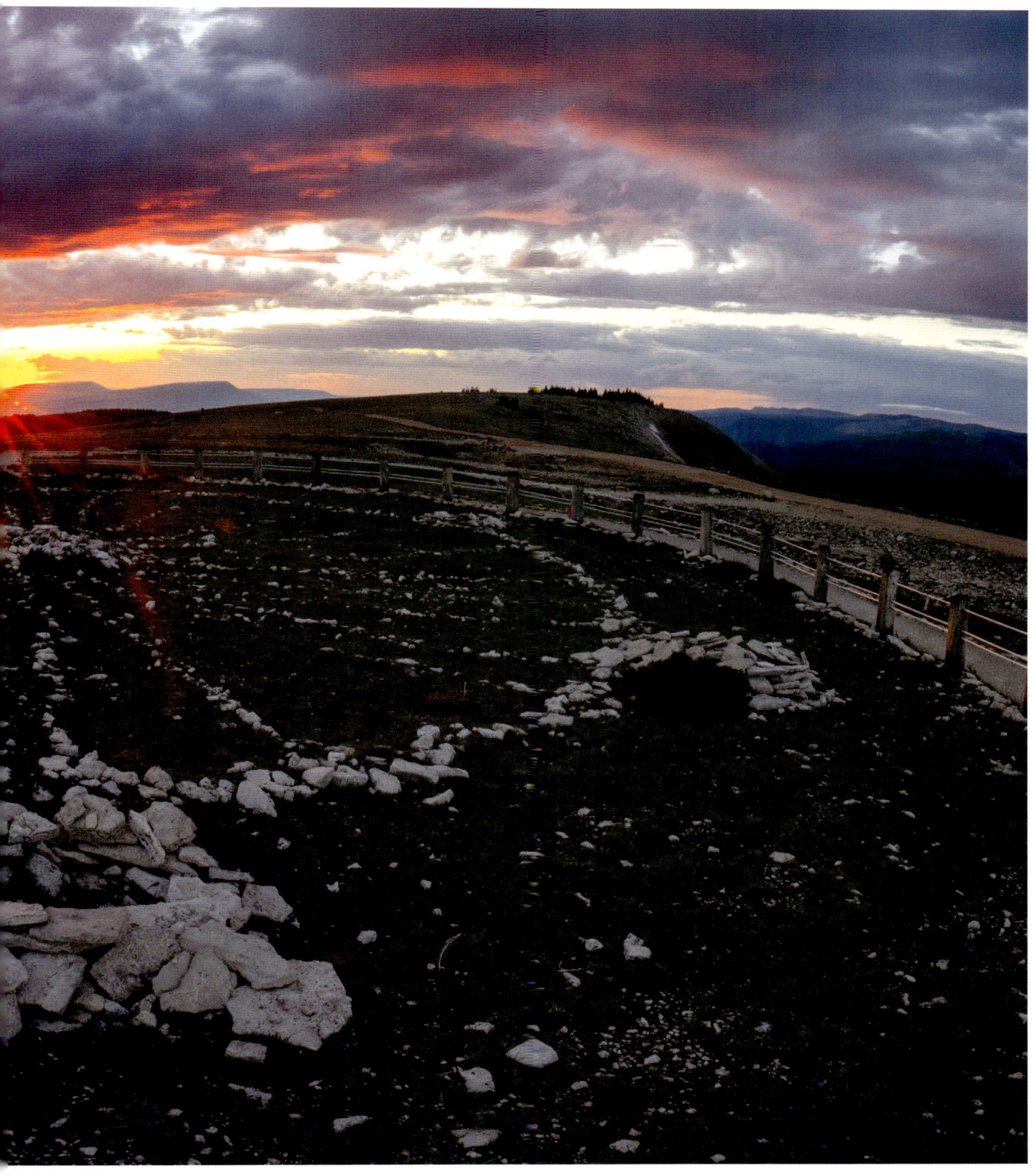

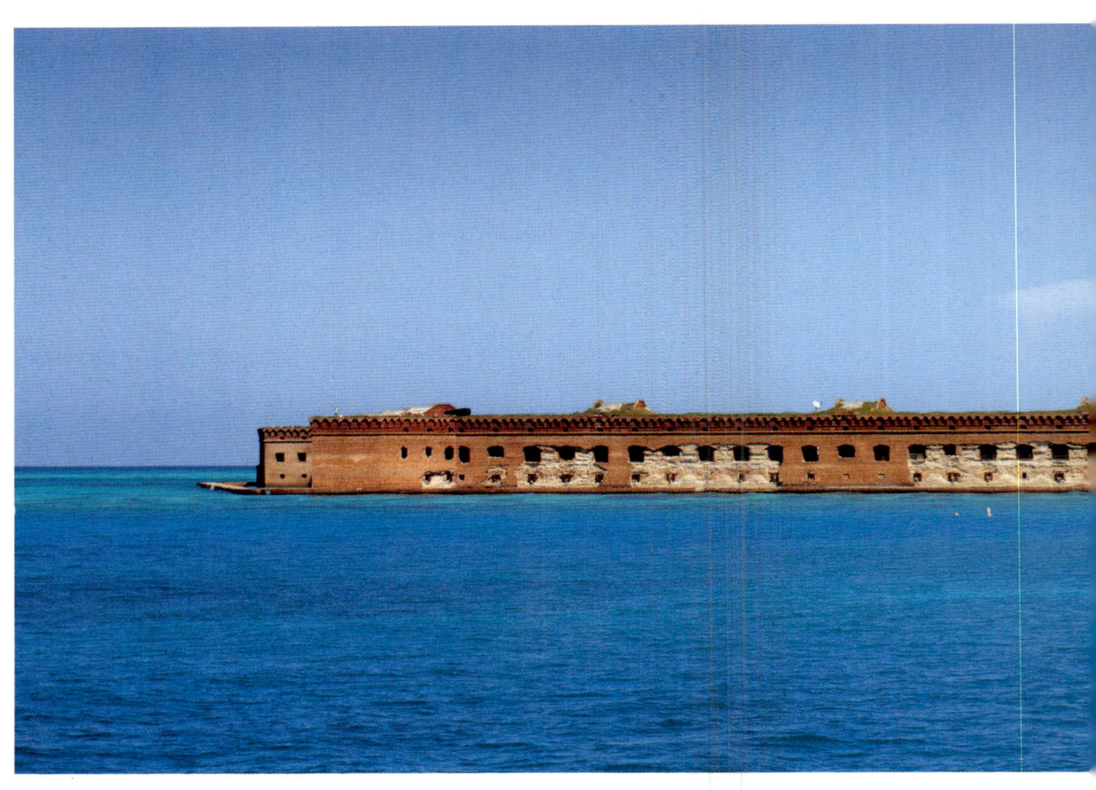

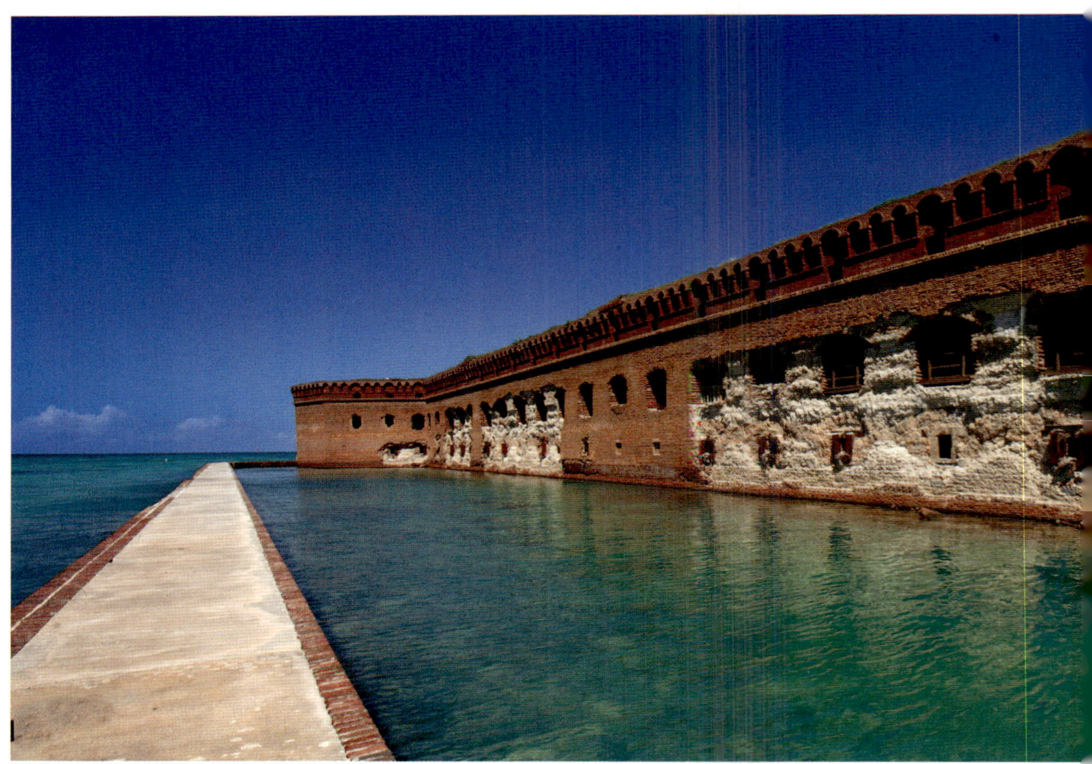

DRY TORTUGAS NATIONAL PARK
Fort Jefferson, located about seventy miles west of Key West, Florida, is accessible only by boat or seaplane. After a smooth boat ride, my friend and I explored the fort's massive brick construction and stunning natural surroundings, before snorkeling in the surrounding pristine waters.

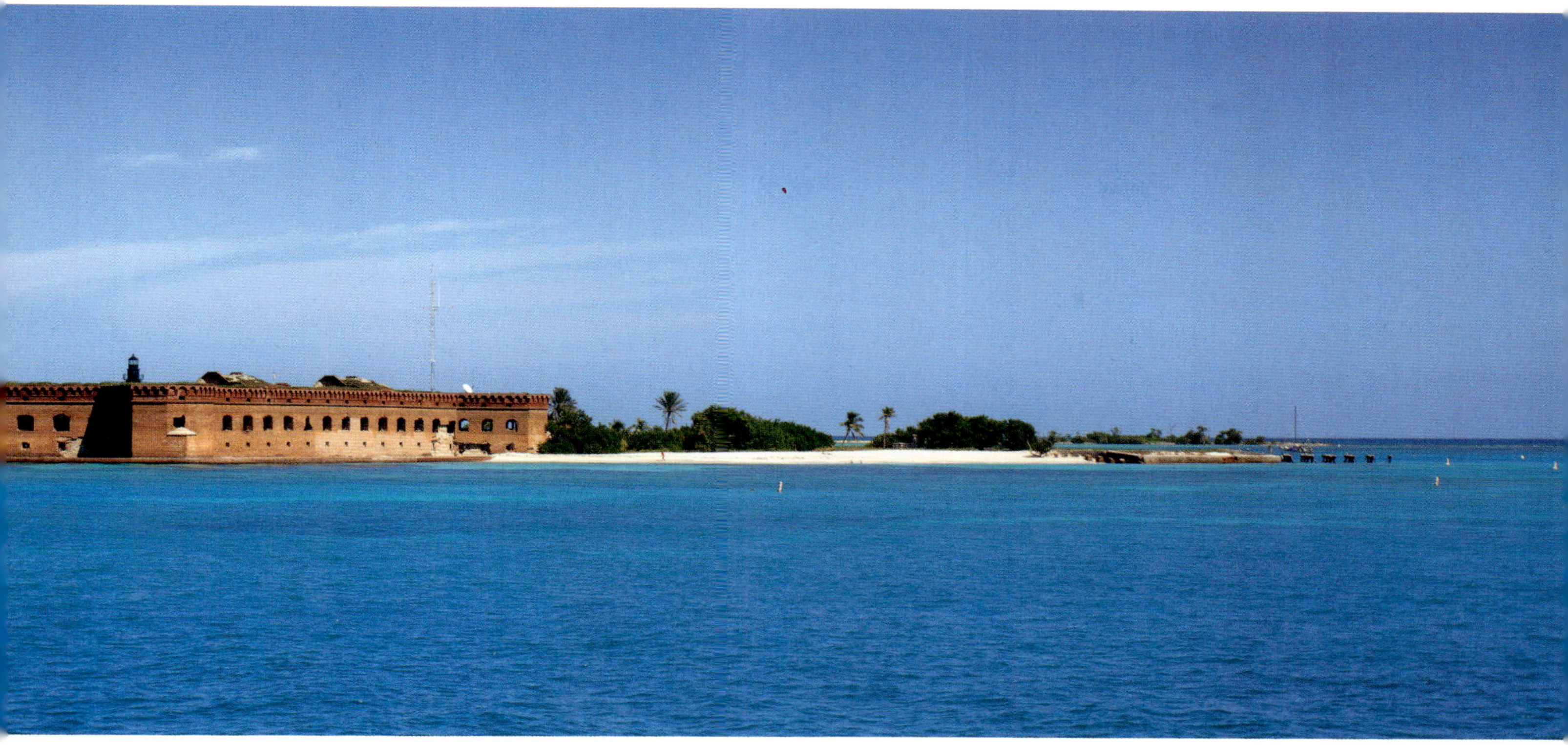

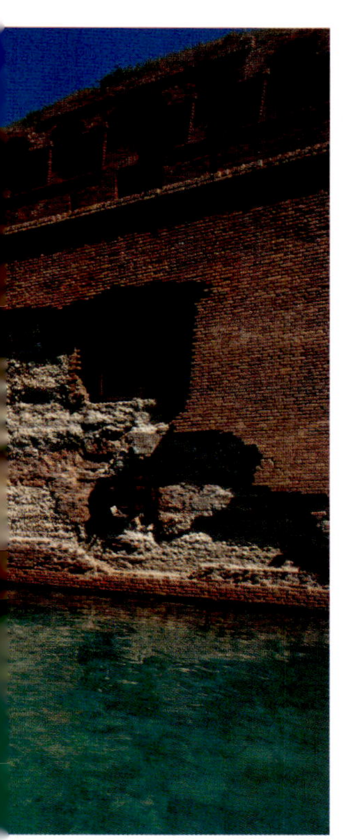

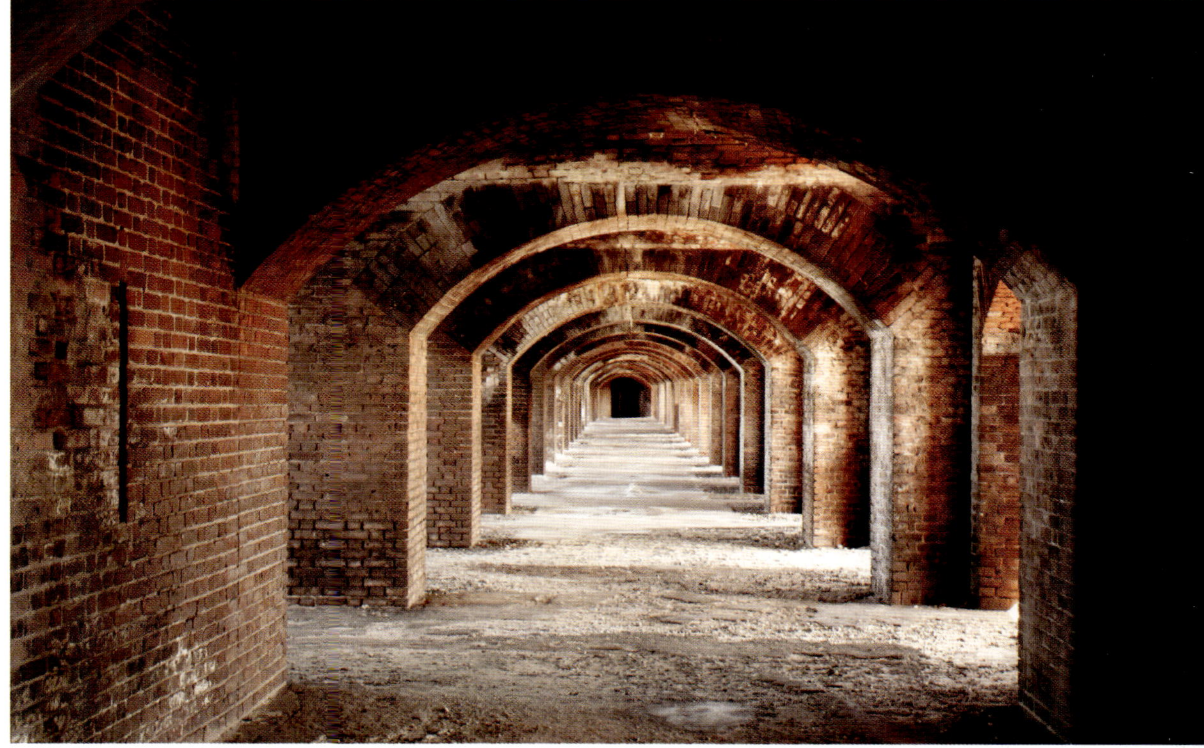

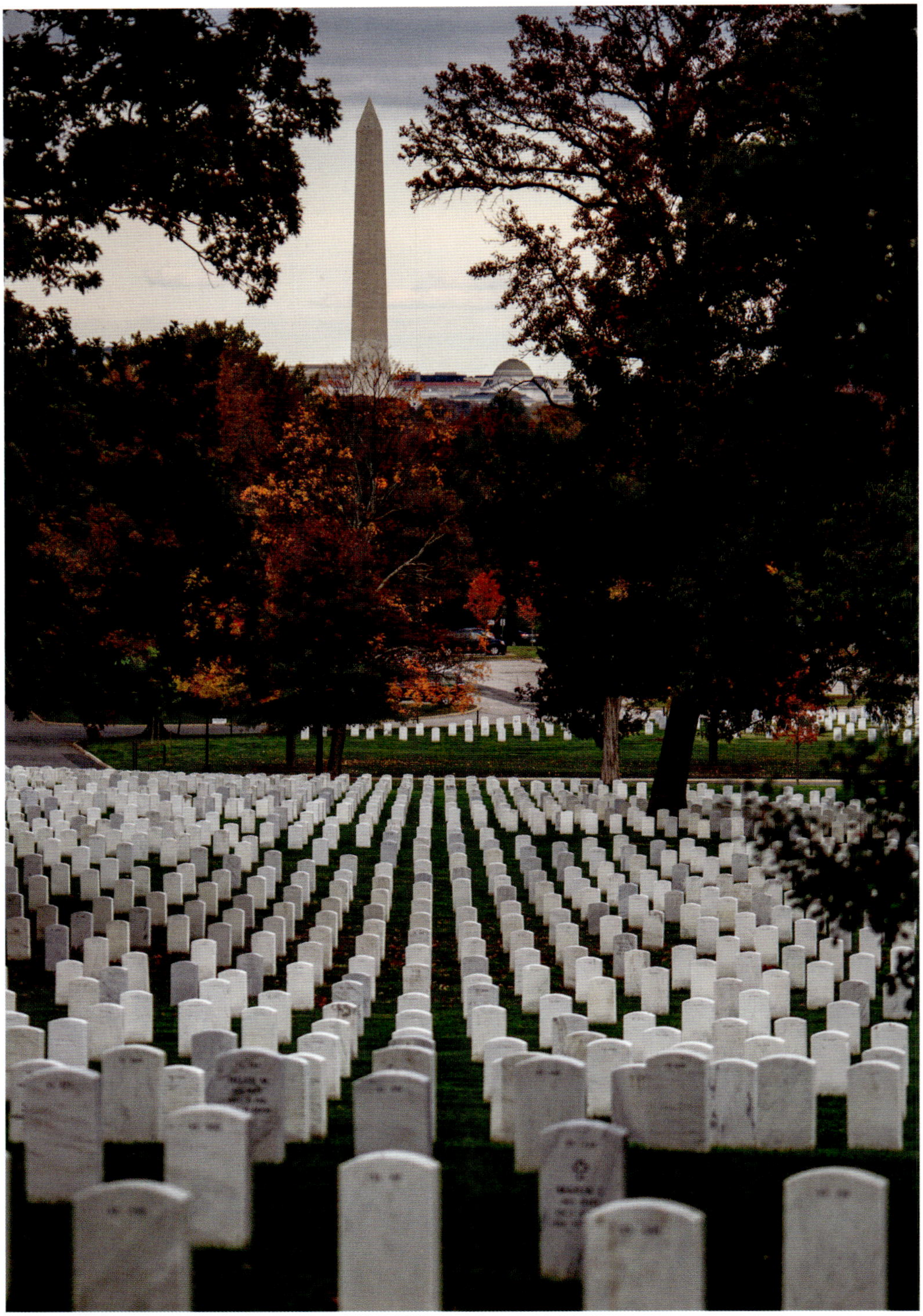

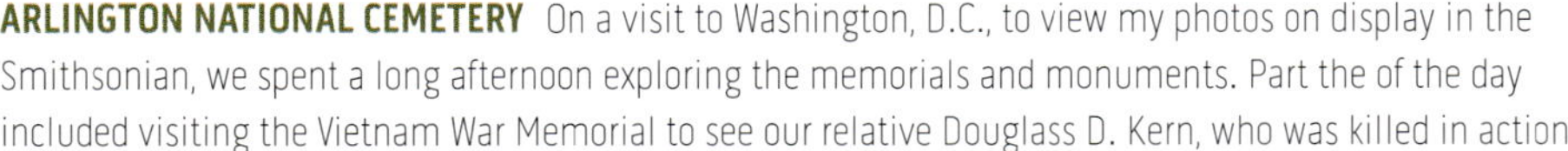

ARLINGTON NATIONAL CEMETERY On a visit to Washington, D.C., to view my photos on display in the Smithsonian, we spent a long afternoon exploring the memorials and monuments. Part the of the day included visiting the Vietnam War Memorial to see our relative Douglass D. Kern, who was killed in action.

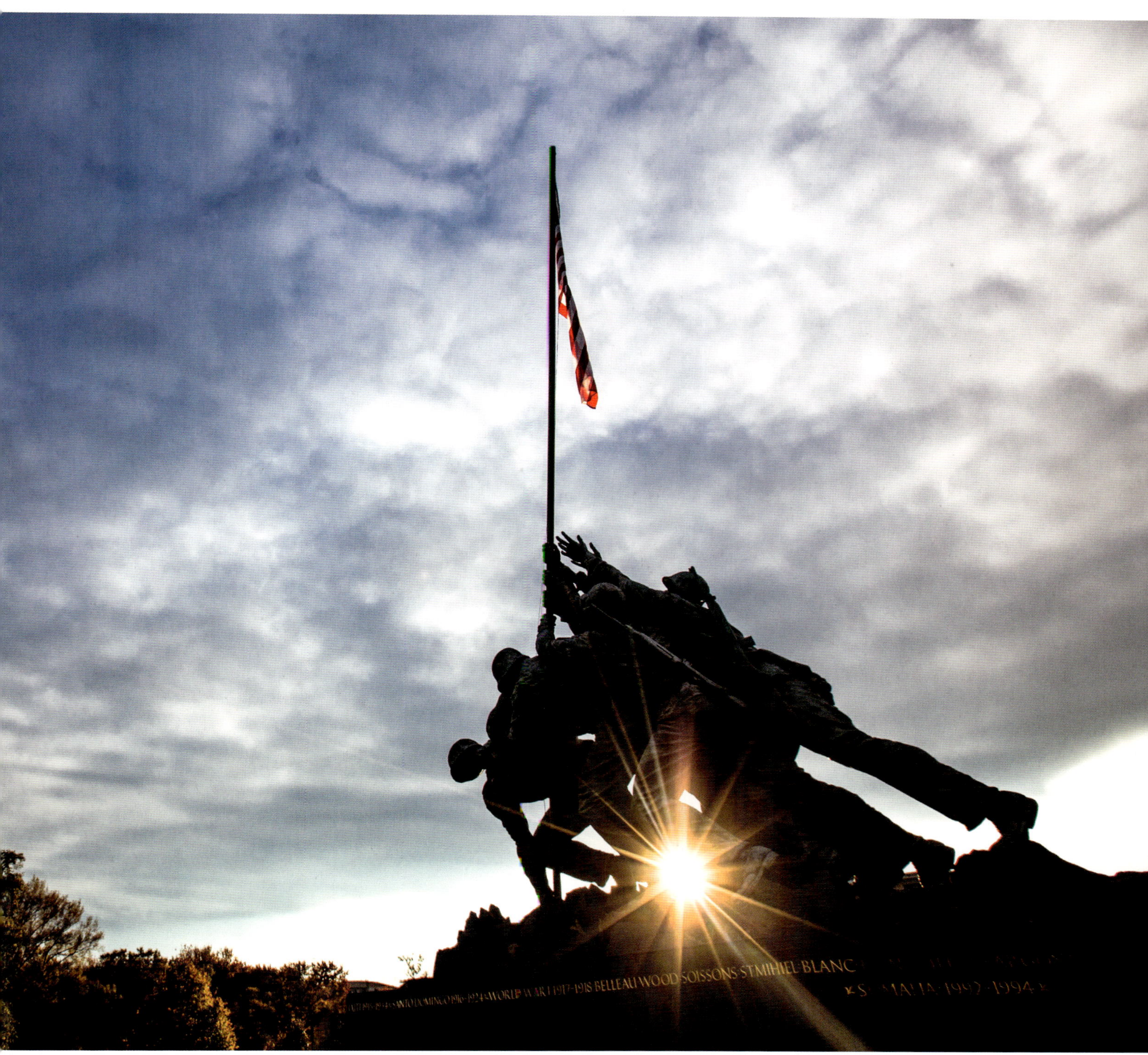

GEORGE WASHINGTON MEMORIAL PARKWAY Sunset at the Marine Corps War Memorial.

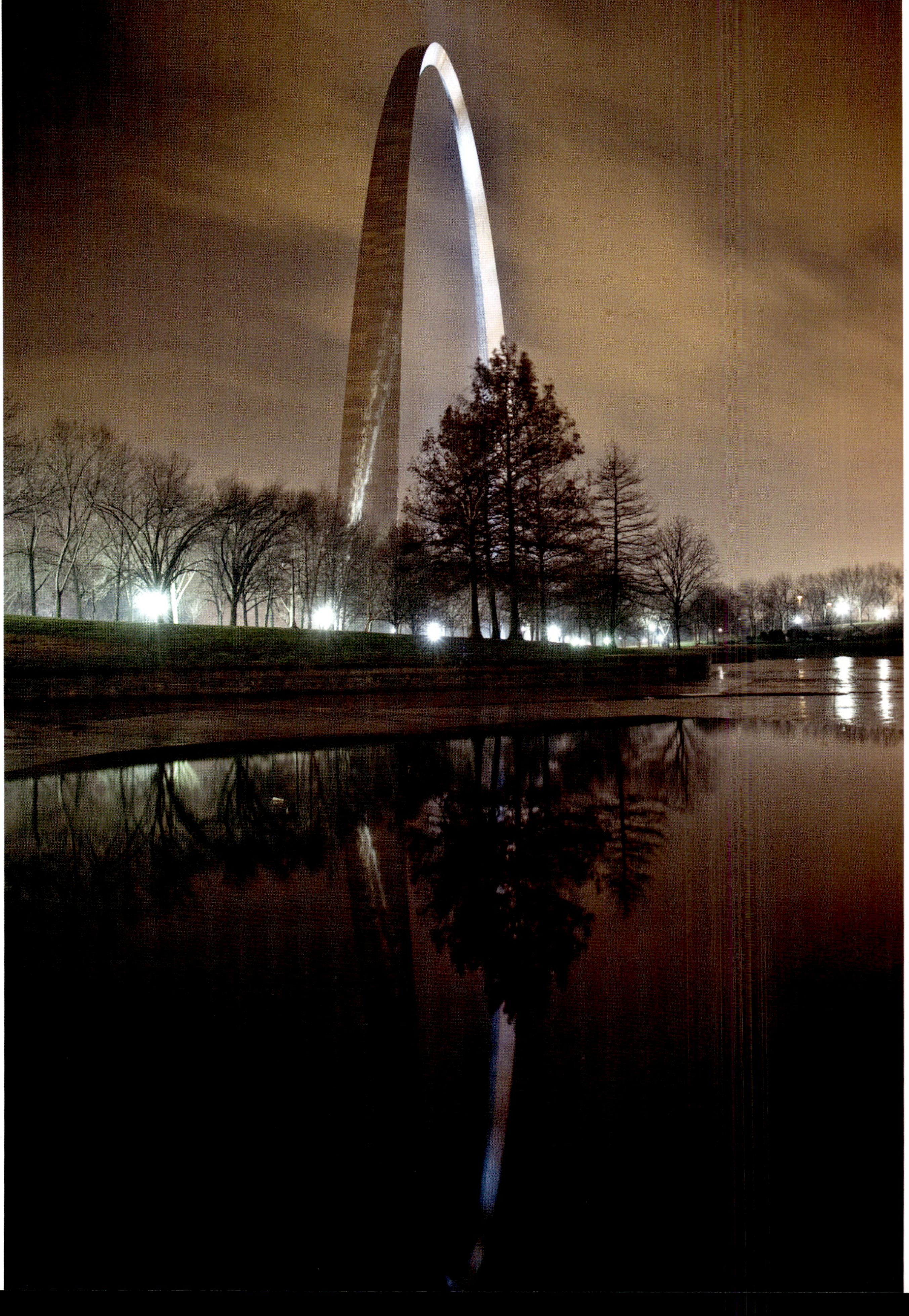

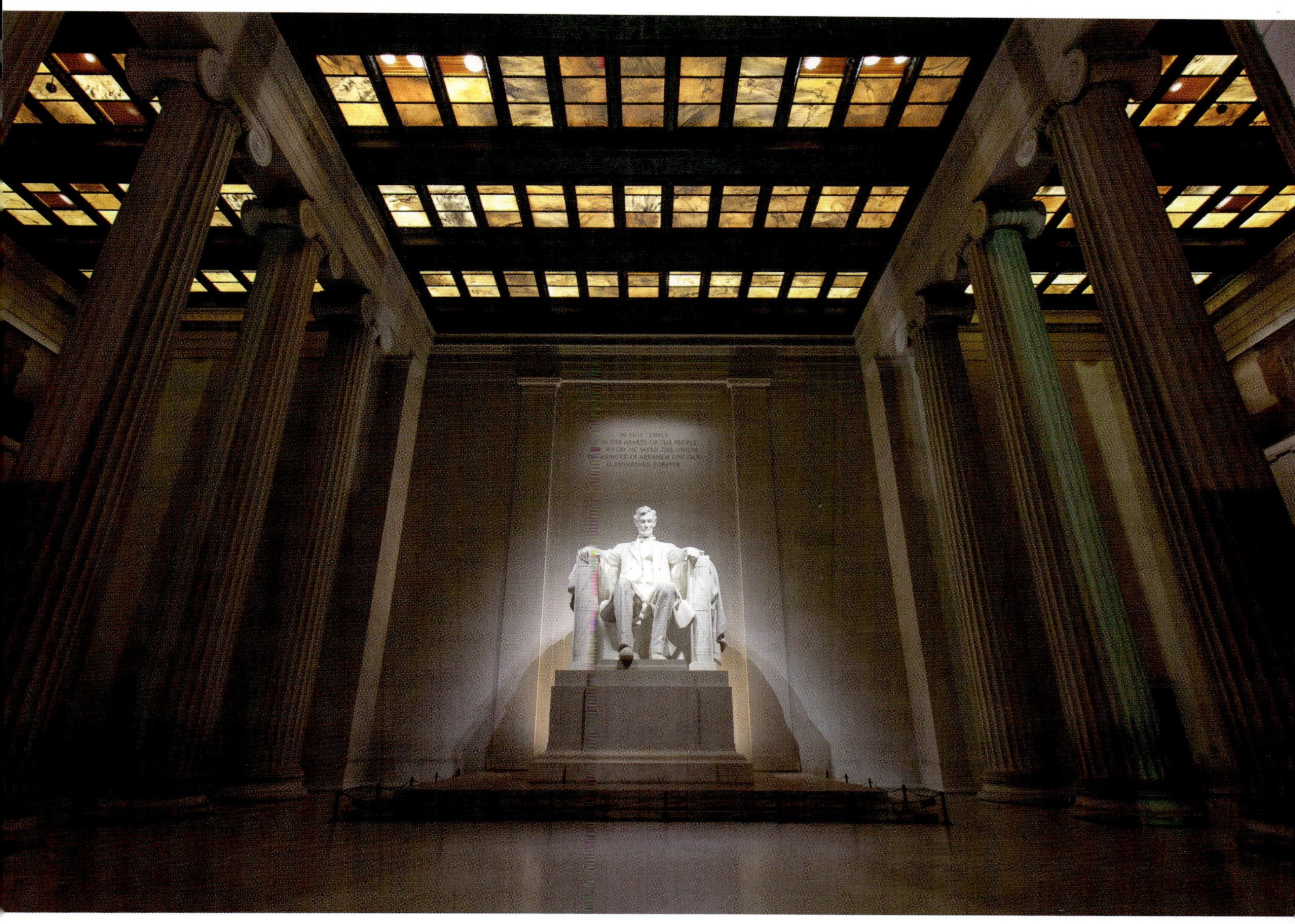

One of my favorite things to do when I visit a city is to explore at night. Many of the sites that are crowded during the day are often empty and you can see them in an entirely different way.

GATEWAY ARCH NATIONAL PARK (OPPOSITE)

LINCOLN MEMORIAL, NATIONAL MALL AND MEMORIAL PARKS (ABOVE)

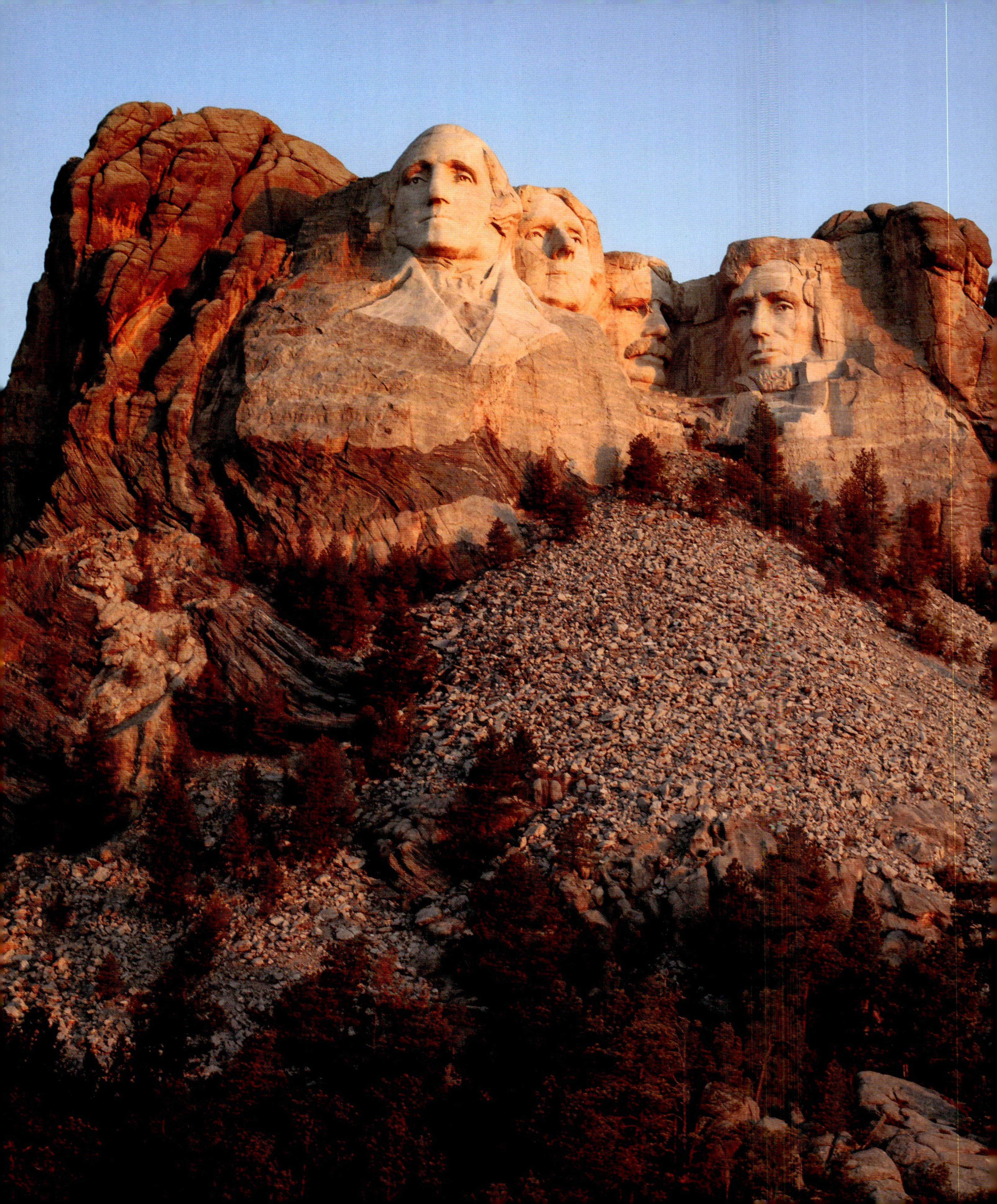

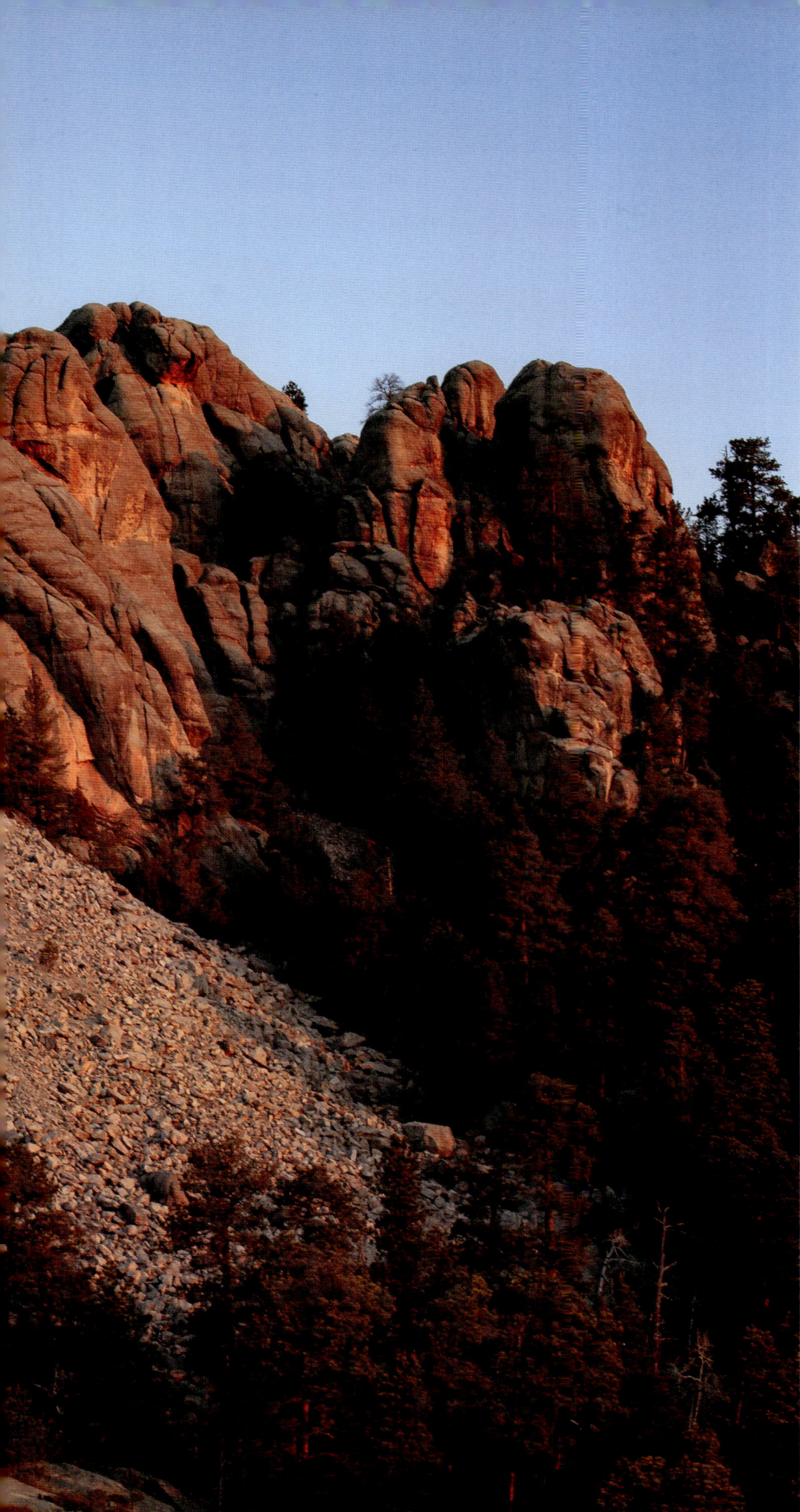

MOUNT RUSHMORE NATIONAL MEMORIAL
While road-tripping to Denali to start my new job, I stopped to visit my friend while she was working at the memorial. I had the opportunity to watch the sunrise all by myself, a moment I won't forget.

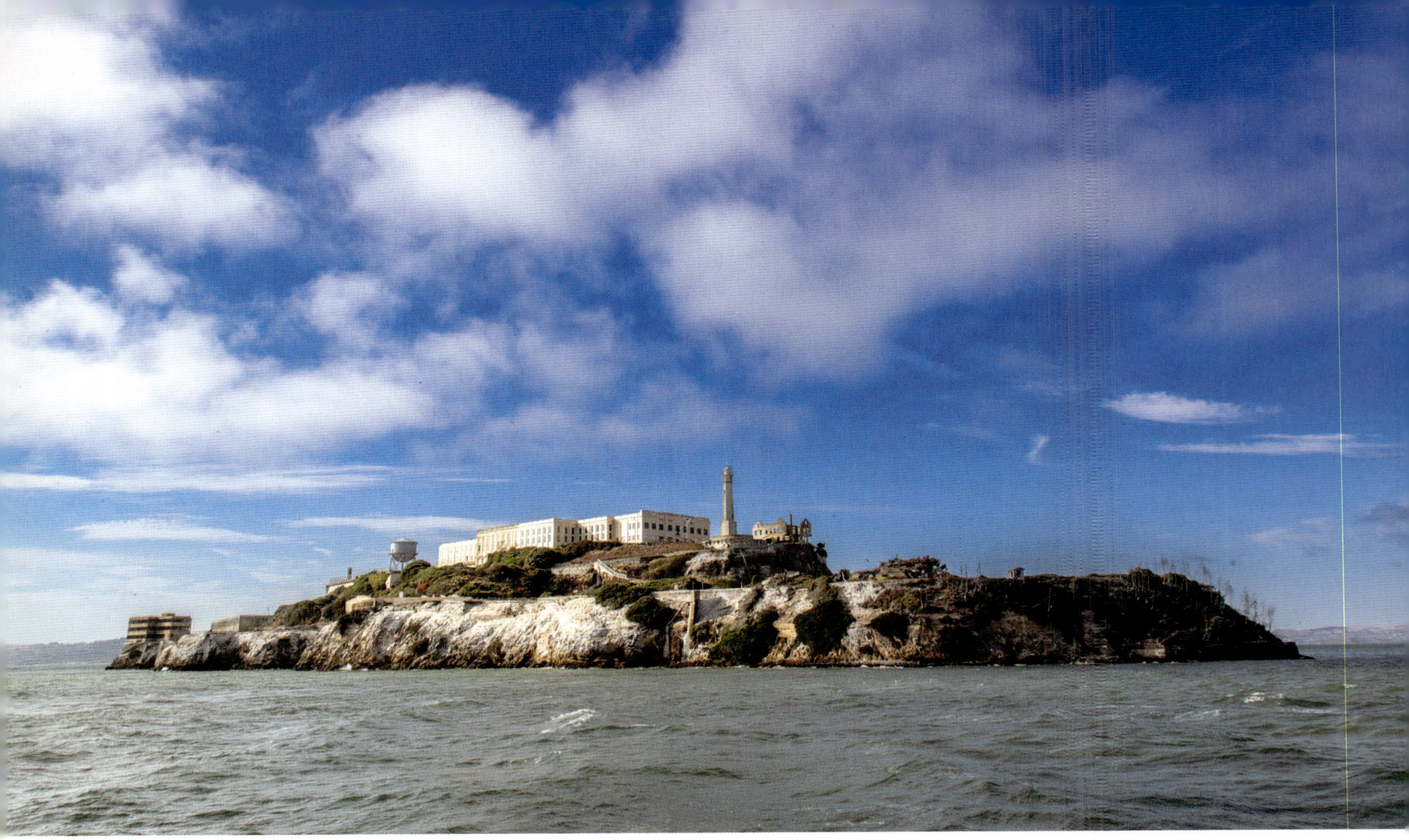

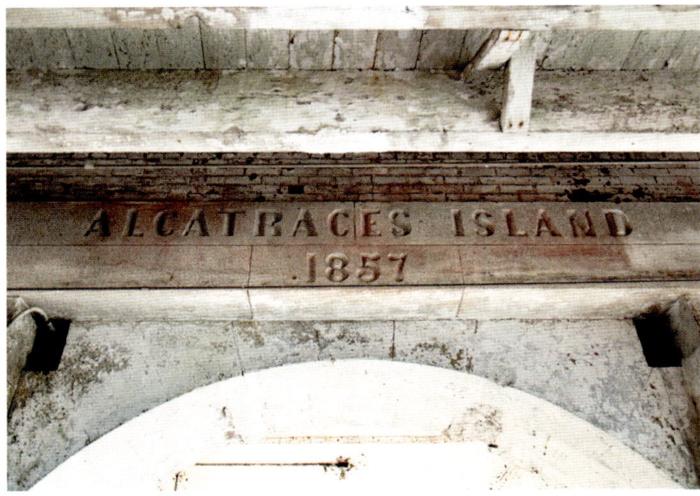

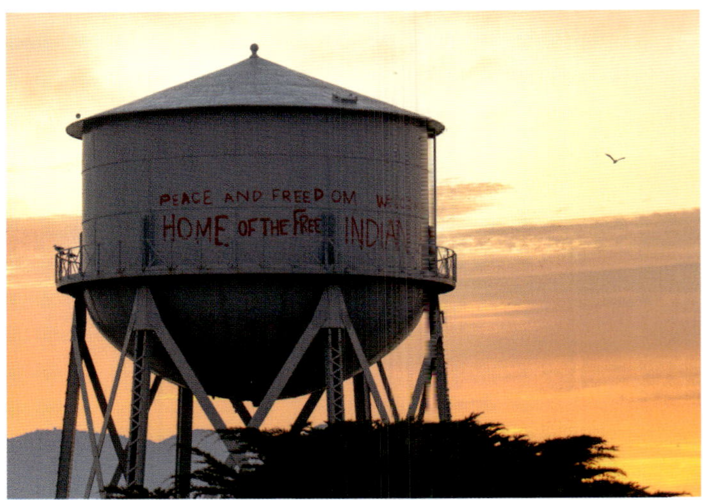

GOLDEN GATE NATIONAL RECREATION AREA While in San Francisco for a wedding, Corrie and I visited Alcatraz Island and were given a private tour by a friend who was working there at the time. The highlight was taking in the view from the lighthouse. A close second was the Nicholas Cage cutout they keep in the offices.

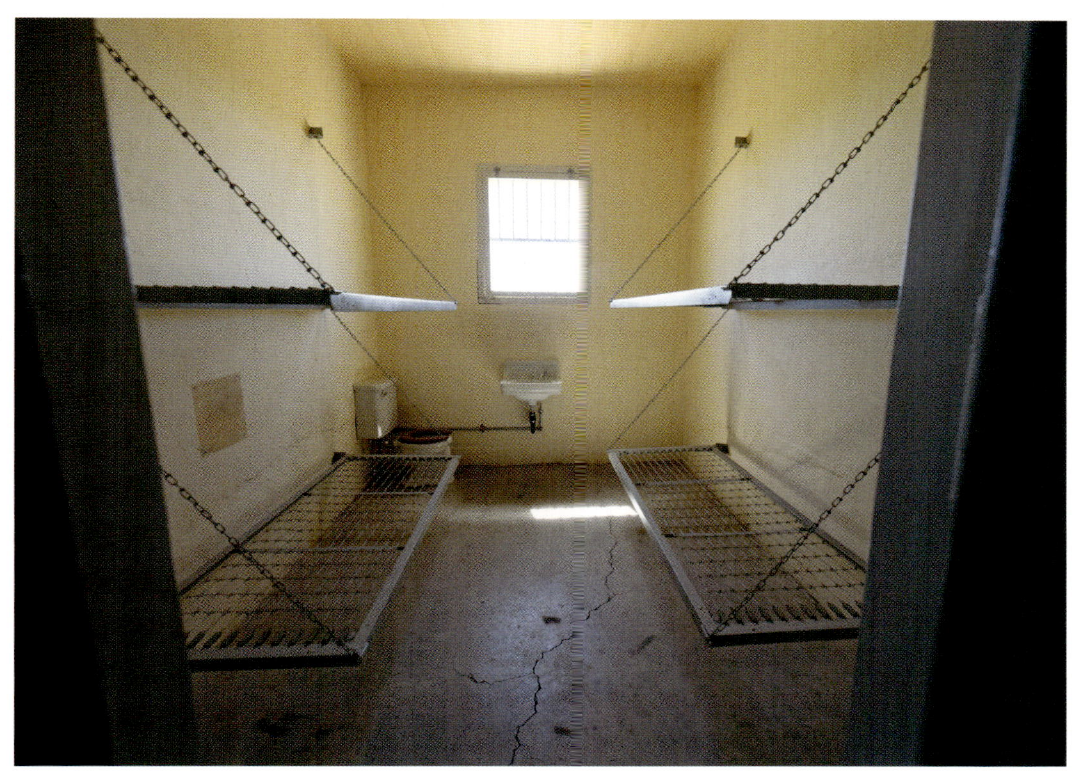

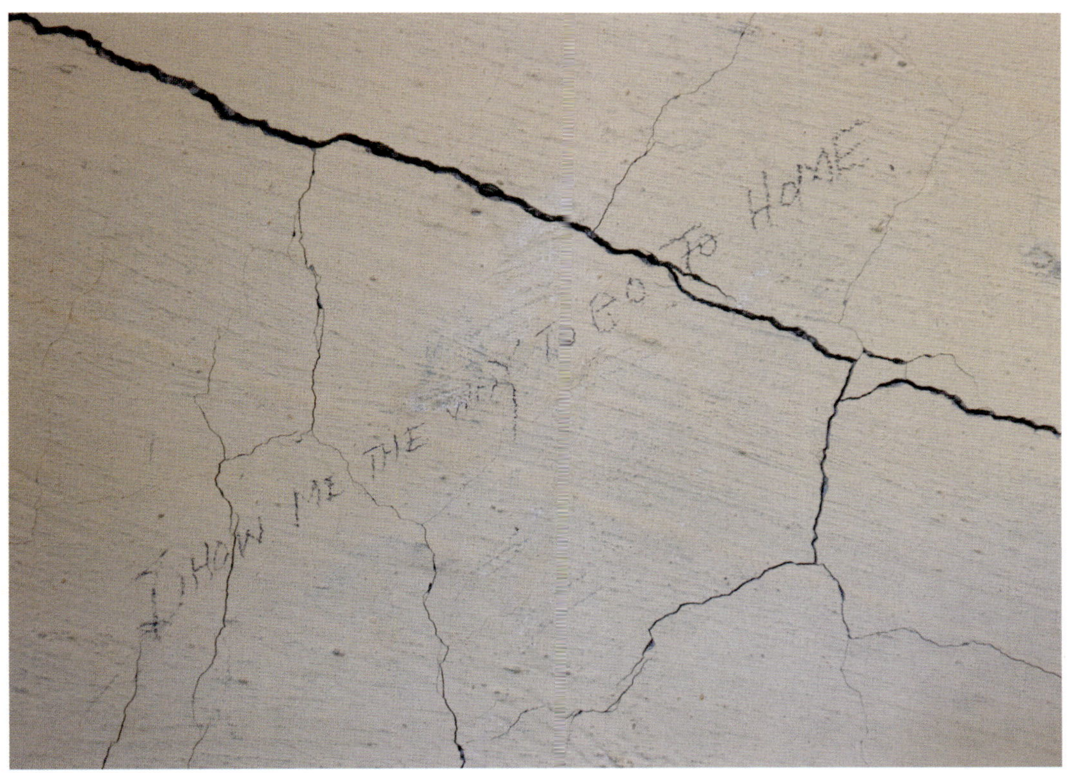

TULE LAKE NATIONAL MONUMENT Before our visit, I didn't know much about the history of World War II Japanese segregation centers. We toured the jail and were able to read the inscriptions of some of the prisoners. It was an enlightening and moving experience.

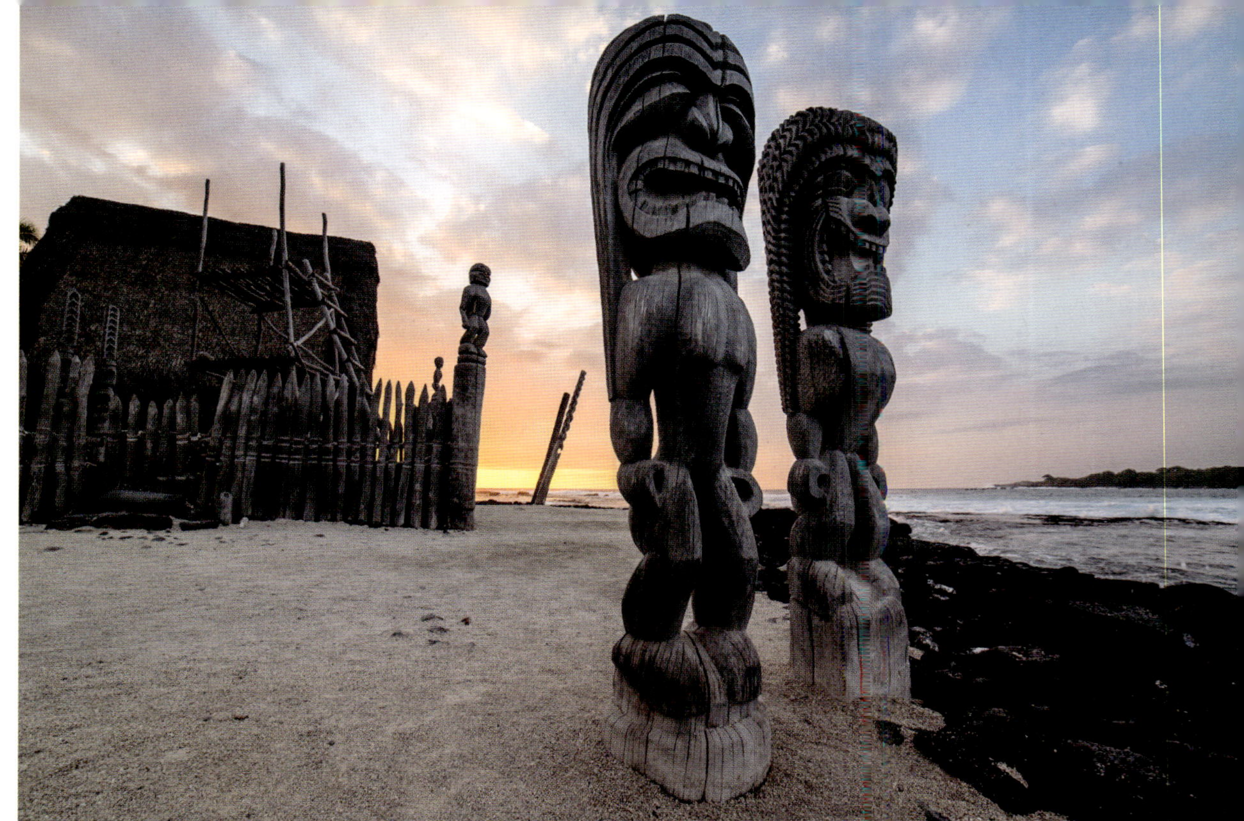

PU'UHONUA O HŌNAUNAU NATIONAL HISTORICAL PARK One of my favorite things to do while on the Big Island is to watch a sunset from the park. It never disappoints.

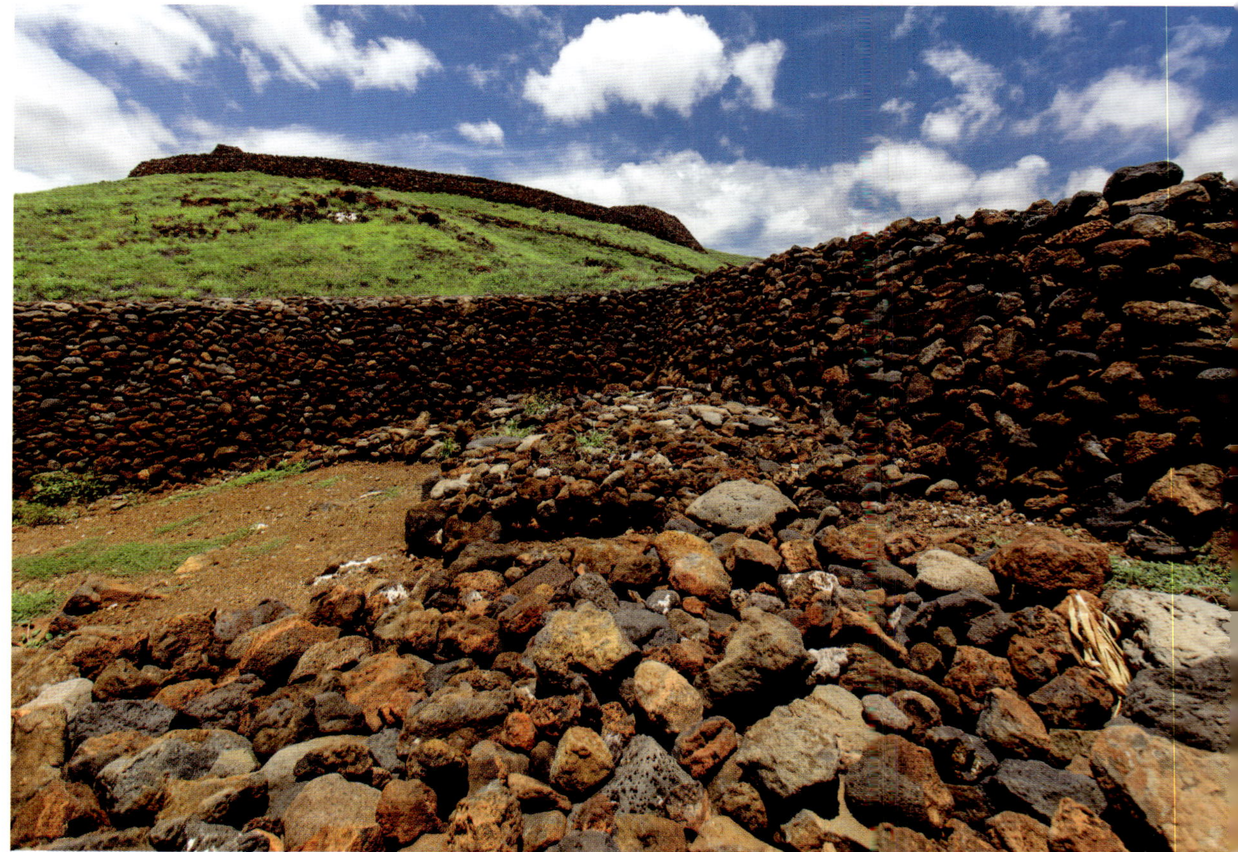

PU'UKOHOLĀ HEIAU NATIONAL HISTORICAL SITE On the northern end of the Big Island is the great temple of Kamehameha the Great, Pu'ukoholā Heiau. During our visit we saw many gifts at the temple, offerings to the most renowned king of Hawai'i.

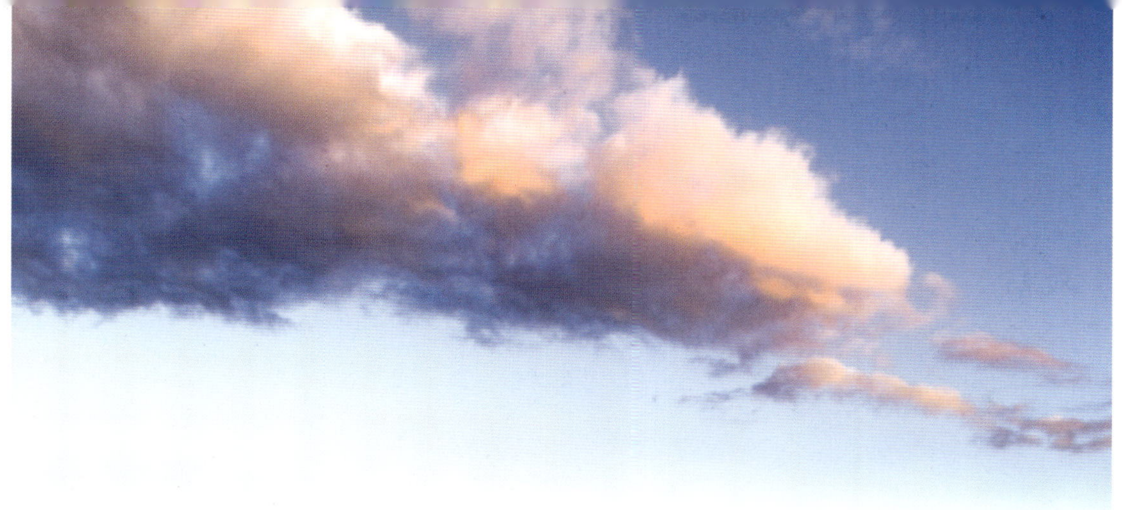

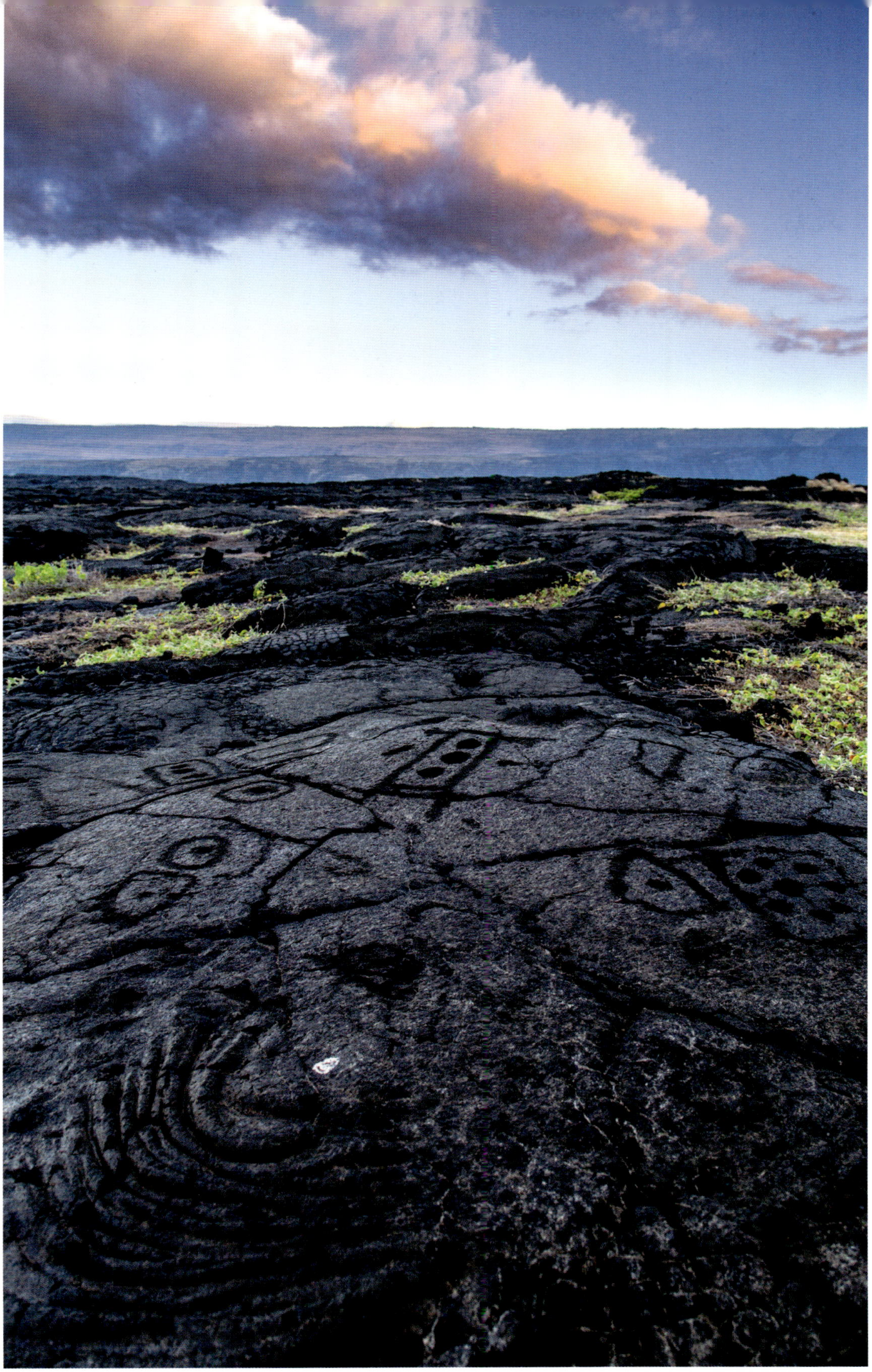

HAWAI'I VOLCANOES NATIONAL PARK On the last day of our four-day backpacking trip along the coast, we started hiking at sunrise to beat the heat of hiking across miles of lava fields. Shortly after leaving camp at Apua Point, we came across these petroglyphs along the trail.

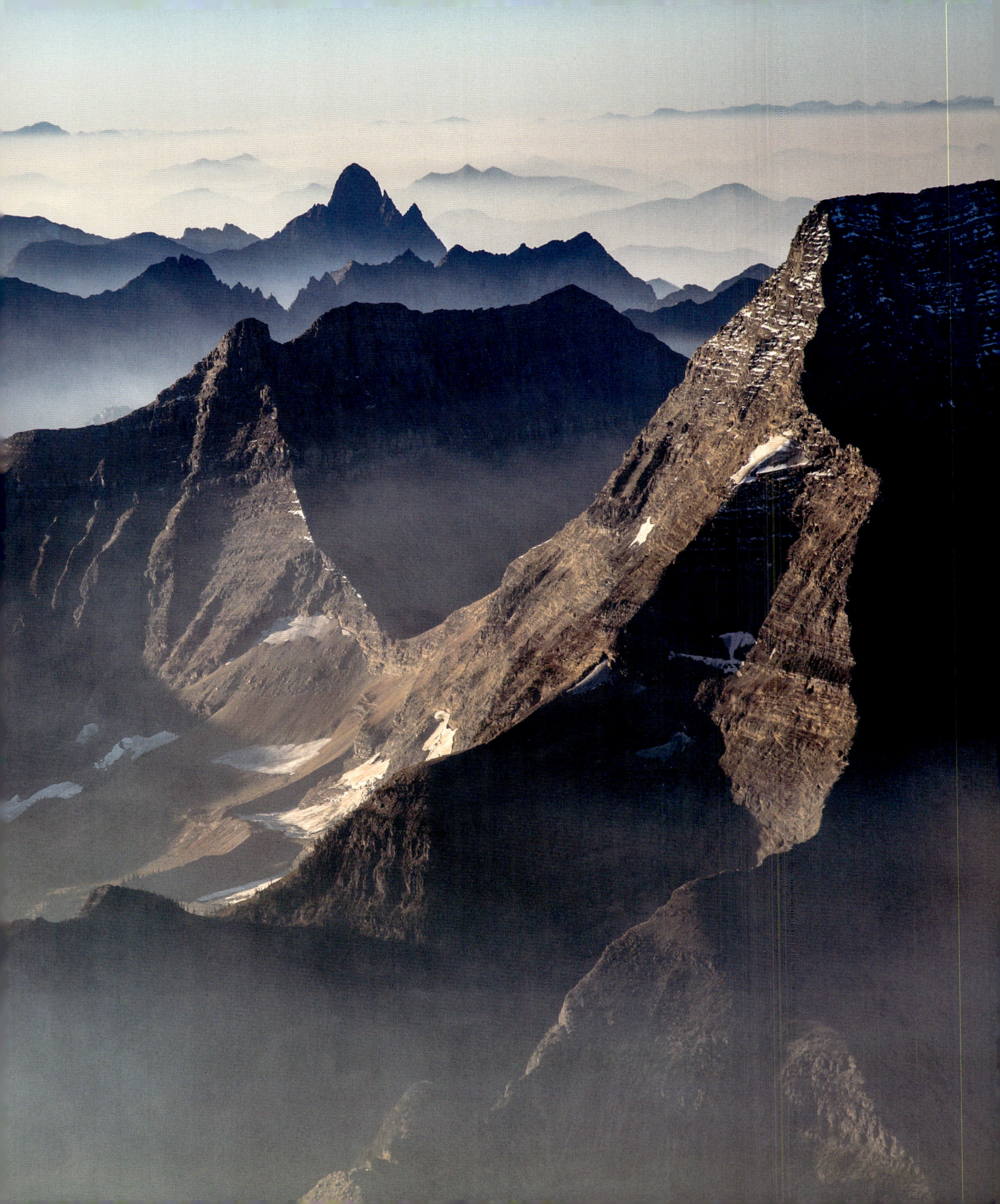

EPILOGUE

TODAY, OUR PUBLIC LANDS are more popular than ever and providing adequate funding to our land management agencies is critical. Proper funding enables conservation and restoration efforts, allowing agencies to acquire and protect wildlife habitats and manage invasive species effectively, through programs like the Land and Water Conservation Fund.

Additionally, public lands play a significant role in the outdoor recreation economy, generating over $887 billion annually in consumer spending and supporting over 4.5 million jobs. Well-funded agencies can maintain trails, campgrounds, and facilities, ensuring safe and enjoyable experiences for all who visit. Access to public lands promotes physical health and environmental education. Spending time in nature positively affects mental well-being, and adequately funded programs can facilitate educational opportunities for local communities.

Our public lands also provide vital ecosystem services. Ecosystem valuation is an economic process that assigns value—whether monetary or otherwise—to an ecosystem and its associated services. This process quantifies benefits, such as how a forest can help reduce flooding and erosion, sequester carbon provide habitat for endangered species, and absorb harmful chemicals. By monetizing these benefits, ecosystem valuation offers tools for policymakers and conservationists to evaluate the impacts of management decisions and conduct cost-benefit analyses of potential policies. Properly funding our land management agencies can enhance these services, benefiting public health and safety while also addressing the effects of a changing climate.

GLACIER NATIONAL PARK
On a morning flight over the park to photograph the disappearing glaciers, I had the opportunity to fly with Keith Ladzinski, who was on assignment for *National Geographic*.

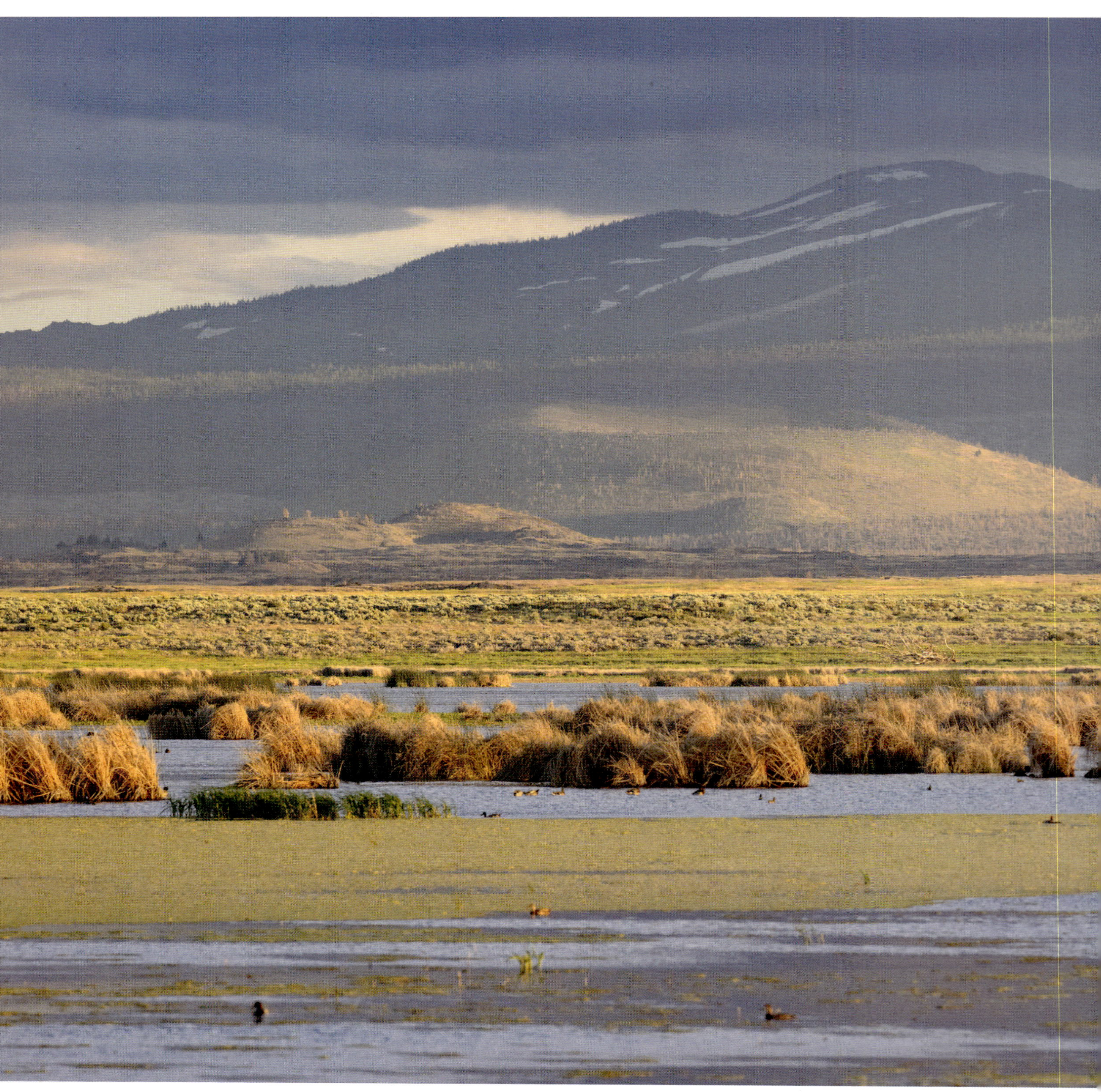

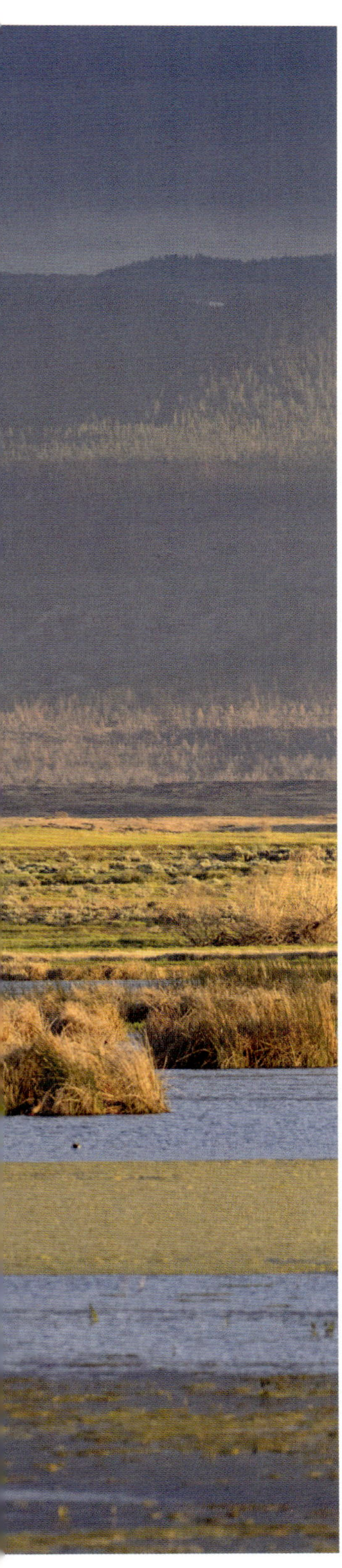

While the benefits provided by natural ecosystems are widely recognized, they are not fully understood. Even so, experts in the field have calculated that worldwide ecosystem services are worth $44 trillion, adjusted for today's dollars, annually. As the climate continues to change and we see more extreme weather events, it's only logical to assume that the importance and value of these services will continue to appreciate over time, if the ecosystems remain intact.

CALL TO ACTION

I challenge you to get involved in protecting and promoting the importance of public lands. One of the most impactful ways to contribute is by volunteering, just as I did when I started. You can volunteer directly with land management agencies or partner organizations that offer hands-on opportunities like restoration projects, cleanups, and educational programs. Citizen science initiatives also provide a meaningful way to engage by contributing to essential research and monitoring efforts.

Stay informed about relevant legislation and advocate for public lands by contacting your representatives. Support your local conservation initiatives. Many states have programs focused on preserving public lands, so consider connecting with land trusts or conservation groups in your area.

If you're able, contribute financially. As land management agencies face funding challenges due to budget cuts and inflation, donations to nonprofit organizations can help bridge the gap in resources and support critical conservation work.

Lastly, share your passion for public lands with others. Educate your friends and family, join or lead outdoor groups, and use social media to share your experiences, responsibly taken photos, and the importance of preserving these special places.

While no single action will guarantee the protection of public lands, our collective efforts can ensure that these treasured spaces endure for future generations to enjoy. Together, we can safeguard the natural beauty and cultural heritage that define our public lands.

TULE LAKE NATIONAL WILDLIFE REFUGE We spent a few hours exploring the lake and observing the waterfowl. The highlight of the day was discovering the eared grebe rookery, where hundreds of birds nested along the water's edge.

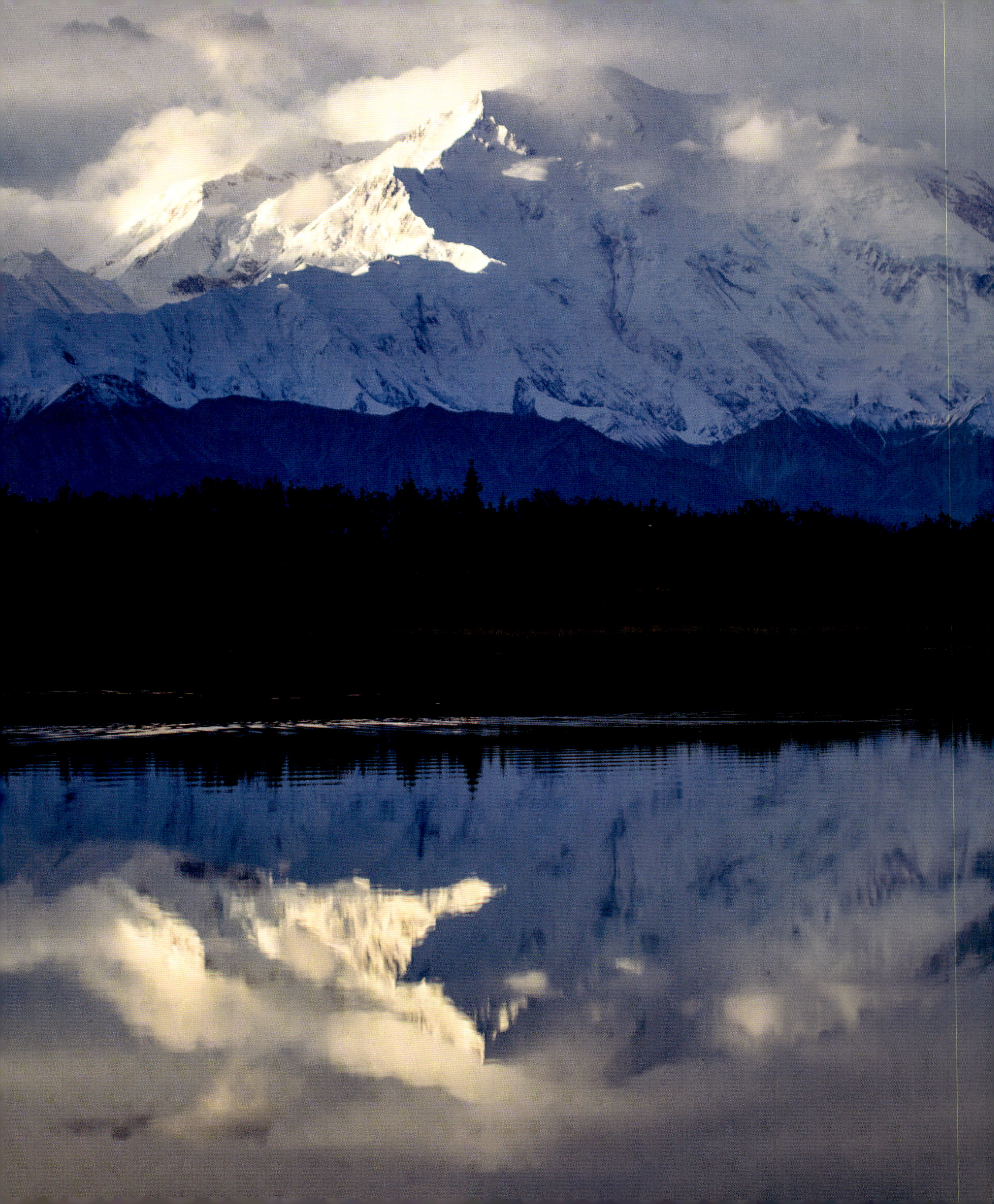

ACKNOWLEDGMENTS

MANY PEOPLE HAVE PLAYED A PART in my photographic journey, but my wife, Corrie, has been by my side through most of it. From early mornings to late nights out shooting, she has shared countless moments behind the lens with me. Her support was invaluable in creating this book—from selecting photos to recalling the stories behind our adventures. Without her, this endeavor would not have been possible.

I am also grateful to my friends and family for their support over the years and especially to those who were with me when I captured the photos featured in this book: Andy Austin, Kass Bissmeyer, Lery Bonnin, Chris Burkard, Annie Carlson, Brian Cohen, Greg Colligan, Adam Conn, Rebecca Crastnopol, Matt Daniel, Amber DeBardelaben, Geni DeKiel, Kaycee DeRisi, Mike DeRisi, Bill Ferrante, Chris Ferrante, Sharon Frank, Christian Graham, Natalie Graham, Pat Graham, Sarah Hayes, Warren Hansen, Neal Herbert, Cristos Ifantides, Heather Jameson, Jennifer Jerrett, Connie Johnson, Jerry Johnson, Kacie Kamp, Ryan Kamp, Monica Koenig, Keith Ladzinski, William Leggett, Christein Leiper, Forrest Mankins, Ken Molestina, Jake Morey, Janet Ross, Alex Rowton, Eric Stearns, Amy Spieker, Susan Tooch, Quinton Tolman, Ali White, and Kara Wang.

DENALI NATIONAL PARK AND PRESERVE Locally known as Reflection Pond, the small kettle pond near the Wonder Lake Ranger Station can offer a spectacular view of North America's highest mountain.

ABOUT THE AUTHOR

SINCE 2008, PHOTOGRAPHER JACOB W. FRANK has boated, climbed, caved, hiked, biked, skied, dog mushed, backpacked, snowmobiled, flown over, and driven through some of the most scenic public lands the United States has to offer.

After receiving a BS and MS in Recreation, Parks, and Tourism at the University of Florida, Jake moved from Florida out West to pursue his career working with the National Park Service. He worked seasonally at Grand Teton, Glacier, Carlsbad Caverns, Denali, Rocky Mountain, and Yellowstone National Parks. He spent a short time living and working on the Colorado Plateau for a nonprofit as a social media manager, videographer, and photographer working with members of the Navajo Nation before accepting his first permanent, year-round National Park Service position.

Frank's photography has been widely featured in books, magazines, and national news outlets, and was showcased in two major exhibits at the Smithsonian National Museum of Natural History: *Wilderness Forever: 50 Years of Protecting America's Wild Places* and *100 Years of America's National Park Service: Preserve, Enjoy, Inspire.*

Jake, his wife, Corrie, and their dog, Toklat, spend most of their free time recreating on public lands.

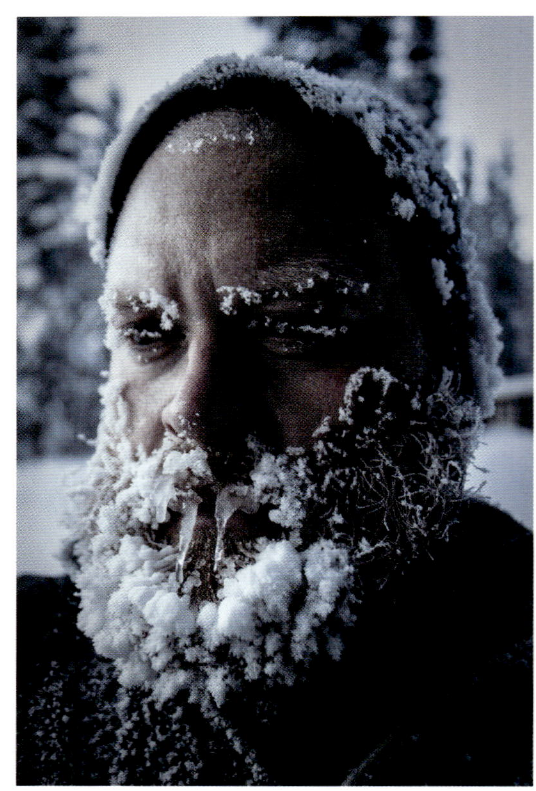

DENALI NATIONAL PARK AND PRESERVE After a week of -40°F temperatures, Corrie and I were starting to feel a bit of cabin fever. We decided to head out for a ski, despite the cold, and after an hour of skiing I was transformed into a yeti.